THE FERGUSON LIBRARY

3 1118 02389

W9-BNL-100

The Ferguson Library
Weed

The Mathews Men

THE
MATHEWS
MEN

SEVEN BROTHERS AND THE WAR
AGAINST HITLER'S U-BOATS

WILLIAM GEROUX

VIKING

THE FERGUSON LIBRARY
ONE PUBLIC LIBRARY PLAZA
STAMFORD, CONNECTICUT 06904

VIKING
An imprint of Penguin Random House LLC
375 Hudson Street
New York, New York 10014
penguin.com

Copyright © 2016 by William Geroux
Penguin supports copyright. Copyright fuels creativity, encourages diverse voices, pro-
motes free speech, and creates a vibrant culture. Thank you for buying an authorized edition of this book and for complying with copyright laws by not reproducing, scanning, or
distributing any part of it in any form without permission. You are supporting writers and
allowing Penguin to continue to publish books for every reader.

ISBN 978-0-525-42815-2

Printed in the United States of America
10 9 8 7 6 5 4 3 2 1

Set in Warnock Pro
Designed by Daniel Lagin
Maps by Jeffrey L. Ward

For my mother, Genevieve Blake Geroux

CONTENTS

CONTENTS

A Gift from the Predators

One night in late July 1942, a hardscrabble Cuban fisherman hauled in a hulking shark from the Nicholas Channel off Cuba's northern coast. He gutted it and tore open its stomach with a knife. Out into the humid air spilled a mass of human remains. The fisherman, whose last name was Carillo, would have been surprised but not shocked.

The Nicholas Channel had been the Carillo family's prime shark-fishing grounds for years. The narrow passage branched off the Old Bahama Channel and the Straits of Florida, where the Gulf Stream ran deep and fast. Its dark-blue water teemed with fish. The sharks preyed on them, and the Carillos in turn preyed on the sharks. They set deep lines in the channel, suspending bloody chunks of meat on six-inch hooks from floating oil drums. When they caught big, dangerous sharks—tiger sharks or snout-nosed bull sharks—they beat them to death with long clubs or drove metal spikes through their gills. They gutted them to keep the meat fresh. The sharks made dinners for the fishermen, who could sell any extra to neighbors.

In recent months, a new predator had joined the sharks and the fishermen in these killing grounds. German U-boats crept among the islets

1

and mangroves. The submarines did not waste time or torpedoes on fishing boats, but they attacked American merchant ships with single-minded focus. The fishermen had glimpsed the U-boats' thin silhouettes at dawn, and heard the rumble of their diesel engines in the dark. They had seen torpedoed vessels flaming like giant torches. And they had seen the U-boats' human victims. Only the previous day, another Cuban fishing boat had picked up survivors of the torpedoed American freighter *Onondaga*. Other men from that ship were still missing.

The Carillos spread out the contents of the shark's belly on the deck of the *Donatella*. They discovered two rings. One was a nondescript pale-yellow band of bone. The other was a heavy gold signet ring, cracked on the underside, bearing the initials "G.D.H." The Carillos could have simply crossed themselves and washed their discovery away with a bucket of seawater. Instead, they pulled in their lines and pointed the *Donatella* toward the stone quays of Havana harbor, to hand over the remains to the authorities.

Port officials in Havana thought at first that the remains were leg bones, but closer analysis would reveal they were forearms. Word about them quickly spread around the harbor to the offices of shipping companies and other businesses. Several cargo ships had been torpedoed in nearby waters, including most recently the *Onondaga*.

The *Onondaga*'s captain—known as the ship's master—George Dewey Hodges, had understood the danger of sailing in the waters off Cuba. Dewey, as he was called, hailed from the tiny seafaring enclave of Mathews County, Virginia, on the western shore of the Chesapeake Bay. Mariners from Mathews had sailed the world's oceans since colonial times. Now, in the summer of 1942, seven months after the United States entered World War II, Mathews mariners were under attack by U-boats in the Atlantic Ocean, the Caribbean Sea, the Gulf of Mexico, the Mediterranean Sea, and the frigid Barents Sea in the Arctic Circle.

For the Mathews men aboard the *Onondaga*, the U-boat war was personal. Dewey's brother Leslie had been killed in a U-boat attack off Cuba

MATHEWS COUNTY

MIDDLESEX
COUNTY

Chesapeake Bay

Piankatank River

Godfrey Bay

Cherry Point

Hills Bay

Gwynn's Island

Cobbs Creek

Hallieford

Callis Wharf

Queens Creek

Milford Haven

Point Breeze

MATHEWS COUNTY

Redart

Hole in the Wall

Stutts Cr.

Hudgins

Gales Neck

Moon

14

Chapel Neck

Mathews Courthouse

Garden Creek

Put-in Creek

North River

Onemo

14

Winter Harbor

East River

Port Haywood

Horn Harbor

GLOUCESTER
COUNTY

Shadow

New Point

Pepper Cr.

Mobjack Bay

Motorun

0 Miles   2   4

0 Kilometers   4

New Point Lighthouse ◆

© 2016 Jeffrey L. Ward

only eleven days before the *Onondaga* was attacked. Dewey's father and four of his six brothers were aboard merchant ships in waters already littered with torpedoed ships and the remains of men who had sailed them. The *Onondaga*'s second officer, Genious Hudgins Jr., also a Mathews man, had already survived one torpedoing, as had the bo'sun, William Hammond, whose two brothers were also at sea. Another Mathews sea captain, Mellin Respess, was sailing home aboard the *Onondaga* as a passenger after having had two ships torpedoed out from under him. The only Mathews man on the *Onondaga* who had not previously encountered a U-boat was the third officer, Russell Dennis. All the men had known the master, Dewey, for most of their lives.

Everyone seemed to know Dewey, a broad-shouldered man with an ever-present Lucky Strike cigarette burning between his fingers. Dewey was a veteran captain for the Ford Motor Co., which operated a fleet of ships that in peacetime delivered autos and auto parts from Ford plants on the East Coast to customers in the Caribbean and South America. At age forty-two, Dewey was a robust man with an infectious grin and a natural gift for conversation. He clapped men on the back and asked about their families. He tossed his spare change to children. "How he loved life!" a former shipmate wrote of him. "Possessing the happy faculty of making and keeping friends—friends the world over." Dewey loved to sing, although he was well aware he could not carry a tune. As a joke on his crew, he once cut a record of himself crooning his favorite song, "Mexicali Rose," a ballad about a man setting out on a journey without his beloved.

Dewey might well have been singing about his wife, Edna, and their four children. He was seldom home but doted on them from distant ports. "My darling and babys [sic]," he wrote in his last letter home. "I am not expecting anything to happen to me, but if it does, you should have enough with my insurance property to take care of you for a long time." He told Edna, "What you do with whatever I leave is all right with me as long as you take care of yourself and the children. I leave all of that to your judgment." He asked that his son finish college if the Army did not draft him first. He repeated, "Don't think that I think anything is going to happen. I am not even worried about it."

But he was worried about it. Everything about the trip felt wrong. It would be Dewey's first voyage after being idled for months by a serious illness. The *Onondaga* was not even his ship. He was substituting for her regular captain on a short but dangerous run from Mobile, Alabama, to Cuba. Dewey took time to inspect the *Onondaga* closely after flying into Mobile. The ship was a tiny freighter, only 231 feet long and displacing 2,309 tons. She was a "laker," designed for the Great Lakes rather than the open sea. Dewey noticed that the *Onondaga*'s life rafts were held to the deck by wire clamps. He replaced the clamps with ropes that could be cut with quick swipes of a knife to free the rafts in an emergency.

The *Onondaga* sailed out of Mobile on June 24, 1942, and made an uneventful passage from Mobile to the industrial port of Nuevitas on Cuba's northeast coast. She took on a load of heavy manganese ore, an ingredient of flares and incendiary bombs. Dewey waited until first light the next morning to leave Nuevitas. He was determined to reach the safety of Havana while the sun was still up. U-boats seemed to spend the daylight hours hiding on the bottom and then rise at night to hunt.

The *Onondaga* chugged through the Nicholas Channel between the Grand Bahama Bank and a string of barrier islands dotting the Cuban coast. Dewey posted two lookouts, though he knew the ship was doomed if a U-boat got close enough for them to spot it. The *Onondaga* was slow and unarmed. If she was unlucky enough to encounter Germans, her only real defense was her relative insignificance. She was such small fry that some U-boat commanders might hesitate to waste a precious torpedo on her.

The U-129's commander, Hans-Ludwig Witt, was not the type to hesitate. Witt was the most aggressive U-boat commander in the Caribbean. He had sunk ten merchant ships in six weeks, including a freighter commanded by another Mathews sea captain. Witt was not afraid to attack ships in daylight or close to shore. On July 23, he was ending his successful mission to the Caribbean. The U-129 was only passing through the

PRINCIPAL ALLIED CONVOY ROUTES AND MERCHANT SHIPPING LANES, 1942

Nicholas Channel en route to the open Atlantic, and back to its base on the coast of Nazi-occupied France. But Witt had saved a torpedo in case a kill presented itself on the trip home. A little before 4:30 p.m., he spotted the *Onondaga* through his periscope as she passed Cayo Guillermo, a sparsely inhabited clump of sand where Ernest Hemingway later set the climax of a novel involving U-boats.*

The U-129 approached the *Onondaga* at periscope depth, unspotted by the lookouts. Witt ordered the sub slowed to its attack speed of 5 knots. He called out the target's range, speed, and course, and the depth to which the torpedo was to run. His torpedo officer entered the data into a steering system built into the torpedo tubes. Witt called *"Rohr los!"*—"Launch!"— and the U-boat shuddered as a torpedo burst from one of its bow tubes on a jet of compressed air. The torpedo raced through the water at approximately 50 miles per hour. Its tip contained an explosive charge of TNT, cyclonite, and aluminum flakes. It struck the *Onondaga* just below the waterline, with a bang and a white flash, and blew a hole in her three-quarter-inch-thick steel hull. The sea poured in and the heavy manganese ore she carried quickly pulled the little ship under.

"As soon as I heard the explosion I ran up to the boat deck," Third Officer Russell Dennis from Mathews told Navy investigators. "It was only six steps up a ladder from where I was standing, but by the time I got there, water was already rushing over the sides. The second mate [Genious Hudgins] hollered, 'Abandon ship,' and then jumped. I was right behind him." Dennis caught a glimpse of Dewey descending a ladder from the bridge, and saw Captain Respess "sawing at one of the ropes holding the life rafts to the deck." The *Onondaga* sank out of sight in less than a minute. "She went down like a brick," Dennis said. Nothing remained on the surface but some debris and three life rafts. Dennis and eight of his shipmates

---

* Hemingway's novel *Islands in the Stream* features a Hemingway-like protagonist, Thomas Hudson, who hunts U-boats off the coast of Cuba and dies in a firefight with a U-boat crew marooned on Cayo Guillermo.

swam to the life rafts and clambered aboard. They made it safely to an uninhabited barrier island, where they were spotted by a search plane, but Dewey and seventeen other men were listed as missing.

Thanks to the shark fishermen, however, Dewey was no longer missing.

The discovery of the rings caught the attention of R. M. Jenkins, who managed a business on the Havana waterfront. Jenkins knew Dewey and knew that he had been lost aboard the *Onondaga*, and recognized the initials "G.D.H." Jenkins examined the ring personally, and came away more convinced, but he was not sure who to tell. He wrote letters to the U.S. ambassador and various steamship companies, asking that someone contact Dewey Hodges's family. "If the widow of the good old man who went down with his ship knows this ring," he wrote, "I imagine it would be of great sentimental value to her."

He was wrong. It was not that simple. The rings would prove to be a thorny gift from the predators that took Dewey Hodges.

CHAPTER ONE

Born to the Water

Mathews County, Virginia, is not on the way to anywhere. "One only goes to Mathews when going to Mathews," the local saying went. The county is a peninsula spreading deep into the Chesapeake Bay, in the shape of a tattered sail. It clings to the western shore of the Bay by a four-mile border with Gloucester County. But the rest of Mathews's boundaries are tidal water.

To the east lies the Chesapeake Bay, one of the world's largest estuaries, which opens out like an inland sea from the outermost edges of the county. To the north, Mathews's shores are bathed by the brackish Piankatank River, and to the south by the North River and Mobjack Bay. That smaller bay joins the Chesapeake at a long shoal marked by the New Point Lighthouse, which was commissioned by President John Adams and completed in Thomas Jefferson's administration. The lighthouse stood on the mainland until August 24, 1933, when a ferocious hurricane flooded much of Mathews and carved a channel that stranded the lighthouse on its own rocky island. The interior of Mathews is gashed by dozens of creeks and streams, including the East River, which cuts a jagged swath through the geographic center of the county.

While Mathews lies only seventy miles from Virginia's capital city of Richmond, mileage never adequately captured the county's isolation. For much of Mathews's history, its roads were so awful that many citizens avoided them entirely and traveled by boat to shop, socialize, and attend church. Bad roads had literally forced the creation of Mathews in the first place. The county had been a parish of Gloucester County until 1791, when citizens complained that the thirteen-mile trip to the Gloucester court-house was too daunting, especially in the mud of winter and early spring. "Those who have business in court [must walk] or resque their lives often over a wide & dangerous Bay in canoes," read a petition by a member of the Virginia House of Delegates, Thomas Mathews. He argued that the far-flung citizens should have their own county with a courthouse less perilous to reach. The Virginia legislature agreed, and the citizens of the new county thanked Thomas Mathews by naming it after him. The signers of the petition included men named Callis, Hudgins, Powell, Billups, Fos-ter, Hunley, Marchant, Forrest, and Borum, whose descendants still live in the lonely community and sail in the Chesapeake and beyond.

By 1941, as the war in Europe was about to explode into World War II, Mathews was an isolated, tightly knit community of about 7,500 people, scattered in hamlets and tiny villages along the tidal creeks. Mathews was country. Everyone knew everyone else, or at least knew their families. Neighbors pitched in to help one another at harvest time and at hog-killing time—right after the first cold snap in late autumn, when the freshly butch-ered meat would set properly. Many Mathews families ventured into the city of Richmond only twice a year: to buy school clothes, and to take children to see Santa Claus at Thalhimers department store.

The only highway leading into Mathews, State Route 14, veered through thick maritime forest along half-hidden shorelines, past the redbrick Mathews courthouse, and down toward the lighthouse before ending abruptly, as if exhausted by the journey, in a confusion of back roads. The back roads narrowed into dirt lanes bordered by small, wood-frame houses and an occasional rotted-out boat or collapsed shed. Some lanes ended at weather-beaten docks, where workboats swung at anchor or rested in the muck, depending upon the tide. The air was filled with the cries of gulls and the sweet reek of the marsh.

One of about every ten citizens of Mathews was black, living almost completely segregated from the county's white population. Black children attended small schools, most of them connected to black churches. When the children grew up, their dealings with their white neighbors consisted mainly of laboring and cooking for them. Mathews was not spared the prejudices of many rural southern communities in the early twentieth century. The portraits in the Mathews courthouse were of Robert E. Lee and Thomas "Stonewall" Jackson. As late as the 1920s, hooded and robed Ku Klux Klansmen had marched in Mathews's Fourth of July parade.

By 1941, though, attitudes about race in Mathews varied widely from family to family. The Hodgeses were progressive. Dewey's father and mother, Captain Jesse and Henny, would have swatted any child who showed disrespect toward the black neighbors who helped out at Gales Neck. "Animosity toward blacks was not in my family, period," said Louise Hodges's daughter, Stormy Heart.* But the gulf between white and black in Mathews was wide enough that the weekly paper, the *Gloucester-Mathews Gazette-Journal*, relegated all news about blacks to the back pages, under the heading "Among the Colored."

The closest thing to a downtown in Mathews was the Main Street business district, which bordered the grassy courthouse green. About half of the county's 150 businesses were clustered along the adjoining streets in tidy, one-story brick buildings. The businesses included Richardson's Drug Store—whose lunch counter was the social center of the county—as well as the Farmers and Fishermen's Bank, two grocery stores, a dry-goods store, a car dealership, a gas station, a candy shop, two pool halls, and the BeJo theater, which showed films that had already played everywhere else.

---

* Stormy Heart Hodges got her name from a character in a magazine story that her mother, Louise Hodges, was reading while waiting for a midwife to help deliver her.

There was a public library and, in the courthouse green, a jail, a welfare office, and a stone monument with the names of Mathews's Confederate dead. An unimpressed visitor described the town as "straggling."

The only time the courthouse area really came alive was on Saturday nights, when more than two thousand people from all over Mathews put on their best clothes and converged at sunset on Main Street in a swirling promenade. They shopped, gossiped, politicked, did business, settled scores, and looked for romance. After about four hours, they climbed back into their Model A sedans and horse-drawn wagons and returned to their villages along the creeks.

Each village had its post office, usually contained in a general store that sold only those essentials that could not be handmade, grown, or caught in the Bay. Mathews villages were not named for European kings or colonial governors, as in Virginia counties with similar colonial pedigrees, but for the hardworking families who eked out their livings there. Several villages had been named just for the hell of it, including Shadow, Onemo ("one more" post office), Redart ("trader" spelled backward), Motorun (the home of a boat mechanic who could get any motor to run), and Moon (named by a postmaster while sitting on his front step one moonlit night). People in Mathews did not put on airs with names, or with anything else.

Mathews's far-flung communities were bound together by some twenty churches, most of them conservative Baptist, Methodist, and Episcopal, with two small Quaker congregations. The evangelical strains of the Quakers and Methodists held revivals wherein traveling preachers held the devout spellbound. In most Mathews churches, however, the pastors beseeched rather than thundered at their flocks to fill the benches on Sundays. The patriarchs of prominent Mathews families had founded those churches, but their children, by and large, were less devoted, and some already had drifted away. Every Sunday the Reverend Iris Elmon Belch of Gwynn's Island Baptist Church welcomed the visiting mariners he spotted in attendance, but the welcome was wistful. He knew those men probably would not see the inside of another church until they came home to the island again, if then. Life at sea did not lend itself to regular churchgoing.

Mathews was also bound together by its schools. While all white Mathews children attended one of the county's four primary schools, many of them never set foot in Mathews High School. They quit their studies to work to support their families. The Chesapeake Bay was too bountiful to allow anyone in Mathews to starve. But beyond basic sustenance, the prospects in Mathews were limited.

"There wasn't nothing in Mathews but the water," said Bill Callis, who grew up in Mathews on Gwynn's Island, a triangular dot in the Bay at the mouth of the Piankatank River. "You farmed, you fished the Bay, or you went to sea. Those were your only options."

Farming was hard in Mathews. The sandy loam soil was too poor to produce crops on a large scale, except for daffodils, which burst into silvery profusion every spring to be shipped by the thousands to florists in northeastern cities.

Working on the water came more naturally to people in Mathews. Every child in the county grew up handling boats. They learned to sail, and also to scull, a method of propelling a boat by twisting a single oar back and forth rapidly at the stern. Sculling was considered an art in Mathews. A capable sculler could outrace a small motorboat. Bill Callis was a commercial fisherman by the first grade, setting pots in the rivers to catch blue crabs and eels, and then selling them to neighbors. "By the time I was five or six, I could take a boat and make it do as I damn well pleased," Bill said. "I guess you could say I was born to the water."

Mathews fishermen favored pound nets, which were large nets staked into the bottom in a T shape. Fish swam into them and could not find their way out. When bulging nets happened to align with high market prices, fishing was lucrative. But fishing could also break your heart, bankrupt you, or even kill you. Catches plummeted without warning. Expensive gear broke. Fish houses burned. Boats sank. Men flayed or smashed their fingers while driving stakes for pound nets. And every year, the storms that boiled up suddenly on the Bay caught at least one fisherman too far out. Many fishermen never learned to swim, regarding it as a leisure activity.

For more than 250 years, the profession of choice in Mathews had been sailing merchant ships. To a Richmonder, Mathews might seem like a dead end at the water's edge, but to a mariner, Mathews was a portal, a jumping-off point to the world. Mathews had been a tobacco port and then a busy steamboat port. In 1941, steamboats still stopped in Mathews regularly on their way between Norfolk and Baltimore. A young man born to the water, with an urge to explore or simply nothing to lose, could pack some clothes into a seabag, present himself to a ship's captain on the dock, and change his life forever. Generations of Mathews men had done exactly that, running away from home or walking away with their families' blessings. During a grueling fall harvest in 1938, George Hudgins of Mathews announced he was leaving the family farm to go to sea. His father handed him $10 and said, "Good luck." George had never been much help on the farm, but he was a natural at the helm of a vessel. He would retire many years later as chief pilot on the Panama Canal.

The pinnacle of achievement in Mathews was to become a captain, to command a ship at sea. In some Mathews families, it was not enough for a young man to find steady work as a seaman or even a ship's officer. His birthright was to become a captain. Portraits of his ancestors in *their* white captain's caps stared down at him expectantly from the walls of his home.

Captains were celebrities in Mathews. When one came home from his ship for a visit, neighborhood boys orbited his house on their bicycles, hoping for a shout of greeting or maybe even a quarter flung to them. Captains always had money in their pockets, even during the worst years of the Great Depression. In 1941, an experienced captain could earn $350 a month. By most standards, that was hardly lavish pay. Captains were "the poorest paid executives in the country," wrote author and mariner Bruce Felknor. But captains made ten times more than able seamen, whose pay was $32.50 per month, and able seamen earned more than most other people in Mathews.

A few captains in Mathews always stood out from the crowd, either for their skill, their exploits, or their prodigious personalities. Captain Jesse Hodges stood out for all of those reasons and more. The Hodges family of Gales Neck was extraordinary.

In 1884, when Jesse was only ten years old, he had signed on as cabin boy on a neighbor's sailing schooner, the *Clemmie Travers*, which ran between Norfolk, Baltimore, and the Caribbean hauling everything from coal to pineapples. The captain taught Jesse to read by the light of swaying oil lanterns, using newspapers from ports of call as textbooks. According to a family history, Jesse "learned to read other things too, like tides, winds, stars, currents, charts, depth sounders and men."

Jesse could handle large vessels as if they were bathtub toys. He just had the touch. He started with sailing schooners and freighters but gravitated toward tugboats. Two of his brothers followed. At the age of twenty, Jesse was promoted to captain of an oceangoing tug, and he spent most of the rest of his life in the wheelhouse, shepherding ships and barges through busy harbors from New England to the Caribbean.

Captain Jesse had a barrel chest, enormous hands, and a piercing look that seemed to say, "Get off your ass." He would not employ men who drank too much or had too little ambition. He was accustomed to shouting orders and seeing them followed without discussion or delay.

Jesse's wife, Henrietta, was a tall, large-boned woman, as kind as Jesse was hard. Henny, as she was universally known, presided over the family's sixty-acre farm on Gales Neck at the head of the East River. Jesse knew little about the farm or other matters on dry land. He got off the tugboat only three or four times a year, for a few days at a stretch. When he was home, Henny waited on him hand and foot. She fixed him his favorite meal of baked alewives—oily fish that most people refused to eat. Jesse enjoyed a little activity, like hoeing his watermelon patch, but mostly he sat in the shade of a tall cedar near the riverbank, smoking a cigar or his corncob pipe, whittling, and waiting for the call back to his ship. He seemed lost at home in all respects except one.

Between 1895 and 1920, Jesse and Henny had fourteen children—nine sons and five daughters. "It seemed like every time he came home, he'd leave her with another child to care for," observed his daughter Louise. It wasn't enough for Henny, who joked that she wanted enough children for a steamship crew but that he had fathered only enough for a tugboat crew. And indeed, at one point Jesse employed five of his sons as officers on his tug.

The Hodges children accumulated quickly: Raymond, Seth, Dewey, Willie, Leslie, Alice, Elizabeth, Spencer, John, Coleman, David, Henrietta, Louise, and finally Hilda. By the time Hilda, the fourteenth and last child, arrived, Jesse and Henny had run out of names. They christened her Hilda Fourteen Hodges. She was the only one born in a hospital. Jesse lost count of his sons and named the ninth boy David in the mistaken belief he was the biblical "seventh son."

But Captain Jesse's career advice to his boys was as clear as the Gulf Stream. When his oldest, Raymond, turned thirteen, Jesse walked him to the dune at the edge of the Bay and pointed out at a ship chugging north to Baltimore. "When you are 14, you'll be old enough to work on a ship," he told Raymond. "By the time you are 21, I want you to be master of a ship like that."

Raymond would not disappoint. Six of Captain Jesse's sons would, in fact, become ship's captains, and a seventh would quit the sea only after hurting his back in a shipboard accident. Jesse and Henny reared two of their grandsons, who also went to sea. Three of the Hodges daughters married Mathews mariners.

When the seafaring Hodges sons married, they had to move their families to the home ports of their ships in Norfolk, Philadelphia, and New York, but whenever their ships docked for more than a day or two, they came home to Gales Neck to pay their respects to Henny, whom they all called "Mama." Even if they were no longer *from* Mathews, they would always be *of* Mathews. After they retired, they would return to Mathews to live out their final years. They would always be Mathews men.

The Hodges captains hired all the crew members from Mathews they could. Every time Captain Dewey Hodges came home to see his mother, he spread the word around Mathews of any jobs open on his ship or other vessels he knew. Any man who wanted work had only to meet him in front of Richardson's Drug Store at 1 p.m. on Sunday, and Dewey would drive him to the docks and sign him on to the crew. Dewey, like his father, encouraged men to apply themselves and advance. "My father wanted to help men from Mathews," Dewey's daughter Jean recalled. "He knew that with a little help, some of them could get out and make some money and see the world. That was what he had done, and he saw himself in them." Dewey also pushed them to be ambitious and rise through the ranks; he had once threatened to fire his second mate, Clayton Hammond of Mathews, if Clayton did not quit procrastinating and test for his first-mate's license. Hammond did as he was told, and became Dewey's second-in-command. At one of Mathews's darkest moments in the coming U-boat war, Clayton Hammond would repay Dewey's confidence in him.

The Hodges family may have been abundant, but it was only one of a dozen families in Mathews with a tradition of sailing merchant ships. The center of Mathews seafaring, in fact, was not the Hodges's community of Gales Neck but Gwynn's Island. The island was three miles long and a mile wide, heavily wooded, and linked to mainland Mathews by a steel drawbridge spanning a placid anchorage called Milford Haven. Gwynn's Island was home to about six hundred people, who were even more closely tied to the sea than were their neighbors across the water.

Gwynn's Island had been a cradle of merchant sea captains since colonial times, which was a great source of pride on the island. In 1924, the *Mathews Journal* printed a letter from "Father Neptune" listing twenty-four Gwynn's Islanders who were captains of merchant ships. The names included Callis, Hudgins, Borum, and Respess, the first families of island seafaring. The list included six island captains named Callis, including the brothers Homer, Rodney, and Robert Melville Callis, who had sailed the deep ocean for two decades.

Like most islanders, the three Callis brothers had quit school after ninth grade rather than scull across Milford Haven every morning to catch the bus to the high school. The sea seemed far more interesting. "I have seen many queer things and had many queer experiences," Captain Robert Melville Callis once said. He had stopped a ship in a Louisiana canal to let a cow swim across. He had seen a storm strip a man naked. He claimed to have seen mermaids, whose "eyes were blue, blue like the waters of old Milford Haven," and who were "built like the steeple on the Gwynn's Island Baptist Church."

Merchant mariners like the Mathews men were civilians, sailing privately owned cargo ships from port to port. Their employer, the U.S. Merchant Marine, was not a branch of the military, as its name seemed to suggest. It was, and is, an association of privately owned shipping companies operating under the American flag, employing American crews, and fighting like bull sharks over contracts to haul goods by sea.

Merchant shipping dated back to the world's earliest civilizations. Any ambitious nation with even a sliver of seacoast projected its economic strength through merchant ships. The U.S. Merchant Marine is as old as the nation itself. It helped build the United States into a global power. Merchant ships carried American goods abroad and foreign goods to America after the Revolution. They fought the young nation's sea battles, as privateers commissioned by the government to attack enemy ships, until the U.S. Navy grew strong enough to take over that job.

Throughout its history, the U.S. merchant fleet had grown and shrunk according to the laws of supply and demand and the strength of foreign competition. But the government never let it grow too feeble without reviving it through subsidies and exclusive contracts. The nation needed a functioning U.S. Merchant Marine. The need was not so clear during peacetime, when foreign ships could deliver goods to and from U.S. ports just as well and often more cheaply. But in times of war, the Merchant Marine was transformed into a vital part of America's arsenal—a fleet of ships the nation could rely on to carry men and supplies wherever they were needed. The Merchant Marine had always showed its true value to the country when the shooting started.

Most Mathews men joined the Merchant Marine at the lowest rungs of the shipboard job ladder, as cabin boys or ordinary seamen, and learned through experience. Climbing up through the ranks that way, rather than through study at maritime training academies, is called "coming up through the hawsepipe," which means coming up the hard way. A hawsepipe is the opening in a vessel's bow through which the anchor chain passes as the anchor is dropped and weighed; a sufficiently determined man could scramble up the greasy chain through the hawsepipe and onto the ship's deck. A hawsepipe mariner would rise through the ranks by logging enough time at each job on a ship to qualify for the next higher job. If the rank or job they aspired to required a certificate or license, they would sit for an exam by the U.S. Coast Guard to prove their knowledge. The job descriptions on merchant ships were as old as seafaring itself.

In the deck department, where Mathews men tended to work, the entry-level deckhands were Ordinary Seamen, who performed tedious work such as painting, scraping rust, washing the deck, and stowing cargo. After three years, they could become Able Seamen, skilled at handling lines, maintaining deck equipment, standing watch, and other duties essential to sailing a vessel. The deck crew was supervised by the Boatswain, or Bo'sun, the senior unlicensed man on the ship. The Ship's Carpenter, who was always nicknamed "Chips," built cargo containers and other wooden structures as needed. The radio operator, always called "Sparks," was responsible for communications.

The lowest-ranking licensed officer on the ship was the Third Mate, or Third Officer, who oversaw cargo operations and maintenance of safety equipment, including lifeboats. The Second Mate, or Second Officer, was in charge of navigation. He used a sextant to measure the angle from the sun or the stars to the horizon, and then used those readings to find the ship's position and chart its course. The First Mate, or First Officer, was second-in-command on the ship. He supervised the day-to-day perfor-mance of the vessel and the crew.

Roughly equal to the First Mate in rank was the Chief Engineer. He ruled the loud, hellishly hot engine room, which usually was located amid-ships just below the waterline. He oversaw one or more Assistant Engineers as well as the unlicensed Firemen, Oilers, and Wipers, who, respectively, kept the ship's engines fueled, lubricated, and wiped free of spilled oil and grime. The ship's Steward oversaw food service, supervising the Cooks who prepared the meals and the Messmen who served them to the crew and then cleaned up.

Every officer and crewman on the ship—somewhere between twenty-five and forty men—answered to the Captain. The captain was ultimately responsible for everything that happened aboard his vessel. He was not actually a member of the crew but an agent of the ship's owner. His job was to deliver the cargo to its destination as fast as possible, while keeping the crew sufficiently healthy and content to get it there. He did not stand reg-ular watches at sea, as his officers did, but when the ship was in danger, the captain's duty was to stay on the bridge for as long as the threat lasted, or until he was too exhausted to continue. The captain might be easygoing, aloof, or a tyrant hated by every man on his ship. But his standing was undisputed and his authority absolute.

Mathews had a reputation for producing capable mariners, and some shipping companies went out of their way to hire Mathews men. An exec-utive of the New York–based A. H. Bull & Co. shipping line explained in the 1930s: "From the beginning of the Line comes the tradition that natives of Mathews County, Virginia, should be in command of its ships. Appli-cants for positions in the company merely stated they were from [Mathews] and proved their contention, and were immediately employed. On the seven steamers now operated by the line, every deck officer is a native of Mathews County." Much of the Bull Line's hiring in Baltimore was handled by a retired sea captain from Gwynn's Island, Virgil Respess, who simply called around Mathews until he found men for the open jobs. All the hiring was supposed to go through the seamen's unions, with the mariners who had been ashore the longest getting the next available jobs for which they qualified. By 1941, every mariner had to join a union, but the unions were still consolidating their hold on the hiring process, and a savvy captain or hiring agent could still place a favored man on a ship.

Mariners from outside the county who did not enjoy the benefits of the Mathews job pipeline understandably resented it. They viewed Mathews men as clannish and ambitious to a fault. Bill Callis once signed on to a new ship and told the captain where he was from. "Oh, Christ!" the captain muttered. "If you're from Mathews County, I had better be careful or you'll have my job." He was not smiling.

Some Mathews mariners scoffed at outsiders who had impressive licenses or commands but no true feel for a ship. The Mathews captain of the Virginia state patrol boat *Commodore Maury* noted condescendingly that the crew of President Franklin D. Roosevelt's presidential yacht, though "immaculately uniformed," needed three tries to dock the vessel during a visit to Yorktown, Virginia. The *Commodore Maury*, by contrast, "eased up to the dock in perfect form on the first approach."

Mathews mariners who preferred to come home every night chose to work on patrol boats, harbor tugs, barges, and other vessels that stayed in and around the Bay. The more adventurous men chose vessels bound across the ocean. Bill Callis, like his father and uncles, loved bracing against a bulkhead while his ship climbed up and down thirty-foot storm seas. "When you're at the top of one of those seas," he said, "you can look out for twenty miles all around you and not see a speck or a soul, just rows and rows of giant rollers. It's a sight you can't see anywhere else except the middle of the ocean." Bill loved sipping strong coffee on the bridge during the morning watch as the rising sun reignited the colors of the sky.

Not everyone saw romance and adventure in the Merchant Marine, however. Daily life on a cargo ship was Spartan. Seamen often slept in coffin-sized bunks, sometimes twelve to thirteen men to a room, packed in like the cargo in the ship's holds. They bathed in the ocean and washed their clothes in buckets of salt water heated by steam from the ship's boilers. The ships had no doctors. Any ailment that could not be cured with iodine or castor oil had to wait for the next port call. The food on a ship was usually plentiful, but its quality depended on the cook's skills and mood.

A voyage might last for three weeks or six months. Most of the work was tedious and monotonous. Each mariner worked a four-hour watch and got the next two watches off. He had little to do in his free time except sleep, read, write letters, play cards or Chinese checkers, or listen to the same phonograph records over and over. He did not get to choose his shipmates, some of whom were sure to be drunks, idlers, or brawlers. "The unlicensed seamen were a bunch of rounders," said Captain Jesse's grandson, Horace "Brother" Hodges, who went to sea during World War II. "When we'd dock, they'd get drunk and chase each other around the deck with fire axes. In Puerto Rico, a guy came back aboard with a pig." By the time the ship finished a voyage, mariners always knew more than they wanted to know about some of their shipmates.

Mariners were paid in cash at the end of each voyage, the result of a law designed to protect them from dishonest shipowners who might otherwise offer them worthless IOUs. They also had to sign on to voyages—to "sign the articles"—in the presence of port officials, whose job was to make sure they were boarding the ships by choice rather than being taken aboard by force or because they were too drunk to know what they were doing.

"Most of us didn't go to sea because we loved it so much," said Captain Willard Hudgins Jr. of Gwynn's Island, who barely knew his sea captain father and yet followed his path. "It was a way to make a living, and it was better than the alternatives."

For some, going to sea was an act of economic desperation. Guy Hudgins of Mathews quit school and joined the Merchant Marine to support his mother and four siblings after his father disappeared. Joseph William Elliott of Mathews joined the Merchant Marine at age sixteen after his father left his mother with six children to feed. At first, Joseph did not meet the Merchant Marine's minimum weight requirement because he was so malnourished. He made weight two weeks later after gorging on bananas and gulping a gallon of water just before the weigh-in. Walter Stillman was an orphan who had been sent as a boy to live with relatives in Mathews. He spent his weekdays toiling in a sawmill and his weekends toiling on a farm. He earned money for his school clothes by gigging frogs—spearing them with a sharp pole at night in the marshes near his home—and selling the meat to neighbors. One blazing hot summer day, he was plowing a cornfield behind a mule when Dewey Hodges's brother Spencer spotted him and offered him a job on Dewey's freighter, the *East Indian*. Walter had never even been on a skiff, but he decided that nothing could be worse than "looking a mule in the butt."

Mathews mariners ran into one another on the docks of New York, London, Rotterdam, Rouen, Cape Town, and Istanbul. "The sun never sets on Mathews men," people in the county said. Brother Hodges once stepped off a freighter in Odessa, Russia, and saw his uncle Captain Raymond Hodges's ship docked nearby. One of Jesse's sons, Captain Coleman Hodges, was surprised to discover that his new second officer was his own nephew, J. W. Corbett. In a few cases, Mathews men's ships literally met at sea. The freighter *Grecian* and the passenger ship *City of Chattanooga*, both commanded by Gwynn's Islanders, collided in 1932 in dense fog off Rhode Island. Four men were killed, including a Mathews man who was second officer on the *Grecian*.

Collisions in the fog were among the common perils of the sea, which had changed little over time. Some twenty-first-century maritime insurance policies still enumerate those perils in nineteenth-century terms, bordering on poetry:

> They are of the Seas, Men-of-War, Fire, Lightning, Earthquake, Enemies, Pirates, Rovers, Assailing Thieves, Jettisons, Letters of Marque and Counter-Marque, Surprisals, Takings at Sea, Arrests, Restraints, Detainment of all Kings, Princes and Peoples of what

Nation, Condition or Quality Soever, Barratry [sabotage] of the Master and Mariners and of all other Like Perils, Losses and Misfortune.

For mariners, the perils also included malaria, smallpox, typhoid fever, and the like in distant ports. They also included a richer variety of shipboard accidents than even the most seasoned mariner could possibly anticipate. Reginald Deagle of Mathews was bitten in the neck by a half-drowned monkey he tried to pull from the ocean after a typhoon.

The mariners' families tried not to dwell on the dangers. They were used to the men being gone, and to having to wait weeks or even months to hear from them, and with farms and businesses and houses to run, they had little time to sit around and wonder what the men were up to. Mariners' wives learned out of necessity to be energetic and resourceful. Their husbands were absent for every crisis and every triumph, every birth, death, injury, birthday, and graduation, and every strange noise in the house at night. The wives singlehandedly maintained the homes and farms and reared the children. Some women secretly dreaded the return of their husbands, who barked orders at them as if they were ordinary seamen.

Henny Hodges, her daughter Louise recalled, "would work in the fields until dinnertime, put dinner on the table, say 'Give me 15 minutes,' and lie down, then get up and go back to the fields and work until dark. There was nothing she couldn't do. She sewed, quilted, milked the cows, fed the hogs and cured the meat." And when her husband came home, "her schedule didn't change except that he stood around telling her what to do."

Not every woman could stand that life. One lonely Mathews widow wrote a letter to the *Gazette-Journal* seeking a new husband, and expressed no preferences about his looks or his occupation, with one exception: "No man who follows a boat and is away from home for weeks need write."

At least the mariners' wives had known what they were getting into, or had thought they did when they married; they had made their own choices. But it was different for a mother when a son followed his father to sea. Saying good-bye to him was a wrenching experience, in which pride mingled with resignation that her life would be defined thereafter by the boy's absences. He would be gone most of the time. Then one day, he might be gone forever. The sea could create hazards that not even the finest mariner could survive. Every mother in Mathews knew a family that had lost a son to the ocean, if she hadn't lost her own. Scattered among the little cemeteries in Mathews were empty graves with footstones bearing the words "Lost at Sea."

War added perils to the sea, and Mathews mariners had fought in every American war since the Revolution. In 1776, the last British governor of Virginia, John Murray, Lord Dunmore, sailed his fleet to Gwynn's Island in search of a safe harbor. A colonial militia hauled cannons to a hill and opened fire on Dunmore's ships, wounding him with splintered wood. He sailed away, never to return. When the people of Mathews learned that His Lordship had dismissed the militiamen at first as "crickets," they named the hill where the cannons had been mounted "Cricket Hill." In another part of Mathews, a tide mill, powered by the ebb and flow of the tide, is said to have supplied grain to George Washington's troops at the decisive siege of Yorktown.*

In the War of 1812, Mathews carpenters built gunboats for the undermanned Continental Navy. The boatbuilders worked in secluded creek beds to avoid patrols by the British, whose blockade fleet for the upper Bay was anchored just off Mathews. In the Civil War, a swashbuckling Confederate naval officer used Mathews as his base of operations, dispatching two yin-and-yang gunboats, the black-painted *Raven* and the white-painted *Swan*, to raid Union shipping in the Bay. Union troops retaliated against the Mathews "guerillas and river pirates" by fanning out through

---

* In April 1980 the tide mill and the colonial estate to which it belonged, Poplar Grove, were purchased by John Lennon through a real estate company. After Lennon was murdered in December of that year, his widow, Yoko Ono, donated the property to a boys' home.

the county to hit Mathews where it hurt: sinking more than 150 boats and skiffs. Mathews also produced the Confederacy's only female officer, Captain Sally Tompkins. She received an honorary officer's commission to allow her to operate a private hospital for wounded soldiers. During the Spanish-American War, Captain Jesse hauled coal to U.S. troops in Cuba. He so admired the U.S. Navy hero of that war, Admiral George Dewey, that he named one of his boys after him.

During World War I, mariners from Mathews had faced the first generation of U-boats, slower and less powerful than those in World War II, but lethal nonetheless. Coles Frank Hudgins, a seaman from the Mathews hamlet of Laban, was killed when the British tanker *Healdton* was torpedoed in the middle of the North Atlantic in 1917. Soon after, Captain L. P. Borum of Gwynn's Island survived the sinking of his freighter *City of Memphis* off the coast of Scotland.

Borum had been returning from Britain with no cargo when a U-boat surfaced and fired warning shots across his bow. Borum ordered the crew and passengers into lifeboats, and they abandoned ship. The submarine approached the lifeboats and the German commander asked what cargo they carried. None, Borum informed him. "Well, captain," the U-boat commander said, "I have to sink your ship, you know that." Borum did not agree, but was in no position to argue. The U-boat sank the *City of Memphis*, and Borum, his crew, and the passengers endured a frigid night in the lifeboats before a British warship spotted them. When he got back to the United States, he was given command of the freight/passenger ship *City of Savannah*. He crossed the Atlantic eighteen more times, carrying thousands of American doughboys to the battlefields of France. By 1941, Borum was fifty-eight years old and approaching the end of his seafaring career. But he was still captain of a ship, and he was still not afraid of U-boats.

In the waning months of World War I, the Germans sent three U-boats to the coast of the United States to attack merchant ships. They were too late to accomplish much, and they found few choice targets, but in the course of a few weeks they sank a cruiser and dozens of unarmed vessels, including a lightship—a floating lighthouse—off Cape Hatteras, North Carolina. Captain Robert Melville Callis of Gwynn's Island recalled sailing along the East Coast in 1918 and seeing "signs of death and destruction every place. One eight-masted schooner was turned over, her sails set and her masts sticking out . . ." It was a last-ditch attack by a defeated enemy, but it was also a warning that U-boats could easily reach U.S. shores.

The Spanish Civil War, a prelude to World War II, is not remembered for its sea engagements. But Captain Elvin "Bubba" Lewis of Mathews, a fearless, hard-drinking, chain-smoking rooster of a man, ran his oil tanker *Nantucket Chief* through a Fascist blockade in the Mediterranean to deliver fuel to besieged Loyalist forces in Barcelona. The job paid so well that Lewis tried it again, but this time he was captured and thrown into a Fascist prison. He was beaten with rubber hoses every day for weeks until the State Department negotiated his release. "My whole body is a mass of bruises," Lewis told *The New York Times*. "I am fed up with the whole business and will not go to Spain again."

In a separate effort, Mathews captain Stanley Ransome diverted his freighter *Exeter* from a cargo run to evacuate Americans who were trapped in Barcelona as Fascist forces closed in. While warplanes engaged in dogfights over his head, Ransome took aboard 162 American refugees and the *Exeter* steamed out of the war zone through a cross fire between Fascist shore batteries and Loyalist warships.

But nothing in Mathews's two hundred years of maritime conflict prepared the people of the county for the deadly confluence of events of World War II.

By late 1941, fishing in the Chesapeake Bay was in decline. Catches of blue crabs had plummeted for no apparent reason. The Bay's oysters, which once had grown in clumps big enough to pose hazards to navigation, were starting to suffer from diseases that eventually would decimate them. Shad were so scarce that fishermen who had caught them for decades no longer even bothered to set nets. Some fishermen turned to work in the shipyards in nearby Norfolk and Newport News. Those yards had plenty of work, and many of the jobs were vital to the government's shipbuilding program and thus exempted the jobholders from being drafted into the Army.

To men accustomed to working on the water, however, the most obvious place to look for work in 1941 was the Merchant Marine. Experienced sailors had always been able to find regular work, but now jobs on ships were becoming so plentiful that any man who knew a bow from a stern was hired. Men from all over the country were streaming into maritime union halls on East Coast ports. The demand for American ships and mariners kept soaring as the war engulfed Europe.

The United States, while still officially a neutral nation, was already fighting in the Battle of the Atlantic on Britain's side. For two years, shipments of American supplies on British, American, and other nations' ships had kept Britain alive. German U-boats tried to sever Britain's lifeline to the outside world by sinking any vessel hauling food, fuel, and arms to the British Isles. They sank more than a thousand British merchant ships and killed more than twenty thousand British seamen—more than Britain could replace. British prime minister Winston Churchill called on Roosevelt for more help.

In 1940, Roosevelt ordered a government agency, the U.S. Maritime Commission, to build two hundred new cargo ships, which would be owned by the government but operated by private companies at government expense. The president then quickly upped the number to three hundred, and then four hundred. He gave the Commission all the money and political muscle it needed. The Commission built or expanded more than seventy American shipyards and then flooded them with orders for ships. The yards ran around the clock and hired thousands of men and women. The only thing that ever threatened to slow them down was having to compete for steel with the U.S. Navy, which even before Pearl Harbor was building 1.3 million tons of new warships, including aircraft carriers, battleships, cruisers, destroyers, submarines, and smaller vessels for fighting submarines. Some of the new ships were already sliding down the ways of shipyards into the water. They would be part of the greatest shipbuilding campaign in history, and a key to winning World War II, but most of the new ships would not be finished in time for the first and most dangerous phase of the war.

For that phase, the U.S. government requisitioned most of the existing U.S. merchant fleet, some 1,200 merchant ships from 131 shipping companies, and chartered them on a permanent basis to haul war cargo. The government paid the companies to operate the ships as before. But the Maritime Administration, and later the War Shipping Administration, decided what cargo the ships would carry and when and where they would sail. Roosevelt considered merging the Merchant Marine into the Navy, as he had done with the Coast Guard. But the maritime unions opposed it. After fighting for years to improve mariners' dismal pay and shipboard conditions, the unions feared losing those gains and the power they had amassed by winning them. Many rank-and-file union mariners also wanted no part of the Navy, which they associated with pointless rules and spit-and-polish.

So merchant mariners went to war as independent contractors, serving their country through a combination of necessity, patriotism, and collective bargaining. In exchange for giving up their right to strike during the war, they received bonuses for sailing in war zones and hauling hazardous cargo such as ammunition and gasoline. Those bonuses could double their wages, which led to complaints from enlisted military men that the mariners were better paid.

But mariners were compensated very differently than soldiers, sailors, or airmen. They were hired from voyage to voyage, and earned money only when they were sailing. Their wages did not start until they boarded a ship, and stopped as soon as the voyage ended, even if it ended with a torpedo strike in mid-ocean. Mariners would be off the clock when swimming for their lives, fending off sharks, or shivering in lifeboats. When they safely completed a voyage, they had to sign on to another ship within thirty days or become eligible to be drafted into the Army. Their only government benefits were death benefits—a $5,000 check for their next of kin if they were lost at sea.

By December 1941, America was on a knife-edge between peace and war in the Atlantic. U-boats had already sunk eighteen American merchant ships, supposedly by mistake. Hitler at first had made excuses for those sinkings, but eventually he quit bothering. A U-boat also had sunk an American destroyer, the USS *Reuben James*, while it was shielding a convoy of merchant ships en route to Britain. Hitler had made no excuses for the sinking of the destroyer. America seemed certain to enter the war, and the moment she did, any merchant ship flying the American flag would become a prime target.

Those ships—the Mathews men's ships—were mostly freighters and tankers built for the last war. Most of the companies that owned them had been founded between 1900 and 1920 by entrepreneurs, many based in New York, who shifted their vessels' routes from ocean to ocean as they won or lost cutthroat competitions for cargo with their rivals. The A. H. Bull & Co. shipping line, commonly known as the Bull Line, had been started in 1902 by Archibald H. Bull, a character out of a Horatio Alger rags-to-riches story. Sixteen-year-old Archibald had begged a job as a clerk at a New York shipping firm after his father fell to a Confederate bullet at the battle of Fredericksburg, and had hustled his way to ownership of a fleet. One of the largest U.S. shipping companies, Moore-McCormack Lines, bore the names of two founding partners who had gambled everything they owned to open a cargo and passenger service to South America. The shipping companies were generous but demanding bosses. As far as they were concerned, no captain ever delivered his cargo quite quickly enough or deserved time off.

By the 1940s, some of the World War I–vintage cargo ships had deteriorated into rust buckets. Even those in the best shape were past their prime. None of them were built to outrun U-boats, or to stand up against attacks. If a torpedo blew a hole in the hull, no watertight bulkheads would slow the in-rushing sea. The old ships would sink fast.

The old seafaring families of Mathews recognized the danger building. In a sermon at Gwynn's Island Baptist Church in November 1941, the Reverend Iris Belch observed, "The prospect of war is being felt more keenly as our own boys and men go into the danger zone in their ships." The only real surprise was that the event that finally drew America into the war took place in the Pacific.

Mathews was preoccupied when war finally came. One week before Pearl Harbor, fire gutted an entire block of the Main Street business district, destroying a grocery store, a hardware store, and one of the pool halls. Black ash rained down on homes a mile away. The Mathews fire truck refused to start, so the flames spread unchecked until pumper trucks arrived from the neighboring towns of West Point and Urbanna. Firefighters prevented even worse damage by extending a hose to nearby Put-in Creek to draw water. By the next day, the failure of the Mathews fire truck was turning into a political scandal. Most citizens of Mathews were too caught up in the scandal and the growing tension in the Atlantic to pay much attention to Japan. The only harm the Japanese had ever done to Mathews was occasionally driving down the price of blue crabs by flooding the market with cheap Alaskan king crab meat.

For more than a year, however, Japanese soldiers had been rampaging through parts of Southeast Asia, seizing coastal regions of China, killing and raping thousands. Japan had allied itself with Nazi Germany. Japanese leaders spewed anti-Allied propaganda. In July 1941, after Japanese troops occupied former French territories in Indochina, America froze Japanese assets in the United States. A few weeks later, the United States halted the sale of oil and aviation fuel to Japan. The furious Japanese began negotiating to try to reverse those steps, while planning a devastating surprise attack. On the morning of December 7, more than 330 Japanese bombers took off from aircraft carriers in the Pacific Ocean and devastated the U.S.

fleet at the Pearl Harbor naval base in Hawaii. The bombers sank or severely damaged 14 American warships, including 4 battleships, and killed 2,490 people. Fortunately for the United States, all of its aircraft carriers happened to be at sea on that day, beyond the bombers' reach.

News of the attack came to Mathews over the radio as people returned home from Sunday church services in a cold drizzle. Some of the churches reopened for prayer. The next morning, a small group of veterans delivered patriotic speeches at the courthouse square. President Roosevelt called December 7 "a date which will live in infamy" in a speech that did not mention Germany. The *Gazette-Journal* printed a list of men from Mathews who were stationed with the Navy in the Pacific. They included Bill Callis's big brother, Homer Verdayne Callis Jr., who was a quartermaster on the destroyer USS *Hazelwood*. Luckily, the *Hazelwood* had not been at Pearl Harbor.

Hitler did not need to rush into war with America after Pearl Harbor, but he did anyway, declaring war against the United States on December 11. He lifted all restrictions on U-boats' attacking American merchant ships. Given what had happened at the end of World War I, it seemed certain that U-boats would return to the U.S. coast. The Navy asked citizens living along the ocean and the Bay to help watch for them.

No one answered the Navy's call with more dedication than twelve-year-old John Dixon of Gwynn's Island. John's big brother, Boyd, was aboard a merchant ship. John did not know him well because Boyd was mostly at sea. But John wanted to help. Some of his buddies had brothers or fathers at sea. The boys established an observation post at Cherry Point, on the northern tip of Gwynn's Island. Every day after school they hurried to take up the watch. They leaped to their feet, breathless, at every passing chunk of driftwood or trick of the light on the water. They stayed until it was too dark to see, and came back the next day. They were inspired and terrified. Nothing stirred their seafarers' blood like the specter of a U-boat, the embodiment of stealthy death.

CHAPTER TWO

The Devil's Shovel

The first wave of U-boats crossing the Atlantic to America in January 1942 collided with a winter hurricane. Thirty-foot seas struck the steel hulls with audible clangs and swept over the U-boats' exposed conning towers. Men standing lookout on the towers ducked and held on for their lives, tethered to the rail by safety harnesses, their dirty hair and beards rimed with freezing salt water.

Breaking waves "swept away the few things they could seize on," wrote Peter Cremer, the commander of the U-333, which started out with the five U-boats that made up the attack force against the United States, but later split from them. Cremer's submarine "climbed the waves, broke through the crests, hung for a moment with its stern in the air, and plunged down the other side into the trough of the wave. When it buried its nose, the screws (propellers) in its stern seemed to be revolving in the air. The stern dropped down, the screws disappeared into the maelstrom and the exhaust broke off with a gurgle." The lookouts caught only glimpses of the horizon between buckshot bursts of spray.

Diving was an option, of course, but traveling submerged would reduce a U-boat's maximum speed from 17 knots to a plodding 7—from

18.5 mph to 8 mph—and prolong the voyage from two weeks to three or longer. The distances from the U-boats' bases on the coast of occupied France were 3,000 miles to New York and 3,500 miles to the mouth of the Chesapeake Bay.

So the U-boats stayed on the surface and absorbed the pounding until a freak wave engulfed one of the conning towers and wrenched loose an antiaircraft gun from its mounting. The gun spun into one of the lookouts and seriously injured him.* Reluctantly, Cremer and the other U-boat commanders gave the orders to submerge, and the submarines crawled underwater toward the United States, at a rate of about 25 to 30 miles per day.

Weather was the least of the challenges in the U-boats' first mission to America. So far from home, they had nowhere to turn for additional fuel or food, and could expect no help with medical or mechanical emergencies. Even the long-range, Type IXC U-boats carried only enough fuel to operate in U.S. waters for about two weeks between their long transatlantic voyages. Each sub could carry only fourteen to eighteen torpedoes, and circumstances often required a U-boat to fire several torpedoes in a fan-shaped pattern to be sure of sinking a single ship. Some of the torpedoes were virtually guaranteed to malfunction, either veering off course, exploding prematurely, or failing to detonate at all.

The commanders had no idea what antisubmarine defenses awaited them in American waters. They did not even possess detailed maps that showed the topography of the American coastline or the depths of the waters in which they would need to hide. The commander of the U-123, Reinhard Hardegan, carried a tourist guide to the 1939 World's Fair in New York, with a map of the New York coastline on one side and an image of the Statue of Liberty on the other.

---

* Standing lookout on a U-boat in rough seas was dangerous work. More than a dozen lookouts were swept overboard in storms during the war, including an entire four-man watch. But whenever a U-boat was on the surface, its commander had no choice but to post lookouts to watch for enemy planes and ships.

The whole mission to America was so fraught with risks and unknowns that it made sense only if the potential rewards were enormous. Admiral Karl Doenitz, the head of the German U-boat command, believed they were, and Doenitz usually got such calculations right.

At age fifty, Doenitz was a master of twentieth-century submarine warfare. He had served twenty-nine years in the German Navy, including time in the U-boat service during World War I. He had been commanding a U-boat in 1917 when its diving system malfunctioned. "[We] suddenly found ourselves submerged and standing on our heads," he recalled. "The batteries spilled over, the lights went out, and in darkness we plunged on into the depths." Doenitz ordered the water blown out of the ballast tanks, and the sub rocketed to the surface, where it bobbed helplessly in the middle of an Allied convoy. Doenitz was sent to a British prison camp, where he feigned insanity—"playing childish games with biscuit tins and little china dogs that could be bought in the canteen"—until he was transferred to an asylum, where he enjoyed softer treatment than his less devious boatmates.

At the beginning of World War I, U-boats such as the one commanded by Doenitz had come close to severing Britain's supply lines. The British had managed to neutralize the U-boats with convoys, a tactic dating back to Julius Caesar's time, in which groups of merchant ships sailed together under the protection of armed escorts.* At the end of the Great War, Winston Churchill had declared, "The submarine has been mastered," a boast he would regret making.

The Treaty of Versailles, which ended World War I, required Germany to abandon its U-boat program. More than 150 U-boats that survived the

---

* The U-boats' effectiveness in the early stages of World War I captured the public's attention. Sir Arthur Conan Doyle, the British creator of Sherlock Holmes, wrote a short story in which a small nation used submarines to starve Britain into defeat. The American humorist Will Rogers joked that the best way to hunt down the U-boats was to drain the Atlantic Ocean. "How?" he continued. "That is a detail. I am not a detail man."

Great War were destroyed, dismantled, or towed to Allied nations to be displayed like trophies at victory rallies. But Germany, bitter over the terms of the treaty, had no intention of abandoning submarine warfare and soon set out to rearm itself for the next war. In the 1920s, the German government secretly bought a Dutch company that designed and built submarines for other nations. In violation of the treaty, Germany operated the company as a cover to develop faster and more powerful U-boats. That new generation of U-boats would lead the assault across the Atlantic.

Doenitz was slender and pale, with birdlike features, but he projected authority with a rigid bearing and an incisive mind. Later, prosecutors at the Nuremberg trials said he had an IQ of 138, just short of "genius or near genius." Doenitz was given the task of running the U-boat force. He used his personal experience to teach his commanders how to take advantage of light and sea state to approach ships unseen, and how to outwait and outsmart pursuers. He cultivated personal relationships with his men in order to motivate them. He recruited pretty nurses to welcome them home at the docks with garlands of flowers, and treated them to dinners of lobster and champagne. When a child was born to a U-boat man at sea, Doenitz personally radioed the news to the new father in a code that referred to a newborn boy as an "arrival with a periscope" and a girl as "an arrival with no periscope." Doenitz promoted the U-boat force to the German public as the nation's elite warriors. One of his U-boat aces, Gunther Prien, enjoyed such rock-star status in Germany that after his submarine was lost, Germans for years reported sightings of Prien, the way Americans years later would report sightings of the long-departed Elvis Presley.

On a tactical level, Doenitz was a master improviser. He constantly shifted his subs and his tactics to capitalize on his U-boats' lethal capabilities and hide their glaring weaknesses.

U-boats were not submarines in the modern sense. They were not equipped to remain underwater for long periods without surfacing. Rather, they were diving vessels. They functioned far better on the surface, but could submerge for short periods to get into position to attack, elude pursuers, or escape rough weather. On the surface, they could outrun most merchant ships and some warships, but not destroyers and certainly not planes. When submerged, they were slow and nearly blind, but they could strike without warning and then withdraw without ever showing themselves, leaving their victims unsure whether they had been attacked or had struck a mine.

A U-boat was a cigar-shaped cylinder of high-tensile steel plates welded together. It had a raked bow, inclined at an angle to the water line and blunted at the tip. The standard Type VII C U-boat, the workhorse of the German submarine fleet, was 220 feet long and highly agile and maneuverable. The larger, long-range Type IXC was 250 feet long and more sluggish, but also more stable in heavy seas and capable of carrying more fuel and torpedoes. Doenitz much preferred the smaller subs.

U-boat hulls were designed to withstand depths of 500 feet, where the water pressure was roughly 16 tons per square foot, but U-boats dove deeper when desperate to avoid attack. On at least one occasion, a U-boat survived a dive to 850 feet. The U-boat hull's structural integrity was compromised by the hatches, air intakes, and exhaust vents necessary to sustain life inside. When a U-boat went deep, the water pressure on those weak points sent eerie creaks and groans echoing through the boat.

When on the surface, a U-boat ran on two thundering, 1,160-horsepower diesel engines located near the stern. The diesels gulped air from outside through an induction pipe high on the conning tower, and drew fuel from saddle tanks outside the hull. When the U-boat submerged, the diesels were shut down and the sub switched over to a pair of battery-powered 375-horsepower motor/generators. The batteries ran out of juice quickly when the sub had to maneuver or run at full speed underwater. Every day, the submarine had to surface and crank up its diesels to recharge the batteries. A full charge took more than two hours. No daily activity was more vital than charging the batteries, without which the sub could not keep its crew alive while submerged.

A typical U-boat commander spent his days in the *Zentrale*, or control room, just forward of the engine room. He peered up at the surface world through angled mirrors in the U-boat's two periscopes, which were mounted on a long metal shaft. He sat in a harness straddling the base of the shaft, and could spin the periscopes 360 degrees. He navigated while looking through the larger periscope but attacked while looking through the smaller one, which left almost no telltale wake on the surface. If a commander felt safe in a stretch of ocean, he might order the sub to surface so that he could look around and enjoy the sweet taste of fresh air.

When the U-boat was surfaced, as many as six lookouts peered through high-powered Zeiss binoculars at their assigned quadrants of the sky and sea. Men with the keenest eyesight were chosen to stand watch at dusk and dawn, when the light played tricks. Every seagull looked like a plane at first glance. A moment's delay in spotting an approaching ship or plane could doom them all. A crash dive, or emergency dive, took twenty-five to thirty seconds. U-boats crash-dived at any hint of trouble. The U-boat commander's manual advocated erring on the side of caution: "It is better to dive too soon, than too late—and [thus] to lose forever the chance to dive."

The U-boat's signature weapon was the torpedo, which resembled a miniature U-boat. Torpedoes were 23.5 feet long and 21 inches in diameter, with fins and a propeller at the tail. They were launched from horizontal tubes with blasts of compressed air, and traveled at speeds of 45 to 50 miles per hour. Torpedoes were named for the electric ray fish, genus *Torpedo*, which delivers a paralyzing shock to its prey, but U-boat crews called them "eels." Commanders were taught to fire them from a distance of 600 yards, calculating the target's speed and bearing and firing at a point in front of it, as a duck hunter fires ahead of a duck in flight. The first torpedoes were designed to explode on contact with a target, but they sometimes failed to detonate unless they hit straight on. The Germans developed magnetic torpedoes that exploded when they entered the magnetic field surrounding a ship's hull, sending shock waves through the water to "break the ship's back." Magnetic torpedoes proved unreliable, too, however, and the British learned to counter them by wrapping electrical cables around ships' hulls to neutralize their magnetic fields, a process known as degaussing.

Toward the end of the war, the Germans would introduce acoustic torpedoes, which honed in on the sound of a ship's propellers. The British would counter them with noisemakers called Foxers, which generated more noise than the propellers and could be towed behind ships to draw acoustic torpedoes harmlessly astern. The continuous chess game in which the Germans developed new kinds of torpedoes and the British found ways to neutralize them typified the technological side of the U-boat war. Each engineering breakthrough gave one side an edge for only as long as it took the other side to counter it. "Strange how little time one side or the other can hold the upper hand thanks to a new weapon," observed the fictitious U-boat commander in Lothar-Günther Buchheim's classic World War II novel, *Das Boot*. "Nothing stimulates the brain cells like a desire to wipe out the other side."

As deadly as torpedoes were, they were undependable and hard to aim. The most successful U-boat of the war, U-48, launched 126 torpedoes and scored only 55 hits. U-boat commanders tried to conserve torpedoes by sinking merchant ships whenever possible with their deck cannons, fearsome-looking 88mm guns mounted on the sub's main deck, forward of the conning tower. The deck cannons could be used only when the U-boat was on the surface and the sea was calm enough for gun crews to venture out onto the narrow deck to man them and aim them. Each U-boat was also armed with an antiaircraft gun on the conning tower, two hand-held machine guns, and various small arms.

U-boats were equipped with defenses designed to thwart antisubmarine weapons, the most formidable of which was the Allies' sonar. Sonar (an acronym for SOund Navigation And Ranging) beamed sound waves through the water that bounced off any solid surfaces and sent back echoes. The speed of an echo's return revealed an object's distance from the ship, and the angle of its return revealed the object's bearing, or direction. Significantly, sonar could not determine an object's depth. All kinds of submerged objects besides U-boats returned sonar echoes, including schools of fish and thermal layers between warm and cold water. An experienced sonar operator could tell the echoes apart.

U-boats were equipped with passive sonar. It did not broadcast a sonar pulse—which could be traced back to the sub—but it gave warning when the U-boat was being detected by another vessel's sonar. The warning came in the form of a metallic "ping" that tolled ominously through the U-boat like a phone call in the depths of the night. If the ping was loud, the hunter was close to its prey, and the next sound in the ears of the U-boat's sonar operator might be the churning of a destroyer's propellers and the splash of depth charges into the ocean overhead.

Depth charges, invented by the British in World War I, haunted submariners' dreams. They were metal canisters about 18 inches in diameter and twice as long. Each contained about 300 to 500 pounds of explosives and could be set to blow up at a specific depth, such as 50, 100, 150, or even 500 feet. Sailors on destroyers called them ash cans. They could be rolled off racks on the stern or fired to either side. Destroyers dropped them in patterns to bracket a sonar target. The cans sank in silence at a rate of 8 to 12 feet per second until they reached their preset depth and then detonated, hurling plumes of water into the air and shock waves through the water. A depth charge exploding within 25 feet of a U-boat would cripple it, and a blast within 14 feet would crack its hull and send it to the bottom, usually with all hands.

Sonar's inability to detect an object's depth posed problems for U-boat hunters. They could only guess at how deep to set their depth charges to explode. In addition, a ship could not drop depth charges while performing delicate maneuvers; it had to drop them while racing full speed, in order to get beyond the range of the explosions. Depth-charge blasts also jumbled the water and "blinded" the sonar long enough to give the U-boat a chance to escape. A U-boat might also throw off its pursuers by activating its *Pillenwurfer*, or "bubble-thrower," which released a jet of sodium hydride that reacted with seawater to create a large chemical bubble with a sonar signature similar to a U-boat's.

If the U-boat did not escape, the pinging would start again. The cat-and-mouse game could last for hours. The air inside the pressurized hull would grow progressively thinner. Every underwater maneuver would further deplete the U-boat's batteries, which could only be recharged on the surface. Former U-boat commander Herbert A. Werner described one such experience:

> A series of 24 [depth] charges detonated in quick succession. The bellowing roar slammed against our boat. The explosions again pushed her into a sharp down tilt while the echo of the detonations rolled endlessly through the depths . . . A new spread [of depth charges] deafened us and took our breath away. The boat listed sharply . . . The steel knocked and shrieked and valves were thrown into the open position. The shaft packings leaked, and a constant stream of water soon filled the aft bilges. Pumps spouted, the periscope packings leaked, and water trickled into the cylinders, water everywhere. Its weight forced the boat deeper into the depths. In the meantime the convoy crawled in a thunderous procession over our boat.

The strain was too great for some submariners, who became hysterical during depth-charge attacks. Their boat-mates said they suffered from *Blechkiller*, or tin-can neurosis—a condition similar to the breakdowns that men on the waters above them suffered while sailing under the constant threat of a torpedo attack.

The Allies' sonar could not detect U-boats on the surface, but radar could. Radar, or RAdio Detecting And Ranging, operates on the same principle as sonar, beaming radio waves through the air—rather than the water—in search of solid objects. Radar could see through darkness and storms and spot a U-boat on the surface from a distance of seven miles. The Germans did not realize how effective radar was until after numerous U-boats had been ambushed by planes and ships.

American submarines were superior to U-boats in the critical capability of detecting and jamming enemy radar, and in other ways as well. The *Gato*-class American subs, which did most of the fighting in World War II, were faster and larger than U-boats and could carry more fuel and torpedoes. U.S. subs were also vastly more comfortable, with roomier living quarters and even air-conditioning. U-boats, on the other hand, were more nimble, especially when under attack. They could crash-dive faster, dive deeper, and run more quietly while submerged. They required fewer crewmen—fifty-five rather than the American subs' seventy to eighty-five. And the Germans' torpedoes, for all their persistent problems, were more reliable than American torpedoes.

U-boat crews had orders to prevent their vessels from being captured at all costs. If a U-boat was forced to the surface, the crew was trained to rig it with explosive charges and open valves to flood it. Then they were to fight off the enemy with small arms until the U-boat plunged into the depths, out of the reach of enemy salvage divers. Every measure designed to prevent the U-boat's capture also reduced the U-boat's crew's chances of surviving.

The crew comprised approximately fifty officers and men. Most of them had come up through the ranks of Nazi youth programs, which since the early 1920s had provided young Germans with physical training and psychological indoctrination. An angry Germany had been preparing for World War II while its victorious foes licked their wounds from World War I. But Germany's navy lagged behind its army and air force, which attracted most of Hitler's attention as well as German money and resources. Doenitz had hoped to start World War II with three hundred active U-boats, but ended up with only forty-four. As he slowly added U-boats to his fleet, he made the most of the relative few he had. Doenitz tried to confuse the Allies by giving U-boats numbers much larger than the number of U-boats he had. The U-506 and U-507, for example, would be operating in American waters long before Doenitz had five hundred U-boats.

The men of the German U-boat force ranged from hard-core believers in the Nazi philosophy to men who doubted Hitler's leadership but who resolved nonetheless to fight for their country. "Very few U-boat captains cared about all those dogmas of the Third Reich," U-boat commander Hans Georg Hess asserted. Another U-boat commander disparaged the Nazi leadership to his crew while at sea, only to be denounced by a subordinate upon his return, and then convicted of treason and executed by a firing squad.

The narrow confines of a U-boat offered no room for privacy, reflection, or even hygiene. Men slept in shifts, tuning out the pounding of the diesel engines and the hiss of the sea sliding past the hull. They never saw the sky or breathed fresh air except on lookout duty. They did not bathe or shave because freshwater was too precious; each man was allotted just enough of it to brush his teeth once a day. Crewmen wore black underwear to hide their filth, and used scented soap to mask their stink. A week or so into the voyage, the heat and humidity inside the hull broke down the fresh food. Fluffy white mold engulfed loaves of bread, and mildew coated sausages and fruit. The cook would scrape off the unwelcome layers and serve the food until no one could bear it. The air inside the hull was a miasma of spoiling food, unwashed bodies, diesel fumes, and overburdened toilets.

U-boat toilets were particularly despised. They did not work when the sub ran deep because the outside water pressure kept them from flushing. They could not be used when the sub was under attack, because the enemy might hear them flush. When the toilets did work, they demanded a precise operating sequence. The waste had to be transferred from the bowl to an intermediate chamber, then to an outer chamber, and then into the sea. Any deviation from that sequence could back up the toilet into the sub in a foul gush of waste and seawater. If the seawater reached the U-boat's batteries, it could react with battery acid to form poisonous chlorine gas.

At least one U-boat was sunk by just such a toilet malfunction. Forced to the surface to ventilate the poisonous chlorine, it was bombed by a British plane.

Few of the U-boat's operational systems tolerated error. If the engine crew failed to shut off the diesels before closing the main hatch in a dive, the exhaust system would suck all the oxygen from the hull. A malfunctioning fan could allow hydrogen to build up to explosive levels in the hull. Maintaining the U-boat's trim—the horizontal balance between its bow and stern—required constant readjustments for even small shifts in weight, such as a torpedo launch. The U-boat's operating systems were so interconnected that a mistake by anyone could kill everyone. Doenitz liked to call a U-boat crew a *Schickselgemeinschaft*—a community bound by fate. U-boat crews had a variety of descriptive names for their vessel, but the most unflattering—and also the most sinister—was "the devil's shovel."*

The main battleground in the Battle of the Atlantic was the North Atlantic convoy routes, a 2,400-mile wilderness of frigid, stormy ocean between Maritime Canada and the British Isles, where the water depth was measured not in feet but in miles. Mariners tried to avoid those waters even in peacetime. The North Atlantic run was known for gales that lasted for entire voyages, mountainous waves, shrieking winds, cold, snow, and ice. U-boats could attack at any point during the voyage, but the most dangerous segment was the "air gap," a 600-mile stretch of sea south of Greenland that was too far from either shore for Allied planes to reach. U-boats could operate freely in the air gap without fear of attack from above.

The convoys, organized by the British Admiralty and the Royal Cana-

---

* An American seaman from Texas named Archie Gibbs got a close look at life aboard a U-boat when he was taken prisoner aboard one for four days after his ship was torpedoed in the summer of 1942. Gibbs said the Germans acted like men who "knew they had a dirty job to do and wanted to get it over with and go home."

dian Navy, departed every eight days from either Halifax in Nova Scotia or Argentia in Newfoundland. A large convoy contained as many as sixty merchant ships loaded with food, arms, fuel, and supplies for Britain. The night before departure, the commodore in charge of the convoy, usually a retired British naval officer, called all the merchant captains and radio operators to a meeting on shore. He explained the convoy's structure, planned course, and precautions for avoiding U-boats. Those precautions always included a total blackout of the ships, as well as periodic zigzagging or changes of course to avoid torpedoes.

The next morning, the ships left the safety of the harbor and took their assigned positions in the convoy, which formed into a rectangle perhaps 6 miles wide and 2 miles deep. Convoys were designed to be much more wide than deep, with as few ships as possible following in a row, because a ship presented its biggest target from the side, and a long line of vessels presented a target few U-boats could miss. Inside the convoy, ships were to maintain distances of 600 feet from the vessels in front of and behind them, and distances of 1,000 yards between ships in the adjacent columns. Freighters full of ammunition and tankers full of oil or gasoline were assigned to the convoy's interior columns for added protection. Ships with less volatile cargo sailed closer to the edges. The exposed positions at the four corners of the convoy's rectangle were called the "coffin corners."

Once a convoy got under way, it was screened by a half dozen or more Allied destroyers, Coast Guard cutters, and smaller escort vessels such as corvettes, all of them equipped with sonar, depth charges, and deck guns. Each escort vessel guarded an assigned segment of the convoy's perimeter. Sometimes, larger Allied warships such as cruisers and even battleships formed an outer ring of protection against German surface warships and planes.

A convoy's best defense, however, was the vastness of the ocean. Even the largest convoys were just dots on the North Atlantic. The U-boats first had to find them, and then find a way past the escorts. Doenitz's answer was the *Rudeltaktik*, or wolf pack strategy. A wolf pack, consisting of eight to fifteen U-boats, spread out like a net across the North Atlantic convoy routes, with gaps of twenty miles between subs. Each U-boat stayed on the surface, weather permitting, watching for the telltale smoke or masts of an approaching convoy. When a U-boat found a convoy, the commander radioed its location to Doenitz, who directed a wolf pack to converge on it. The pack waited until dark and then struck as a unit to confuse and overwhelm the escorts. U-boats often attacked on the surface, darting through gaps in the escort screen into the heart of the convoy and rapid-firing torpedoes in all directions to hit as many ships as fast as possible. A wolf pack could strike a convoy repeatedly over the course of a single night, and then attack every night afterward until the convoy reached port. One wolf pack tore into two convoys heading in opposite directions through a remote stretch of ocean and sank a total of thirty-two ships.

Merchant seamen could only go about their duties and pray they would not be the next target. If their ship went down and they ended up in the water, the other ships in the convoy would not stop for them. Their only hope was that the single rescue vessel assigned to the convoy could reach them in the few minutes they could expect to stay alive in the icy water.

Behind the scenes, the Battle of the Atlantic turned back and forth on clandestine electronic surveillance and code breaking. Almost since the start of the war, the British had been able to pinpoint the locations of U-boats at sea by intercepting their daily radio transmissions. Doenitz required each U-boat to check in with headquarters every day by radio. Those radio transmissions were picked up by a British network of direction-finding stations scattered all along the Atlantic coast. Once two stations picked up the same U-boat's transmission, they could use the cross-bearings to pinpoint the sub's location. The British used the information to route convoys away from U-boats. Doenitz did not think the radio transmissions posed any risk unless the Allies broke the German Enigma code and could read the coded messages—something he thought could never happen. He and the rest of the German high command considered Enigma unbreakable.

The code relied on Enigma machines, which resembled complicated typewriters, to encrypt messages in a way that only other Enigma machines, set identically, could decrypt. The German Navy used an extra layer of encryption in its variation of the Enigma code, which made the naval Enigma code even more difficult to break. Each U-boat carried an Enigma machine, and Doenitz confidently sent all his orders to his U-boats through Enigma. British cryptologists broke the code in early 1941 after a captured U-boat yielded up an Enigma machine and codebook. By May, the British could read the Germans' most secret communications. That capability was so precious that the British used it sparingly to avoid giving the Germans any reason to suspect the code had been compromised. Unfortunately for the Allies, the Germans would soon seize the advantage in the code-breaking war.

Germany's conquest of France in 1940 had extended the U-boats' reach. Until France fell, U-boats had operated out of bases in Germany and occupied Norway. They had had to dodge British patrols in the North Sea just to reach the ocean. The coast of France, however, offered U-boats direct access to the North Atlantic. The Germans built U-boat bases in French fishing villages along the Bay of Biscay, including Lorient and Saint-Nazaire. The German construction firm, the Todt Organisation—the builder of the Autobahn— built three-foot-thick, steel-reinforced concrete bunkers to protect the U-boats from Allied bombs. Doenitz appropriated the waterfront estate of a sardine tycoon in Lorient and set up an operations center nearby. The walls of the center were papered with maps pinpointing the locations of all U-boats and all known or suspected convoys, as well as weather reports, tide charts, and up-to-date statistical breakdowns of U-boat kills and, especially, tonnage.

A ship's tonnage is the volume, in cubic meters, of all its enclosed spaces—its cargo capacity. Tonnage was the best measurement of a merchant ship's size and value. Doenitz called the U-boat campaign a tonnage war, or *Tonnageschlacht.* He maintained that if U-boats could sink 700,000 tons of Allied shipping per month, Germany would win the Battle of the Atlantic.

The U-boats had yet to hit Doenitz's target, but between 1939 and 1941, they had sunk more than 1,100 Allied merchant ships and killed 9,200 men. They had also sunk several British warships, including a battleship. The U-boat force had lost 50 submarines and about 2,200 men. It had come close several times to choking off Britain's lifeline.

The fall of France also set the U-boats on a collision course with the United States. Throughout the first two years of the war, most Americans had favored leaving the fight to the Europeans. Memories of American dough-boys dying by the thousands in World War I were still vivid, and all those deaths had purchased only twenty years of peace for Europe. Roosevelt had won a third term as president in 1940 by promising to keep America out of the war. But the newsreel images of German armored divisions rumbling down Paris's fair boulevards and Hitler posing in front of the Eiffel Tower raised questions about how much of the world the Führer might actually be able to conquer.

The isolationist spirit in America faded with the fall of France. Congress quickly supported Roosevelt's proposals for billions of dollars' worth of new warships and cargo ships. In March 1941, Roosevelt signed the Lend-Lease Act, which committed the United States to lending Britain and China millions of tons of supplies and weaponry—"all possible aid short of war." Roosevelt downplayed the significance of the Lend-Lease Act with the famous analogy that America was simply lending a garden hose to a neighbor whose house was on fire. He never really imagined America would get the fire hose back.

In August 1941, Roosevelt met with Churchill in Newfoundland and agreed that in case of war with Germany and Japan, they would focus on beating Germany first. Roosevelt and Churchill also signed the Atlantic Charter, agreeing to defend "freedom of the seas"—a euphemism for

America's freedom to haul war supplies across the ocean without attacks by U-boats. The following month, the U.S. Navy assumed responsibility for escorting North Atlantic convoys halfway across the ocean to a point south of Iceland—the so-called mid-ocean meeting point—where British warships met the convoys and escorted them the rest of the way to the British Isles. The U.S. Navy's expanded role led to increasingly deadly encounters between U-boats and "neutral" U.S. warships on the North Atlantic convoy routes.

Hitler had ordered his U-boats not to attack American warships and cargo ships despite the obvious aid they were providing Britain. Hitler was in no hurry to add America to his growing list of enemies so soon after invading his old ally Russia in May. But events overtook his uncharacteristic caution.

In the first week of September 1941, the World War I–vintage American destroyer *Greer* encountered a submerged U-boat en route to Iceland and tracked it with sonar. The U-boat commander, thinking he was under attack, fired two torpedoes at the *Greer* but missed. The *Greer* responded with a barrage of depth charges. The U-boat sustained minor damage but escaped.

In October, a U-boat mistook the U.S. destroyer *Kearney* for a British warship in the confusion of a nighttime wolf pack attack on a convoy south of Iceland, and torpedoed the *Kearney*, killing eleven American sailors and injuring twenty-four—the first American military casualties of the Atlantic war. The damaged *Kearney* limped into port in Iceland. Over the course of the next two weeks, the Germans sank two American merchant ships and damaged the U.S. Navy oiler *Salinas*—all with no loss of life.

But the crew of the old U.S. destroyer *Reuben James* would not be so fortunate. On October 31, the *Reuben James* was escorting a convoy near the mid-ocean meeting point when a torpedo from the U-552 smashed into its hull. The blast ignited the destroyer's magazine and blew the ship apart. Of the *Reuben James*'s 159 crew members, 115 were killed, some of them by the destroyer's depth charges, which exploded in the water beneath them as the *Reuben James* plunged into the depths. "Whether the country knows it or not, we are at war," the U.S. chief of naval operations, Admiral Harold R. Stark, told a fellow admiral.

Folksinger Woody Guthrie wrote a ballad titled "The Sinking of the *Reuben James*," with the chorus:

> *Tell me what were their names*
> *Tell me what were their names*
> *Did you have a friend*
> *On the good* Reuben James?

Five weeks later, the Japanese attacked Pearl Harbor. Hitler was as surprised as the Americans, but he seized his chance. Within four days, Germany and America were at war. The two nations' armies would not meet on the battlefield for almost a year—after the Allied invasion of North Africa—but the U-boats could carry the fight to America immediately.

Doenitz proposed sending fifteen of his ninety-one operational U-boats immediately into U.S. waters. But his superiors had other ideas. Hitler insisted on dispatching a large force of U-boats to Norway, wrongly expecting a British invasion there. Doenitz's immediate boss, Grand Admiral Erich Raeder, the head of the German Navy, ordered twenty-five U-boats into the eastern Mediterranean to support Germany's Afrika Corps against the British in North Africa. Still more U-boats were assigned to operate as weather spotters for German bombing raids on Britain. Doenitz privately stewed. His U-boats were wasted on such support missions. They were purely ship-sinking machines, and they were at their best against weak and inexperienced defenses, as America's were certain to be. But after satisfying all his superiors' demands, Doenitz was left with only six U-boats to send to the United States, and one of those broke down at the last minute.

Still, Doenitz believed that five U-boats could cause enough havoc to shock America and persuade Hitler to send more. He felt so confident that he code-named the mission to America *Paukenschlag*, which translated to a "roll of the kettledrums"—melodrama in the extreme.

During Christmas week, 1941, Doenitz called the five U-boat commanders he had chosen for *Paukenschlag* into his office for one-on-one conferences. The commanders were not his aces; two of the five had never led U-boats into combat. He assigned each commander a patrol area between New England and Cape Hatteras, North Carolina. Commander Hardegan took the U-123 out before Christmas and celebrated the holiday at sea. He wrote in his war diary:

> U-boat Christmas in the Bay of Biscay. Trees were placed in all compartments, decorated by the crew and provided with electric candles. Later the real trees were in some cases replaced by artificial trees. After a collective ceremony and subsequent meal, the letters, packets and goody bags were distributed. It was celebrated in the individual compartments and one could hear the old Christmas songs performed by the crew. The war was forgotten for a few hours by this simple but impressive Christmas festival.

Yuletide sentiments notwithstanding, Doenitz told the commanders to get into position off the U.S. coast and wait for his signal. He wanted all five to strike in unison at different points along the coast for maximum effect. The Americans would think their waters teemed with U-boats. Just after midnight on January 1, 1942, Doenitz broadcast a coded message to his crews: "Men of the U-boat Service: In the year anew we want to be like steel, harder, fiercer, stronger. Long live the Führer."

The winter hurricane that struck the first wave of U-boats en route to America kept them submerged for two days. The weather finally abated on January 10, and the subs resurfaced and resumed their voyage at top speed. The British direction-finding stations pinpointed their locations from their radio transmissions and decoded enough of their messages to determine where the subs were going. The British warned the U.S. Navy that five U-boats would be in American waters by January 13.

That was, in fact, the day Doenitz had chosen for the coordinated attack. The day before, however, Hardegan in the U-123 spotted the British freighter *Cyclops* steaming unprotected off Cape Cod, and could not resist torpedoing her. The *Cyclops* carried a crew of 30 and 151 British merchant mariners riding as passengers to meet their new ships. Ninety-eight of those men died, most from exposure in lifeboats on the wintry sea. Their shipmates survived by stacking the corpses of the dead to shield their own bodies from icy rain and spray.

Hardegan sank his second ship on the morning of January 14, torpedoing a Panamanian oil tanker 60 miles off Montauk Point on Long Island, New York. "I think the Americans are going to be very surprised to see us," he told his crew. The U-123 intercepted the tanker's radio distress call. The radioman said the ship was sinking after being struck by a torpedo or possibly a mine. "They're saying a mine?" Hardegan cried. "What assholes."

In the predawn hours of the following morning, the U-123 reached the shallow waters off Long Island. Hardegan, who had visited New York before the war, recognized the Ferris wheel at the Coney Island amusement park and the glow of New York City against the low clouds farther west. The U-123 cruised along the surface among fishing boats and harbor tugs, whose crews did not recognize the enemy in their midst. Every vessel in the harbor was burning its lights as if America were still at peace. Merchant captains talked freely over the radio about their ships' locations and the routes they planned to follow. Hardegan shook his head at their cluelessness.

He was about to bring the U-boat war home to Mathews County.

CHAPTER THREE

Missing

Henny Hodges was "a crier," all her children agreed. Four or five times a day, while she was cooking or working the family farm, her green eyes would glisten behind her Coke-bottle glasses and tears would slide down her cheeks. She cried softly, but eventually her broad shoulders shook and gave her away. "Mama, what's the matter?" the children would ask. Henny would cite a recent trivial event, such as an argument among her daughters, who argued all the time. But just as often, she cried without any provocation, and deflected questions with a shake of her head. Then she threw herself back into her chores until the feeling passed. Her children regarded her crying as just part of her makeup, like her big bones and her coarse brown hair. What the tears did not mean was that Henny Hodges was soft.

On the contrary, she worked harder than anyone they had ever seen. She had reared fourteen children and several of her twenty-seven grand-children with little help from her husband, Captain Jesse, who rarely came home from the sea. She ran the family's sixty-acre farm, which included forty acres of crops, a barn full of horses and cows, a hog pen and smoke-house, a chicken house, and two docks. Henny maintained the Hodges home, a two-story, white clapboard farmhouse that rose like a citadel from a marshy bank on the East River. The house offered a panoramic view of the river and its tributary creeks, but few other amenities. It had no electricity, running water, or indoor plumbing. Every drop of water for cooking, washing, and bathing had to be pumped from a well fifty feet from the house and lugged inside. The family outhouse had three seats angled for a pretty view of the river, but it was always wise to rattle a broom handle before entering, to dislodge the spiders. None of the Gales Neck inconveniences seemed to faze Henny, who had grown up just across the river in a log cabin with dirt floors.

Henny got up at three o'clock every morning, tied on an apron and a floppy, wide-brimmed bonnet, and rekindled the fire in the woodstove to start breakfast. Then for the next seventeen hours, she worked. Henny grew or raised all the food the extended family needed—corn, butter beans, collard greens, turnips, cucumbers, peppers, and tomatoes, as well as hogs, chickens, and cows for meat. The only items she ever bought at the store were salt, pepper, and coffee. Their self-sufficiency had insulated the Hodges, like a lot of Mathews families, against the Great Depression. The Depression's impact was muffled throughout the county, where most families already grew their own food and made do with little work that brought in wages. "People who grew up in Mathews during the Depression thought they were poor because of the Depression, but Mathews was poor before and afterward," said Roland Foster III, whose father went to sea.

Between Henny's cooking, child rearing, and toiling on the farm, she found time to carry on running quarrels with the U.S. Department of Agriculture over milk prices and limits on the amount of wheat she could grow. Jesse Carroll Thornton, who lived with her when he was a child, thought she was superhuman: "I really believed that if I had accidentally cut my arm off, she could have fixed it." Henny was the only person in the family—maybe the only person, period—who did not hesitate to buck Captain Jesse, even when he was in a nasty mood. Nothing in her makeup explained her tears.

But Henny's family sometimes wondered if her tears brimmed out of a reservoir of sadness too deep inside her for them to see. She had seen three of her children die in horrific ways. One stifling-hot summer day, her two oldest sons had raced into the house parched from working in the yard and snatched up containers of a white liquid they assumed was milk. It was toxic lye, which Henny used to make soap. The older boy, Raymond, recognized his mistake just in time and spat out the poison. But four-year-old Seth Hodges drank his down and died in agony while Henny watched helplessly. Captain Jesse was at sea, so Henny washed and dressed her son's body while her father-in-law fashioned a little casket from lumber he had brought from Savannah, Georgia, for building boats. Henny sewed a cloth lining for the casket. Six years later, the Hodges's one-year-old son, John, died, very likely of tuberculosis but possibly from fatal burns after falling into the family's fireplace. Jesse and Henny never spoke of him after his death. Fourteen years later, in 1918, their two-year-old daughter, Martha Henrietta, was killed when the car driven by her brother Leslie overturned while passing a truck on a sharp curve. Little Henrietta, who had been asleep on the seat, was thrown from the car and died two hours later at a hospital without ever regaining consciousness.

In addition to losing three children, Henny had lost a home. The family's previous house on Tick Neck, across the East River from Gales Neck, had burned to the ground in 1931. No one was in the house when the fire started in the chimney. Henny was outside hanging up clothes when she saw smoke pouring from an upstairs window. The family managed to salvage only a few pieces of furniture and a wooden shoe from a pair that one of the boys had brought back from a voyage to Holland.

Jesse and Henny immediately purchased the farm at the tip of Gales Neck. The land was not flat but a series of ridges and swales, like gentle waves on an ancient seabed. The East River once had been lined with wharves, shipyards, and seafood packinghouses, but by the 1940s the river was so silted in that only small boats could navigate its upper reaches. Some of Captain Jesse's neighbors wondered what had possessed him to settle his family in such an isolated place. "Maybe he saw himself becoming a gentleman farmer," said his grandson Horace Hodges. "The Hodges were always dreamers." But it was not the sort of question one asked Captain Jesse. And Henny seemed happy at Gales Neck.

Over the course of a decade, she had transformed Gales Neck into a working farm and the focal point of the family. The Hodges built a large kitchen onto the front of the house, lined with windows because Henny loved the sun. The aroma of fresh bread and biscuits hung perpetually in the air. The children loved the farm's secret places and idiosyncratic animals. The bad-tempered mule was terrified of storms and would scoot under the house into the crawl space at the sound of thunder. The Hodgeses' enormous sow crashed out of the hog pen every so often and, for reasons only she understood, led her piglets swimming across a creek to root in a neighbor's yard. The Hodges children would take a skiff to capture her, tie her front legs together, and tow her back across the creek, with the piglets again thrashing behind, while other family members cheered the flotilla from the dock. Henny's grandchildren often spent entire summers with her at Gales Neck.

Henny watched out for her friends and neighbors. She was tight with money, in the Hodges tradition, but gave freely of the family's time and possessions. When her sons were younger, Henny sent them around the neighborhood as a volunteer work team to help people at critical junctures in the year, such as hog-killing time, the onset of winter, and harvest season. She gave away clothes even if her family was still wearing them if she met someone who needed them more. She gave one son's only dress clothes to a poor black farm laborer to wear to the Mathews Farmers and Fishermen's Bank to apply for a loan to buy a home. Henny also accompanied him to the bank and vouched for him to make sure he got the loan.

It wasn't all work, all the time, though. Sometimes when Captain Jesse or one of the boys came home to Gales Neck from a voyage, Henny would order all the furniture moved out of the main downstairs room of the house and organize square dances. The man who drove the ice truck in

Mathews played the fiddle, accompanied by two of his cousins. Henny called the figures if no one else wanted to. Fishermen came in skiffs and clomped to the music in their work boots. Dancers competed to see who could stay on the floor the longest without collapsing. Across the creek, Edwin Jarvis's pious parents shook their heads at the unholy racket emanating from the Hodges place. Edwin only wished he could be there.

By the winter of 1942, however, Gales Neck was a lonely place. Chill northeast winds blew across the long fetch of the Bay. Captain Jesse was gone as usual on his tug, towing barges through the Caribbean. He had taken along his sixteen-year-old grandson J. W. Corbett as a member of his crew. Most of Jesse and Henny's sons had moved to port cities where their ships regularly docked. Raymond and Dewey commanded freighters. Willie was the captain of a seagoing tug. Leslie and Coleman were officers on Ford Motor Co. freighters, working their way up the hawsepipe. David worked in a Norfolk shipyard. All of them were exempt from being drafted into the Army because the nation needed capable mariners and shipyard workers more urgently than it needed a few more infantrymen. Spencer Hodges was the only brother to remain in Mathews, where he worked in a creamery. He had been forced ashore by a shipboard back injury, which also exempted him from the draft. All four of the Hodges daughters had married and moved, though they tended to move back in with Henny between marriages.

Henny's only constant companions at Gales Neck were her three-year-old grandson, Jesse Carroll Thornton, and Ammon Gwynn, a wiry black man with a frosting of gray in his hair. Ammon had worked for the family for years. He lived in a cabin several miles away and walked to the Hodges farm every day through the woods, checking his traplines for rabbits and other game. Ammon was a character. "He could curse the mule for a half hour and never use the same word twice," Jesse Carroll recalled. "He called the horse everything but a horse." But Ammon was kind to the Hodges children and respectful to Henny, with whom he worked side by side in the fields.

Twice a week, Ammon hitched the Hodgeses' horse and mule to a wagon and drove Henny to Main Street. She always took along a few clothes in case a telegram had arrived from Captain Jesse instructing her to meet him in a port somewhere. If no telegram awaited her, Henny settled into the rear booth at the Richardson's Drug Store lunch counter and held court for a couple hours. Friends from all over Mathews stopped to exchange the latest news and gossip with her.

Henny's trips to Main Street were her only regular contact with the world beyond Gales Neck. The farmhouse had no telephone or radio. Henny did not drive (or own) a car. The Hodges lived at the end of a mile-long dirt driveway that ran razor-straight through a dense forest and was riddled with deep ruts and potholes. Neighbors wondered whether the family simply neglected the driveway or kept it that way on purpose to discourage visitors. From the farmhouse at night, the headlights of a car bobbing up and down through the potholes resembled the lights of a ship pitching in heavy seas. Any news for Henny that was too urgent to wait for Saturday—any bad news—would come jouncing down the driveway.

Henny insisted she did not worry about Captain Jesse or her boys. The sea had been dangerous long before the U-boats. If a man's time was up, her worrying about him would not help him. "It's just the way of life that everybody dies," she told Jesse Carroll. "We're all going to die."

Once, when the boy had jumped off a dock and cut his knee on an oyster shell, Henny and her daughter Alice cleaned the wound and then caught a June bug and tied it to his finger with a piece of thread. He got so caught up watching the June bug trying to fly free that he forgot all about his knee. That was the Hodges way of dealing with pain: Turn your mind somewhere else.

Their detachment was about to be tested.

By late January 1942, the war had disrupted the rhythms of life in Mathews in ways that were impossible to ignore. The absence of so many young men at sea and in the military had left Mathews an enclave of women, old men, and children. Volunteers shivered around the clock in the Mathews fire tower and other observation posts, watching the skies for enemy planes. Each observer had a guide sheet showing the silhouette shapes of German warplanes. A Luftwaffe pilot would have to be very lost indeed to bomb Mathews, but a civil-defense film titled *Fighting the Fire Bomb* drew a large crowd at the high school. The annual Mathews daffodil show and formal ball were canceled "due to war conditions." Mathews held blackout drills, spreading the word by air-raid sirens and by church bells in hamlets too far from the sirens to hear them. The drills never went well because too many people in Mathews lived too far out to hear either the sirens or the church bells.

Life on the Bay had changed too. Lighthouse keepers could no longer broadcast weather reports to fishermen for fear the information would aid U-boats. The Navy said a U-boat had picked up a report of blue skies over Duluth, Minnesota, and used it to plan subsequent attacks in the shipping lanes. Commercial fishermen had to get special ID cards in order to take their boats offshore. But not all of them wanted to keep fishing, despite good catches. Many of the trawlers in the lower Bay stayed in port because they kept spotting U-boats in their fishing grounds.

Then, in the last week of January, the first Mathews mariner was killed by a U-boat. He simply vanished along with his ship.

Captain Ernest Jefferson Thompson was the forty-year-old son of a farmer from the Mathews hamlet of Hallieford, at the mouth of the Pianka-tank River across a bay from Gwynn's Island. At age fifteen, he had written a letter asking for a job from a neighbor who owned the sailing schooner *Clemmie Travers*—the same ship on which Captain Jesse had gone to sea at age ten. The shipowner told Thompson to meet the schooner in the Chesapeake Bay's main channel on her daily run to Baltimore. A friend sailed Thompson to the rendezvous point and he climbed aboard. He quickly rose through the ranks to become captain of the 253-foot freighter *Norvana,* operated by the North Atlantic and Gulf Steamship Company.

Thompson was a rugged, confident man with dark hair and eyes. He treated his crews fairly and showed a playful side. He always trailed a big meat hook in the water behind his ship, baited with a chunk of beef, to try to catch big sharks. But at home in Mathews, Captain Thompson was neither patient nor playful. "He was a very determined man, and when he made up his mind about something, he was going to do it," his son Ernest Travers Thompson said. "He had a habit that if anything went wrong, he'd whack you, and he did worse than whack me a couple of times. He had an iron fist, and you feared him, you didn't want to get beat by him. He'd beat the hell out of you." Travers had been relieved when his father divorced his mother, moved out of the house, and remarried.

On January 14, 1942, Captain Thompson sailed the *Norvana* out of Nuevitas, Cuba, bound for Philadelphia with a load of raw sugar. Some of the sugar was destined for American cooks and kitchens, but it was also an ingredient in the C rations produced for the troops. Cuban sugar was especially precious because the Japanese had cut off the sugar supply from the Philippines. The freighter's northern deep-ocean route took her hundreds of miles off Hatteras.

The *Norvana*'s sole link to the rest of the world, in a time before Global Positioning Systems (GPS) and Emergency Position-Indicating Radio Beacons (EPIRBs), was her wireless radio, which could broadcast a distress call for hundreds of miles. But if the radio operator failed to get the message off in time, or if no vessel was near enough to help, the sinking ship was alone on the face of the sea.

When the *Norvana* had been overdue in Philadelphia for a week, her owners started to worry. They could only hope she had been forced to put into a port unexpectedly along the way. The steamship company and the Navy inquired at all the ports the ship could possibly have reached. No one had seen the ship. First the *Norvana* was listed as "overdue," a term the seafaring novelist Joseph Conrad described as "an ominous threat of loss and sorrow trembling yet in the balance of fate . . . There is something sinister to a seaman in the very grouping of the letters which form this word, clear in its meaning, and seldom threatening in vain." There was no set timetable for declaring a ship overdue or missing; it depended on the ship, the weather, and the length of the voyage.

Next, the *Norvana* was classified as "missing"—an even more foreboding term for the insurers and next of kin. Conrad wrote, "Nobody ever comes back from a 'missing' ship to tell how hard was the death of the craft, and how sudden and overwhelming the last anguish of her men." Only one ship had ever returned safely from the "missing" list—a sailing schooner in the Pacific that had been delayed five months by unfavorable winds.

On the day the *Norvana* finally was declared lost, Thompson's son Travers was at Navy boot camp in Norfolk, having enlisted right after Pearl Harbor. He was standing in line to be issued his uniform when an officer called out his name, took him aside, and told him in a surprisingly gentle tone to call his mother. She came on the line sobbing and told him his father's ship was believed to have been sunk by a U-boat with the loss of all hands. She still thought the world of her husband. Travers could not muster any grief over his father's death, but he was "young and stupid and wanted revenge." He decided on the spot to join the American submarine force. He would spend the rest of the war on a U.S. sub in the South Pacific, stalking Japanese cargo ships in much the same way a U-boat had stalked his father's.

The only trace ever found of Ernest Thompson's ship was a battered lifeboat that drifted in, empty, among the shoals north of Hatteras. In Mathews, Thompson was described as "lost," which he literally was. But even when a mariner's body was found, or the cause of his death at sea was clear, people in Mathews would always call him lost, a term cloaked in ambiguity, hope, and faith.

U-boat logbooks captured after the war showed that Hardegan of the U-123 torpedoed the *Norvana* on January 22. Hardegan wrote that the torpedo jumped out of the water twice but blew up the ship with such force that men on the U-boat's bridge heard "the whistling of debris flying past and falling all around the [U-boat] into the water."

The *Gazette-Journal* article about Thompson's "loss" contained a piece of unrelated good news: Captain Bernard Blake of Mathews, whose ship had been rumored lost with all hands, had turned up safe with his vessel. A few weeks later, another ship rumored to have been sunk with two Mathews men aboard also reached port. Rumors of sinkings raced through the county with the terrifying speed of a marsh fire.

Some of those rumors proved true. Just as the news of Captain Thompson's death reached Mathews, a second Mathews man disappeared with his ship. George Ernest Harrison of Port Haywood was forty-five years old, powerfully built, with blue eyes and close-cropped black hair. He had fought in France during World War I and come home to Mathews to fish pound nets in the Bay with his father. But after a run of poor catches in 1935 he joined the Merchant Marine. He caught on with the Bull Line and was working his way up to second officer of the freighter *Major Wheeler* when America entered the war. In one of his last letters, he wrote his sister:

> I was in hopes I would never see any more wars in my time. But we have to make the best of things. How are the children making on? . . . I sure wish I could be home with you all Christmas. [My wife and I] have been married 19 years and this is the first time I haven't been home with the family. I shouldn't say this but I sure hate this going to sea. It is sure a dog's life. The work is not hard but being away from home all the time is bad . . . Think of me when you all are eating that old ham at Christmas. I will probably have a tough piece of cod.
>
> Lovingly, Bro.

Like the *Norvana*, the *Major Wheeler* was on the sugar run between Philadelphia and the Caribbean. She had been held in Puerto Rico for three days because of reports of U-boats along her route. She was finally allowed to sail on February 3, alone and unarmed. The Navy advised the captain to stay well offshore to avoid submarines. The *Major Wheeler* was never seen again. Not even a battered lifeboat remained of her. After the war, captured

U-boat records would reveal that the U-107 had torpedoed her in the deep ocean off Hatteras. She had sunk in only two minutes, taking the lives of all thirty-five officers and crew. Their killers were the only witnesses.

As with the *Norvana*, the first signs that the *Major Wheeler* would not return were an empty berth in Philadelphia and the ominous silence of her crew. Harrison's family had not heard from him since Puerto Rico. After a week, they and the family of Everett Callis, another Mathews man who was believed to have been on the ship, called the Bull Line office in New York. The company could tell them nothing. On February 17, the Bull Line manager, W. A. Kiggins Jr., wrote to Navy secretary Frank Knox about the *Major Wheeler*:

> Even allowing for an unduly long voyage, due to special routing instructions, this vessel is now considerably overdue, and no word has been received from her. Relatives and friends of personnel aboard the *Major Wheeler* are calling on us daily for information. The purpose of this letter is to inquire whether the Navy Department can give us any information as to the *Major Wheeler*, or advise us as to what we may tell the next of kin.

Declaring a vessel sunk with all hands was not a step to be taken hastily. On rare occasions, mariners who had been given up for dead reappeared months or even years later, after having been marooned or hospitalized with serious injuries. Everett Callis's family rejoiced when he telephoned them to report he had never boarded the *Major Wheeler*. He had, in fact, just gotten off a different ship before *that* ship was torpedoed. For Harrison's family, the silence continued. His wife drove to Baltimore and checked into a hotel near the docks. After two weeks of staring at the ship's empty berth, she went home to Mathews. The Navy informed the Bull Line that the *Major Wheeler* had not been seen at any port where she conceivably might have stopped. The ship first was classified as overdue and then as "missing— presumed sunk by a submarine."

The ship's disappearance received only a brief mention in the big-city newspapers, which were far more concerned about the possibility of America being bombed, invaded, or betrayed from within. On the East Coast, the FBI hunted spy rings. On the West Coast, the government prepared to force thousands of innocent Japanese Americans out of their homes and into bleak internment camps for the duration of the war, to prevent them from covertly aiding the enemy.

On February 20, another Bull Line ship popular with Mathews men, the *Lake Osweya*, vanished with all hands in the North Atlantic. She had been en route from New York to the Navy's new base in Iceland with a load of ammunition. Captured U-boat documents would later show she was torpedoed hundreds of miles off the northeast coast by the U-96. No Mathews men had sailed on the *Lake Osweya*'s last voyage. Louise Hodges's husband, Ralph Brooks, however, had been a regular member of the ship's crew. Brooks had made two trips to Iceland aboard the vessel, but had decided at the last moment to sit out what was her final trip. Brooks was so shaken by his close call that he quit the Merchant Marine and took a job splicing cables at a shipyard. Several other Mathews men who regularly sailed on *Lake Osweya* but had skipped her last voyage contacted the *Gazette-Journal* to spread the word they were still alive.

These would be no random incidents in the coming U-boat war. By war's end, 33 U.S. merchant ships would just vanish in the war zones, along with their 1,499 officers and crew. Some of the ships probably left no trace because they carried ammunition and were blown to bits. Most of them, however, were torpedoed in remote reaches of the ocean. Any survivors were left to die of exposure, thirst, hunger, or madness in open lifeboats. No other sinkings so clearly illustrated how U-boats were changing the traditional rules of war at sea.

Since the Age of Sail, maritime tradition had called for the captain of a ship that defeated another ship at sea to capture her as a "prize" rather than sink her, and to ensure the safety of her crew. Even at the height of a war, the captain of the victorious ship would dispatch a "prize crew" from his own vessel to sail the captive ship into port, where a judge could award it to a new owner or sell the vessel and divide the proceeds among the captors. If circumstances prevented a victorious captain from taking a defeated ship as a prize, he still had to ensure the safety of the crew before sinking her. As quaint as the prize rules may seem today, they had prevailed for centuries, preserving a degree of mercy in war at sea. But submarines simply could not follow the prize rules.

U-boats could survive only if they struck fast and then hid or fled. They could not expose themselves by leading captured prizes into harbors. They had no room to take aboard captured crews. "Submarine warfare, whoever wages it, will always be a ruthless, cold-blooded business following no rules except expediency," wrote U.S. Navy admiral Daniel V. Gallery, who hunted U-boats in World War II. Gallery regarded any effort to impose rules on submarine warfare as "pious hypocrisy . . . It was like agreeing that from now on when we drop bombs on cities we will kill only combatant males. Such rules of warfare make no more sense than a set of rules for rape."

Gallery's attitude prevailed in the Pacific war, on both sides. U.S. Navy submariners targeted Japanese merchant ships, recognizing that the island nation of Japan depended just as heavily on shipping as Britain did. Over the course of World War II, American subs would sink more than a thousand Japanese merchant ships—63 percent of the Japanese merchant fleet—and rarely offer help to the survivors. U.S. submarines would even copy Doenitz's wolf pack tactics against Japanese convoys. After the war, the brutal similarities between the German and American submarine campaigns would be part of Doenitz's defense at his war crimes trial at Nuremberg.

Japanese submarines did not routinely target Allied merchant ships. They were assigned primarily to protect Japanese warships. But when they happened upon unprotected Allied cargo ships, they sank them without regard for the safety of the crews, and sometimes tortured and murdered mariners. The commander of the Japanese sub I-8, Tetsunosuke Ariizumi, ordered his men to line up American seamen from the torpedoed freighter

Jean Nicolet on the sub's narrow deck, tie their hands, and assault them with bayonets and rifle butts. When a lookout spotted a plane, the I-8 crash-dived, leaving the bound and helpless prisoners on the sub's deck to drown.*

Hitler wanted his U-boats to kill as many merchant mariners as possible, gunning them down in lifeboats if necessary. "Once it gets around that most of the seamen are lost in the sinkings, the Americans will have great difficulty in enlisting new people," the Führer told the Japanese ambassador soon after Pearl Harbor. "We are fighting for our existence and cannot therefore take a humanitarian viewpoint." Hitler backed off after Doenitz assured him that new triggers on magnetic torpedoes would sink Allied ships faster and cause mariners' casualties to soar without forcing U-boat commanders to commit such overtly murderous acts. Doenitz was right: About 70 percent of the merchant ships sunk between 1940 and 1944 went to the bottom within fifteen minutes. But the moral question of how to treat survivors of sunken ships persisted in the U-boat force. In the historical novel *Das Boot*, a drunken U-boat officer complains to friends, "The whole thing is a farce . . . As long as a man has a deck under his feet you can shoot him down, but if the poor bugger is struggling in the water, your heart bleeds for him. Pretty ridiculous, isn't it?"

In the end, Hitler and Doenitz had little impact on the moral choices their U-boat commanders made thousands of miles from Berlin. Many U-boat commanders balanced their cold-blooded orders with the dictates of their consciences, and provided lifeboat survivors with food, water, medical attention, and directions to the nearest land. The U-boat ace Otto Kretschmer posted a standing order aboard his U-99: "Survivors are to be assisted if there is time and by doing so the submarine is not exposed to

---

* The ruthless commander of the I-8 rose through the ranks of the Japanese submarine force. At the time Japan surrendered he commanded a giant submarine designed for special missions. He shot himself as his sub was being escorted into port by American warships.

undue danger. The crew of U-99 . . . would expect to be rescued by the enemy, and that is precisely what the enemy have the right to expect from us." Circumstances also dictated how much help a U-boat crew offered its victims. One U-boat was en route to its assigned patrol station off the coast of the United States when it torpedoed a freighter far from land. The U-boat commander stuck to his schedule and did not stop to help survivors who had escaped the sinking ship in a lifeboat. But two weeks later, the U-boat was en route back to its base when it happened upon the same lifeboat. This time, the U-boat commander had no schedule to keep and plenty of supplies to get home. He stopped to give the men in the lifeboat food, water, chocolates, and cigarettes.

Another U-boat commander, Friedrich Guggenberger of the U-513, astonished a lifeboat full of survivors by asking how the Brooklyn Dodgers baseball team had been doing. Guggenberger had lived in Brooklyn with his parents before the war. Still another U-boat commander, Werner Winter of U-103, subjected lifeboat survivors to tirades against President Roosevelt. "I am sorry but you can thank Mr. Roosevelt for this," he told castaways from one torpedoed ship. On a different occasion, Winter refused a plea by lifeboat survivors for drinking water, telling them, "Roosevelt is to blame for this, he will give you water."

The U-boat captain was not far wrong. Roosevelt was partly to blame for the castaways' predicament, but the blame extended well beyond the White House, to the U.S. Navy and even the American public. The U-boats had taken over American coastal waters with little interference from the U.S. military. After three-quarters of a century of peace on its shores, the United States was unprepared to defend itself. The first of the Navy's new warships were just emerging from the yards. Half of the Navy's existing warships were in the Pacific, trying to hold back the Japanese, who had overrun Borneo, Singapore, Burma, Bali, Timor, and the Solomon Islands, and had cornered thousands of exhausted, starving American and Filipino troops on the Bataan peninsula in the Philippines.

The Navy had compounded its shortage of warships in 1940 by giving Britain fifty old World War I–vintage destroyers in exchange for ninety-nine-year leases for U.S. military bases on British territory in Newfoundland, Bermuda, and the British West Indies, which provided the United States with an outer ring of defense against a German attack on the American continent. Without those fifty destroyers, the only U.S. warships left to defend the East Coast were a dozen other old destroyers and a wide variety of smaller craft, including Coast Guard cutters, wooden-hulled sub-chasers from World War I, and pleasure boats of dubious value in a war. The Coast Guard's vessels at Ocracoke Island, North Carolina, included a sailboat rigged to drop depth charges from its stern. The sailboat's crew suspected the boat was too slow to get clear before the depth charges exploded, and that they would blow themselves up if they ever dropped them. Fortunately for the crew, the sailboat never got anywhere near a U-boat.

The Navy had no planes on the East Coast capable of flying patrols over distant sea lanes to protect merchant ships. The Army Air Forces was only slightly better equipped. Its assets included one long-range bomber, three torpedo bombers, three fighters, and various patrol and training planes incapable of carrying bombs or depth charges. Most of the planes lacked the radio equipment to communicate with American ships. Further compounding the problem, Army leaders did not want their planes flying routine patrols. They wanted them out hunting U-boats, which seemed like a more aggressive approach than babysitting coastal convoys. It would take the U.S. military months to figure out that the surest way to find and engage the elusive U-boats was to stay close to the merchant ships the subs had traveled thousands of miles to attack. For U-boats, merchant ships were irresistible bait.

A shortage of ships and planes was only part of the Americans' problem. Their sailors and aviators had no experience in antisubmarine warfare. Regular Navy and Army Air Forces training was of little use against seasoned U-boat commanders in the specialized world of sonar, magnetic torpedoes, and *Pillenwurfers.*

Before America entered the war, the Navy had handed the task of protecting U.S. coastal waters to Vice Admiral Adolphus Andrews, a capable, energetic officer with friends in Roosevelt's inner circle. Andrews struck some fellow officers as windy—"senatorial in port and speech," wrote the distinguished naval historian Samuel Eliot Morison. But Andrews was savvy, and he recognized at once that he had nowhere near enough forces to protect his assigned area of responsibility. That area encompassed 28,000 square miles of the Atlantic, extending from Maine to Florida, and for 200 miles out to sea. The Navy dubbed that zone the Eastern Sea Frontier, and set up other sea frontiers for the Caribbean and the Gulf of Mexico. They would be wild frontiers.

The shipping lanes in the sea frontiers were crowded with Allied merchant ships hauling every kind of war cargo. Tankers loaded with Venezuelan crude oil lumbered up the coast to Halifax to join North Atlantic convoys. Old freighters hauled manganese from Caribbean mines to defense plants in the United States, where it was used to harden steel. Other freighters carried powdery bauxite ore, an ingredient of aluminum, from open-pit mines in Brazil to American aircraft factories. Still other freighters carried staples of everyday American life such as rubber, sugar, and coffee—all of which would soon grow scarce enough to require rationing.

Andrews did not mince words with his superiors. Two weeks before Pearl Harbor, he wrote to them, "There is not a vessel [under my command] that an enemy submarine could not out-distance when operating on the surface. In most cases, the guns of [my] vessels would be out-ranged by those of the submarines. It is submitted that should enemy submarines operate off this coast, this command has no forces available to take adequate action against them, either offensive or defensive." Andrews set out to remedy the problem, shuttling between his headquarters in Manhattan and Washington, D.C., trying to leverage his connections into additional ships and planes. But his requests usually died at the desk of his formidable boss, Admiral Ernest J. King, the commander in chief of the U.S. fleet, who had operational control over the entire U.S. Navy.

King, a classmate of Andrews's at the Naval Academy, was on the cusp of a legendary career. He was a workaholic with a keen intellect. He had broad experience, having commanded a submarine base, a squadron of seaplanes, and an aircraft carrier. He had overcome career setbacks that would have discouraged many ambitious officers. But King was no sympathetic figure. He was an arrogant bully, a heavy drinker, and a strict disciplinarian—a "sundowner" in Navy slang. Roosevelt, who liked his toughness, joked that King "shaved with a blowtorch." But General Dwight D. Eisenhower, who found King difficult to work with, wrote in his diary that America would win the war faster if someone shot King. One of King's daughters described her father as "the most even-tempered man I know—always in a rage."

King faced the enormous challenge of managing wars in two oceans with a Navy unready to fight in even one. In the Pacific, he had to rally the U.S. fleet after the devastating losses at Pearl Harbor, and to prevent Japan from conquering still more territory. In the Atlantic, King had to defend the United States against a possible German invasion by sea, which seemed possible in 1942, and to provide destroyers and other escort vessels to protect the big North Atlantic convoys as far as mid-ocean. He also had to protect the troopships that were starting to carry American soldiers to Britain.

With so many demands on his resources, King did not regard protecting merchant ships in America's coastal waters as a priority. He was adamant in refusing to assign his few available ships and planes permanently to that task. King and his inner circle of advisers believed in running convoys only if those convoys had powerful enough escorts to fight off or scare off U-boats. In King's view, organizing convoys with weak escorts only made the U-boats' work easier, by assembling their targets in one place for them. King thought merchant ships were better off sailing alone, relying on luck to keep them from ever crossing paths with a U-boat. The Navy would help them by routing them away from waters where British intelligence and recent sinkings showed U-boats were operating.

At a glance, King's view seemed logical. But the British had learned over the course of two world wars that even the weakest escort was better than none. Lone, unarmed ships were the U-boats' favorite targets. They and their cargoes could be destroyed quickly with little risk. The only reason Doenitz was willing to send his U-boats all the way across the Atlantic to American waters was that the kills were so easy there. Any step the United States took to make those kills more difficult would force Doenitz to recalculate the costs versus benefits of the long-range mission.

King had misread the enemy, and he would stick to his misguided course for seven months—long after the terrible losses of merchant ships had proven him wrong. But he was adamant, and in case Admiral Andrews still had not gotten his message, King emphasized in a memo that the Eastern Sea Frontier's prospects for acquiring new escort ships and planes were "dependent on future production" of those ships and planes.

The U-boats wasted no time in confirming that the Eastern Sea Frontier was as vulnerable as Andrews had predicted. In January 1942, they sank thirty-five ships totaling more than 200,000 tons within the frontier's boundaries—three times the tonnage sunk on the North Atlantic convoy routes over the same period.

The American defenders were game but overmatched. At times the U.S. coastal defense resembled a deadly comedy of errors. Inexperienced American pilots often bombed and strafed whales, thinking they were U-boats.* An American submarine traveling from New London, Connecticut, to Norfolk to help with antisubmarine training was mistaken for a U-boat and attacked by two different U.S. warships. The submarine returned fire but none of the combatants hit anything. One dark night near the mouth of the Chesapeake Bay, jittery Navy gunners on a merchant ship

---

* The writer Theodore Taylor concluded, "The extent to which whales were machine-gunned, depth charged and subjected to aerial bombardment during World War II was such that their . . . survival was little short of miraculous. So many of the mammals were sent to the bottom that pilots, to ease their mortification, organized the 'Royal Order of the Whale Bangers,' and its members were legion."

opened fire on what they thought was a U-boat but was, in fact, the destroyer USS *Dickerson*. The rounds tore into the *Dickerson's* bridge and critically wounded the captain. After the *Dickerson* raced into Norfolk to take the wounded to a hospital, the freighter that had mistaken the *Dickerson* for a U-boat was torpedoed by a real U-boat.

The United States neglected to employ even the most obvious antisubmarine measures. The merchant ships sailed blacked out at night in order to blend in with the darkness, but the glow of American coastal cities silhouetted them like targets in a carnival shooting gallery. U-boats had only to sit on the surface to the seaward side of the shipping lanes and wait for ships to reveal themselves against the lights. One U-boat commander wrote that "against this floodlight glare of a carefree new world," merchant ships were "recognizable in every detail and sharp as the outlines in a sales catalogue. Here they were formally presented to us on a plate: Please help yourselves! All we had to do was press the [torpedo launch] button."

Britain and Germany had blacked out their coastal cities since the start of the war, but American business owners complained a blackout would cost them money. Police warned it would increase crime. Roosevelt clearly understood the danger of coastal lights. On February 16, 1942, he signed an executive order giving the military the authority to control "all lighting on the seacoast as to prevent the silhouetting of ships and their consequent destruction by enemy submarines." But King took no steps to implement a blackout. He possessed all the real power in the Navy, and his opinion, and his orders, were the only ones that mattered.

U-boats attacked helpless merchant ships every night and sometimes by day. During February, they sank twenty-five Allied merchant ships in American waters. The victims included the tanker *W.D. Anderson*, which was torpedoed on February 22 within sight of the Florida coast. A crewman on the fantail of the tanker felt the ship shudder, and then glanced up to see a mass of fire racing along the length of the ship toward him. He saw a shipmate's hair burst into flames, and dove over the side. He would be the only survivor of the *W.D. Anderson*'s thirty-six officers and crew. Tourists in beachfront hotels watched the tanker burn.

Unlike the *W.D. Anderson*, most merchant ships were torpedoed too far offshore for their destruction to be seen or heard from land. But the losses were too severe to remain secret from the mariners. In New York, some ship sailings were delayed due to shortages of crews. The press and public started asking the government why the sinkings could not be stopped or at least reduced. The Navy and the White House responded with secrecy and lies.

The Navy began to withhold the names of torpedoed ships, citing a need to keep that information from the Germans. Even official U.S. government telegrams announcing merchant mariners' deaths to their next of kin included a plea for secrecy: "TO PREVENT POSSIBLE AID TO OUR ENEMIES PLEASE DO NOT DIVULGE THE NAME OF HIS SHIP." But the Germans had their own sources of information. U-boat commanders took pains to find out the torpedoed ships' names, cargoes, and tonnages because Doenitz wanted that information. Some U-boats carried copies of Lloyd's of London's *Register of Ships*, which listed the specifications of the world's vessels. If all else failed, a U-boat commander would pry the information from men in lifeboats at the point of a machine gun. The only people kept in the dark by the government's secrecy were American citizens, who, in their enforced ignorance, had to assume their leaders knew what they were doing.

The government's iconic "Loose Lips Sink Ships!" campaign, launched in 1942, focused on a problem that barely existed. German spies did haunt some squalid waterfront taverns to try to coax drunken seamen to blurt out ship schedules and cargoes. But America's coastal waters were so crowded with merchant ships that U-boats needed no whispered secrets to find them. Spies would only have slowed the U-boats down. Most merchant mariners knew little about their own ships' cargo or itinerary anyway. "The total knowledge of one million seamen, sounding off in as many bars with 'scraps of information,' could never equal the sum of German Naval Intelligence knowledge of Allied merchant ship movements in World War II," the mariner and writer "Ferocious" O'Flaherty (S. J. Flaherty) declared.

The Allies' most damaging security breaches occurred far from the pierside bars. In February 1942, the Germans added a fourth rotor to the naval Enigma machines, complicating the encryption system and abruptly cutting off the Allies from reading the Germans' coded radio messages. A few weeks later, the German Navy's code-breaking service, B-dienst, penetrated a British code through which Allied convoy plans were transmitted. Soon the Germans knew most of the convoys' routes and could shift U-boats into position to intercept them. For the Allies, the one-two punch of suddenly losing access to the Germans' most sensitive messages while the Germans gained access to theirs was devastating. Tipsy seamen talking in dockside bars or among their friends in places like Mathews were the least of the Allies' worries.

The White House and Navy were not content to merely stonewall the public. Only two weeks after America entered the war, Navy Secretary Knox—the publisher of the *Chicago Daily News*—declared that U.S. warships "probably" had sunk or damaged at least fourteen U-boats. In fact, they had not sunk or even damaged any. Knox based his claims partly on wildly optimistic reports from Navy warships and Army planes. As the weeks passed, the Navy kept adding phony U-boat kills to Knox's total, even affecting a winner's swagger. "Some of the recent visitors to our territorial waters will never enjoy the return trip," the Navy bragged in a news release on January 23. A widely published news story described an Army pilot sinking a U-boat and then announcing his kill over the radio with a jaunty "Sighted sub—sank same." But he had only thought he had sunk a sub, and he had never spoken those memorable words. A military public affairs officer had made them up.

Rear Admiral Manley H. Simons would set a standard for malarkey when he declared in a speech in Elizabeth City, North Carolina, "I can tell you this—we have sunk plenty of submarines . . . the Axis has paid a terrible price in both submarines and men for the sinkings on the Atlantic Seaboard." In fact, at that point, the Axis had yet to pay any price at all, as Doenitz well knew from his daily radio communications with his U-boats.

Rear Admiral John Howard Hoover, Admiral Andrews's counterpart in the Caribbean Sea Frontier, maintained his credibility by refusing to make any public statements whatsoever. His standard comment to reporters was, "Gentlemen, I have nothing to say."

The Eastern Sea Frontier's war diary, an official record not accessible to the public, provided a more candid assessment of the U-boat war in the winter of 1942. The diarist Elting Morison, a naval reservist, professor at the Massachusetts Institute of Technology, and cousin of naval historian Samuel Eliot Morison, wrote that no antisubmarine strategy could possibly overcome America's shortage of escorts. Merchant ships and their crews would remain easy prey for U-boats until America produced enough new ships and planes to protect them. In the meantime, Morison wrote, "Whatever possible grounds there may be for optimism must be found in the hope that the forces available can be used in such fashion as to limit losses to bearable proportions."

To Morison and to America's military and political strategists, "bearable" losses meant losses of ships and cargo in small enough proportions that America could keep its factories and defense plants humming. Bearable losses meant losing no more ships than could be replaced by the new ships emerging from American shipyards. Bearable losses meant losing few enough mariners that their shipmates would be willing to keep sailing. All of those calculations were critical to winning the war.

But to seafaring families in Mathews and hundreds of other communities from Maine to Texas to California, the losses were not merely proportions or calculations, but husbands, fathers, sons, and brothers. Already, mariners' families had begun to dread the jangle of the telephone, the trip to the post office, and the clump of footsteps on the front porch. On Gwynn's

Island, nine-year-old Clarence Collier Jr., whose father and grandfather were both at sea, "prayed to the Lord every night to watch over my daddy, bring him home." It seemed to the boy that every ship on the sea was getting torpedoed.

A mariner's family would receive no letters for weeks, and then receive a thick stack of them. Any details a mariner might have written about his ship's voyage or his own activities would have been cut out of the letters by a censor. The letters were always too old to be of any comfort. The only time Lottie Mise of Gwynn's Island ever stopped worrying about her fiancé, Lester Smith, was when he telephoned her from a port. The moment he hung up, she resumed worrying. Lottie moved in with Lester's parents for company, but they were even more worried about Lester than she was. She would hear them in their bedroom at night, their voices hushed and anxious.

The losses in Mathews had just begun, and Henny Hodges and her neighbors would have to make their own calculations of what was bearable.

CHAPTER FOUR

Professional Survivors

Two months into the war, Raymond Hodges paid a rare visit to Gales Neck. Henny could not stop beaming. If she had a favorite son, he was Raymond. He was her first, and the only one of her children widely considered to be his father's equal at handling ships. And while Captain Jesse was rough and taciturn, Raymond was handsome, charming, and savvy in business. He was a senior captain with Moore-McCormack Transportation Co. of New York, one of the nation's most prominent shipping lines, and the master of the freighter *Mormacmoon*—the loftiest position any Hodges had ever achieved. "Raymond was above us," a family member recalled without a trace of sarcasm. And Raymond had a flair for the spotlight.

He mingled with shipping executives. A Hollywood studio chartered his ship as the set for the movie *His Woman*, starring Gary Cooper and Claudette Colbert. In 1936, Raymond nearly started his own war in the upper reaches of the Amazon jungle on behalf of the Colombian Navy. As he explained to *The New York Times*, the Colombian government bought his ship, the freighter *Commercial Traveler*, from Moore-McCormack in order to strengthen its navy for a border clash with Peru. The Colombians had no vessel anywhere near as big as the freighter, and they offered to double Raymond's salary if he stayed at the helm to lead their forces up the Amazon to a disputed patch of jungle. Command of the ship came with the temporary title of Admiral and Commander in Chief. After Moore-McCormack agreed to let Raymond stay aboard, he recruited a crew of American seamen in Philadelphia to sail the ship, which was renamed the *Cucata*. He sailed her down to the coast of South America and then more than 2,000 miles up the Amazon. Along the way, Raymond picked up Colombian troops, ammunition, and pompom guns to be fired from the deck of the freighter. The *Cucata* arrived at its destination and reinforced a small garrison of Colombian troops, but the League of Nations stepped in and resolved the border dispute before the Peruvian Navy arrived to join the fight. Raymond collected his pay, surrendered his title, and returned to Moore-McCormack. "It was fun, but I'm glad we never fired a shot," he told the *Christian Science Monitor* years later. "I don't know how I would have made out as an admiral." He charmed the *Monitor* reporter, who wrote that Raymond looked less like a sea captain than "a tycoon, a new ambassador off to some South American post, or perhaps a noted archaeologist southward bound to prod among Inca ruins."

When Raymond arrived at Gales Neck in February 1942, he wore a coat and tie, as usual. He wore a tie whenever he went out in public. "The only man I ever saw who went fishing with a tie on," one of his nieces joked. Raymond cared about appearances. When he caught his young sons slouching, he whacked them in the small of their backs with a paint-stirring stick. He once chewed out his brothers Dewey and Willie for dressing sloppily aboard his father's ship, only to see Captain Jesse clump into the wheelhouse in a grimy, sleeveless T-shirt, gnawing on a cigar.

Raymond had a barrel chest and a trim waist, unlike his brothers and sisters, who were squarely built, even pear-shaped. At his side was his wife, Ethel, whom the family had nicknamed Dolly. Dolly had grown up in New York City. She was tall and slender. She was not beautiful, but she wore elegant dresses and puffed cigarettes through a silver holder. The Hodges girls whispered that she had been a dancer for the Ziegfeld Follies. In fact, Dolly came from a prosperous family on Long Island but had been working as a telephone operator in Manhattan when Raymond first met her. After they married, he tried to talk her into moving to Mathews but she vetoed the idea, saying the county was "all marsh and salt water and ticks and dirt roads." The couple compromised and bought a home in neighboring Gloucester County on a bluff overlooking the York River. By late 1941 that home stood mostly empty. Raymond lived aboard his ship in New York Harbor; Dolly had moved back in with her parents. They sent their son Bill to boarding school in upstate New York.

Henny cried when Raymond arrived at Gales Neck, and cried harder when he rose to leave. He told her not to worry. He said he had not seen a single U-boat in several voyages between New York and South America, and if one came after him, the *Mormacmoon* was fast enough to outrun it. The *Mormacmoon* was only two years old, one of the newest American freighters on the ocean, and could make 18 knots. Raymond's easy confidence was contagious. Even in a war, he seemed in total control of events. Henny wanted to believe him.

About the time Raymond returned to his ship, the focus of the U-boat war on America shifted south. Doenitz sent his next wave of U-boats to Florida, the Caribbean, and the South Atlantic. Despite Admiral King's intransigence, Admiral Andrews had mustered enough Coast Guard cutters, smaller craft, and patrol planes to pose a nuisance to the U-boats, at least in the Atlantic. The sight of any plane usually forced a U-boat to crash-dive; the Germans did not have the luxury of waiting until they got a close look at the aircraft and determined how much of a threat it posed. Doenitz figured the waters farther south would have fewer defenses, and that the hunting would be just as good, if not better.

The Caribbean was a crossroads for ships hauling oil and raw materials from South America to North America. Britain had come to depend almost entirely on South American oil since the Germans had cut off the oil supply routes from the Middle East. Getting South American oil to

Britain was a challenge. The crude oil was pumped out of the vast fields under teardrop-shaped Lake Maracaibo on Venezuela's northern coast, and then hauled by shallow-draft tankers across a lagoon to refineries on the Dutch islands of Aruba and Curaçao. The refineries processed the crude oil into gasoline, aviation gas, and other essential fuels. Large, deep-ocean tankers then carried the refined products across the Caribbean, up the U.S. coast, and across the North Atlantic. The last, transatlantic leg of that journey was the only one protected by convoys.

The Caribbean and South Atlantic were also the sources of more than half the dry-cargo tonnage entering the United States, including bauxite, manganese, and other raw materials for American factories building ships, tanks, and planes. Manganese was precious to both sides. One of Hitler's main reasons for invading Russia had been to seize its manganese resources. Sir Thomas Holland, head of the University of Edinburgh, declared in 1942 that Germany needed manganese more than oil.

The six Caribbean U-boats announced their presence in the predawn hours of February 19, 1942, with the kind of coordinated mayhem Doenitz loved. One U-boat slipped into a coral lagoon at Aruba and shelled the refinery and the British base with its deck cannon, but had to retreat after a round exploded in the cannon barrel and killed a crewman. Another U-boat, commanded by a former merchant sea captain who knew the Caribbean well, squeezed into the harbor at Curaçao through a shallow inlet named the Dragon's Mouth and sank two ships right under the British guns. By daybreak, the six German submarines had sunk four ships and damaged three others. Over the next two weeks, they sank eighteen more ships in the Caribbean. The shaken Allies temporarily halted all tanker traffic. That left the U-boats to hunt lesser prey, such as the little Bull Line freighter *Mary*.

The *Mary* had long been a favorite of Mathews men. Captain Holly Bennett of Mathews had commanded her for years before switching to a different ship weeks before. The *Mary*'s final crew included two twenty-one-year-old Gwynn's Islanders, Robert Lee Brown and Allenby Grimstead. Grimstead's father had died on a ship in Puerto Rico, and Grimstead eventually would suffer the same fate. But he and Brown would outlive the *Mary*.

The *Mary* had sailed out of New York on February 3 loaded with food, supplies, and airplanes—still unassembled in crates—for British troops in North Africa. The ship stopped in San Juan, Puerto Rico, and then steamed down the coast of South America. She eventually was to cross the ocean to Cape Town, South Africa, and then sail around the Cape of Good Hope and continue up the east coast of Africa and through the Suez Canal to Egypt. Instead, late in the morning of March 3, 160 miles off the coast of Brazil, she was struck by two torpedoes from the U-129.

Brown, an able seaman, was resting in his quarters when the first torpedo hit. He got up and struggled into his pants. Then a second torpedo shook the ship, and he took off his pants. He did not know why. Instinct may have told him he was going to have to swim for his life. But first he had to escape from his room. The force of the second explosion had thrown his bunk and locker against the exit door. Brown cleared a path to the door but found it jammed shut. Cold seawater gushed into the room through gaps in the bent door frame and swirled around his bare feet. Brown gave no thought to his belongings. He kicked out a panel in the door. A phonograph somewhere on the ship continued to play music as if nothing had happened, filling the passageways of the doomed ship with the twang of a cowboy love song by Gene Autry, "Be Honest with Me."

Brown reached the main deck and beheld "an awful sight." The 5,104-ton *Mary* was dead in the water and sinking. The weather was fair, but heavy swells persisted from a recent storm. The first torpedo had sent a mass of water flying into the air and thundering down onto the ship's bridge. It had wrecked the radio before a distress call could be sent, caved in part of the crew's quarters, and smashed one of the lifeboats, which hung in splinters from its davits. The *Mary* had two other lifeboats and six rafts. The rafts were nothing more than wooden platforms nailed to empty, buoyant barrels, but they were better than swimming.

Grimstead was the *Mary*'s third assistant engineer. He had been on watch in the engine room when a torpedo blew a hole in the hull big enough to "drive a truck into." Grimstead shut down the ship's engines, stopping the vessel so that the lifeboats could be launched safely. Then he scrambled up a ladder out of the engine room, just ahead of the rising water.

The *Mary*'s crew cut free the life rafts from the lines holding them to the deck, and lowered the rafts into the ocean near the ship. Brown and some other men leaped overboard and swam to the rafts, but the captain called them back to help launch the two intact lifeboats. The *Mary* was listing steeply, which complicated the launching process. Brown saw a friend, Edwin Fleming of Gloucester County, standing on deck wearing only his underclothes. Fleming had been asleep when the impact of the first torpedo threw him out of his bunk. He had stumbled to his feet, grabbed a life preserver, and run. Now, it occurred to him for the first time that he might have to survive a long voyage in an open boat. Fleming ran back inside his quarters and grabbed his seaman's papers, some clothing, and a hat. The captain also risked returning to his cabin. He fetched the secret Navy routing codes, stuffed them in a weighted bag, returned to the main deck, and threw the bag into the ocean.

The crew lowered two lifeboats and got into them without anyone falling overboard. That was critical, Grimstead said, because the turmoil in the water had attracted a large number of sharks, and anyone in the sea at that point "would have been devoured." A fire in the cargo holds was burning its way up through the main deck and engulfing the *Mary*. The oarsmen in the lifeboats pulled hard, but the waves kept driving the boats back to the freighter. A sinking ship was a deathtrap that could kill a man in a thousand ways. Falling masts and guy wires snagged mariners and pulled them under. Jagged debris swirled through the water. The ship's hot boilers could explode from contact with cold seawater. The *Mary*'s crew feared the ship would capsize onto the lifeboats.

A third torpedo drove the *Mary* under fast. The ship's whistle sounded two long, shrill blasts, followed by a short one. It seemed to repeat that sequence twice more. At first, the men in the lifeboats assumed the whistle cord had caught on something. Then they noticed that one of their shipmates was not in either lifeboat. Just before the first torpedo explosion, he had entered the crew's quarters to wake men for the next watch. Brown thought he had seen the man on deck afterward but was not certain. Had the man gotten trapped inside the ship? Was he blowing the whistle, calling them back to save him? They would never know.

The U-129 remained submerged and cruised slowly past the lifeboats. Its commander, Nicolai Clausen, swiveled the periscope to examine the castaways as he passed. Clausen had hunted convoys in the North Atlantic. Stalking lone, defenseless ships in the turquoise waters of the Caribbean was child's play for him. He brought the sub to the surface only twenty-five feet from the nearest lifeboat, nearly capsizing it. The U-boat's conning tower was a kiosk of painted messages, including "Westward Ho" written in English, "Das Kampf" ("the struggle"), and the U-129's unofficial symbol, a deck of playing cards. Clausen emerged from the main hatch, shirtless in the tropical heat and holding a submachine gun. He was described by the survivors as about thirty (he actually was thirty-one), blond, rugged, and speaking good English with a German accent. Three other Germans followed Clausen out onto the U-boat's bridge. They glared down at the Americans. Clausen demanded in English the name of their ship, its tonnage, cargo, and intended destination. The crew lied that they were carrying "general cargo" to Rio de Janeiro. Clausen probably did not believe them. The Germans could not have failed to notice the pieces of airplanes floating among the wreckage. But Clausen signaled they were free to go. He called out an incongruous "Cheerio" and waved as the Germans retreated down the hatch. The U-129 submerged and left the thirty-three castaways to their own devices.

The two lifeboats had plenty of room and supplies for the *Mary*'s survivors. A standard World War II–era lifeboat was twenty-eight feet long with a ten-foot beam, and could hold as many as thirty-six people. Most merchant ships carried at least four lifeboats. Both sides of each lifeboat were lined with buoyancy tanks, atop which lay wooden thwarts that served as benches. Four perpendicular cross-thwarts provided seats for the oarsmen. Each boat had four oars to a side, as well as a twenty-foot mast that could be stepped and fitted with a small sail. The boat was steered with a tiller in the stern. Unlike modern lifeboats, those in the 1940s were open at the top, offering no protection from the sun, rain, snow, wind, and spray.

Each lifeboat was required by the U.S. Bureau of Marine Inspection and Navigation to carry fifteen gallons of drinking water, the basic sustainer of life. A healthy adult requires at least three six-ounce cups of water a day. Without water, digestion begins to slow, toxins accumulate in the body, the blood thickens, circulation stops, and death arrives in as little as four days. Each lifeboat also was required to contain two weeks' worth of protein-rich foods such as biscuits, chocolate, dried milk, and pemmican, a concentrate of dried beef, flour, and molasses. The *Mary* castaways had extra food, because the captain had had the presence of mind to collect the supplies from a wrecked lifeboat before abandoning ship. The captain also had remembered to bring his compass and sextant for navigation. Unfortunately for the castaways, they could not bring the radio.

The rough seas made it hard to keep the two lifeboats together. Brown found rowing against the strong current exhausting. The wind came up, and the boats rigged their sails and set a course for the coast of French Guiana, almost 300 miles away. The sun and wind burned the men's skin. Nightfall brought a cold wind. Brown wished he had risked going back to his quarters to get more clothing. Big waves ambushed the lifeboats from unexpected directions in the dark, drenching everyone and jarring awake those who had managed to doze. During the second night, the men noticed a blinking red light in the water that seemed to be following them. They theorized it was a U-boat using them as bait to attract another ship. On the third night, a blue parachute flare lit up the sky and the object with the blinking light appeared to exchange signals with another vessel. Then the lights disappeared for good.

The wind and current kept pushing the lifeboats off course. By the fifth day, they had traveled and drifted for more than 540 miles. The captain rationed the food and water. One man in his boat caught a flying fish, tore off its scales with his teeth and ate it.* Grimstead got plenty to eat but never enough to drink. For years afterward, an intense thirst would seize him every time he thought about his lifeboat voyage.

The castaways finally drifted into the sea lanes off British Guiana—now Guyana—and were picked up by an old bauxite freighter, which looked to Brown "like a million-dollar hotel." The freighter dropped them at the U.S. Navy base in Trinidad. The island of Trinidad had become an ad hoc refugee camp for mariners whose ships had been sunk out from under them. At one point, more than seven hundred survivors of dozens of torpedoed ships were stranded at Trinidad, waiting for transportation back to the United States, living on burlap pallets in tents, swatting at insects and vermin.

The *Mary* survivors spent several weeks in Trinidad before a ship carried them and the survivors of seven other vessels to Miami. When Brown got back to Gwynn's Island, he visited his mother and then joined the Navy. He wanted to serve on a ship that could defend herself. Grimstead stayed in the Merchant Marine, as did the *Mary*'s captain, who kept sailing even after he lost two more ships to U-boats.

Less than a week after the *Mary* sinking, her sister ship the *Barbara* approached the Windward Passage under a bright Caribbean full moon.

The Windward Passage is a deep, fifty-mile-wide strait between Cuba and the island of Hispaniola, which Haiti and the Dominican Republic share. From the lush, green hills on either side of the strait, the lights on

---

* Throughout the war, castaways caught birds or fish to eat after their food ran out. The most obliging creatures were flying fish, which glided over the waves on winglike pectoral fins and sometimes slammed into the sides of lifeboats and knocked themselves senseless. Eating any sea creature other than fish was a gamble. Seaweed was plentiful and nutritious, but too salty if the water supply was unreliable. One starving mariner ate a jellyfish, became deathly sick, and then jumped out of his lifeboat and disappeared.

the other side are visible at night. The Windward Passage was the most direct sea route between the Caribbean and the U.S. East Coast. Its remoteness had made it a haven for eighteenth-century pirates, including Henry Morgan, Charles Vane, and Jack "Calico Jack" Rackham. Two centuries later, the Windward Passage attracted U-boats for the same reason it had attracted the pirates: It was an isolated chokepoint for merchant shipping.

The *Barbara*'s master was Captain Walter Gwynn Hudgins of Gwynn's Island. Walter was part of a vast network of Hudgins mariners that reached into every neck of Mathews, and seemingly onto every ship on the sea. Three Hudgins captains from Mathews once sailed their ships out of Baltimore harbor in a single afternoon. Walter was a big man with a balding pate and a ruddy complexion. He wore glasses that lent him a grandfatherly air. He was fifty-five and had been denied an officer's commission in the Navy because of his age. Besides, the Navy had informed him in a letter, "Your services [as a merchant captain] will be of just as much value to the war effort as if you were serving on some man-of-war."

Walter spoke commandingly at sea but softly at home. His son Elliott was shocked when he accompanied Walter on a voyage and heard him bellow at a crewman. Walter had moved his family from port to port while he worked his way up through the hawsepipe. He worked on colliers—coal ships—before landing a job with the Bull Line, which promoted him to master in 1918. By the time America entered World War II, he and his family had settled in Baltimore, though Walter seldom was there. His children wrote of him, "His one regret about his calling to sea was that it required him to be away from his family for extended times."

Walter's chief officer on the *Barbara* was twenty-one-year-old Charles Harold Davis, a slightly built bachelor from the hamlet of Bavon near the southeastern tip of Mathews. Harold chain-smoked Camels and closed out every day ashore with a six-pack of beer. He made a point of knowing every scrap of gossip in Mathews and buffeted his friends and family with jokes and silly stories about life at sea. But Harold was shy and soft-spoken among people he did not know well. He had no ambition to command a ship, and was content to sail under Walter, whom he had known most of his life.

The *Barbara* was a freight/passenger ship, built to carry cargo in its holds and dozens of passengers in private berths. Even in wartime, the ship employed three women as stewardesses to wait on the passengers. The passengers on the current voyage included twenty-seven military personnel en route to their duty station at the new U.S. Navy base in Guantanamo Bay, Cuba. Walter and Harold were both on the bridge on the night of March 7 as the ship approached the Windward Passage. Walter followed the Navy's routing instructions to the letter, zigzagging and hugging the coast of Haiti on the Hispaniola side of the strait. He kept the ship blacked out, even though the full moon illuminated the water and every ship on it in sharp relief.* Neither Walter nor Harold noticed the U-126 sitting on the surface a half mile ahead of them.

The U-126 commander, Ernest Bauer, was a veteran of the North Atlantic like Nicolai Clausen. He had sunk twelve ships, including a British warship, under much more difficult conditions than those in the Caribbean. He coolly watched three vessels enter the Windward Passage ahead of the *Barbara* before choosing her. He somehow mistook the *Barbara* for a tanker, to her great misfortune.

Bauer's first torpedo hit the *Barbara* amidships, blowing thirty feet of metal plating off the hull. The blast killed every man in the engine room, which was always the most dangerous place on a merchant ship because U-boats typically aimed their first torpedoes at engine rooms to disable their prey. The explosion also killed two of the *Barbara*'s three stewardesses, whose berths were directly above the engine room. The *Barbara*'s fuel tanks exploded, showering the ship with flaming bunker oil and set-

---

* The Caribbean full moon helped U-boats in early 1942, when the United States had only a few float planes and wooden-hulled subchasers to patrol the Windward Passage. But once the United States had enough ships and planes to patrol the strait regularly, the full moon made U-boats so easy to spot that Doenitz kept them out of the Windward Passage until the moon waned.

ting all four lifeboats on fire. Flames towered mast-high above the bridge. The fire bell clanged incessantly. Passengers flung open their cabin doors and were engulfed by fire and superheated gases. The radioman wrapped a stewardess's fur coat around his nose and mouth to keep out the smoke and ran into the crew's quarters to check if everyone had gotten out. Walter tried to retrieve the secret codes from the radio room but was driven back by the heat. He gave the order to abandon ship. The lifeboats were gone, but the crew managed to throw three rafts into the water. Some men jumped overboard without life preservers or vests. A Navy report cited "a complete lack of discipline and order" on the part of the crew, but a messman found no fault with his shipmates: "Some [were] plenty scared but behaved all right."

Three swimming men pulled themselves onto a floating gangway. It was barely buoyant enough to stay afloat beneath their weight, but they dared not let go of it. Sharks flashed through the water around them. The men splashed and kicked at them to keep them back.

Walter and Harold were the last men to leave the ship. They swam to different rafts and took command of them. All around, men thrashed in the water, crying for help. Harold tried to paddle his raft to them, but the paddles were too small and the raft too unwieldy to maneuver. Some of the drowning men recognized Harold on the raft by the light of the burning ship and cried out to him by name, pleading with him to save them. Several of them "went down screaming for help before the rafts could get to them," he recalled.

The men on the rafts picked up all the swimmers they could. The other men left in the water soon fell silent. The survivors rowed the rafts toward a thin sliver of Haitian coast, barely visible in the distance. They could hear the dull booms of the U-126 firing its deck cannon at one of the ships that had preceded the *Barbara* into the Windward Passage. On Harold's raft, the men lay piled on top of one another so precariously that he was afraid to sleep for fear he would tumble off the pile into the sea. On Walter's raft, the only surviving stewardess, a middle-aged woman nicknamed "Grandma," took her turns at the paddles. She had survived the sinking by jumping overboard and then swimming to a raft, and she knew how to row. "The men would row for awhile and when they got tired, the woman would row and put them to shame," Walter recalled.

On the third day, the pilot of a Navy seaplane spotted Walter's raft, landed the plane on the ocean, and took all the people on the raft aboard, ignoring regulations against overloading the plane (and earning a medal for doing so). The other two rafts, including Davis's, drifted for another day before scraping ashore on the northern tip of Tortuga Island, a mountainous, turtle-shaped mass of rock and jungle that once had been a pirate stronghold. One seaman hiked for eighteen hours through the jungle to a native village for help. Harold was given a ride on a mule into the village, and then on a bus to Santo Domingo in the Dominican Republic, where he was entertained in the home of a wealthy family "in a way fitting to royalty."

The three men on the floating gangway were not so lucky. They had no water and were coated with thick bunker C fuel oil—"the blood of dead ships," in the words of the Caribbean historian Gaylord T. M. Kelshall. The oil weighed the men down and magnified the effects of the sun. On the second day, one of the men swam off in quest of food and drink that existed only in his mind. He apparently was a victim of heat stroke, which can disrupt the body's heat-regulating mechanisms and cause lethal fevers and bizarre visions.

Heat-stroke hallucinations often drove castaways in lifeboats to suicidal acts. Two men in one lifeboat joined hands and walked over the side into the ocean, saying, "We're going down to the hospital." In a lifeboat of the torpedoed freighter *Blink*, the first mate recalled, "One by one the men went mad. They would talk of a comfortable bed or a cup of coffee. [The captain] talked of his family just before he died. Several men tried to jump overboard but we kept them inside." One young seaman repeatedly jumped into the water to haul the hallucinating swimmers back into the lifeboat.

The two men on the *Barbara*'s floating gangway kept seeing planes fly directly overhead, but could not attract the pilots' attention; the gangway rode too low in the water. Finally, on the third day, a ship picked the men up. They had survived without food or water.

Hudgins's wife, Bessie, who worried about him constantly, first learned of the *Barbara*'s sinking in a phone call from a friend. The friend did not know if anyone on the ship had survived. Bessie was beside herself for several hours until the Bull Line called to report Walter was alive. Two days later, she received a postcard from Walter saying only that he was "well and happy" and asking her to tell Harold's mother that he, too, was safe. Walter had come through the sinking without a scratch. Even his gold pocket watch still kept time: His skin-tight life vest had kept any water from reaching it.

In all, thirty-seven of the *Barbara*'s eighty-eight crew and passengers died and fifty-one lived. The Bull Line flew Walter home from Santo Domingo and booked Harold a comfortable stateroom on a ship for the ride back. But Harold felt trapped inside the stateroom and barely set foot inside it. He spent his days on the ship's bridge and his nights on deck, sleeping in his clothes with his life vest fastened around him. Weeks later, a *Gazette-Journal* reporter interviewed him at home in Bavon and wrote that Harold "showed signs of having gone through a great struggle," and seemed haunted by the memories of drowning shipmates calling to him for help: "His thoughts were mirrored in his eyes." But as soon as the Bull Line assigned Walter a new ship, Harold signed back on with him and returned to sea, where another U-boat encounter awaited them both.

Hundreds of merchant mariners went right back to sea after harrowing experiences such as Walter's and Harold's. One hard-luck mariner, John Stanizewski, had a total of ten ships sunk out from under him over the course of the two world wars. The survivors of the ore carrier *Marore*, torpedoed off Norfolk in February, included two old seamen who had survived a total of seven sinkings. One of them told reporters he had tried driving a taxi and a streetcar but concluded "life was too short for such uninteresting professions." The experience of being torpedoed was so common that the president of the Boston Seaman's Club founded a "40-

Fathom Club" for men who had survived sinkings. "I hope the membership won't become too large," he added. But it grew larger every day as rescue ships brought exhausted, oil-soaked survivors to the docks of St. John's, Halifax, Boston, New York, Norfolk, Morehead City, Miami, and Havana.

Twenty-seven ships from six Allied nations were sunk off U.S. shores in March 1942. Statistically, U.S. coastal waters had become the most dangerous on earth, the scene of half the world's sinkings. The U-boat war was forcing mariners to become professional survivors. Their job description had expanded from navigation and cargo stowage to escaping from shipwrecks, avoiding fire and sharks, and surviving days or even weeks in open boats with no guarantee of rescue.

Surviving a sinking could be absurdly easy or agonizingly hard. All eighty-four men on one torpedoed ship made it into the lifeboats without even getting their feet wet, and spent their time adrift being entertained by a young seaman who played the flute. When a ship picked them up, the captain had a cow slaughtered in order to feed them a steak dinner. But the survivors of a Belgian freighter drifted in a lifeboat for three weeks in the North Atlantic cold. "Those of us who lived saw wounds, hunger, thirst and cold take 24 men one-by-one," the chief mate reported. "Two men went insane, stood up screaming and jumped overboard during that 25-day eternity, but men willingly gave up their rations to those weaker than themselves. They say there's an animal streak in all men. That's a damn lie."

All a merchant captain could do was to follow the route assigned to him by the Navy, and hope the Navy had gotten it right. The Navy received daily updates from the British Admiralty about the locations of U-boats in the Atlantic, and kept track of U-boat sightings and sinkings in U.S. waters. But the Navy's methods of tracking U-boats were still disjointed, and many ships, including the *Barbara*, followed their Navy routing instructions straight to the bottom of the sea.

Merchant captains also were told to keep their ships zigzagging in dangerous waters to make it harder for U-boats to line them up for torpedo strikes. But zigzagging extended a voyage, widening the window of opportunity for the ship to encounter a U-boat, and a ship might just as easily zigzag into a torpedo's path as out of it. "For every ship saved by a fortuitous zig, another is lost by an unfortunate zag," an American submariner concluded.

No captain was more conscientious than Homer Callis of Gwynn's Island. Homer, a trim man with a carefully groomed moustache, was one of three brothers commanding freighters for the Bull Line. Homer and his brothers Robert and Rodney all had reputations as fine seamen, but Homer stood out. He was a natural ship-handler like Jesse Hodges. But unlike Captain Jesse, Homer was a soft-spoken and benevolent boss. He took care of his crews and treated them with respect. Two of his crew members named their sons Homer after him. Shipowners and even the sea unions held Homer in high regard. Some mariners said that until they sailed with Captain Callis, they had never realized a sea captain could also be a gentleman.

Homer and his wife, Nancy, lived on Gwynn's Island in a white, two-story clapboard house on the shore of Milford Haven, near the drawbridge. Nancy named the house "Dunrovin'," as in the place Homer came when he was "done rovin'." The couple's two sons, Homer Jr. and Bill, had learned to sail and scull almost as soon as they could walk. Homer kept the captain's launch from his ship, the *Mae*, anchored in Milford Haven for the boys to use. Homer also took Homer Jr. and Bill on voyages to the Caribbean aboard the *Mae*, where they worked alongside the crew. Homer's crews always included several Mathews men. When Homer came back to the island, he always rounded up the local boys to play baseball, and then afterward treated them all to Cokes at the general store.

Since Pearl Harbor, Homer had sailed the *Mae* on short voyages in the Caribbean and Gulf of Mexico. He diligently followed the Navy's routing instructions, monitored all radio traffic, conducted daily lifeboat drills, and assigned extra lookouts. He was well aware that the *Mae* was on its own against U-boats. One day, a Coast Guard vessel escorted the *Mae* along the coast until nightfall, when the Coast Guard captain announced his ship was returning to port. Homer held his tongue, but as the Coast Guardsmen sped off, he said to himself, "But now is when I need you."

Homer spent every night on the bridge. At any hint of trouble he sounded the ship's general alarm, rousing the crew from their bunks to stand by the lifeboats. "Sometimes when you sailed with him you wouldn't get no sleep at all," said Jack Rowe of Gwynn's Island. "He'd call you to the lifeboats three or four times a night, the alarm going beep, beep, beep. I got so I would rather get torpedoed than wake up again and stand by the lifeboat. But I and all the other men on the crew appreciated Capt. Homer. He treated his ship and his crew like he was their daddy. He was an A-No. 1 captain, the best captain I ever sailed with." Mothers in Mathews wanted their sons to go to sea with Homer.

The only time Rowe ever saw Homer angry was on a gloomy night in the Caribbean in early 1942. The *Mae* was steaming blacked out through Stygian darkness when a light started blinking about a half mile away. The ship's third officer started to signal back with his own light in reply. "Stop, Goddamn it," Homer roared at him. "That light could be a trap by a U-boat." Homer ordered the *Mae* to run at full speed, zigzagging. He called down to the engine room to tell the firemen to keep the fuel temperature steady so the ship would not produce exhaust smoke.

Not every merchant captain took Homer's approach. Captain Jesse Hodges followed the Navy's instructions only when they did not conflict with his instincts. He tried to think like U-boat captains, who used the weather and the changing light to their advantage. "Twilight, that's when you've got to watch the boogers," he told a reporter. "That's when there's shadows. Early mornings, too."

The freewheeling Captain James Elvin "Bubba" Lewis of Mathews completely ignored the Navy and took his own precautions. Lewis—who had been captured by the Fascists in the Spanish Civil War and beaten with rubber hoses—did not trust the Navy to protect him. He avoided convoys even when assigned to them. He always sailed at night and alone. He never told the crew more than a couple hours in advance of when he planned to leave port. He was the kind of merchant captain who infuriated the Navy. But he sailed tankers across the Atlantic and Pacific throughout the course of the war without ever encountering an enemy submarine.

So many ships were being torpedoed that a publisher of mariners' textbooks hurried into print a 144-page book titled *How to Abandon Ship*, whose purpose was to reduce fatalities. One of the coauthors, John Banigan, had survived a torpedoing. The writers interviewed dozens of mariners who had lived through explosions, fires, and lifeboat voyages. They interviewed Navy survival experts, doctors, professors of chemistry and physiology, search-and-rescue coordinators, the inventor of the life suit, and even a polar explorer. *How to Abandon Ship* was a step-by-step primer for surviving a torpedoing, with vivid examples of self-sacrifice and ingenuity, including the case of a ship's engineer who saved everyone in his lifeboat by cobbling together plastic scraps and rubber tubing to build a still that converted seawater into drinkable water. *How to Abandon Ship* sought to encourage readers by evoking the eighteenth-century British captain William Bligh, who sailed a small boat 3,618 miles across the Pacific after being set adrift by mutineers on the HMS *Bounty*, and Sir Ernest Shackleton, who guided three lifeboats 346 miles through Arctic waters in 1915 after polar ice crushed his ship, the *Endurance*.

How to Abandon Ship stressed in its opening chapter that the best way to survive was to prepare for the worst. The U-boat war punished those who flouted that rule, including Captain Levy Morgan of Gwynn's Island and the crew of the freighter *Colabee*.

Morgan was descended from an oysterman, a sailor, and a tugboat captain—his rough-hewn father, Napoleon Vaudie Morgan. Levy and his brother quit school to go to sea. Levy rose through the ranks to become a captain for the Hawaiian American Line. A family photo of him shows a big man flashing a grin beneath a wide-brimmed straw hat, as if on holiday.

The *Colabee*, however, was not a happy ship. Morgan's treatment of his crews had prompted the shipping line to take the unusual step of ordering him to "lean [over] backward in the treatment of the crew," his first officer said, and that leniency "ruined shipboard discipline." The crew never practiced launching the lifeboats.

The *Colabee* sailed out of Nuevitas, Cuba, on March 12 on the sugar run to Baltimore, laden with 38,600 bags of raw sugar. She crept along the northern coast of Cuba for two days before turning north. Morgan kept two lookouts posted, but the sea was choppy and they failed to spot the U-126 waiting in ambush on the surface ahead of them. The submarine drilled a torpedo into the *Colabee*'s starboard side, blowing a hole in the hull and raining sugar down on the deck. Steam pipes in the engine room ruptured, scalding the chief engineer as he tried to stop the engines. Morgan gave the order to launch the only remaining intact lifeboat. He lowered a suitcase full of documents to the boat on its way down. But the crew had committed the cardinal sin of launching the lifeboat while the ship was still moving. As soon as the boat reached the water, its bow nosed under and it flipped violently, hurling its occupants into the sea. Seven of them never came up. The briefcase sprang open and spilled the documents across the water. Some of the crew struggled to right the lifeboat. Others panicked and jumped overboard without life rings or life vests. "Leadership was lacking," one survivor recalled. "Each man looked out for himself." The *Colabee*'s momentum carried the ship into the shallows, where she ran aground. The U-126 prowled alongside the stranded freighter, shining a searchlight on the superstructure. The badly scalded chief engineer flattened himself against the deck as the searchlight beam swept back and forth over his head. The Germans fished one of the *Colabee*'s crew from the ocean and interrogated him. One U-boat officer spoke perfect English, having lived in America before the war. Bauer, the U-boat commander, expressed annoyance that the *Colabee* had been carrying only sugar. He let his prisoner slide down the U-boat's hull into the water near the lifeboat, which the men had finally managed to right. Then the U-126 submerged.

There was no sign of Levy Morgan. Several men said they had seen the captain jump into the ocean.

The Navy took possession of the damaged *Colabee* the next day. Intelligence officers searched in vain for her secret codebooks, and speculated ominously that the Germans had boarded the ship and captured them. The codes more likely had been in the briefcase and now lay at the bottom of the sea, but Morgan was not available to ask, and the night had been a debacle. Twenty-five of the *Colabee*'s thirty-seven officers and crew were dead, even though the ship had not sunk. A Navy report blamed the high death toll on "great confusion and lack of discipline among the crew." The Coast Guard was even more unsparing: "Had the crew remained onboard [*sic*] instead of trying to cast off precipitously in the port lifeboat, they would have all been saved, or could have left at their leisure in the [other] boat." It was a harsh critique from a government that had sent Levy Morgan and his volunteer crew into harm's way alone and unarmed. And it hinted at America's ambivalence toward the men of the 40-Fathom Club.

After the war, the merchant mariners' independent status would shut them out of a lifetime's worth of military veterans' benefits, including health care, money for a college education, and low-interest loans for homes and businesses. The mariners' reputation, and the Navy's wariness about them, was already a problem even as they faced the U-boats in 1942. "The sailor from the merchant ships was in those days known to America as a bum," the former mariner and author Felix Riesenberg wrote. "He was associated with rotgut whiskey, waterfront brawls and quickie strikes that held up big passenger ships at New York, New Orleans and San Francisco . . ." Mariners had been in such short supply at the start of the war that shipping companies had lowered their standards and hired drunks, idlers, thieves, brawlers, and card sharps to fill out their crews. The antics of those "performers," as the unions called them, had tarnished the Merchant Marine's reputation. The presence of Communists in the sea unions further eroded the mariners' public image, although most mariners, and certainly the Mathews men, had no interest in radical politics. Navy admirals deplored the mariners' refusal to bend to military discipline. Critics in the press railed that wartime bonuses raised mariners' pay higher than that of military men—ignoring the facts that mariners earned wages only when at sea, paid income tax, and received no government benefits. The Hearst newspaper columnists Walter Winchell and Westbrook Pegler, whose influence with the public far exceeded their understanding of the war, attacked mariners as greedy and unpatriotic. Pegler asserted in a column that merchant seamen had refused to unload supplies at Guadalcanal, forcing sick Marines to do the work—a baseless and easily disproven claim for which Hearst ended up paying libel damages. *Time* magazine declared that new recruits to the Merchant Marine greeted one another as "slacker," "draft-dodger," and "profiteer"—at a time when mariners were dying at a higher rate than men in any branch of military service except the U.S. Marines.

Not everyone piled on. President Roosevelt praised the Merchant Marine in speeches, and his wife, Eleanor, credited mariners with "supreme courage" and suggested they be issued uniforms. Helen Lawrenson, a writer for *Collier's* magazine, waded into a dingy seamen's bar in Greenwich Village and was charmed by a group of mariners who went by the names of Low Life McCormick, No Pants Jones, Screwball McCarthy, Foghorn Russell, Soapbox Smitty, Riff Raff, and Whiskey Bill. Ten of the twelve mariners she met had been torpedoed at least once, and one of the other two complained, "I feel so out of place. I'm a wallflower, a nobody." Lawrenson wrote that the mariners cut decidedly unromantic figures, guzzling "vast and formidable quantities of beer" while belting out sea ditties with raw lyrics. But beneath that surface, she found them intensely patriotic, casually fearless, and wise to the workings of the world. "They were the best informed, the most widely traveled, and the most truly sophisticated men I have ever met," she concluded.

The New York Times characterized merchant mariners as the war's unsung heroes: "No one steps up to the bar to buy them drinks. No moist-eyed old ladies turn to them in the subway to murmur 'God bless you.' The cop on the beat, gentle with the tipsy soldier or the unsteady gob [Navy man], is apt to put his nightstick to the britches of a merchant sailor who has tippled heavily in the town's bars to celebrate his rescue from the sea."

Few of the Mathews men read the columnists or listened to the Communists, the admirals, or the politicians. They were too focused on trying to reach the next port with their ships still beneath their feet. The tedium of sailing was now overlaid with a constant, corrosive fear of being attacked without warning. When their ships delivered badly needed supplies or arms, most of them felt as if they had achieved something. "The stuff had to go overseas," said J. W. Corbett. "It had to be done. We were the only ones who could do it, and we did it."

The fear receded in port but returned to the pit of the stomach as soon as the ship left the dock again. U-boats often waited just outside busy Allied harbors and sank ships at the start of their voyages. Standing lookout was nerve-racking at any time, but especially around dawn and dusk, when the colors of the sea and the sky merged into a gray haze, and any flash of color or ripple of motion might signal a U-boat waiting in ambush.

"I just tried to relax and think, if we get hit, we get hit," recalled Jack Rowe of Gwynn's Island. "You were taking a chance, that's for sure, but a lot of people were taking chances. You couldn't just say, 'Why me?' Somebody had to sail the ships." Raymond Edwards, a Gloucester mariner who survived a torpedoing, said of his shipmates: "[M]ost of them act as if they are not worried about or even thinking about submarines. Occasionally a man will get the jitters and will be noticed walking the deck at night when he should be asleep . . . usually the men laugh and joke, go through the routine of life aboard a ship as they did before the war, except for the precautions for lifesaving that are now required."

When a ship is torpedoed, Edwards added, "Even two seconds could mean the difference between life and death for any member of the crew. Running in the wrong direction might cut a sailor off from all means of escape. Jumping overboard at the wrong spot or at the wrong instant might easily cost a life. If a sailor is lucky enough to be alive after a torpedo hits his ship, it takes quick thinking and fast action to get him off the ship and into a lifeboat. Many are saved by sheer luck."

The job of professional survivor seemed to grow tougher all the time. The risk extended not only to men on freighters and tankers but to fishermen and tugboat men like Captain Jesse Hodges, his son Willie, and his grandson J. W. Corbett. If Henny Hodges had ever taken comfort in the idea that tugboats were too small for U-boats to attack, an incident in late March 1942 dispelled that assurance. On a misty night off a lonely uninhabited barrier island on the Virginia coast, a U-boat chased down the tug *Menominee*, blew it out of the water with point-blank blasts from its deck cannon, and then attacked three barges the tug had been towing. The attack killed sixteen men, including several from Virginia's Northern Neck, a peninsula on the Bay north of Mathews. The Hodges family had known several of the dead.

Henny's sons Raymond, Leslie, and Coleman were on freighters in the Caribbean, which was arguably the most dangerous place in the world to sail. Her son Dewey was at home with a serious illness, but he would soon be back at sea. In Dewey's absence, his ship the *East Indian*, commanded by a substitute captain, was shuttling between austere ports on the coast of West Africa, from Cameroon to Nigeria, Ivory Coast, Liberia, and Sierra Leone, stalked not only by U-boats but by malaria. The odds that all of the seafaring Hodges men would be lucky enough to survive the U-boat war seemed to grow longer every day.

No mariner in Mathews, however, would face longer odds than Captain Mellin Respess of Gwynn's Island, whose fate was soon intertwined with the Hodges family's.

Mellin had grown up on the island, the grandson of an oysterman and the son of a pound net fisherman. He had been named Mellin after a favorite brand of baby food, but everyone on Gwynn's Island called him "Choc" because he loved chocolate, and many islanders knew him by no other name. Mellin grew up fishing with his father but switched to the Merchant Marine in his late twenties. He was handsome, with dark hair and a sparkle in his brown eyes that women liked. "He was a ladies' man, sort of took life as a joke," recalled Bill Callis. Mellin traveled the world as a young man, leaving the island for years at a time. The only surviving photo of him shows him sitting on a camel in Giza, Egypt, with the Great Sphinx and the Second Pyramid in the background. But Mellin always came home to Gwynn's Island. In 1935 he took a job on a freighter commanded by a neighbor on the island, Captain J. T. Powell, who lived just down a dirt lane from the house where Mellin grew up. The ship hauled a load of ice from Baltimore to Fort Pierce, Florida, and returned with a cargo of fresh oranges. Mellin must have impressed Powell, because soon after they returned to the island, he married Powell's daughter Eleanor, whom he had barely known growing up. Eleanor was a pretty, whip-smart brunette with a serious demeanor. She taught math and later French at Mathews High School, where the boys nicknamed her "Poker" because she maintained a poker face no matter what pranks they pulled on her.

By 1942, Mellin was twenty-six years old and a licensed master. He sailed for the Bull Line—for which his cousin Virgil did the hiring—but worked for other companies too. Like many young masters, Mellin sometimes sailed as a first officer for lower pay while he waited for a ship of his own. He and Eleanor moved to Baltimore and hoped to start a family, but she miscarried. Once America entered the war, Eleanor moved back into her parents' two-story home at Cherry Point on the island's northern tip, not far from where twelve-year-old John Dixon and his friends kept watch for U-boats in the Bay. Eleanor rented rooms to the wives of Bill Callis and two other mariners, and the women fortified one another against the rumors and loneliness.

Mellin's first and lightest brush with death had come in February 1942. He had been among the half dozen Mathews men who got off the *Major Wheeler* just before it vanished. Even Eleanor had sailed on the *Major Wheeler*, having joined her husband on a harbor cruise before the war. Mellin had left the *Major Wheeler* to become first officer of the *Oakmar*, a 5,766-ton freighter owned by Calmar Steamship Co. of New York.

In late February, 1942, the *Oakmar* had steamed from Baltimore across the Atlantic and around the Cape of Good Hope to Calcutta, India, where she had taken on a cargo of leather and burlap. The ship recrossed the ocean to Trinidad to pick up a load of manganese ore. By mid-March, U-boats had sunk several ships in the waters off Trinidad, and the Navy, hoping to spare the *Oakmar* from a similar fate, instructed her captain to stay well offshore on the homebound voyage to Baltimore. The captain did as he was told. But on the morning of March 20, about 300 miles off Hatteras, the ship steamed into the crosshairs of the U-71.

The *Oakmar* was so alone and helpless that the U 71's commander, Walter Flachsenberg, decided to save his torpedoes and sink her by other means. The sea was too rough for the Germans to aim the deck cannon. So the U-71 charged the *Oakmar* and raked the freighter's bridge with machine-gun fire. The *Oakmar* was too slow to outrun the sub, so the captain gave the order to abandon ship. Flachsenberg had the U-71 hold its fire until the crew got away in two lifeboats. Despite his show of mercy, two of the freighter's crew members drowned while trying to board the lifeboats.

Flachsenberg reluctantly decided to spend a torpedo to sink the *Oakmar.* His first torpedo missed—or possibly was a dud—so he ended up having to use two. He did not stop to engage the men in the lifeboats. The boats became separated and the one without Mellin was never seen again. Mellin and twenty-nine of his shipmates drifted in the second lifeboat for two days before a Greek freighter picked them up and took them to Bermuda. Mellin spent almost a month in Bermuda "quite ill in a hospital" before finally catching a Pan Am flying boat to New York. He took a bus home to Gwynn's Island, arriving just in time for his twenty-seventh birthday. His family and friends held a birthday dinner for him.

After a couple of weeks, he had to start looking for a new ship. In Mathews, the thirty-day deadline for a mariner to either go back to sea or be drafted was strictly enforced. A representative of the local draft board, Ms. Moody, had a preternatural sense of how long each mariner had been back in Mathews. She sent them official letters when their time was near, and if they stayed too long, she reported them to the Selective Service and also gave their names to the newspaper. "She acted like it was her privilege and pleasure," fumed Charles "Pete" White of Mathews, who received a letter from her. His eyes still flashed at the memory seventy years later, at the age of ninety-two. During the war, some Mathews mariners took pains to avoid the courthouse area, where Ms. Moody worked in a lawyer's office.

Mellin did not hesitate when, after two weeks on the island, the Bull Line offered him command of the Liberty ship *Thomas McKean*. Getting torpedoed, coming home for a break, and then going back out into the war zone had become part of his job description.

The night before Mellin left Gwynn's Island to join his new ship in Baltimore, he stopped by the L.M. Callis & Son general store near the courthouse, where old-timers gathered around a woodstove every day to play cards and pass the time. Mellin was sharply dressed in a suit and hat, and lighthearted as always. Everyone wished him a good voyage. Nobody mentioned U-boats. Mellin shook hands all around and returned to the island for a last night with Eleanor.

His encounters with U-boats were only beginning. He would never see Gwynn's Island again.

CHAPTER FIVE

"Off Hatteras
the Tankers Sink"

T he oil tanker *E.M. Clark* was approaching Cape Hatteras early on the
morning of March 18, 1942, when a lightning storm swept across the
Outer Banks of North Carolina. The tanker was running without
exterior lights, and her portholes and passageways were draped with heavy
curtains to prevent any light from leaking out and betraying the ship's
position. But the storm made a cruel joke of the crew's precautions. The
lightning flashes lit up the big tanker from bow to stern every few seconds,
like a giant strobe light. Every man aboard the *E.M. Clark* knew U-boats
haunted Hatteras, and that they were in grave danger. It is hard to imagine,
however, that Boyd Dixon of Mathews was afraid.

Boyd led a hustling, devil-may-care life. He was a tinkerer and an en-
trepreneur. He built the fastest Soap Box Derby cars in Mathews. He built
a telescope, grinding and polishing his own lenses. He grew miniature
vegetables and raised a family of raccoons. He was a good student but a
brilliant billiards player, and steadily gravitated from the classroom to his
father's pool hall near the courthouse. By age fifteen he was playing exhi-
bition matches against adult billiards champions in front of crowds in
Richmond and elsewhere. When he lost, he laughed about it. In high

school, he managed a local boxer, whom he insisted could challenge heavy-weight champ Max Baer. Boyd set up a ring in the local Odd Fellows Lodge. After his fighter won a couple of bouts, he talked the principal of Mathews High School into setting up a ring on the baseball diamond, with seating for hundreds of paying customers. He arranged for a doctor to oversee the fight and a man "with traveling-circus and professional ring experience" to referee. The upcoming fight was the talk of Mathews until the local prosecutor, a friend of the Dixon family, pointed out that sixteen-year-old Boyd was not a licensed boxing promoter.

After high school, Boyd signed on with the Bull Line as an able seaman. He loved the ocean and devoted his time ashore to smoking, drinking, and hustling pool to finance those vices. He lived too hard to ever rise above the rank of seaman, but he was no hoodlum. He "believed in the idea of helping everyone that he could, and to never hurt anyone or an animal," his brother John wrote of him. Boyd sailed on several voyages through war zones before signing on to the *E.M. Clark*, a 9,647-ton Standard Oil Co. tanker that carried heating oil from refineries in the Gulf of Mexico to cities in the Northeast.

Some mariners sailed exclusively on tankers, but others avoided them like the plague. Tankers offered roomy quarters, good food, and steady employment with chances for advancement. Tanker crews did not have to manhandle cargo or quarrel with stevedores on the docks. They had only to connect the hoses and turn on the valves and wait for the cargo to flow. The process was so fast that the crews complained they rarely got to spend any time in port. Tankers docked at remote piers at safe distances from the bustling waterfronts, in case their volatile cargo ignited or exploded.

The downside of serving on tankers was that their cargoes of oil and its refined products such as gasoline, aviation fuel, and kerosene, gave off flammable vapors that readily ignited.* Gasoline has a flash point of minus-

---

* Vapor is the only form of a substance that burns, because fire occurs when molecules of a flammable substance are virtually surrounded by oxygen molecules. The mole-

45 degrees Fahrenheit, which means a spark can ignite it under virtually any weather conditions. Crude oil has a far higher flash point of 400 degrees, but a fire burning out of control can reach that temperature quickly. An oil fire can generate temperatures exceeding 2,500 degrees, along with dense, black smoke laden with soot, particulates, and compounds like sulfur dioxide and carbon monoxide. The smoke alone can kill, wrecking a victim's lungs and causing chemical pneumonia or convulsions. Any oil spilled into the sea floats and gives off fumes that also can ignite, creating a moat of fire around the ship and sealing off escape. After one wreck, two mariners were burned to death when the self-igniting calcium flares on their life vests, designed to attract rescuers in the dark, ignited oil slicks around them. Other men fought fires in their lifeboats when oily water sloshing around their feet suddenly burst into flame from sparks or intense heat. One tanker captain recommended equipping lifeboats with fire extinguishers.

A quarter-inch-thick layer of oil can burn for thirty minutes, boiling the water under and around it. Even if spilled oil does not ignite, it can incapacitate swimmers by clogging their noses and mouths and plastering their eyelids shut. Even a man rescued from an oil slick might suffer long-term illness because of oil lodged in his lungs or eyes. Men drowned in 1942 because the oil coating their bodies made them too slippery for rescuers to pull from the water. No peril of the sea conjured more nightmare images than a tanker on fire.

Oil companies installed safety features such as fire-retardant chemical sprays to reduce the risk of catastrophe. Those features were fine for peacetime, but they could not stop torpedoes from transforming tankers into floating volcanoes. And that was exactly what Doenitz wanted his U-boats

---

cules of solids and liquids are too tightly packed to allow such encirclement. Heat applied to solids and liquids releases vapors into the air where they can ignite. Increasing heat releases more and more vapor, degrading the substance as the fire burns. That is why fire consuming an object often appears to be hovering just above the object. In fact, it is.

to do. He made it clear to his commanders that tankers were their No. 1 targets. Sinking a tanker was the single most telling blow a U-boat could strike against the Allies, and the surest path to medals and glory for a U-boat commander. No one understood that better than Johann Mohr, the cocky, twenty-eight-year-old commander of the U-124.

Mohr had entered American waters in early March 1942 as a part of a wave of eleven U-boats. Doenitz had given him the plum assignment of patrolling off Hatteras, where strong currents and the ever-shifting Diamond Shoals created a bottleneck for shipping. Mohr had sunk two ships on his way to Hatteras and two more after arriving on March 16. He had brazenly attacked in daylight and within sight of a U.S. destroyer and a Coast Guard cutter. The American ships had not pursued him, choosing instead to pick up survivors, but a plane had dropped depth charges that rattled the U-124 as it crash-dived. Mohr kept the sub on the bottom for several hours until night fell. He had just brought the U-124 to the surface when the lightning storm presented the *E.M. Clark* to him as a gift.

The U-124's first torpedo hit the tanker amidships on the starboard side, blowing a hole in the hull below the water line and leaving the *E.M. Clark* rattling "like a bunch of tin cans," a seaman recalled. The 118,725 barrels of heating oil in her tanks did not ignite. Dixon and his shipmates were climbing down rope ladders into the lifeboats when a second torpedo hit and the tanker sank fast. The men in the lifeboats felt hot rain patter down on them. Except it was not rain. The ship's cargo of heating oil, blown high into the air, was falling in a fine spray. "It seemed a miracle that the ship had not caught fire," the radioman said. The oil overspread the water around the ship. The fumes made some men vomit, but the crew was lucky. Had the oil been a few degrees hotter, or exposed to an open flame, they might all have died in a rain of fire. As it was, the oil calmed the ocean around them.

The *E.M. Clark*'s captain ordered the two lifeboats to circle the spot of the sinking, in case any survivors were still in the water. All they found was a shark floating belly up, apparently killed by the torpedo explosion.

The U-boat lingered at the scene and shined a spotlight in all directions, but the cresting waves concealed the lifeboats, and the submarine left after an hour. The men in one lifeboat were picked up a few hours later by a Venezuelan tanker. The occupants of the other boat were picked up shortly after dawn by a U.S. destroyer.

Forty of the *E.M. Clark*'s forty-one officers and crew survived, including Boyd Dixon. He went home to Mathews, collected some new clothes and a new pool cue, and soon went cheerfully back to sea. He would sail on tankers and freighters throughout the war, injuring his leg while abandoning ship after a torpedoing in the Caribbean, and suffering a shrapnel wound from a German bomb on the docks of North Africa.

Sinking Dixon's ship was only a warm-up for Mohr. In the space of five days off Hatteras, the U-124 sank five tankers and damaged three more. One of the victims, the tanker *Naeco*, loaded with kerosene and heating oil, ignited in a fireball that rose three hundred feet into the air and showered burning oil on the crew, killing twenty-four of the thirty-eight men—the fate the *E.M. Clark*'s crew had been so lucky to avoid. Mohr did not stop sinking tankers until he ran out of torpedoes. Before turning for home, he radioed Doenitz a poem he had composed to celebrate his success:

> *The new-moon night is black as ink.*
> *Off Hatteras the tankers sink,*
> *While sadly Roosevelt counts the score—*
> *Some fifty thousand tons*—by Mohr*

Mohr's departure did not slow the U-boats' assault. Throughout late March and early April 1942, tankers were being sunk at a rate of almost one a day—a litany of death for merchant mariners. Jobs on tankers grew harder to fill, as stories about the horrors of flaming tankers spread.

---

* The five tankers Mohr sank on the cruise actually displaced less than 40,000 tons combined, although his total for all his war cruises exceeded 100,000 tons.

Nathaniel "Nat" Foster Jr. was not dissuaded. Nat's ancestors had set-tled in Mathews along Mobjack Bay before the American Revolution, and had fought with a colonial militia against the British. Nat's grandfather had run a shipping company. Nat had quit high school to work on Bull Line freighters commanded by two of his neighbors, Captains Holly Bennett and Ellis Hudgins. Nat had married a girl from the seafaring community of Belfast, Maine, on Penobscot Bay, and settled there. Soon after Pearl Harbor, he had signed on to the *Muskogee*, which was part of the tanker fleet hauling Venezuelan crude oil to Britain. His first voyage had been tense from start to finish, and his wife, Ruth, asked him to stay ashore. But Nat signed on for another voyage.

As the *Muskogee* steamed south off Cape May, New Jersey, on Febru-ary 1, her captain, William Betts, heard distress calls over the radio from torpedoed ships. He saw flares from their lifeboats, but did not dare stop for fear his ship would be torpedoed next. He wrote to his wife, "If I live to have grandchildren I will have plenty of exciting stories to tell them." Captain Betts guided the *Muskogee* safely to Venezuela, where the ship took on 67,000 barrels of heavy bunker C fuel oil, so viscous it had to be preheated to flow through the hoses. The tanker recrossed the Caribbean and stopped at Trinidad for routing instructions to New York. The Navy sent her alone and unarmed on a course roughly 600 miles offshore. On March 22—four days after Johann Mohr composed his poem off Hatteras—the *Muskogee* disappeared with all hands, including Third Of-ficer Nat Foster.

The shipping company classified the tanker as missing. Nat's parents, Capt. and Mrs. Nathaniel Foster, drove from Mathews to the company's main office in New York, in the hope that their physical presence would pry loose information their phone calls had not. But the company had no information. The Fosters finally went home to Mathews, where their fears slowly crystallized into the certainty that Nat was dead. Nat's parents and his widow would go to their graves not knowing any more. It would be thirty-six years before the details of the *Muskogee's* end would be revealed in dramatic fashion.

Two days after the *Muskogee* vanished, the tanker *Dixie Arrow* burst into flames after being torpedoed off Hatteras and sank in a conflagration that evoked every tanker crewman's worst nightmares. Samuel Dow of Mathews, rowing for his life in a charred lifeboat, looked back at the dying ship and witnessed a sacrifice that was seared into the memory of every man who lived through that day.

The *Dixie Arrow* was an 8,046-ton tanker owned by the Socony-Vacuum Oil Co. of New York—later to become Mobil Oil Corp. Early on the morning of March 26, the *Dixie Arrow* approached Hatteras from the south, carrying 96,000 barrels of crude oil from Texas to a refinery in New Jersey. The *Dixie Arrow* was alone and unarmed, but her captain took every precaution, zigzagging and timing the voyage so that the tanker could round Hatteras while the sun was up. It was almost enough. The U-71—which had torpedoed Mellin Respess and the *Oakmar* the week before—was just preparing to dive after a night on the surface when a lookout spotted the tip of the *Dixie Arrow's* masts on the southern horizon. The U-boat submerged to periscope depth and waited.

The first torpedo tore into the *Dixie Arrow* amidships, wrecking the deckhouse and killing most of the ship's officers. The captain emerged from his cabin in full uniform—the first time the crew had ever seen him wearing it—and started up a ladder to the bridge. But a second torpedo jolted the ship and sent the captain hurtling through the air in a mass of flying debris. A third torpedo quickly followed, cracking the *Dixie Arrow* in half. Fire engulfed the fore half, and oil gushed from the cargo tanks onto the water's surface, where it too rippled into flame.

Dow, a thirty-six-year-old fireman, had just emerged from the engine room and sat down to eat breakfast in the mess hall near the stern. He jumped up and "ran like hell. Every man had to look out for himself, for there was no time to think about anything else." None of the officers were alive to give the order to abandon ship, "but it was plain there was nothing else to do." For the first time he could remember, Dow was scared.

The *Dixie Arrow* was only 15 miles offshore—close enough for onlookers to witness her destruction. The concussion of the torpedo explosions rattled windows in the Hatteras Island village of Buxton at the point of the cape. Children on the way to school stopped to see a pillar of black smoke boiling out of the sea. They forgot about their classes and ran toward the beach. Coast Guard rescue vessels raced for the sinking ship.

Two of the *Dixie Arrow*'s four lifeboats were on fire and a third hung over flaming oil. Dow and several shipmates hurried to lower the only remaining lifeboat before it too was cut off from the open water. The lifeboat swung wildly, crushing a man to death, and then splashed into the sea empty. Dow and the others dived after it, climbed in, and grabbed the oars, two of which were broken and useless. Other crew members threw a raft into a patch of open water, but it landed upside down. The men struggled onto the raft anyway, but they could not reach the paddles, and could not stop the raft from drifting toward burning oil. All of them jumped off except the *Dixie Arrow*'s old cook, who could not swim and was paralyzed with fright. The cook was beloved—"He was the only cook whose soup ever quite suited me," one seaman noted. His shipmates in the water pleaded with him to jump. One even tried to demonstrate how a nonswimmer could stay afloat by lying on his back and kicking. The cook could not budge. "He stayed on the raft and burned to death there right in front of our eyes," a crewman said. On the fore end of the *Dixie Arrow*, eight more crewmen were cornered by fire. The wind whipped the flames from the deckhouse toward them; the water below them shimmered with flaming oil. They agreed to share a last cigarette but nobody had a light. Only one man was in a position to save them. A skinny blond able seaman named Oscar Chappell, from the East Texas railroad town of Normangee, stood alone in the wreckage of the ship's wheelhouse. He had taken the helm just before the attack, working a shipmate's watch in exchange for a few extra hours of sleep. The men on the bow saw blood on Chappell's head and shoulders. They could not tell how badly he was injured or whether he could have saved himself. He did not try. "He stayed there at the wheel," a shipmate recalled. "He put the helm hard over into the wind to keep the flames from spreading to the bow where we were." Then Chappell swung the bow clear of the flaming oil so that the men could jump into open water. "When we jumped overboard, he was still at the wheel, with flames all around him," another seaman said. "All of us . . . owe our lives to Chappell."

Dow watched from his lifeboat and wondered what was going through Chappell's mind. Dow's lifeboat drifted on the fringe of the burning oil slick until a Navy destroyer rescued him and the boat's other occupants. Eleven men on the *Dixie Arrow* died, including the captain and Chappell, who was posthumously awarded the Merchant Marine Distinguished Service Medal. Dow returned to Mathews unscathed. A *Gazette-Journal* reporter described him as "calm and composed . . . One would not know to look at him that he had suffered such an experience." He went back to sea in time to satisfy Ms. Moody of the Mathews draft board, and sailed through the end of the war in the North Atlantic, the Caribbean, the Indian Ocean, and the Arabian Sea. But no records show him ever sailing on another tanker.

In March, oil company executives traveled to Washington, D.C., to plead with the Navy for better protection for their tankers. U-boats had sunk more than forty tankers in the Eastern Sea Frontier, the Caribbean, and the South Atlantic. Those were not bearable losses. Boston and other East Coast cities had barely enough oil for heat. Trains carrying oil in tanker cars were diverted from city to city to plug temporary gaps in the supply. The oil men said they were growing alarmed. If tankers kept being sunk at the current pace, one-third of the U.S. tanker fleet would lie on the seabed by the end of 1942, three thousand tanker crewmen would be dead, and the Allied war effort would stall.* The situation on the water was more

---

*When America entered World War II, the fleet of U.S-flagged tankers comprised roughly 350 vessels.

desperate than the Navy seemed to realize. The ship's carpenter of the tanker *Esso Baton Rouge* built fake guns out of wood and painted them gray to make it look as if the tanker could fight back, but the *Esso Baton Rouge* was torpedoed anyway.

The oil executives told Admiral King that if convoys still were not possible, the Navy should at least install real guns on the tankers and enlist the help of civilian pilots to patrol the shipping lanes. Shell Oil Co. offered to fly its own small planes from the decks of tankers to scout for U-boats. The oilmen also called for a blackout of U.S. coastal cities—an extraordinary request from an industry whose profits were tied to keeping the lights on.

King immediately agreed to start arming tankers and stationing Navy Armed Guard crews on them to operate the guns. The arming of merchant ships progressed throughout the war, although no Armed Guard crew on a merchant ship would ever sink a U-boat. King dismissed the idea of organizing civilian pilots to patrol the coast as "unworkable." He still did not order a blackout, instead asking on March 14 for a "dimout" of unnecessary lights. That half measure set off a debate over which lights were necessary, and while the debate went on, most shore lights continued to blaze. The night of King's call for a "dimout," an American freighter was torpedoed off Atlantic City, New Jersey, with the loss of twenty lives, and a survivor complained that shore lights had betrayed the ship to a U-boat: "It was lit up like daylight all along the beach."

King continued to withhold destroyers from the Eastern Sea Frontier, insisting he needed all of them to escort North Atlantic convoys and troopships to Britain. Admiral Andrews kept hustling. On March 12, he asked King and Roosevelt for blanket authority to requisition small craft of all kinds to help patrol the coast. Roosevelt pounced on the idea and warned the Navy not to impede it with red tape. The small craft were a meager line of defense. But Andrews also had Coast Guard vessels at his disposal, and he was starting to receive the first of two dozen armed fishing trawlers from the British. The 170-foot trawlers were coal-fired vessels armed with depth charges and deck guns for antisubmarine duty. They were manned by veteran British sailors. The fact that hard-pressed Britain was willing to lend twenty-four of them to the United States showed how worried the British were about the carnage along the U.S. coast.

The British were especially alarmed about the tanker sinkings. Britain needed an average of four tankers a day to fuel its tanks and planes and heat its homes. Churchill did not understand why the Americans allowed the losses to go on. In March, he wrote to his primary contact at the White House, Roosevelt aide Harry Hopkins: "I am most deeply concerned at the immense sinkings of tankers west of the 40th meridian and in the Caribbean Sea . . . The situation is so serious that drastic action of some kind is necessary."

Roosevelt relayed Churchill's message to Admiral King, who insisted he was doing all he could. He complained that the British needed to do their part by bombing the U-boat bases on the French coast. In fact, the British had missed a chance to bomb the concrete U-boat bunkers while they were still under construction and vulnerable. But by March they were finished, and impervious to British bombs.

Roosevelt remained confident in King, whose job as chief of the Navy encompassed much more than fighting U-boats offshore. But in a response to Churchill's message to Hopkins, Roosevelt distanced himself from King and the Navy. The president told Churchill the Navy had been preoccupied with building powerful warships, at the expense of humble escort ships that could have been protecting U.S. coastal waters from U-boats. "My navy has been definitely slack in preparing for this submarine war off our coast," Roosevelt wrote to Churchill. "You [British] learned the lesson two years ago . . . We still have to learn it."

The president also mentioned to Churchill King's advice that the British target the U-boat bunkers. A few weeks later, British commandos staged a nighttime raid on the bunker and other German naval facilities at Saint-Nazaire. The raid caused only temporary damage and the commandos suffered heavy losses. French partisans in the village mistook the raid for the long-awaited Allied invasion of France and joined in the attack with the commandos, only to be executed by the Germans after the commandos withdrew. The biggest impact of the raid on the Germans was that Hitler ordered Doenitz to move U-boat headquarters from the French coast to the safety of Berlin.

Hitler crowed in public over America's helplessness against his U-boats. He had once scoffed, "What is America but millionaires, beauty queens, stupid records and Hollywood?" Now he was more convinced than ever that America was soft. "The United States kept up the tall talk and left her coast unguarded," Hitler said. "Now I daresay that she is quite surprised."

Nothing the Americans tried seemed to work. At Britain's urging, the U.S. Navy armed three old freighters with hidden 4-inch guns, machine guns, depth charges, and sonar gear, and sent them into the shipping lanes to ambush U-boats. The Q-ships, as they were called, were loaded with pulp wood, which was buoyant enough to keep the ship afloat for a while even after being torpedoed and flooded. The hope was that U-boat captains would grow curious after the ships did not sink and venture close enough to be obliterated in a surprise attack. On March 27, Hardegan in the U-123 torpedoed the Q-ship *Atik*—formerly the freighter *Carolyn*, a favorite of Mathews men—300 miles off the Virginia coast. The *Atik* stopped as if crippled and dispatched men into lifeboats to further suggest a normal sinking. When the U-123 approached to finish off the ship with its deck cannon, the *Atik* opened fire, killing one of Hardegan's crew. The U-boat barely managed to retreat out of range. After dark, Hardegan returned to finish off the *Atik* with a torpedo, killing all 141 men aboard. He made no effort to aid the lifeboat survivors as a storm bore down on them.

The attack by the *Atik* was the closest any Q-ship came to sinking a U-boat. But the idea of ambushing U-boats so fascinated Ernest Hemingway that he persuaded U.S. authorities in his adopted home of Cuba to arm his beloved 38-foot fishing boat *Pilar* with a light machine gun, hand grenades, and dynamite charges. The novelist envisioned luring a U-boat close enough to the *Pilar* to chase its crew down the hatch with machine-gun fire and then toss the grenades and dynamite down after them. Hemingway piloted the *Pilar* on several uneventful patrols along Cuba's northern coast. His estranged third wife, the war correspondent Martha Gellhorn, scoffed that his efforts were "nothing more than a fancy excuse to get gas rations" to fish for marlin. But Hemingway learned enough from the experience to help him write the novel *Islands in the Stream*, which was published after his death.

By the end of March 1942, the tide of the entire war was running in the Axis's favor. Invading German armies in Russia advanced toward Stalingrad and the precious oil fields of the Caucasus region. Panzer tanks rolled across the deserts of North Africa. Jews in Berlin were ordered to mark all homes they owned. In the Pacific, the Japanese drove ever closer to the trapped Allied troops on Bataan. Japanese troops landed on Guadalcanal in the Solomon Islands, which had a primitive airfield within bombing range of Australia. The entry of the United States had done little to change the war's immediate trajectory. Most of the good news on the front pages of American newspapers fell into the category of small victories in the shadows of disasters. But some of those small victories were so extraordinary, they seemed to pierce the gloom and foretell the war's outcome. First among them was the story of the *City of New York* and the lifeboat baby.

The *City of New York* was a combination freighter and passenger ship, owned by the American-South African Line, which ran between New York and Cape Town, South Africa. On the afternoon of March 29—two days after the *Atik* Q-ship disaster—the *City of New York* approached Hatteras on the last leg of a voyage covering more than 6,700 miles. The ship carried eighty-eight officers and crew, nine Navy armed guards, and forty-seven passengers, including a twenty-eight-year-old Yugoslav woman named Desanka Mohorovicic, who was eight months pregnant, and her two-year-old daughter, Vesna.

Desanka personified Europe at the mercy of the Nazis. She and her husband, Joseph, a diplomat from a prominent Yugoslav family,* had fled Europe for the safety of British-held Cape Town. No sooner had they arrived when Joseph was offered a post with Yugoslavia's government-in-exile in New York. Authorities in Cape Town refused to let Desanka sail because she was too far along in her pregnancy. So the family decided Joseph would travel to New York alone and Desanka would follow with Vesna and the new baby when possible. A few weeks after Joseph left, Desanka was told she could sail after all. She booked passage for herself and Vesna on the next passenger ship leaving Cape Town, the *City of New York*. "I did not have to think long on it, I decided to depart," she wrote. "I felt as a wife and mother I wanted to be alongside my husband. It is hard to live separated by continents and in constant uncertainty. I embarked on the voyage with great faith and confidence, and I was not afraid."

The ship was only a day out of New York when it approached Hatteras a little before 1 p.m. on March 29. A storm, which had been building all morning, darkened the sky to the southeast. Lunch was being served in the dining hall, but Desanka, who tired easily due to her pregnancy, had a waiter bring fruit to her cabin. She and Vesna were lying on their bunks when the first torpedo from the U-160 hit. Desanka heard people running outside their door. She looked for life vests, but they were buried under overturned pieces of furniture. The cabin door was stuck. Desanka threw her swollen body against it and forced it open. She and Vesna climbed a ladder to the main deck to find the crew already launching the lifeboats. They passed a young sailor with blond hair who saw they had no life vests and gave them his. Desanka never learned his name or whether he survived that day.

Mother and daughter struggled down a rope ladder into the ship's Lifeboat No. 4. The crew began lowering the boat, but the chain snagged

---

* Joseph's uncle was a world-famous geologist who was credited with discovering the layer between the earth's crust and mantle, the Mohorovicic Disconformity.

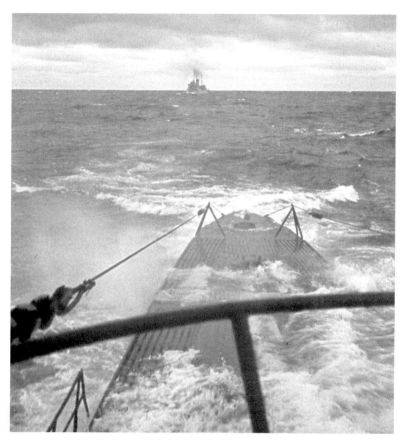

An unidentified U-boat pursues a lone Allied ship in the Atlantic. U-boats were considerably faster when on the surface than most Allied merchant ships.

CREDIT: HUGO JAEGER/THE LIFE PICTURE COLLECTION/GETTY IMAGES

Captain Dewey Hodges's ring. It was discovered in the belly of a shark caught by fishermen near the spot where Dewey's ship was sunk.

CREDIT: COURTESY OF G. DEWEY HODGES III

Captain Dewey Hodges, one of seven Hodges brothers, was lost when his ship the *Onondaga* was torpedoed by the U-129 off Cuba in July 1942.

CREDIT: COURTESY OF THE HODGES FAMILY, VIA JESSE CARROLL THORNTON

The freighter *Onondaga* was built to ply the Great Lakes but was pressed into service during World War II to haul ore and other war cargo.

CREDIT: COURTESY OF HISTORICAL COLLECTIONS OF THE GREAT LAKES/BOWLING GREEN STATE UNIVERSITY

The U-701 returns to its base in France after a patrol. Its final mission ended on the sea bottom off the North Carolina Outer Banks.

CREDIT: THE ALPHEUS CHEWNING COLLECTION, THE OLD COAST GUARD STATION MUSEUM

The Hodges' farmhouse, commanding the family's forty-acre farm on isolated Gales Neck along the East River in Mathews County.

CREDIT: COURTESY OF THE GLOUCESTER-MATHEWS GAZETTE-JOURNAL

A painting of Captain Jesse Hodges. The artist captured Jesse's intensity and his hard gaze, which seemed to say, "Get off your ass."

CREDIT: COURTESY OF THE HODGES FAMILY, VIA JESSE CARROLL THORNTON

Henny Hodges churns butter at Gales Neck. She toiled for long hours running the farm while Captain Jesse essentially lived on his tugboat.

CREDIT: COURTESY OF THE HODGES FAMILY, VIA JESSE CARROLL THORNTON

Several of the Hodges men playing baseball barehanded at Gales Neck. From left, they are J. W. Corbett (Captain Jesse's grandson), David, Dewey (in the background), and Spencer.

CREDIT: COURTESY OF THE HODGES FAMILY, VIA JESSE CARROLL THORNTON

Captain Raymond Hodges, the eldest Hodges son, was widely regarded as having inherited his father's extraordinary skill handling ships.

CREDIT: COURTESY OF HERMAN "BILL" HODGES

Raymond's freighter the *Mormacmoon*. Unlike most merchant vessels of its time, it was fast enough to outrun a U-boat, but that did not guarantee safety.

CREDIT: FROM THE COLLECTIONS OF THE MARINERS' MUSEUM AND PARK, NEWPORT NEWS, VA

Captain Leslie Hodges. He was an outlier among the Hodges brothers, with dark hair, a quiet manner, and a family tragedy weighing on his conscience.

CREDIT: COURTESY OF THE HODGES FAMILY, VIA JESSE CARROLL THORNTON

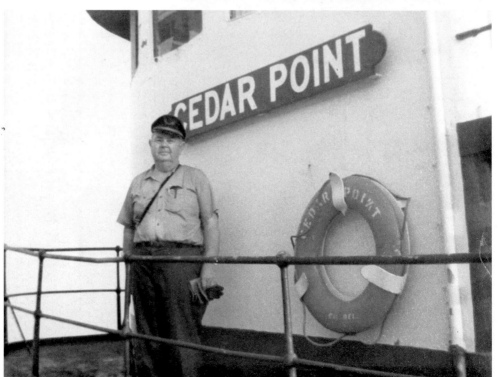

Captain Willie Hodges. He agreed to limit his wartime sailing to safe inland waters for the sake of his heartbroken mother.

CREDIT: COURTESY OF HORACE W. "BROTHER" HODGES, JR.

Captain Coleman Hodges. His lighthearted, joking manner concealed an intensely driven man who was determined to command a merchant ship against the Germans.

CREDIT: COURTESY OF THE HODGES FAMILY, VIA JESSE CARROLL THORNTON

Mr. and Mrs. Spencer Hodges. Spencer was the only Hodges brother not to pursue a career at sea, but he recruited mariners for his brothers' ships.

CREDIT: COURTESY OF THE HODGES FAMILY, VIA JESSE CARROLL THORNTON

Captain David Hodges, the youngest Hodges brother. Known for his piercing wit, he worked in a shipyard during the war but afterward became a pilot.

CREDIT: COURTESY OF HORACE W. "BROTHER" HODGES, JR.

Ammon Gwynn, a black neighbor of the Hodges family. He spent much of his adult life working on the farm at Gales Neck.

CREDIT: COURTESY OF THE HODGES FAMILY, VIA JESSE CARROLL THORNTON

The oil tanker *Dixie Arrow* sinks in flames after being torpedoed off Cape Hatteras. Tankers were the U-boats' favorite targets.

CREDIT: NATIONAL ARCHIVES

This photo of the *Dixie Arrow* was taken just as a young helmsman sacrificed his life to save his shipmates from wind-driven flames.

CREDIT: NATIONAL ARCHIVES

The body of an unidentified mariner floats off the coast of Florida, a prime hunting ground for U-boats in 1942.

CREDIT: NATIONAL ARCHIVES

An unidentified U-boat returns to its base on the French coast. Germany's conquest of France gave U-boats easy access to the Allied convoy routes.

CREDIT: THE OLD COAST GUARD STATION MUSEUM

Admiral Karl Doenitz, the head of the German U-boat force, was a gifted improviser who constantly shifted his submarines into weak areas in the Allies' defenses.

CREDIT: NATIONAL ARCHIVES

Doenitz welcomes a U-boat crew home after a mission. Doenitz took pains to reward returning crews with medals and special perks.

CREDIT: NATIONAL ARCHIVES

Doenitz (fourth from left) with Hitler and other Nazi leaders. In Hitler's will, he named Doenitz to succeed him as Führer.

CREDIT: NATIONAL ARCHIVES

The cocky and capable U-boat commander Reinhard Hardegan, who distinguished himself in the U-boat assault on America. Hardegan's victims included two Mathews men.

CREDIT: NATIONAL ARCHIVES

Admiral Ernest J. King. Though acclaimed for leading the U.S. Navy during the war, he failed to protect merchant ships in U.S. waters in 1942.

CREDIT: NATIONAL ARCHIVES

Admiral Adolphus Andrews. He improvised after being handed the impossible task of protecting the U.S. East Coast from U-boats with aging, poorly equipped vessels and planes.

CREDIT: NATIONAL ARCHIVES

An Allied convoy plows through the North Atlantic carrying desperately needed supplies to Britain. The British called such convoys "the heartbeat of the war."

CREDIT: NATIONAL ARCHIVES

A U.S. Coast Guardsman watches the explosion of depth charges his ship has just dropped in an effort to sink a U-boat.

CREDIT: NATIONAL ARCHIVES

In this sequence of three photos, taken by a Nazi propaganda officer, the American oil tanker *Muskogee* sinks by the stern after being torpedoed by the U-123, and the U-boat approaches a raft carrying seven survivors. The castaways were hundreds of miles from land in the dead of winter and their expressions suggest they know they are doomed. Their families knew nothing of their fates until the late 1980s, when the son of the *Muskogee*'s captain tracked down the retired commander of the U-123, Reinhard Hardegan, who recounted the sinking and provided the photographs.

CREDIT: IMAGES COURTESY OF THE GEORGE BETTS COLLECTION, INDEPENDENCE SEAPORT MUSEUM, PHILADELPHIA, PA

The only surviving photo of Captain Mellin Respess of Gwynn's Island shows him perched on a camel during a prewar voyage to Egypt.

CREDIT: COURTESY OF GWYNN'S ISLAND MUSEUM

Eleanor Respess, the widow of Captain Mellin Respess, christens a just-completed Liberty ship before it is launched at a Baltimore shipyard.

CREDIT: COURTESY OF GWYNN'S ISLAND MUSEUM

and the boat hung suspended over the sea, still tethered to the doomed ship. Then a second torpedo shook the *City of New York* and jarred the lifeboat free. It splashed into the water but did not capsize. Desanka was startled by how much rougher the ocean looked from the low-riding lifeboat than it had from the main deck. The *City of New York* sank right out from under the lifeboats. An outspread mast nearly snagged Desanka's boat on the way down. The U-boat also vanished.

The storm finally broke, drenching the castaways with cold rain. Desanka and Vesna huddled together for warmth on the lifeboat's port-side bench. Fifteen other people occupied the boat, including the ship's doctor, a bespectacled family physician from New York City named Leonard H. Conly. Conly had broken two of his ribs after losing his grip on a rope and falling hard into the boat, and was in considerable pain. The other survivors included a businessman, who wept inconsolably for his missing wife, and a woman who babbled in a voice too soft to hear over the shriek of the wind. A tough old second officer named Charles Van Gordon commanded Desanka's lifeboat. He kept the boat turned into the wind, but the storm roiled the ocean, and waves broke over the boat from all directions. The ocean was surprisingly warm because the boat was in the Gulf Stream, where water temperatures can reach 70 degrees in March. But despite its warmth, the Gulf Stream was not the castaways' friend. It veered northeast at Hatteras, and if they did not escape its grip, it would carry them into the middle of the Atlantic. Crew members and passengers argued over who should row. One passenger called the crew "a bunch of skunks." After dark, cold rain pelted the survivors. Few of them had warm clothes. Desanka wrote later of "bitter, bitter cold and bitter rain" and "dark mountains of water." Across her lap lay Vesna, drifting in and out of sleep.

At around 2:30 the next morning Desanka cried out, "Doctor, the baby is here." Conly was taking his turn at the oars despite his broken ribs. He crawled painfully across other castaways to her side. Van Gordon steadied the boat while other castaways laid the boat's sail over Desanka. "She was awfully courageous," able seaman Leroy Tate recalled. "She never whimpered or cried the whole time. She had her feet in water all the time. She was wet all over." The waves played with the boat while Conly worked. "It was like being on a scenic railway," he told *The New York Times*. "We were swooping up and down on these 15-to-20-foot waves." He delivered a healthy baby boy, and allowed the Gulf Stream to wash him clean. The baby bawled.

"I think it must have been a beautiful sound in that lifeboat," the baby's sister, Vesna, reflected many years later, "because how could you think you were going to die when a newborn baby was crying?" Desanka said some of her boat-mates were "superstitious" and saw the baby as a good omen. Others in the lifeboat were too frightened and preoccupied to care. "I felt sorry for the mother," one recalled, "but there was just so much going on that I really didn't give it much thought."

The doctor worried about the chill wind, and asked a woman if he could wrap the baby in a decorative turban she wore. She hesitated and he snatched the turban off her head, swaddled the baby in it, and presented him to Desanka. She tucked him inside her blue wool dress beneath her life vest, which made Conly think of a kangaroo's pouch. Desanka was exhausted. A seaman let her lean against him. Later, when the clouds briefly parted, the gruff Van Gordon turned grandfatherly and pointed out the stars to the lifeboat baby.

The storm abated by the next afternoon, but the Gulf Stream already had carried Desanka's lifeboat almost 75 miles farther out to sea. The destroyer USS *Roper*—the only destroyer Admiral Andrews had available—had already found another of the *City of New York*'s lifeboats and two of its rafts, rescuing a total of forty-eight people. Just before dawn on March 31—roughly forty hours after the sinking—the *Roper* found Desanka's lifeboat. The destroyer, which was longer than a football field, maneuvered close to the lifeboat and lowered a cargo net. The doctor handed the baby up to a young sailor, who thought he was receiving a bundle of documents and was flabbergasted to be clutching a baby instead. Conly had "never seen such an expression on anyone's face like that on the face of that seaman." The *Roper*'s crew cheered. Desanka would never forget the sight of the sailors in their white uniforms gently passing her son to safety. *Divini hrabni mornari*, she called them in Croatian—"divine, brave sailors." She named her son Jesse Roper Mohorovicic in honor of the destroyer, which itself bore the name of a Navy gunboat captain who died trying to save a member of his crew from a fire.

One of the *City of New York*'s lifeboats was still missing, but the *Roper* was ordered to break off the search and deliver the survivors to Norfolk. A man the *Roper* had picked up from another lifeboat had died in the ship's infirmary, shaking violently, in abject terror of another torpedo strike. As the *Roper* approached the dock, Dr. Conly and Van Gordon devised a birth certificate for the baby in the form of an entry in the *City of New York*'s logbook, listing the place of birth as "At sea in Life Boat." The Navy and the shipping line contacted the next of kin of the *City of New York*'s crew and passengers, including Joseph Mohorovicic, who had no idea his wife had even left Cape Town. Joseph too had had a hard voyage to America. His ship from Cape Town had gotten only as far as the Windward Islands before being torpedoed in the harbor at Port Castries. Joseph had spent three days in a hospital recuperating from cuts and bruises and a punctured eardrum, and then had ridden a Coast Guard vessel to New York City.

Joseph's duties at the Yugoslav embassy in New York included translating dispatches that came over the teletype machine in English. On the morning of April 1, he was shocked by a Navy bulletin that a Yugoslav woman had given birth in a lifeboat. Soon afterward, a telegram arrived for him from the general manager of the American-South African Line:

> THE VESSEL ON WHICH MRS MOHOROVICIC AND
> DAUGHTER WERE RETURNING TO THE UNITED STATES
> IS A WAR CASUALTY STOP AND WERE LANDED AT ST
> VINCENTS HOSPITAL NORFOLK VIRGINIA STOP IN
> ADDITION A BABY WAS BORN TO MRS MOHOROVICIC
> IN A LIFEBOAT AT SEA AND IT IS ALSO IN THE SAME

HOSPITAL WHERE THE DOCTORS REPORT THEY ARE IN
FINE CONDITION STOP OUR REPRESENTATIVES PRESENT
AND ASSISTING THEM

Joseph caught the first train to Norfolk. The next morning he was re-united with his family and then swarmed by reporters. Desanka praised her rescuers and played down her ordeal. "I [had] thought I would have my baby here, in free America," she said, struggling a little with her English. "But it wasn't so badly. He is here, we are well. *Grace de Dieu*."

The story of the "Lifeboat Baby" appeared on the front page of *The New York Times* and dozens of other papers. "The war has yielded few stories as great as this," declared an editorial in the *International Herald Tribune*, "great in its eternal symbolism, great in its simple, almost accidental, state-ment of the deep mysteries of death and life with which we are all sur-rounded." Desanka's story was broadcast over shortwave radio to resistance fighters in Europe. The family moved into a predominantly Jewish neigh-borhood in upper Manhattan, where women called Jesse "the baby Hitler couldn't get." For twenty years afterward, New York tabloids would mark milestones in her son's life with stories such as "Lifeboat Baby Gains Two Pounds," "Lifeboat Baby, Now 11, Loves the Ocean and the Dodgers," and, on his wedding day, "Born in Lifeboat in WWII, He Pipes Life-Mate Aboard."

The press did not dwell on the final chapter of the *City of New York*'s story. Two weeks after the lifeboat birth, the ship's last lifeboat was spotted off the coast of Delaware, more than 300 miles northeast of Hatteras. Of the twenty people who had gotten into the boat, only two remained alive: a seaman and a three-year-old girl. The girl's mother, like Desanka, had sailed with her daughter out of Cape Town to join her husband in New York. The mother had been the last to die of thirst and exposure—only an hour before a plane spotted the boat. The child had begged the seaman not to cast her mother overboard as he had done with the other dead, and he had agreed.

If the story of the lifeboat baby had hinted at a brighter future, the story of the *City of New York*'s last lifeboat more truly reflected the state of the U-boat war in the spring of 1942.

The people of Mathews understood the vagaries of the U-boat war as well as anyone. The county was consumed by it. On April 2, a few days before Easter, the front page of the *Gazette-Journal* carried five separate stories about Mathews men confronted by U-boats. One story reported that Captain Walter Hudgins and First Mate Harold Davis were safe in Baltimore after being torpedoed on the *Barbara*. Other stories confirmed the safe returns of Allenby Grimstead and Robert Lee Brown to Gwynn's Island after the sinking of the *Mary*. Another mariner was quoted as saying his oil tanker had been chased three times by U-boats on a voyage across the Caribbean. And Captain Levy Morgan's brother wrote a letter to the paper saying the family had not given up hope for Levy. A sixth story on the front page reported that a Gwynn's Islander had been killed in a barge accident on the Bay—a reminder that the normal perils of the sea took no vacation in wartime.

Perhaps the most widely read story in the paper that day, however, was a one-paragraph note on a back page that the Ford Motor Co. freighter *East Indian* had returned safely to the Ford docks at Camden, New Jersey, "after a dangerous voyage." If any single vessel on the sea could be called a Mathews ship, the *East Indian* was the one.

The *East Indian* was the flagship of the Ford fleet. Unlike many Ford ships, she was not a tiny laker, small enough to squeeze through the canal between Lakes Erie and Ontario, but a true deep-ocean vessel, 445 feet long and displacing 8,159 tons. Ford had bought her from a Japanese company before the war to carry autos and auto parts from Ford manufacturing plants on the East Coast to customers in the Caribbean and South America.

Since 1930, Ford had entrusted the command of the *East Indian* to Captain Dewey Hodges. Everyone in Mathews knew the *East Indian* as Dewey's ship. Dozens of Mathews mariners had gone to sea for the first time aboard the *East Indian*, at Dewey's invitation. In 1936, Dewey had gotten

Ford's permission to take his wife, Edna, and his four children aboard the *East Indian* for a two-and-a-half-month run to South America, stopping to deliver auto parts at ports in Brazil, Argentina, Uruguay, and Paraguay. Dewey's son, George Dewey Jr., worked as a seaman. The two older girls, Doris and Jean, had their own stateroom and the run of the vessel. The Hodges's baby, Jan, spent her days in a playpen built by the ship's carpenter. The *East Indian* was a menagerie of friendly animals, including an elderly dachshund named Wimpy and more than a dozen canaries that sang in cages in a room designed to cheer up sick and injured seamen. At night, the crew invited the children into the wheelhouse and told them ghost stories under the glittering stars. At every port of call, people greeted Dewey as an old friend and took the family to see the local sights. Dewey's daughter Jean had never wanted the voyage to end. She loved seeing her father in his natural environment. It was the longest period she had ever spent with him.

Dewey had hoped to take his family on another South American cruise in 1940, but as the departure date neared, he decided to leave them at home for their safety. Even though the United States was still neutral at that point, the war already had bled into the South Atlantic. As the *East Indian* steamed past the mouth of the River Plate—the border between Argentina and Uruguay—Dewey had seen the wreck of the German pocket battleship *Graf Spee* lying just upriver. The ship had been crippled in a naval battle with British warships, and then scuttled by her crew. The German captain had shot himself in shame. The sight of the huge, dead warship had cast a pall over the voyage, and Dewey was glad Edna and the children had not been there to see it.

Dewey was normally healthy and robust, but while at home in the fall of 1941 he took severely ill with complications from an old appendectomy. He spent several weeks flat on his back in the hospital, looking so frail that his daughters feared for him. The doctors finally sent him home for a long recuperation, with orders to do as little as possible. He was in no shape to command the *East Indian*, so Ford found a substitute captain for what would be the ship's final voyage before America entered the war.

In November 1941, the *East Indian* set out from the Ford plant on the Delaware River on a 14,000-mile voyage to Calcutta, India. Even without Dewey, there were eight Mathews men aboard. The ship picked up a load of precious rubber in Calcutta, and then turned for home. She was working her way up the west coast of Africa, preparing to recross the Atlantic, when America entered the war. To the crew's chagrin, the *East Indian* was held in Africa all winter, shuttling between remote, barely developed harbors. She managed to avoid U-boats but not mosquitoes. Seventeen of the crew contracted malaria, including two of the Mathews men.

When the *East Indian* finally reached home in April 1942—the homecoming noted briefly by the *Gazette-Journal* on April 2, just before Easter—some of her crew had had enough and got off the ship for good. They included the chief engineer, who had sailed on the *East Indian* for eighteen years. He had been torpedoed twice in World War I and did not want to tempt fate again. Also departing was Walter Stillman of Mathews, who had sailed with Dewey since Spencer Hodges had recruited him from a life of plowing fields while "looking a mule in the butt" four years earlier. Stillman wanted to keep sailing, but he was superstitious and thought it might be bad luck to sail on the same vessel twice.

Seven other Mathews men stayed on the *East Indian*, however, including First Officer Clayton Hammond, whom Dewey had once threatened to fire if he did not quit putting off his first-officer's exam. Clayton and the other Mathews men assumed Dewey would be fully recovered and back on the bridge when the *East Indian* sailed again in a few weeks. Dewey had probably assumed that too.

But during the last week of April, a few nights before the *East Indian* was to depart, Dewey came to the docks to tell the crew he would not be going with them. He felt fine, but his doctors still would not clear him to command a ship on a voyage to the other side of the world. Dewey was disappointed, and so were his men. The ship's carpenter, Stanley MacLean, who had sailed with Dewey for eleven years, was particularly upset. He did not relish going back through dangerous waters without him. MacLean, however, stayed on the ship, and Ford chose a new substitute captain, Ovide St. Marie, to take the *East Indian* across the ocean.

Dewey went back to his home in Norfolk. He was not used to being idle, but he made the most of his time with his family. Dewey was as much of a doting husband and father as a mariner could possibly be. He bought his family a nice home in a leafy Norfolk subdivision, and employed a maid so that his wife, Edna, would not feel tied down at home. Despite the fact that Dewey had not finished grade school—or perhaps because of that fact—he stressed the importance of a wide-ranging education to his children. His son, George Jr., was the first Hodges to attend college. Dewey bought his daughters a piano and insisted they take music and dance lessons. Every night Dewey listened to the popular radio broadcaster Lowell Thomas, whom he considered erudite, and always kept a dictionary handy to look up any unfamiliar words Thomas spoke. Dewey had once brought home a beehive and a wide-brimmed hat with a protective wire screen, and invited the family to learn the science of beekeeping with him. That was more than Edna and the girls wanted to learn. After Dewey went back to sea, they never went near the hive again.

Dewey did not just sit at home after the *East Indian* sailed. Ford apparently found less strenuous work for him, such as overseeing repair work at local shipyards. When he was home, he never bossed his family around the way some captains did theirs. He seemed to enjoy a respite from the burden of command. He played with the children. He sat in the front yard, where he had made friends with a squirrel.

Even though the newspaper printed stories every day about merchant ships being sunk by U-boats, Dewey and his family never talked about it. "We tried to keep everything as normal as possible for my father when he was home," Jean Hodges said. But she and her sister felt their perspective changing. They had never worried about their father when he was at sea all the time. But now that he was spending more time at home, they worried. Sooner or later, he would have to go back out there.

CHAPTER SIX

Killing Ground to Battleground

Just after midnight on April 14, 1942, the radar operator on the destroyer USS *Roper* reported a blip on the screen, in the shallow ocean close to shore. No one on the *Roper*'s blacked-out bridge thought the blip was a U-boat. The *Roper*—the same ship that had rescued the lifeboat baby—had been patrolling the mid-Atlantic coast for weeks without seeing a U-boat. The sailors on the *Roper* had seen only the U-boats' victims. They had found dead bodies, empty lifeboats, and vast fields of floating debris. "Early this morning passed through a large patch of burnt paint where another tanker or supply ship sank last night," *Roper* sailor Robert Gillon wrote in his diary. "Paint about three inches deep on water. Lord only knows what this night will bring."

The *Roper* already had charged at several suspicious-looking radar blips, only to terrify the crews of fishing boats and Coast Guard vessels. A sense of futility was setting in. So the latest blip, only 14 miles from the shore of the Outer Banks of North Carolina, looked initially like yet another false alarm.

Instead, it was the start of a brutal encounter that would show not only how far the U.S. coastal defenses had come, but how far they still had to go.

A few seconds after the blip appeared on the radar screen, the *Roper*'s sonar operator reported a contact, as well as the sound of propellers turning fast—faster than any fishing boat's propellers. The blip and sonar contact came from the same place: two miles off to starboard, between the *Roper* and the darkened shore. The men on the *Roper*'s bridge exchanged glances. The officer of the watch, a young ensign named Kenneth Tebo, sent a sailor to wake his commanding officer.

The *Roper* had been diverted into these waters from its regular coastal patrol to follow up on a tip. The captain of a fishing trawler named the *Sea Roamer* had reported spotting a U-boat in the area. Such tips came over the radio with some regularity, and they never panned out. Even if the tipster had really seen a U-boat, as opposed to a whale or some floating debris, the submarine was likely to be long gone by the time the destroyer reached the spot. Still, pursuing a tip about a U-boat made at least as much sense as just patrolling back and forth along the coast in the hope of bumping into one. Such patrols were so ineffective that President Roosevelt, while a Navy undersecretary in World War I, had compared them to "hunting the hornets all over the farm."* And U-boats hunted back.

The *Roper* had replaced the USS *Jacob Jones*, which had been torpedoed by a U-boat off New Jersey on February 28, 1942, with the loss of 138 of her 149 officers and crew. Some of the men had jumped into the water only to be killed by the shock waves of the *Jones*'s own depth charges, detonating as the warship plunged into the depths. The *Roper*'s men had been warned not to let their ship become the next *Jacob Jones*, but the warning was hardly necessary. Many of them had lost friends on the *Jacob Jones*. They were eager to strike a blow.

---

* Doenitz wrote in his memoirs, "Single destroyers . . . sailed up and down the traffic lanes with such regularity that the U-boats were quickly able to work out the timetable being followed. They knew exactly when the destroyers would return, and the knowledge only added to their sense of security during the intervening period."

The *Roper* was a relic of World War I. She was called a "four-piper" because of her four distinctive slender smokestacks. She guzzled fuel and tended to leak and break down under the pounding of the winter seas. But she was much faster than a U-boat, and bristled with 3-inch guns, machine guns, torpedoes, and depth charges. She had microwave radar that could see farther than the Germans realized. The *Roper* was well equipped to sink a U-boat if she ever found one. And now maybe, at last, she had.

Ensign Tebo ordered the *Roper*'s helmsman to pursue the blip at an angle, as a precaution against torpedoes. His commanding officer, Lt. Cmdr. Hamilton Howe, made his way back to the bridge, half-asleep, still in his uniform. Howe was skeptical about the blip. He ordered the crew to prepare the *Roper*'s powerful 24-inch searchlight. The night was moonless. The only light in the sky was the stars and the rotating flash of the lighthouse on nearby Bodie Island. But the ocean was full of light. The water around the destroyer was bioluminescent—teeming with microscopic plankton that sparkled when stirred into motion.* Every wake and wave crest gave off a bright, bluish glow.

A glowing streak raced toward the *Roper* from the direction of the blip. Howe thought it was a dolphin. Tebo knew it was a torpedo. Its wake drew a bioluminescent line along the *Roper*'s port side. It shot past the destroyer's stern, a near miss. Sailors near the stern shouted. Howe called for the searchlight. The brilliant beam fell upon a gray submarine sitting on the water's surface, apparently recharging its batteries. One *Roper* sailor thought it looked too small to be a U-boat; another thought it "looked as big as the Empire State Building." The U-boat turned away from the *Roper*, and Germans began scrambling out of a hatch onto the deck. They were running toward the deck cannon. Howe "gave the word to fire anything,

---

*Bioluminescence is a common phenomenon in some parts of the ocean. Scientists think bioluminescent zooplankton release a glowing chemical in order to confuse predators and attract mates. Bioluminescence made it more difficult for U-boats to hide and attack, and some U-boat commanders took pains to avoid heavily bioluminescent stretches of ocean.

and we were all scared," a sailor recalled. One of the *Roper*'s guns jammed, and then another. The destroyer's torpedo officer screamed to back up and give him a firing angle. After what seemed like an eternity, the chief bo'sun's mate cleared a jammed .50-caliber machine gun and fired in a sweeping motion back and forth along the U-boat's deck. Every fifth shot was a bright tracer round. Some of the Germans were shot or jumped into the sea. Others took cover behind the conning tower. Still more Germans scrambled out of the hatch. The U-boat's tighter turning radius kept the *Roper* from closing the distance quickly. Finally, one of the *Roper*'s 3-inch guns opened fire. The first shell splashed into the ocean short of the U-boat. The second shell came closer. The third struck the U-boat with a flash and a clang, right at the base of the conning tower, exactly where gunners were taught to aim, where a breach in the U-boat's hull was a mortal wound.

The U-boat slowed and nosed down, still bathed in the searchlight glare. The *Roper*'s officers could not tell if the sub was diving, sinking, or being scuttled. The *Roper* ran straight at it. Tebo was afraid that ramming it would sink the old *Roper* too. But the U-boat submerged just as the destroyer reached it. The water all around was full of Germans, crying out in broken English. Some were treading water in a circle, holding hands. Word came down from the *Roper*'s bridge to release life rafts, but the destroyer was already past the swimmers, and word came down to wait. The sonar operator reported the U-boat was barely moving. Howe wondered if it was dead or playing possum. He had no time to mull it over. The *Roper* was alone in the middle of the night, facing an enemy that struck with no warning and left men to die. Howe ordered the *Roper* to circle back and prepare a barrage of depth charges.

The *Roper* raced to the spot where the U-boat had vanished, and bracketed the sonar target with eleven 500-pound depth charges. Tebo wrote in the ship's log that the nearest swimmers were 200 yards away, but other sailors recalled them being much closer. The *Roper* raced to get clear of the depth-charge blasts. In her wake, more than two and a half tons of TNT erupted in a thundering, bioluminescent plume. The old destroyer shook from stern to bow, rivets popping out of the seams in her hull. One sailor reported seeing some of the Germans blown out of the water.

The *Roper* sent a coded message to Norfolk that she had possibly sunk a U-boat, and was searching for others. Howe believed two U-boats might be working in tandem, but the sonar operator found no other targets. Twice more that night the *Roper* passed close to the spot of the attack, but there were no more cries for help, and no further orders to release the life rafts.

At dawn, an Army plane spotted an oil slick and some floating bodies. Howe sent out lifeboats. The dead Germans were mostly young men in gray and green clothing. Many wore breathing devices, which suggested they had swum out of the sub while it was underwater. The condition of the bodies made it clear they had been broken and battered by the depth charges.

Howe told some of his men that his uncertainty over the U-boat commander's intentions had left him no choice but to drop the depth charges. In the excitement of the moment, Tebo thought the captain had made the right decision. Tebo had not foreseen the result. "I should have known what would happen to those men in the water, but I didn't," he recalled sixty years later, his voice breaking.

The lifeboats delivered twenty-nine dead Germans to the *Roper*, where they were laid out on the main deck. The destroyer crew immediately descended on the bodies. "Our crew is like a pack of hungry animals in its desire for souvenirs," wrote a civilian who happened to be riding aboard the *Roper* that night. He reported that one sailor pulled a ring from a dead German's finger and found a lock of hair in a hidden compartment; another sailor grabbed a pair of boots, which eventually ended up on display in a bar on Michigan's Upper Peninsula. Howe angrily dispersed the souvenir hunters and posted an armed guard over the corpses. The *Roper* transferred the dead to a Navy tug, whose crew also looted the bodies for souvenirs as the tug made it way to the Norfolk naval base. The U-boat crewmen were the first enemy dead to reach American soil since the War of 1812, when a British officer, killed in a naval battle, was buried with honors on the coast of Maine.

After more than four months of false claims, the Navy finally had sunk a U-boat in American waters.* But instead of announcing the kill, the government set out to keep it secret; after all, it was not the first according to their claims. The crews of the *Roper* and the tug were ordered to keep quiet about it. An elite Navy dive team departed from Washington on a fruitless quest to salvage the sub for its Enigma machine and other secrets. FBI agents and Naval Intelligence officers searched the bodies and determined that the submarine was the U-85, under the command of twenty-seven-year-old Eberhard Greger. The U-85 had sunk three merchant ships, including a Norwegian freighter four nights earlier. The personal items recovered from the bodies included the diary of a young crewman named Erich Degenkolb. He had written mostly about girls back home and the unpleasantness of U-boat duty. His earliest entries included:

Seasick—Oh Neptune.

Severe vomiting.

It continues.

Slowly improving.

Frightful seas.

Food tastes good again.

But by the end, Degenkolb had grown accustomed to the hardships and was enjoying the experience.

---

* American planes based in Newfoundland had sunk two U-boats in Canadian waters in March.

Noon   magnificent sunshine just off America. Thoughts of home.

Abominable heat—all stripped bare.

Sighted a steamer and sank it.

Ready for attack—During the day heard three steamers.

We lie on the bottom all day. All is asleep off New York.

And Degenkolb's last entry:

American searchlights and beacons visible at night.

The U.S. Army Quartermaster General's Office in Washington contacted the nearest military cemetery, in Hampton, Virginia, and ordered
twenty-nine graves dug quickly and quietly. At dusk the next day, a convoy
of trucks delivered the bodies to the cemetery. The mid-April evening was
unseasonably warm, and a curious crowd gathered from a neighborhood
next to the cemetery. The Army said the bodies were those of American
merchant seamen—an all-too-plausible lie. The crowd fell into respectful
silence as an honor guard carried the dead from the trucks and laborers
lowered the caskets by ropes into the graves. Catholic and Protestant chap-
lains offered prayers and a Navy bugler blew taps. The graves were left
unmarked. The Navy promised to provide a chart later showing which
Germans lay in which graves.

The sinking of the first U-boat in American waters hardly changed the
course of the U-boat war. By mid-April, Doenitz had three hundred operational U-boats, including more than a dozen in U.S. and Caribbean waters. They sank thirteen Allied merchant ships within a week of the U-85's
loss. Their victims included the tanker *Gulfamerica*, which Hardegan torpedoed only five miles off the beach at Jacksonville, Florida. The *Gulfamerica* was one of the first tankers to be armed, as the oil executives had
suggested, but the Navy gun crew did not get off a shot. The U-123 surfaced

and shelled the crippled tanker with its deck cannon in front of a crowd of tourists and sailors on leave from the nearby Navy base. "A rare show for the tourists," Hardegan wrote in his log. On April 18, four days after the U-85 sinking, the reeling Allies halted all tanker traffic north of Florida.

But if the *Roper*'s victory was no turning point, it was at least a sign that the United States was learning to defend itself. Even the sardonic Hardegan, who had sneered at the Americans' weak defenses in January, acknowledged they had improved by the time he and the U-123 returned to U.S. coastal waters in April. "Some ships were beginning to sail without lights, and the coast was only brightly lit close to the big seaside resorts," Hardegan wrote. "When a ship was sunk, planes arrived quickly. They had woken up a bit." The waters off the U.S. coast were changing from a killing ground into a battleground.

By mid-April, Admiral Andrews had assembled an escort force in the Eastern Sea Frontier of about sixty vessels, including an increasing number of World War I–vintage destroyers, which Admiral King was releasing to the Eastern Sea Frontier for longer stretches. King even allowed Andrews to set up a partial convoy system along the coast known as the "bucket brigades." The name came from the firefighting method in which a line of people pass buckets of water hand to hand from a water source to the fire. In bucket brigade convoys, small groups of merchant ships steamed along the coast in a series of daylight-only voyages, spending nights in protected harbors or anchorages. The ships were protected on each leg of the journey by a group of escorts manning that stretch of coastline. The bucket brigade convoys forced the U-boats to operate more cautiously. But the convoy escorts were not formidable enough to deter the U-boats from attacking, or to fight them off when they did. The Eastern Sea Frontier remained a wild frontier, losing at least one merchant ship a day to U-boats.

On April 19, 1942, the Royal Navy sent Rodger Winn to Washington. Winn was the head of Britain's highly organized U-boat tracking center, which integrated daily intelligence reports, U-boat sightings in the field, and radio contacts. Winn's mission was to persuade Admiral King to re-organize the U.S. Navy's U-boat tracking center along similar lines. King was reported to view the British as know-it-alls. His deputy chief of staff, and gatekeeper, Rear Admiral Richard S. Edwards, tried to brush off Winn by telling him the U.S. Navy preferred to learn its own lessons about fight-ing U-boats. Winn replied, "The trouble is, Admiral, it's not only your bloody ships you're losing, a lot of them are ours. And we're not prepared to sacrifice men and ships to your bloody obstinacy." Edwards agreed Winn had a point, and set up a meeting with King. King agreed to start upgrading the Navy's U-boat tracking center immediately. He said he would set up a convoy system as soon as he had enough ships. The Navy had a plan for a fully interlocking convoy system to protect ships from Maine to the Caribbean to the Gulf, but so far it had received only a frac-tion of the new escort ships necessary to put it into effect. King's interlock-ing convoy system would eventually prove itself, but his timetable for implementing it was based on obtaining enough ships to run convoys his way, not on the urgency of the situation offshore.

America's production of new merchant ships was finally hitting its stride. By the spring of 1942, new vessels were joining the merchant fleet at a rate of one per day—about the same rate as the U-boats were torpedo-ing ships out of the fleet. Most of the new merchant ships were Liberty ships—slow, blocky freighters, 441.5 feet long, with two large boom cranes and five cavernous holds with room for 9,000 tons of cargo. The first Lib-erty ship had taken 217 days to build, but the shipyards constantly stream-lined the construction process. In a publicity stunt, one yard completed the Liberty ship *Robert E. Peary* in 4 days, 15 hours, and 30 minutes. Amer-ican shipyards would produce 746 Liberty ships by the end of 1942, and more than 2,700 before switching to faster Victory ships in 1944.*

---

* So many new ships were entering the merchant fleet that finding names for them became a challenge. Liberty ships would bear the names of a broad spectrum of peo-ple, including Big Foot Wallace, Sun Yat-sen, Frederick Douglass, Betsy Ross, Edgar

Liberty ships could be built quickly because they were built assembly-line style, like cars. Ships traditionally had been constructed by laying a keel and then building upward, riveting new sections onto the frame. But Liberty ships were built in prefabricated sections at factories outside the shipyards. Those sections then were hauled to the yard as needed and welded rather than riveted into place. Welding was much faster than riveting. The shipbuilders also saved time and money by powering the Liberty ships with old-fashioned three-cylinder steam engines. Those engines were easy to repair partly because they were interchangeable. An engineer who learned how to fix one could fix any.

Speed and ease of construction came at a cost to the men who sailed the Liberty ships. The vessels had one propeller rather than two, which increased the chance of a dead-in-the-water breakdown. Welding the hull together made it more rigid and susceptible to cracking in rough seas. The old-style steam engines could drive a Liberty ship at a maximum speed of only 11 knots—even slower than the old Ford and Bull Line freighters, and much slower than a U-boat on the surface. Liberty ships, however, were built to lumber along in protected convoys. The only speed that mattered with them was the speed at which they could be built.

The U.S. strategy for winning the Battle of the Atlantic was straightforward: Build more merchant ships than the U-boats could sink. Admiral Emory S. Land, the folksy, pipe-smoking chief of the Maritime Administration, would title his memoir, *Winning the War with Ships*. The United States also set out to produce more merchant mariners than the U-boats could kill. By the end of the war, a nationwide recruitment and training program for merchant mariners would expand their ranks from the prewar total of 55,000 to more than 250,000.

A strategy of overwhelming the enemy through sheer numbers made sense for a nation that could produce the ships at a pace no other nation

Allan Poe, Johnny Appleseed, Wyatt Earp, and Pocahontas, as well as Oscar Chappell, the helmsman who had died at the wheel of the tanker *Dixie Arrow*.

could approach. But pursuing that strategy while failing to protect the ships and mariners already on the water created the sense that they were expendable—easier to replace than to protect. The author Stephen Budiansky called America's approach to the Battle of the Atlantic "a brutal calculus, a naval war of attrition at its most elemental." The Mathews men and their shipmates bore the brunt of that strategy.

At the end of April, the German intelligence service reported that America was building ships at three times the anticipated rate. The U-boats would have to increase their sink rates accordingly. Doenitz, for the first time in the war, had the resources to answer such a challenge. He had enough U-boats to send a dozen to the Americas at the same time, the largest force to date. He also had the means to resupply those U-boats at sea. Big, lumbering supply submarines, which the Germans called "milch cows," or milk cows, rendezvoused with U-boats in remote stretches of the ocean to replenish their fuel and deliver food and spare parts. A visit from a milch cow could extend a U-boat's mission by two weeks. That extra time was especially precious in the Caribbean, where Doenitz sent most of the latest wave of U-boats.

The Caribbean was a plum assignment for U-boat crews. Targets were plentiful enough to make a U-boat commander's career, and Allied patrols were so rare that U-boat crews occasionally slipped ashore on remote islands to sunbathe, swim, fish, and even hunt. "It is a wonderful day today, and flying fish fall onto our deck," one U-boat crewman wrote in his diary of a Caribbean voyage. "At noon one of our pith helmets is blown into the water, and we jump in to get it and have a nice swim." U-boat commanders in the Caribbean—perhaps inspired by the laid-back lifestyle—tended to be more magnanimous toward lifeboat survivors in those waters than anywhere else.

William Hammond of Mathews would experience that phenomenon firsthand. William was the youngest of three brothers who had followed their friends the Hodgeses to sea. William's brother Clayton was Dewey Hodges's first officer on the *East Indian*; his brother Stacy served with

Leslie Hodges on the Ford freighter *Oneida*. William was an able seaman on the little freighter *Norlindo*, which shuttled around the Caribbean and the Gulf.

On May 4, 1942, the *Norlindo* was steaming through calm seas about 80 miles northwest of the Dry Tortuga islands, along the watery border between the Caribbean and the Gulf. The ship had sailed empty from Mobile to pick up cargo in Havana. Several men who normally would have been on lookout duty had been sent below to prepare the holds to receive cargo. Just before sunset, a torpedo from the U-507 struck the *Norlindo* with enough force to topple the mainmast into the sea. All five of the men working in the holds were killed. The *Norlindo* sank so fast that no lifeboats could be launched. The crew threw the ship's four life rafts into the ocean and jumped in after them. William had no sooner clambered onto a raft than the U-boat broke the surface about a mile distant and headed for the castaways. A face-to-face encounter with the Germans was surely the last thing William and his shipmates wanted, but they were in for a surprise.

The U-507 was freshly painted light gray and its conning tower bore an image of a laughing boar with flared pink nostrils. Several Germans emerged from the main hatch. The enlisted men wore nothing but blue swim trunks and the officers, khaki shorts and pith helmets. One German took photos of the castaways while another swept the horizon with binoculars. The U-boat crew did not bother to man the sub's deck cannon or machine gun. The U-507's commander, Harro Schacht, was a big man with sandy hair and a reddish beard. "Sorry we had to sink you, but this is war," he explained in English with only a slight German accent. He asked the men if they needed medical attention. They said they needed only cigarettes and drinking water. Schacht ordered his men to pull the raft alongside the sub with a boat hook. Then the Germans began handing out supplies: forty packs of German cigarettes, several boxes of French matches, a four-pound box of French cookies, and a ten-gallon water jug wrapped in a wicker apron like a Chianti wine bottle. Before handing over the water jug, one of the Germans squeezed fresh limes into it, apparently to fortify the castaways with vitamin C to prevent scurvy. "Be careful of the cigarettes and water as you are the same as ten thousand miles from home," Schacht cautioned. "Sorry we cannot give you a tow or send out a message for you, but we do not dare." As the U-507 pulled away from the rafts, Schacht called out, "Come over and see me sometime after the war is over."

William and twenty-three shipmates drifted on the rafts for three days, lacking nothing in the way of food and drink, but severely burned by the sun, whose rays were intensified by the spilled bunker oil coating the men's bodies. A passing freighter finally picked them up and took them to the port of Balboa on the Pacific side of the Panama Canal. Their account of Schacht's generosity drew keen interest from Navy intelligence officers, who speculated the U-boat had gotten the fresh limes from Nazi sympathizers in the Caribbean.* William made it back to the United States without a scratch. He went back to sea, where he soon would encounter another U-boat under circumstances far less cordial.

One day after the *Norlindo* sinking, Captain William Callis of Gwynn's Island was torpedoed off the coast of Florida in the old Bull Line freighter *Delisle*. The ship was only a few miles off Jupiter Inlet, north of Palm Beach, and Callis thought fast and ran the ship aground to keep her from sinking. The *Delisle* ended up being towed to Miami and repaired. But her days were numbered.

Less than twenty-four hours after the *Delisle* was torpedoed, the little Ford freighter *Green Island* was passing through the Gulf into the Caribbean en route from New Orleans to the oil-refinery island of Aruba. Third Officer Genious Hudgins Jr. of Mathews was worried. Genious was an

---

* In fact, the U-507 had brought the limes from France. But the U.S. Navy worried throughout the war that U-boats were being aided by sympathizers on the French island of Martinique, which was under the control of the German puppet Vichy government. No German records suggest U-boats ever received help on Martinique or any other island in the Caribbean, though U-boats sometimes raided passing boats to steal fresh food.

atypical Mathews mariner—trim, handsome, polite, and an impeccable dresser. His father, Genious Hudgins Sr., had been sheriff of Mathews and captain of a state oyster patrol boat. The family stressed honesty and duty. At age five, Genious Jr. had slipped a candy bar into his pocket at a general store. His grandmother found it when they got home and made him walk four miles back to the store by himself to return the candy bar and apologize. Genious and his wife, Salome, had been sweethearts since the fifth grade, breaking up only once for a couple of days. When Genious was still in high school, his parents signed for him so that he could marry Salome. "To me, he was almost perfect," Salome would recall seventy years later. "He was truthful, and you could depend on him."

But the U-boat war was tearing at Genious and Salome's marriage. Genious disliked the long periods away from his family. He did not see his daughter, Vicki, until she was six months old. The problem was that no shore job in Mathews paid nearly as well as the Merchant Marine, and Genious needed money. He was supporting not only his wife and daughter, but also his parents. His father had quit working well before retirement age after contracting tuberculosis. But his father and mother were prominent in Mathews, and were accustomed to a certain way of life, including having nice things and hosting parties. They did not hesitate to ask Genious and his brother Russell for the money they needed to maintain their social position. When Russell moved out of Mathews, Genious wrote Salome of the "bad news"—the burden of supporting his parents was now his alone. Salome understood her husband's loyalty but thought Genious should rein in his parents' spending. As things stood, Genious could only support them by continuing to sail through war zones.

Genious wrote Salome every day he was at sea. "There is no man on earth who would rather be home with his wife and children than I do, darling," he declared, "but please don't ask me to quit." He felt a sense of duty to both his parents and his country. "Darling I believe and truly believe that I should do what I set out to do and help what little bit I can. It hurts me an awful lot when I say goodbye to you and all at home when I leave, but it would hurt me an awful lot worse if we had to live under Hitlerism or the Japanese."

Genious's ship the *Green Island* had narrowly escaped a U-boat in February off Florida by hiding in a blinding tropical rain squall. Then the freighter mistook a U.S. destroyer for the U-boat and rammed her. The *Green Island* was due for an overhaul in a dry dock in Norfolk, and Genious cherished the prospect of a long stay with Salome and Vicki. But the overhaul was postponed at the last minute, and the *Green Island* was dispatched to pick up a load of lumber in New Orleans and haul it across the Caribbean to Aruba.

Genious wrote reassuringly to Salome about the voyage, but he revealed his true feelings in a letter to his sister. "Don't say anything to mother or Salome about it, but this is about the worst place we can go," he wrote. He told his sister to make sure Salome received the insurance money due her if he did not come back. "Not that I think I won't," he added. "If I thought that, I wouldn't go at all, but you can never tell, you know." Genious promised to call his sister when he reached Aruba safely. At that point, she was to destroy his letter to make sure Salome never saw it.

Genious was dressing for breakfast in his room on the morning of May 6 as the *Green Island* steamed south through the Gulf, about 80 miles south of Grand Cayman Island. The ship was not zigzagging because she was low on drinking water and the captain wanted to reach port before it ran out. A torpedo exploded into the ship's hull, buckling the freighter amidships. Genious raced out onto the main deck with only the clothes he wore. Then he ran back inside to save a sextant his father had handed down to him. Waves were breaking over the main deck by the time he reemerged. He and the ship's twenty-one other officers and crew got away in two lifeboats. The U-125 surfaced to make sure the ship was done for, and a German officer waved farewell to the castaways before the submarine submerged. Genious and his shipmates spent a night in the lifeboats, firing flare guns every few hours, before the British freighter *Fort Qu'Appelle* picked them up and took them to Miami. The *Fort Qu'Appelle* then set out for Bermuda, where she was torpedoed with the loss of fourteen officers and crew.

Genious wrote to Salome from a hotel in Miami, downplaying the sinking and boasting playfully about some clothes that had been donated to him: "I have on an Irish linen suit and I look great." He went home to Mathews and obtained a new set of mariner's papers to replace the ones he had lost. To Salome's consternation, he began looking for a new ship.

If any waterway in America still seemed inviolable in May 1942, it was the Mississippi, the nation's main artery, the river of Tom Sawyer and Huckleberry Finn. But on May 10, Harro Schacht, who had treated the *Norlindo* survivors with such generosity, guided the U-507 to the mouth of the great American river. It was not shock value or symbolism he was after. It was oil. Huge tankers of 10,000 tons or more passed constantly in and out of the Mississippi. The river mouth was not a single, wide, bustling channel, but a spider's web of narrow passes through the dense marshlands of the Mississippi Delta. The passes were lonely places, inhabited chiefly by "bar pilots and millions of fiddler crabs," as the author Theodore Taylor put it. Before a tanker was allowed to head upriver, it had to anchor at a buoy just outside one of the passes and wait for a bar pilot, who would scramble up a ladder and guide the ship around the inevitable sandbar at the mouth of the river and then up a narrow channel into the main stem of the Mississippi.

On the morning of May 12, the 10,731-ton tanker *Virginia* sat at anchor at a buoy only 1.5 miles off the Southwest Pass, the westernmost of the Mississippi passes, waiting for a pilot. The *Virginia*'s holds were loaded with 180,000 barrels of high-octane gasoline. Thousands more barrels of gasoline sat in steel drums lashed to the ship's main deck, along with dozens of airplanes, tanks, and jeeps. The *Virginia* had been waiting for the pilot for more than two hours, due to a mix-up ashore, but there had seemed to be no hurry, because U-boats had never dared to venture so close to the river mouth.

The *Virginia*'s crew included Merritt Frank White of Mathews, whose life already had been shaped by fire. White's father had run a general store near Mathews courthouse until it burned down. He used the insurance money to build a new store, only to see it also burn down. White was still a boy when the family left Mathews in search of a better life, or at least better fire protection. They took everything they still owned, including a Holstein cow named Buttercup, and bought a dairy farm in Norfolk. Frank worked on the farm and in his brother's cigar store before deciding to follow two of his older brothers into the Merchant Marine. Whenever Frank or one of his brothers came home, the men in the family gathered in the barn to drink and sing along with the radio. The White brothers— like the Hodges, Callis, and Hammond brothers—rarely all came home from the sea at the same time. Frank came home least of all. He was the only brother who sailed the deep ocean. He wrote letters from foreign ports to a friend, Norfolk newspaper reporter Harry P. Moore, declaring, "When I come home, I'm going to stay." But he always ended up deciding, "I believe I will go back to sea for just one more voyage."

The *Virginia*'s pilot still had not shown up at 3:06 p.m. when a torpedo from Harro Schacht's U-507 exploded into the tanker's port side, igniting the gasoline in the holds. Two more torpedoes hit, and a fiery mass engulfed the ship. Any men who could still move leaped overboard without even looking, because it was obviously their only prayer. The men who jumped off the tanker's lee side landed in flaming oil and died in agony. Some who jumped off the windward side found a narrow path through the flames. "Great courage and bravery were exhibited by certain crew members who saved the lives of two or three men who were able to get off the ship but were so badly burned that they could not swim," the Coast Guard reported. The *Virginia* burned furiously and settled onto the shallow bottom, her blackened masts sticking up out of the Gulf to mark the mass grave she had become. Twenty-five of the *Virginia*'s forty officers and crew were lost, including Frank White, whose body was never found. A footstone on his empty grave in Mathews reads, "DIED AT SEA 1942."

More U-boats followed Schacht's U-507 into the Gulf and enjoyed similar success. A Louisiana man driving along the coast stopped to examine fresh wreckage on the beach and was aghast to discover an oil-smeared oar bearing the name of the oil tanker *William C. McTarnahan*—his son's ship. His son had survived the torpedoing of the *McTarnahan* hours earlier but had not had a chance to contact his family.

Eight days after the *Virginia* sinking, the U-506 torpedoed the tanker *Halo* less than 50 miles from the mouth of the Mississippi. Twenty-four men—exactly half the crew—made it into the water. But all the lifeboats and rafts had gone down with the ship, along with all the food and water. Some of the men had no life vests or life rings and had to tread water to stay afloat. The men held on to one another and vowed to stick together. They thought their nearness to land would lead to a quick rescue. They could not have been more wrong.

The first man to die had been suffering from severe burns on both legs. Without a word, he slipped out of his life preserver, pushed it to a man who did not have one, and swam off. On the second day, a seaman who had been helping the severely burned man drank salt water and lost his mind. He announced he was going to dive down to the wreck to bring up some canned pears. He dived three times and did not come up from the third. Two other men followed his mad example and dived in search of orange juice. They too vanished after a few attempts. Drinking salt water had swollen their tongues to the point where they no longer fit in their mouths. Late on the second day, the *Halo*'s fuel tanks ruptured under the crushing water pressure on the sea bottom, and a mass of heavy, black bunker oil burbled up from the wreck and engulfed the survivors in a vast slick. Pieces of the ship came up too. Two mariners from Gloucester County, Joseph "Pat" Shackelford and Jesse D. Hogge, pulled themselves onto a floating slab of wood. The Gulf sun bore down through a cloudless sky. Planes kept flying over the men in the water, low enough that the men could see the U.S. stars on their wings, but the pilots never spotted them. Several ships passed maddeningly close.

As night fell on the third day, the nineteen remaining men vowed to stay close and look out for one another. But by first light, only seven were left. Shackelford was too spent to move. He could not even raise his head to check on Hogge, who had fallen silent next to him. Shackelford promised himself not to drink salt water no matter how thirsty he got. But every time he lost consciousness, oily seawater splashed into his mouth and he woke up coughing. The oil had plastered his hair over his eyes. He left it there.

On the fifth day, the crew of a Mexican freighter spotted the oil slick from ten miles away. The Mexican seamen explored the floating wreckage and found Shackelford and Hogge still on the slab of wood. Hogge was dead. Shackelford was barely alive. There were only two other survivors, and one of them, John S. Gietek, died soon after being taken to a hospital. Doctors said he died from exposure and ingestion of toxic oil. Shackelford wrote Gietek's parents in Massachusetts that their son was buried "on a beautiful hill" in Tampico, Mexico, with full military honors, beneath a stone slab inscribed with his name and covered with flowers picked by local villagers. Shackelford and Gietek had pledged that if only one of them lived, he would visit the other's family and tell them as much as they cared to know. When Shackelford recovered enough to travel, he kept that vow. He eventually went back to sea and sailed through the end of the war. He wrote to his sister, "We get up to hot spots once in a while but I am OK."

"They can't hurt me."

The failure of the patrol planes and passing ships to find the *Halo* survivors prompted an official inquiry and some informal soul-searching. A Coast Guard report called it "strange that patrol planes which passed over the area daily made no effort to discover the source of the tremendous oil slick which came to the surface after this vessel was sunk . . ." The Coast Guard noted without comment that some sea captains steered away from any oil slick or lifeboats for fear a U-boat might still be in the vicinity. A Mexican oil company official wrote a letter to the U.S. Maritime Administration pointing out that if any of the *Halo* castaways had possessed a handheld mirror, they could easily have attracted the attention of passing pilots.

On the same day the Halo was torpedoed, Captain Walter Hudgins and First Officer Harold Davis, who had survived the sinking of the *Barbara* in the Windward Passage in March, approached the strait in a different ship, the Bull Line freighter *Elizabeth*, which Walter had commanded before the war.

The *Elizabeth* had set out from New York with forty trucks and various construction materials for the new U.S. Navy base at San Juan, Puerto Rico. The ship had enjoyed the protection of canals and bucket-brigade escorts for most of the voyage, but her last escort had put into port at Key West, leaving her to finish her voyage alone. The *Elizabeth* followed two other ships around the western tip of Cuba, only 100 miles from where the *Barbara* lay on the sea bottom. Just after 10:30 p.m., Harold was asleep in his bunk—he no longer slept on deck in his life vest, as he had for a week after the *Barbara* sinking—when a shipmate shook him awake. The ship in front of the *Elizabeth* had just been torpedoed.

Harold joined Walter on the bridge just as a U-boat fired a star shell with a flare that floated down on a fireproof parachute, illuminating the water around them as if it were daytime. From the darkness ahead, the U-boat opened fire with its deck cannon. Walter and Harold saw the muzzle flashes, which looked round because the cannon was aimed at them. One 88mm shell whistled over their heads and knocked down the ship's smokestack. Then a torpedo exploded into the *Elizabeth*'s engine room, killing every man inside and stopping the freighter dead in the water.

For the second time in two months, Walter gave the order to abandon ship and Harold oversaw the launching of the lifeboats. Once again, Walter and Harold were the last to leave the ship. The *Elizabeth* "settled just like a lady," as the Navy Armed Guard report put it, and the survivors rowed toward the coast of Cuba. After two days, the lifeboats crunched ashore on a remote beach near the Cape San Antonio lighthouse. The castaways bushwhacked twenty miles through a "desolate landscape" to a tiny settlement. The natives dressed the castaways' injuries and the owner of a "barkee"—a small fishing schooner—agreed to sail them to a larger village. There they were treated to "a big feed" and put on a bus to Havana. The Bull Line flew them home. Walter was given a few months of safe duty ashore, though he had not asked for it.

Harold sent his family in Mathews a telegram: "This is getting ridiculous."

The *Gazette-Journal* agreed. "The loss thus far suffered has been appalling," the paper editorialized, "not only because of the value of the ships and cargoes sunk and the precious lives sacrificed, but because of the humiliation of what amounts to a blockade of our shores and the injurious effect on our war effort."

The U.S. supplies of rubber and sugar had been cut off by the Japanese conquests in the Pacific. The rationing of rubber affected everyone in Mathews. Shipments of new tires to Mathews garages simply ceased, as all the available rubber was needed for tires for new warplanes, trucks, and other military vehicles. Gasoline was rationed initially to reduce wear on automobile tires and make them last longer. People were allowed to drive to work, to the grocery store, or to the doctor, but forbidden to drive for recreation or pleasure. Anyone caught "pleasure driving" had to forfeit some of their future gas rations. Every week, alleged violators were summoned to appear before a specially appointed panel at the Mathews courthouse to justify why they had been on the road.

The ban on pleasure driving virtually shut down Mathews's only regular public event, the traditional Saturday night gatherings on Main Street, because most participants came by car. On one Saturday night alone, Virginia State Police and federal investigators swooped into Mathews and cited more than two hundred motorists for defying the pleasure-driving ban. The number would have been much higher had the authorities not run out of tickets. The *Gazette-Journal* reported the busts, while noting somewhat defensively that other communities received their share of tickets and that "Mathews County was not exactly in a class alone with regard to pleasure driving."

Even the self-sufficient and resourceful cook faced problems—canning vegetables required sugar, which was rationed, and Henny Hodges cut way back on the hundreds of jars of vegetables she normally canned in preparation for the winter. As rationing expanded, the government urged Americans to start "victory gardens" to grow their own food. Most families in Mathews, of course, had been growing their own food in gardens long before the war.

Job opportunities in Mathews had never been so plentiful. Buses circled through the county several times a day to pick up and drop off shift workers for the shipyards in Newport News and Norfolk and the Navy Mine Depot in Yorktown, which produced mines to protect American rivers and harbors from U-boats. Mathews women who had never even considered taking jobs outside the home were being courted by the military, the defense plants, and even the crab-picking and oyster-shucking houses, whose male workers were gone. One of the Hodges daughters, Elizabeth, would join the Army Air Forces as a medical technician, and care for wounded soldiers in stateside hospitals.

Every week brought new reports of Mathews men being torpedoed, and for every ship actually sunk, two or three were falsely rumored to have gone down. Captain Stanley Hodges, Captain Jesse's distant cousin, survived the sinking of the tanker *Gulfpenn* near the mouth of the Mississippi. Floyd West escaped the torpedoed tanker *Harry F. Sinclair Jr.*, off Hatteras. The entire county was on edge. The Reverend Iris Belch of Gwynn's Island Baptist Church told his flock, "[W]e have been impressed by the anxiety in the hearts of the families of these brave men, that it requires courage on their part to endure, in keeping the home fires burning."

Amid all the gloom and uncertainty, the *Gazette-Journal* found cause for optimism in a report that a large Allied convoy had fought its way to the port of Murmansk in North Russia with arms and ammunition to help the beleaguered Red Army hold off the Nazis. That convoy, the paper explained, "had to not only evade the enemy forces in the Atlantic but elude a large naval force . . . in Northern waters." The Mathews mariners who had heard of the Murmansk Run at all knew it only by its evil reputation. But that was about to change.

CHAPTER SEVEN

"Avoid Polar Bear Liver"

B efore setting out on the *Green Island*, Genious Hudgins Jr. had called the Caribbean the worst possible place for a merchant ship to sail in 1942. But that distinction belonged by general agreement to the Murmansk Run. The voyage to the bleak northern coast of Russia was a 5,000-mile gauntlet of diabolical weather, air raids, and U-boat attacks. And the Murmansk Run was as much about politics as it was about delivering supplies to the Russians.

Russia had joined the Allied cause only after Hitler broke his pact with Russian dictator Joseph Stalin and invaded the Soviet Union in 1941. By the spring of 1942, millions of Russians had died fighting on the eastern front—roughly 1 million at Kiev alone—and the Nazis were still advancing. Stalin complained to his new allies that Russia was doing most of the fighting against Germany, which at that point was true. The Russian dictator demanded that Britain and the United States relieve pressure on Russia by opening a second front with an amphibious invasion of France. Roosevelt and Churchill did not think their troops were ready. But they worried that if they ignored Stalin's complaints, he might negotiate a separate peace with Hitler.

Stalin's messages to Churchill left no doubt that he was absolutely ruthless. Stalin did not see why his allies balked at suffering heavy casualties. He reminded Churchill to send him fresh newsreel footage of a German city bombed to ruins. He accused his allies of standing by and allowing the Nazis and the Russians to destroy one another. It was true that Roosevelt and Churchill already saw Russia as a future threat. Churchill had called Bolshevism "foul baboonery and a plague-bearing infection," and said he did not think the Russians needed to be thanked for "fighting in their own country for their own lives." But he was willing to help anyone who stood against Hitler.

The best way to help Russia, short of invading France, was to ship weapons and supplies to the Red Army. The most direct route was through the Mediterranean, which was blocked by the Germans. The next best route was through the Arctic to Murmansk, a bleak port on the frigid Barents Sea. Murmansk was only a thousand miles from the North Pole, but its harbor stayed free of ice all year because the tail of the warm Gulf Stream ended there. The British had been sending convoys to Murmansk since 1941. In May 1942, Roosevelt, in an effort to keep Stalin in the Allied fold, added U.S. ships to the Murmansk convoys.

The route to Murmansk led north from Britain through the North Atlantic to Iceland, and then farther north into the Arctic Circle, east through the Strait of Norway, past Bear Island, and into the stormy Barents Sea. The trip subjected ships and men to some of the most extreme weather on the planet. Gales built mountainous waves. Sea spray froze so fast on ships' hulls and superstructures that men had to chip off the ice constantly to keep the ship from becoming top-heavy. The water was so cold that a man who fell in would be dead in minutes. Polar bears glared from caves in drifting icebergs. Collisions of cold and warm currents created dense fog, as well as thermal layers in the water that confused sonar. The nearness of the magnetic North Pole skewed compass readings. A ship could steam blindly for days before the navigator was able to fix her position by the stars. Ships had to be fortified for the Murmansk Run, their bows reinforced with cement and their bronze propellers replaced with steel ones less likely to shatter if they struck ice. *How to Abandon Ship* offered advice about life-boat survival in the Arctic, including a section on how to kill and eat polar bears. Among its key points: "Avoid polar bear liver."*

But the Germans posed greater hazards than the weather. U-boats painted white to blend in with the ice waited for the convoys in the fjords of Nazi-occupied Norway, as did the battleship *Tirpitz* and other German warships. But the worst threat by far to the Murmansk convoys was from German bombers. The North Cape of Norway was home to six Luftwaffe air bases, one of which was only thirty-five miles from Murmansk. The Arctic sun never set in spring or summer, which allowed the bombers to attack twenty-four hours a day.

The first Mathews man to set out on the Murmansk Run was Captain Guy Hudgins, a distant cousin of Genious Hudgins Jr. Guy Hudgins was a rugged mariner with a taste for the good life. Guy had been born in Portsmouth, Virginia, but moved to Mathews to live with relatives after his father vanished from a ferryboat in a storm. Guy always wondered if his father had faked his death and abandoned the family. Whatever the truth was, Guy quit school in the sixth grade to support his mother and sisters. He fished and crabbed and delivered newspapers on horseback. He became friends with Dewey and Leslie Hodges and worked on a tug and then on steamships. During a visit home to Mathews in 1926, he plunged into the Saturday night crowd on Main Street and locked eyes with Dorothy Powell, the pretty daughter of a Mathews sea captain. They married after Guy was promoted to captain by the American Export Lines, and bought a duplex in Jersey City, New Jersey, where the company docked its ships.

Guy commanded ships on voyages all over the world. He visited Beth-

---

* The booklet recommended shooting a polar bear in "a place just behind the shoulder, so that the bullet will pierce the heart. Do not shoot a polar bear while it is in the water. You will not be able to haul it out." The authors suggested eating bear meat raw, frozen, or half frozen because it becomes stringy when cooked. No records indicate a lifeboat crew ever ate a polar bear, or vice versa.

lehem and King Tut's tomb, and carried mail to Malta and Syria. Dorothy enjoyed life in Jersey City with plenty of free time and spending money. Friends from Mathews stopped in when their ships arrived in port, and Dorothy and Guy entertained them, though sometimes Guy could party too hard. Dorothy kept after him to cut back on his drinking, and he kept promising to. Guy's politics could seem conservative; he hated Franklin and Eleanor Roosevelt for championing social programs, which Guy had not needed to make his way. But Guy was open-minded toward the world at large. "My father did not care if you were a laborer or the Queen of England, he treated every person the same," his daughter Diana recalled. Guy became friends with two gay mariners in his crew and had a glossy photograph of one of them, an underwear model, oiled up and wearing leopard-skin briefs. He liked to joke that all radio operators and second assistant engineers were gay. Guy attended church, mostly out of habit, but his faith had limits. He did not believe in life after death.

Guy began the war as captain of the Liberty ship *Zebulon B. Vance*. After several uneventful voyages, he was ordered to pick up military supplies in New York, including 400 tons of TNT, and join convoy PQ-15, bound for Murmansk. Convoys to North Russia in 1942 bore the designation PQ—the initials of a British convoy planner—followed by the sequential number of the convoy. PQ-15 was the fifteenth major convoy to Murmansk. Merchant ships bound for Murmansk always traveled in convoys, like those crossing the North Atlantic to Britain.

Guy sailed the *Zebulon B. Vance* across the Atlantic to Scotland to join convoy PQ-15. The convoy was about half the size of the big North Atlantic convoys, which could have as many as sixty ships. This one comprised twenty-five merchant ships, which formed a rectangle five miles wide and two miles deep. They were surrounded by antisubmarine vessels, mostly trawlers and minesweepers, which used sonar to screen the water around them for U-boats. An outer ring of destroyers and other warships kept watch for enemy ships and planes.

The convoy headed north into the Arctic Circle. The sea ice reached down into the shipping lanes, forcing the convoy even closer to Norway and the German bombers. The escorts spotted a cluster of German mines bobbing in the swells in front of the convoy and blew them up with shell fire. The convoy was 300 miles from Bear Island at the entrance to the Barents Sea when a German surveillance plane appeared overhead. The plane was a big, long-range Focke-Wulf Condor. Mariners called them the vultures. The plane kept pace with the convoy, flying just out of range of the ships' guns, as the pilot radioed the convoy's size, speed, and bearing to the bombers.

A few hours later, a faint bumblebee-like drone filled the air, and four black dots materialized in the sky astern. The *Zebulon B. Vance*'s dog, a black-and-white mongrel named Zebbie, barked a warning. The dots resolved themselves into German torpedo bombers, which launched small torpedoes from low altitude. The escort ships threw up a wall of antiaircraft fire. The planes broke formation and veered toward the convoy at different angles, flying so low that they seemed to skim the waves. All their torpedoes missed. Guy stepped out of the bridge to see the planes roar overhead, then watched as one plane crashed into the ocean. Some of the escorts began dropping depth charges, which meant they had found U-boats. Soon Zebbie resumed barking and five more dots raced toward them. This time, a torpedo bomber scored a direct hit on the British freighter *Cape Corso*, which was directly ahead of the *Vance*. The *Cape Corso* exploded. The *Vance* swerved to miss her. Guy saw men thrashing in the icy water, but the convoy could not stop without endangering everyone else on board the ships. Only nine men on the *Cape Corso* survived.

Next came Stuka dive-bombers, whose flared wings made them resemble birds of prey. They were equipped with sirens to emit piercing screams as they dived. The first Stukas hit no ships, but over the next few days, the planes attacked in waves that began to feel like one endless siege. "We did not take our clothes off during the entire trip through the Arctic region," Guy recalled. "We slept whenever and wherever we could. There were so many alarms I lost count. We were on the alert all the time." On the fourth day, the convoy was picking its way through a field of small chunks of floating ice known as growlers when a storm hit. The ships rode huge waves. Heavy snow piled up on their decks. The German air bases were socked in. The storm persisted until Russian destroyers emerged from the gloom to escort the convoy into Murmansk.

Guy had never been anywhere like Murmansk. It had an apocalyptic feel. Fires continuously burned throughout the city. German bombers attacked five or six times a day. Russian fighters rose to meet them, and engaged in dogfights with German fighters. Antiaircraft guns crackled from sandbagged bunkers in the rubble of buildings. A bomb hit the docks close enough to the *Vance* to rain debris onto her deck. The Russians quickly repaired any damage to the docks with lumber delivered daily by train. Salvage teams roamed the harbor, blowing up hulks of bombed ships to make way for new arrivals. Guy wrote that Murmansk "was almost deserted but for the soldiers, and only necessities are obtainable." He was impressed by the Russians' toughness, but when a friendly Russian asked him what he thought of Murmansk, he stood speechless.

The *Vance*'s cargo was unloaded by Russian women and Red Army soldiers on leave from the eastern front. The soldiers were hard-looking characters, and their presence so agitated Zebbie that she had to be shut up in the galley. The process took twelve days, during which Guy counted forty-five air raids. A plane crashed into the marshes a quarter mile away but Guy could not tell whose it was. Despite the hair-raising prospect of the return voyage, the scene in Murmansk was grimmer, and he was glad when the convoy re-formed to set out for home.

German bombers attacked the returning convoy almost immediately, but were driven off by a British fighter plane. The British pilot's mission was to take off from one of the merchant ships when the convoy needed air cover, fly for as long as his fuel lasted, and then ditch the plane in the ocean and be picked up from the water—the ship had no room for the plane to land again. The pilot ended up dying when his parachute failed to open. Months would pass before Guy would see his first escort carrier—a miniature aircraft carrier for convoys, with room for planes to take off *and* land.

Hardly one for military discipline, Guy stepped on a few toes during the voyage. He infuriated the convoy commodore by racing the *Vance* ahead of the rest of the ships, and he angered the Navy gun crew on the *Vance* by sticking them with the worst bunks and declining to order his crew to spell them in the gun tubs. But he got the ship home. Twenty-two of the twenty-five ships in PQ-15 delivered their cargo in Murmansk and got back safely. The convoy was considered a success, and the Allies decided to send even more ships in the next one, PQ-16. Four Mathews men would make that run, but only two would survive it.

PQ-16 formed off Halifax, Nova Scotia, in mid-May, crossed the Atlantic to England, and, like its predecessor, headed north into the Arctic Circle. On May 25, a Condor pilot spotted PQ-16 off Norway and called in the bombers. The first wave of bombers failed to hit a ship, but two bombs exploded in the water close enough to the old freighter *Syros* to cause damage in her engine room. The *Syros* straggled behind the convoy.

Her crew of thirty-nine included William Cecil Ripley Jr., an able seaman from the Mathews village of Susan. Cecil, as his family called him, was twenty-eight years old, tall and rail thin. He had quit fishing pound nets with his father in 1936 to join the Merchant Marine. Cecil had deep-set eyes that lent him a sorrowful aspect, but he had a wry sense of humor and plenty of girlfriends. A month before, he had written his family in Mathews that he had just been to India and thought his next stop was Russia. His family did not know the name of his ship.

Cecil had been at sea long enough to know that the bomb damage had placed the *Syros* in grave danger. The U-boats followed behind Arctic convoys just to pick off stragglers like her. Like many ships bound for Russia, the *Syros* was a floating bomb. Her holds were packed with explosives and ammunition. At around 1 a.m. on May 26, in hazy Arctic daylight, the U-703 crept to within a thousand yards of the *Syros* and launched a torpedo. Men on other ships saw the torpedo racing toward the *Syros* and fired machine guns at it to try to detonate it prematurely. But the torpedo struck the *Syros* just below the smokestack. Nothing happened for a second or two. Then a deafening explosion split the freighter in half. Both halves sank, leaving dozens of men thrashing or clinging to wreckage in 29-degree water. A rescue vessel picked up thirty of the crew, but ten others, including Cecil Ripley, were never seen again.

When Cecil's mother received her telegram from the government, she climbed the stairs to his old room and opened the door for the first time since his last visit. Cecil had left a coat and hat on the bed. She closed the door and told her daughter not to touch them because "they're all I have left of him."

Charles V. "Bud" Majette of Mathews watched the *Syros* explode from the deck of the freighter *Alamar*, which was sailing just ahead in the same column. Majette had left a $3-a-week job at an ice plant to join the Merchant Marine. He had just turned twenty-one and gotten his third-officer's license. He had known Cecil Ripley from grade school but had not known he was on the *Syros*. The explosion reminded Majette that the *Alamar* was carrying 350 tons of TNT in her holds. In addition, her main deck was crowded with planes, tanks, train locomotives, and drums of highly flammable aviation fuel. Majette did not like to think about what would happen if the ship got hit. He could stay calm only by working constantly, even when he was off watch. Some of his shipmates were so unnerved by the constant air attacks that they flailed their hands at the swooping planes as if swatting at wasps.

As the convoy approached Bear Island, Stukas attacked from several directions at once. Majette looked up to see a Junkers 88 light bomber dart through a gap in the wall of antiaircraft fire and drop a bomb squarely on the *Alamar*'s deck. The drums of aviation fuel burst into flames. The ship's deck cracked open. The crew coolly lowered two lifeboats and climbed down Jacob's ladders into them. Majette was on his way down the ladder when a new eruption of flames panicked the men in the lifeboat below him, and they pulled away too early. Majette splashed into water so cold it took his breath away. The lifeboat immediately picked him up. All thirty-six men on the *Alamar* got away safely and were picked up by other ships. The convoy struggled on to Murmansk. Majette thought he was lucky the bomb had found the aviation fuel rather than the TNT in the holds. But his voyage was far from over. The ships of PQ-16 still had to survive their stay in Murmansk, and then their trip home.

By June 1942, the war in the Pacific was starting to turn. The U.S. fleet had halted the Japanese advance across the Pacific at the Battle of the Coral Sea, in which the United States and Japan each lost an aircraft carrier. The U.S. and Japanese fleets collided on June 4 in the Battle of Midway. Torpedo bombers from U.S. carriers sank two huge Japanese carriers, reversing the balance of naval power in the Pacific. Admiral King distinguished himself in the Pacific as a strategist, halting the Japanese advance through skillful deployment of carrier task forces. He also disrupted the Japanese supply lines through aggressive submarine attacks on the Japanese merchant fleet, which was as poorly protected as America's.

But the war against Germany, which Roosevelt and Churchill had agreed to win first, was being lost. The Red Army continued to hemorrhage men and surrender Russian soil. In North Africa, German Field Marshall Erwin Rommel's Afrika Corps routed the British in a tank battle at Tobruk, Libya. In the Mediterranean, two Allied convoys trying to reach the strategic British-held island of Malta were pummeled by German bombers. Nazi storm troopers in a Czechoslovakian village responded to the killing of a German officer by executing every man and boy in the village and then torching it. Reports came from Eastern Europe that Jews were being killed with poison gas. The U-boat force was expanding by thirty submarines a month. Doenitz sent U-boats to attack Canadian vessels in the Saint Lawrence estuary, the river road to the Great Lakes.

U-boats had sunk forty-four merchant ships in U.S. waters in May 1942, the highest monthly total of the war to date. The U-701 added insult to injury on the night of June 9 by sneaking into the main channel at the mouth of the Chesapeake Bay and laying a string of mines. The mines went undetected for five days until an inbound Allied convoy blundered into them. William Coles Forrest Jr. of Mathews was sleeping in his bunk on the tanker *Robert C. Tuttle* when the ship triggered one of the mines. The impact knocked Forrest onto the deck. He grabbed a life vest and climbed down a ladder into a waiting lifeboat. Two other ships in the convoy also detonated mines. Black smoke from the damaged ships billowed into the sky. Wide-eyed tourists emerged from Virginia Beach hotels to watch. Firefighters saved the *Robert Tuttle*. Navy planes and ships raced back and forth in ferocious pursuit of a U-boat that was long gone.

Since the start of the war, jittery coastal residents had feared U-boats landing spies or saboteurs in their midst. Mysterious lights were reported on empty beaches. Dead Germans were rumored to have been found with ticket stubs from local movie theaters in their pockets. Now some of the fears would come true, as the U-boats grew bolder still.

On the night of June 13, the U-202 landed a team of four would-be saboteurs in dense fog on a beach at Amagansett, Long Island. Their mission, code-named Operation Pastorius, was to choose a vital industrial plant and wreck it, but their plans went wildly off track from the start. The Germans were spotted as soon as they arrived on the beach by a twenty-one-year-old Coast Guardsman named John C. Cullen, who was patrolling the beach on foot. The Germans first told Cullen they were clamming—in an area with no clams. Then the Germans' leader, George Dasch, abandoned the charade. He pointedly asked the unarmed Cullen if he had a mother and father, and added, "I wouldn't want to have to kill you." He offered Cullen $100 in cash to just go away and forget he had seen anything, then quickly upped the offer to $300. Cullen pretended to accept. Dasch told Cullen to look him in the eyes. Cullen did so, half afraid that Dasch intended to hypnotize him. Dasch asked, "Would you recognize me if you saw me again?" Cullen—no fool—said no, and Dasch let him walk away. Cullen ran to his station and reported the encounter to his superiors.

The Long Island saboteurs managed to reach Manhattan by train and melt into the crowds, but Dasch's confidence in the mission had evaporated. He gave himself up and provided the FBI with enough information to arrest the other members of his team, as well as a second four-man team of saboteurs who had landed on the beach near Jacksonville, Florida. Two of the Florida saboteurs made it to Cincinnati, and two others to Chicago, but no one got as far as picking a target. All eight of the Germans would be tried by a special military tribunal and convicted of espionage. Six would be hanged; Dasch and another man who informed on his partners would receive long prison terms, commuted after the war by President Harry Truman. No U-boat would ever land a sabotage team on American soil again, although two spies were landed on a beach near Bar Harbor, Maine, in late 1944. Both were quickly apprehended.

Most U-boats stuck to torpedoing ships, and those in the Caribbean continued to find easy prey. A rising star among U-boat commanders, Hans-Ludwig Witt viewed his assignment to the Caribbean as a chance to rack up kills against weak defenses. He would in fact sink ten Allied ships in the Caribbean, including Dewey Hodges's *Onondaga*. Witt took command of the U-129 from Nicolai Clausen, who had used it to sink several American ships, including Captain Walter Hudgins's freighter the *Mary*.

Witt guided the U-129 from the Atlantic into the Caribbean through the narrow Nicholas Channel between Cuba and the Grand Bahamas Bank. He probably did not expect to find his first victim right there in the channel, before he even reached the Caribbean. But when Witt spotted a heavily loaded freighter through his periscope, he knew what to do.

The U-129 drilled a torpedo into the freighter amidships, causing an explosion that blew men into the air. The ship plunged down by the stern. One lifeboat got free. Witt guided the U-129 alongside it. He pointed a machine gun at the castaways and demanded their ship's name, cargo, and destination. The men said their ship was the Bull Line freighter *Millinocket*. She had been hauling bauxite ore from the Virgin Islands to Mobile,

Alabama. Her captain, Lewis Callis of Gwynn's Island, was among the eleven men missing.

The castaways asked Witt for a first-aid kit, and the U-boat commander gave them one. Witt did not make small talk. He did not wish the survivors good luck. The U-129 submerged and headed into the Caribbean with one kill already to its credit. The castaways fired rockets until a Cuban fishing boat picked them up.

Lewis Callis's body was never found. He had sailed the Caribbean for the Bull Line for more than twenty years. His wife and children lived on Gwynn's Island, and he always took time at sea to write to them. One of his letters included a poem he had written about home:

There is an Island in Old Virginia,
Down on the Chesapeake,
It's my old home town,
And I'm going there this week
Yes, I'm going back tomorrow,
If I can steal, beg or borrow
I just want enough for fare
For you won't need money there.
Down on my old Gwynn's Island home

The *Millinocket* was the thirty-seventh merchant ship sunk in U.S.-patrolled waters that June, which was shaping up as yet another record month for ships lost. James Ashberry of Mathews survived the torpedoing of the freighter *City of Alma* in the deep ocean off Puerto Rico. Ashberry, a tough, hard-drinking seaman, came home to Mathews to rest up but feared dying of boredom. He said, "I had rather be in the Atlantic Ocean, for it is just as alive as Mathews." John Elmo Godsey Jr. of Mathews survived a U-boat assault on the Bull Line freighter *Manuela* off the Outer Banks of North Carolina. Godsey was knocked cold by the torpedo explosion but revived when cold seawater swirled over him on deck. He made his way into a lifeboat with a deep gash on his head and two black eyes. The ship stayed afloat and Godsey went back aboard to search for two shipmates who had been on watch in the engine room, but the door to the engine room was sealed shut in a misshapen way that ended all hope.

The sinkings prompted Army chief of staff George C. Marshall to write Admiral King: "The losses by submarines off our Atlantic seaboard and in the Caribbean now threaten our entire war effort . . . We are all aware of the limited number of escort craft available, but has every conceivable improvised means been brought to bear on this situation? I am fearful that another month or two of this will so cripple our means of transport that we will be unable to bring sufficient men and planes to bear against the enemy in critical theaters to exercise a determining influence on the war."

The pointed question from a respected colleague appeared to pierce King's detachment. He replied to Marshall that the Navy's resources were stretched thin with escort duty for the North Atlantic convoys and troop transports to Britain. As far as protecting coastal shipping, King wrote, "We had to improvise on a large scale . . . We took over all pleasure craft that could be used and sent them out with makeshift armament and untrained crews. We employed for patrol purposes aircraft that could not carry bombs, and planes flown from school fields by student pilots. We armed our merchant ships as rapidly as possible. We employed fishing boats as volunteer lookouts . . ."

King concluded his letter by professing a devotion to convoys. "I might say in this connection that escort is not just one way of handling the submarine menace; it is the only way that gives any promise of success."

In fact, King had shown little enthusiasm for any of the improvisational methods of protecting coastal shipping, such as pleasure craft and unarmed air patrols, for which he was now taking credit. And he had shown little interest in coastal convoys until he could accumulate enough new ships and planes to operate the kind of powerful convoys he favored. King did not acknowledge that to Marshall, but he apparently gave in to the latter's pressure. King began releasing more old destroyers to the bucket-brigade convoys for longer periods. Two weeks after Marshall's memo, the first convoy from Key West sailed for Panama. For the first time, a merchant ship could theoretically travel the length of the U.S. coast and into the Caribbean with an armed escort. Roosevelt wrote King that he was pleased, but added, "I think it has taken an unconscionable time to get things going." The convoy system still had a lot of holes for U-boats to exploit. It offered little or no protection in less traveled waters between small ports. But the open season on merchant ships in U.S. waters was finally over.

At the end of June, Captain Jesse came home to Gales Neck for the first time in months. He and his grandson J. W. Corbett had spent the last four months on a tug in the Caribbean, towing and pushing barges between ports. A torpedo whizzed past the tug's stern one day, but nothing further came of it, and Jesse said nothing to Henny about it. He had a reputation for fearlessness at sea. He once rescued two men from a leaking barge in a howling blizzard that blew off his tug's smokestack. He taunted men who cowered when seas swept the tugboat's deck, but when he came home, he just wanted to relax. He would sit for hours at a table in the stifling kitchen, cheating at solitaire in a blue haze of cigar smoke. Henny treated him like a king. He awoke every morning to a hot breakfast, a set of freshly cleaned and folded clothes, and a basin of warm water next to his razor. Nevertheless, he always found something to complain about, and Henny cried.

Captain Jesse's four-year-old grandson, Jesse Carroll Thornton, who lived at Gales Neck with Henny, reverted to his best behavior when his grandfather came home. He might get yelled at or even smacked by Henny if he acted up, but Jesse had a short fuse and meted out punishment with a belt. For all of that, Jesse Carroll was always glad to have his grandfather safely home. The boy saw a side of him that most people could never imagine. Jesse would comfort him when he woke up from a bad dream. He remembered being pulled in a wagon by Jesse as he and Henny walked the property at Gales Neck, talking about the farm, holding hands.

Henny celebrated Captain Jesse's visit home in June 1942 with a huge family gathering and feast, which she called a dining. The guest list for a Hodges dining included all members of the family, including every son who was in port. The list also included dozens of neighbors and friends. The turnouts always exceeded fifty and sometimes one hundred. Henny spent days cooking in a big woodstove with a firebox on one side and a tank for heating water on the other. She fixed fish, fried chicken, ham, spoon bread, and biscuits with fried hog parts. A Washington newspaper reporter who attended a dining described a meal "of such dimensions that the dessert course calls for three freezers of ice cream."

The Hodges dinner table seated only sixteen, so the guests at a dining ate in shifts. The men were served first, starting with Jesse, who sat at the head of the table facing east toward the sea. After the men ate, the women took their turn. The children went last. David, the youngest Hodges son, joked that he learned to drink coffee black because the milk never once got to him.

Though Henny loved to cook, her true pleasure in the dinings came from bringing her family together. They and the farm were her only interests. She loved to talk with her children, and soak up all the details of their families' lives. She liked it when her children stayed behind in the kitchen to sit with her after the commotion died down. These gatherings were the best times of her life. The dining in June 1942 stood out because four of her six seafaring sons happened to be home.

Captain Dewey Hodges brought his family from Norfolk. He was still recovering from his illness, but he never missed a dining if he was home. Dewey felt a responsibility to help keep the family together because he was the second oldest and Raymond rarely came home. The trip from Dewey's house in Norfolk to Gales Neck took five hours and included two ferry rides. On a hot summer day, it was nothing short of an ordeal. But Dewey piled Edna and the three girls into their Buick Zephyr and set out for Mathews. He sang all the way, as he always did, crooning "Mexicali Rose"

and "You Are My Sunshine" until the girls started giggling and then singing along. Even Edna joined in.

At the dining, Dewey greeted his brother Leslie Hodges, and his wife,
Cecile. Leslie was a licensed captain but did not have his own ship. He was
serving as first officer on the Ford freighter *Oneida*, a laker running cargo
between the Caribbean and the Gulf of Mexico. Leslie was something of
an outlier in the Hodges family. He was the only son with dark hair, and
wore a moustache that his brothers said made him look like Hitler. Leslie
took the joking well but never joked back. He was also the only quiet
Hodges son. Cecile was a slender, dark-haired firecracker from Mobile,
Alabama, who had a sweet nature but swore like a stevedore. Leslie and
Cecile lived in Norfolk and attended dinings when Leslie was in port, but
they never seemed quite comfortable at them and hung at the edges. Leslie
once told his sisters he never felt the same coming home after he caused
the car crash that killed his two-year-old sister, Henrietta.

The guests at the dining included Willie Hodges, the captain of an
oceangoing tug that guided ships and barges along the coast and into the
Bay. Willie was a jolly man whose waistline was expanding as fast as Jesse's.
His brothers joked that Willie had stayed at the table for the women's and
children's shifts. Willie and his family lived only two houses away from
Dewey in Norfolk, and the families often got together to share a bushel of
steamed crabs or a bag of fresh oysters.

The three youngest Hodges brothers, Spencer, Coleman, and David,
were so much younger than their older brothers, they were almost a separate generation. Spencer lived in Mathews with his wife and son and
worked at the local creamery, making ice cream. He had started going to
sea but injured his back while working for Dewey on the *East Indian*, and
went ashore for good. Spencer became the only Hodges brother to graduate from high school. Though he stayed on land, he helped his seagoing
brothers by recruiting Mathews men for their ships.

Coleman Hodges was tall and almost gangly, with a pronounced

Adam's apple and a grin like his brother Dewey's. He was a dedicated jokester. He could squirt milk from a cow's udder accurately for long distances. Only Coleman's wife and daughters saw his serious side. He was working his way up through the officer ranks at the Ford fleet and was determined to command a ship in time to serve his country in the war.

David Hodges, the youngest of the seven Hodges sons, lived with his family in Norfolk, where he worked in a shipyard as a rigger, securing heavy objects to be moved. David aspired to become a pilot in the Bay, guiding ships up the channels between Norfolk and Baltimore. He mentioned his goal to his father one day while working on the farm, and Captain Jesse replied, "Why don't you start by piloting that manure over here?" David and Coleman were best friends. David could make anybody laugh, and he sometimes used his wit to cut people he disliked.

The only Hodges boy absent from the dining that June was Raymond. He was ferrying American soldiers across the Atlantic on the *Mormacmoon*. Raymond's wife, Dolly, came to Gales Neck, however, along with her sons, Raymond Jr. and Bill. Fourteen-year-old Bill was impressed by the sight of many fine sea captains in one place. They included not only his grandfather and uncles but his cousin Will Hunley, who was about to be given command of a ship.

After the meal, the men strolled across the wide front yard to the point of Gales Neck, where several lawn chairs encircled a table near the water's edge. The men lit cigars and passed around a bottle of Jack Daniel's whiskey. The jokes flew and the captains told preposterous stories about one another and everything else. Dewey claimed to have grown a tomato so big that it had to be sliced with a crosscut saw. As David put it, "The only difference between a fairy tale and a sea story is that a fairy tale begins, 'Once upon a time,' and a sea story begins, 'Look, this ain't no bullshit.'" About the only subject that did not come up was the U-boat war. Nobody wanted to talk business. The brothers wanted to leave the war behind, and just enjoy their mother's cooking and the pleasures of an early summer evening on Gales Neck.

Inside the farmhouse, the four Hodges daughters directed the cleanup. Though overshadowed by their brothers, they were a formidable group. They answered only to Henny. The eldest daughter, Alice, was as tall and broad-shouldered as her brothers. She was a young widow with three children. She waited tables at a restaurant at the end of a fishing pier. The place got rowdy at night, and Alice was said to have picked up a man by his collar and belt loops and thrown him out the door. Alice was the most pious of the Hodges children, and frowned upon some of her sisters' activities, particularly those of Hilda Fourteen, who went to the dance halls.

Alice and her middle sisters, Elizabeth and Louise, had booming voices and argued all the time. They could go back and forth for hours over trivial points such as when it had rained last. They once got into a ferocious debate over what color sweater a woman had been wearing in her casket at her funeral. None of them ever conceded a point, and they held grudges for months. Their endless bickering made Henny cry, but Jesse sometimes egged them on for entertainment.

The men stayed out on the riverbank until the fireflies came out and the wives called that it was time to go. Each guest usually took home some freshly picked vegetables and sometimes a live chicken. Henny cried as each of her sons kissed her good-bye. One by one, they got into their cars and started down the driveway, back to their homes, and then to their ships. Dewey, Leslie, Willie, and Coleman would rejoin Raymond in the U-boat war. Jesse and J.W. would be close behind.

At Murmansk, the surviving ships of convoy PQ-16 finished unloading their cargo and were organized into a new convoy for the long trip home. Bud Majette and the others who had been pulled from the water after the *Alamar* sinking were given bunks on her sister ship, the *Massmar*. Naturally, Majette found a couple of Mathews men on the *Massmar*'s regular crew. The ship's first officer, Captain Sam Jones Diggs, who was named for the nineteenth-century evangelist Sam Jones, had left Mathews at age sixteen and sailed the world for almost three decades. Sam rarely returned to

Mathews, but he wrote to his family from every port. He addressed all his letters to his half sister Helen, the postmistress in the Mathews hamlet of Laban.

Sam's last letter from the *Massmar*, on April 26, had been cut to pieces by the censors. "Dear Sister," it began. "Arrived here today from _____. _____ just called for orders. Will go _____. _____ don't know how long we will be here." Sam told his sister not to write, "as we don't have any forwarding address. We don't know where we will go or be."

The other Mathews man on the *Massmar*, Charles Edwards, might have been the only mariner in the convoy excited about sailing to Murmansk. Edwards had been at sea for five years and was still intoxicated by travel. He kept a map of the world on his wall at home, and every time he got back from a voyage, he marked the route. The Murmansk Run would be an impressive addition to the map if he lived to add it.

The Germans ignored the *Massmar* and the other empty PQ-16 ships on their return trip from Russia. They threw all their U-boats and aircraft at the next Murmansk-bound convoy, PQ-17. Majette got a glimpse of PQ-17 when the two convoys passed at a great distance on the Fourth of July. PQ-17 was sailing beneath a fiery cloud of bombers and antiaircraft fire. Majette compared it to a Fourth of July fireworks display. He had no inkling that PQ-17 was about to turn into the worst convoy disaster of the war.

PQ-17 was the largest Arctic convoy yet, with thirty-eight merchant ships and forty-five escort ships, including thirteen British cruisers and destroyers. Soon after PQ-17 passed out of Majette's sight, the British Admiralty abruptly withdrew all of the escorts. The British believed, wrongly, that the German battleship *Tirpitz* was emerging from the Norwegian fjords to attack the convoy. The British escort ships could not match the *Tirpitz*'s firepower, and the British could not allow the *Tirpitz* to destroy them. So the Admiralty took the desperate step of ordering the escorts to abandon the convoy and save themselves. The merchant ships were ordered to "scatter" and run for Murmansk. The Germans could not catch them all.

But the Germans, as it turned out, came close. Over the next six days, the Condors tracked the scattered cargo ships into remote stretches of the Barents Sea, and then guided U-boats to sink them. One German Condor pilot radioed the captain of a merchant ship the exact time a U-boat would arrive to sink it. Men who had escaped their sinking ship in a lifeboat refused to be picked up by a second ship, reasoning that they would just have to get into another lifeboat when the second ship was torpedoed. They were right. The crews of the two ships met again later on the beach of a remote island. The *Tirpitz* never attacked the convoy, but the faulty intelligence and the decision to withdraw the escorts enabled the Germans to sink twenty-four of the thirty-eight merchant ships in PQ-17, killing 153 mariners. The Allies suspended all convoys to Murmansk.

After passing the ill-fated PQ-17, the *Massmar* and the other ships returning from the previous convoy encountered no threat except the weather. But the weather was enough. They were only a day out of the safety of the harbor at Reykjavik, Iceland, when a storm engulfed them. Two days of dense fog followed. Navigators could not take the stars and lost their bearings. A senior officer mistook an iceberg for land and, in his confusion, directed the convoy into the Allied minefield protecting Reykjavik. No one could see the mines bobbing in the rough seas.

Charles Edwards was oiling the steering gear on the *Massmar*'s main deck when a mine detonated against the hull with enough force to blow the ship's bow out of the water. The *Massmar* sank fast. Majette helped lower a lifeboat, but a huge wave caught it and threw it right back on the deck beside them, upside down. Majette, who could not swim, saw a hatch cover floating by and jumped toward it. The cold water hit him like a punch and quickly sapped his strength. A sailor on a Free French escort ship threw him a line but he was too weak to reach for it. "All I wanted to do was go to sleep," he recalled. The French sailor dove into the water and tied the line around him, and he was pulled to safety. Sam Diggs was not so lucky. He apparently was trapped in his stateroom and went to the bottom with the ship. His sister, the Laban postmistress, opened the government's official letter of regret. Forty men died on the *Massmar*, including twenty-three survivors of the *Alamar*.

Charles Edwards and Majette came home to Mathews. Edwards marked the route on his wall map but took no joy in it. He told a reporter that "[I] still can't get out of my mind the sight of so many men perishing." He had seen other men reduced to quivering wrecks by the constant air raids. "If I have my choice, I think I won't go back to Russia," he said. "The boys in the Caribbean have had it bad. But at least [the Germans] don't pound away at you there, and break up your rest for a couple of weeks before they finally get you."

Majette, who had survived two plunges into subfreezing water, agreed. He wanted to sail in southern waters, where at least "if I hit the water again, it would be warm."

Caribbean voyages were shorter, and the weather most of the year was perfect. Mathews men who had sailed before the war on Ford, Bull Line, or Moore-McCormack ships knew the Caribbean well and had friends in most of the ports. Everyone's favorite destination was Cuba, where the port authorities were laid-back, the rum was cheap, and the women were lovely and prone to suggestion. Every mariner had a story about a magical night in Havana with a girl on his arm or a gang of shipmates at his side, raising hell. But those were peacetime memories. In 1942, Cuba had asked for U.S. help in ferreting out Axis spies, and outlawed the Nazi and Communist parties (Fidel Castro's revolution was more than a decade away). Cuban president Fulgencio Batista welcomed the construction of two American air bases and a seaplane base on Cuban soil to help patrol for U-boats, which had torpedoed merchant ships all around the island. The warm, turquoise waters off Cuba were no longer quite so inviting.

CHAPTER EIGHT

Catastrophe

Dewey Hodges had been back home in Norfolk for only two weeks after Henny's big June dining when the telephone rang. His boss at the Ford Motor Co. fleet wondered if Dewey felt well enough to serve as the substitute captain of a ship on a short run. The freighter *Onondaga*, a laker of just 2,309 tons, was being sent by the government from Mobile to Havana and back. The ship was to leave Mobile in late July.

Dewey felt fine. He had been surprised when his doctor had not cleared him three months before to command his own ship, the *East Indian*. But the *East Indian* was leaving on a six-month voyage halfway around the world, and the *Onondaga* would only be gone for a few weeks. His doctor had no objection, and Dewey called his boss and said he would go. Dewey followed the news enough to know that a run to Cuba was dangerous, but a lot of runs were dangerous in July 1942.

Dewey asked his brother Spencer in Mathews to help him fill out the *Onondaga*'s crew with Mathews men if possible. William Hammond signed on as bo'sun, returning to sea for the first time since being torpedoed on the *Norlindo*. Russell Dennis signed on as third officer. Genious Hudgins Jr. had been home only a week after being torpedoed on the *Green*

Island when he heard Dewey needed a second officer. Genious had just gotten his second-officer's license. Here was a chance to start his new job working for a captain he had known for years, and whom Genious trusted to bring them home. He gladly signed on.

Edna and the girls tried to make the days leading up to Dewey's departure feel normal, but they felt Dewey's anxiety. He was setting out on his first voyage in months—his first since America had entered the war. He was commanding an unfamiliar ship about one quarter the size of his *East Indian.* He did not say a word about it to his family. At the airport, he kissed Edna and the girls good-bye, bent down to the girls and smiled at them and said, "Be good for your mother." Then he got on a plane to Mobile.

The Navy destroyer USS *Corry* was approaching the eastern tip of Cuba near the Windward Passage on July 4 when a lookout spotted a raft bearing four oil-soaked men. They said they were the only survivors of the Bull Line freighter *Ruth*, torpedoed five nights earlier. The torpedo ignited she ship's magazine and blew off the entire stern of the ship. The *Ruth* sank so fast that thirty-four of her thirty-eight officers and crew never got out. Five were Mathews men.

The Navy sent word by telegraph to the Bull Line. That night at nine o'clock, the telephone rang at the home of Captain Robert Melville Callis on Gwynn's Island. The *Ruth* was—had been—Mel Callis's ship. He and four other Mathews men in his crew were among the missing. Mel was one of the best-known captains in Mathews, the brother of Captain Homer Callis and Captain Rodney Callis. Mel was the eldest of the three brothers, and the most carefree. It was he who had described seeing mermaids with "eyes as blue as the waters of old Milford Haven," who were "built like the steeple of Gwynn's Island Baptist Church." Mel had been a stalwart of the Bull Line for over twenty years. He lived with his wife, Lucy, whom everyone called Luna, in a house set back from the water in a patch of woods.

The Callis house stood literally within shouting distance of the homes of two of the other missing men.

Perry Collier, the *Ruth*'s carpenter, was one of the oldest mariners in Mathews at sixty years. He was tall and angular, with close-cropped gray hair. He was a devout man who sang like a songbird in the choir at Gwynn's Island Baptist Church. He gave all his spare change to children because no one had ever given him spare change when he was a child. "As long as I've got it," he told his wife, "I'm going to give it to them." Perry had known the Callis family most of his life. He fished pound nets and made runs on the *Ruth* when the fishing was poor. Perry's son Clarence had planned to ship out with him on the *Ruth* but was taken aback by the sight of new 3-inch guns installed on the old ship. "Dad, let's get off," Clarence said, but Perry replied, "No, I'm going to go ahead." In Perry's last letter, which arrived after the ship had sunk, he wrote he was excited about getting home to see a newborn grandchild.

The *Ruth*'s second officer, Howard Morris, had grown up with the Callises too. Only minutes before the torpedo struck, he had taken over the bridge from Mel, who was exhausted after several straight watches. Morris left behind a wife and a grown daughter. The *Ruth*'s bo'sun, Robert Belvin, grew up in the Mathews hamlet of Port Haywood, south of the courthouse, but the sea had been his home for the last nine of his twenty-eight years. He wrote regularly to his mother, who had just received a letter from him postmarked at Trinidad, the *Ruth*'s last port. His mother said she would not give up hope for Robert. "He was my only boy."

The fifth Mathews man killed on the *Ruth* was Ashley Clinton Williams, a black messman who had grown up in the village of Hallieford, just across Milford Haven from Gwynn's Island. Ashley was one of the few black Mathews men employed on a steamship. Blacks in 1942 were unwelcome in most of the sea unions—the National Maritime Union was an exception—and at many large U.S. shipping companies, including Moore-McCormack. The companies that did employ them relegated them to menial jobs such as steward and messman. Ashley served food to the officers and crew and did the dishes. He would have found no better opportunities in the Navy, where segregation still prevailed, and the few jobs open to black sailors were much like those open to black merchant mariners.

Ashley was the grandson of a Baptist preacher and the son of a fisherman. His family left Mathews for good in the 1930s and moved to Baltimore, where Ashley worked as a stevedore before obtaining a seaman's certificate and joining the Merchant Marine. His Mathews background may have helped him get the job on the *Ruth*. Mel Callis very likely knew that Ashley was from Mathews.

The families of Mel Callis and the other men missing from the *Ruth* were still awaiting official word from the government when the news reached Mathews that Captain Mellin Respess had been torpedoed a second time.

After his good-byes in the Mathews general store in March, Mellin had taken command of the Liberty ship *Thomas McKean*, operated for the government by Calmar Steamship Line of New York. The *Thomas McKean* spent much of June loading munitions to take to Russia. Convoys to Murmansk had been suspended since the PQ-17 debacle. Until they resumed, the only open sea route from the East Coast to the Russian front led 13,000 miles across the South Atlantic, around the Cape of Good Hope, north through the Indian Ocean, around the Horn of Africa, and through the Persian Gulf to Basra, Iraq. From Basra, trains carried the cargo thousands more miles to the front.

The *Thomas McKean* carried enough firepower to wage a small offensive. Her holds were packed with ammunition, small arms, and gasoline. Her main deck was crammed with tanks, trucks, and eleven medium-range bombers. The ship followed canals and convoys as far south as Norfolk. But from there, Mellin was directed to take her across the Atlantic alone. She was 245 miles north of Antigua on the morning of June 29 when a torpedo crashed into her hull. The explosion killed three members of the Navy Armed Guard crew who were assigned to the merchant vessel, and injured two other men.

Mellin stayed calm. He had been through the torpedoing of the *Oakmar* only three months earlier. "How hard are we hit?" he asked the chief engineer. "It looks to me like the whole stern is gone," the chief replied. He took a closer look and declared the *Thomas McKean* "finished." Mellin gave the order to abandon ship. He disappeared into his cabin and emerged with a weighted bag containing secret Navy codes, which he threw into the sea, and a case of cigarettes, which he tossed to the chief engineer for the lifeboat voyage.

Four lifeboats escaped the ship. The U-boat commander gave them time to get a safe distance away, and then finished off the *Thomas McKean* with the sub's deck cannon. Round after round smashed into the empty vessel. The men in the lifeboats counted fifty-seven shots. Finally, the ammunition in the cargo holds ignited, and flames engulfed the *Thomas McKean* as she sank by the bow. She was one of the first Liberty ships sunk.

Mellin commanded one of the four lifeboats. Another Mathews man, Roland Foster Jr., the second officer, also commanded a boat. Roland was short and wiry with enormous hands. As a boy in Mathews, he had struggled to stay in school, but at sea, Roland read every book he saw, including the Bible twice. He was thoughtful and opinionated, and never afraid to speak his mind.

The U-505 approached Roland's lifeboat. The sub's conning tower bore the painted images of a lioness and a swastika.* The U-boat commander, Peter Zschech, called through a megaphone in English, "Please come alongside," and then handed the megaphone to an officer with a bushy red beard and shorts. The officer asked about the *Thomas McKean*, and Roland said she was American. "Good," the officer said. He asked Roland if the castaways needed anything. Roland asked for medicine for a badly injured

---

* Mariners were instructed to pay attention to U-boats' markings and report them to Naval Intelligence agents as a way of tracking U-boats' movements. Foster obviously took that task seriously. He wrote in his report that the lioness figure on the conning tower "was standing on its hind foot, the left one I believe, and in its front paw it had a big hammer, and in its tail a torch."

mariner in his boat. The mariner had been found motionless on the deck by some Navy Armed Guard men, who risked their lives to carry him into the boat. Roland did not think he would live for long. The U-boat officer sent over a first-aid kit and apparently a sedative to ease the man's pain.

The German asked Roland and his boat-mates, "You are carrying munitions? Yes?" and, according to Roland, "looked at every one of us in the lifeboat with that wicked eye he had, as much as if to say that none of you had better say 'No' to that." Roland changed the subject, asking for the course to the nearest land. The German apparently thought Roland was asking for a tow, and replied, "We haven't got the time." Roland said he only wanted a course. "Steer with the wind," the German said, by way of ending the discussion. The U-505 pulled away and submerged, on its way to a dubious place in history.

The oarsmen had to work hard to keep the lifeboats from drifting apart. Roland called over to Mellin's lifeboat to ask his opinion about the severely injured man, who lay silent and still. Mellin told Roland to burn the man's foot with a cigarette to see if he reacted. He did not, so Roland tried burning his fingers. When he did not respond to that either, he was eased into the ocean. There was nothing more they could do for him. The survivors in all the boats had plenty of pemmican, chocolate, and malted milk tablets to eat. But the drinking-water casks in one boat had been built with green wood, which turned the water so dark that the men were afraid to drink it.

They made an effort to steer as a small convoy, heading south toward the Virgin Islands, but wind and current finally overpowered the oarsmen and separated the lifeboats. After five days, two of the four boats reached shore in the Virgin Islands. A week later, Roland's boat reached an uninhabited stretch of Anguilla Island in the Leeward Islands. Two more days later—fourteen days after the sinking—Mellin's boat finally landed on the coast of the Dominican Republic. Fifty-five of the sixty men on the *Thomas McKean* survived, but all the bombers, tanks, and ammunition lay on the sea bottom. Roland came home to Mathews and spoke his mind. "We're not getting anywhere like this," he told the *Gazette-Journal*. "We're simply throwing ships and valuable cargoes away, sending them over the southern route without convoys. The odds against us are too heavy." But he went right back to sea.

The *Thomas McKean* sinking prompted a Navy investigation into "possible leakage of information" about her route and cargo. The investigator concluded the U-boat had simply stumbled upon the ship. He added that a possible leak could not be ruled out, though, because the ship's schedule had been known to more than forty-five people in various offices from New York to London. In addition, the investigator noted, anyone walking along the pier while the *Thomas McKean* was loading had only to read the words on the cargo crates to determine their contents, or look up at a big sign reading, "*Thomas McKean*, Basra."

The day after the *Ruth* and *Thomas McKean* were sunk, Captain L. P. Borum of Gwynn's Island was torpedoed in his second world war. Borum, who was fifty-eight years old, had lost a freighter to a U-boat off the coast of Scotland in 1918, but had sailed a troopship across the Atlantic for the rest of that war. Once, while bringing the ship back empty from England, he had stopped in dangerous waters to pick up twenty-six lifeboat survivors from a torpedoed Belgian freighter, desperate after three weeks at sea. When World War II started, Borum picked up right where he'd left off, running his freight/passenger ship, the *City of Birmingham*, between the East Coast and Bermuda, hauling people and supplies to the new U.S. Navy base on the island. In May 1942, he stopped the *City of Birmingham* in mid-ocean to pick up twenty-five British seamen who had been adrift in a lifeboat for two weeks. Borum was not the kind of captain who left castaways in a lifeboat for someone else to save.

On the *City of Birmingham*'s final voyage, Borum's ship was escorted by the Navy destroyer USS *Stansbury*, steaming alongside at a distance of a mile. They were 250 miles short of Bermuda when the *Stansbury* received a radio report of a U-boat sighting well ahead of them. The *Stansbury* signaled in Morse code for the *City of Birmingham* to shift course. For some reason, no one on Borum's ship understood the signal, and the *City of Birmingham* had no signal light with which to reply; the vessels most likely had been communicating by whistles and, during daytime, by signal flags. Ten minutes later—too early for the change of course to have mattered— two torpedoes struck Borum's ship only seconds apart. A U-boat had fired a long-range shot and then fled while the torpedoes were still en route.

Borum knew as soon as the torpedoes hit that the *City of Birmingham* was doomed. For him, the stakes were much higher than they had been in World War I, when he lost an empty ship. The *City of Birmingham's* cargo was 381 human beings, including the passengers, crew, and 261 men and women reporting to the base at Bermuda.

Borum made his way to the side of the ship and helped guide hundreds of people down cargo nets and into lifeboats. Each boat was filled and rowed to the *Stansbury*, which took the occupants aboard. The evacuation was fast and smooth. Borum and his officers were the last to leave. In all, 372 of the 381 people aboard the *City of Birmingham* survived and were landed at Bermuda. The Coast Guard afterward classified the sinking as a "noteworthy case" because of the unusually high survival rate. Borum was credited with helping to avert a catastrophe.

But another was coming.

Three days after Borum was torpedoed on the *City of Birmingham*, Captain Herbert Callis of Mathews, a cousin of Mel, Homer, and Rodney Callis's, was torpedoed near the Windward Passage. Herbert was a stout, taciturn man who expected everyone to do his or her duty. He did not have a fun side. He had sailed for thirty years and survived a sinking in the mid-1930s after his ship was hit by an ocean liner. More recently, in March 1942, he had stopped his ship, the freighter *Norlandia*, off Cape Lookout, North Carolina, to pick up lifeboat survivors of a torpedoed ship. Herbert had expected the *Norlandia* to be torpedoed eventually.

So when it happened, Herbert was calm. But he was also woozy from the torpedo blast, which had killed five men. He ran into his cabin to get his sextant but failed "because of his dazed condition." He missed both of the lifeboats pulling away from the ship, and had to jump off the bow and swim to one of them and be helped in. The U-575 surfaced and its commander, Gunther Heydemann, questioned the men in the boats. Heydemann was disappointed to learn the *Norlandia* had been small and empty. He apologized for having had to sink an American ship, and asked if the castaways needed anything. They said no, but Heydemann tossed them a bottle of German brandy. He had one of his men keep a flashlight trained on the bottle as it flew through the air so the men would be sure to catch it. He shined the light along the length of the U-boat so the survivors could see what it looked like. Heydemann obviously had no fear of antisubmarine patrols.

The *Norlandia* lifeboats reached the coast of the Dominican Republic two days later. The men in one of the lifeboats complained angrily about its unseaworthy condition. The mast had snapped at its base when the men tried to rig the sail. The matches in the survival kit were wet. The drinking water containers had not been replaced in so long that the water "smelled like putrefied rats." The lifeboat was certified to have passed a recent inspection, but that inspection obviously had not taken place. Unseaworthy, ill-equipped lifeboats were a common problem on merchant ships in World War II, and *How to Abandon Ship* advised crews to take it upon themselves to examine the lifeboats whenever they boarded a new ship, report any missing items to the captain, and buy the items themselves if necessary: "A few dollars from your pocket may mean all the difference between your becoming a 1943 casualty or a 1983 veteran."

Herbert complained about the way the *Norlandia* had been routed. He said confusion between two Navy commands delayed his departure needlessly for two days, and ended up delivering him straight to the U-boat. He also "stated emphatically" that the Navy should stop sending merchant ships east along the coast of Cuba, where they had to fight a strong westerly current. The current slowed ships down, Callis said, and they had to move fast around Cuba, because U-boats were prowling all around the island.

At that moment, both Dewey's and Leslie Hodges's ships were entering the same Cuban waters. Leslie's vessel, the *Oneida*, was on the sugar run, hauling raw sugar from the southern coast of Cuba to ports in the Gulf. Dewey's little *Onondaga* was hauling war supplies between ports in Florida, Cuba, and Hispaniola. Both ships made short, daylight runs to avoid U-boats.

When the *Onondaga* arrived in San Juan, Puerto Rico, the Mathews men on the ship—Dewey, Genious, William Hammond, and Russell Dennis—welcomed aboard a familiar passenger. Captain Mellin Respess of Gwynn's Island had arranged to ride aboard the *Onondaga* as a passenger back to Mobile. Mellin had spent twelve days in a hospital after being torpedoed on the *Thomas McKean* and drifting in a lifeboat for two weeks. He had earned a few weeks at home on Gwynn's Island with Eleanor. Mellin passed up a ride home on another ship in order to ride with Dewey on the *Onondaga*. Mellin would help out, of course, if an emergency arose.

The *Onondaga*'s radio brought warnings of U-boat sightings and attacks all around them. The weather was stormy and sultry. Genious wrote to his wife, Salome, from San Juan that he had been up all the previous night dealing with drunken seamen. He lamented that Russell Dennis had not returned to the ship from a night on the town, which left Genious to oversee cargo loading. Genious had not even had time for a haircut. But what seemed to eat at him the most was not getting letters from Salome. He and Salome were still at odds over Genious's sailing to support his parents. When Genious received no letters from her, he imagined the worst. "Do you love me, darling?" he wrote. "I love you with all my heart, soul and body and always shall. If sometime something should happen and I don't get back, remember I always loved you truly whether you think so or not. I am yours forever, Salome."

The *Onondaga* had sailed alone since its initial departure from Mobile. Genious had seen no convoys or patrol planes. He no longer pretended he was not worried. "You hear a lot about the protections they have, darling," he wrote Salome, "but it's a lie, every word of it so far as I can see." Later he wrote, "I had much rather be running to Russia or England, Salome, than [around the Caribbean] . . . I guess the censor will cut this part out, but this is suicide, Salome, and nothing else."

While Dewey Hodges waited in San Juan to learn the *Onondaga*'s next destination, his brother Leslie approached the Windward Passage on the *Oneida*. The *Oneida* was empty, en route south around Cuba's eastern tip to pick up a load of raw sugar at Punta Gorda. Leslie served as first officer under Captain Walter Deal, a veteran captain from Gloucester County, next to Mathews. Leslie had written to his wife, Cecile, that he planned to stay home from a voyage soon and spend time with her. The *Oneida*'s second officer was Stacy Hammond, another of blacksmith Harry Hammond's sons. Unlike some of his shipmates, Stacy had yet to be torpedoed, but he counted himself lucky to be alive. He was one of several Mathews men who had gotten off the *Lake Osweya* before she vanished in the North Atlantic in February.

In the early morning hours of July 13, the *Oneida* was approaching Cape Maysi, Cuba, when one of the lookouts shouted. The feathering plume of a torpedo was heading straight for the ship. The helmsman swung the wheel, but it was too late. The torpedo slammed into the *Oneida* just below the water line, blowing a gaping hole in the hull. The sea barreled in, and the *Oneida*'s boilers exploded.

Leslie Hodges had stopped in the galley for a cup of coffee on his way to the bridge when the torpedo hit. Stacy Hammond caught a glimpse of Leslie struggling to launch a lifeboat in a cloud of steam. Captain Deal remembered Leslie running up to him to say he was going into the crew's quarters to search for the cook. Deal told him there was no time. Leslie went anyway. He was never seen again.

The *Oneida* sank by the stern, its bow rising high out of the water. Stacy dived off the bow from a height he estimated at sixty feet. He forgot to remove his glasses, and they smashed when he hit the water, leaving him with a bloody gash above his eyes. He swam with all his strength to get away from the suction of the sinking ship. He spotted an empty raft, climbed on, and picked up two other men. They rowed to a coral island only two miles away. Two other rafts arrived with more of their shipmates, and the men hiked for about five miles to a village. Stacy, who had lost his shoes, lacerated his feet on the jagged coral. The castaways eventually caught a ride to a larger village aboard a sailing schooner, and then traveled to Havana by bus. Most of the *Oneida*'s twenty-three survivors suffered severe sunburns. Leslie and five other men were missing.

Afterward, Captain Deal and Stacy Hammond vented their frustration to the Coast Guard, which routinely interviewed survivors of sinkings about how to improve safety measures. Deal complained that the fledgling coastal convoy system was full of holes. "Put the ships in convoy and stop sending them around without protection," he said. "Since this war has started . . . all the airplanes I have seen protecting ships you could put on one hand and all the destroyers could be put on one hand and you would have a whole lot of fingers left." Stacy agreed. "We saw no planes or nothing until about probably an hour after [the torpedoing], then I saw three or four different planes," he said. "We should be convoyed. Have no business running alone like that."

Stacy wired his wife in Mathews that he was safe. Leslie's wife, Cecile, apparently learned of her husband's death in a call or telegram from Ford. The next person who would have to be told about Leslie was Henny Hodges. And the person to tell her was her son Spencer.

Spencer had always been the one to whom the family turned to calm tempers and resolve disputes. He had a gift for reasoning with people. The family respected Spencer for having finished high school. He was the only one who could mend hard feelings between the quarreling Hodges daughters. His job got him out and about in the community. Spencer not only made ice cream at the creamery but drove a truck to deliver it to homes and general stores in a fifty-mile radius. He often took along his four-year-old son, Spencer Jr., in order to expose him to a wide variety of people and situations. The boy seemed to enjoy it, and always handled himself well.

At suppertime on Thursday, July 16, the telephone rang at Spencer's house. It was one of the few telephones in that part of Mathews, installed years before when Spencer's father-in-law was sheriff of Mathews. Spencer picked up the phone and his son could tell by his expression that something was wrong. Spencer thanked the caller and hung up. He told the family his brother Leslie was lost. He said he had to go to Gales Neck and tell Henny. He got to his feet and looked at Spencer Jr., and the boy got up too. "My father used to carry me to a lot of places that I wouldn't take my kids," Spencer Jr. said years later.

Father and son got into the family's black Chevrolet sedan. Neither spoke. Spencer drove out to the main highway and then turned onto the long driveway to Gales Neck. The car bobbed slowly through the holes and ruts. It was hot in the late afternoon and the car windows were down. Spencer parked on the left side of the house near the kitchen door. He told Spencer Jr. to wait in the car while he got out and walked to the door, tapped, and let himself in.

A cry came from inside the house and built into a wail. The sound of a second female voice told Spencer that Alice or one of his other aunts was home. The wailing continued for what seemed to the boy like an impossibly long time. It finally subsided, and a few minutes later his father came out of the house and started the car. He did not speak all the way home. Neither did Spencer Jr., who still heard the wailing in his head.

Leslie was the thirteenth Mathews man killed by U-boats since January. At least one man from the county seemed to die every week. "It was happening so much that you wondered it if was ever going to end," said the Hodgeses' cousin and neighbor Edwin Jarvis. "You were tired of it all. You expected more bad news every day. You were just numb." For the most part, families dealt with their sorrow privately. Every Sunday, Mathews pastors led prayers for the lost.

The losses of so many Mathews men on the *Ruth* in June prompted the Reverend Belch of Gwynn's Island Baptist Church to organize a memorial service for Mathews County. He may have assumed the *Ruth* disaster was the worst the war could inflict on Mathews. The service was held on

July 19, the hottest day of the summer, with the temperature rising into the nineties by nine o'clock in the morning. People from all over Mathews overflowed the church an hour before the service. The crowd sang hymns with images of the sea:

I've anchored my soul
In the Haven of Rest,
I'll sail the wide seas no more;
The tempest may sweep
O'er the wild storms deep
In Jesus I'm safe evermore.

Pastors of several Mathews churches took turns at the pulpit. Belch called merchant mariners "the unsung heroes of this war." He said he constantly heard of brave deeds by military men, who deserved all honors, but no less honors were due to the men on merchant ships. "Perhaps [I] feel more strongly because of the fact that so many of our Mathews men have helped man those ships, and many have made the supreme sacrifice."

From the church, the families of Mel Callis, Howard Morris, Perry Collier, and Robert Belvin Jr. led a procession down Old Ferry Road, the island's main thoroughfare, past the Gwynn's Island cemetery to the steel drawbridge over Milford Haven. The sheriff closed off traffic, and the crowd lined both sides of the 728-foot span. The next of kin tossed flowers from the center of the drawbridge into Milford Haven, where a falling tide carried them toward the Bay.

Robert Belvin's sisters wrote later:

Brother it was so hard to scatter your flowers here on the sea
And knowing your sweet form lies way out on the deep

None of the Hodges family attended the ceremony. Eleanor Respess did. She had known Mel Callis and most of the other men lost on the *Ruth*.

But her thoughts must have strayed to her husband, Mellin. She had almost lost him twice, but now he was headed home on the *Onondaga* with Dewey Hodges. He was to be at her side in a matter of days.

After Mellin came aboard the *Onondaga* in San Juan, Dewey was ordered to sail the ship to Nuevitas, the industrial port on Cuba's northern coast, to pick up a load of magnesium ore. The ship headed west along the coast of Hispaniola, across the northern end of the Windward Passage, and along the coast of Cuba to Nuevitas. The *Onondaga* docked, and began using her boom cranes to lift the heavy ore on wooden pallets and lower them into the cargo holds.

It's possible Dewey learned about his brother Leslie's death at Nuevitas. Loading the magnesium took three days, and Leslie's ship was sunk only 200 miles away. But Dewey did not mention Leslie in a letter to his family, dated July 23, 1942.

"My darling and babys," Dewey wrote. "Well, here I am all ready to go, but now they won't let me, as the port is closed until further notice . . . Gee is it hot here and am I working. I thought my Bees were busy but they haven't a thing on me, from 5 a.m. yesterday until midnite last night, and all day today, and the mosquitoes just eat you up at night." He wrote he was enclosing all his cash in the letter because "I do not want to carry any money to sea with me in these times."

"Darling, I am not expecting anything to happen to me," he continued, "but if it does, you should have enough with my insurance property to take care of you for a long time, and above all I want [our son] George to finish college unless the army takes him. What you do with whatever I leave is all right with me as long as you take care of yourself and the children. I leave all of that to your judgment."

Dewey reviewed the family's savings accounts and described how Edna could gain access to them without him. He suggested that if he did not return, his boss at Ford might feel an obligation to give George Jr. a job on a ship.

Dewey suggested Edna take the girls to Gales Neck, which he called "the country," and stay with Henny. "Hope you go up the country for a month, think you should if Mama wants you," he wrote. "Think the change will do you good, also the children." Dewey wrote that he might not be able to contact them for a while, "but if you don't hear from me, don't worry as no news will be good news . . . Kiss the children for me and tell them to be good girls. With all my love & kisses for my sweetheart & babys, from your true & loving husband, from daddy."

The *Onondaga* finally was allowed to leave Nuevitas on July 23. Dewey headed west with the current along the northern coast of Cuba, steering along the 100-fathom line, where the shallow continental shelf drops off into the depths. The ship stayed within 5 miles of a string of barrier islands lining a remote stretch of the coast.

Had Dewey waited at Nuevitas for a few hours, the *Onondaga* could have joined a convoy with armed escort ships and even air cover, passing Nuevitas en route to Havana. But Dewey had had no way of knowing the convoy was coming. Those convoys on that route were the latest link in the expanding U.S. Navy convoy system, which extended all the way up the East Coast. But the system still had flaws. It was not yet set up, for example, to notify merchant captains in Nuevitas of approaching convoys.

Dewey kept the *Onondaga* running at top speed, which in her case was barely 8.5 knots. He did not zigzag. His only concern was reaching the safety of Havana before dark. The *Onondaga* passed through the Old Bahama Channel and into the Nicholas Channel, approaching the Straits of Florida. Dewey posted lookouts on the bridge and the "monkey island" above it. He did not need to remind Mellin, Genious, and William Hammond to stay alert. The *Onondaga* chugged into the glare of the late afternoon sun. The weather was fair and the sea was calm, and dotted with small fishing boats. Dewey had the time to beat the sunset to Havana, but not the luck.

Heading straight at the *Onondaga* from the opposite direction was Hans-Ludwig Witt in his U-129. The sub was passing through the Nicholas Channel on its way out of the Caribbean after sinking eight merchant ships in four weeks—a performance that would earn Witt an Iron Cross. The U-129's voyage had been productive from the start, when Witt had stumbled upon the freighter *Millinocket* in the channel on his way *into* the Caribbean and torpedoed the ship, killing Captain Lewis Callis of Gwynn's Island. Now, as the U-129 departed the Caribbean, Witt had saved a torpedo in case he got lucky in the channel again. At 4:30 p.m., the *Onondaga* appeared in the U-129's periscope. It was almost too easy. Witt maneuvered the sub into position for a torpedo strike and waited for the little freighter to come closer.

Dewey was on the bridge and apparently saw the torpedo coming. He looked astern and shouted, "Everybody aft stand clear!" and "Here she comes!" A seaman turned to look but "a white flash and sharp explosion" knocked him unconscious into the ocean. Another seaman recalled a geyser of seawater and "things shooting up into the air. Everything went sky high." Third Officer Russell Dennis of Mathews was in his room when he heard the shouts and felt the jolt of the torpedo. He ran out onto the main deck to see Dewey descending a ladder from the bridge. Captain Respess was "sawing at a rope that held one of the life rafts." The *Onondaga*'s main deck already was awash. Genious shouted, "Everybody jump overboard." Dennis dove. When he came up, the *Onondaga* was gone. The heavy ore had pulled her under in less than one minute.

The U-129 was gone too, resuming its trip home. Dennis swam to a raft and then moved to a different raft occupied by eight of his shipmates. They said they had been looking for survivors but had almost lost hope. They had not seen Dewey, Mellin, Genious, or William Hammond. The men rowed to a barrier island and lay on the beach. At daybreak, an American search plane spotted the *Onondaga*'s oil slick and then the men on the beach. The pilot found another raft with six more survivors. Eighteen of the thirty-three men on the *Onondaga* were missing, including Genious, William Hammond, Dewey, and Mellin. "Both captains went down with the ship," Dennis said.

The American vice consul in Nuevitas wrongly blamed the sinking on the *Onondaga*'s crew, who supposedly talked so loosely that "practically everyone in Nuevitas knew the ship's destination and time of departure."

Dennis, as the sole surviving Mathews man on the ship, was bound by Mathews tradition to get word about the sinking and the casualties to the county at once. He sent a telegram from the Exchange Hotel in Miami to the telegraph office across from the Mathews courthouse saying: "Arrived in Miami OK. Capt. Hodges Respess Hudgins and Hammond failed to return."

It's unclear who telephoned Dewey's family. Telegraph operators in Mathews usually passed bad news to family members, if they could be reached, or consulted the courthouse crowd of lawyers and businessmen to choose a suitable messenger. The system was efficient but not always compassionate. The phone rang at Dewey's house in Norfolk and Edna answered. A man whose voice she did not recognize said the *Onondaga* had been lost and that Dewey "was not one of the survivors." Then the caller hung up.

Edna, characteristically, showed little emotion. She repeated the caller's statement to the girls, and told them she would try to determine if it was true. They could tell she believed it was. Edna telephoned Ford, the Navy, and the Coast Guard, but it was late and she could not reach anyone. She was furious at the caller for delivering such news and hanging up before she could ask questions. She and the girls wondered if the call had been a malicious prank.

The phone also rang in Spencer Hodges's home, and he took the call as he had taken the call eleven days before. He hung up and told his family that now Dewey had been lost. He got up and looked at Spencer Jr., and the boy got up too.

To four-year-old Spencer Jr., everything about the second trip to Gales Neck seemed exactly like the first one, eleven days earlier: the silent ride in the black Chevrolet, the long crawl up the driveway, his father parking by the kitchen door and stepping inside. The only change was that, this time, the wailing began the moment his father stepped in the door. More than seventy years later, Spencer Jr. would feel a chill at a TV news broadcast of Filipino mothers wailing after a ferryboat disaster. "It was exactly the same sound," he said.

The night after the *Onondaga* sinking, the Cuban fishermen named Carillo set out in their boat, the *Donatella*, to fish for shark in the Nicholas Channel. Most of the Cubans on the water were poor, subsistence fishermen, catching shark to eat or barter. Their boats generally had sails but no motors, and their shark-fishing rigs were floating oil drums dangling heavy lines with fist sized hooks, baited with bloody fish. The bait hung just above the bottom, where the big sharks hunted.

The Carillos caught a big tiger or bull shark, at least six feet long. They killed it and gutted it right on deck, and found human remains—and two rings. They apparently set out directly for Havana, about a day's sail away, to turn in their discovery.

Authorities in Havana took custody of the remains and the rings. They inspected the rings and discovered that one of them, a heavy gold signet ring, was engraved with the initials "G.D.H." Word of the discovery spread along the docks. It reached R. M. Jenkins, who managed an office in Havana. Little is known about Jenkins. He knew Dewey well enough to know his full name was George Dewey Hodges. Jenkins took the trouble to get the story from the Carillos personally and to examine the ring. He was convinced it was Dewey's, but was not sure whom to tell. He wrote letters to U.S. government offices in Havana and to steamship companies. He mistakenly thought the *Onondaga* was owned by the Lykes Brothers Steamship Company.

Months would pass before one of Jenkins's letters would find its way to Dewey's family. But news of Dewey's death spread quickly among mariners whose careers and lives he had influenced. His longtime crewman M. Stanley MacLean wrote of Dewey, "To me, George Hodges, the seagoing diplomat and my friend, is not dead, only away."

In Mathews, anger at the federal government festered. The *Gazette-*

Journal's account of the *Onondaga* sinking included the observation that "the people [of Mathews] are becoming more and more critical of the seeming lack of effective effort to protect the Merchant Marine . . . against the submarine force. The sending of merchant ships through submarine-infested waters, alone and entirely unprotected, is being bitterly decried in this county, which supplies the Merchant Marine with more men, perhaps, than any other area of comparable population."

In August 1942, the *Gazette-Journal*'s complaints drew a reply from the region's congressman, Rep. Schuyler Otis Bland, who was chairman of the House Merchant Marine and Fisheries Committee. Bland wrote to the paper that he had spoken personally with Navy leaders and believed they were doing everything possible. He said he wished the Navy were more forthcoming about its successes against U-boats because "I think the Navy has done a much better job than they have been given credit for." The editors replied that while they believed Bland was sincere, they stood by their view that the nation "had failed . . . to give the most effective aid possible to our merchant marine and the men who operate it."

In the same issue of the paper, a Mathews fisherman who had just returned from a trawler off the mid-Atlantic coast said the trawler crew had been accosted and questioned by two U-boat captains and had seen two merchant ships torpedoed.

Captain Jesse Hodges came home to Gales Neck in late August from another long voyage on his tug in the Caribbean. Henny broke the news to him that two of his sons had been lost, only eleven days apart. Jesse's immediate reaction to the news was not recorded. But a few days later, he curtly told a reporter, "There's been a whole lot of slack in this business, mister." He was home only a few days when Ford sent him a telegram summoning him to sail a freighter. He showed the telegram to a photographer, who arranged a photo of him sitting on the couch and displaying the telegram to Henny. She looks as though she is about to cry.

Jesse returned to sea. For the first time in the war, however, he and his ship could expect to be protected from U-boats. After seven months of horrific losses, Admiral King finally had enough ships and planes to establish a strong, interlocking convoy system, extending from along the U.S. East Coast and through the Gulf of Mexico and Caribbean. Convoys moved along feeder routes in the Gulf and Caribbean to the main routes, which ran from Trinidad to Cuba to New York. New York replaced Maritime Canada as the departure point for North Atlantic convoys to Britain. All the convoys moved on a tight schedule, arriving at intervals to avoid clogging up ports. The convoys were guarded by destroyers and smaller escorts, as well as Army and Navy aircraft, and few ships were left to make their solo voyages alone and unguarded.

Even coastal lights at East Coast ports finally had been extinguished, after much wrangling, long after the time of greatest need had passed. Admiral Andrews called those who had fought the blackout "selfish, greedy and unpatriotic." Morison, the Navy historian, concluded, "Ships were sunk and seamen drowned in order that the citizenry might enjoy business and pleasure as usual."

By midsummer, American planes and escort ships were no longer easy foils for U-boats. Many pilots had radar, as well as training in how to bomb U-boats. Navy crews on escort ships had learned that killing U-boats took patience and strategy. It was a chess game with depth charges.

In the Gulf of Mexico, a Navy patrol vessel depth-charged and sank the U-166, which had torpedoed the *Oneida* and killed Leslie Hodges. The U-boat's entire crew was killed, as was often the case when a U-boat was sunk. The U-153, which had torpedoed the *Ruth* and killed five Mathews men, was depth-charged by a destroyer off Panama, with no survivors. The U-701, which had embarrassed the Navy in June by laying mines at the mouth of the Chesapeake Bay, was depth-charged by an Army plane off Hatteras. The U-boat commander and three other survivors were rescued from the ocean and taken prisoner.

Just like that, Admiral King's interlocking convoy system put an end to the U-boat successes in U.S. waters. Sinkings of merchant ships along the East Coast plummeted from twenty-three in April to four in May. They rose to thirteen in June, but dropped back to four again in July. Admiral Andrews, who had suffered through a miserable winter and spring, noted in his war diary for July: "This month is the most significant in operations in the history of this Frontier, since it demonstrates that the increasing success of past weeks rests upon a solid basis of strong forces properly used."

Doenitz tracked the numbers too. The time had come to pull back his subs from the U.S. Atlantic coast. He was not wistful. He had expected the Americans to chase him off long ago. For seven months the U-boats had had their way in American waters, sinking more than three hundred merchant ships and killing thousands of merchant seamen. They had sunk millions of tons of Allied food, supplies, munitions, and fuel into the sea, playing havoc with the enemy's supply line. Doenitz already knew where he wanted to shift the U-boats. He kept a few in the Caribbean, the Gulf, and the South Atlantic, but sent most to the North Atlantic air gap, beyond the range of Allied planes. Doenitz thought an all-out attack in the air gap could win the Battle of the Atlantic for Germany. Ending the assault on America's coast did not end the U-boats' assault on merchant shipping.

Nor did it end the U-boats' war-within-a-war against the Mathews men.

CHAPTER NINE

"Please Don't Tell Me"

C aptain Homer Callis of Gwynn's Island, who proved that a sea captain could also be a gentleman, quit the bridge of the old Bull Line freighter *Mae* in August 1942 to become assistant port captain for the Bull Line in Baltimore. The job was a promotion, and Homer had earned it. He had commanded Bull Line ships for twenty years, and he enjoyed a sterling reputation among mariners, fellow captains, his bosses, the Navy, and even the unions.

The port job in Baltimore kept Homer from having to face U-boats, which had killed his brother Mel and had almost gotten Homer on his last trip on the *Mae*. On a stormy night in the Windward Passage, several U-boats had attacked the *Mae*'s convoy and sunk ships all around her, five in all. One had been so close to the *Mae* that Homer had to turn sharply to avoid hitting the sinking vessel. Another ship exploded with such force that pieces of it clattered against the *Mae*.

Homer's new job allowed him, for the first time at age forty-five, to live full-time with his wife, Nancy. Nancy commanded the Callis home at Dunrovin' the way Henny Hodges commanded the Hodges farm at Gales Neck. Nancy was tall and slender, with shoulder-length brown hair. She drank her coffee black and her whiskey neat, and told friends, "I hate old people." She was a Diggs, a family known on Gwynn's Island for producing women who were outspoken, even brassy. She and the deliberative Homer seemed to be polar opposites, but they were close. The U-boat war weighed on Nancy. She had one of the few telephones on Gwynn's Island, and knew everyone. She often received the first phone call from a survivor of a sunken ship or a representative of a shipping company that a man from the island had been lost. Nancy had begun to feel that neighbors shrank from her approach "as if I was the angel of death."

Homer and Nancy's two sons were nearly grown. The elder, twenty-one-year-old Homer Jr., was a quartermaster on a Navy destroyer in the Pacific. He took after his father, with a quiet, thoughtful attitude. The younger son, Bill, had a rowdy Diggs demeanor. Bill was seventeen and bursting to get out of Mathews. His brother warned him to stay out of the Navy, which had more regulations than Bill could possibly follow. Homer Jr. suggested Bill try the Merchant Marine.

When Homer Sr. left the *Mae*, the Bull Line followed its longstanding tradition and replaced him with another captain from Mathews. Their choice, Captain Willard Hudgins, was a veteran captain from a seafaring family. He had commanded military transport ships in World War I and merchant ships ever since. He was an officer in the U.S. Naval Reserve, but was needed more as a merchant captain than as a naval officer. Though no one could replace Homer, Willard was a solid successor. He had the approval of the only other Mathews man on the *Mae*, the irrepressible Thomas Lester Smith.

Lester, as he was called, was a compact pile driver of a man. He was good company, although he sometimes drank and fought. Bill Callis once saw him whipping a man twice his size. Lester was a fisherman's son who joined the Merchant Marine for the adventure and the money. By the time he turned eighteen, he had saved enough to buy a red Buick convertible, which he drove around Mathews High School with the top down, flirting with all the girls. Then he met Lottie Mise, who knew at age sixteen that

Lester was the one. He knew it too. "When he came home, the first thing he made for was me," Lottie said, "and I was waiting for him."

Lester had sailed on the *Mae* with Homer since before Pearl Harbor. Even though he had been on the last trip, with ships blowing up all around them, Lester stayed on the ship for its first voyage under Captain Hudgins. He and Jack Rowe of Gwynn's Island had talked about taking that trip off. Jack decided he could afford to sit out one voyage, but Lester had blown all his pay from his last voyage and decided to stay on the ship. The *Mae* was being sent to the port of Georgetown, British Guiana—today, simply Guyana—to pick up a load of bauxite ore. As the *Mae* prepared to leave Mobile, she was armed for the first time with a 3-inch gun and a .50-caliber antiaircraft gun, operated by a Navy Armed Guard crew.

The *Mae* sailed from Mobile empty, in ballast, and alone. She encountered no U-boats en route to Cuba and then to Trinidad. After she turned south for the final leg of the voyage, the captain ordered a zigzag course and assigned men extra watches as lookouts. Lester was too excited to close his eyes. Finally he flopped down exhausted on his bunk, with his feet at the end where he normally laid his head. That deviation from normal saved his life. Just after midnight on September 17, one of the *Mae*'s lookouts saw a blinking light ahead of them. He was turning to report it when a torpedo bore into the freighter's starboard side, blowing up the magazine holding the shells for the new guns. The magazine was located directly beneath Lester's bunk. The explosion mangled his legs and hurled him against a bulkhead, unconscious.

The *Mae* was sinking. The U-boat approached the ship and trained a spotlight on the Armed Guard crew, which was trying to fire the 3-inch gun. Captain Hudgins warned them to stop or get shot, then gave the order to abandon ship. The cook was rushing to the main deck when he saw Lester motionless in the wreckage of his bunk. The cook called for Captain Hudgins and another man to help pull Lester free. Lester's legs were a gruesome mess, but there was no time even to examine them. The captain tied some lines into a makeshift cradle, and Lester was lowered into one of the three lifeboats.

On closer inspection, Lester's left leg appeared to be shattered at the knee, and his right leg was broken or worse. His shipmates used a tourniquet to cinch off the bleeding in his left leg, but not before Lester's blood had pooled at their feet. Lester faded in and out of consciousness. The U-boat broke the surface and drilled several rounds from its deck cannon into the *Mae* to finish her off. The U-boat captain asked the men in the lifeboats the usual questions, then left them alone on a rough, windy sea.

Lester's blood attracted sharks, which shot past the lifeboat and sometimes tested it with their snouts. A frightened seaman said Lester would get them all eaten, and that he was going to die anyway. He wanted to throw Lester overboard. Captain Hudgins said they were going to do all they could for Lester. It was clear, though, that Lester would not survive for long in the lifeboat.

Only three hours after the sinking, a Norwegian freighter on its way out of Georgetown spotted the lifeboats and began taking the survivors aboard. As soon as Captain Hudgins found the Norwegian captain, he asked him to turn the ship around. He pointed out Lester and said his only chance was to get to a hospital, and Georgetown had a small one. The captain changed course and ran full-speed back to Georgetown. A Navy teletype about the *Mae* sinking mentioned Lester by name and summed up his status as "severely injured, hospitalized, recovery doubtful."

Lester awoke on a stretcher on the beach at Georgetown and began talking rapidly and smoking cigarettes "like they were going out of style." He kept passing out and waking up. Once he awoke to find a sheet had been pulled over his head. Later, at Mercy Hospital, he heard one nurse whisper to another that they must at least comfort him because "he is some mother's son."

To some in Mathews, the loss of the *Mae* felt almost like the loss of a family member. Like the *Ruth* and the *East Indian*, the *Mae* had never sailed without several Mathews men in the crew. Homer had taken dozens of young men from Mathews to sea for the first time on the ship. When Homer heard about the *Mae* and about Lester, he went to his boss in Baltimore and told him he no longer wanted to work on shore. He wanted a new ship.

The latest man to join the brotherhood of Mathews sea captains was Will Hunley, a Hodges cousin who was practically a brother. Childhood friends with David Hodges, Will never thought about going to sea until one afternoon in 1930 when David announced he was going to work on his brother Raymond's ship. Will, who was seventeen, decided to go along. He sold his bicycle to Henny Hodges for $10 for bus fare to New York Harbor. He was so homesick that David had to beg him not to jump ship in every port, but Will ended up staying with it long after David left. He idolized Raymond Hodges and kept his photograph on his desk. Will had a booming voice, a feel for ships, and a fine eye for a vessel's finances. Moore-McCormack promoted him up through the ranks and in August 1942 named him captain of the freighter *Commercial Trader*. At age twenty-eight, Will was probably the youngest captain in Mathews. He had been a captain for three months. Now came his trial by fire.

On the morning of September 16, 1942, the *Commercial Trader* was about 75 miles from Trinidad when a torpedo exploded into the hull, throwing up a geyser of water that knocked Will off the bridge onto the deck below. He got to his feet and realized his pants were gone. He gave the order to abandon ship and plunged into his cabin for the secret codes. The water was three feet deep in the cabin and he was struck by floating furniture, but he got the codes and threw them overboard in their weighted bag. The *Commercial Trader*'s cargo had been magnesium ore, with large bags of castor beans piled on top. Will called out to his men to be careful not to swallow seawater, because the beans released castor oil that could make them sick. Castor oil contains a deadly poison, ricin.

Will got into the last lifeboat. A line from the sinking ship snagged on the lifeboat and flipped it, throwing Will and the other occupants into the water. Will, who could not swim, clung to the side of the overturned boat with a few others. They saw a man on a raft in the distance. He was trying to paddle to them but was being swept away. A Norwegian seaman named Nils Antonsen volunteered to swim to the raft and help the man. His shipmates warned he would be eaten by sharks or carried away by the current, but Antonsen set out through a heavy swell. He reached the raft and helped the man paddle back to Will and the others; on their way, they picked up two other men from the water. All the men heaved together to right the lifeboat, and then climbed in. They also rescued the ship's dog, a mongrel named Hendrick Wilhelm Berg Johanson that was floating past on a bag of castor beans.

Will ordered the lifeboat's sail rigged, and used a compass to guide the boat to the island of Tobago in only four hours. The boat landed on the beach estate of a British oil executive, who met the castaways "with a bottle of rum in each hand and several servants to help them ashore," Will said. The injured, including a man with mild castor oil poisoning, were taken to a hospital. Will and the others spent a comfortable night at the executive's estate. Twenty-eight of the *Commercial Trader*'s thirty-eight officers and crew survived the sinking. Moore-McCormack commended Will for showing such presence of mind at his young age. Like Homer Callis, Will immediately asked for a new ship.

On Gwynn's Island, Lester Smith's parents and his fiancée, Lottie, prayed constantly. They knew only that Lester was fighting for his life at Mercy Hospital in Georgetown, British Guiana, a place they had not known existed until a few weeks before. Traveling to Georgetown was too dangerous. They could only wait. Then letters from Georgetown began arriving in the mailbox, with reports on Lester from nurses and representatives of the Salvation Army. At first the letters were bleak. Lester had lost so much blood that doctors and nurses at the hospital had to donate their own blood to keep him alive. Both his legs were crushed and his left foot had been blown off. A surgeon had amputated his left leg at the knee. "He is very brave and although suffering, never murmurs," a Salvation Army officer wrote of Lester. "I feel very distressed for him, but he is taking it all like a man. I know that this will be a terrible blow to you, but you must try to be as brave as your Lester is."

But weeks passed and Lester stayed alive. One day, a letter noted his "wonderful improvement." A young Filipina nurse who tended to Lester wrote, "I am with him all the time and try to keep him at rest. One night, asleep, he called to his mates. I think he dreamed he was at sea. He is not changed but still carries the heart of gold. Today we sat him up in the bed and he had the smile of a conqueror and said he would soon be coming back home to Gwynn's Island."

The *Gazette-Journal* printed updates on Lester's recovery for all of Mathews to read. Captain Willard Hudgins surprised Lester's family by bringing three of his shipmates from the *Mae* to Gwynn's Island. They said Lester was brave even in his times of great suffering. Lester's mother was overwhelmed: "I think it is so wonderful that with all the fighting and killing going on that there is still so much kindness and sympathy," she said. "I think it wonderful that far away in a strange land, my boy should receive so much attention . . ."

News of a different kind arrived for the families of the men lost on the *Onondaga*. Salome Hudgins's telegram about Genious read:

THE NAVY DEPARTMENT DEEPLY REGRETS TO INFORM YOU THAT YOUR HUSBAND GENIIS [SIC] THOMAS HUDGINS IS MISSING FOLLOWING ACTION IN THE PERFORMANCE OF HIS DUTY AND IN SERVICE OF HIS COUNTRY. THE COAST GUARD APPRECIATES YOUR GREAT ANXIETY AND WILL FURNISH INFORMATION PROMPTLY WHEN RECEIVED. TO PREVENT POSSIBLE AID TO OUR ENEMIES PLEASE DO NOT DIVULGE THE NAME OF HIS SHIP.

Salome, however, refused to believe Genious was dead. She told neighbors he was marooned on an island or hospitalized in a foreign country, like Lester Smith. Salome insisted Genious would walk in their front door any day. When two men from the government came to the door with Genious's $5,000 life insurance payout, she refused to take the envelope. A friend persuaded her to hold on to it, "just in case," for her daughter, Vicki.

Unlike Salome, Dewey's widow, Edna Hodges, harbored no false hope that he was alive. Edna, in fact, was trying to prove Dewey was dead. Much of the family's savings was in bank accounts under only Dewey's name. Edna and the children could not access it unless a judge declared Dewey legally dead. Edna filed a petition in Norfolk Circuit Court, and offered the official government letters of regret as evidence. But the case dragged on for lack of witnesses. All of the *Onondaga* survivors had gone back to sea. Edna's lawyers finally tracked down Russell Dennis and two other crew members. None of them had seen the U-boat or the torpedo. But they had seen Dewey on the ship during her last moments afloat, and they had searched for survivors afterward in the wreckage. They knew Dewey could not swim. That was enough evidence for Judge Alan R. Hanckel, who declared Dewey dead on October 15, 1942. The judge ruled that since Dewey had left no will, his last letter to his family—the one that began, "My darling and babys"—would serve as his last will and testament.

Dewey's story was not quite over, though. His old ship, the *East Indian*, was nearing the end of the odyssey his illness had forced him to miss. The ship had sailed across the South Atlantic, around the Cape of Good Hope, and north through the wild Mozambique Channel to avoid *Japanese* subs. She rounded the Horn of Africa and transited the Persian Gulf to Basra, where her cargo of ammunition was transferred to trains for the rest of the trip to the Russian front. The men endured fifty-five days in the Persian Gulf, cursing the heat, the sand fleas, and the dust storms that rolled up like rogue waves and blotted out the horizon. Some men were so desperate for relief that they jumped into the bathtub-warm Gulf, only to be chased from the water by a swarm of yellow-banded sea snakes, which the locals warned were venomous.

The *East Indian* sailed to Colombo, Ceylon (now Sri Lanka), whose harbor was full of charred shipwrecks from a Japanese bombing raid. The ship steamed up the Ganges River, the sacred river of the Hindus, where clusters of worshippers waded in the shallows. The *East Indian* took on a load of rubber and burlap in Calcutta, where the tension was palpable. India's British governors had just jailed the Indian spiritual leader Mohandas Gandhi, and protests had degenerated into bombings, arson, and other violence that left more than a thousand people dead. The mariners were happy to leave India and even happier to reach Cape Town, which they assumed was their last stop before crossing the Atlantic to New York.

Instead, the men were crestfallen to learn at Cape Town that the *East Indian* was to take a long roundabout route home. To avoid U-boats, she was to cross the South Atlantic to Chile, pass through the Strait of Magellan into the Pacific, then pass back through the Panama Canal into the Caribbean, and then sail up the East Coast to New York. Captain St. Marie could hardly believe it. He thought the U-boats had abandoned the South Atlantic. But the Navy and the War Shipping Administration made the decisions. At noon on November 3, 1942, the *East Indian* sailed out of Cape Town's picture-book harbor, heading southwest toward Tierra del Fuego. She carried a total of seventy-three people, including forty-five officers and crew, twelve Navy gunners, and twelve passengers.

Cape Town was a meeting point for Allied convoys heading around the Cape of Good Hope for the Persian Gulf. Doenitz dispatched U-boats to the waters off Cape Town when the convoy traffic surged, and he had just sent four subs, including the U-181, commanded by Wolfgang Luth. Luth was a U-boat ace, with twenty-seven Allied ships to his credit. He was also an ardent promoter of Nazism. He gave weekly talks to his men on such topics as "racial and population problems" and "the struggle for the realization of the Reich." On Hitler's birthday, Luth told the crew stories about the Führer's life.

The U-181 was sitting on the surface off Cape Town, and Luth spotted the *East Indian* almost as soon as she cleared the breakwater. He ordered the U-181 to periscope depth and watched. The *East Indian* was zigzagging. Luth timed her changes of course with a stopwatch, and when he thought he had figured out her path, he fired two torpedoes from long range. The ship changed course unexpectedly, and the torpedoes missed by such a wide margin that no one on the freighter noticed them. The *East Indian* continued on its way, oblivious to Luth. He gave chase. The U-181 pursued its quarry for nine hours and more than 200 miles to get into position for a second attack. Luth made this one count. Two torpedoes struck the *East Indian* on the starboard side only seconds apart.

Vernon Davis, an able seaman from Mathews, had just gotten up from breakfast and headed out to the stern to smoke a cigarette. He was never seen again. Captain St. Marie was eating with Clayton Hammond, Dewey's hand-picked first officer, when the ship shook and ceiling tiles crashed down on the table between them. They ran out to the main deck. The ship already was listing so steeply they could barely stand up. Noxious smoke filled the air and made it hard to breathe. The captain climbed a ladder to the bridge, possibly to get the secret codes. Clayton ran to his cabin, grabbed a life vest, and jumped. The sinking vessel tugged him toward the bottom but he broke free and swam to an empty raft.

Marion Capers of Mathews, the *East Indian*'s bo'sun, managed to launch a single lifeboat. He and about a dozen other men got in. They looked up to see the U-181 coming to the surface nearby. Luth and four other Germans emerged from the hatch on the conning tower. Luth and every other U-boat commander had just received fresh orders from Doenitz to stop helping survivors of torpedoed ships. "Rescue contradicts the most fundamental demands of war for the annihilation of enemy ships and crews,"

Doenitz ordered. "Be harsh, having in mind that the enemy takes no regard of women and children in his bombing attacks on German cities."*

Luth was a big man with reddish hair and a thick beard. He glared down at the men in the *East Indian*'s only lifeboat.

"Are you Limeys?" Luth asked.

"Americans," a mariner replied.

"Why are you helping the Limeys and the black Russians?" Luth asked. "We have nothing against you."

Luth added a disparaging crack about Roosevelt, and some of the other Germans chimed in. The Americans said nothing. Luth said if the *East Indian* had not been zigzagging, they would have been sunk hours before and within sight of land. "As it is, you are now 300 miles from Cape Town, and there is nothing for you to do but row," Luth said. "I'm sorry, for you had a beautiful ship. But this is war." Luth asked to speak to the captain, first officer, or chief engineer. Clayton was the only one of those three still alive, but he lay silently on his raft, worried that if he identified himself he would be taken prisoner. His shipmates protected him by claiming all three of the ship's top officers were dead. Luth asked if the castaways needed food, water, or medical treatment. They said no, afraid if they got close to the sub they would be taken aboard. In fact, Luth, the most ardent Nazi in the U-boat force, was disobeying a direct order by trying to help them.

Luth questioned the castaways about their ship and cargo. He seemed to mark their answers on some kind of checklist. His questions prompted the *East Indian*'s third officer to ask Luth if he had known their ship was about to leave Cape Town. Luth said he came upon the *East Indian* purely

---

*Doenitz's message was prompted by the bombing of a U-boat that had been towing lifeboats to shore. The U-boat had torpedoed the armed British troopship *Laconia* only to discover she was carrying 1,800 Italian prisoners of war. The U-boat crew was trying to save as many of them as possible when an Allied bomber spotted the sub and damaged it with depth charges. Doenitz's order to offer no aid to castaways would later become one of the prosecution's chief pieces of evidence at his war-crimes trial at Nuremberg.

by accident.* He wished the castaways "Godspeed," and clasped his hands above his head in a gesture of farewell. The other Germans on the conning tower gave the castaways a "Heil Hitler" salute as the U-181 prepared to submerge. Luth later claimed an *East Indian* crewman returned the Hitler salute and wished the Germans, "Good luck and good hunting." This seems to have been his fantasy, though; none of the survivors' accounts mention an American making any such response.

The men in the lifeboat rowed to Clayton's raft and took him aboard. As the highest-ranking officer alive, he was in command. Clayton was the personification of self-control. As a boy, he awoke one night and looked out the window to see his school on fire down the street. He went back to bed and said nothing until his mother called for him to get up for school. "There won't be any school today," Clayton told her. "It burned down." On another occasion, Clayton walked calmly into the living room and told his parents his grandfather was trying to hang himself from the apple tree in their back yard. They leaped to their feet but Clayton said there was no hurry. None of the limbs was strong enough to support his grandfather.

Now Clayton faced the challenge of his life. A head count showed twenty-three men from the *East Indian* dead or missing, including Vernon Davis and Second Officer Lemuel Marchant of Mathews. The survivors numbered fifty-one, including seventeen in the only lifeboat and thirty-four scattered among four rafts. One of the men in the lifeboat was Bernard Pierson of Gwynn's Island, a husky able seaman known for his temper. He would be remembered instead for an act of sacrifice. Pierson saw that one of the men on the rafts was badly injured, and gave up his seat in the boat to the man and took his place on the raft. He must have known the exchange could cost him his life.

---

* Luth's denial did not convince Navy intelligence officers, who always looked for more complicated explanations for sinkings than the simple fact that the ships had been sent into harm's way unescorted. In this case, the Navy suggested a "Nazi-controlled vice ring" in Cape Town had pried information about the *East Indian*'s schedule from crewmen "under the influence of passion and intoxicants."

Clayton had no charts and only a compass with which to navigate. Based on the ship's position before the sinking, he estimated the castaways were 317 miles southwest of Cape Town. The lifeboat had oars and a sail and enough provisions for two weeks. If the weather was favorable, it might reach Cape Town within a week. The rafts, on the other hand, could do little but stay afloat. Clayton decided the survivors' best chance was for the lifeboat to run for Cape Town and send help.

The thirty-four men on the rafts understood the decision, and its ramifications for them. They would be left alone in the deep ocean to hope for a miracle. None of them flinched. "I remember that not any of the boys left on the four rafts acted panicky," wrote M. Stanley MacLean, who was in the lifeboat. The men on the rafts included Bernard Pierson; Andrew Dennis, an orphan living with relatives in Mathews, who had found a home at sea; and Wilson Forrest, whose brother Coles's ship had been mined at the mouth of the Chesapeake Bay.

Clayton's hopes for favorable weather were obliterated on the second day by a howling storm that blew the lifeboat all the way around the Cape of Good Hope into the Indian Ocean. A week passed. A pod of whales surrounded the lifeboat one night and MacLean worried they would capsize it: "Whenever one surfaced and made its mournful sound, a chill went up my spine." Clayton rationed the food and water. Each man received a small quantity of pemmican and five ounces of water per day. The men were perpetually thirsty. They regretted not having collected rainwater during a recent downpour. Every time a rain squall approached, they prepared to catch the rain in a sail and with "our mouths open like young birds," as MacLean put it. But the squalls bypassed the boat. Tempers grew short, and two men stood up in the boat to throw punches, but Clayton got them to sit down. Clayton announced he had a .45-caliber pistol on his hip, and would use it if anyone endangered the boat. The men could see a holster under his shirt, but Clayton never displayed the gun, if, in fact, he really had one.

On the second day, the radioman became delusional. He was wracked with guilt for not having gotten off an SOS call. He called the lifeboat a prison ship. Men held him down to keep him from jumping overboard. They finally had to tie him up. He passed out and never woke up. The drinking water ran out, and the men regretted having refused the water Luth had offered from the U-181.

On the lifeboat's thirteenth day adrift, a British merchant ship spotted it and took the survivors to Cape Town. Clayton reported the last known position of the rafts, but after two weeks of rough weather, they might be anywhere, or nowhere. Search planes flew grid patterns for three days but found nothing. Six months later, in June 1943, one of the *East Indian*'s rafts would turn up off the coast of Brazil, more than 2,500 miles from the sinking, bearing an unidentified set of remains.

Five Mathews men had died on the *East Indian*—the same number killed on the *Ruth* five months earlier. This time, there was no memorial service, no symbolic tossing of flowers in the water. Mathews was in shock. In the nine months since the United States entered the war, twenty-two Mathews mariners had been killed. At least twice that many had been torpedoed. Seven Mathews men had been torpedoed at least twice. Mellin Respess was torpedoed three times on three different ships in a little over three months before he finally was killed. And the war was only starting.

Just days after the *East Indian* sinking, Edna Hodges received a call from her lawyer. He had finally received a copy of one of R. M. Jenkins's letters from Havana about the ring in the shark's belly. On October 22, 1942, Jenkins had written:

> I have come in touch with a matter which might be of great sentimental value to some person, and I will explain the matter to you thinking you might care to and be able to contact who might be the interested party. In the vicinity of where the *SS Onondaga* was torpedoed and several of the crew lost is a great shark fishing ground. Around there for years, a family by the name of Carillo has fished commercially for sharks.

A short time after the sinking of the ship, according to them and as told to me by the one I think the most reliable, they caught a shark that had in its belly the flesh and bones of a human being. They say they took out and saved the bones from the hip to the ankle. Also at the same time they found with the rest two rings. They have shown me the rings and I have carefully examined them.

I thought they would be of interest mainly because the outside initials on the heavy gold signet ring are G.D.H. As it was my understanding that the captain who went down with the ship was G.D. Hodges, it has occurred to me that it might be his ring. On the inside of this same ring it [is] engraved as follows: "E.R.G. '17." The bottom of the ring is broken.

The other ring seems to be made of some such material as bone and is of light yellow color with a large dark top imitating a stone of some kind.

If the widow of this good old man who went down with his ship knows this ring, I imagine it would be of great sentimental value to her. I am giving you this information for you to do with as you think best.

Edna knew instantly that the ring with the initials G.D.H. was Dewey's. She had given it to him as an engagement present in 1917. Her initials and the date were engraved inside the band. Her head surely spun. "Since it all had to be, I'm glad to know about the rings because they relieve a lot of anxiety and wondering," Edna told a British magazine. But the discovery raised the question of whether Dewey had been killed by a shark—unanswerable but hard to let go. The discovery also raised a practical question: Did Dewey's family want the remains shipped to Norfolk? Edna called her daughters together. She told the girls she had never seen the second ring before. She assumed it was not Dewey's. That meant the remains might not be all Dewey's. They might not be his at all. She did not want to bury a stranger. Dewey had wanted to be buried at sea anyway. "I think we have been through enough," Edna told her daughters, and they agreed. The family asked for the return of only the ring with Dewey's initials.

The Norfolk newspapers got wind of the story, and soon it made headlines all over the state and around the country. Two days later, on November 7, Henny Hodges's young cousin Edwin Jarvis, who lived across a creek from Gales Neck, rowed over to visit. He walked into the kitchen and found Henny sitting back in a chair sobbing, with a newspaper laid on a table in front of her. For a second the boy wondered if a third Hodges son had been torpedoed. Henny's daughter Alice showed him the headline: "Death of Captain Hodges Confirmed by Ring Found in Shark's Belly." Edwin thought Henny had just learned the news from the paper. It seems more likely that she already had been told, but was upset all over again by the headline.

Henny could not stop crying. She could not even work. She told her daughters, "If anything else happens, please don't tell me. I couldn't stand to hear it." Her daughters for once agreed: Their mother could not take another blow. Alice, Elizabeth, Louise, and Hilda Fourteen decided to act. They went to Captain Jesse and their brothers Willie and Coleman and asked them to stop sailing in war zones, if not for their own sake, then for Henny's.

The Hodges men were not used to taking orders on seafaring matters from their sisters, and the request was complicated. The idea of retreating from danger in wartime was hard to swallow. No one in Mathews would think ill of the Hodges family for thinking they had sacrificed enough after the deaths of Leslie and Dewey. But small communities had long memories. Almost seventy years after World War II, Clarence Collier Jr. of Gwynn's Island, who was eleven years old when his grandfather Perry Collier was lost on the *Ruth*, rattled off the names of five islanders who quit sailing steamships when the U-boats attacked. "Those sons of bitches," Clarence Collier Jr. said. "They were draft dodgers and they died draft dodgers."

The Hodges daughters could not have known what to expect when they asked their father to find safer work. Captain Jesse could find work on the water anywhere he wanted, and he agreed at once to work on tugs that stayed in the Bay.

Captain Willie Hodges discussed his sisters' request with his wife over the dinner table. Willie and his family lived only two houses from Dewey's family in Norfolk. Willie had yet to encounter a U-boat while working offshore on his tug, but he knew it could happen. Willie too decided to honor his sisters' request. Like Captain Jesse, he could easily find work on tugs inside the Bay.

David Hodges already was ashore, working in the shipyard. Spencer was ashore too. That left Raymond and Coleman Hodges still sailing the deep ocean.

The only way for the sisters to reach Raymond would be to send him a letter and hope it found him halfway around the world in a war zone. Raymond had taken the *Mormacmoon* to Suez, Egypt, with tanks, planes, and ammunition for the Russians. Off the Cape of Good Hope, the *Mormacmoon* was swept by huge seas known as cape rollers, which opened a three-inch crack in the hull. The crew patched it with cement, wire, and caulk. After the *Mormacmoon* finished unloading its cargo, the ship was placed under temporary command of the British Admiralty, for a special mission. Raymond was not told what it was.

Coleman Hodges simply refused his sisters' request. Coleman was driven to command a ship in the war, and he was almost there. He had a reputation as a light-hearted jokester, but at home, when he got angry, his eyes flashed. His wife, Ethel, and daughters froze until he relaxed. Coleman never laid a hand on his family. In fact, he left all discipline to Ethel. But "you got this feeling that he was running and couldn't run fast enough," his daughter Betty said of him.

Coleman was a dutiful son to Henny. He and his family lived in Norfolk, but he came home to Gales Neck often. He fetched wood for Henny's stove and found other ways to help her without being asked. When he stayed at the farm, he sat up with her for an hour every night before she went to bed, telling her about his family and hearing her complaints about

Jesse's slights. Coleman "was a mama's boy," his daughter Betty said. But he was not going to stop sailing offshore. His brothers' deaths would only have hardened his resolve. Coleman was stubborn enough to do the opposite of whatever his sisters or anyone else wanted him to do.

Coleman and Raymond would join a new phase of the U-boat war. For ten months after Pearl Harbor the U.S. Merchant Marine had kept the war from being lost. They had kept Britain supplied with the oil, munitions, and food it needed to continue fighting the Nazis. They had delivered enough oil and raw materials such as manganese and bauxite to keep American factories churning out ships, planes, tanks, and other weapons. They had carried tens of thousands of American troops to England for future invasions. They had endured the cold of the Murmansk Run and the heat of the Persian Gulf to deliver supplies to the Red Army and keep Stalin in the Allied camp.*

By the fall of 1942, the number of merchant mariners had almost tripled, to 150,000. The rate of new Liberty ships being launched had nearly doubled to two per day. The Merchant Marine was still "America's cross-eyed stepchild," as Admiral Land of the Maritime Commission said, but it was growing into a juggernaut. Its role in the war, like America's role, was about to shift from defense to offense. The Merchant Marine would sustain the great Allied amphibious invasions to liberate Europe from the Nazis.

The first of those invasions was Operation Torch, the Allied invasion of North Africa, set for the first week of November 1942. The strategic objectives were to capture Tunisia, trapping German armies in Libya, and to reopen part of the Mediterranean to Allied shipping. Roosevelt and Churchill had chosen North Africa largely because it was a softer target for their untested troops than France, or any territory defended by the

---

*Fifty years after the end of World War II, in the spirit of *Glasnost*, Soviet president Mikhail Gorbachev decided to award medals to U.S. merchant mariners who took part in the Murmansk Run. The medals would end up being awarded under the presidency of Boris Yeltsin, who replaced Gorbachev after a coup removed him from power. Some Mathews families still have the Russian medals.

Germans. The defenders of North Africa were mostly Vichy French. They officially served the German puppet government in France, but might not follow its orders. They might even lay down their arms and welcome the invaders ashore. If not, the invasion force was strong enough to overrun them.

Operation Torch would employ nearly four hundred merchant vessels and troop transports, in addition to three hundred warships, to deliver more than 100,000 troops to the beaches of North Africa. Three-quarters of those troops would be American—the first American armies to join the European war. Once those men started pouring into North Africa, the United States was committed to supporting them for months, even years. They would need not only guns, ammunition, tanks, planes, artillery, trucks, jeeps, and ambulances, but food, clothing, shelter, medicine, blankets, and insect repellent. Each American soldier serving overseas in World War II would need between seven and eight tons of supplies. They would also need reinforcements. Cargo ships were the only way to move everything.

The invading Allied troops were most vulnerable on the beaches, where a moment's interruption in the flow of supplies could bring disaster. But even when the troops were far inland, they would depend on a long skein of freighters, tankers, and Liberty ships, plowing across the ocean in giant rectangles, hunted by an increasingly desperate enemy.

CHAPTER TEN

Counterattack

C aptain Guy Hudgins had returned from the Murmansk Run with a big, fur-lined hat with long ear flaps. He modeled it for his wife and daughter, and for guests who dropped by for a drink at their duplex in Jersey City. Guy was enjoying catching up on the good life when he and his Liberty ship, the *Zebulon B. Vance*, were temporarily assigned to the British Admiralty in August 1942 for a special mission. He would be told the details later.

Guy was ordered to sail the ship to Liverpool, England, where her holds were filled with U.S. Army tanks and trucks, guns, and ammunition. Two big landing barges were lashed to the main deck. The barges were so heavy that special cranes had to be brought to the wharf to lift them onto the ship. A British gun crew came aboard, followed by fifty American soldiers. No one was allowed to leave the ship. The *Vance* sailed to a rendezvous point at sea, where ships stretched in all directions, farther than Guy could see. Sixty merchant ships were protected by a ring of warships, including the British escort carrier HMS *Avenger*. Guy had never seen an escort carrier before. The carrier was a floating airfield with enough planes to maintain air cover for the convoy all across the ocean. The *Avenger* sent a boat to collect Guy and the other merchant captains for a conference. It was there that Guy learned the *Vance* was part of Operation Torch.

The invasion force to North Africa was divided into three prongs. One, Task Force 34, commanded by General George S. Patton, was sailing from Norfolk across the Atlantic to land troops on the ocean coast of Morocco. The two other prongs of the invasion force were sailing from the British Isles through the Strait of Gibraltar to the Mediterranean coast of Oran and Algeria. All three prongs followed their plans perfectly, and the invasion took place on the night of November 8.

The invaders were welcomed with artillery fire, not open arms. Hutson Hudgins of Mathews, an eighteen-year-old Navy sailor, drove landing craft full of soldiers to the beach at Morocco, and compared the scene to "Christmas at home, with plenty of Roman candles and pop crackers . . . With the ships blazing away at the planes and shore batteries, the planes bombing, dropping flares and firing at each other, the shore batteries firing as fast as they could be handled, the sky afire with tracer bullets and bursting shells and bombs—boy it was some show!"

Guy Hudgins's prong of the invasion force landed near the Algerian port of Arzeu. He saw Allied warships exchange long-range volleys with shore batteries. No one shot at the *Vance*, so Guy brought her to her assigned anchorage and started unloading cargo. The crew rigged one of the heavy landing barges to the *Vance*'s largest boom crane and prepared to lift it. The British crew climbed into the barge, saying they wanted to get underway as soon as it hit the water. The crane lifted the barge and swung it out over the sea. Then the crane bent and broke. The barge splashed into the water from a height of fifteen feet. It stayed upright but a crewman was injured. The falling end of the broken crane just missed two men on the pier.

Later that day, another of the *Vance*'s cranes broke and dropped a five-ton Army truck into a cargo hold. The falling truck knocked a young American soldier into the hold, killing him. The truck tumbled into the hold after him, killing a second man and injuring two others. The *Vance* had suffered two deaths and three injuries in Operation Torch without encountering the enemy.

After those accidents, the *Vance* was moved to a newly captured dock, where unloading was easier. Guy had sailed in these waters before the war and had Arab friends and business associates in Oran. He caught a ride on a jeep to pay them a visit. The roadside was littered with dead livestock and charred Vichy French vehicles. Many of the buildings were pockmarked with bullet holes. Guy's friends welcomed him, and the invasion. His favorite ship chandler in Oran told him, "Get this war over with, captain! Come back and see us, the sooner the better!" Other residents were more hostile; the Vichy French fought for two days in North Africa, killing more than 800 Allied soldiers, before signing an armistice.

Operation Torch caught the Germans by surprise. They had not thought the United States was ready to launch a large-scale invasion. Doenitz fumed that the German intelligence apparatus "had failed completely." His U-boats had made no contact with the invasion force. After the Allies had landed in North Africa, Doenitz belatedly sent out his U-boats. They torpedoed four troop transports returning from the beaches off Morocco, killing 111 Americans. But the U-boats had failed to prevent the buildup for the invasion, or stop it. Guy took the *Vance* back to the United States, picked up another load of supplies for the troops, and joined another convoy to North Africa. Once again, he encountered no U-boats.

While the Germans were reeling from Operation Torch, Captain Raymond Hodges was dispatched on a different special mission for the British. The *Mormacmoon* was ordered from Suez, Egypt, where it had dropped off supplies for the Russians, to Port Sudan, where it was loaded with food, coal, ammunition, and gasoline. The gas was stored in scores of small five-gallon containers. A seaman asked the ship's agent in Suez where they were going, but he "refused to tell us our destination, but said he did not think we would return."

Raymond, ever a stickler for routine and detail, insisted the crew practice launching the lifeboats every day, even when the wind blowing off the desert made rowing an ordeal. He was a consummate professional who would never think of questioning his orders, but he was accustomed to being in control of events, and could not have liked not knowing where he and his ship were headed next. Finally, on the night of November 16, the *Mormacmoon* was ordered to sail out through the northern end of the Suez Canal into the eastern Mediterranean. Three freighters that had been taking on cargo near the *Mormacmoon* followed. The four ships entered the Mediterranean at dawn and were quickly encircled by British warships. At that point, Raymond was told he and the *Mormacmoon* were part of Operation Stoneage, a convoy to Malta.

Malta is a tiny limestone island in the Mediterranean 50 miles south of Sicily. It is famous for its stone towers and medieval knights, but in 1942 it was better known as one of the most bombed places on earth. Malta was a base for British planes and submarines that attacked the Germans' supply lines to Africa, frustrating the Germans' attempts to capture Egypt and the Allied oil fields in the Mideast. The Germans were desperate to drive the British from Malta, and bombed the island daily from air bases in Sicily and North Africa. They reduced entire villages on Malta to rubble. Malta's 250,000 citizens and 20,000 British defenders lived in caves and tunnels carved into the limestone hills. Their greatest danger was not bombs but starvation. Malta produced little food. Any Allied ship trying to deliver supplies to the island was attacked by German bombers and U-boats. Shortages of food and aviation fuel became critical. The most recent convoy to Malta, Operation Pedestal, had delivered enough supplies in August to save the islanders from having to surrender. But Malta remained isolated and vulnerable, and any ship approaching the island was sure to be attacked.

Raymond's four-ship convoy was escorted by four cruisers and seven destroyers—nearly three times as many warships as cargo ships. That reversal of the normal balance of warships to merchant ships in a convoy showed how much trouble the British anticipated, and how vital the cargo was to Malta. British fighters flew overhead. The *Mormacmoon* led the other merchant ships west through a calm sea at a speed of 15 knots. Malta was four long days away. The only question was when the first attack would come.

Less than four hours after the escorts had joined the convoy, five German light bombers flew directly overhead and dropped bombs. One bomb exploded in the water close enough to the *Mormacmoon* to make the whole ship rattle. Other German planes passed ahead of the convoy, and the British planes pursued them. At dusk, a German torpedo bomber severely damaged a British cruiser in the escort force, killing 129 men. The convoy kept going.

After dark, the greatest danger was accidentally colliding with another ship. Every ship was blacked out, and commands to zigzag were transmitted by signal light or whistle. If a ship missed one of those commands, it might smash into a ship in the next column. Raymond stayed on the bridge with his binoculars. On the third day, gales swept across the Mediterranean and grounded the German bombers. The storms blew until the next day, when the convoy was close enough to Malta for British Spitfire fighters based on the island to fly out and provide air cover.

That night, the *Mormacmoon* led the three other merchant ships into Grand Harbor at the Maltese port of Valetta. Submarine nets opened to admit the convoy, and depth charges were dropped behind it to make sure no U-boats followed it in. Amphitheater-like Grand Harbor was blacked out, but people lined the stone walls under a full moon and cheered the convoy in. Malta's governor, General Sir William Dobbie, went aboard the *Mormacmoon* to welcome Raymond. The confident, debonair Raymond was perfectly comfortable in the presence of high-ranking officials.

British soldiers started unloading the *Mormacmoon* and discovered gasoline had leaked from the little containers and pooled two feet deep in the holds. A spark could blow up the ship. Raymond set the whole crew to work. They hauled out the leaky gas containers and pumped out the spilled gasoline. The fumes in the hold were overpowering. Men held their breath, scrambled down a ladder for a few seconds of work, and then scrambled back up to breathe. An air-raid alarm sounded every few hours, as if to remind the men to hurry. Neither Raymond nor any of his officers took a break until the job was finished.

Once the crisis was over, Raymond accepted an invitation to dine with Governor Dobbie. The view from the governor's home was impressive, but daylight had revealed the bombed hulks of several ships in Grand Harbor, and the meal was little more than "a dish of beans and a glass of wine." Raymond felt guilty eating any of the islanders' scarce food. Unloading took a little over two weeks. On December 7, one year after Pearl Harbor, the *Mormacmoon* led the convoy out of Grand Harbor through the submarine nets.

The Germans were waiting. Torpedo bombers damaged a British escort ship and killed three seamen. Their funeral services had just begun the next morning when two waves of Junkers 88 bombers attacked. A British fighter chased them off, but more attacked at dusk. Bombs exploded in the water all around the *Mormacmoon*. One bomber roared right over the ship, barely higher than the masts, and dropped a bomb just astern. Later in the day, four planes headed straight for the *Mormacmoon*. The first officer saw Raymond drop to his knees, apparently in prayer. The planes passed directly over the ship and kept going. They were unarmed transport planes, probably evacuating German troops from North Africa to Italy.

The *Mormacmoon* and the other ships got back to Suez unscathed, and Raymond set out on the long trip home. The bombers did not follow. On Christmas Day, the *Mormacmoon* was steaming south through the Indian Ocean. One of the lookouts spotted two submarines in the distance off Tanzania, but the subs showed no interest in their ship.* The *Mormacmoon* stopped in Portuguese East Africa to take on a load of chrome ore. Ray-

---

* The submarines may have been Japanese. Japanese subs patrolled the waters off Tanzania, but did not pursue merchant ships as aggressively as the U-boats did, mainly because Japanese subs were constantly being diverted to other missions by Japanese admirals. German submariners sometimes exhorted their Japanese counterparts to attack more merchant ships.

mond decided to wait for a high tide to take the ship through the tricky Mozambique Channel. Some of the crew took the opportunity to go on safaris, hunting predators in the African bush—a surreal end to the first full year of the U-boat war on America.

The year had treated merchant mariners cruelly. A preliminary Navy summary of losses in the western Atlantic in 1942 included 548 Allied and neutral ships sunk, and more than 3,000 American mariners killed. The Allies had lost 2.2 million tons of cargo, more than half of it in the Caribbean.

The war had treated Mathews cruelly too. Some mariners' families were bitter. "We had some animosity toward the government for leaving my father unprotected," Dewey Hodges's daughter Jean said. The U.S. government seemed to consider merchant ships and mariners expendable. Would Admiral King spend the lives of his Navy men so freely?

Christmas was always a subdued time in Mathews. Families of mariners at sea hung special ornaments on the tree, set symbolic plates before empty dinner chairs, and wrapped Christmas presents to sit unopened for weeks or even months. The melancholy penetrated even deeper than usual in 1942. "Those of us who live in small towns are able to see more clearly the suffering caused by war," the *Gazette-Journal* said. "We have a friendly, personal interest in each other. The spirit of neighborly love and devotion has eased many a saddened heart . . ." Captain Jesse's new job on a tug in the Bay allowed him to come home on Christmas, which was also his and Henny's wedding anniversary. Coleman happened to be in port and brought his family to Gales Neck for a few days. Most of his brothers were on the water.

Captains of ships at sea on Christmas tried to boost the crews' spirits. The benevolent Captain Robert Gayle of the collier *Achilles* set up a Christmas tree in the ship's dining room and canceled all routine duties. The cook outdid himself with a huge turkey dinner with gravy. The crew of the *Achilles* was lucky to be alive to enjoy the meal. In dense fog off the coast of

Rhode Island, the *Achilles* had nearly collided with a U-boat. Gayle could hear the Germans shout and smell their cigarettes. The fog swallowed the vessels again before either could react. Gayle ordered the *Achilles* to steam at full speed the rest of the night despite the fog.

The new year of 1943 began promisingly for the Allies. In the Pacific, the U.S. Marines were driving the Japanese off Guadalcanal after months of bloody fighting over a strategic jungle airstrip. In Europe, the German Sixth Army was bogged down in the freezing ruins of Stalingrad, and American and British bombers were pummeling German cities night and day. The Allied campaign in North Africa was progressing so well that Roosevelt and Churchill traveled to Casablanca in January for a meeting to decide their next step. They declared the Allies would accept nothing less than "unconditional surrender" from the Axis nations. Stalin once again was demanding that the United States and Britain launch an amphibious invasion of France to siphon German troops away from the Russian front. But Roosevelt and Churchill still were not ready to hurl their troops across the English Channel at the fortifications Hitler called the "Atlantic wall." The Allied armies needed a new target to maintain their momentum. Churchill persuaded Roosevelt it should be Sicily, the island at the end of the Italian boot.

Sicily was not so important strategically as it was there for the taking. It was only a day's voyage from North Africa. Its defenders were mostly Italians, who might not fight any harder than the Vichy French in North Africa had. Where the Allies would go after capturing Sicily was left open, but the most obvious choice was invading mainland Italy. Sending thousands of Allied troops to Sicily, and then possibly to mainland Italy, would require a larger and more complex supply chain. It would take thousands of ships steaming up and down the U.S. coast, through the Gulf and Caribbean, back and forth across the Atlantic between New York and Britain, Italy and North Africa, and between North America and Italy. No supply operation on that scale had ever been attempted.

———

U-boats continued to pick off ships from the fringes of convoys. Johnie Hall, a twenty-eight-year-old mariner from Gwynn's Island, survived a sinking after his ship, the *Steel Navigator*, straggled behind a convoy in the fog. Roland Howard Garrett of Mathews lived through the sinking of the Liberty ship *Benjamin Harrison*, torpedoed in a convoy en route to North Africa. In January, Alton Hudgins of Mathews survived the torpedoing of the little freighter *Collingsworth* in a convoy off Dutch Guiana.

But ships sailing alone were always in the greatest danger, as Alton Hudgins's cousin Allen Hudgins discovered. Late on the night of February 3, 1943, his vessel, the Liberty ship *Roger B. Taney*, was steaming alone through the middle of the South Atlantic. The ship was empty, en route to Brazil to pick up a load of bauxite ore. The lookouts shouted that a torpedo was coming. It missed the ship's bow by 10 feet. The *Taney* ran, but a Liberty ship's maximum speed was 11.5 knots; a U-boat on the surface could make 17. The U-160 quickly overtook the *Taney*. An hour after missing with its first torpedo, the submarine fired a second torpedo straight into the *Taney*'s engine room, killing all three men on watch there, and buckling the ship's deck. The rest of the crew got away in two lifeboats.

The U-boat surfaced and the commander asked the men in the boats about their ship. No one responded and he barked, "It doesn't matter, we know all about your ship." He offered to tow the lifeboats closer to land, but the mariners were suspicious and declined. The U-boat left them alone. Both lifeboats were nearly full, with twenty-eight men in one and twenty-six in the other. The *Taney*'s captain, Thomas J. Potter, decided they should rig the sails and ride the southeast trade winds to Brazil. The lifeboats became separated in rough weather the first night. The breeze kept dying and the castaways cursed the calm. They had plenty of water because rain squalls kept drenching the boat. Days passed, and then weeks. The men in Allen's lifeboat kept each other's spirits up by talking constantly about thick steaks and ice cream. In the absence of those choices, they speared a fish, drank its blood, and cooked it over a fire in a metal bucket in the boat, smashing up a spare oar for firewood. After three weeks adrift, the twenty-eight men in Allen's lifeboat were picked up by a British ship on March 1.

Captain Potter's lifeboat drifted for another week. Finally, the captain saw birds and knew they were nearing land. Frigate birds and storm petrels nested on land but ranged far out to sea, so the sight of them meant land was only a few days away. Then Potter "saw one dragon fly and one butter fly [sic] and I was definitely sure that land was near." He could tell from the small fish in the water that they had reached the shallow banks south of Trinidad. Potter may even have been able to smell the coast. Land gave off distinctive smells that carried long distances across the sea. The Cape Verde Islands off Africa smelled like oranges, and some tropical isles, like coconuts. All land gave off a sweet smell after a rain.

Three nights after spotting the birds, the men in the lifeboat saw the glow of a city against the clouds in the western sky just before dawn. The captain said it was Rio de Janeiro. Sunrise revealed a mountaintop in the distance. The breeze quit again. The captain worried the current would sweep them south, away from land. He handed out extra rations of water and crackers and urged everyone to take a turn at the oars and row with all their strength. The lifeboat drew close to a wild shore. The captain thought the exhausted men might have to row to the beach through thundering surf. But a half mile from the Brazilian coast near the city of Santos, a steamship picked them up. In the 42 days since the *Taney* sinking, their lifeboat had traveled more than 2,600 miles.

The U-boat attacks in the South Atlantic in the first months of 1943 were only a prelude to the main event. Despite the Allied victories and the new defenses mounted for convoys, the decisive clash of the Battle of the Atlantic was about to begin. Doenitz could hardly wait.

Doenitz believed U-boats could still win the war if they sank enough Allied merchant ships, and for the first time, he had enough influence in Berlin to put that theory to the test. Doenitz had been promoted to Grand Admiral of the German Navy, replacing his old boss Erich Raeder, who was tired of Hitler's red-faced tirades. Unlike Raeder, Doenitz had Hitler's ear, and money and resources for U-boat construction flowed. By early 1943, Doenitz had 430 U-boats in service, of which roughly a hundred were always on active patrol. The U-boat force had never been larger.

Doenitz believed he could stagger the Allies by launching his wolf packs in an all-out assault on the North Atlantic convoy routes, the regular supply runs to Britain that the Royal Navy called "the heartbeat of the war." The main point of attack would be the air gap, the 600-mile stretch of ocean south of Greenland where Allied planes could not reach. When the weather finally cleared at the start of March, Doenitz sent forty-eight U-boats into the air gap and surrounding waters—too many for Allied convoys to avoid. Convoy after convoy plunged into the submarine gauntlet. What had been a contest of hit-and-run, hide-and-seek had turned into a brawl.

Clashes between the U-boats and the convoy escort ships were ferocious. One British escort rammed a surfacing U-boat, only to be sunk by a second U-boat, which in turn was sunk by a French escort ship. In mid-March, wolf packs attacked two convoys passing in opposite directions through the air gap and sank nineteen ships, killing 740 mariners and sending 82,049 tons of cargo to the sea bottom. The ebullient Doenitz called the attack "the greatest success that we had so far scored against a convoy." He did not see disaster approaching, as the Allies began for the first time to seize the initiative against the wolf packs.

The counteroffensive against the U-boats did not erupt suddenly from a single event or invention. It had been building slowly for years, as improvements in Allied strategy, technology, and weaponry coalesced into a critical mass.

Almost from the start of the war, the British had engaged some of their most brilliant scientists to analyze U-boats' vulnerabilities. Physicists such as Patrick Blackett advised pilots and seamen on topics ranging from the most productive settings for depth charges—30 feet—to the best routes and times of day for aerial patrols. British engineers developed microwave radar that could spot U-boats on the surface at a distance of 10 miles, even at night or in thick clouds and fog. That radar, which could be installed in planes and escort ships, robbed the U-boats of the only sanctuary they enjoyed at sea. A U-boat commander could no longer relax on the water's surface at night, enjoying a glimpse of the sky and a few gulps of fresh air while the sub's batteries were recharging. Now, he might look up to see an Allied bomber racing at him out of the darkness, shining a blinding spotlight in his eyes. The searchlights, named Leigh Lights after Humphrey de Verd Leigh, the British squadron commander who invented them, were designed to pick up where radar left off. A bomber approaching a U-boat at night would lose the submarine's image on radar about three-quarters of a mile from the drop point—not close enough for the pilot to see his target in the dark. At that point, he would switch on the Leigh Light, whose brilliant beam guided him the rest of the way. U-boats were equipped with rudimentary radar detectors, but they were clumsy to set up and dismantle, prone to buzzing constant false alarms, and incapable of detecting microwave radar.

Night or day, planes enjoyed a clear advantage over U-boats. A sharp-eyed U-boat lookout might be able to spot an approaching plane from a distance of three miles. But the plane could cover that distance in less than fifteen seconds, while the U-boat needed at least twenty-five seconds to crash dive. Doenitz, who once had boasted that a plane "can no more kill a U-boat than a crow can kill a mole," had come to recognize the plane as the U-boat's nemesis. U-boats rarely received air cover from German planes, partly because Doenitz and the chief of the Luftwaffe, Field Marshal Hermann Goering, loathed each other.

Radar combined with sonar enabled convoys to detect U-boats approaching on the surface or underwater. New technology combined with new escort ships and planes meant that large, well-protected convoys, like those crossing the North Atlantic, no longer had to be content with fending off U-boats. Once they found them, they could hunt them down and destroy them.

Convoys increasingly were accompanied by new, American-built

Navy destroyer escorts (DEs), inexpensive versions of destroyers, which were fast enough to outrun U-boats, built to withstand winter seas, and armed with new Mark 9 and Mark 10 depth charges, which sank fast and could be set to explode at 600 to 800 feet—the depth to which a desperate U-boat captain might take his sub as a last resort.

The DE was designed by Rear Admiral Edward L. Cochrane, a naval architect and the future chief of the Navy's Bureau of Ships. Cochrane had failed to persuade Admiral King and others in the U.S. Navy hierarchy to build DEs, so he pitched the design to the British, who ordered some of them built at American shipyards through the Lend-Lease program. When Roosevelt learned about the British orders, he diverted the DEs to the U.S. Navy, and then ordered more DEs. Later, Roosevelt and Admiral King would each blame the other for not building DEs sooner.

American shipyards also produced escort carriers like the one that had impressed Captain Guy Hudgins in Operation Torch. The "baby flattops," as they were called, were miniature versions of the aircraft carriers anchoring the U.S. fleet in the Pacific. Escort carriers operated 28 planes compared to a big aircraft carrier's 103. Some escort carriers were embedded in convoys to provide a moving umbrella of protection wherever the convoys went. Their planes patrolled the convoys' paths and flanks, searching for U-boats on the surface. When they found one, they either attacked it or forced it underwater and radioed its location to the escort ships.

The U.S. Navy pioneered the use of escort carriers as the nuclei of "hunter-killer groups," designed to destroy U-boats. A typical hunter-killer group consisted of an escort carrier and four destroyers. The group prowled the convoy routes, beaming radar and sonar in search of submarines. It also chased down leads from the Allied radio direction-finding network, which used Doenitz's daily radio communications with his U-boats to find his subs for the hunter-killers. What made hunter-killer groups so lethal was that they never had to break off from attacks in order to keep up with a convoy, as escort ships did. When a hunter-killer group found a U-boat, it could take all the time necessary to destroy it. The group's sole purpose was hunting down one U-boat after another. From early 1943 to the end of the war, they would be the most prolific destroyers of U-boats.

By late March 1943, the counteroffensive against the U-boats had tilted the convoy battles in the North Atlantic in the Allies' favor. Captain Raymond Hodges saw the change firsthand when the *Mormacmoon* was assigned to the first big North Atlantic convoy of April. Raymond had returned only a few days earlier from his voyage to Malta. On the way home from Malta, he had first learned of his brothers' deaths from a six-month-old newspaper clipping. He wrote to Captain Jesse and Henny:

> I heard about Dewey and Leslie after we left Cape Town. One of my mates gave me a Norfolk paper to read, and I happened upon the sad news while we were at sea. You know how shocked I was. I suppose one must expect such things when the whole crazy world is fighting, like, as you used to say, 'a passel of Arabs.' We shall have to bear our losses until it is all over. If I am not mistaken, very few of us will come out of this war free from some sort of damage. It has not really started yet. Day in and day out, our people are losing their lives on every sea, even more so than on the land. As I see it, no one stands to gain much from this everlasting fighting. I hope it will end before we suffer more losses. I am about to go on another trip and this time think I shall go to England.

The *Mormacmoon* left New York Harbor on April 2 in Convoy HX-232,* the latest in the long series of huge North Atlantic convoys, and typical of them: thirty-nine merchant ships carrying oil, aviation fuel, steam locomotives, landing barges, sugar, grain, and lumber, along with 200 U.S. Army soldiers. Several ships in the convoy carried passengers, including the *Mormacmoon*, which also carried thirty-eight precious bags

---

* The HX designation referred to Halifax, Nova Scotia, where many transatlantic convoys to Britain originated.

of mail for American soldiers in Britain. The escort force included three destroyers and four corvettes, but no escort carrier and therefore no air cover.

The Germans tracked the formation of Raymond's convoy by reading coded Allied messages, and assembled wolf packs to intercept it. The Allies, who had broken back into the German Navy's Enigma code in December, tracked the U-boats tracking the convoy. Allied code breakers would continue to read secret German messages through Enigma, with few interruptions, through the end of the war. As HX-232 made its way across the Atlantic, neither side suspected the other had tapped into its secrets and knew most of its moves in advance. This didn't necessarily mean either side was in a better position to attack or defend its vessels.

The first vessel in convoy HX-232 to be sunk was a Liberty ship that had straggled far behind the convoy, alone. The U-615 fired four torpedoes in a fan pattern. Only one torpedo hit the ship, and it was a dud. The U-boat chased the ship down and sank her with two more torpedoes. All sixty-nine of the Liberty ship's passengers and crew were killed.

Halfway across the Atlantic, the main body of Convoy HX-232 ran into a storm. The *Mormacmoon* scaled mountainous waves. She hung momentarily on the wave crests, and then slid down into the troughs. That kind of roller-coaster motion placed a strain on ships' hulls. One of the escort ships developed cracks in her deck plates and had to turn back. The commodore in charge of the convoy received a radio warning of a wolf pack dead ahead. He briefly changed course, but decided there was no avoiding the U-boats. Convoy HX-232 would have to run through them.

On April 11, the wolf pack code-named *Lerche*—"Lark"—attacked the convoy. A destroyer spotted a U-boat on the surface but did not bother to fire because the destroyer was rolling violently, and any shell aimed at the U-boat from the warship's guns might end up flying wildly into the air or straight into the sea. The escorts detected other U-boats by radar and sonar. Some escorts darted out from the convoy to drop depth charges on sonar targets. Every such foray by an escort left a temporary gap in the screen around the merchant ships. Early the next morning, an Australian destroyer left her position in the screen to investigate a radar contact, which turned out to be nothing. The destroyer was hurrying back into place in the screen when the U-563 sneaked into the gap she had left and fired a spread of torpedoes into the heart of the convoy.

Explosions shook three freighters. The first two sank quickly, leaving dozens of survivors adrift in lifeboats, including a group of women. Raymond was horrified that he could not stop for the survivors, but a rescue ship trailing the convoy picked up most of them. A fourth ship was torpedoed, bringing the toll to five, including the straggler. The *Mormacmoon* and the rest of the convoy kept going.

First light brought the convoy air cover in the form of Very Long Range (VLR) B-24 Liberator bombers based in Newfoundland. Liberators could fly at 290 mph, with a range of 3,000 miles—long enough to reach the air gap and essentially close it. Admiral King had not assigned the VLRs to convoy duty until March, when Roosevelt, alarmed by the surge in convoy losses, asked where the VLRs had been. The Liberators provided air cover for HX-232, scouring the ocean ahead of the convoy and forcing any U-boats in its path underwater. The planes thoroughly disrupted the wolf pack attack. One U-boat commander in the *Lerche* group complained, "Am continually being harassed by aircraft." Another U-boat was forced to crash-dive three times in the course of a few hours. By night, when the planes had to return to Newfoundland, the U-boats had fallen far behind the convoy. Doenitz urged them over the radio to race ahead and strike the convoy again before the planes returned at first light. But the U-boats did not catch the convoy that night, or ever. The *Mormacmoon* and thirty-three other merchant ships of HX-232 unloaded their cargo safely at Loch Ewe, Scotland.

The Allied antisubmarine forces built on their successes. The next major North Atlantic convoy, HX-233, lost only one ship. The convoy after that, HX-234, did not lose any.

The U-boats' losses, however, were soaring. Fifty-five U-boats were sunk in the first three months of 1943—the worst losses since the start of the war. Doenitz recalled many of his subs to their bunkers in April to repair the damage from a winter of pounding seas and near-miss depth-charge explosions. He sent the U-boats back out in May, hoping for a fresh start and a return to glory. But the Allied defenses had simply grown too strong. Another forty-one U-boats were sunk in May—"Black May" as U-boat men afterward called May 1943. The Germans were losing a U-boat for almost every ship they sank.

Part of the reason was that U-boat men were no longer Germany's warrior elite. The mounting casualties had reduced the number of top-flight volunteers, forcing Doenitz to increasingly fill his submarines with inexperienced men who did not want to serve in submarines. Studies after the war would show that a core of twenty U-boat commanders accounted for nearly a fourth of all the Allied tonnage sunk, and that many commanders accomplished little or nothing. Not every U-boat commander had what it took to charge into a convoy, wreak havoc, and slip away in the confusion.

Because U-boats often suffered their death blows deep underwater, their entire crews often died with them and were entombed in them. The growing list of U-boats lost with all hands included the U-124, whose young commander, Johann Mohr, had written a poem about sinking tankers off Hatteras. The list also included the U-507 and commander Harro Schacht, who had squeezed fresh limes into a jug of drinking water for the *Norlindo* survivors and told them to "come see me after the war." Lost as well were the U-125, which had torpedoed Genious Hudgins Jr. on the *Green Island*, and the U-563, which had slipped through the gap in the screen of convoy HX-232 and torpedoed three ships. And sunk too was the U-954, whose crew included Doenitz's twenty-one-year-old son, Peter.*

---

*Doenitz's older son, Klaus, was allowed to withdraw from the German military as a result of his brother's death, and was studying to become a doctor. A year after his brother, Peter, was killed on the U-954, Klaus Doenitz tagged along with some old friends from the military on a mission across the English Channel on a torpedo boat, and died when the torpedo boat was sunk.

Doenitz took each U-boat loss hard. When one was reported, he "would sort of go into his private room and sort of cry about it," his former chief of operations recalled. At month's end, shaken and most likely heartsick, Doenitz withdrew all his U-boats from the North Atlantic convoy routes. The Battle of the Atlantic, far from his defining victory, seemed to be lost, or at least slipping away from him. Black May had demonstrated how far behind the U-boats had fallen in tactics and technology. U-boats urgently needed technological upgrades, especially a defense against airborne radar. Without them, they were so vulnerable that Doenitz considered whether he should send them back out at all.

He ultimately decided he owed it to the Third Reich to keep going. Even though U-boats were no longer effective—even though they had become death traps—they still posed a threat that tied up hundreds of Allied escort ships and planes. If those ships and planes no longer had to worry about U-boats, they surely could be diverted to other missions against Germany. "I finally came to the conclusion that we had no option but to fight on," Doenitz wrote. Hitler agreed. "There can be no talk of let-up in submarine warfare," he declared. "The enemy forces tied up by our submarine warfare are tremendous, even though the actual losses inflicted by us are no longer great." The U-boats had become bearable losses.

Doenitz tried to rally the U-boat force with a message promising better days ahead. He said new radar-jamming equipment was coming. U-boats would be equipped with snorkels, long retractable tubes through which subs could draw fresh air while submerged. Conning towers would be better armored. Torpedoes would finally stay on course and blow up when they were supposed to. A new generation of U-boats would run faster and stay submerged all day. "The time will come," Doenitz promised his men, "in which you will be superior to the enemy with new and stronger weapons, and will be able to triumph over your worst enemy—the aircraft and the destroyer." But promises did not help the U-boat crews setting out on patrols in the spring of 1943. The predators were becoming prey.

CHAPTER ELEVEN

The Conveyor Belt

Eighteen-year-old Navy sailor Bernard Stansbury squinted up into the bright afternoon sun over the island of Sicily and saw two dozen planes approaching in a V formation. Bernard was a spotter for a Navy Armed Guard gun crew on the Liberty ship *Robert Rowan*. It was July 11, 1943, and the *Robert Rowan* was one of the first cargo ships to unload supplies after the Allied invasion of Sicily.

The ship sat at anchor in the harbor at Gela, on Sicily's southern coast, amid dozens of other vessels of the invasion fleet. Bernard's job was to watch for enemy planes. Normally, the sight of a large V formation would have spurred him and his gun crew into action. But they had been warned that Allied planes would fly over in a V formation en route to drop paratroopers farther inland. They were to hold their fire. One Allied parachute drop in Sicily already had turned disastrous when Allied ships mistakenly shot down 23 of their own planes, killing or wounding 229 men. So Bernard did nothing but watch the planes through his binoculars. They were passing at about 12,000 feet, like bombers. They were nearly overhead when Bernard saw swastikas on their tails.

"Those are German planes. Shoot!" he shouted to his gun crew. The gunners on other ships also recognized the truth. A wall of antiaircraft fire took shape, but it was too late. The men on the *Rowan* saw bombs tumble from the planes directly above them.

The Allied invasion of Sicily, code-named Operation Husky, had begun two days before. The invasion armada sailed from North Africa. It comprised seven Allied divisions and 3,300 ships—a larger force than even the one that would land at Normandy on D-Day. "There is no way of [describing] the size of that fleet," the war correspondent Ernie Pyle wrote of the Sicily armada. "On the horizon it resembled a distant city. It covered half the skyline and the dull-colored, camouflaged ships stood indistinctly against the curve of the dark water, like a solid formation of uncountable structures blending together. Even to be part of it was frightening. I hope no American ever has to see its counterpart sailing against us."

U-boats did not confront the invasion force on the 90-mile voyage from North Africa to Sicily, but German bombers from the Italian mainland took aim at Allied ships. German and Italian soldiers fought hard at Gela and at other pockets in the landing zone, but the invaders moved inland. The *Rowan* carried mostly artillery shells, with crates of small-arms ammunition piled on top, on the theory that an invading army would need bullets before artillery shells. The captain ran the *Rowan* right onto shore to get as close as possible for the Army DUKW vehicles. The "Ducks" were two-and-a-half-ton Army trucks balanced on flotation tanks and powered by propellers. They operated as floating shuttle barges, receiving cargo from the ships' cranes and then carrying it to the docks and up onto land.

Soon after the *Rowan* arrived at Gela, German tanks in the brown hills three miles above the harbor began shooting at the ship. Every minute or so a tank round fell into the water around the *Robert Rowan*. The shells arrived with a rush of air and a splash but did not explode when they hit the water. A few landed close to the ship. A tugboat towed the *Rowan* into deeper water, out of the tanks' range. The unloading had just resumed when Bernard Stansbury spotted the planes in the V formation.

Bernard was not a Mathews native but a "come-here," a vaguely dismissive term for anyone not born in the county.* He had grown up in Richmond but spent his boyhood summers and weekends at his family's cottage on Gwynn's Island. He sailed and sculled with some of the Callis boys, but joined the Navy instead of the Merchant Marine. He envisioned himself on a warship charging across the Pacific to trade volleys with the Japanese. But he was assigned instead to the Navy Armed Guard, a branch of the sea service established in 1942 to operate the guns being installed on merchant ships. Among Navy men, an assignment to the Armed Guard was widely considered undesirable, partly because of the danger of serving on merchant ships. Navy nicknames for Armed Guard units were "Sitting Ducks" and "Clay Pigeons." Armed Guard men recited a facetious motto, "Sighted sub, glub, glub"—a parody of "Sighted sub, sank same," the widely quoted comment of an Army pilot hunting U-boats. Bernard kept an open mind about the Armed Guard. He wanted to stay positive.

The delay in shooting at the German bombers proved disastrous for the *Robert Rowan*. Three bombs fell directly on the ship. They were falling too fast for Bernard to see them, but he heard a faint whistle and felt a rush of air. One of the bombs was a dud. It flew in through a cargo hold and was going so fast, it poked a hole in the hull on its way back out of the ship, into the water. The other two bombs fell directly into the sixteen-foot-square opening of the No. 3 cargo hold. The *Rowan* gave a slight jolt, and black smoke began streaming from the No. 3 hold. The bombs were incendiaries and had started a fire. Crew members wrestled two thick fire hoses across the deck, lowered the nozzles into the hold, and turned on the water. The fire was detonating the small-arms ammunition on top of the artillery shells. Live rounds ricocheted around the hold and flew out of the hatch in bursts. The men were afraid to get close enough to the edge of the hold

---

*Even a person brought to Mathews as an infant was regarded by the natives as a "come-here," although after long years of residence, he or she might jokingly be promoted to a "been-here."

to direct the hoses. The black smoke thickened and formed a smudge in the sky over the harbor. Every man on the ship was thinking about the artillery shells under the small-arms ammunition. Bernard and his gun crew stayed at their posts, watching an empty sky and stealing glances at the No. 3 hold.

After thirty anxious minutes, the captain gave the order to abandon ship, and men scrambled down cargo nets into Ducks, which ferried them to ships a safe distance away. The abandoned *Rowan* simmered for another hour and then exploded in a sheet of flame and a boiling cloud, with pieces of the ship pinwheeling thousands of feet in the air. The roar was audible for miles. The Liberty ship split in half and settled onto the shallow bottom with much of her superstructure still above water. The wreck burned furiously all night, lighting the harbor for enemy pilots. Bernard came away from the experience energized and feeling lucky. But the crew of Liberty ship *Timothy Pickering*, moored on another side of Sicily, was unlucky. A bomb landed directly in one of the ship's cargo holds and detonated tons of ammunition in one sudden, devastating blast, killing twenty-two crew members, eight Navy gunners, and one hundred British soldiers traveling on the ship. Flaming pieces of the *Timothy Pickering* flew across the harbor and hit other ships, killing three men on one vessel and starting a fire that blew up an oil tanker.

On July 27, 1943, the Hodges family suffered another blow with the death of Captain Jesse's father, John Thomas Hodges, at the age of ninety-three. John, who had grown up in Mathews, listed his profession in Census forms as farming. But like many in Mathews, he had eked out a living from farm work, carpentry, boatbuilding, and whatever other work he could find. He had lived through the Civil War in Mathews. He had founded the Macedonia Baptist Church there. Since the death of his wife, Sarah, years before, he had lived alone in a small brick house across the creek from Gales Neck. He was a frail man with a long white beard who sat on his porch with his chin perched on the tip of his cane. He liked to tell stories, and he credited his longevity to "hard work, good food, and abstinence from hard liquors." He was a gentler sort than his son Jesse, but not a man of means. In his will, he left six children and three of his grandchildren $10 apiece.

The Allies took Sicily by the end of July after losing 25,000 men, including nearly 10,000 Americans. They carelessly allowed three retreating German divisions to escape Sicily by crossing the narrow Strait of Messina to the mainland. Roosevelt reluctantly agreed with Churchill that the Allies should invade mainland Italy next, while building up another invasion force for France.* The Allied armies would land in far southern Italy and fight their way up the 750-mile-long Italian boot to liberate Rome.

The focus of the war in Europe had shifted to the Mediterranean. The clear, shallow, crowded Mediterranean was a nightmare for U-boats. Doenitz called it a "mousetrap." Just entering the Mediterranean through the Strait of Gibraltar was so challenging for U-boats that it was called "breaking in." Staying alive in the sea was almost as difficult. Allied planes were so numerous that U-boats had to stay submerged, blind to much of what was happening above them. But with the Allied victory in Sicily and eyes clearly turning toward Italy, Doenitz had no choice but to send U-boats into the Mediterranean. His men recognized what he was asking of them. Herbert Werner of the U-203 was crestfallen at first to be ordered to break into the Mediterranean. "But what difference did it make where we sailed?" he concluded. "It was all the same everywhere—furious attempts to destroy [the enemy] combined with desperate attempts to avoid being bombed, mutilated and sunk. It was like committing slow-motion suicide. The end was the same, only the name of the sea would change."

Captain Homer Callis of Gwynn's Island arrived in the Mediterranean in August. He had quit his desk job with the Bull Line in Baltimore after his old ship, the *Mae*, was torpedoed on its first voyage without him, leav-

---

* The Army chief of staff, General George C. Marshall, disagreed with the Allies' entire Mediterranean strategy and pressed for an immediate invasion of France.

ing Lester Smith maimed. He had taken the job ashore because it was a promotion, and to reduce the family's risk after his brother Mel was killed on the *Ruth*. But the *Mae* sinking had changed his thinking. He could not sit at a desk when the country needed sea captains. When he asked for a new ship, the Bull Line gave him the freighter *Cape Mohican*. His schedule was busy. The stops included Panama and Cape Town. He sailed up the Red Sea, briefly running aground on a sandbar not on the maps. The *Cape Mohican* hauled everything from ammunition to soldiers' mail.

Homer was unaccustomed to such long voyages and missed talking with his wife, Nancy. He and Nancy worried about their older son, Homer Jr. He never complained but they could tell from his letters that he did not like serving on a Navy destroyer in the Pacific. When his ship docked in San Francisco, Nancy flew all the way out to see him. Homer wrote to Nancy:

My Darling,

There never was anything as pleasant to me as that which happened last night when I was told your letter was waiting for me. It was such a swell thing for you to do, Darling, for it has seemed so many eternities since I left and not a word from you or anyone in that time. That has been the toughest part of my journey, and now I'm happy to know that you and my boys are alright and soon I shall have that greatest of all joys of seeing you again. I wish I knew how to say how badly I've missed you. I'll try to tell you when I come back and say all the other things that I've penned up in my heart to wait that happy hour. I know how long and hard these days are for you, but please God may you enjoy many more happy years with Homer Jr. and Bill. I'm so glad that he could [get leave from his ship and] come to see you. I wondered about that and I'm so anxious to hear about him. We've made out alright and are feeling swell with the knowledge that we will be home before very long. I wish I could notify you, Darling, but I can't send any messages so I'll have to wait until I reach a phone. I'll save all the other things I have to tell you until then too. All of my love to you and to Bill. Always.

Homer commanded the *Cape Mohican* through the Mediterranean with the same careful attention to detail he'd shown throughout his career. He took every precaution against U-boats and enemy bombers. But he was not expecting an attack by his own side. On the night of August 21, 1943, the *Cape Mohican* was sailing in a convoy between Sicily and Malta. One of the escorts picked up a U-boat on sonar and sounded a general alarm. The warships maneuvered, looking for the enemy. A torpedo exploded into the *Cape Mohican*, breaking the rudder and the main propeller shaft, and flooding the engine room. A Navy gunner was seriously injured. The ship stayed afloat but sat dead in the water. Homer assumed a U-boat had torpedoed them, but an inquiry later determined that a British destroyer had fired the torpedo after mistaking the *Cape Mohican* for a U-boat. The torpedoing was the fourth for the *Cape Mohican*'s radio operator, Jay Lopez, who had been sunk on the *Barbara* with Captain Walter Hudgins.*

The *Cape Mohican* was declared repairable, and towed to Malta and then through the Strait of Gibraltar toward a shipyard in Scotland. The tugboat's tow line snapped in a gale and the fully manned but crippled *Cape Mohican* drifted for fifty-two hours in heavy seas before the tug could retrieve the ship and finish the voyage. The ship needed major repairs, and the Scottish yard was already overburdened. Overseeing the work would take months. Homer's hopes of a quick family reunion were gone. He sent a telegram to Nancy saying, "Am OK All Love."

---

* Lopez was quoted in a magazine as saying, "I've sat in a lifeboat and made a vow that if I ever put my foot on dry land again I'd stay there. But when I get home, most of my friends are at sea, and I remember the friends who didn't get back. I guess it's a sort of personal fight with me."

Homer's headstrong sixteen-year-old son, Bill, reacted to his father's torpedoing by promptly joining the Merchant Marine. "I wasn't doing so good in school, and my father and brother were in the war, and I just figured I might as well be with them," he recalled. Nancy had seen it coming. She drove Bill to Norfolk to sign for him because he was underage. Bill filled out forms at the union hall, and someone at the Bull Line arranged for him to receive an able-seaman's license. He set out on a freighter hauling supplies to U.S. troops in North Africa, while Homer made the daily rounds at the shipyard in Scotland.

In Russia, the Red Army had finally stopped the German invasion and was driving Hitler's armies west, out of Russia, along a thousand-mile front. The Russians had revived some of their bombed-out defense plants but still needed weapons and munitions from their allies. Mathews men continued to make the dangerous, unpredictable run to Murmansk. None of them saw more of Russia than Captain Herbert Callis, a distant cousin of Captain Homer Callis.

Herbert, who had survived the sinking of the freighter *Norlandia* off Puerto Rico in July 1942, had set out in a convoy for North Russia in January 1943, in command of the Liberty ship *Thomas Hartley*. The voyage to Murmansk was rough. A bomb hit close enough to the ship to crack steam pipes in the *Hartley*'s engine room. Nonstop air raids reduced one crew member to a "mental case." After they reached Murmansk, the *Hartley* and the other ships in the convoy were held in port for months awaiting a convoy back home.

Herbert got so tired of sitting around Murmansk that he hitchhiked almost a thousand miles to Moscow just to have a look around. The fact that he could not speak a word of Russian did not trouble him in the least. While strolling through the streets of Moscow in August 1943, he happened to bump into the famous Russian correspondent for *Collier's* magazine, Quentin Reynolds. Reynolds was amazed to find a Virginia sea captain wandering the streets of Stalin's capital. He gave Callis a tour of the city and then quoted him in an upbeat article about how Russians coped with the rigors of war:

> Recently, Captain Herbert Callis, skipper of an American merchant ship temporarily anchored in a Russian port, came to Moscow for a week's vacation. I showed him around town. Captain Callis, whose home is in [Mathews], Virginia, made a rather profound observation on Russia's capital. "Friendliest town I ever did see," he declared enthusiastically in his Southern drawl. "And it's the truth that anyone in this town big enough to walk is wearing a uniform."

Reynolds concluded that Moscow "is a strange town, but it's a town of friendly people. No foreigner, and very few Russians, understand this country of paradox where the unusual is typical." The city "has not allowed the scanty food, the lack of fuel and the horror of a battlefront only an hour away by air to dampen its spirit or to shake its faith in its eventual destiny."

When the *Collier's* story ran, Herbert's family in Mathews was deluged with copies of the magazine from friends, relatives, and total strangers. The magazines were still arriving in September, when the Allies finally organized a homebound convoy. Herbert brought the ship into New York Harbor eleven months and twenty-six days after having set out for Murmansk. They became known as the "forgotten convoy." He and each of the others who took part were given hand-drawn certificates by the U.S. naval attaché in Murmansk saying they "did suffer 8 months confinement in North Russia and did undergo all privations connected therewith, that he did shiver through the Arctic winter and bask in the rays of the Midnight sun and by virtue of these facts is herewith declared to be a member of the forgotten convoy." When Herbert got home, he told his family he had rarely accepted food from the perpetually hungry Russians, and had subsisted for the entire eight months mostly on Spam, the canned meat "product" with a gelatinous glaze. Herbert told the family he "never wanted to see Spam again."

The Allies invaded the Italian mainland in the first week of September 1943. Italy's government quickly surrendered. Many Italians were weary of war and realized their leaders had picked the wrong side. The German occupation was harsh and unforgiving. The Allied invasion force came ashore at Salerno, just south of the great port of Naples, and raced to seize the port. No other port in Italy could handle the flow of cargo necessary to support the invasion. A U.S. soldier in Italy required at least half a ton of supplies every month, and more than 750,000 American soldiers would fight in Italy.

The Germans understood the importance of Naples. German field marshal Albert Kesselring, assigned to defend Italy, dispatched demolition teams to render the port unusable. They wrecked 130 vessels in the harbor, blew up 73 cranes, and toppled piers and dockside buildings into the water. They wrecked virtually everything in the waterfront area except churches, and planted booby traps. They set bombs with delayed-action fuses in un-damaged buildings, to explode after the Allies moved in. One such bomb detonated forty-two days after the Germans abandoned Naples.

The Allies went to work clearing the wreckage. Liberty ships unloaded their cargo into Ducks until docks were uncovered or rebuilt. After two weeks, 3,500 tons of cargo a day was flowing through Naples. After two more weeks, that number doubled.

Benny Fitchett of Mathews arrived in Naples in November 1943 on a Liberty ship to find the harbor still crowded with wrecks. German planes bombed the docks every night and sometimes strafed them during the day. Benny and his shipmates pulled on their gas masks in case the Germans dropped poison gas. The Allies thought Hitler might resort to poison gas, and shipped mustard gas to Italy so they would be able to retaliate in kind. Hitler, it turned out, used poison gas on the helpless in concentration camps but never on enemy troops. The Germans nonetheless unleashed the Allies' mustard gas against them by accident. On December 2, 1943, the gas was stored in the cargo holds of the Liberty ship *John Harvey*, docked at the port of Bari on Italy's Adriatic coast. The port was attacked by German bombers, and the *John Harvey* exploded, releasing the mustard gas over the waterfront. The gas contributed to the casualties, which exceeded 2,000 merchant mariners and military personnel. Secrecy by the U.S. and British governments prevented an accurate accounting of how many died from the gas.

As horrific as the losses at Bari were, they did not interrupt the flow of Allied cargo. America's war machine was running at full speed. New Liberty ships were entering the U.S. fleet at a rate of 140 per month. The average construction time for a ship had shrunk to 42 days. A total of 1,896 new Liberty ships would be launched in 1943, more than twice as many as in 1942. The Merchant Marine had evolved into an enormous conveyor belt of ships hauling supplies to every theater of the European war. Convoys crisscrossed the Atlantic and shuttled across the Mediterranean between North Africa and Italy. The belt kept running despite the German bombers and U-boats. During the fourth week of October alone, 363 Liberty ships unloaded their cargo in eastern Mediterranean ports. A new loop of the conveyor belt began delivering U.S. troops and supplies to Britain for the invasion of France, which was scheduled for the late spring of 1944. The final outcome of the war seemed less in doubt every day. But winning the war was no guarantee that your loved ones would come home alive. The war and the sea were too unpredictable.

On a chill night in October 1943, off the coast of Newfoundland, Paul Grubb of Mathews took part in a rescue that skirted the edges of myth. Grubb was first officer on the Bull Line freighter *Delisle*, which had been repaired and returned to service after Captain William Callis of Gwynn's Island ran her aground in May 1942 to keep her from sinking. Now the *Delisle* was in a small convoy heading south along the coast of Newfoundland when two ships near her were rattled by explosions. Grubb turned to the captain, William Clendaniel of Brooklyn, New York, and said, "I guess we will be the next." The men assumed a wolf pack had found the convoy, but, in fact, they had stumbled into a string of mines released by a U-boat.

As the last ship in her column, the *Delisle* drew the perilous duty of picking up the survivors of any ships sunk ahead of her. Captain Clendaniel and Grubb saw the red flashes of men's life vests in the water. The captain called down to stop engines. Before a lifeboat could be lowered, the *Delisle* struck a mine. The force of the explosion blew the little freighter's bow out of the water. The foremast crashed down on the bridge, knocking the captain unconscious and pinning him in the wreckage. While the rest of the crew abandoned ship, Grubb and Third Officer Alberto Galza struggled to free Captain Clendaniel, whose leg was trapped. They could see by matchlight that his trapped leg was a wooden leg. Grubb said he grabbed a fire axe and cut off the leg to free the captain, but Galza said he was able to unstrap the wooden leg. The men carried the captain to the main deck and lowered him by rope onto a raft. Galza said he then returned to the bridge, where the wreckage had shifted and released the wooden leg. He grabbed the leg and two puppies in training to become the ship's dogs, and brought them to the lifeboat. But a wave tore the leg and the puppies out of his hands and carried them overboard.

Captain Clendaniel spent several weeks in the hospital in St. John's, Newfoundland, recuperating from broken bones and pneumonia. He faced a long wait for a new wooden leg, the war having consumed the inventory. But a few days before he was to be sent home, his old leg was delivered to his hospital bed, "done up like a Christmas present, wrapped up in a fancy paper with a ribbon around it." Exactly how the leg got there was in dispute. The captain's hometown newspaper, the *Brooklyn Eagle*, reported that the leg had been picked up at sea by commercial fishermen, who passed it to the crew of a Canadian escort vessel. But a press release from the Maritime Commission said the leg washed up on shore near St. John's and was taken to the hospital by a beachcomber. The Maritime Commission awarded Galza the Distinguished Service Medal for saving the captain, and also noted that Galza had rescued a different shipmate with a wooden leg when the *Delisle* was damaged by a torpedo five months earlier.

After the mine sank the *Delisle* in October 1943, Paul Grubb went home to Mathews to recuperate. While he was there, an accidental explosion leveled a warehouse at the Navy Mine Depot in nearby Yorktown, killing six men. The sound of the blast carried across the lower Bay to Mathews, and Grubb threw himself on the floor of his living room. He would go back to sea, but for years afterward, any loud noise made him jump.

On the same day the *Delisle* sank, the tanker *Esso Providence* was unloading gasoline at Malta when a fire broke out in the ship's magazine. The magazine held .50-caliber antiaircraft rounds, artillery shells, and powder. The steel door blew open and flames and .50-caliber rounds flew out of the opening, setting fire to an abandoned hulk the *Esso Providence* was using as an anchor. The tanker's first officer, Leslie Winder, of the Mathews village of Hudgins, ignored the bullets and the fire and ran for the valve that would flood the magazine. The valve was in a padlocked box that was too red-hot from the fire to touch. Winder grabbed an ax from a lifeboat station and smashed the padlock. He pried open the hot box and turned the valve, burning his hands. He very likely saved the ship and many of the crew. "Windy" Winder was a big, florid man who liked to tell outlandish stories, but when a war correspondent interviewed him, he said, "Nothing interesting happened on the voyage. There was a fire and it was put out." He changed the subject. "I'm going on my vacation down home in Hudgins, Virginia. My father is going to kill a hog for me."

By October 1943, some of the gloom had begun to lift from Mathews. No Mathews mariner had been killed in almost a year. The convoy system had sharply reduced sinkings and deaths on ships that were sunk. A mariner whose ship was bombed or torpedoed in a convoy in Allied-controlled waters stood a good chance of being quickly picked up. The war stories on the front page of the paper were finally about Mathews soldiers, sailors, and airmen earning medals, and only sometimes dying in combat.

The danger of Mathews itself being bombed was declared officially over, and the volunteer plane spotters who had shivered in the Mathews fire tower were thanked for their "useful and worthwhile service" and sent back home.

Eleanor Respess was invited to the Bethlehem-Fairfield shipyard in Baltimore to christen the Liberty ship *John Russell Pope* as a tribute to her late, thrice-torpedoed husband, Mellin. She broke the bottle of champagne with one swing, and the *Pope* slid down the shipyard's ways and into the war. The sheer number of ship christenings forced the events to be shortened from lavish formal affairs to a few perfunctory speeches and the crash of a bottle on the hull. But the tradition ran too deep in the superstitious ranks of shipbuilders and mariners to be abandoned altogether in the name of efficiency. It was said that a ship denied her drink at christening would drink her crew's blood instead.

The Germans and the winter mud halted the Allies midway up the Italian boot, creating a bloody stalemate that dragged on for months, consuming thousands of lives and tons of supplies. Merchant mariners with free time in Naples caught rides inland and saw sides of the conflict others missed. Seventeen-year-old Jack White, who had never left Mathews before the war, rode a Liberty ship full of ammunition to Sicily and explored the ancient ruins of Syracuse and Augusta. In Naples, White borrowed a jeep and drove to the front lines. He was shocked to see how many Italians had been reduced to begging.

Another Mathews mariner, Jack Ward, hitched rides to the Italian front and spent time with American soldiers. They thanked him for bringing them food and ammunition, and always asked how people in America felt about the war. Jack said the public was fully behind it. He was impressed by how resolute the soldiers seemed, even after months of fighting. On one of Jack's forays inland, two officers in a jeep picked him up just ahead of a German counterattack. He spent the night with an artillery team and slept in a haystack. On his way back to Naples, he passed a house where an Italian family insisted on feeding him dinner. They had little to eat, and apologized for the poor quality of their wine. On the docks, Jack saw two beggars who collected rubbish together beat each other bloody over an empty coffee tin. One hot night when the ship was in port, Jack dragged his mattress up on deck in search of a breeze, and awakened to an air raid. Hot shrapnel from flak exploding above him as Allied guns fired at German planes whistled down in the dark and rattled onto the deck around him. He pulled the mattress over him and went back to sleep.

The Allies tried to break the stalemate in Italy in January 1944, by landing an invasion force on the beach at Anzio, the birthplace of the Roman emperor Nero. Anzio was behind the German lines and only thirty-five miles south of Rome. The strategy was to land troops behind the German lines and spread the lines so thin that they broke. The Allies poured 36,000 troops and 3,200 vehicles into Anzio the first day. But the Germans reacted quickly and pinned the invaders in a crescent-shaped expanse of beach. The Germans could not throw them into the ocean despite repeated attempts, but the Allied troops could not break out of the beachhead. Weeks passed. Churchill later wrote about Anzio, "I had hoped that we were hurling a wildcat onto the shore, but all we got was a stranded whale."

The survival of the Allied troops on the beach at Anzio depended on a stream of Liberty ships. They anchored a few miles offshore and sent the cargo to the beach in Ducks. For the crews of the merchant ships, being anchored off Anzio was a white-knuckle experience. Several times every day, the Germans fired at them with huge railroad guns hidden in tunnels in the hills above the beach. The guns, which the Americans nicknamed "Anzio Annie" and "the Anzio Express," flung six-hundred-pound shells at the Liberty ships. No ship had been hit, but every shot sent a spectacular geyser of water two hundred feet into the air. Nervous merchant captains demanded the freedom to move their ships if the shots got any closer. A high-ranking Navy admiral replied, "The chances of being hit by a shell from a shore battery are negligible . . . If shells are falling near you, there is no objection to your moving a few hundred yards, but remember that you are just as likely to move into as you are out of the path of the next shell."

Every night German planes attacked the anchorage off Anzio. They began each attack by dropping parachute flares. John Frederick Livesay of Mathews admitted he would "tremble with fear" when the flares illuminated his Liberty ship. The drone of bombers always followed. Livesay was relieved when his ship finished unloading at Anzio and sailed back to the relative safety of Naples.

The Allied invasion of Italy had forced the Germans to concentrate their aircraft in the Mediterranean, leaving few to attack convoys to Murmansk. But a ship on the Murmansk Run could still count on being attacked by the U-boats based in the Norwegian fjords, as Bernard Stansbury, returning to sea with the Navy Armed Guard, would see.

After escaping the fireball of the *Robert Rowan* off Sicily, Bernard was given command of a Navy Armed Guard unit on the Liberty ship *Penelope Barker*. In New York Harbor, the entire crew was issued heavy winter coats, boots, and mittens. His shipmates whispered they were going to Murmansk. Bernard had never heard of it. The *Penelope Barker* carried tanks, locomotives, steel, food, and containers of acid. The ship crossed the Atlantic to Scotland, joined a convoy, and headed north into the worst storm Bernard had ever seen. The *Barker* would climb to the top of a huge wave, then tilt down the back side of the wave, her propeller spinning crazily in the air, shaking the ship as if to pull it apart. Other ships in the convoy turned back to Scotland, but the *Barker*'s captain was afraid to turn. He thought the *Barker* might turn too slowly and be broadsided by the next huge wave. He rode out the storm, keeping the bow turned into the seas and wincing every time the propeller vibrated. The storm abated on the third day, and the convoy reassembled and set out for the Arctic. The convoy entered the Barents Sea on January 24, 1944. The ocean was relatively calm but the air temperature was below freezing, and the ship passed through snow squalls. Bernard finished his watch in the starboard gun tub and stopped to warm himself against the smokestack, which funneled hot exhaust from the ship's engines into the air. He leaned on the stack for about a minute, trying to decide whether to go for some coffee in the galley.

The ship was rocked by two torpedoes exploding only seconds apart. Bernard hit his head and lost consciousness. He awoke on his back with the heavy steel rim of the smokestack lying across his legs. He struggled out from under it and looked around. The gun tub he had just left was gone, blown to pieces. The ship was sinking. Bernard decided to check the crew's quarters to make sure everyone was out. He was going through the door when a merchant mariner shouted to him that everyone was out and the lifeboats were leaving. Bernard hurried to one of the boats. Two other men ignored the mariner and went into the crew's quarters, never to come out. The ship sank suddenly. Some men had no time to find life vests and jumped into the subfreezing water with only the clothes they wore.

The U-boat did not show itself. Sailors in an escort ship called to the men in the lifeboats to switch off the blinking red lights on their life vests. They said a rescue ship would return to the lifeboats after dark to pick them up. The rescue ship indeed arrived, and fifty-four of the sixty-nine men on the *Barker* survived. Bernard was one. It was his second sinking in six months, but this one affected him. Men had been killed. He had narrowly missed dying three times in only five minutes: being relieved from the gun tub just before the torpedo destroyed it, being struck with the smokestack rim, and then almost joining the two doomed men for a last search of the crew's quarters. Seventy years later, the memory would bring tears to his eyes.

The Allied troops at Anzio clung to the beachhead all winter, fighting off German attempts to push them into the sea. The Liberty ships not only kept them supplied, but continually delivered artillery shells to be stock-piled for an all-out attack to break out of Anzio. One of the Liberty ships helping to build the stockpile was the *Paul Hamilton*, which set out for Anzio from North Africa in April 1944, carrying 7,000 tons of ammunition and 504 American soldiers. Most of the soldiers were to be handed the task of clearing land mines the Germans had planted around the beachhead. The *Paul Hamilton*'s convoy was sailing along the coast of Algeria on April

20 when the convoy commander warned that an attack by German torpedo bombers was likely that evening.

The *Paul Hamilton*'s third assistant engineer was Charles Ogletree Billups Jr. of Mathews. Billups was thirty-two years old and came from an old Mathews family living on land granted to them by the King of England. Charles Billups had sailed on merchant ships in his twenties, but had gone ashore to work in a shipyard. When America entered the war, he obtained his engineer's license and went back to sea. The *Paul Hamilton* was his first ship in wartime.

Just after sunset, three German torpedo bombers flew toward the convoy at wave-top height. The Naval Armed Guard gunners threw up a wall of antiaircraft fire, but a light bomber slipped through a hole in the wall and released a torpedo at the *Paul Hamilton* at point-blank range. The ship exploded in a cloud of fire and black smoke that boiled 1,000 feet into the air, looming over an empty spot on the ocean where the ship had been. Nothing was left of the *Paul Hamilton* or the 580 passengers and crew. "The ship was observed to explode with such violence," a Navy report said, "it is now concluded there were no survivors." Charles's family received a telegram declaring him "missing and presumed lost in the performance of his duty and in the service of his country," but no other details.

On May 25, 1944, the Allied troops at Anzio pulverized the German lines with their stockpiled artillery shells, and broke out of the beachhead. They ran through the retreating Germans toward Rome. British and American troops broke the German lines farther inland. American and British armies literally raced to be first to liberate Rome. The world's attention, however, was about to shift to the Normandy coast.

On the eve of the D-Day invasion of France, tens of thousands of Allied soldiers, sailors, and merchant mariners sat on ships at anchor in the British Isles, waiting for the order to cross the English Channel. The invasion fleet comprised more than 5,300 vessels, including 1,213 warships and 4,100 cargo ships, troopships, and landing craft. The Allies originally had planned to invade southern France at the same time as Normandy, but had to postpone that part of the invasion because all the available vessels were needed at Normandy. The D-Day armada was the second-largest amphibious invasion in history—the one that had landed at Sicily was actually larger—but it was the invasion that all the others had been building toward, and the one that could fail. Among those waiting for the order to cross the Channel to France was Homer Callis's younger son, Bill.

Bill Callis had just returned to Gwynn's Island in May from his first deep-ocean voyage as an able seaman when Virgil Respess at the Bull Line office called. A job was waiting for Bill on a freighter that was preparing to sail from Norfolk. "I can't tell you where she's going," Virgil said, "but you might get a chance to see your father." Homer was in Scotland, still overseeing repairs on the *Cape Mohican.* Bill could guess that the ship was heading to a Scottish port, and he also guessed it would take part in the long-anticipated invasion of France. Bill packed a bag and his mother, Nancy, drove him to Norfolk.

The ship took on a full load of C rations in Norfolk and then sailed to Nova Scotia in a small convoy, which was then folded into a much larger convoy. Warships appeared at the far edges, barely visible. Bill had never seen so many ships. They telescoped out beyond the horizon in every direction. Bill's ship was near the center, as best he could tell. He heard reports of U-boat alarms on the convoy's perimeter, but never saw or heard anything. He was impressed by the choreography of the convoy. "It was amazing to me to see that many ships all sailing in formation," he said. "They would communicate changes of course by signal flags. The flags would go up, and all the ships would make the change at the same time. It was like a dance. Planes were flying overhead of us. We had more escort ships than I had ever seen before, even a teeny little escort carrier." For the rest of Bill's life, he would shake his head at the memory of the sheer size of the convoy. It was a pure expression of America's power, no longer restrained by the U-boats.

Two days before the Normandy invasion, on June 4, 1944, an American hunter-killer group off South Africa captured the U-505, which had torpedoed Captain Mellin Respess on the *Thomas McKean.* The Americans forced the U-boat to the surface with depth charges and sent a boarding party to secure the sub before the Germans could scuttle it. The commander of the hunter-killer group, Admiral Daniel Gallery, thought he had achieved a great feat by seizing the sub. But Admiral King was furious that Gallery had not just sunk it. King worried that if the Germans learned the U-505 had been captured, along with its Enigma machine, they might change the Enigma system again and cut off the Allies' access to their secret messages on the eve of the Normandy invasion. That did not happen. The Germans suspected from time to time that Enigma had been compromised, but always managed to reassure themselves that it was secure.

On D-Day, June 6, the narrow Channel was jammed with the Allied invasion fleet. Thousands of landing craft churned back and forth between troopships and the beaches. Allied warships pressed close enough to shore to shell the German coastal fortifications. Tugboats towed 75 old merchant ships into the shallow waters off the invasion beaches, and volunteer mariners scuttled the vessels to create breakwaters to absorb the Channel waves. The volunteers rigged the old merchant ships to sink, and then jumped onto tugs for a ride back to England. More than 5,800 Allied planes flew over the invasion fleet in the Channel.

"Every ship in the world seemed to be there," the captain of the Liberty ship *Cyrus McCormick* recalled. "There wouldn't be enough room to squeeze in another ship. You have to be constantly alert to avoid hitting somebody, or being hit . . . Constantly overhead are hundreds of our own bombers and fighters . . . Air power is overwhelming."

The overcrowded Channel was no place for U-boats, whose survival depended on their ability to hide. But Doenitz sent them anyway. He had expected for months that an Allied invasion force would one day fill the Channel, and had decided that when that day came, the stakes would be so high that "the U-boats must be there," no matter the cost. When the attack came, he quickly assembled thirty U-boats that were equipped with snorkels, which allowed them to draw fresh air while submerged, and sent them into a meat grinder. His orders made the mission sound like a suicide attack, which was not far from the truth: "Every vessel taking part in the landing . . . must be attacked regardless of risk. Every boat that inflicts losses on the enemy while he is landing has fulfilled its primary function even though it perishes in so doing." During the assault, the Allies sank twenty of the thirty U-boats in the invasion zone, killing 750 German submariners. The U-boats sank twelve Allied merchant ships, five escorts, and four landing craft—boats filled with men, but far too few of them to have any impact on the D-Day invasion. Morison, the naval historian, concluded, "The Allies were able to pull off the greatest invasion in modern history . . . and to sustain it by sea, with insignificant interference by U-boats. No more striking evidence of the collapse of Hitler's policy and Doenitz's strategy could be adduced."

Several days into the invasion, Randolph Payne of Mathews, a young messman on a Liberty ship, got a chance to go ashore at Omaha Beach. Young and perhaps naïve, he was excited, but he had not expected to see the bodies of scores of American soldiers, wrapped in white, awaiting burial, and he wished afterward that he had stayed on the ship. He told his family, "No one should ever have to see that."

Bill Callis's ship ended up being held in reserve off the coast of Scotland, in a lovely harbor beneath green hills dotted with sheep. The pastoral scenery was wasted on Bill, who wanted to be at D-Day. He learned about the invasion by reading a notice posted on the ship by the captain, who had received the news during a trip ashore. Three weeks later, Bill's ship finally unloaded its C rations at the great French port of Cherbourg. The Allies had just captured Cherbourg, which the Germans had left in the same ruined, booby-trapped condition as they had left Naples the year before. Bill's ship had to weave among sunken hulks to reach the dock. The ship was directed to a spot where Allied demolition teams had blasted away just enough wreckage for a ship to squeeze in. Bill walked out on the dock and picked up a German gas mask for a souvenir, but got right back on the ship. He was worried about mines in the rubble.

The Ducks unloaded Bill's ship at such breakneck speed that they kept sinking from overloading or careless handling. The men who drove them did not seem to care. They all wore life vests, and whenever a Duck sank, its crew climbed aboard the next Duck and got back in the rotation. Their lack of concern about the tons of cargo piling up on the floor of the harbor gave Bill a sense of how vast the D-Day supply operation was. By the end of June, the Allies had landed 200,000 troops on Omaha Beach alone, along with 68,799 tons of supplies and 27,340 vehicles.

Rome had been liberated in D-Day's shadow. In early July, the streets of the Eternal City were full of soldiers on leave, and full of rubble from bombed buildings. Jack Ward and a friend caught a ride from a port into Rome and wandered through the city to the Vatican, which had been spared from the bombs. The Liberty ships brought food not just for Allied troops but for starving Italians whose homes had been plucked clean by the retreating Nazis.

German armies were in retreat all across Europe, beaten down by a never-ending flow of American troops and supplies. The Germans would keep fighting for another year, but the U-boats were growing less and less relevant. The D-Day invasion troops forced the U-boats out of their bomb-proof bunkers in France and back to Norway, and they were being sunk everywhere. By the final months of 1944, three out of every ten U-boats that went out on patrol never came back.

Off the coast of France, a plane depth-charged the U-107, which had killed Ernest Thompson on the *Major Wheeler*. Off Africa, near the Azores, a bomber from an American escort carrier sank the U-575, which had torpedoed Captain Herbert Callis on the *Norlandia*. In the South Atlantic, a hunter-killer group sank the U-515, which had torpedoed the *Mae* and ruined Lester Smith's legs.

Lester, for his part, was back at home on Gwynn's Island. He had been re-leased from the hospital in British Guiana in June, and flown home. His fiancée, Lottie, had prepared herself to see his mutilated legs for the first time, but they were worse than she had expected. His left leg was artificial below the knee, and his right leg was heavily wrapped and still painful. A surgeon in British Guiana had grafted silver plating into the leg, but infection kept developing around the plating. Lester nonetheless was in excellent spirits. He was excited to be back in Mathews. He wanted to get married immediately. Lester had learned to drive with his artificial leg, and he and Lottie took rides in his red convertible just like before. He was already talking about going back to sea. Lottie couldn't believe he was serious.

CHAPTER TWELVE

War's End

Coleman Hodges, who had refused his sisters' pleas to quit sailing in war zones, had finally achieved his goal and was promoted to captain of the Liberty ship *Edward A. Savoy* in late 1943, at the age of thirty. He took the *Savoy* on a couple of short runs along the East Coast, and then was ordered to sail her to New York to take on cargo for a deep-ocean voyage. He was surprised to find that his new second officer was his nephew J. W. Corbett.

J.W., the son of Coleman's sister Elizabeth, was a quiet, slightly built young man. He had grown up on Gales Neck with Henny, and gone to work as a teenager on Captain Jesse's tugs. J.W. regarded his grandfather Jesse and his uncle Raymond as consummate mariners. He used one of Jesse's old sextants to take the ship's position by the stars, which was his favorite activity. J.W. had grown up watching his uncle Coleman running around Gales Neck with his brother David, playing pranks, raising hell. J.W. considered Coleman "a good, jolly fellow." But Coleman was all business on the bridge of the *Savoy*, and he would need to be. The crew was issued heavy winter clothing, which told the story: They were going to Murmansk.

Murmansk convoys had been suspended for most of the summer because of the pressing need for ships for the Normandy invasion and its immediate aftermath. The Russians were driving the Germans back, but the Red Army needed arms and food as badly as ever. The *Savoy*'s holds were filled with guns, ammunition, and food. Two narrow-gauge locomotives were lashed with steel cables to the ship's main deck.

The Murmansk run had grown less lethal for mariners since the first years of the war. The rate of sinkings of merchant ships fell from 12 percent in 1943 to 1 percent in 1944. But those were statistics. Murmansk was still the last place most men wanted to go. The Arctic weather and the U-boats, which were plentiful in the Norwegian fjords, still made for an anxious voyage.

On the eve of the convoy's departure from New York, Coleman and the other merchant captains were summoned to port headquarters on Battery Place in Manhattan to meet the port captain and the convoy's commodore. The merchant captains all affirmed their ships could maintain the convoy's planned speed of 10 knots for the entire Atlantic crossing. A large blackboard showed each ship in its assigned column and row. The *Savoy* was near the front, in the middle. The port captain handed out folders with sealed orders, codes, and other documents and the captains returned to their ships.

The next morning, December 19, 1944, the *Savoy* and seventy-one other merchant ships streamed out of the harbor at intervals of one ship per minute. They formed a line 19 miles long that took three hours and twenty minutes to clear the last channel buoy. Offshore, the convoy was joined by Canadian and British escort ships, as well as several merchant ships that had been delayed by a storm. The convoy formed into a rectangle nearly 7 miles wide and 1.5 miles deep, covering more than 10 square miles of ocean.* The convoy encountered no U-boats on its eight-day crossing until, almost within sight of the Irish coast, a British tanker was torpe-

---

* The convoy was not close to being the largest HX convoy; an earlier convoy had included 168 ships and 7 escorts and presented a front 9 miles wide.

doed, as was a rescue ship searching for survivors of the tanker. One hundred and twenty-five British seamen died.

The convoy split at the British Isles, as planned, with the *Savoy* and eleven other ships joining a larger group of ships at Loch Ewe, Scotland. Together, they formed a new convoy of thirty-one merchant ships, bound for Murmansk. They were surrounded by an unusually large escort force, including twelve destroyers, two escort carriers, a cruiser, and even the British battleship HMS *Rodney*. The *Rodney* was insurance against another PQ-17 debacle. If the *Tirpitz* or another German warship emerged from the fjords to attack the convoy, the *Rodney* had enough firepower to fight her. The escorts would not be told to withdraw. The merchant ships would not be told to scatter.

From Scotland, Coleman's convoy set out through heavy weather into the Arctic Circle. No German planes appeared, but nineteen U-boats in the *Panther* group waited for the convoy in the Barents Sea just east of Bear Island. The escort ships surprised the U-boats by racing out ahead of the convoy, forcing the U-boats to submerge. The escorts held the U-boats down with depth-charge attacks while the merchant ships steamed past the ambush. Five U-boats managed to fire torpedoes at the escorts, with no success. The convoy reached Murmansk intact.

As soon as they'd landed and J.W. was free to come ashore, he hiked up a hillside in the wrecked city to the only place that sold alcohol. All they had was cheap vodka. "It was rough stuff, barely drinkable, but they weren't stingy with it," said J.W., who choked down two glasses and then quit. Unloading the ships went quickly. As the date neared for the convoy to set out for home, the Nazi propagandist Axis Sally addressed the mariners over the radio. "We missed you on the way in," she purred, "but we'll be waiting for you to return." The *Panther* U-boats waited just outside the narrow Kola Inlet, the passage to Murmansk. The escorts tried the same tactic, racing out of the inlet ahead of the convoy and forcing the U-boats to dive. This time, one U-boat torpedoed the British frigate *Mounsey*, forcing her to quit the convoy and struggle back into Murmansk. But once again, the merchant ships escaped the U-boats' ambush. They plowed west through the Barents Sea in the direction of home. One gale after another swept down on them from the Arctic. No German plane could fly. J.W. had never been so glad to see bad weather. The skies did not clear until the convoy was approaching Scotland. From there, the *Savoy* returned to the United States. Coleman brought the ship into New York Harbor on December 17. He felt satisfied finally that he had done his duty to the country and his brothers.

Coleman did not make it from New York to Gales Neck in time for a festive dining on Christmas Day, 1944, to celebrate Captain Jesse and Henny's fiftieth wedding anniversary. The guests included 125 family, neighbors, and friends. Henny and her daughters cooked for days, preparing four turkeys, two hams, and platter after platter of fish and crackling biscuits. Henny enjoyed getting dressed up for parties, and the *Gazette-Journal* reported that she was in "a two-piece afternoon dress of grey crepe, with which she wore black accessories and a corsage of orchids." She and Captain Jesse cut a three-tiered wedding cake and exchanged rings a second time. Five of their nine surviving children were present—David, Alice, Elizabeth, Louise, and Hilda Fourteen—along with most of their twenty-four grandchildren.

After the guests had finished their shifts at the kitchen table, Henny gave the order to clear the living room for a square dance. The ice truck driver and his cousins played fiddle tunes. The dancers formed a circle and people took turns in the middle showing off. Hilda Fourteen "trucked"—a dance that included strutting while waggling the index finger. Sheriff W. E. Aldrich, a friend of the Hodges family, danced an old-fashioned jig.

No one at any point raised a glass to the Allied cause, or even brought up the war. No one mentioned Leslie or Dewey, whose framed photographs had been placed on the mantel above the fireplace. No one had told their seven-year-old niece, Stormy Heart, that they had been killed by U-boats. She assumed they were alive on ships at sea.

Raymond also was absent, though he really was on a ship at sea. Afterward, he wrote his sister Louise that he had just docked the *Mormac-moon* in New York on Christmas Eve after his latest trip to Europe, and was forced to remain on the ship to await orders. He wrote:

> Have just returned from a trip to France where things are not so very nice. We are in the habit of taking many of our boys over, so I see lots of our fighting men. Leaving in a few days for England or perhaps the north part of France and hope we have good luck again.

Captain Homer Callis spent the holidays at home on Gwynn's Island after eighteen months overseas. He had sailed the *Cape Mohican* halfway around the world only to be torpedoed by mistake and then stuck in a shipyard in Scotland. The *Cape Mohican* was finally back in service, and being loaded for her next voyage. Homer's wife, Nancy, picked him up at the docks in New York and they drove home to Dunrovin'. Nancy took Homer to see a new stained-glass window in the Gwynn's Island Baptist Church dedicated to his brother Mel. Mel's wife, Luna, had chosen an image of Christ praying for strength in the garden of Gethsemane as storm clouds swirl overhead. Nancy had contributed money on behalf of their side of the Callis family.

The couple talked about their sons. Bill seemed to be thriving in the Merchant Marine, but Homer and Nancy were not sure about Homer Jr., who was still on the destroyer USS *Hazelwood* in the Pacific. One of Homer's old crew members on the *Mae*, Jack Rowe of Gwynn's Island, had seen Homer Jr. at a supply pier in the Marshall Islands. Homer Jr. looked thin. He told Jack the Navy chow did not agree with him. Jack took him aboard his supply vessel and got him a huge meal. Homer Jr. protested but cleaned his plate. As he was leaving, he told Jack he was worried. The *Hazelwood* had experienced several close calls and he confided, "I feel like we are going to run out of chances." Jack was caught off guard by the comment and said they would all just have to hope for the best. He suggested Homer Jr. put in for a transfer to a different ship. But Homer Jr. smiled and said,

"No, I don't think I'll mess with it." Jack could not get over how much he looked like his father, whom Jack called Big Homer. When Jack got back to Mathews from the Pacific on leave, he told Nancy her son seemed fine. He did not see what good the truth would do her.

After his Murmansk run, in January 1945, Coleman Hodges set out in the *Edward A. Savoy* for Antwerp, Belgium. His nephew J. W. Corbett stayed on as second mate. Antwerp was the newest link in the conveyor belt carrying Allied supplies to Europe. The Belgian port on the North Sea was one of the largest in Europe, crowding the mouth of the Scheldt River with more than six hundred cranes, dock space for hundreds of ships, and rail connections to any part of Western Europe. Antwerp's cargo facilities and location made it the ideal supply port for the drive into Nazi-occupied Belgium and Holland, and then into Germany itself. The Allies had captured Antwerp largely undamaged, thanks to Belgian resistance fighters who harassed the German demolition teams trying to wreck the port. Hitler understood the importance of Antwerp. He had made Antwerp the final objective of the German counteroffensive in December 1944 that became famous as the Battle of the Bulge. After the Germans were stopped short of Antwerp, Hitler rained a special kind of destruction on the city, and it was still coming as the *Savoy* came into port

J.W. was standing watch on the *Savoy*'s gangway in Antwerp when he heard a growling noise behind him. Over his head flew a black object resembling a torpedo with wings. It was a German V-1 flying bomb, more commonly called a buzz bomb. Hitler, who called them "cherry stones," ordered dozens of them launched at Antwerp every day. The V-1 was not accurate enough to aim at specific targets, but its randomness magnified its power to frighten. The "V" in V-1 stood for *Vergeltungswaffen*, or "weapons of revenge." A buzz bomb flew until it ran out of fuel, and then dropped onto whatever was under it. The V-1 that flew over the *Savoy* stopped growling and fell onto a building a block away. The blast's concussion knocked J.W. off his feet. He got up, checked himself for injuries, and resumed standing watch. Black smoke rose from the building the buzz bomb had hit. A few days later, J.W. was in a hotel in another part of Antwerp when he saw a buzz bomb fly past the window.

The Germans also fired V-2 rockets, which carried more powerful payloads. V-2s were too fast to shoot down and made no sound as they were about to hit. A V-2 struck a movie theater in Antwerp and killed 567 people, including many merchant mariners and American military personnel, who were watching Gary Cooper star in the western film *The Plainsman*. The Germans continued pouring V-1s and V-2s into Antwerp even after they had been pushed back onto their home soil. The only city hit by more V-1 and V-2 rockets than Antwerp was London.

Captain Raymond Hodges finally came home to Mathews in the first week of March 1945. He had not been to Gales Neck for three years. Although the war was still going on, and he would soon return to it, Raymond's visit felt like a harbinger, a sign the war was nearing its end. There were other signs. The *Gazette-Journal* devoted most of the front page to the danger of forest fires rather than the war. A story described Representative Bland's effort in Congress to develop a postwar plan to sell off some of the nation's surplus war vessels without hurting the shipping industry. The front page even had a sports story about the Mathews High School baseball team sweeping a doubleheader.

Raymond invited the entire family to dinner at his farm in Gloucester. Captain Jesse, Henny, and about a dozen children and grandchildren put on their best clothes. Dolly had decorated the house in a style the Hodges had seen only in movies; to young Stormy Heart, visiting her aunt and uncle was "like going to the White House." The dining room had a big picture window overlooking green, rolling hills, where Raymond's cattle roamed. Raymond had taken an interest in raising beef cattle, though his sons did all the work.

Raymond greeted his guests in a coat and tie, of course. He was as confident and self-assured as ever. But the family could not help but stare at his hair, which had turned from brown to snowy white. Raymond told his sisters his hair had changed color overnight after a scare on one of his convoy runs. A ship ahead of him had been torpedoed, and he nearly ran over a lifeboat full of women and children. Raymond gave no further details. Navy records show that a ship with female passengers was torpedoed in convoy HX-232, in which Raymond's *Mormacmoon* sailed. The records do not mention a near miss between a ship and a lifeboat. All the women in the lifeboat were rescued.

Raymond assured Henny he would come through the rest of the war unharmed, and this time, it was easier to believe him. Henny acted like her old self most of the time, but since Dewey's and Leslie's deaths, her crying spells came more frequently. "When times were hard, she would cry a lot," said her grandson Jesse Carroll Thornton.

Captain Jesse still commanded tugboats, as did his son Willie, both of them staying in inland waters as the Hodges daughters had asked. Willie, in fact, would never sail offshore again. David Hodges had been promoted to head rigger at the shipyard. Spencer Hodges had quit the creamery to become a Mathews deputy sheriff. He would carry Spencer Jr. on his patrols as he had carried him on his ice-cream deliveries. Spencer would go on to become sheriff of Mathews, and Spencer Jr. would succeed him. Raymond and Coleman were still the only Hodges brothers at sea, Raymond ferrying U.S. soldiers across the Atlantic in the *Mormacmoon*, and Coleman hauling cargo on the *Edward A. Savoy* with J. W. Corbett as second officer.

Two more of the next generation of Hodges men had gone to sea, and to war—the sons of Willie and Raymond. Willie's son Horace, who was known as Brother, told his mother on the day he turned seventeen that he was joining the Merchant Marine. Brother was a serious young man who had driven a dump truck in Norfolk since he was fifteen without a driver's license. He told his mother he would be safe at sea. The U-boats "were pretty well whipped," and he would avoid getting drafted into the Army. His mother agreed. His father was on his tug and unreachable.

Raymond's younger son, Bill, also joined the Merchant Marine when he turned seventeen. Raymond suggested it. He did not challenge Bill to become a captain by age twenty-one, the way Jesse had challenged Raymond a half century before. Raymond told Bill only that the Merchant Marine needed men who knew how to handle ships. Bill had little interest in school and seized on the idea of following in the Hodges seafaring tradition. By the spring of 1945, just as many Hodges men served on merchant ships as on the day the United States entered World War II.

In February 1945, Bill Callis, Big Homer's younger son, signed on with a Liberty ship in Norfolk and was astonished to see Lester Smith employed as an able seaman. Lester had hounded the Bull Line and the union to let him go back to sea almost since the day he came out of the hospital in British Guiana. The Bull Line finally agreed to give him a chance to show he could still perform the physical work. Bill did not think Lester looked ready to come back. Lester's one whole leg hurt and sometimes bled. It did not slow Lester down, however. Bill noted that the new Lester, much like the old Lester, "would fight a tomcat after a few drinks." The ship sailed for the Pacific.

After the *Rowan* and then the *Penelope Barker* were sunk out from under him, Bernard Stansbury was offered a shore job, but he told his superiors in the Navy Armed Guard he would rather go back to sea. He ended up on another Liberty ship, carrying pack mules to India, where they would haul supplies across the Himalayas for General Joseph "Vinegar Joe" Stilwell's forces, descending into China to fight the Japanese. Several mules died on the voyage. The crew watched to make sure the carcasses were thrown to the sharks and not smuggled into the galley.

On April 12, 1945, President Roosevelt died at his retreat in Warm Springs, Georgia. His death shocked a nation he had led through the Depression and to the brink of victory in World War II. Part of the shock was due to the fact that he never allowed the public to see how ill he was. His death had special meaning for merchant seamen and sailors, who considered

Roosevelt a mariner at heart. "To the men of the sea Franklin Delano Roosevelt was a blood brother," the Masters, Mates & Pilots (MMP) maritime union declared. "His love of the sea, his pride in our Navy, his concern for our Merchant Marine and the welfare of 'the men who go down to the sea in ships' were part of his very life."

But the union's regret cut deeper. The unions had counted on Roosevelt to see that the government rewarded mariners for their service in the war. Congress had excluded merchant mariners from the G.I. Bill of Rights, passed in 1944 to provide military veterans with free college tuition and low-interest loans for homes and businesses. Some Navy and some veterans' groups opposed including the Merchant Marine. Roosevelt had signed the G.I. Bill despite its exclusion of mariners, but he had been pushing legislators to produce a new bill giving mariners at least some postwar benefits. "I trust Congress will soon provide similar opportunities to members of the Merchant Marine who have risked their lives time and time again for the welfare of our country," Roosevelt said. But Congress had not acted quickly, and Roosevelt's successor in the White House, his vice president, Harry S. Truman, was a midwesterner with no ties to the Merchant Marine, and different priorities. The sea unions now saw trouble coming. The MMP predicted that at war's end, "the scramble for land, jobs, new businesses, new merchandising methods will obscure and dim the heroism of the Merchant Marine. The public has a short memory." The MMP encouraged mariners to look out for their interests by steadfastly supporting the union. Unfortunately for the mariners, that would not be nearly enough.

Roosevelt's death did not change the course of the war. The Axis powers were collapsing. Allied troops crossed the Rhine River into Germany. The Red Army pressed toward Berlin from the east. In the Pacific, the Navy sank three Japanese carriers in the Battle of the Philippine Sea. U.S. forces recaptured the Mariana Islands and forced the Japanese back ever closer to their home islands. The news reaching Mathews from the Pacific was not all good. Shortly after Christmas, 1944, the parents of Wendell Hudgins, a young Navy sailor on the destroyer USS *Monaghan*, received a telegram saying his ship had been sunk in the South Pacific—by a typhoon. The *Monaghan* and two other ships in a Navy task force had been capsized by enormous waves in Typhoon Cobra after Admiral William S. "Bull" Halsey refused to allow the ships in the task force to break out of a refueling formation and maneuver to save themselves. Halsey had brushed aside warnings about the typhoon's growing intensity. On the three capsized ships, 756 men lost their lives.

The Japanese grew more desperate as the war turned more lopsidedly against them. On the island of Saipan, thousands of Japanese soldiers died in suicidal assaults on heavily defended Allied lines. As the Allies closed in on the Philippines, the Japanese turned to the suicide plane, the kamikaze.

Kamikazes flew directly into ships. They often carried bombs and extra fuel for added explosive power. The planes were mostly the fast and nimble Japanese Zero fighters. The pilots ranged from fanatical veterans to wide-eyed teenagers. Kamikaze attacks were well organized and used diversions. A decoy formation of planes would draw the attention of the targeted ships. Then three or four kamikazes—the designated killers—would race at the ships from a different direction. They would skim the ocean to avoid radar and bear down on their targets with machine guns hammering. The pilots were taught to aim at a ship's bridge, to kill as many officers as possible. Kamikaze attacks grew more and more frequent as U.S. warships approached Okinawa, which was just 350 miles from Japan.

Homer Callis Jr.'s destroyer, the USS *Hazelwood*, was off Okinawa on April 29, 1945, protecting the flank of an aircraft carrier, when a radio message warned of a possible kamikaze attack. Homer Jr. was on the bridge, possibly steering the ship. Three planes came into sight but banked away. Navy Hellcat fighters from the carrier rose to pursue them. The radio said two more enemy planes were inbound. A kamikaze roared low along the side of a second destroyer, the USS *Haggard*, and exploded into the hull near the water line. The *Hazelwood* was untouched, but was ordered to stand by the damaged ship to offer help as needed. She was still standing by an hour later when a kamikaze appeared without warning and raced straight at her. The *Hazelwood*'s gunners knocked the plane into the sea. Another kamikaze came at the ship from astern, almost brushing the wave-tops, strafing. The plane's right wing clipped the destroyer's aft smokestack, and the plane spun into the bridge. It exploded in a fireball, killing forty-six men, including Homer Callis Jr. His remains, like most of those in the blackened hulk of the bridge, were never identified. The crew put out the fire and saved the ship.

Nancy Callis received word of Homer Jr.'s death while she was alone at Dunrovin'. Her close friend Eleanor Respess was with her when her younger son, Bill, happened to telephone from San Francisco, where his and Lester Smith's ship was preparing to sail for the Philippines. Nancy broke the news to Bill with no emotion in her voice. Bill asked if she wanted him to come home, and she said, "No, I'll be all right." She contacted the Bull Line to get word to her husband, Homer, who was at sea. Homer wrote to her from the middle of the North Atlantic:

My Darling,

I am going to try to write a few lines to you every once in a while until I reach my next port and perhaps my effort might lessen the endlessness of these days and if possible bring to you a semblance of comfort insofar as may be possible for us to get comfort from the thoughts that are in our minds and hearts.

I've hoped and prayed for some word each day that would give back to us the joy of living again and with each message that comes to me from our Radio Room there is a silent prayer that it may be the one that we most want from life. What earthly joy it would be for me to have the happiness of telling you that all is well with our wonderful Son. The greatest day of life would be so small to compare with such a glorious event. We must hope even against hope, My Darling, until we know that there is none left.

Forgive me if the words I write are causing you a greater grief, but I can't seem to think of anything but that fate has turned its eye away from us and I hate the knowledge that it has hurt so much you, who have been such a wonderful mother. We love you, Darling, but I know that a mother's love is so great that no other love can erase or minimize the pain of the loss of her son. But if our love and devotion to you can help to salvage anything that is left to bring you peace and comfort I know that the rest of my life is justified. You have always been a wonderful wife and mother and it has been with gratitude always that we have been privileged to belong to you. For us there couldn't have been a greater glory and we know that you will always be wonderful even in your sorrow. Good night, Darling.

The Navy confirmed Homer Jr.'s death a few days later.

The day after the kamikaze killed Homer Jr., Hitler committed suicide in his bunker in Berlin. In his will, he designated Doenitz as his successor as leader of the Third Reich. Hitler at the end seemed to see Doenitz as a loyal professional on a staff of traitors and cowards. Doenitz told the German people in a speech that Hitler "has fallen," and exhorted them to fight on. He knew Germany had lost the war, but wanted to give retreating German troops time to escape a massacre by the Russians. Sixty-two U-boats remained at sea, and they continued to sink ships and be sunk. On May 4, 1945, Doenitz finally ended the U-boat war with a terse message to his commanders: "All U-boats cease fire at once. Stop all hostile action against allied shipping."

One U-boat did not receive his message immediately. The U-853 was at periscope depth off the coast of Rhode Island, lining up a torpedo strike, when Doenitz broadcast his cease-fire message. A submarine could not receive radio transmissions while submerged. The U-boat commander fired a torpedo into the starboard side of the collier *Black Point* as she passed Point Judith, Rhode Island, with a load of coal. The ship sank quickly, taking twelve crewmen with her. The *Black Point* got off a distress call that brought two destroyer escorts and a Coast Guard vessel. The three ships located the U-boat with sonar and depth-charged it until its insides burst to the surface in a mass of debris, including a U-boat officer's cap. There were no survivors.

Four days later, on May 8, the Bull Line's main office in New York sent a radiogram to all the company's ships at sea:

> GERMANY HAS SURRENDERED UNCONDITIONALLY.
>
> CEASE FIRE HAS BEEN ORDERED FROM 10 P.M. EIGHT MAY.
>
> PENDING FURTHER ORDERS ALL EXISTING INSTRUCTIONS REGULATING THE DEFENSE SECURITY AND CONTROL OF MERCHANT SHIPPING ARE TO REMAIN IN FORCE.
>
> MERCHANT SHIPS AT SEA WHETHER IN CONVOY OR SAILING INDEPENDENTLY ARE TO CONTINUE THEIR VOYAGES AS PREVIOUSLY ORDERED.

Doenitz had hoped the U-boat force would be allowed to destroy its submarines in a symbolic ceremony. The Allies, however, insisted that all U-boats be surrendered intact. Doenitz told his commanders to hoist black flags of surrender and sail to the nearest Allied or neutral port. U-boats surrendered at the docks of Cape May, New Jersey, and Portsmouth, New Hampshire. One defiant U-boat commander committed suicide in a Boston prison by smashing his eyeglasses and cutting his wrists with the shards of glass. U-boats surrendered at Halifax, Nova Scotia; St. John's, Newfoundland; Bergen and Narvik, Norway; Gibraltar, Spain; Loch Foyle, Scotland; and Liverpool, England. Two U-boat commanders let their crews vote on whether to surrender. They voted to run for Argentina to try to escape capture. Argentine authorities turned over the rogue U-boats and crews to the U.S. Navy.

Numerous damaged and mothballed U-boats were discovered by Free

French troops entering the abandoned concrete U-boat bunkers on the French coast. Among those U-boats were Hardegan's U-123, which had killed Ernest Thompson on the *Norvana* and Frank White on the *Muskogee*, and the U-129, which had sunk the *Mary*, *Millinocket*, and *Onondaga*, killing Dewey Hodges, Mellin Respess, Genious Hudgins, William Hammond, and Lewis Callis.

Months after the war ended, the British destroyed most of the surrendered U-boats in a naval gunnery exercise. But as after World War I, a few U-boats were given to other Allied nations for testing and publicity. One was secretly towed up the Chesapeake Bay, right past Mathews. The U-505, which had torpedoed Mellin Respess on the *Thomas McKean* and then had been captured just before D-Day, was sailed up and down the U.S. East Coast by American sailors, docking at coastal cities to serve as an attraction for War Bond rallies. The U-505 drew 13,200 people during a five-day visit to Norfolk.

Germany's surrender ended only the Atlantic war, of course, and much of the Merchant Marine's work simply shifted to the Pacific. "The end of organized resistance in Germany brings no lessening of any of the tasks of the United States Merchant Marine," the Maritime Commission told mariners in a radiogram. "Closing of hostilities in the European theater means . . . a situation unchanged basically except for a shift in emphasis in time and places. There will be no lesser demand for ships or for men to sail them." The Maritime Commission estimated that 70 percent of the surplus war equipment in Europe would be shipped 13,000 miles to the Pacific.

But the end of the Pacific war was near as well. In April 1945, Captain T. O. Rainier of Mathews docked his troopship *Cape Victory* at Seattle, Washington, and took aboard 1,400 Army Air Forces personnel in an atmosphere of great secrecy. The *Cape Victory*'s crew was confined to the ship, and Rainier was allowed ashore only in the company of an Army Intelligence officer, who listened to his phone calls. Rainier had to use a private phone because all the pay phones on the pier had been disconnected. Finally, he was ordered to take the airmen to the remote island of Tinian in the Marianas chain. The elaborate secrecy puzzled Rainier. He had been ferrying troops across the Pacific for three years. He saw from the airmen's uniforms that they were B-29 bomber personnel with specialized ratings. He finally asked a colonel from the squadron what was up. The colonel deflected his question and told Rainier, "Give us four and a half months, and if Tokyo isn't flat, then turn your guns on us." Rainier had no idea what the colonel meant. He would not realize for years that he had delivered most of the crew and support personnel of the B-29 Superfortress *Enola Gay*, which would fly from Tinian to drop the first atomic bomb on Hiroshima, Japan, on August 6, 1945.

Another Mathews man helped deliver the uranium-235 for the atomic bomb to Tinian. William Franklin Hale, a Navy seaman 2nd Class, served aboard the heavy cruiser USS *Indianapolis*, which stopped at Tinian to drop off a vial of the subcritical uranium. Then Hale and the *Indianapolis* were sent across the Philippine Sea alone, with no equipment for detecting submarines. A Japanese sub torpedoed the cruiser, casting approximately 900 American sailors into the North Pacific. Many had only life preservers to keep them afloat. The Navy inexcusably lost track of the *Indianapolis* and did not know she was missing until four days later, when a patrol plane spotted the oil slick. In the meantime, the men in the water died of thirst, exposure, drowning, and ferocious attacks by oceanic whitetip sharks, which pulled men screaming from the cluster of swimmers. As many as 80 men may have been killed by the sharks. Only 316 of the 900 *Indianapolis* sailors who went into the water survived. William Hale was among the lost.

The Navy withheld news of the sinking until after Japan surrendered. Hale's daughter Betsy was only two years old at the time. She would know nothing about the circumstances of the *Indianapolis* sinking until decades later, when she started attending reunions for *Indianapolis* survivors and their families. She met a close friend of her father's. He showed her a snapshot of the two of them in a photo booth. Betsy asked him if he knew how her father died. She wanted to hear he had died in the ship and not in the water. The man said he did not know how her father died, but his expression made Betsy wonder.

The second atomic bomb was dropped three days after the first, on August 9, 1945, on Nagasaki. Japan surrendered on August 15. The war's end set off wild celebrations in New York, Norfolk, and other cities across the United States. Mathews did not celebrate. A few drivers tooted their horns as they passed the courthouse on Highway 14. The stores on Main Street closed at 7 p.m. when President Truman announced Japan's surrender, and stayed closed the next day, even though it was Wednesday. The *Gazette-Journal* soberly welcomed the end of anxiety "which shadowed practically every home." The paper observed:

> With so many local boys still far away from home, the general attitude seemed to be one of quiet, thoughtful thanksgiving, that with the war's end they are no longer in great danger. Many remembered, too, those fine fellows who, having given their lives in the war, will not return. And so, it was not difficult to restrain any urge there might have been to blow off in any extremely hilarious celebration at this time.

The Merchant Marine losses in the war were staggering. The official mariner death toll announced by the Maritime Commission at the war's end was 5,662, but government records on mariners' deaths were spotty and did not include deaths of American mariners on foreign ships. Subsequent tallies by merchant mariners' support organizations turned up more than 3,500 additional deaths, for a total of roughly 9,300. The exact number of American merchant mariners killed in World War II may never be known.

Mathews County—population 7,500—lost 23 mariners to torpedoes, bombs, fires, explosions, shark attacks, drowning, exposure, hunger and thirst, and other violent ends as their ships plunged into the depths. None of their families learned exactly how they died, or had the opportunity to bury them. The deaths touched every corner of Mathews. Every family in the county lost a member, relative, or friend.

The U.S. Merchant Marine's fatality rate in World War II was approximately 3.9 percent—one of every 26 mariners who sailed on a merchant ship. The only branch of the U.S. military with a comparably high fatality rate was the U.S. Marines. The casualty rate for the U.S. Navy was 1.49 percent—less than half the casualty rate of the Merchant Marine. British seaman had borne the brunt of the U-boat war for two years before America entered. The British lost 32,000 merchant seamen in World War II, almost a quarter of Britain's total war deaths.

The most staggering losses, however, belonged to the German U-boat force. Of the roughly 39,000 men who served in U-boats during the war, more than 27,000 were killed. That fatality rate of nearly 70 percent was, and is, the highest for any fighting force in modern warfare. Of the 830 U-boats commissioned to serve in World War II, 717 were sunk.

American merchant ships delivered more than 300 million tons of war cargo, including ammunition, explosives, aircraft, aviation fuel, tanks, trucks, landing craft, jeeps, ambulances, locomotives, food, clothing, and medicine. No Allied invasion force was ever thrown back for want of arms, food, supplies, or munitions. "Our merchant seamen displayed their highest qualities," Churchill wrote, "and the brotherhood of the sea was never more strikingly shown than in their determination to defeat the U-boat." Even Admiral King had praise for the Merchant Marine: "During the past three and a half years, the Navy has been dependent upon the Merchant Marine to supply our far-flung fleet and bases. Without this support, the Navy could not have accomplished its mission. Consequently, it is fitting that the Merchant Marine share in our success as it shared in our trials."

King prepared to retire and reap praise for his role in winning the war. In September 1945, he rode at the head of a two-and-a-half-mile-long victory parade through the streets of his hometown of Lorain, Ohio. An estimated one hundred thousand people lined the parade route, and confetti swirled through the streets. Warplanes flew in formation overhead. Ohio governor Frank J. Lausche praised King as "Ohio's most illustrious son, one of the leaders who helped pave the way" to victory. King had indeed done just that, but historians on both sides of the Atlantic would call his failure to protect merchant ships and mariners in coastal waters in 1942 a terrible error. The German naval historian Jürgen Rohwer called King's slowness in setting up coastal convoys "one of the greatest mistakes in the Allied conduct of the Battle of the Atlantic." The British historian Martin Middlebrook called it "almost criminal." American historian and author Michael Gannon compared the sinkings in the first half of 1942 to "an Atlantic Pearl Harbor" that dragged on for six months. A few historians have defended King, including the late Clay Blair, who said King did all he could and that suggesting otherwise was "absurd."

In the midst of the victory celebrations, the United States set out to dismantle the huge fleet of merchant ships it had built to win the war. The nation could not afford to sustain that fleet. America had finished World War II with more than five thousand merchant ships—five times as many as at the start of the war, and 54 percent of all the merchant ships in the postwar world. Most of those ships were owned by the government. So in 1945, the Maritime Commission began selling off the Liberty ships and other vessels for as little as one-third the construction price. The ships were sold not just to American companies and investors, but to buyers in Britain, Norway, and other Allied nations whose merchant fleets had been decimated by the U-boats. Among the beneficiaries of the sell-off was the Greek businessman Aristotle Onassis, Jacqueline Kennedy's future husband, who bought tankers from the United States. Helping rebuild the Allies' merchant fleets was a worthy goal, but dumping almost two thousand new ships on the global market was a gamble. The new owners would use the ships to compete directly with established American shipping companies. The sell-off would be the first step in the U.S. Merchant Marine's long decline.

At the war's end, however, merchant ships and mariners were busy, busier in fact than they had been at any point *during* the war. The nation's first priority was bringing home more than 1 million soldiers from overseas. Raymond Hodges carried six loads of troops from Liverpool to New York on the *Mormacmoon* in late 1945 and early 1946 without stopping on either side of the ocean for more than a few days. Captain Frank G. Boyer of Mathews brought home 5,000 soldiers on three consecutive trips to the Pacific on a troopship, stopping in Mathews only to spend New Year's Day in 1945 with his family. The soldiers came home to brass bands and red-white-and-blue bunting. The mariners who delivered them receded into the background. When they arrived in port, they got a couple of days off and then a call to return to the ship to pick up another load of troops.*

On their return trips to Europe, merchant ships hauled food and supplies to the European nations devastated by the war. They carried grain, steel, chemicals, tools, construction equipment to repair bombed cities, and explosives to level what could not be saved. Cargo would continue to surge in 1948 when Secretary of State George C. Marshall announced the Marshall Plan to ship an additional $17 billion worth of supplies to help rebuild Europe and forestall the spread of Communism. Norfolk became an export center for American livestock to Eastern European countries whose native animals were eaten or slaughtered by passing armies.

Brother Hodges made several trips to Poland on Liberty ships hauling chickens, cows, and horses. On one voyage, the horses began suffocating due to poor ventilation in the holds, and the captain abandoned caution and steamed full speed through the fog all the way to port. On another trip, Brother arrived at the docks in Odessa, Russia, on a ship carrying mostly horses. The horses were kept on deck in wooden stalls. A company of cowboys from Pennsylvania fed them and shoveled their shit overboard. Brother got off the ship and saw his uncle Raymond's *Mormacmoon* docked

---

* Two years later, merchant ships would bring home the bodies of many of the 150,000 Americans who were killed overseas but whose families wanted to bury them in American soil.

a few berths away. Raymond went to the gangplank and spoke to a black messman he recognized as a Mathews man. Raymond was dealing with an oil spill but the messman promised to get word to him. Later, Raymond sent a seaman to invite Brother to dinner. Raymond and his officers all dined in uniforms and jackets; Brother's best clothes were dungarees and a sweater. Brother was surprised to be served a steak and fresh milk; most of the food he ate was canned. After dinner, Raymond and Brother smoked cigars while looking out over the Black Sea.

CHAPTER THIRTEEN

Legacy

No sooner had the war ended than Captain Jesse and Henny Hodges sold their farm on Gales Neck. The Hodges children were surprised but they understood. Henny was seventy-one years old. She simply could no longer handle the work. Jesse was seventy-four. His legs were no longer strong enough to carry him up and down ships' ladders. He tried working on tugs and even fish steamers in the Bay, but it was no use. After more than six decades at sea, he had to stay ashore. "I'm dying," he complained to his niece Stormy Heart.

Jesse and Henny bought a large, wood-framed house in the village of Hudgins. The new house was only a few miles from Gales Neck, but it was dramatically different. It had four acres to farm instead of forty. It stood right on State Route 14, the main road through Mathews, and was only a five-minute walk from a country store. The new house had no indoor plumbing, but it had electricity, oil heat, and a well much closer to the kitchen than the well at Gales Neck.

As soon as they were set up in their new home, Captain Jesse and Henny held a dining. Henny did what she had always done at Gales Neck: prepared a huge meal, orchestrated all the activity in the house, and withdrew from time to time to cry. Her sons Willie, Coleman, and David brought their families, as did her daughters Alice and Louise. Leslie's widow, Cecile, did not attend. Although she remained in close touch with Henny, Cecile had never felt comfortable at the boisterous dinings. Dewey's family did not come either. The long trip from Norfolk to Mathews by car and ferry was too arduous without Dewey behind the wheel of the Buick Zephyr, cracking jokes and crooning "Mexicali Rose."

Other Mathews families felt the war's aftershocks as well. The father of Bernard Pierson, who had died on the *East Indian*, looked up one day from the counter of a store he ran on Gwynn's Island to see an unfamiliar young man standing in front of him, struggling to speak. The man finally said, "Your son gave his life to save me." He was the seaman who had been badly injured and lying on a raft when Bernard insisted on giving him his spot in the *East Indian*'s only lifeboat, hundreds of miles off Cape Town. Only the men in the lifeboat had survived; Bernard and the others on the rafts were never seen again. The young man had traveled down from New York to tell the story to Bernard's father.

In October 1945, the family of a young Navy machinist's mate named William Burton Gay, who had been missing since the fall of Bataan, learned in an official telegram that he had died two years earlier, in the brutal Japanese prison camp at Cabanatuan in the Philippines.

A month later, Captain Otis Levering Callis of Gwynn's Island, who had spent the war sailing the Liberty ship *Benjamin Chew* back and forth across the Atlantic without incident, was killed in a car accident thirty minutes from Mathews. His ship had just returned a few days earlier from India.

After more than a year, Salome Hudgins finally abandoned hope that her husband, Genious, had survived the sinking of the *Onondaga* in July 1942, and would return to her from a foreign hospital or deserted island. Salome had kept every letter Genious ever wrote. As a last farewell to him, and perhaps a symbolic new start for herself, she carried most of his letters into the backyard and burned them.

The official verdict on the U-boats' conduct of the war against merchant shipping came in 1946 near the end of the Nuremberg trials, in which twenty-two former Nazi leaders, including Karl Doenitz, were tried for war crimes by a military tribunal. Doenitz maintained a rigid dignity throughout the proceedings. He resented his jailers for taking his razor away. "I wouldn't commit suicide," he said. "That would be cowardly."* Doenitz and his lawyers convinced the judges that he had been promoted late into Hitler's inner circle and knew nothing about the death camps and other atrocities the Nazis perpetrated on land. But for Doenitz's conduct of the U-boat war, he was charged with "murder and ill-treatment of persons on the high seas"—specifically, with ordering his men to kill the survivors of torpedoed ships and to leave other survivors to die without hope of rescue. Doenitz testified in his own defense. He expressed no regrets. He pointed out that he had insisted in the final days of the war that all the U-boat force's records be kept intact, while other branches of the German military were destroying theirs. He argued that Allied merchant ships had forfeited all claim to noncombatant status by carrying guns and depth charges, and by radioing the locations of U-boats to Allied antisubmarine forces. Doenitz's lawyers introduced evidence showing that British warships had sunk German ships they could easily have seized and brought into port under the so-called prize rules. The defense's most powerful evidence was a sworn affidavit from Admiral Chester Nimitz, commander in chief of the U.S. Pacific Fleet during the war, acknowledging that American submarines had routinely sunk Japanese merchant ships without trying to aid survivors. One of the American judges on the Nuremberg tribunal, Attorney General Francis Biddle, favored acquitting Doenitz because his U-boats had "waged

---

* Doenitz may have been referring to Heinrich Himmler, who oversaw the Nazi death camps. While Doenitz and other leaders of the German government were being arrested, Himmler was caught trying to slip out of Germany on a phony passport. When a doctor tried to examine his teeth, Himmler committed suicide by swallowing a cyanide pill hidden in his mouth.

a cleaner war than we did." But a majority of the judges convicted Doenitz and sentenced him to ten years in Spandau prison—the lightest sentence for any of the nineteen defendants convicted at Nuremberg.* The judges added somewhat ambiguously that Doenitz's sentence was "not assessed on the grounds of his breaches of the international law of submarine warfare," given the Allies' conduct of the sea war. Admiral Gallery, who had scoffed at the idea of trying to hold U-boats to the prize rules, would later accuse the Nuremberg tribunal of "barefaced hypocrisy" in convicting Doenitz. Gallery said Doenitz's only offense was "almost beating us in a bloody, but fair, fight."

Doenitz would live in Germany until his death on Christmas Eve, 1980. A long line of old U-boat men filed past his casket.

The real verdict on unrestricted submarine warfare, however, was handed down in the corridors of power in Washington, D.C., and Moscow even before World War II ended. Submarines already were evolving into a role in the Cold War more significant than anything Doenitz had ever imagined. By 1946, Travers Thompson of Mathews, who had joined the American submarine force after a U-boat killed his father, was in a sub patrolling the North Pacific for Soviet subs. His next submarine would carry long-range ballistic missiles, preprogrammed to strike Russian cities in the event of a nuclear war with the Soviet Union.

Mathews men felt the first chill of the Cold War on the docks in Eastern Europe. Benny Fitchett of Mathews got his introduction on a wintry afternoon in the Baltic Sea port of Gdynia, Poland. The Russians had seized Poland from the Germans during the war, and made it clear they intended to keep Poland. Benny arrived in Gdynia on a Liberty ship delivering horses. While the ship was being unloaded, he noticed a huge warship at

---

* Three of the twenty-two Nuremberg defendants were acquitted of all charges. Twelve other defendants, including Field Marshal Hermann Goering, the head of the *Luftwaffe*, were sentenced to hang.

the end of a long stretch of empty wharves. He and a friend had time to kill, and hiked to the vessel for a closer look. The warship was the old German battleship *Schleswig-Holstein*, scuttled by her crew on the shallow bottom before the Russians took the port. The warship looked deserted. Benny noticed a red flag on the stern, which caused him to pause but not stop. He and his shipmate walked across a gangplank onto the vessel and then down a passageway with a low overhang, which gave the passageway the feel of a long tunnel. Within seconds, Benny realized they had made a dangerous error. A man's silhouette crossed the opening at the far end of the passageway, followed by a second silhouette. Benny whispered to his friend to keep walking and hand him all his cigarettes. When the mariners reached the opening at the end of the passageway, two uniformed guards carrying rifles stepped in front of them. One of the guards held out his hand for the mariners' identification documents. Benny tried to explain that he and his friend meant no harm and just wanted to get back off the ship. He felt his heart banging in his chest. If he was taken prisoner on this derelict vessel, no one would ever know what had happened to him. Benny handed over all of his and his friend's cigarettes to the guards, who accepted them without a word or a change of expression. The guards spoke to one another in Russian. Then they returned the men's documents, and gestured toward the gangplank. Benny had to fight the urge to run across it to safety.

Mathews slowly regained its prewar rhythms as the restrictions imposed by the war fell away one by one. The end of rationing of gas and rubber revived the Saturday-night gatherings on Main Street. The Mathews County Fair resumed, as did the Mathews High School graduation ceremonies. The first postwar commencement ceremony in 1946 attracted more than one thousand people, the largest turnout anyone in Mathews could remember. The county held a four-day series of sailboat races that drew large crowds. Plans were laid to establish a Mathews yacht club, of which Lester Smith eventually would become president.

Captain Walter Hudgins. Denied an officer's commission in the Navy for being too old, he commanded merchant ships and survived two sinkings.

CREDIT: COURTESY OF ELLIOTT HUDGINS
© 2015 ELLIOTT HUDGINS

This wartime poster, produced by the War Shipping Administration, dramatized the fact that thousands of merchant mariners chose to keep sailing despite the dangers.

CREDIT: NATIONAL ARCHIVES

"YOU BET I'M GOING BACK TO SEA!"

Register at your nearest U.S. Employment Service Office

U.S. MERCHANT MARINE

War Shipping Administration

MAN THE VICTORY FLEET

Dead crewmen of the U-85—the first U-boat sunk in American waters—piled unceremoniously on the deck of the American destroyer USS *Roper*.

CREDIT: NATIONAL ARCHIVES

The "lifeboat baby," Jesse Roper Mohorovicic, with his mother, Desanka, and four-year-old sister, Vesna, after his birth in a lifeboat off Cape Hatteras, North Carolina.

CREDIT: BETTMAN/CORBIS/AP IMAGES

UNITED STATES COAST GUARD
42 BROADWAY
NEW YORK 4, N. Y.

ADDRESS REPLY TO
~~DISTRICT COAST GUARD OFFICER~~
REFER TO FILE:

5 April 1944

M/V CITY OF NEW YORK - Of UNITED STATES REGISTRY

The following is a copy of the entry made in the Official Log Book
of the M/V CITY OF NEW YORK, under date of 30 March 1942:

"March 30, 1942:
2:30 AM - At Sea
In Life Boat:

"This is to certify on this date and hour
set forth a male child was born to Mrs Desarka
Mohorovicic, a passenger aboard the vessel.
The Birth occurred in lifeboat after the
vessel was destroyed by enemy action. At
approximately 4 AM March 31, 1942, the U. S.
Navy Destroyer "JESSE ROPER" picked up all
survivors in said lifeboat. The mother and
child were placed in care of Lieut. Johnson,
Surgeon aboard the "JESSE ROPER. All sur-
vivors of this lifeboat were landed at Norfolk,
Virginia. Upon arrival at Hospital, Norfolk,
Va. the mother of the child named him Jesse
Roper Mohorovicic."

(SGD) Leonard H. Conly, MD   (Sgd) G. T. Sullivan
Ship's Surgeon   Master

Witnesses:

(SGD) Charles O. Van Gorden - 2d Officer

"   Miguel P. Davila - Oiler

                    (Signed) John J. Daly
                    U. S. Shipping Commissioner."

The above is a true and correct copy of entry
as shown in the Official Log Book of the M/V
CITY OF NEW YORK.

Raymond A. Shea
Acting Shipping Commissioner.

The birth certificate of the lifeboat baby, copied from an entry in the *City of New York*'s log book after the ship was torpedoed.

CREDIT: COURTESY OF JESSE ROPER MOHOROVIC

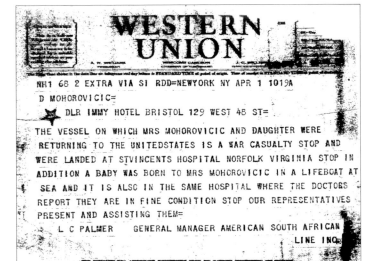

A copy of the telegram that informed a shocked Joseph Mohorovicic that his wife had given birth to his son in a lifeboat at sea.

CREDIT: COURTESY OF JESSE ROPER MOHOROVIC

The destroyer USS *Greer* contends with ice while on convoy escort duty in the North Atlantic.

CREDIT: NATIONAL ARCHIVES

NAVAL MESSAGE — NAVY DEPARTMENT

DRAFTER	EXTENSION NUMBER	ADDRESSEES	PRECEDENCE

FROM COMNAVEU LONDON — OPNAV — PRIORITY

RELEASED BY — RRRRR

DATE APRIL 30 1942 — DEFERRED

TOR CODEROOM 2241/29 — PRIORITY

DECODED BY MALONE — ROUTINE

PARAPHRASED BY BALL — DEFERRED

INDICATE BY ASTERISK ADDRESSEES FOR WHICH MAIL DELIVERY IS SATISFACTORY.

ROONEY 291616 NCR 8189

UNLESS OTHERWISE INDICATED THIS DISPATCH WILL BE TRANSMITTED WITH DEFERRED PRECEDENCE.

ORIGINATOR FILL IN DATE AND TIME	DATE	TIME	GCT

TEXT PAGE 1

FOLLOWING IS SUMMARY OF REPORT OF COMMODORE OF QP13. CONVOY LEFT KOLA INLET 1900/13 APRIL WITH SURFACE ESCORT AND AIR ESCORT OF RUSSIAN FLOWN HURRICANES UNTIL 2300. THROUGHOUT PASSAGE AROUND NORTH CAPE FORCED TO SOUTH BY PACK ICE AND GROWLERS. AT 0300/11 6 JU 88'S CARRIED OUT 11 ATTACKS DROPPING 4 BOMBS ON EACH ATTACK. EMPIRE COWPER SUNK AT 1410. 1 JU 8 SHOT DOWN BY MERCHANT SHIP INSIDE CONVOY. HITS SCORED ON AT LEAST 2 MORE. ATTACK ENDED 1500. LONG RANGE FIGHTER SUPPORT WHICH HAD BEEN PROMISED BY RUSSIANS DID NOT MATERIALIZE. 0300/12 SIGHTED BY ENEMY AIRCRAFT BUT HEAVY WINDS APPARENTLY DETERRED THEM AS ONLY 1 FUTILE ATTACK WAS MADE AT 2130. AT SAME TIME SUBMARINE WAS REPORTED ON SURFACE WHILE CONVOY WAS MANOEUVER- ING THROUGH GROWLERS. TWO SHIPS TORPEDOED PROBABLY BY TWO SUBMARINES ONE OF WHICH THOUGHT TO HAVE BEEN SUNK BY ESCORT. WEATHER MODERATED SOMEWHAT AND AT 0530/13 15 TO 20 JU 88'S BEGAN 2 GROUP ALTERNATE ATTACKS. 30 TO 40 ATTACKS OF 4 BOMBS EACH WERE MADE. 1ST 5 WERE LEVEL BOMBING ATTACKS AND 1 JU 88 WAS SHOT DOWN WITH SHRAPNEL AT CLOSE RANGE AND SEVERAL MORE PLANES HIT. ENEMY AIRCRAFT THEN CHANGED TO DIVE BOMBING ATTACK FROM 6,000 TO 90

SECRET

DECLASSIFIED Authority NND 96/5/33

Make original only. Deliver to communication watch officer in person. (See Art. 76 (4) NAVREGS)

This U.S. Navy report describes the rigors of the Murmansk Run, the notorious 5,000-mile voyage from the U.S. East Coast to North Russia.

CREDIT: NATIONAL ARCHIVES

A ship taking part in the disastrous Allied convoy PQ-17 to Murmansk is struck by an aerial torpedo from a German torpedo bomber.

CREDIT: NATIONAL ARCHIVES

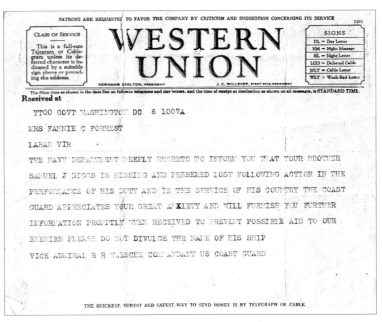

The official telegram from the Navy to the parents of Captain Sam Diggs expressing regret at his death on a convoy run to Murmansk.

CREDIT: COURTESY OF GARY W. BROWNLEE

Captain Sam Jones Diggs, who was killed when his ship struck a "friendly" mine in dense fog on a return trip from Murmansk.

CREDIT: COURTESY OF GARY W. BROWNLEE

The freewheeling Captain Guy Hudgins, with his daughter Diana. He sailed in the invasion of North Africa and on the Murmansk Run.

CREDIT: COURTESY OF DIANA GWYNNE HUDGINS SWENSON

Captain Mellin Respess's ship *Thomas McKean* under attack by the U-505 in the Atlantic. The U-505, later captured, is displayed today in a Chicago museum.

CREDIT: COURTESY OF GWYNN'S ISLAND MUSEUM

Captain Herbert Callis. He survived a torpedoing, rescued castaways at sea, and endured eight months in Murmansk with the Forgotten Convoy.

CREDIT: COURTESY OF BOB AND JOAN MARBLE

Captain Lewis Callis, who was killed when his ship was torpedoed off Cuba. He left behind a poetic tribute to Gwynn's Island, his lifelong home.

CREDIT: COURTESY OF GWYNN'S ISLAND MUSEUM

The *Zebulon B. Vance*—Guy Hudgins's future ship—is prepared for launch in Baltimore. American shipyards built more than 2,700 Liberty ships during the war.

CREDIT: NATIONAL ARCHIVES

Firefighters work to save the tanker *Robert C. Tuttle* after it struck a mine laid by a U-boat at the mouth of the Chesapeake Bay (above and below).

CREDIT: NATIONAL ARCHIVES

Stacy Hammond, one of three seafaring sons of a Mathews blacksmith. All three were torpedoed, on separate ships, over a four-month span in 1942.

CREDIT: COURTESY OF STACY L. HAMMOND

William Hammond, the youngest Hammond brother. He survived one sinking, with help from a generous U-boat captain, only to die aboard the *Onondaga*.

CREDIT: COURTESY OF STACY L. HAMMOND

Genious Hudgins Jr. at home in Mathews with his wife, Salome, and daughter, Vicki, a few months prior to his death aboard the *Onondaga*.

CREDIT: COURTESY OF VICKI HUDGINS PRITCHETT

Genious Hudgins Jr. with his daughter, Vicki, and his brother Russell.

CREDIT: COURTESY OF VICKI HUDGINS PRITCHETT

The unstoppable Lester Smith, who returned to sea after nearly being given up for dead when both of his legs were mangled in a torpedo explosion.

CREDIT: COURTESY OF LOTTIE MITCHEM

Russell Dennis, the only Mathews man to survive the sinking of the *Onondaga*. He later testified in two court cases about the sinking.

CREDIT: COURTESY OF THE DENNIS FAMILY

Homer's elder son, Homer Verdayne Callis Jr., who served in the Pacific on a U.S. Navy destroyer and was killed in a kamikaze attack.

CREDIT: COURTESY OF LISA CALLIS AND MAVA MILES

Captain Homer Callis, the "gentleman captain," aboard the Bull Line freighter *Mae*. He was one of three Callis brothers commanding merchant ships during the war.

CREDIT: COURTESY OF LISA CALLIS AND MAVA MILES

Homer's younger son, Willie "Bill" Callis (right), at a waterfront bar. He joined the Merchant Marine to follow his father and brother into the war.

CREDIT: COURTESY OF LISA CALLIS AND MAVA MILES

Crewmen from the U.S. Coast Guard cutter USS *Spencer*, hunting a submerged U-boat while on convoy escort duty, watch as the ship's depth charges explode astern.

CREDIT: NATIONAL ARCHIVES

Captain Robert Melville "Mel" Callis, Homer's brother, who was killed along with four other Mathews men when the freighter *Ruth* was torpedoed off Cuba.

CREDIT: COURTESY OF LISA CALLIS AND MAVA MILES

The freighter *Commercial Trader*. She was torpedoed off Trinidad only four months after Will Hunley was promoted to serve as her captain.

CREDIT: COURTESY OF REBECCA HUNLEY LOVE

Captain James Wilber "Will" Hunley. A cousin of the Hodges brothers, he sold his bicycle to get enough money to follow David Hodges to sea.

CREDIT: COURTESY OF REBECCA HUNLEY LOVE

Charles Ogletree Billups Jr. left a safe shoreside job to go to sea in the midst of the war and died aboard the *Paul Hamilton*.

CREDIT: COURTESY OF GWYNN'S ISLAND MUSEUM

The Liberty ship *Robert Rowan* erupts in a spectacular explosion off Sicily after being bombed by a German plane. Bernard Stansbury escaped the blast.

CREDIT: NATIONAL ARCHIVES

A Navy memo describes the atomizing of the Liberty ship *Paul Hamilton* by a German bomb. The ship carried explosives and hundreds of U.S. soldiers.

CREDIT: NATIONAL ARCHIVES

DECLASSIFIED
Authority NND 968133

NAVAL MESSAGE

DRAFTER   EXTENSION NUMBER   ASTERISK (*) MAILGRAM ADDRESSEE   PRECEDENCE

FROM   COMGEN USAF NORTH AFRICAN THEATER OF OPERATIONS

RELEASED BY   ALGIERS

DATE   6 MAY 1944

TOR CODEROOM   1628

DECODED BY

PARAPHRASED   SAMUEL

ROUTED BY   HARRINGTON

AGWAR   **DECLASSIFIED**   PRIORITY

NO F 37846

PEMBARK; HRPE; ADNAP; MAAF; COMGEN SOS NATOUSA

NO F 37846   26 APRIL 1944   NCR 12957

(RECEIVED BY PRINTER FROM ARMY)

F 37846 SIGNED DEVERS CITE NATPM TO AGWAR FOR ACTION
WAR PASS TO PEMBARK AND HRPE, AND ADNAP FOR DOCT
AAFSC/MTO AND MAAF AND COMGEN SOS NATOUSA FOR INFO.

LIBERTY PAUL HAMILTON SUBJECT FHTPN NUMBER F 35297
APRIL 21 AND NATPN NUMBER F 35567 APRIL 22, REFERRED
TO FURTHER. NO SURVIVORS HAVE BEEN FOUND. THE SHIP
WAS OBSERVED TO EXPLODE WITH SUCH VIOLENCE, IT IS
NOW CONCLUDED THERE WERE NO SURVIVORS.

NOTE: 35297 IS CM-IN-15412 (21 APRIL 1944) ASF
        35567 IS CM-IN-16446 (22 APRIL 1944) ASF

CM-IN-19769

COMINCH....COG.

FX37....16....BUPERS....23....39....NAVAIDE....OPR....

SECRET

Make original only. Deliver to Code Room Watch Officer in person. (See Art. 76 (6) NAVREGS.)
OPNAV-NCH-15

An unidentified U-boat under attack by an Allied plane. After Allied pilots acquired radar and proper training, planes became the U-boats' nemeses.

CREDIT: NATIONAL ARCHIVES

An Allied convoy moves across the Atlantic escorted by warships and a blimp. As the war progressed, U-boats became increasingly helpless to stop convoys.

CREDIT: FROM THE COLLECTIONS OF THE MARINERS' MUSEUM AND PARK, NEWPORT NEWS, VA

Captain Jesse and Henny Hodges in retirement.

CREDIT: COURTESY OF THE HODGES FAMILY, VIA JESSE CARROLL THORNTON

Scores of military veterans returned to Mathews, giving the county less of a ghost-town feel. Many of those veterans signed up for college and other educational opportunities under the G.I. Bill. Veterans returning to the farm were given the inside track in buying new farm equipment. None of the merchant mariners were eligible for those benefits.

Nor were merchant mariners included in the "Gold Star Honor Roll" compiled by the Commonwealth of Virginia to honor men who had given their lives for their country. The citizens of Mathews created their own Gold Star Honor Roll to include mariners, who accounted for roughly half of the county's war dead. Henny Hodges was chosen to unveil a small monument in front of a Mathews school bearing the names of all the Mathews men killed in the war—with the exception of the black mariner Ashley Clinton Williams, who had been lost on the *Ruth*. Although it's impossible to be certain, every indication is that those who designed the monument were unaware of Williams's roots in Mathews.

More than a dozen new businesses sprouted in Mathews, including some run by former mariners. Roland Foster Jr., who had survived the sinking of the *Thomas McKean*, opened an auto dealership with his brother. Boyd Dixon, who had survived the torpedoing of the tanker *E.M. Clark* in a lightning storm off Hatteras, opened a service station not far from the Hodgeses' new home. Captain Will Hunley, who had survived the sinking of the *Commercial Trader* and its cargo of castor beans, took a job sailing steamships on the Bay between Norfolk and Baltimore. Will bought a house on the Bay near the tip of New Point, where only ten miles of water separates Mathews from Virginia's Eastern Shore. Will's ship passed within sight of his home every night at the same time, and Will always blinked the lights on the ship's bridge to say goodnight to his children. They blinked the lights in their bedrooms in reply.

Commercial fishing in the Bay rebounded, as if rejuvenated by the war's end. The catch of blue crabs in 1946 was the best in more than a decade. The market for Virginia oysters expanded with a new air freight service that could deliver them fresh to Chicago and other midwestern cities. Striped bass, which the locals called rockfish, were plentiful. Even a few shad showed up in fishermen's nets. The good fishing, of course, would not last.

World War II had been over for more than a year by the time Mathews felt like celebrating. In September 1946, the county held a two-day festival to welcome the return of peace to Mathews. The assault transport ship USS *Mathews*, which had been named to honor the county's war losses, anchored just off Gwynn's Island as a centerpiece. The festivities included a seafood feast, a baseball game, and water sports. Eleanor Respess won one of the motorboat races, and more than five hundred people gathered on the riverbank to listen to a speech by Congressman Bland, who was still trying to persuade Congress to offer postwar benefits to merchant mariners. Bland evoked Mathews's seafaring history and pointed out that Mathews mariners had refused to let U-boats chase them from the sea. "Wherever you go, the world over, in far distant ports, there you will find men at sea from Mathews," Bland said. He recalled that on a voyage he had taken to Brazil, he discovered that the ship's captain was from Mathews. The celebration attracted the attention of the *Richmond Times-Dispatch*, which declared in an editorial: "Mathews mourns its losses, but it has long been reconciled to the furies and hazards of the sea. It is a certainty that a good proportion of its sons will continue to make their living from it, just as did their fathers and grandfathers before them."

A month after the ceremony, Captain A. G. Gaden of the USS *Mathews* wrote a letter to the *Gazette-Journal* from the Pacific. Gaden reported that the *Mathews* was encountering Mathews mariners everywhere the ship went. He confessed being "dumbfounded" when a Panama Canal pilot who came aboard to guide the warship through the canal introduced himself as a Mathews man. At least six other Mathews men worked on the canal as pilots or tug operators. Gaden concluded, "[I]t is impossible to get away from Mathews County people if one is in the seafaring business!"

One final act remained in the saga of the ring found in the belly of the shark. In 1948, Dewey Hodges's widow, Edna, petitioned the New York Life

Insurance Co. to double a $10,000 payout the family had received after Dewey's death. (Dewey apparently bought more life insurance than the government's basic coverage for mariners.) Edna contended the *Onondaga* had been sunk not by a U-boat but by accident. She asked the company to honor a double-indemnity clause in the insurance policy that doubled the payout if the death was accidental.

New York Life rejected her claim, and Edna filed a lawsuit and took her case before a jury in Norfolk's federal court. Her lawyers argued that the cause of the *Onondaga*'s sinking was unclear, since none of the survivors actually had seen a sub or a torpedo. Russell Dennis of Mathews, the ship's former third officer, returned to the witness stand to reiterate he had seen nothing. The insurance company responded that all available evidence pointed to the ship having been torpedoed, and that Edna had argued as much in 1942 when she had persuaded a judge to declare Dewey legally dead. How, then, could the jury allow Edna to claim six years later that the sinking was accidental? The jury sympathized with the widow, however, and ordered New York Life to pay Edna an additional $10,000.

Immediately after the jury's verdict was read, the insurance company's lawyers asked U.S. District Judge John Paul to reject it as "plainly contrary to the evidence." Such requests were standard for the losing side in a jury trial, and judges usually let the verdict stand. Judge Paul, however, agreed to consider the request. A month later, in a written ruling, he threw out the jury's verdict and made it clear in his ruling that he had found Edna's case entirely unpersuasive. Edna did not dwell on the defeat. She made use of the money Dewey had left to buy a beauty shop in Norfolk, then sold it and ran a Norfolk hotel, and then bought a motel and restaurant in what is now Virginia Beach. She remarried, and died in 1960 at age sixty-three. Her pallbearers included Dewey's brothers Willie, Coleman, and David Hodges.

Edna and Dewey's son, George Dewey Jr., finished college as Dewey had wished, though the Navy interrupted his studies and deployed him on a warship to China, where he contracted malaria. He served his stint in the Navy and then came home and got his degree, becoming the first member of the Hodges family to graduate from college. Edna never asked Dewey's old boss at Ford to give her son a job. Dewey Jr. had no interest in the Merchant Marine. He built a successful insurance business. He inherited his father's initialed ring, and then passed it on to his son George Dewey Hodges III. None of Dewey's descendants ever went to sea.

Captain Homer Callis sailed merchant ships until the end of his life. He never again considered working ashore. He stayed with the Bull Line, which kept him busy hauling freight around the Caribbean. Homer took every opportunity to come home to Gwynn's Island. His wife, Nancy, was never the same after Homer Jr. was killed by the kamikaze. She made a shrine of sorts to her son in the house, using photographs and some of his letters. Nancy, who had always loved the Christmas holidays, never celebrated them again after the war. She and Homer installed a marble bench in Homer Jr.'s memory in the Callis section of the Gwynn's Island cemetery. It says, "To live in our hearts is not to die."

Homer's visits home to Dunrovin' sometimes came when younger son Bill was also home from the sea. Bill was moving up through the ranks toward captain. On one of Bill's visits home to Gwynn's Island, he saw young Kathryn Hudgins on the beach in a blue bathing suit, and that was that. They married and had a baby girl named Lisa. She was Homer's first grandchild. He proudly showed her picture to his crew and his passengers, and wrote letters to the infant on Bull Line stationery. One of Homer's letters to Lisa, early in 1955, read:

> Granddaddy surely feels bad because he could not come home from New York to see you last week. He is just counting the days until someone comes to relieve him of this job so he can come home to play with you. . . . I hope you can dance for me when I come home again, and I know that Mommy and Grandmother will let you stay up and watch the television with me when you are not real sleepy. You make them let you do the things you want to do, or Granddaddy will fuss up a storm when he comes home . . .

In May 1955, Homer experienced chest pains while sailing the Bull Line ship *Jean* up the East Coast to Philadelphia. He had suffered a heart attack. The ship stopped in Baltimore so that Homer could be rushed to a hospital. He spent a week there before he felt better and was allowed to go home. Being at Dunrovin' always seemed to reenergize Homer, and his family assumed he soon would return to sea. But on the afternoon of May 19, he lay down on the couch for a nap and never woke up. He was sixty-two years old. Homer was buried in the Callis family plot in the Gwynn's Island cemetery, next to the marble bench dedicated to Homer Jr. The inscription on Big Homer's headstone reads: "We know that the waters he sails on now will be peaceful, as he was a pilot and our God needs good pilots."

Nancy Callis would live on the island well into her eighties. She drove a pickup truck with a bumper sticker saying "To Hell with Japan." Her close friend Eleanor Respess—Mellin's widow—also would live well into her eighties. Eleanor would become something of a Renaissance woman, serving on various civic boards, and becoming a gourmet cook and a master gardener. She would wage a long, lighthearted, and ultimately successful campaign to persuade state and federal mapmakers to add an apostrophe to "Gwynn's" in Gwynn's Island. Guy Hudgins sailed merchant ships for years after the war. He had always wanted to command a cruise ship but never was chosen for one of those jobs. He came to believe it was because the steamship companies thought he had too many rough edges, and maybe he did. Guy would retire from the Merchant Marine at age sixty-two and move to Ormond Beach, Florida, where he drowned in the surf while on a morning swim at the age of eighty-two.

Lester Smith ended up walking on two artificial legs, but he never stopped working. He bought a fishing boat and hauled seine nets in the Bay, often working alone on his boat at night with his artificial legs jammed into hip boots. At least Lester knew how to swim. Lester also opened an ice plant and seafood store. He was a relentless boss but an affectionate husband and father. In the last year of his life, he spent summer mornings crabbing in a skiff in the creeks near Gwynn's Island with his daughter Ellen and granddaughter Kim. Ellen said catching crabs was secondary to spending "quiet time with my daddy."

Captain Jesse Hodges had settled into a landsman's life at his new home in Hudgins. He and Henny worked their four acres as a small farm, raising vegetables, corn, chickens, and hogs, much as they had on Gales Neck, but on a smaller scale. Jesse mostly spent his time tending his prized watermelon patch and visiting with other sea captains who dropped by to ask his advice or just to reminisce.

One day in August 1957, Jesse felt strange and checked into the Marine Hospital in Norfolk. The U.S. Marine Hospitals were a network of hospitals operated by the federal government to provide free care for sick or injured merchant mariners. Mariners helped pay the cost of operating them with deductions from their wages. Until the Marine Hospitals were closed in the 1980s by President Ronald Reagan, they were the merchant mariners' equivalent of the Veterans Administration hospitals, which were open to veterans of the armed forces but not to veterans of the Merchant Marine. Most of the Marine Hospitals were large, imposing buildings with an institutional feel.

The Marine Hospital in Norfolk was a long trip from Mathews, but the distance did not deter Henny. She got up before dawn several days a week, cooked Captain Jesse a big breakfast of fried fish or whatever he wanted, and brought it to his hospital bed. He always complained it was too cold, or too bland, and made Henny cry.

Jesse died in the hospital on August 22, 1957, with his daughter Hilda Fourteen at his side. His funeral service was held in Mathews Baptist Church, less than three hundred yards from the Hodges house in Hudgins. Henny would not leave the house to attend the funeral, because she could not stop crying. The rest of the Hodges family turned out in force. Captain Jesse's grandchildren lined the walkway to the church, carrying armloads of flowers. The pallbearers included Spencer; Dewey's son George Jr.; Raymond's oldest son, Raymond Jr.; and Elizabeth's son J. W. Corbett. More than a hundred people came to say good-bye to Jesse, including dozens of Mathews mariners who had learned to sail from him.

His star pupil, the oldest Hodges son, Raymond, was promoted by Moore-McCormack after the war to captain of the cruise ship *Brazil*, which carried tourists from New York to Rio de Janeiro and Buenos Aires, Argentina. Commanding a cruise ship required not just fine seamanship but a knack for charming the wealthy passengers, with whom the captain dined each night. Raymond took dancing lessons before starting the job. Photos taken aboard the *Brazil* show him dancing in conga lines with bejeweled matrons, and posing with his arms around their lovely daughters.

The *Brazil*'s passengers typically included diplomats, captains of industry, and celebrities. Raymond dined with the actor Cesar Romero, and with the Catholic archbishop of New York, Francis Cardinal Spellman, who in 1955 rode the *Brazil* with hundreds of other Catholics to the 36th International Eucharistic Congress in Rio de Janeiro. On the way to Rio, Raymond steered the *Brazil* out of the path of Hurricane Diane. "That's one lady I really wanted to get away from," he joked.

Raymond seemed to have been born to command a cruise ship. He especially loved visiting Argentina, where he had good friends dating back to before the war. His son Bill said Raymond bought a small cattle ranch in Argentina and hired a woman to oversee it for him. He continued to pay his sons to raise his cattle in Gloucester.

The *Brazil* was retired in 1957 and Raymond was offered the job of captain of her replacement vessel, which was under construction in a shipyard in Pascagoula, Mississippi. Raymond was sent to Pascagoula to supervise the work. He stayed in a hotel and took a taxi to the shipyard every morning to deal with the contractors. One morning on his way up the gangplank, he lost his balance and nearly fell. It was the first sign that Raymond suffered from Parkinson's disease. His condition rapidly worsened. On December 23, 1960, three years after his diagnosis, Raymond died peacefully at his farm in Gloucester. His last wish was that he be buried at sea, off the coast of Argentina. After a memorial service in

Mathews, his body was released to Moore-McCormack, which loaded it on the first cruise ship heading for South America. The ship stopped its engines off the coast of Argentina, and the crew slid Raymond's casket into the South Atlantic.

Coleman Hodges quit sailing the deep ocean as soon as the war ended. He felt he had done his duty, and wanted to go home to Mathews. He bought a house in the woods near the drawbridge to Gwynn's Island, and piloted tugs for a lumber company, which allowed him to come home most nights. He kept five beagle-mix hounds in a kennel, and spent every Saturday fox hunting with his brother David. His daughters asked how Coleman could stand the dogs' howling. "Have you ever heard the birds sing?" he said. "Well, this is music to my ears." Coleman bought a small boat and fished in the lower Piankatank River and the Bay. He loved the outdoors and especially the stars. He showed his daughters how to use his sextant. "This'll always get you home," he told them.

Coleman continued to entertain his family and friends with his jokes, but he occasionally made comments that revealed a gloomy view of life in general. He did not understand how a just God could have allowed U-boats to kill his brothers Dewey and Leslie. He never forgave the Germans or the Japanese. He once smashed a knickknack against a wall because it had been made in Japan. He shouted at his wife, Ethel, "Don't you know that they attacked us?"

In 1964, Coleman was diagnosed with renal cancer. He clung to life for months in the Marine Hospital on Staten Island, which specialized in cancer treatment, but which his daughter Betty recalled as being "like an asylum, a big, brick, drafty place with steel beds, ice everywhere. It was a very poor picture." Coleman died on February 13, 1965, at the age of fifty-one, with his wife and his sister Elizabeth at his side. His brother David was vacationing in Hawaii, and felt guilty for not having been with Coleman at the end. On the first Christmas Eve after Coleman's death, David left his home on Gwynn's Island without telling his family where he was going. Hours passed. David's children found him standing before Coleman's grave.

Henny Hodges did not attend Raymond's or Coleman's funeral services. She moved in with her daughter Louise, who set up a bed for her in the living room. Her children and grandchildren were always coming in and out, and her friends dropped by to see her every day. She died at Louise's house on March 19, 1965, at the age of eighty-six, having outlived seven of her fourteen children as well as her husband. Members of her extended family filled the funeral home. They included seven children, twenty-six grandchildren, forty-eight great-grandchildren, and two great-great-grandchildren. She was buried in the cemetery of the Episcopal Church, next to Captain Jesse. Henny left $134 to each of her surviving children.

The grandson Henny reared at Gales Neck, Jesse Carroll Thornton, saw a basic difference between his grandparents, whom he called Mama and Papa: "I loved both of them," he said. "If there is a heaven, I know Mama is there. Papa, maybe not."

The physical remains of the U-boat war on America are scattered along the coast for those who know where to look.

A periscope salvaged from the U-190 is installed in the Crow's Nest Officers Club in the old section of St. John's, Newfoundland. Patrons at the bar can peer through the periscope at the city's magnificent harbor, from which convoys set out across the North Atlantic to Britain.

An anchor from the destroyer USS *Roper*—which rescued the lifeboat baby and then sank the first U-boat in U.S. waters—is displayed at the entrance to the Pratt School of Naval Architecture and Marine Engineering at the Massachusetts Institute of Technology in Cambridge, Massachusetts. MIT had no particular connection with the *Roper* but requested an anchor at a time when the destroyer was about to be scrapped.

Two Liberty ships that sailed in World War II still operate today as floating museums that take visitors on harbor cruises out of Baltimore and San Francisco. The Baltimore-based *John W. Brown* offers lunch and tours, with flyovers by World War II–vintage warplanes. Other surviving Liberty ships sit in mothballs in the U.S. government's reserve fleets, collecting dust and seagull droppings, waiting their turns in the scrap yard.

The U-505, which torpedoed Mellin Respess on the *Thomas McKean* and then was captured by a hunter-killer group two days before D-Day, is a marquee attraction at the Museum of Science and Industry in Chicago.* Every year, approximately 2 million museum visitors squeeze through the narrow, dimly lit U-505 for a sense of what life was like on the devil's shovel.

The U-85's main hatch and the Enigma machine it carried are on display in the Graveyard of the Atlantic Museum in Hatteras Village, on the southern tip of Hatteras Island on the North Carolina Outer Banks. A few elderly residents of the island still remember waking up at night to the rattling of their windows from torpedo strikes on ships offshore.

The sea continues to reveal secrets of the U-boat war.

Off the Outer Banks in 1965, the scallop boat *Snoopy* hauled up a live torpedo in its nets. When the crew attempted to disentangle it, the torpedo exploded, killing eight of the twelve men on board. A decade later, another fishing boat pulled up a torpedo in its nets off Rhode Island. A U.S. Navy ordnance disposal team blew it up at a safe distance from the boat. Other live ordnance from the U-boat war surely waits on the ocean bottom for the unlucky.

In September 1992, a group of elite divers discovered the wreck of a U-boat about 60 miles off the coast of Point Pleasant, New Jersey. How it ended up there was not clear from either the Allied or German war records. The wreck lay in 230 feet of water, and diving it was especially dangerous because of strong, shifting currents and blinding silt, but the divers were determined to identify it. Two divers lost their lives over the course

---

* Admiral Gallery, the commander of the hunter-killer group that captured the U-505 off South Africa two days before D-Day in 1944, was a Chicago native who pulled strings with the Navy to have the sub spared from destruction and made available to the museum. An American crew sailed the U-boat up the St. Lawrence River and across four of the five Great Lakes to the shore of Lake Michigan, where it was hauled a short distance overland to the museum.

of a five-year search before an artifact from the sub identified it as the U-869, which had vanished in December 1944. The sub may have been sunk by one of its own malfunctioning acoustic torpedoes, a "circle runner" that circled back to its source after being launched.

In 2014, oceanographer and shipwreck archaeologist Robert Ballard explored the wreck of the U-166 in the Gulf of Mexico off the Louisiana coast and changed the Navy's conclusions about who sank the sub. Ballard and his team of explorers used unmanned, remotely operated vehicles (ROVs) to dive down to the wreck, 5,000 feet deep, and send up high-resolution images. The images showed devastating damage to the U-166's bow, which suggested a depth charge had exploded against it, as the commander of a Navy patrol vessel had claimed in 1942.

The Navy had originally discounted the patrol vessel's claim of sinking the sub, and further criticized the vessel's commander, Herbert G. Claudius, for errors in conducting the depth charge attack. The Navy had credited the sinking to a Coast Guard bomber. The wreck of the U-166 sat undiscovered until 2001, when an oil company stumbled upon it while exploring the gulf bottom for a route for a natural gas pipeline. No one closely examined the U-166 wreckage until Ballard in 2014. After he presented his findings, the Navy shifted credit for the sinking of the U-166 to Claudius and posthumously awarded him a medal for heroism in battle. His son accepted it on his behalf.

Also in 2014, a research team with the U.S. National Oceanic and Atmospheric Administration (NOAA) found the wreck of the U-576 about 30 miles off the North Carolina Outer Banks. The U-576 was bombed by a U.S. plane after sinking the Nicaraguan freighter *Bluefields*, whose wreckage lies only 240 yards from the sub's.

The U-576 and the *Bluefields* are only two of hundreds of World War II shipwrecks resting on the seabed of America's shallow continental shelf. More than eighty such wrecks lie off the Outer Banks of North Carolina, which is sometimes called the Graveyard of the Atlantic. For thirty years those wrecks were ignored by everyone except fishermen, who took note of them because they attracted fish. Recreational divers discovered the World War II wrecks in the 1970s, creating a cottage industry of dive shops, charter boats, and historical guidebooks. Divers had gradually stripped the U-boats and other wrecks of all recognizable artifacts by the beginning of the twenty-first century, when NOAA began discouraging the practice.

Jim Bunch, a veteran diver from North Carolina, said divers had long assumed they could keep whatever they found in the old wrecks. He had gone on dive trips with off-duty FBI agents and North Carolina state investigators. Bunch took pictures, mostly, but brought up several artifacts, including the U-85's Enigma machine. "We did it for the thrill, crawling into narrow spaces, fighting the current and the low visibility, and then the fun of showing pieces to our friends," said Bunch, who is now in his seventies. "No one was in it for the money."

Then, in 2004, President George W. Bush signed the Sunken Military Craft Act, which made it clear that any sunken military vessel belonged to its nation's government, and that disturbing the dead or removing artifacts was illegal. Jim Bunch donated the Enigma machine to the Graveyard of the Atlantic Museum in Hatteras, which obtained permission from the German government to display it.

NOAA is considering adding the U-boats and some of the sunken merchant ships to its marine sanctuary program, which protects historic wrecks such as the Civil War ironclad *Monitor* off Cape Hatteras. Some divers are angry over what they consider government overreaching, but Bunch said the issue is moot: All the World War II wrecks that remain undisturbed are either too deep or too hazardous for divers, and chemicals in the seawater are breaking down the old ships into unrecognizable piles of metal.

The U-boat war has continued to stir emotions.

In the late 1960s, George Betts of Milo, Maine, was reading a German book about the U-boat war and found a clue to the fate of his father's ship, the Marine Transport Lines oil tanker *Muskogee*, which had vanished in 1942 with all hands, including Nat Foster of Mathews. According to the book, Reinhard Hardegan and the U-123 had sunk a tanker named the *"Muscogcc"* on March 22, 1942. Betts contacted a U.S. Navy archivist who examined newly declassified records, including the captured logbook of the U-123. The records showed Hardegan's sub had indeed sunk Betts's father's tanker, the *Muskogee*. Betts tracked down Hardegan, a retired businessman in Bremen, West Germany, and the two exchanged cordial letters.

"I'm glad that you are not angry at me," Hardegan wrote, "and you have the right idea, that all soldiers did their duty. The single persons were not our enemies and when we sunk a ship, the sailors etc. were comrades and we tried to help them as much as we could. In the case of *Muskogee* I was not able to [take] the crew on board, because we were westbound and had no place for so many people." Hardegan told Betts the *Muskogee* sank so fast that her crew only had time to launch two rafts. The U-123 approached the rafts and offered the men food, water, and cigarettes. But the castaways were hundreds of miles from land, Hardegan wrote, "and it was bad for us all to let them alone with the wind and sea . . . This personal contact with men probably condemned to death was one of the moments which shows me that this must be the last war . . ."

Hardegan gave Betts copies of photos the U-123's propaganda photographer had taken of the *Muskogee* sinking, as well as a series of photos of the U-boat approaching the rafts. The last photo in the series is one of the most haunting images of the U-boat war. It shows seven doomed castaways facing the U-boat. Two of them appear to be shouting, but others stare hollow-eyed, knowing they can expect no salvation from the Germans, or from anyone.

Betts was relieved to know at last what had happened to his father, and he figured that family members of the thirty-three other men killed on the *Muskogee* would feel the same. He set out in the late 1980s to share his knowledge with them, including the relatives of Nat Foster. Betts tracked down children, grandchildren, nephews, cousins, and great-nieces. The NBC TV show *Unsolved Mysteries* publicized his quest. Most of the family members he contacted thanked him. "After all these years, due to your perseverance, we now know what happened," one wrote. But not all the families wanted to revisit the past. Betts identified two of the seven men on the raft in the photograph, and suspected Nat Foster was one of the others. He mailed a copy of the photo to Foster's sister, Lucy Marchant. She thanked him but concluded, "I do not need further information. I am unable to identify my brother in this picture."

German relatives of the crew of the U-85 gather occasionally on April 14 in the Hampton National Cemetery in Virginia, where the twenty-nine bodies recovered in 1942 were buried in unmarked graves. Today the U-boat men's graves are marked in the same style as the American graves, though they are kept separate from them. A cousin of the U-85's captain called the killing of the sub's crew in the water by the *Roper*'s depth charges "murder." But the families of other U-85 crewmen apologized for Germany's actions in the war.

Farther south, on Ocracoke Island, North Carolina, a memorial service is held every May for four British sailors from the armed trawler HMT *Bedfordshire*, who are buried on the island. The *Bedfordshire*, one of the twenty-four antisubmarine trawlers lent to the United States by the British to help protect the East Coast, was torpedoed by a U-boat off the Outer Banks on May 14, 1942, with the loss of all hands. The bodies of two of the trawler's Royal Navy crew washed up in the surf at Ocracoke—one of very few cases in which the bodies of U-boat victims washed up on American beaches. Two more bodies of the *Bedfordshire* crew were found in the shallow water just offshore. All four of the Brits were buried with military honors in Ocracoke's cemetery. Today, the sailors' graves are enclosed by a wooden picket fence and shaded by live oaks. Two more of the *Bedfordshire* sailors are buried in a rural part of Virginia Beach.

Two British merchant mariners from the British freighter *San Delfino*, whose bodies washed up on Hatteras Island, are buried a short distance from the iconic, candy-striped Cape Hatteras Lighthouse. The men's graves are adorned with flowers and seashells.

The lifeboat baby, Jesse Roper Mohorovicic, who was born after the

City of New York was torpedoed in 1942, gradually escaped the scrutiny of the tabloid press and became a shipping company executive. He shortened his last name to Mohorovic, shaving off the last "ic" for easier pronunciation in the business world. Jesse never mentioned the circumstances of his birth unless someone asked him directly where he was born. "It's really my mother's story," he would tell people. "I didn't do anything." In fact, he felt like "the football at the Rose Bowl." His mother never talked about how hard it had been for her in the lifeboat. She never lost sight of the fact that she had been one of the lucky ones. Jesse felt a lifelong attachment to the U.S. Merchant Marine. He had been born in the midst of its finest hour. Before he died of lung cancer in 2009, he would witness firsthand its steep decline.

The U.S. merchant fleet shrank steadily after the sell-off of vessels after World War II, despite temporary revivals during the wars in Korea, Vietnam, and the Persian Gulf. One by one, the Bull Line, Moore-McCormack, and other American companies went bankrupt or were swallowed up by competitors. By the 1980s, U.S. flag ships had become so costly to operate that they could no longer compete for international trade. Unionized U.S. mariners were paid three and four times as much as their counterparts from Eastern Europe and the Philippines. U.S. flag ships were subject to U.S. taxes and U.S. Coast Guard safety regulations, which added still more overhead costs. A shipowner who wanted to avoid paying the high wages, taxes, and costs of complying with U.S. safety regulations could simply switch the flag of his vessel to that of a country with no such requirements. Nations such as Liberia, Panama, and the Marshall Islands offered "flags of convenience" under which merchant ships, in exchange for registration fees, could sail with low-paid, foreign crews and avoid taxes and many safety requirements.

The U.S. government did not allow the U.S. Merchant Marine to disappear, as most private businesses would after pricing themselves out of the market. The federal Jones Act restricts the shipment of cargo between U.S. ports to U.S. flag vessels built in American shipyards, giving American mariners and shipyard workers a near monopoly on coastal shipping. The

U.S. government also continues to use subsidies to sustain a fleet of U.S. flag vessels capable of hauling supplies overseas for America's next war. The current subsidies include longstanding Cargo Preference laws, which require a percentage of America's food aid to foreign countries to be shipped on U.S. flag ships, even though the cost is higher than hauling those supplies on foreign-flagged vessels. In addition, the government's Maritime Security Program pays yearly stipends to the private owners of sixty U.S.-flagged cargo ships to keep those vessels flying the U.S. flag and available immediately to the government if needed. The vessels in the Maritime Security Program comprise the bulk of the eighty-one privately owned U.S.-flagged commercial ships that are still engaged in international trade.

The number of U.S. merchant mariners actively sailing internationally has plummeted from a high of about 250,000 at the end of World War II to roughly 11,000 today. Those 11,000 mariners compete for only about 5,000 jobs. The number of mariners and jobs has been shrinking fast for almost a decade, with little apparent prospect of a reversal. But more than 200,000 American merchant mariners are licensed or certified to sail along the coast or in inland waters on smaller vessels, ranging from tugboats to fishing boats, dive charter boats, and water taxis. Most Mathews men still working on the water are fishermen and tugboat operators. One of Captain Jesse and Henny's great-grandsons, David Callis, is captain of a tug in the Gulf of Mexico and returns to Mathews when he has time ashore. David revels in the Hodges family seafaring history and tells salty tales about Captain Jesse and his boys. Jimmy Hunley, son of Captain Will Hunley and a cousin of the Hodges brothers, is captain of a tug in New York Harbor. He said well over a dozen Mathews men work on tugs. "I can't go anywhere in the tugboat crowd without people asking me if I know other tugboat men from Mathews."

It took Congress forty-three years after Roosevelt's request to extend veterans' benefits to World War II merchant mariners, which lawmakers finally voted on in 1988. Most of the mariners who faced the U-boats were dead by then, but some of those still alive were grateful for access to Veterans Administration hospitals after the old Marine Hospitals were shuttered.

Joseph Elliott of Mathews, who had seen action on a Liberty ship during the war, sought treatment at VA hospitals for post-traumatic stress disorder. When he was eighty years old, he would awaken his wife and daughter in the middle of the night, believing he was back in the engine room with U-boats and bombers closing in. At those moments, Joseph seemed to move about in a claustrophobic trance. He would usher his wife and daughter out of the house into the yard, even in the dead of winter. They would stay out with him until he regained his senses and led them back into the house.

One national veterans' organization, the Veterans of Foreign Wars, prohibits merchant marine veterans of World War II from joining, although some individual chapters ignore the rule.

For the past twenty years, a nonprofit advocacy group for World War II merchant mariners has tried to persuade Congress to distribute cash payouts to them. For years the group argued that each mariner who served in the war should receive $1,000 per month for the rest of his life. But in 2015 the group changed its request to a one-time $25,000 payout for each mariner. There are approximately 5,000 World War II mariners still alive, which means the payout would cost U.S. taxpayers roughly $125 million. Other Allied nations, including Britain and Canada, have made similar one-time payouts to their World War II–era merchant mariners. But the bill's chances of going anywhere in the gridlocked U.S. Congress appear low.

Mathews is still not on the way to anywhere. It remains one of Virginia's smallest and least populous counties. It is still a place young people leave in search of opportunities. Instead of jumping onto merchant ships, they move to Hampton or Newport News for jobs at medical offices and technology companies. Mathews still has no stoplights, four-lane highways, or motels. "If you come to Mathews, you are either lost or visiting somebody," said Sonny Richardson, a realtor who grew up in Mathews. Mathews still feels like the country. On Main Street, farmers leave pickup trucks full of fresh produce, for sale by the honor system. Drivers wave to one another on the back roads. Most of those back roads still narrow into country lanes, and end at the water's edge.

The story of the Mathews mariners in the U-boat war lives mostly in two small museums with irregular hours, the Gwynn's Island Museum and the Mathews Maritime Foundation's museum. The old mariners themselves are almost gone. One of the last, Bill Callis, died in December 2014.

Bill had sailed the world's oceans for forty years. He had been to the Arctic and the Antarctic, and to every country except China. When Bill came home from the sea to visit Gwynn's Island, he was unpredictable. He once tumbled drunk down the steps of his plane and landed in a heap on the tarmac. His angry wife spun around on her heels and got into the car, leaving Bill's daughters to help him up. Bill lost track of his daughters' ages while he was at sea, and sometimes brought home gifts that were ten years out of date—a giant stuffed animal, a tiny child's kimono. But Bill just as often was funny and charming on his visits. He was never dull. He loved Dunrovin' and left it to his daughters. He found it incomprehensible that anyone who owned property on the island would sell it to outsiders for vacation homes, although many of his neighbors did just that.

Louise Hodges Leigh, the last surviving child of Captain Jesse and Henny's fourteen children, died in 2011, but the Hodges family still gathers periodically in Mathews for dinings that recall Henny's celebrations at Gales Neck. A reunion of Hodges family and friends in an American Legion hall in the fall of 2014 attracted more than a hundred guests, including descendants of Raymond, Dewey, Willie, Spencer, Coleman, David, Alice, Elizabeth, Louise, and Hilda Fourteen Hodges.

Some of the Hodges grandchildren have revisited Gales Neck, which is now owned by a historic trust. The farmhouse is long empty, but well maintained. Despite a number of additions and alterations, the property looks much as it did in 1942. Willie's son, Brother Hodges, and Hilda Fourteen's son Jesse Carroll Thornton had no trouble remembering the locations of the well pump, the barn, the hog pen, the smokehouse, and the chicken house. The years seemed to fall away as they stood in the kitchen, which still had a big iron cook stove like Henny's; and in the dining room, where the furniture had been shoved aside to clear the way for square dancing. The most striking change at Gales Neck was that the farmhouse no longer commanded the headwaters of the East River. It was hidden behind a wall of marshes and foliage that had grown up along the riverbank.

The visit to Gales Neck took Brother Hodges, now in his late eighties, back. He had lost two uncles to U-boats, but he had joined the Merchant Marine in 1944 as soon as he turned seventeen. He had gone to sea not out of duty or a desire for revenge, but because the Merchant Marine offered opportunities for a young man comfortable on the water—the same reason Mathews men had always gone to sea. He said the U-boats took a toll on his family but never cowed or deterred them.

"The Hodges kept going to sea like they always had. Men all over Mathews County kept going to sea like they always had. They didn't do anything different during the war. The torpedoes just got in the way."

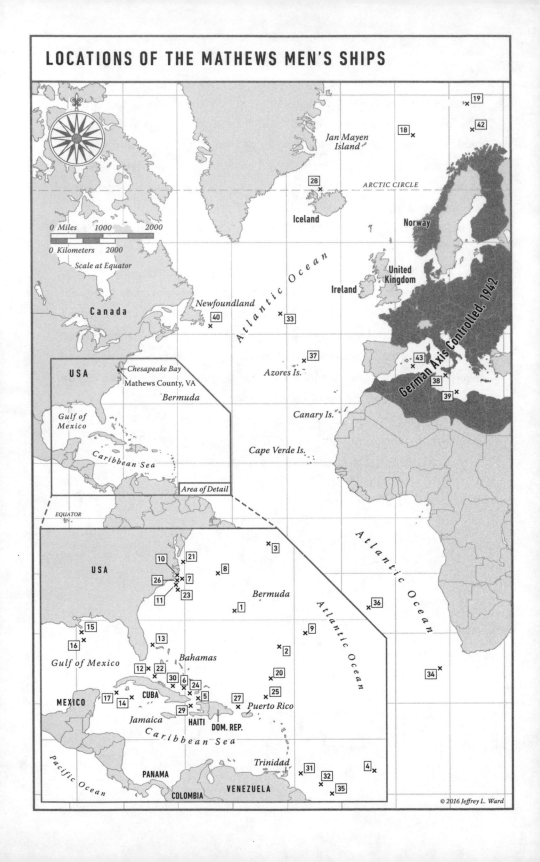

SUNK OR DAMAGED IN WORLD WAR II

1. **NORVANA**, General location: off coast of North Carolina
   Position: unknown
   Sunk – January 22, 1942

2. **MAJOR WHEELER**, General location: East Coast of United States
   Position: unknown
   Sunk – February 6, 1942

3. **LAKE OSWEYA**, General location: North Atlantic
   Position: 43.14 N/64.45 W
   Sunk – February 20, 1942

4. **MARY**, General location: 250 mi. NE of Paramaribo, Dutch Guiana
   Position: 8.25 N/52.50 W
   Sunk – March 3, 1942

5. **BARBARA**, General location: 9 mi. NNW of Tortuga Island
   (Dominican Republic)
   Position: 20.10 N/73.05 W
   Sunk – March 7, 1942

6. **COLABEE**, General location: 10 mi. off Cape Verde, Cuba
   Position: 22.14 N/77.35 W
   Damaged – March 12, 1942

7. **E.M. CLARK**, General location: 22 mi. SE of Cape Hatteras, NC
   Postion: 34.50 N/73.35 W
   Sunk – March 18, 1942

8. **OAKMAR**, General location: 300 mi. E of Cape Hatteras, NC
   Position: 36.22 N/68.50 W
   Sunk – March 20, 1942

9. **MUSKOGEE**, General location: 450 mi. SE of Bermuda
   Position: 28 N/58 W
   Sunk – March 22, 1942

10. **DIXIE ARROW**, General location: 12 mi. off Cape Hatteras, NC
    lighted buoy
    Position: 35 N/75.33 W
    Sunk – March 26, 1942

11. **HARRY F. SINCLAIR JR.**, General location: 7 mi. S of Cape Lookout, NC
    Position: 34.25 N/76.30 W
    Damaged – April 11, 1942

12. **NORLINDO**, General location: 200 mi. NE of Havana, Cuba
    Position: 24.57 N/84 W
    Sunk – May 4, 1942

13. **DELISLE**, General location: 15 mi. outside of Jupiter Inlet, FL
    Position: 27.05 N/80.05 W
    Damaged – May 4, 1942 (the same ship appears later in this list,
    sunk this time, on October 19, 1943)

14. **GREEN ISLAND**, General location: 80 mi. SW of Grand Cayman Island
    Position: 18.25 N/81.30 W
    Sunk – May 6, 1942

15. **VIRGINIA**, General location: 1.5 mi. from the mouth of
    the Mississippi River
    Position: 28.53 N/89.29 W
    Sunk – May 12, 1942

16. **GULFPENN**, General location: 30 mi. from the entrance to
    the Mississippi River
    Position: 28.29 N/89.12 W
    Sunk – May 13, 1942

17. **ELIZABETH**, General location: 30 mi. S of Cape Corrientes, Cuba
    Position: 21.36 N/84.48 W
    Sunk – May 20, 1942

18. **SYROS**, General location: Barents Sea, 200 mi. SW of Bear Island
    Position: 72.35 N/5.30 E
    Sunk – May 26, 1942

19. **ALAMAR**, General location: 100 mi. SE of Bear Island,
    Position: 74 N/20 E
    Sunk – May 27, 1942

20. **CITY OF ALMA**, General location: 400 mi. NE of San Juan, Puerto Rico
    Position: 23 N/62.30 W
    Sunk – June 2, 1942

21. **ROBERT C. TUTTLE**, General location: within 5 mi. of Virginia Beach, VA
    Position: 36.51 N/75.51 W
    Damaged – June 15, 1942

22. **MILLINOCKET**, General location: off La Isabella Island, Cuba
    Position: 23.12 N/79.58 W
    Sunk – June 17, 1942

23. **MANUELA**, General location: 75 mi. E of Cape Lookout, NC
    Position: 34.30 N/75.40 W
    Sunk – June 24, 1942

24. **RUTH**, General location: 100 mi. N of Cape Maysi, Cuba
    Position: 21.44 N/74.05 W
    Sunk – June 29, 1942

25. **THOMAS MCKEAN**, General location: 350 mi. NE of Puerto Rico
    Position: 22 N/60 W
    Sunk – June 29, 1942

26. **CITY OF BIRMINGHAM**, General location: 250 mi. E of Cape Hatteras, NC
    Position: 35.16 N/74.25 W
    Sunk – June 30, 1942

27. **NORLANDIA**, General location: 25 mi. NE of Cape Samana,
    Dominican Republic
    Position: 19.33 N/68.39 W
    Sunk – July 3, 1942

28. **MASSMAR**, General location: NW coast of Iceland; Allied minefield
    Position: 66.39 N/22.33 W
    Sunk – July 5, 1942

29. **ONEIDA**, General location: 2 mi. N of Cape Maysi, Cuba
    Position: 20.17 N/74.06 W
    Sunk – July 13, 1942

30. **ONONDAGA**, General location: 5 mi. N of Cayo Guillermo, Cuba
    Position: 22.40 N/78.44 W
    Sunk – July 23, 1942

31. **COMMERCIAL TRADER**, General location: 75 mi. E of Trinidad
    Position: 10.30 N/60.15 W
    Sunk – September 16, 1942

32. **MAE**, General location: 100 mi. N of Georgetown, British Guiana
    Position: 8.03 N/58.13 W
    Sunk – September 17, 1942

33. **STEEL NAVIGATOR**, General location: North Atlantic
    Position: 49.45 N/31.20 W
    Sunk – October 19, 1942

34. **EAST INDIAN**, General location: 275 mi. SW of Cape Town, South Africa
    Position: 37.23 S/13.34 E
    Sunk – November 3, 1942

35. **COLLINGSWORTH**, General location: 100 mi. NE of Paramaribo,
    Dutch Guiana
    Position: 7.12 N/55.37 W
    Sunk – January 9, 1943

36. **ROGER B. TANEY**, General location: South Atlantic
    Position: 22 S/7.45 W
    Sunk – February 3, 1943

37. **BENJAMIN HARRISON**, General location: 150 mi. FNE of Terceira, Azores
    Position: 39.09 N/24.15 W
    Sunk – March 16, 1943

38. **ROBERT ROWAN**, General location: Harbor of Gela, Sicily, 5 mi. from shore
    Position: unknown
    Sunk – July 11, 1943

39. **CAPE MOHICAN**, General location: off the coast of Libya
    Position: 33.42 N/16.43 E
    Damaged – August 21, 1943

40. **DELISLE (AGAIN)**, General location: off the coast of Newfoundland
    Position: 47.19 N/52.27 W
    Sunk – October 19, 1943

42. **PENELOPE BARKER**, General location: 115 mi. from North Cape, Norway
    Position: 73.22 N/22.30 E
    Sunk – January 24, 1944

43. **PAUL HAMILTON**, General location: off the Algerian coast
    Position: 37.02 N/3.41 E
    Sunk – April 20, 1944

THE MATHEWS MEN AND WOMEN

The Hodges Family

Capt. Jesse Hodges
Tugboat and steamboat captain, and patriarch of the Hodges clan. He survived the war. Six of his sons would become merchant sea captains.

Capt. Raymond Hodges
The eldest of the fourteen Hodges children. Captain of the Moore-McCormack deep-water freighter *Mormacmoon*, crossing the North Atlantic in numerous large convoys under attack by U-boat wolf packs. He lived to become captain of a luxury cruise ship.

Capt. Dewey Hodges
Second oldest of the Hodges children, he was captain of the Ford Motor Co. flagship *East Indian*. Temporary captain of Ford freighter *Onondaga* on July 23, 1942, when it was torpedoed by the U-129 off Cuba. Dewey and three other Mathews men were killed.

Capt. Willie Hodges

The jolly and highly skilled captain of oceangoing tugboats, he sailed in dangerous waters until his sisters asked him to stay ashore after two of his brothers had been killed. He survived the war.

Capt. Coleman Hodges

The fourth son, driven by ambition and a sense of duty to become captain of a ship during the war. Commanding the Liberty ship *Edward A. Savoy*, he sailed on the notorious Murmansk Run through the Arctic Circle to North Russia, and to Antwerp, Belgium, where German V-1 buzz bombs rained down. He survived the war but died of illness at age fifty-one.

Capt. Leslie Hodges

An outlier among the seven Hodges brothers, dark and quiet, he became a captain but was serving as first officer aboard the freighter *Oneida* on July 13, 1942, when it was torpedoed by the U-166 off Cuba. Leslie died, apparently while trying to rescue another man.

Spencer Hodges

The only Hodges son to choose a career ashore, after he severely injured his back as a teenager while working on his brother Dewey's ship. Served as a recruiter in Mathews for crewmen for his brothers' ships. Became sheriff of Mathews.

Capt. David Hodges

The youngest of the Hodges brothers, he quit going to sea before the war and spent World War II working in one of the scores of U.S. shipyards racing to build new ships. After the war he became a captain and worked as a federal pilot guiding ships up and down the channels and into the ports of the Chesapeake Bay.

Horace "Brother" Hodges

The son of Willie Hodges, he went to sea toward the end of the war, as soon as he reached the qualifying age of seventeen. He sailed on Liberty ships in war zones but none of his ships were hit. He survived the war.

Herman "Bill" Hodges

The younger son of Captain Raymond Hodges, Bill joined the Merchant Marine toward the end of the war, when he turned seventeen, and sailed on Liberty ships to the Mediterranean and the coast of France. He survived the war.

James Wilber "Will" Hunley

A Hodges cousin, he followed his cousin and boyhood friend David Hodges to sea on Raymond Hodges's ship. Will went on to become captain of the freighter *Commercial Trader*. On September 16, 1942, the ship was torpedoed off Trinidad by the U 558. He survived and went back to sea, sailing through the war's end and long afterward.

Henrietta "Henny" Hodges

The matriarch of the Hodges family of Gales Neck, she reared fourteen children and ran the family's forty-acre farm, with little help from her husband, Captain Jesse Hodges, who was always on a tugboat.

The Hodges daughters

Alice, Elizabeth, Louise, and Hilda Fourteen Hodges rarely agreed on anything, but after two of their brothers were killed by U-boats, they took the unusual step of asking their father and brothers to stop sailing in war zones.

Edna Hodges

Dewey Hodges's wife, she received word of his death in a jarring manner, and afterward struggled with the court system to get the money to support her family. She received Dewey's ring.

The Callis Family

Capt. Homer R. Callis

One of three sea-captain sons of Willie and Lucy Callis of Gwynn's Island, Homer guided the freighter *Mae* through a ferocious U-boat attack in the Caribbean in 1942, but his new ship, the *Cape Mohican*, was torpedoed by accident by a British warship in the Mediterranean in 1943. He survived the war but lost a son and a brother.

Homer Callis Jr.

The twenty-one-year-old son of Captain Homer Callis, he served as a U.S. Navy quartermaster in the Pacific and was killed when the bridge of his ship, the destroyer USS *Hazelwood*, was struck by a kamikaze off Iwo Jima on April 28, 1945.

Willie "Bill" Callis

The younger son of Captain Homer Callis and little brother of Homer Callis Jr., he went to sea after his father's ship was torpedoed, and sailed throughout the war and long afterward.

Capt. Robert Melville "Mel" Callis

Brother of Captains Homer and Rodney Callis, he was killed when his ship, the *Ruth*, was torpedoed by the U-153 off Cuba on June 29, 1942. Four other Mathews men also were killed on the *Ruth*.

Capt. Rodney Callis

Brother of Captains Homer and Mel Callis, he sailed throughout the war and served as captain of two Liberty ships. He survived the war without serious incident and sailed for years afterward.

Capt. Lewis Callis

A distant cousin of the three Callis brothers, who also lived on Gwynn's Island, he was killed when his freighter, the *Millinocket*, was torpedoed by the U-129 off Cuba on June 17, 1942.

Capt. Herbert Callis

Another Callis cousin, he survived the torpedoing of the freighter *Norlandia* on July 3, 1942, and also a trip to Murmansk in the so-called Forgotten Convoy, which was stranded for eight months in Murmansk.

Capt. William W. Callis

A Callis cousin from Gwynn's Island, he saved his freighter, the *Delisle*, from sinking by running it aground after it was torpedoed off Florida on May 4, 1942, by the U-564. He survived the war and sailed on different ships for years afterward.

Capt. Otis Levering Callis

Brother of William Callis, he sailed between the United States and Britain throughout the war on the Liberty ship *Benjamin Chew* without serious incident. Only days after he returned to Gwynn's Island from the war, he was killed in a car accident.

Nancy Callis

The wife of Captain Homer Callis of Gwynn's Island, she managed the family home and often served as the reluctant bearer of bad news when islanders were killed in the war. She lost a son to a kamikaze attack in the Pacific.

The Hudgins Family

Capt. Guy Hudgins

He commanded the Liberty ship *Zebulon B. Vance* on the Murmansk Run and during Operation Torch, the invasion of North Africa, in November 1942. He survived the war and sailed for years afterward. At age eighty-one he drowned during a morning swim in the Atlantic Ocean off Florida.

Genious Hudgins Jr.

A member of the large network of Hudgins cousins in Mathews, he survived the torpedoing of the freighter *Green Island* on May 6, 1942, by the U-125, but was killed when the *Onondaga*, under the command of Captain Dewey Hodges, was torpedoed off Cuba on July 23, 1942.

Capt. Walter Hudgins

A Gwynn's Islander, he survived the torpedoing of the *Barbara* in the Windward Passage on March 7, 1942, by the U-103, and also the torpedoing of the *Elizabeth* in nearby waters on May 20, 1942. He survived the war and sailed for years afterward.

Capt. Willard Hudgins

Another Gwynn's Islander, he took over the freighter *Mae* from Captain Homer Callis, only to have it torpedoed on his first voyage, on September 17, 1942, off British Guiana. He helped rescue Lester Smith of Mathews, whose legs were severely injured by the torpedo explosion.

Alton Hudgins

He survived the torpedoing of his freighter, the *Collingsworth*, off South America on January 9, 1943.

Allen Hudgins

He survived a sinking and a 2,400-mile lifeboat odyssey after the Liberty ship *Roger B. Taney* was torpedoed in the middle of the South Atlantic on February 3, 1943, by the U-160.

Wendell Hudgins

A Navy enlisted sailor, he died when the destroyer USS *Monaghan* was sunk by Typhoon Cobra off the Philippines on September 18, 1944.

Salome Hudgins

The wife of Genious Hudgins Jr., she tried to persuade him to stop sailing in war zones, and refused to accept his death.

The Hammond Family

William Hammond

One of three seafaring sons of a Mathews blacksmith, William survived the torpedoing of the *Norlindo* in the Gulf of Mexico on May 4, 1942, by the U-507, but was killed in the torpedoing of the *Onondaga* off Cuba on July 23, 1942, along with three other Mathews men.

Stacy Hammond

The brother of William and Clayton Hammond, he survived the torpedoing of the freighter *Oneida* off Cuba on July 13, 1942, by the U-166. Captain Leslie Hodges was killed in the sinking.

Clayton Hammond

The oldest of the three seafaring Hammond brothers, he survived the sinking of the freighter *East Indian* off South Africa on November 3, 1942, by the U-181, and was forced into a terrible choice to try to save his shipmates' lives.

The Respess Family

Capt. Mellin Respess

He was torpedoed three times on three different ships in 1942. He survived the sinking of the freighter *Oakmar* off Cape Hatteras, North Carolina, on March 20, 1942, as well as the sinking of the Liberty ship *Thomas McKean* off the British West Indies on June 29, 1942. But he was killed along with three other Mathews men when the *Onondaga* was torpedoed off Cuba on July 23, 1942, by the U-129.

Capt. Virgil Respess

Retired from the sea, he did most of the hiring for the Bull Line steamship line in Baltimore during World War II, and went out of his way to employ as many men from Mathews as possible.

Eleanor Respess

The wife of Captain Mellin Respess, she suffered as death came closer and closer to him before she finally lost him when he was torpedoed a third time in six months.

Other Mathews Men and Women

Wallace M. Albertson

A Navy electrician's mate 2nd class, he was killed after Japanese bombers sank the airplane tender USS *Langley* off Java on February 7, 1942.

James Ashberry

He survived the torpedoing of the freighter *City of Alma* in the mid-Atlantic on June 2, 1942, by the U-159.

Robert Lee Belvin Jr.

A seaman, he was killed when the *Ruth* was torpedoed by the U-153 off Cuba on June 29, 1942.

Charles Ogletree Billups Jr.

He quit a safe job in a shipyard to go to sea and was killed on his first voyage when the Liberty ship *Paul Hamilton* exploded after being torpedoed by a bomber in the Mediterranean on April 20, 1944.

Capt. Lewis P. Borum

A Gwynn's Island native, he survived a torpedoing in each world war—first in the freighter *City of Memphis* off Ireland in 1917, and then in the troopship *City of Birmingham* off the Outer Banks of North Carolina on June 30, 1942, by the U-202. Borum also rescued men in lifeboats in both wars. He survived the wars and sailed for years afterward.

Robert Lee Brown

A twenty-one-year-old seaman, he survived the torpedoing of the freighter *Mary* off South America on March 3, 1942, by the U-129. Immediately afterward, he joined the Navy.

Marion Capers

He survived the torpedoing of the freighter *East Indian* off South Africa on November 3, 1942, which killed five Mathews men. He sailed throughout the war and afterward, but was killed in 1951 when his ship sank in a hurricane.

Perry Collier

He was killed along with four other Mathews men when the freighter *Ruth* was torpedoed off Cuba on June 29, 1942, by the U-153.

Harold Davis

Along with Captain Walter Hudgins, he survived the torpedoing of both the *Barbara* in March 1842 and the *Elizabeth* three months later. Like Hudgins, he went back to sea and served throughout the war and afterward.

Vernon Davis

A seaman, he was killed when the freighter *East Indian* was torpedoed off South Africa on November 3, 1942, by the U-181.

Reginald Deagle

A young engineer, he sailed on several Liberty ships during the war. He survived without serious incident and continued sailing after the war.

Russell Dennis

He was the only survivor among the five Mathews men on the *Onondaga*, torpedoed off Cuba on July 23, 1942, by the U-129. He survived the war and sailed for years afterward.

Capt. Sam Jones Diggs

The veteran mariner was killed when the freighter *Massmar* struck a mine en route home from Murmansk on July 5, 1942.

Boyd Dixon

He survived the torpedoing of the oil tanker *E.M. Clark* off Cape Hatteras, North Carolina, on March 18, 1942, by the U-124, and apparently survived another sinking in the Gulf of Mexico and a bombing attack on the docks of southern France.

Samuel Dow

This seaman survived the torpedoing of the tanker *Dixie Arrow* off Cape Hatteras, North Carolina, on March 26, 1942, by the U-71, and witnessed an ultimate sacrifice by one of his shipmates.

Charles Edwards

A young Mathews seaman, he survived the sinking of the *Massmar* by a mine off Iceland on July 5, 1942. He continued sailing throughout the war and afterward.

Joseph Elliott

He joined the Merchant Marine to help feed his family and served on several Liberty ships. He survived the war and continued sailing afterward.

Benny Fitchett

This young mariner joined the Merchant Marine in the middle of the war and sailed on Liberty ships to the Mediterranean and the Pacific. He survived the war and continued sailing long afterward.

William Coles Forrest Jr.

A seaman, he survived the mining of the tanker *Robert C. Tuttle* at the mouth of the Chesapeake Bay on June 15, 1942. He survived the war but lost a brother, Wilson, on the *East Indian* on November 3, 1942.

Wilson Forrest

A seaman, he was killed after the torpedoing of the freighter *East Indian* off South Africa on November 3, 1942, by the U-181.

Nat D. Foster

A Mathews native living in Maine, he was killed when the oil tanker *Muskogee* was torpedoed off the mid-Atlantic coast on March 22, 1942, by the U-123.

Roland Foster Jr.

He survived the sinking of the freighter *Thomas McKean* in mid-ocean on June 29, 1942, by the U-505, and apparently survived the bombing of another ship in the Pacific later in the war. He sailed for years afterward.

Roland Harold Garrett

He survived the torpedoing of the Liberty ship *Benjamin Harrison* in the Mediterranean off Algeria on March 16, 1943, by the U-172.

William Burton Gay

A Navy machinist mate 1st class, he was reported missing early in the war after the fall of the Philippines, and was later discovered to have died in the Japanese prison camp Cabanatuan on July 16, 1942.

Capt. Robert Gayle

The captain of the collier *Achilles*, he survived a close encounter with a U-boat in dense fog off Rhode Island in 1942. He sailed throughout the rest of the war without serious incident.

John Elmo Godsey Jr.

He survived the torpedoing of the freighter *Manuela* off the Outer Banks of North Carolina on June 24, 1942, by the U-404, and later survived a collision between his ship and another vessel near the mouth of the Chesapeake Bay.

Allenby Grimstead

A shipmate of Robert Brown's, he also survived the sinking of the *Mary* off South America on March 3, 1942, by the U-129. He kept sailing merchant ships throughout the war and afterward.

Paul Grubb

He survived the mining of the freighter *Delisle* off Newfoundland on October 19, 1943, and helped to rescue the ship's captain by separating him from his trapped wooden leg.

William Franklin Hale

A Navy seaman 2nd class, he was killed after the cruiser USS *Indianapolis* was torpedoed off the Philippines by a Japanese submarine on July 30, 1945, after delivering the uranium-235 for the first atomic bomb to the island of Tinian.

George Ernest Harrison

He was killed when the freighter *Major Wheeler* was torpedoed off the mid-Atlantic coast on February 6, 1942, by the U-107.

Capt. Stanley Hodges

A distant relative of Captain Jesse Hodges, he survived the torpedoing of the tanker *Gulfpenn* near the mouth of the Mississippi River on May 13, 1941, by the U-506. He went back to sea.

Capt. Elvin "Bubba" Lewis

He got a head start on World War II when he tried to drive the oil tanker *Nantucket Chief* through a Fascist blockade during the Spanish Civil War, and was captured and whipped with rubber hoses. He survived that experience and sailed tankers throughout World War II and afterward.

Victor "Bud" Majette

A young seaman, he survived the bombing of the freighter *Alamar* on the Murmansk Run on May 27, 1942, and then the mining of *Alamar*'s sister ship, the *Massmar*, on the way home from Murmansk, off Iceland, on July 5, 1942. He sailed for the rest of the war and afterward.

Lemuel Marchant

Second officer of the *East Indian*, he was killed after the ship was torpedoed off South Africa on November 3, 1942, by the U-181.

Capt. Levy Morgan

The Gwynn's Island captain was killed when the freighter *Colabee* was torpedoed off Cuba on March 13, 1942, by the U-126.

Howard Dale Morris

The second officer of the *Ruth*, he was killed when the ship was torpedoed by the U-153 off Cuba on June 29, 1942.

Bernard Pierson

He died after the torpedoing of the freighter *East Indian* in the deep ocean off South Africa on November 3, 1942. He gave up a safe seat in the ship's only lifeboat to an injured man, and took the man's place on a raft.

Capt. T. O. Rainier

The commander of the troopship *Cape Victory*, he delivered the crew and support staff of the B-29 Superfortress *Enola Gay* to the island of Tinian in 1945 for the mission of dropping the first atomic bomb on Hiroshima, Japan.

William Cecil Ripley Jr.

A seaman, he was killed when his freighter, the *Syros*, was torpedoed on the Murmansk Run on May 26, 1942.

Lottie Smith

The fiancée and then wife of mariner Lester Smith, she worried constantly about him while he was at sea and helped him recover from devastating injuries.

Thomas Lester Smith

He suffered severe injuries to his legs when the freighter *Mae* was torpedoed off British Guiana on September 17, 1942, by the U-515. He went back to sea and sailed for the rest of the war and afterward.

Bernard Stansbury

A gun captain in the Naval Armed Guard, he survived the bombing and explosion of the Liberty ship *Robert Rowan* off Sicily on July 11, 1943, and, on his very next voyage, the torpedoing of the Liberty ship *Penelope Barker* on the Murmansk Run on January 24, 1944, by the U-278.

Walter Stillman

He went to sea before the war to escape farm work, and sailed throughout the war and for years afterward.

Capt. Ernest Thompson

He was the first Mathews man killed by a U-boat in World War II when the freighter *Norvana* was torpedoed off the Outer Banks of North Carolina on January 22, 1942, by the U-123.

Capt. Jack Ward

He served on several Liberty ships and often caught rides inland to visit soldiers on the battlefields of Italy. He sailed throughout the war without serious incident, and became a tanker captain afterward.

Floyd West

A young seaman, he survived the torpedoing of the tanker *Harry F. Sinclair Jr.* off Cape Hatteras on April 11, 1942, by the U-203.

Charles "Pete" White

A young seaman who joined the Merchant Marine during the war, he sailed on Liberty ships to ports in Europe. He survived the war without serious incident, and continued to sail afterward.

Merritt Franklin White

A Mathews native, he died in the inferno caused by the torpedoing of the gasoline tanker *Virginia* near the mouth of the Mississippi River on May 12, 1942, by the U-507.

Ashley Clinton Williams

One of the few black Mathews mariners, he was killed when the *Ruth* was torpedoed by the U-153 off Cuba on June 29, 1942.

Leslie Winder

He served on tankers throughout the war and distinguished himself on October 19, 1943, when he risked his life to extinguish a fire on the oil tanker *Esso Providence* at the docks in Valetta, Malta.

This list does not include all the Mathews men who sailed against the U-boats in World War II. Merchant Marine records are scattered, and some Mathews men moved to distant cities, where their connections to Mathews faded. Others left no descendants to tell their stories. Still other descendants chose to keep their stories to themselves.

AUTHOR'S NOTE

The idea for this book dates back to 1991, when as a reporter I covered a forum at which old men recalled watching merchant ships explode into flames right off the beach in my home city of Virginia Beach. I was astonished, and began reading all I could find about the U-boat war on America. A few good books told parts of the story, but they left me wanting to know more, particularly about the men on the sinking ships. They had exhibited a different type of courage than what I was used to reading about in war stories.

In 2005, I wrote two historical pieces about the U-boat war for my newspaper, the *Richmond Times-Dispatch.* But I still hadn't gotten enough of the topic, and I began to wonder if I could write the book I had not been able to find in the stacks. Six years later, while working for Maersk Line, Limited, a shipping company based in downtown Norfolk, Virginia, I was wandering around the Kirn Memorial Library (since demolished and replaced by the Slover Library) on my lunch break and ended up in a section devoted to old books on local history. I started thumbing through a dusty, forty-three-year-old edition of a yachtsmen's guide titled *A Cruising Guide to the Chesapeake*, and noticed a section about Mathews County, Virginia, where I once had lived, a short distance from tiny Gwynn's Island. One paragraph stood out from all the descriptions of the channels and shoals: "According to a local authority on the [Mathews] fish wharf who talked convincingly, 5 of the first 61 merchant marine captains whose ships were torpedoed in World War II came from Gwynn's Island—out of a population of 700 . . . [I]n 1942, 57 men from the Island were serving the Nation in some capacity, including 19 sea captains."

I wondered if that was true (it was close). And I wondered if it would be possible, seventy years after World War II, to recover enough information to tell the story of the Mathews men's experiences in the U-boat war. I called the little museum in Gwynn's Island and got a few names and phone numbers.

At that point, no one in Mathews had any reason to believe anything would come of my inquiries, but everywhere I went, old mariners took the time to tell me their stories, and their children and grandchildren dug through trunks and closets for old letters, photos, and documents. They had long ago accepted the idea that the mariners and their sacrifices had been forgotten. But they were not angry or indignant. They just seemed to enjoy the opportunity to tell the stories. I'm not sure any of them truly expected to see them in print.

Every person who spoke with me gave me a few more names and numbers. Several also told me, "Hurry." Most of the Mathews mariners from World War II were dead, and the surviving ones were in their late eighties and early nineties. Parts of the story would not be there for the telling much longer. But most of the old mariners were razor-sharp and crudely funny. They were unfailingly modest and self-effacing. Their children, grandchildren, and other family members were much the same way. They said they hoped the stories would help show what the mariners went through, how they helped to win the war. If this book does that, most of the credit belongs to them.

I am particularly indebted to the members of the Hodges family: Dewey's daughter Jean McFarlane and her husband, Mac; Coleman's daughter

Betty Fernald; Bill Hodges, the keeper of his father Raymond's memory; Louise Hodges's daughter, Stormy Heart Romaniello; Jesse Carroll Thornton, who provided great insight into the characters of his beloved grandparents, Captain Jesse and Henny; and Horace "Brother" Hodges, Willie Hodges's son, who opened doors for me with members of his family and others in Mathews.

Bill Callis informed me and entertained me with tales of his family over the course of numerous interviews. I only wish he were alive to see the result. After his death, his daughter, Lisa, picked up where Bill left off.

I am grateful to Elsa Verbyla, the longtime editor of the *Gloucester-Mathews Gazette-Journal*, who shared the paper's files and photos with me, and frequently used her encyclopedic knowledge of Mathews to put me in touch with relatives of long-lost mariners. I received valuable help from Jean Tanner at the Gwynn's Island Museum, Toni Horodysky at usmm.org, and Nathaniel Patch at National Archives II in College Park, Maryland.

This book is the product of years of support and inspiration from a long list of friends and former colleagues. The names at the top include Paul Tyler and Bill Graves, as well as Tom Kapsidelis, Bill Tangney, Rex Bowman, and Carlos Santos. Those at the *Times-Dispatch* who indulged my interest in the U-boat war include Bill Milsaps, Louise Seals, Dave Burton, Tom Silvestri, and John Dillon. Colleagues at Maersk Line, Limited, in Norfolk, including David Sloane and Bob Bowers, taught me a lot about merchant shipping.

My agent, Farley Chase, took the time to show me how to turn a concept into a book proposal. My editor at Viking, Wendy Wolf, then showed me how to turn a draft into a book. Between them, they made writing *The Mathews Men* more enjoyable than I had imagined it could be. Others at Viking I'd like to thank include Jason Ramirez, Daniel Lagin, Jeannette Williams, Ted Gilley, Melanie Tortoroli, Carolyn Coleburn, Shannon Twomey, Kate Stark, and Georgia Bodnar. Thanks also to Jeff Ward for the fine maps.

AUTHOR'S NOTE

I could not have written this book without the love and support of my family. My wife, Kema, has read every sentence a half-dozen times. My son Cody plowed through early drafts with care and good humor. My son Nick and daughter, Sarah, also offered suggestions, while never letting me take myself too seriously.

NOTES ON SOURCES

I use the following abbreviations of frequently mentioned sources:

The National Archives and Records Administration (NARA) Record Group 38, kept at the Archives II branch in College Park, Maryland, contains the files of the Chief of Naval Operations and the Tenth Fleet antisubmarine command, and thus many of the documents relating to merchant ship sinkings in World War II. NARA's Record Group 26 in the main Archives building in Washington, D.C., holds Coast Guard records, including interviews with the survivors of torpedoed ships. In these notes, those two sources will be described as NARA Record Groups 38 and 26.

I use *GJ* for the *Gloucester-Mathews Gazette-Journal*, and *GJ* notes for the reporters' drafts and notes, which often contained details and comments edited out of the published articles.

Prologue: A Gift from the Predators

The description of the shark fishermen finding the ring comes primarily from a letter written by a businessman in Havana harbor on October 22, 1942, as part of his efforts to find the owner of the ring. The letter finally found its way to Dewey Hodges's family in Norfolk, Virginia, and was to be entered into court. The story was so unusual that both Norfolk newspapers, the *Virginian-Pilot* and the *Ledger-Dispatch*, printed the letter in its entirety in their November 7–8 editions. Dewey Hodges's daughter Jean also provided details of the discovery of the ring.

The description of the fishermen's experience with U-boats and their attitude toward them is based on numerous accounts of sinkings in the National Archives. As a rule, U-boats attacked fishing boats only when the fishermen radioed warnings about them. U-boats in the Caribbean also raided fishing boats for fresh food.

Dr. Jack Musick, a biologist and expert in sharks and shark fishing, provided details about the shark fishermen's operations. Musick, a professor emeritus at the Virginia Institute of Marine Science (VIMS) in Gloucester Point, Virginia, said the Carillos most likely were poor and living hand to mouth on shark and whatever they could get in trade for them. He said the *Donatella* most likely had no motor and a single sail.

Details about the rescue of some of the *Onondaga*'s crew came from NARA Record Group 38. The file for each sunken ship typically contains a summary of the statements by survivors describing the sinking and their rescue; a two-sided card with the official Navy summary of the sinking; and any number of other documents, including investigations by Naval Intelligence, crew lists, and charts.

I found the detail about Dewey Hodges replacing the wires holding the life rafts on the Onondaga with ropes for faster launching, in NARA Record Group 26, which contains Coast Guard interviews with survivors of sunken ships about how to improve lifesaving equipment.

The descriptions of Captain Dewey Hodges were drawn from interviews with his daughter Jean and several other people in Mathews who knew him, including Horace C. "Brother" Hodges, Bill Hodges, and Edwin Jarvis. The quote beginning, "How he loved life!" came from the book *13 Days Adrift*, self-published in 1943 by M. Stanley MacLean, Dewey's longtime ship's carpenter aboard the *East Indian*.

Dewey's last letter to his family is contained in the Chancery section of Norfolk Circuit Court, where the letter is filed as Dewey's last will and testament.

Details of the *Onondaga's* voyage came from the vessel's Ship Movement Card in NARA Record Group 38. Such cards document each ship's port calls, including the dates of arrival and departure. Genious Hudgins's letters to his wife, Salome, provided other details. Genious's daughter, Vicki, shared her father's letters.

The information about U-129 commander Hans-Ludwig Witt came from Kenneth Wynn's *U-boat Operations of the Second World War, Vol. I* (1998). Wynn's book, in two volumes, is an extraordinary piece of work, offering encapsulated histories of individual U-boats during World War II.

The firefight between Hemingway's protagonist Thomas Hudson and a stranded U-boat crew takes place at the climax of Ernest Hemingway's novel *Islands in the Stream* (1970), which was published after his death.

Russell Dennis's descriptions of the sinking came from *GJ* articles after he returned to Mathews, and from reporters' drafts of the articles, which frequently contain more details. Dennis also is quoted in a Navy account of the sinking, and in a federal judge's ruling in the case in 1948.

Chapter One: Born to the Water

I first got to know Mathews in 1985, while I was working as a newspaper reporter for the *Newport News Daily Press* in Gloucester, Virginia. I rented the upper floor of a house on Stutts Creek in Mathews, where I could see through a gap in the barrier islands—the Hole in the Wall—out to the Chesapeake Bay. The owner, a retired Navy rear admiral, had crab pots in the creek and a dock where I would sit on warm evenings and gaze into the water at a scrum of tiny fish, crabs, jellyfish, oysters, and other creatures. I lived in Mathews for only about a year before I got a better job, but I liked the place so much that afterward I often went out of my way to visit (you always had to go out of your way to reach Mathews). The opportunity to write a book about Mathews was a special treat.

Descriptions of the poor roads in early Mathews are from articles in the *GJ*. Many of the newspaper's stories are collected in *History and Progress: Mathews County, Virginia*, published by the Mathews County Historical Society in 1982. Mathews roads remained poor well into the twentieth century. A newspaper headline in 1954 read: "Mathews County Marooned When Three-Day Rain Turns Main Roads into Quagmire."

Several people who grew up in Mathews during the 1940s described the community's way of sharing labor at harvest and hog-killing time. Benny Fitchett of Mathews told me his parents regularly sent him around to the homes of elderly and needy neighbors to lend a hand, especially when winter was approaching. His efforts on behalf of one elderly neighbor paid off when she turned out to be the beloved aunt of a girl Benny wanted to ask out. The aunt spoke glowingly of Benny, and the girl not only went out with him but ended up becoming his wife.

Descriptions of "downtown" Mathews came from interviews with people who lived in the county during the 1940s. A feature story in the *Richmond Times-Dispatch* on December 21, 1941, described the Mathews courthouse area in detail, and as "straggling." The *Times-Dispatch* published a story on the Saturday night gatherings on Mathews's Main Street on July 17, 1938.

A photo of hooded and robed Klansmen at a Mathews Fourth of July parade in 1925 appears in *Mathews County Panorama* (2000). The description of the Hodgeses' views on race relations comes from interviews with several members of the family, including Brother Hodges, Stormy Heart Romaniello, and Jesse Carroll Thornton.

The circumstances of Captain Jesse's first going to sea were described by numerous members of the Hodges family, including Brother Hodges, Jesse Carroll Thornton, Jean Hodges McFarlane, and Bill Hodges. The family history quoted was written by Raymond Hodges's granddaughter Marie Hodges.

The comment about Captain Jesse by his daughter Louise came from a taped interview with her and her brother David in 1999. The comment that Captain Jesse "played out" came from Louise on the tape too. The interviewer, Charlotte Crist, hunted down the tape for me. David Hodges found humor in having been erroneously named for the "seventh son," and had a vanity license plate of 7TH SON.

Captain Jesse's skills as a tugboat captain were lauded by several Mathews men who sailed with him, including his grandson J. W. Corbett, in an interview in 2011. J.W. said no one but Raymond Hodges could handle a ship the way Captain Jesse could.

Jean and Bill Hodges recalled Captain Jesse employing five of his seven sons on a tugboat as officers. Jean described her father Dewey Hodges's efforts to recruit men from Mathews for jobs on his ship when he came home.

The descriptions of the Callis family came from the late Bill Callis, as well as from islanders Jack Rowe and Lottie Mitchem. The "Father Neptune" article appeared in the *Mathews Journal* on February 7, 1929.

Captain Mel Callis's reflections and sea tales appeared in the *GJ* on August 4, 1938.

As a newspaper reporter, I wrote stories about the drowning deaths of fishermen who had never learned to swim. Sadly, such deaths continue to happen.

The anecdote about George Hudgins leaving home during the fall harvest came from Stacy Hammond Jr. of Mathews.

The descriptions of the various jobs on a merchant ship are based on interviews with officers and crew, but a good overall explanation can be found in Glenn A. Knoblock's *African American World War II Casualties and Decorations in the Navy, Coast Guard and Merchant Marine* (2009).

The description of a hawsepipe came from David Sloane, a former cruise ship captain and now vice president, Maersk Line, Limited, Norfolk, Virginia.

The comments about the Bull Line's preference for Mathews men were released in a prepared statement by the company and printed in the *GJ* on February 7, 1929.

The cozy arrangement by which the Respess brothers from Gwynn's

Island did all of the Bull Line's hiring was described by Bill Callis, Jack Rowe, Clarence Collier Jr., and others in interviews. Bill Callis described Virgil Respess, and the process of getting a ship.

The account of the docking of FDR's presidential yacht came from the *GJ* on July 12, 1936.

The lonely widow's letter appeared in the *GJ* in March 1926.

The accounts of Mathews men going to sea out of desperation come from Guy Hudgins's daughter, Joseph Elliott's widow and daughter, and Walter Stillman's widow.

The list of perils of the sea came from boilerplate language in a maritime insurance policy I stumbled upon while working at Maersk Line, Limited, in Norfolk in 2009.

Reginald Deagle told me the monkey story in an interview in 2014. The submarine story came from the *GJ* on September 9, 1920.

The account of Lord Dunmore's defeat at Gwynn's Island is drawn from several sources, including *History and Progress*.

The information about the tide mill at Poplar Grove and John Lennon's subsequent purchase of the property is from the *GJ* on December 11, 1980, and November 3, 1983.

The accounts of Mathews's roles in America's wars are drawn largely from the *GJ* files through *History and Progress*. The reference to Mathews being rife with "guerillas and river pirates" came from a story from the *Philadelphia Inquirer* on October 13, 1863, and was reprinted in a compilation of Gloucester and Mathews newspaper articles by Joan Charles of the Gloucester Historical Society of Virginia in 2014.

Details about the belated German attempt to blockade the U.S. coast with U-boats in World War I came from John Terraine's *Business in Great Waters* (2009), pages 133–34.

Details of the story of Captain L. F. Borum's torpedoing in World War I came from a written account by Borum's family in the Gwynn's Island Museum in Mathews. Details of Captain Elvin "Bubba" Lewis's adventures during the Spanish Civil War came from an interview with his nephew

Raymond Owens, of Mathews, in 2014; and from articles in the *GJ* on January 27 and February 3, 1938.

I examined Mathews census records for 1910, 1920, 1930, and 1940 via www.ancestry.com.

I based my descriptions of the prewar and wartime Merchant Marine on interviews with mariners including Bill Callis, Brother Hodges, and Jack Rowe, and on books including Felix Riesenberg's *Sea War* (1956), Robert Carse's *The Long Haul: The U.S. Merchant Service in World War II* (1965), John A. Butler's *Sailing on Friday: The Perilous Voyage of America's Merchant Marine* (1997), John Bunker's *Heroes in Dungarees* (2006), and *The U.S. Merchant Marine at War 1775–1945*, edited by Bruce L. Felknor (1998). My information on the U.S. Navy's wartime shipbuilding program comes from Samuel Eliot Morison's *The Battle of the Atlantic, 1939–1943* (1947), pages 27–28.

My brief descriptions of the histories of the Bull Line, Moore-McCormack Lines, and the Ford Motor Company fleet come from, respectively, the article "Bull Line," by Lt. John K. Tennant of the U.S. Maritime Service, in the November 1949 *The Mast* magazine, published by the Maritime Service; a profile of Moore-McCormack on www.moore-mccormack .com, a Web site devoted to the history of the defunct company; and interviews with Jean Hodges and other family members of Mathews men who served on Ford ships.

The report on the Reverend Belch's sermon comes from the *GJ* on November 20, 1941. The current pastor of Gwynn's Island Baptist Church, the Reverend Ed Jordan, provided background on the church and a tour.

Accounts of the fire appeared in the *GJ* on December 4, 1941. A story about Japanese crab meat flooding the market and depressing blue crab prices for Mathews crabbers appeared in the *GJ* on January 23, 1941.

Chapter Two: The Devil's Shovel

Several commanders in the first wave of U-boats wrote about encountering the storm, but the quote is from Peter Cremer's *U-boat Commander* (1984), pages 38–39. The information about the losses of U-boat lookouts to the sea came from Timothy Mulligan's *Neither Sharks Nor Wolves* (1999), pages 19–20. Mulligan's book uses extensive research to humanize the U-boat men and puncture myths about U-boats.

Commander Reinhard Hardegan's use of a tourist map and guidebook in his attack on U.S. shores is described in Michael Gannon's *Operation Drumbeat*, page 137. Gannon's groundbreaking book surprised me with its descriptions of the ease with which the U-boats operated in American waters and the Navy's slowness to act to protect merchant ships.

The description of Germany's secret use of a Dutch company to design and build the next generation of U-boats comes from Brayton Harris's *The Navy Times Book of Submarines* (1997), page 265.

Doenitz describes his thinking about sending U-boats to America in detail in his *Memoirs: Ten Years and Twenty Days* (1959), page 196. Doenitz's recollections of his experience in a sinking U-boat are found on pages 3 and 4. The characterization of his behavior at the asylum comes from Wolfgang Frank's *The Sea Wolves* (1955), page 16. Frank was Doenitz's propagandist during the war. Germany's maneuvers to continue developing submarines after World War I are described in Harris's *Navy Times Book of Submarines*, page 265.

The account of Doenitz reporting births to his men at sea comes from Mulligan's *Neither Sharks Nor Wolves*, page 184.

Among the books and documents I consulted for descriptions of U-boats and their workings were Cremer's *U-boat Commander*; Doenitz's *Memoirs*; E. B. Gasaway's *Grey Wolf, Grey Sea* (1970); Herbert A. Werner's *Iron Coffins: A Personal Account of the German U-boat Battles of World War II* (1969); Gannon's *Operation Drumbeat* (1990); Clay Blair's *Hitler's U-boat War* (2000); Harris's *Navy Times Book of Submarines*; and Wynn's *U-boat Operations of the Second World War* (1998). A good layman's explanation of the workings of sonar and radar in the U-boat war can be found in Admirel Daniel Gallery's *Twenty Million Tons under the Sea* (1956), pages 49–57. The book recounts the capture of the U-505.

The admonition that it is better to dive too soon comes from Gordon Williamson's *U-boat Tactics in World War II* (1990), page 56. The statistic about the ineffectiveness of torpedoes on the U-48 also comes from Williamson, page 43.

The wry observations of the fictitious U-boat commander in Lothar-Gunther Buchheim's novel *Das Boot* (1975) appear on page 52 of that book.

The information about Sir Arthur Conan Doyle's and Will Rogers's commentary on U-boats came from Harris's *Navy Times Book of Submarines*, page 234.

Werner's description of a depth charge attack is from his *Iron Coffins*, page 124.

Tin-can neurosis is described by Barrie Pitt in *The Battle of the Atlantic* (1977), page 72.

The fact that Doenitz gave his U-boats artificially high numbers to make the Allies think he had more than he did came from Edwin P. Hoyt's *The U-boat Wars* (2002), page 94.

My characterization of U-boat crews' political views is drawn in part from Mulligan's *Neither Sharks Nor Wolves*, as well as from U-boat commander Hans Georg Hess's recollections in Melanie Wiggins's *U-Boat Adventures: Firsthand Accounts from World War II* (1999), page 169. The account of a U-boat commander being denounced and executed comes from *Neither Sharks Nor Wolves*, pages 232–33.

The comparison of U.S. and German submarines comes from several sources, including an essay by Bernard Zimmermann on www.uboat.net.

The account of the U-boat's fatal toilet malfunction comes from Ronald Spector's *At War at Sea* (2001), page 243.

The account of Archie Gibbs, the American seaman who spent four days as a prisoner in a U-boat, comes from the *Virginian-Pilot* of Norfolk, July 27, 1942.

The figures on the Allied shipping losses at that point in the war come from Blair's *Hitler's U-boat War*, pages 418–19. The story about the "sightings" of Gunther Prien after his disappearance comes from Spector's *At*

War at Sea, page 239. The story about another U-boat officer checking on Prien in a prison camp came from Andrew Williams's *The Battle of the Atlantic*, pages 125–26.

My information about relatively few U-boat commanders accounting for most of the losses comes from Bernard Ireland's *The Battle of the Atlantic* (1993) and Mulligan's *Neither Sharks Nor Wolves*, pages 64 and 71.

Descriptions of how convoys are formed and structured came in part from interviews with Mathews mariners and from Felknor's *The U.S. Merchant Marine at War*, page 248.

My information about the role code breaking played in the U-boat war came from Stephen Budiansky's *Blackett's War* (2013); Spector's *At War at Sea*, page 239; Hugh Sebag-Montefiore's *Enigma: The Battle for the Code* (2000); John Winton's *Ultra at Sea* (1988); and Harris's *Navy Times Book of Submarines*, page 236.

The structure of a wolf pack is described, among many other places, in Doenitz's *Memoirs* and Williamson's *U-boat Tactics of World War II*.

Descriptions of the Germans' U-boat bunkers on the French coast can be found in Doenitz's *Memoirs*, notably on page 129, and in Randolph Bradham's *Hitler's U-boat Fortresses* (2003).

For a starting point and perspective on what was happening in the United States and elsewhere at stages of the U-boat war, I used Winston Groom's *1942* (2005).

Admiral Stark's comment that America was already at war in the autumn of 1941 comes from Gannon's *Operation Drumbeat* (1990), page 92.

Doenitz describes his frustration at not being able to send more U-boats to the United States in his *Memoirs*. Another good description of the U-boat force being pulled in all directions appears in Lisle A. Rose's *Power at Sea: The Breaking Storm, 1919–1945* (2007), page 308.

Hardegan's meeting with Doenitz and his preparations for departure to America are described in Gannon's *Operation Drumbeat*, and by Hardegan himself in his war diary, translated from German to English on www.uboatarchive.net. The text of Doenitz's message to his crews came from Ed Offley's *The Burning Shore* (2014), page 69.

The account of Hardegan's attack on the *Cyclops* and the U-123's cruise past New York comes from Williams's *The Battle of the Atlantic*, page 166, and Gannon's *Operation Drumbeat*, page 213.

The account of Hardegan's crude response to his victims' failure to realize they had been torpedoed comes from Thomas Parrish's *The Submarine: A History* (2004), page 253.

Chapter Three: Missing

The description of Henny Hodges is drawn from interviews with family members and neighbors, including Jesse Carroll Thornton, Jean Hodges, Brother Hodges, Stormy Heart Romaniello, Marlene Callis, and taped interviews with Louise and David Hodges. Jesse Carroll Thornton lived with Henny alone at Gales Neck in 1942, though he was only four years old.

Most of the Hodges family had been told that Jesse and Henny's infant son James Hodges died of tuberculosis. But Stormy Heart Romaniello said her mother, Louise Hodges, told her the toddler had died of burns after falling into the fireplace at the Hodges home in Norfolk. Death certificates including causes of death were not required by the Commonwealth of Virginia at the time.

The account of little Henrietta Hodges's death in an automobile accident comes from interviews with family members and a story in the *Mathews Journal* on May 30, 1918. My description of the fire comes from interviews with family members; a taped interview with Louise Hodges; and the *Mathews Journal* on December 3, 1931.

My information about Captain Ernest Thompson comes mainly through an interview with his son Ernest Travers Thompson, a retired U.S. Navy submariner from Mathews. Accounts of the sinking of the *Norvana* come from the NARA Record Group 38. Little documentation exists about the *Norvana* sinking because the ship vanished. But other ships' sinkings are described in survivors' statements, intelligence reports, and other documents. The movements of ships between ports during the war can be tracked through Ship Movement Cards, also in NARA Record Group 38.

Joseph Conrad's description of "overdue" and "missing" appear in his *The Mirror of the Sea*, pages 49 and 52. The exception to the grim record of "missing" ships comes from John R. Stilgoe's *Lifeboat* (2007), page 22. Hardegen described the torpedoing of the *Norvana* and her violent explosion in his war diary, translated into English on www.uboatarchive.net.

The *GJ* article on Thompson's loss and Blake's survival appeared on February 5, 1942.

The description of George Ernest Harrison comes partly from U.S. Census records, the *GJ*, and an interview with his relative, Grady Powell of Mathews. Powell also provided the letter from Harrison to his sister.

The account of the *Major Wheeler* sinking comes mainly from NARA Records Group 38. The description of the family's effort to get information comes from the *GJ*. The excerpt from the letter from the Bull Line to the navy secretary comes from Captain Arthur Moore's *A Careless Word . . . A Needless Sinking* (1998), page 330. Captain Moore's book is indispensible to anyone writing about the U.S. Merchant Marine in World War II. Another vital source of information is Robert M. Browning Jr.'s *United States Merchant Marine Casualties of World War II* (2011).

Accounts of mariners coming home after being thought dead can be found in John Bunker's *Heroes in Dungarees* (2006), pages 294–95.

The sinking of the *Lake Osweya* is described in NARA Record Group 38. Louise Hodges described her then husband's response to the sinking in a taped interview.

I obtained the list of vanished ships from Moore's *A Careless Word*, page 559, and tallied up the losses through Moore's book and NARA Record Group 38.

Thoughtful explanations of how submarines obliterated the prize rules can be found in Thomas Parrish's *The Submarine* and Bragton Harris's *Navy Times Book of Submarines*. Admiral Gallery's assertion about the cold-bloodedness of submarine warfare can be found in his *Twenty Million Tons Under the Sea*, page 12.

Much of my information about the Japanese submarine force came from interviews with Dr. Carl Boyd, history professor emeritus at Old Dominion University in Norfolk, Virginia, and coauthor of *The Japanese Submarine Force and World War II* (1995). Information about the U.S. submarine force's approach to Japanese merchant shipping came from Theodore Roscoe's *United State Submarine Operations of World War II* (1956) and Ann and John Tusa's *The Nuremberg Trial* (2010).

The account of Hitler's comments to the Japanese ambassador about killing merchant seamen came from Harris's *Navy Times Book of Submarines*, pages 302–3.

According to Timothy Mulligan's *Neither Sharks Nor Wolves*, page 213, historical records show only one instance of a U-boat commander's embracing Hitler's wishes. In March 1944, Heinz Eck of the U-852 opened fire on survivors on life rafts after interrogating them. Three of the castaways hid behind their rafts and survived to testify against Eck, who was hanged.

U-boat commander Otto Kretschmer's order to show mercy came from Mulligan's *Neither Sharks Nor Wolves*, page 196.

The information that 70 percent of merchant ships between 1940 and 1944 sank within fifteen minutes comes from Harris's *Navy Times Book of Submarines*, pages 302–3.

The accounts of U-boat captains offering help to lifeboat survivors come mainly from NARA Record Group 38. Moore's *A Careless Word* often describes such offers of aid in its summaries of ship sinkings.

The death of Wallace Albertson on the USS *Langley* was described in the *GJ* on April 9, 1942. The descriptions of the shortages of defenses for the East Coast of the United States come mainly from the Navy's *Eastern Sea Frontier War Diary*, from Michael Gannon's *Operation Drumbeat*, and Felknor's *The U.S. Merchant Marine at War*, pages 210–26. The description of the sailboat rigged to fire depth charges came from a 2004 interview with retired Coast Guardsman Theodore Mutro of Ocracoke Island, North Carolina.

Descriptions of Admiral Andrews's overwhelming responsibilities and his unsuccessful efforts to get help come from the *Eastern Sea Frontier War Diary*, Gannon's *Operation Drumbeat*, and Theodore Taylor's *Fire on the Beaches* (1958).

Morison's description of Admiral Andrews appears in Samuel Eliot Morison's *The Battle of the Atlantic*, volume 1 of his history of the U.S. Navy in World War II (1947), page 208. Descriptions of King come in part from Morison, page 130, as well as Gannon, Blair's *Hitler's U-boat War*, and Felknor. King's reluctance and slowness to organize convoys is described in Felknor, pages 210–26, as well as Gannon, Williams's *The Battle of the Atlantic*, Harris's *Navy Times Book of Submarines*, Bunker, Taylor, and Ed Offley's *The Burning Shore*. Blair defends King, saying he could not possibly have acted quicker than he did. Andrews's comment about his forces' helplessness against submarines can be found in the Preface to the *Eastern Sea Frontier War Diary*.

The strafing and bombing of whales was reported in the *Virginian-Pilot* on April 14, 1942. Theodore Taylor's comment in the footnotes comes from his *Fire on the Beaches*, page 36. The debacle of the USS *Dickerson* being attacked by a U.S. merchant ship is described in Homer H. Hickam Jr.'s *Torpedo Junction* (1989), pages 91–93. The U-boat commander's gleeful comments about shore lights on the U.S. East Coast came from Cremer's *U-boat Commander*, page 69; Morison's comment about shore lighting appears in his *The Battle of the Atlantic*, page 130. Felknor's *The U.S. Merchant Marine at War*, page 216, contains the text of Roosevelt's executive order giving the military the right to control "all lighting on the seacoast." The *GJ* editorial on coastal lights appeared on May 21, 1942.

U-boat commanders, including Reinhard Hardegan, wrote about taking pains to identify the vessels they sank, so that they could report back to Doenitz. Hardegan was one of those who carried a reference book from Lloyd's of London. The captured logbooks of U-boats show no indication of the commanders' receiving useful intelligence from spies on shore. The writer and former merchant mariner S. J. Flaherty, who wrote as "Ferocious" O'Flaherty, punctures the myth of loose lips sinking ships in his wry book *Abandoned Convoy* (1970). The telegram with the warning about not divulging the name of the missing man's ship came from Salome Hudgins of Mathews.

The double-whammy against the Allies of losing their access to secret German messages while the Germans gained access to theirs is described in Offley's *The Burning Shore*, page 83, as well as Stephen Budiansky's *Blackett's War*, Hugh Sebag-Montefiore's *Enigma: The Battle for the Code*, and John Winton's *Ultra at Sea*.

Navy Secretary Knox's absurd claims about U-boat sinkings appeared in newspapers all over the country, including *The New York Times*, March 22, 1942. Not all Americans bought into the propaganda. *Times* columnist Hanson W. Baldwin suggested that "the very nature of submarine warfare makes it difficult if not impossible to determine whether or not a submarine raider has been sunk. Frequently the Navy Department reports of encounters between surface ships and submarines have been misleading and overoptimistic." Admiral Simons's speech was covered by the *Virginian-Pilot* on April 2, 1942. Admiral Thomas Hoover's minimalist press remarks are described in Taylor's *Fire on the Beaches*, page 172.

The "bearable losses" assessment appears in the *Eastern Sea Frontier War Diary*, page 31.

The descriptions of the early war days in Mathews came from interviews with Clarence Collier Jr. and Elliott Hudgins.

Chapter Four: Professional Survivors

My description of Raymond Hodges comes mostly from interviews with members of the Hodges family, including his son Bill, Brother Hodges, Jesse Carroll Thornton, Stormy Heart Romaniello, Marlene Callis, and Louise and David Callis on tape. I also relied on several newspaper clippings tracking Raymond's career, including: the *Mathews Journal*, February 4, 1932; the *Mooremack News*, with permission from the *Christian Science Monitor*, December 1947; *Time* magazine, November 19, 1934; *The*

New York Times, September 1951; and *Critica*, of Buenos Aires, February 16, 1955.

Everyone in the Hodges family agreed Raymond dressed up when he went out, although his son Bill said Raymond dressed in jeans and denim shirts around the house. Bill Hodges described being whacked by his father with paint sticks. David Callis described Raymond's dressing-down of his brothers.

The Hodges girls may have been goaded by Raymond's son Bill, who tired of their questions and began concocting elaborate stories to watch their eyes widen. Bill may have originated the story that Dolly was formerly a dancer in the Ziegfeld Follies.

Numerous books describe the shipping lanes in World War II. Among the best are Gaylord T. M. Kelshall's *The U-boat War in the Caribbean* (1988); Melanie Wiggins's *Torpedoes in the Gulf: Galveston and the U-boats, 1942–1943* (1995); and Kenneth Wynn's *U-boat Operations of the Second World War*.

The description of the coordinated attack comes from Stanton Hope's *Tanker Fleet: The War Story of the Shell Tankers and the Men Who Manned Them* (1948), which on pages 54–55 describes the Dutch island of Aruba. Sir Thomas Holland made his remarks about the importance of manganese at a speech in London, reported by the Associated Press on July 24, 1942.

The descriptions of the *Mary*'s voyage and ultimate sinking are drawn from NARA Record Groups 38 and 26, and from interviews given by Robert Lee Brown and Allenby Grimstead to the *GJ* on April 23, 1942. Details are contained in the *GJ* notes. The notes are hundreds of pages of typewritten 1942 *GJ* reporters' notes and first drafts of stories, containing details not in the paper.

Details about Nicolai Clausen came from Kelshall's *The U-boat War in the Caribbean*, page 46, and Wynn's entry for the U-129.

Particulars of lifeboats, their food and water supplies, and other equipment, came from Phil Richards and John Banigan, *How to Abandon Ship* (1942), page 3. I recommend *How to Abandon Ship* for a wide range of interesting observations about lifeboat survival in the U-boat war. Banigan survived the sinking of the first U.S. ship in World War II, the *Robin Moor*.

The details about the refugee camp for mariners on Trinidad comes from Felix Riesenberg's *Sea War*, page 18.

The information about pirates in the Windward Passage comes from Angus Konstam's *Scourge of the Seas* (2001), pages 23–24, 80, and 97.

The description of Captain Walter Hudgins comes mainly from an interview with his son Elliott Hudgins, and from a testimonial to him that his family wrote for the Gwynn's Island Museum. The description of Charles Davis comes mainly from his cousin Amelia Minter of North Carolina. The description of the attack on the *Barbara* is drawn from NARA Record Groups 38 and 26, and from accounts in the *GJ* on April 9, 1942.

The dangers of working in the engine room are described in numerous books. In Buchheim's novel *Das Boot*, the fictitious U-boat commander tells his crew: "What a job working ten feet below the water line, knowing that at any second a torpedo may tear open the ship's side without the slightest warning? How often when on convoy the men must measure the thin plates that divide them from the sea. How often they must surreptitiously try out the quickest route to the deck, always with the taste of panic in their mouths, and in their ears the rending scream of iron, the blast of the explosion, and the roaring inrush of the sea. Not one second's feeling of security. Always scared shitless, always waiting for the clanging of the alarm bell."

The account of radioman Lopez's experience came from www.usmm .org, a Web site devoted to the U.S. Merchant Marine.

The information about the U-boat commander Ernest Bauer came from Wynn's entry for the U-126.

The report that the Eastern Sea Frontier was the scene of half the world's sinkings in March 1942 comes from the Navy's *Eastern Sea Frontier War Diary*, page 102. The interviews with the survivors of the *Marore* appeared in the *Virginian-Pilot* of Norfolk on March 36, 1942. The description of the easy lifeboat voyage appeared in the *Virginian-Pilot*, May 5, 1943. The account of the nightmarish voyage of the survivors of the Belgian freighter appeared in the *Virginian-Pilot* on February 24, 1942. The tally of ten sinkings for Stanizewski comes from www.usmm.org. The account of a ship's engineer constructing a still to produce drinking water from seawater appears in Bruce Felknor's *The U.S. Merchant Marine at War*, pages 319–20. The quote about the fortuitous zig comes from Roscoe's *United States Submarine Operations of World War II*, page 214.

Captain Jesse Hodges described his approach to avoiding U-boats to the *Washington Sunday Star* on September 6, 1942. Captain Homer Callis's approach was described by Jack Rowe and Lottie Mitchem of Gwynn's Island, as well as by Homer's son Bill Callis. Captain Elvin Lewis's approach was described by his nephew Raymond Owens of Mathews.

How to Abandon Ship also included a prayer for committing the dead to the sea: "Unto Almighty God we commend the soul of our brother departed, and we commit his body to the deep; in sure and certain hope of the Resurrection unto eternal life, through our Lord Jesus Christ; at whose coming in glorious majesty to judge the world, the sea shall give up her dead; and the corruptible bodies of those who sleep in him shall be changed, and made like unto his glorious body; according to the mighty working whereby he is able to subdue all things unto himself."

The information about Captain Levy Morgan comes from Jack Rowe of Gwynn's Island, U.S. Census records, and a memorial his family wrote to him in the Gwynn's Island Museum, as well as the *GJ* on March 26 and April 2, 1942. The complaint about Morgan's having to treat the crew carefully came from the first officer's interview with the Coast Guard in NARA Records Group 26, and the descriptions of the torpedoing and the grounding come from NARA Record Group 38, which in this case includes an intelligence report.

The descriptions of the merchant mariners' unique civilian, free-agent status come from numerous mariners, including Bill Callis, Jack Rowe, J. W. Corbett, and Brother Hodges. Riesenberg's comment appears in *Sea War* on page 22.

The information about Pegler's allegations about the Merchant Marine and the resulting libel case come from www.usmm.org, and the information about *Time*'s criticism of the Merchant Marine came from Riesenberg's *Sea War*, page 151. Helen Lawrenson's article in *Collier's*, "They Keep 'em Sailing," appeared on August 8, 1942. *The New York Times* editorial praising the U.S. Merchant Marine appeared on June 22, 1942.

My description of Captain Mellin Respess comes from interviews with Bill Callis, Jack Rowe, and Benny Fitchett of Mathews; Eleanor's friend Edward Judson; and U.S. Census records. Ship crew manifests accessed on www.ancestry.com show Mellin had sailed on the *Major Wheeler* several times in 1941.

The description of the voyage and sinking of the *Oakmar* came largely from NARA Record Group 38, and from the former German submariner Jochen Brennecke's *The Hunters and the Hunted: German U-boats 1939–1945* (2003), page 166.

The account of Mellin Respess visiting Eleanor's family on Gwynn's Island after being "quite ill in a hospital" comes from the *GJ* on April 30, 1942. The account of Mellin's last visit to the general store came from Benny Fitchett of Mathews, who also remembered being taught math at the island's only school by Mellin's wife, Eleanor.

Chapter Five: "Off Hatteras the Tankers Sink"

The account of the *E.M. Clark*'s sinking comes from NARA Record Group 38, and *Ships of the Esso Fleet* (1946), pages 144–48; Gerald Reminick's *Patriots and Heroes, Vol. 2* (2004), pages 72 and 183–84; and Bruce Felknor, *The U.S. Merchant Marine at War*, pages 200–201. The background on Boyd Dixon comes from an interview with his brother John Dixon of Gwynn's Island.

The description of the positive aspects of sailing on tankers comes from John Bunker's *Heroes in Dungarees*, page 188; Stanton Hope's *Tanker Fleet*; and Philip Kaplan's and Jack Currie's *Convoy* (1998) as well as from interviews with Captain Bill Callis and Jack Ward of Mathews, who commanded tankers after the war.

The descriptions of the dangers of burning oil and oil slicks come from the *Fire Fighting Manual for Tank Vessels* (1974) and Hope's *Tanker Fleet*, page 95, which describes the dangers of oil slicks to swimming men. The accounts of added perils in the footnote come from accounts of tanker sinkings in Captain Arthur Moore's *A Careless Word . . . A Needless Sinking.*

My accounts of the successes of Mohr and the U-124 are based in part on NARA Record Group 38 and Wynn's descriptions of U-124's activities. Mohr's poem also is quoted in several books, including Thomas Parrish's *The Submarine*, page 257.

My information about Nat Foster comes from U.S. Census records, letters in the George Betts collection at the Independence Seaport Museum in Philadelphia, and the *GJ* on March 22, 1942. The account of the *Muskogee*'s disappearance is based in part on documents in NARA Record Group 38, the Betts collection, and Wolfgang Frank's *The Sea Wolves.*

My description of Sam Dow comes mainly from U.S. Census records, crew manifests, and the *GJ* on April 9, 1942. The description of the sinking of the *Dixie Arrow* comes from NARA Record Groups 38 and 26; the *Virginian-Pilot* on March 29, 1942; *The New York Times* on March 29, 1942; Wynn's *U-boat Operations of the Second World War*; and the Maritime Commission's description of Oscar Chappell's actions in its award to him posthumously of the Merchant Marine Distinguished Service Medal. The description of the children of Hatteras seeing the pillar of smoke from the *Dixie Arrow* on their way to school comes from a 2004 interview with Gibb Gray, who was a boy on Hatteras Island in the village of Buxton in 1942.

The toll of tankers by the end of March comes from Clay Blair's *Hitler's U-boat War*, page 765. The accounts of fuel shortages in the northeastern United States come from Theodore Taylor's *Fire on the Beaches*, page 219. The information in the footnote about the tanker fleet comes from Blair, page 468.

The tanker losses prompted the construction of pipelines to carry oil from the Gulf of Mexico to the northeastern United States. The largest pipeline, nicknamed the Big Inch, was built in less than a year and finished in July 1943, according to Nathan Miller's *War at Sea*, page 294.

The account of the oil companies' concerns and suggestions comes from Michael Gannon's *Operation Drumbeat*, page 343. The description of the fake guns on the *Esso Baton Rouge* comes from Taylor's *Fire on the Beaches*, page 68. The fact that the tanker was sunk anyway came from Moore's *A Careless Word*, page 90. The account of Admiral King's request for a dimout rather than a blackout, and of the subsequent sinking off Atlantic City, New Jersey, comes from Gannon's *Operation Drumbeat*, page 344.

The account of Admiral Andrews organizing an escort fleet of small craft, and of Roosevelt's enthusiasm for it, comes from Parrish's *The Submarine*, page 258.

The text of Winston Churchill's comment to Harry Hopkins comes from Churchill's *The Hinge of Fate* (1950), the second volume of his five-volume series about World War II, page 110. The text of King's complaint about the British not bombing the U-boat pens comes from Edwin P. Hoyt's *U-boats Offshore* (1978), page 76.

The accounts of the British commando raid on the U-boat bunkers and the subsequent executions of French partisans come in part from Churchill's *The Hinge of Fate*, pages 121–22, and *The New York Times* on March 29, 1942.

The account of Rodger Winn's encounter with Admiral King and his staff is described in several books, including Stephen Budiansky's *Blackett's War*, pages 182–83. The report of the Navy's convoy plans comes from the *Eastern Sea Frontier War Diary*, page 111. Gaylord T. M. Kelshall points out the focus of the plan on available forces rather than need in *The U-boat War in the Caribbean*, page 17. Hitler's remark about "millionaires" and "beauty queens" came from Richard Overy's *Why the Allies Won* (1995), page 205. Hitler's boast came from Gannon's *Operation Drumbeat*, page 339.

My account of the *Atik* disaster came from Gannon's *Operation Drumbeat*, pages 322–28. My description of Hemingway's efforts to turn his fishing boat into a Q-ship came from Michael Reynolds's *Hemingway: The Final Years* (1999), pages 64–69, and Hilary Hemingway and Carlene Brennen's *Hemingway in Cuba* (2003), page 78.

I researched the story of the "lifeboat baby" in late 2004 and early 2005 while working for the *Richmond Times-Dispatch*. I got much of the story from interviews with the lifeboat baby, Jesse Roper Mohorovic, and his sister, Vesna Jurick, who was kind enough to translate from Croatian to English an account by her mother of the sinking and birth. Jesse had all the Navy documents about the sinking; the telegram his father received announcing his birth in a lifeboat; a copy of his ad-libbed birth certificate; and a map someone had given him showing the route his lifeboat had traveled between the sinking of the *City of New York* and the rescue of the lifeboat survivors by the USS *Roper*. Several members of the *Roper*'s crew talked with me, including Rhodes Chamberlain of New Mexico, who had a copy of the *Roper*'s logbook, a shipmate's diary, and other documents. The commander of the *Roper*, Hamilton Howe, left an oral history of his war experiences at East Carolina University. The story is also based on NARA Records Groups 38 and 26 and news accounts in *The New York Times*, the *International Herald Tribune*, and the *Virginian-Pilot*, as well as various tabloids. I interviewed Larry Atkinson, an oceanographer at Old Dominion University in Norfolk, about the characteristics of the Gulf Stream. The family of George Orner, who was in the lifeboat with the baby, sent me his account of the journey after my story was published in the newspaper. A Methodist missionary, Sarah King, also survived the sinking and published an account in the June 1942 issue of *The Methodist Woman* magazine, "My Experiences off Cape Hatteras." The fate of the last of the *City of New York*'s lifeboats was described in Felix Riesenberg's *Sea War*, page 75.

Lottie Mitchem described her nervousness in an interview on Gwynn's Island. Harry Hammond's respite from worry was described in the *GJ* on March 19, 1942.

The *East Indian*'s return was reported in the *GJ* on April 3. My description of the ship is based on interviews with Jean Hodges. The *East Indian*'s arduous voyage was described in M. Stanley MacLean's *13 Days Adrift* and reconstructed through the vessel's Ship Movement Card in NARA Record

Group 38. The departures of the crew are described by MacLean and in an interview with Walter Stillman's widow, Claire Stillman.

Dewey Hodges's illness was described by his daughter Jean. My description of Dewey Hodges comes significantly from Jean, but also from others who knew him in Mathews, including his nephews, Brother Hodges and Bill Hodges.

Chapter Six: Killing Ground to Battleground

I researched the story of the sinking of the U-85 in 2004–2005 while working on a story for the *Richmond Times-Dispatch*. I interviewed retired naval officer Kenneth Tebo, in Alexandria, Virginia. He was the young officer who first decided to pursue the radar and sonar target, and was on the bridge during the attack on the U-85 and the immediate aftermath. I also interviewed Rhodes Chamberlain of New Mexico, who provided a copy of the *Roper*'s logbook, the Navy's reports on the encounter, two shipmates' diaries, and other documents. I interviewed former *Roper* crewman Jacob DeWitt. I read the transcribed oral history of the *Roper*'s commander, Hamilton Howe, at East Carolina University. The civilian's account of the looting of the German bodies came from an article by John S. Van Gilder in the *Knoxville News Sentinel*'s Sunday Magazine on November 29, 1942. Doenitz comments about the ineffectiveness of destroyers patrolling for U-boats in his *Memoirs*, page 202.

The account of the *Gulfamerica* sinking comes from NARA Record Group 38; Hardegan's war diary translated on www.uboatarchive.net; Michael Gannon's *Operation Drumbeat*; Bruce Felknor's *The U.S. Merchant Marine at War*, page 205; and other sources. Hardegan's comment about improving Allied defenses came from Andrew Williams's *The Battle of the Atlantic*, page 176.

A great deal has been written about Liberty ships. I found some of the most interesting facts in Jim Marshall's article in *Collier's* magazine, "Hulls in a Hurry," on July 11, 1942. The material in the footnote about christening comes from another *Collier's* article, this one by Josef Israels II, "A Ship

Is Born," on August 28, 1943. I also drew from interviews with several Mathews mariners, including Bill Callis, Benny Fitchett, Reginald Deagle, Pete White, and Jack Ward; and from John Gorley Bunker's *Liberty Ships: The Ugly Ducklings of World War II* (1972), A. A. Hoehling's *The Fighting Liberty Ships* (1996), William F. Luthmann's *At Liberty* (1995), and Philip Kaplan and Jack Currie's *Convoy*.

Stephen Budiansky's quote about a "brutal calculus" comes from *Blackett's War*, page 185. The long list of World War II Liberty ship names is an entertaining read, at www.usmm.org/libertyships.html.

The information that Germany's intelligence service tripled its estimate of America's shipbuilding capacity comes from Ronald H. Spector's *At War at Sea*, page 239. Doenitz describes his new options in his *Memoirs*. The advantages of the milch cows are described in Wolfgang Frank's *Sea Wolves*, page 169.

The information about most of the ships lost in World War II dating back to the previous war comes from Axis Roland, W. Jeffrey Bolster, and Alexander Keyssar's *The Way of the Ship* (2008), page 303.

My description of the potential pleasures of a Caribbean mission comes from Gaylord T. M. Kelshall's *The U-boat War in the Caribbean*, page 85, and Melanie Wiggins's *U-boat Adventures*, page 50.

The account of the *Norlindo*'s sinking comes from NARA Record Group 38, which includes an intelligence report examining the Germans U-boat commander's level of generosity, and from Harro Schacht's war diary, translated from German into English on www.uboatarchive.net. The account of Schacht's subsequent torpedoing of the two tankers comes from Captain Arthur Moore's *A Careless Word*, pages 161 and 198.

The account of the torpedoing and grounding of the *Delisle* comes from NARA Record Group 38 and the *GJ* on August 20, 1942.

Much of my description of Genious Hudgins Jr. comes from interviews with his widow, Salome, and daughter, Vicki, as well as from others in Mathews. Salome and Vicki provided access to more than a dozen of Genious's letters, including the letter in which he reveals his fears to his sister.

The account of Genious surviving the sinking of the *Green Island* comes from his letters and from NARA Record Group 38. The account of the *Green Island*'s previous narrow escape comes from Felix Riesenberg's *Sea War*, pages 72–74.

Theodore Taylor offers a description of the 1940s Gulf Coast and the Mississippi River passes in *Fire on the Beaches*, pages 149–50.

The account of the *Virginia* sinking comes from NARA Record Groups 38 and 26; Schacht's war diary translated into English on www.uboat archive.net; Wynn's *U-boat Operations of the Second World War*; Robert Carse's *The Long Haul*, page 56; and Riesenberg's *Sea War*, page 114. Information about Frank White came from his nephew J. Edgar White of Portsmouth, and a tribute to White in the *Virginian-Pilot* on June 13, 1942, by reporter Harry P. Moore, with whom Frank White corresponded. The account of the courage of the swimming men comes from Wiggins's *Torpedoes in the Gulf*, page 56. The account of the *William C. McTarnahan* comes from Wiggins, page 85.

The account of the *Halo* sinking comes from NARA Record Group 38, including a six-page statement by Joseph Shackelford describing his experience, and a letter from the Mexican Gulf Oil Company suggesting ways to prevent future such disasters; the *GJ* on June 4, 1942, and July 2, 1942, in which Shackelford is quoted at length; on December 30, 1999, the *GJ* reporter's drafts; U.S. Coast Guard record of tanker losses; and Taylor's *Fire on the Beaches*, pages 163–67.

The account of the sinking of the *Gulfpenn* comes from NARA Record Group 38, the *GJ* on May 27, 1942, and *GJ* notes.

The account of Captain Borum's rescue of Belgian seamen in World War I comes from the *Mathews Journal*, May 5, 1919. The account of his rescue of the British seamen in World War II comes from the entry for Borum's ship, the *City of Birmingham*, on www.uboat.net, and from a brief history provided by the Borum family to the Gwynn's Island Museum.

The account of the *Elizabeth* sinking comes from NARA Record Group 38, which includes a Navy Armed Guard report on the voyage and an interview with Captain Walter Hudgins's son Elliott. The contents of the Davis telegram to his family came from an interview with his cousin Amelia Minter.

The *GJ* editorial complaining about the lack of a blackout appeared on May 21, 1942. The account of the pleasure-driving bust in Mathews came from the *GJ* on May 16, 1943. The *GJ* editorial finding reason for optimism in the Russian convoy's success appeared on April 16, 1942.

Chapter Seven: "Avoid Polar Bear Liver"

In writing about the rigors of the Murmansk Run, I drew from an interview with Bernard Stansbury, records on Russian convoys from NARA Record Group 38, and several other sources, including S. J. Flaherty's *Abandoned Convoy* (1970); Paul Kemp's *Convoy!* (2004); Theodore Taylor's *Battle in the Arctic Seas* (1976); B. B. Schofield's *The Russian Convoys* (1964); and Robert Carse's *A Cold Corner of Hell* (1969).

The political backstory to the Murmansk Run is described in detail in Churchill's *The Hinge of Fate*, which includes telling communications between Churchill and Stalin on pages 257 and 270–71. Churchill's comment that Bolshevism was "foul baboonery" came from Nicholas Bethell's *Russia Besieged* (1977), page 136, and the famous quote about being willing to help any enemy of Hitler's is printed on page 137.

The instructions for killing and eating polar bears are found on pages 139–40 of Phil Richards and John Banigan's *How to Abandon Ship*.

My description of Captain Guy Hudgins is drawn from interviews with his daughter Diana Swenson and her husband, Art, in Mathews. The account of Guy's voyage to Murmansk with PQ-15 comes from that interview; a detailed account of the trip in Samuel Duff McCoy's *Nor Death Dismay* (1944); Felix Riesenberg's *Sea War*, page 139; Carse's *A Cold Corner of Hell* and *The Long Haul*; Kemp's *Convoy!*; NARA Record Group 38; and the *GJ* on July 2, 1942.

The account of PQ-16's voyage to Murmansk comes from *GJ* interviews with Charles Edwards and Charles Majette on August 6, 13, and 27,

1942, and *GJ* notes; my interview with Pearl and Fay Hutchinson, Cecil Ripley's sister and niece, of Mathews; Riesenberg's *Sea War*, page 139; Carse's *A Cold Corner of Hell* and *The Long Haul*; Kemp's *Convoy!*; and NARA Record Group 38. Joe Diggs's letters were provided by his relative Gary Brownlee of Mathews.

My description of James Ashberry came from an interview with his younger brother, Vernon, in Mathews. The account of the *City of Alma*'s sinking came from a *GJ* interview with James Ashberry on August 20, 1942; NARA Record Group 38; and the U.S. Maritime Administration's account of the actions of a third mate who won a medal for heroism for helping Ashberry right the boat and then rescue several shipmates. The *GJ* reporter's notes contained Ashberry's disparaging remark about Mathews, which did not appear in the paper.

A detailed account of the U-701's mine laying appears in Ed Offley's *The Burning Shore*. The details about the mining of the *Robert C. Tuttle* come from NARA Record Group 38. The description of Forrest's experience on the *Tuttle* comes from an interview he gave the *GJ* on June 25, 1942, and *GJ* notes. Forrest still believed at the time that his ship had been torpedoed rather than mined. Several residents of Virginia Beach still remember watching the mined ships exploding offshore. Doenitz's boast came from Taylor's *Fire on the Beaches*, page 177.

Descriptions of the U-boat landings of saboteurs, and the results, appear in Clay Blair's *Hitler's U-boat War*, pages 602–05, and many other books, as well as on the FBI's Web site.

The account of the *Millinocket*'s sinking comes from NARA Record Groups 38 and 26, Wynn, and the *GJ* on July 9, 1942. The paper subsequently printed the poem Captain Lewis Callis had written about Gwynn's Island.

The account of the *Manuela*'s sinking comes from NARA Record Group 38 and an interview by the *GJ* with Godsey on July 7, 1942. Captain Rodney Callis recalled the summer of 1942 along the coast in an interview with the *GJ* on December 30, 1999.

Marshall's message to King and King's reaction came from Michael

Gannon's *Operation Drumbeat*, page 391, and Carse's *The Long Haul*, page 100. Roosevelt's comment comes from Felknor, page 226.

Numerous members of the Hodges family, including Brother Hodges, Jesse Carroll Thornton, Jean Hodges, and David Callis described a Hodges "dining" to me. The size of a Hodges meal is described by John A. Fox in "Virginia Seamen Give Their Lives to Keep Our Ships Afloat," in the *Washington Sunday Star* on September 6, 1942. Bill Hodges remembered the dining in June in particular, and the large number of sea captains present. Jean Hodges recalled her father's call back to the sea from Ford and his efforts to get the *Onondaga* crewed and ready. Genious Hudgins Jr.'s daughter, Vicki, found a document in which her father is offered a different job at lesser pay just before signing on with Dewey Hodges.

The disaster of PQ-17 is described in numerous books, one of the best being Flaherty's *Abandoned Convoy*.

The description of the return trip of Convoy PQ-16 from Murmansk comes from *GJ* interviews with Charles Edwards and Charles Majette on August 6, 13, and 27, 1942; *GJ* notes; Carse's *A Cold Corner of Hell* and *The Long Haul*; NARA Record Group 38; and Navy Armed Guard reports. Information about Captain Joe Diggs came from interviews with Pearl Hutchinson and Gary Brownlee of Mathews. Brownlee provided a letter from Charles Edwards about Diggs's death, as well as some of Diggs's heavily censored letters to his family in Mathews.

Chapter Eight: Catastrophe

The account of the *Ruth* sinking came from NARA Record Groups 38 and 26; *GJ* notes; a *Richmond Times-Dispatch* article on July 22, 1942; and *GJ* articles on July 16 and 23, 1942. Information about Mel Callis came from his nephew Bill Callis, as well as Benny Fitchett, Clarence Collier Jr., and Jack Rowe of Mathews. Mel Callis's comments about Mathews and mermaids appeared in the *GJ* on August 4, 1938. Information about Perry Collier came from his grandson, Clarence Collier Jr.

I learned of the existence of Ashley Clinton Williams from Glenn A.

Knoblock's *African American World War II Casualties and Decorations* (2009), pages 542–43, and found more about him in U.S. Census records for 1920 and 1930. Knoblock's book describes the discrimination African American mariners faced in the first half of the twentieth century.

The account of the attack on the *Thomas McKean* comes from NARA Record Group 38, which includes lengthy reports on an intelligence investigation that led nowhere, and the official statements of Roland Foster and the ship's first assistant engineers, printed in their entirety in Daniel Gallery's *Twenty Million Tons Under the Sea*, pages 125–40. Gallery wrote his book when the official statements of hundreds of ships' officers were in NARA's records. NARA has since destroyed those statements, retaining only summaries of the statements of the survivors of sunken ships. The account of the attack also draws on *GJ* notes and the *GJ* on July 23 and August 6, 1942.

Captain L. F. Borum's second sinking in two world wars was described in NARA Record Groups 38 and 26, including a Navy Armed Guard report, and through information provided by the Borum family to the Gwynn's Island Museum.

The account of the *Norlandia* sinking comes from NARA Record Groups 38 and 26 and an interview with Captain Herbert Callis's daughter Joan Marble. The description of Callis's previous rescue of men from another ship comes from Captain Nicholas Manolis's *We at Sea* (1949).

Information about the *Onondaga*'s voyages through the Caribbean comes from her Ship Movement Card in NARA Record Group 38 and in Genious Hudgins's letters to his wife, Salome. Mellin Respess's joining the *Onondaga* as a passenger in Puerto Rico was described by Jean Hodges and Jack Rowe, among others.

The descriptions of Leslie Hodges are based on interviews with several members of the Hodges family, including Jean Hodges, Brother Hodges, Jesse Carroll Thornton, Betty Fernald, and Stormy Heart Romaniello, as well as family friends such as Edwin Jarvis, and a taped interview with Louise Hodges. The description of Stacy Hammond comes in part from interviews with his son Stacy Hammond Jr. in Mathews. The account of the sinking of the *Oneida* comes from NARA Record Groups 38 and 26, *GJ* notes, and the *GJ* on July 30, 1942.

My description of Spencer Hodges comes from interviews with his son Spencer Jr. as well as other members of the Hodges family, and others in Mathews who knew him later as the county sheriff. Spencer Jr. remembered the trips with his father to break the news of Leslie's death to Henny.

Accounts of the memorial ceremony at the Gwynn's Island drawbridge come mostly from *GJ* notes and the *GJ* story on July 23, 1942.

I reconstructed the *Onondaga*'s voyages through her Ship Movement Card in NARA Record Group 38, Genious Hudgins's letters to Salome, and Dewey Hodges's last letter to his family on July 23, 1942. Dewey's letter, as noted earlier, is entered in Norfolk Circuit Court in Norfolk, Virginia, as Dewey's last will and testament.

The sinking of the *Onondaga* is described from interviews with Russell Dennis's son Russell Dennis Jr., who provided the text of Dennis's telegram to Mathews after the sinking. The account relies on NARA Record Groups 38 and 26; Wynn's *U-boat Operations of the Second World War*; *The New York Times*; the *Virginian-Pilot*; *GJ* notes and the *GJ* on July 30, 1942; Norfolk Circuit Court Probate case files for October and November 1942; and the U.S. District Court decision by Judge John Paul in *Hodges v. New York Life Insurance Co.*, March 2, 1948.

Jack Musick, a shark biologist and author from Virginia, provided background about sharks and shark fishing economics and methods for particulars about the Carillos and the *Donatella*.

The surviving records do not specify exactly when the shark fishermen found the remains. Jenkins's letter says the fishermen found them shortly after the sinking and that they included flesh and bone. A large shark would digest flesh in its stomach within a day or two of consuming it, but the shark's digestive tract could contain flesh for as long as a week, and fishermen gutting a shark would open its digestive tract as well as its stomach. The exact timing of the fishermen's catch does not affect the chain of events.

The family's reaction to the anonymous call came from Jean Hodges, who was present when the call came. Spencer Hodges Jr. recalled accompanying his father to break the news of Dewey's death to Henny, as he had done with Leslie's death.

The story on Mathews in the *Washington Sunday Star* appeared on September 6, 1942. A *Baltimore Sun* feature on the losses on Gwynn's Island had appeared on August 9, 1942. The *Sun* story, "Torpedoes Strike on Gwynn's Island," by William B. Crane, prompted a Mathews man to write to the paper to point out that the island was not the only part of Mathews that had suffered terrible losses.

The descriptions of the evolution of the interlocking convoy system come from Samuel Eliot Morison's *The Battle of the Atlantic*, pages 254–57 and 260. The statistic about the decline in sinkings in the Eastern Sea Frontier comes from Michael Gannon's *Operation Drumbeat*, pages 388–89. Admiral Andrews's remarks come from the Navy's *Eastern Sea Frontier War Diary*.

Doenitz's reflections on withdrawing his U-boats from U.S. waters are described in his *Memoirs*, pages 236–38.

Chapter Nine: "Please Don't Tell Me"

The account of Homer's last voyage on the *Mae* comes from the *Mae*'s Navy Armed Guard commander's report on convoy TAW-12 in NARA Record Group 38. The description of Captain Homer Callis and his short-lived effort to go ashore comes from interviews with his son Bill Callis, Jack Rowe, Benny Fitchett, and Lottie Mitchem on Gwynn's Island. The description of Nancy Callis comes from the same people, as well as Bill Callis's daughter, Lisa Callis. Nancy Callis told the *GJ* on December 30, 1999, that she had felt that her neighbors regarded her as the angel of death. Bill Callis recalled his big brother, Homer Callis Jr., advising him to choose the Merchant Marine over the Navy.

The information about Homer Sr.'s replacement, Captain Willard Hudgins, comes from his son, Buster Hudgins, as well as Lottie Mitchem, Bill Callis, and Jack Rowe.

The description of Lester Smith is based on interviews with his widow, Lottie Mitchem, and his friends Bill Callis and Jack Rowe. The account of the *Mae* sinking comes from NARA Record Groups 38 and 26 and interviews in the *GJ* with Lester Smith.

The account of Will Hunley's going to sea comes from his children, Jimmy and Rebecca Hunley; from an interview in the *GJ* with Hunley and David Hodges upon their joint retirement from the sea on January 11, 1979; and from an interview Hunley gave the *Glo-Quips* paper in Gloucester County, Virginia, on August 14, 1974. The account of the sinking of the *Commercial Trader* comes from NARA Record Groups 38 and 26, including a Navy Armed Guard report; a detailed written account of the sinking by Captain Hunley, provided by his son, Jimmy; *GJ* notes; the *GJ* stories on November 19, 1942, and January 11, 1979; and the *Glo-Quips* account.

The account of the *Steel Navigator* sinking comes from NARA Record Group 38; *GJ* notes; a *GJ* interview with Hall on November 24, 1942; Robert M. Browning Jr.'s *United States Merchant Marines Casualties of World War II*, page 188; and Wynn's *U-boat Operations of the Second World War*.

The letters noting Lester Smith's recovery were shared with me by his widow, Lottie Mitchem, and in some cases printed in the *GJ*.

Genious Hudgins Jr.'s widow, Salome, and daughter, Vicki, shared the letters she received from the Navy and from well-wishers. They also described Salome's reaction and refusal to believe Genious was dead.

Edna Hodges's attempts to have her husband, Captain Dewey Hodges, declared legally dead so the family could access accounts in his name are described in the October 15, 1942, proceedings in the Probate section of Norfolk, Virginia, Circuit Court.

The description of the first part of the *East Indian*'s voyage comes from M. Stanley MacLean's forty-page *13 Days Adrift* and a detailed account by Charles Edwards of Gloucester; *GJ* notes; and the *GJ* on January 14, 1943, and December 30, 1999. The sea snakes are indeed highly venomous but pose little threat to humans because their teeth are not designed for biting us.

The description of Wolfgang Luth comes from Jordan Vause's *U-boat Ace: The Story of Wolfgang Luth* (1990); Jocher Brennecke's *The Hunters and the Hunted*, pages 196–99; and Timothy Mulligan's *Neither Sharks Nor Wolves*. The account of the sinking and subsequent lifeboat voyage comes from NARA Record Group 38, including a Naval Armed Guard report; Brennecke, pages 196–99; *GJ* notes; the *GJ* on November 26 and December 3, 1942, and January 7, 1943; my interview with Clayton's son Rick Hammond; and MacLean's *13 Days Adrift*.

The text of Doenitz's *Laconia* order comes from Ann and John Tusa's *The Nuremberg Trial*, page 186.

A lifeboat crammed with frightened, hungry, thirsty people was an incubator for conflict. Writers and filmmakers have turned the lifeboat drama into a genre. A short story by John Steinbeck formed the basis for Alfred Hitchcock's 1944 film *Lifeboat*, in which American, British, and German castaways schemed and struggled to the death. More recent examples include Charlotte Rogan's novel *The Lifeboat*, in which a woman chooses sides between a ship's officer and others who challenge his leadership, and Yann Martel's novel *Life of Pi*, in which a young Indian man shares a lifeboat with a ferocious Bengal tiger.

The letter from R. M. Jenkins describing the Carillos's discovery of the rings in the shark's belly is dated October 22, 1942—almost three months after the sinking. The letter makes it clear that Jenkins investigated the situation as soon as the Carillos brought the rings and remains into port. The most likely explanation for the time lag is that Jenkins initially wrote to the wrong shipping companies. Edna Hodges's lawyer first heard about the letter from a law school classmate who worked for the Lykes Brothers shipping line.

The entire text of Jenkins's letter was printed by both the *Virginian-Pilot* and the *Ledger-Dispatch* of Norfolk on November 7, 1942. The story was picked up by United Press and the Associated Press and reprinted in newspapers around the country, including the *Richmond Times-Dispatch*, where Henny Hodges most likely read it under the headline, "Shark's Body

Yields Rings, Man's Remains." The *American Weekly* of Great Britain printed a story on the ring in the shark in 1943.

The account of Edna discussing the family's options with her daughters comes from her daughter Jean, who took part in the discussion.

The descriptions of the Hodges daughters come from members of the Hodges family, including Brother Hodges, Jesse Carroll Thornton, Louise and David Hodges (on tape), Stormy Heart Romaniello, Marlene Callis, and Betty Fernald, as well as Edwin Jarvis.

The account of the Hodges daughters' approaching their father and brothers to ask them to stop sailing the deep ocean comes from Brother Hodges, who overheard his parents discussing the daughters' request at the dinner table.

The description of Coleman Hodges comes largely from his daughter Betty Fernald, but also from members of the Hodges family, including Brother Hodges, Jesse Carroll Thornton, Louise and David Hodges (on tape), Stormy Heart Romaniello, and Marlene Callis, as well as Edwin Jarvis.

Roosevelt's and Churchill's strategy sessions have been described in numerous books. My favorites are Churchill's *The Hinge of Fate* and Rick Atkinson's *An Army at Dawn* (2002). Atkinson's great trilogy about the American armies in the European war never overlooks the role of the Merchant Marine in sustaining them.

The estimate of the supply needs of American soldiers in Europe comes from Benjamin W. Labaree et al., *America and the Sea: A Maritime History* (1998), page 582.

Chapter Ten: Counterattack

The account of Captain Guy Hudgins's voyage in Operation Torch comes from NARA Record Group 38, including a Naval Armed Guard report; Samuel Duff McCoy's *Nor Death Dismay*; and an interview with Guy's daughter and son-in-law, Diana and Art Swenson. Rick Atkinson's *An Army at Dawn* offers a detailed account of all three prongs of the North Africa invasion. Hutson Hudgins's excited accounts of the invasion came from *GJ* notes and the *GJ* article of December 10, 1942. The account of the German intelligence failure regarding Operation Torch and the U-boats' preoccupation with attacking a routine convoy instead comes from Doenitz's *Memoirs*, pages 275–77. The account of the four troop transports being torpedoed off Morocco comes from Robert Carse's *The Long Haul*, page 151.

The account of Captain Raymond Hodges's voyage to Malta on the *Mormacmoon* comes from interviews with Raymond's son Bill; the "Malta War Diary," which I accessed at www.naval-history.net/xDKWD-Malta1942a.htm; and Jim Whalen's *Last of the Boom Ships* (2000).

The descriptions of Malta draw in part on Philip Kaplan and Jack Currie's *Convoy* and Sam Moses's *At All Costs* (2007). Raymond's austere meal with the governor was described by his son Bill Hodges. The dismal success rate of ships trying to reach Malta between February and August comes from Kaplan and Currie's *Convoy*, page 165. Dr. Carl Boyd, the specialist on Japanese submarines from Old Dominion University in Norfolk, offered perspective on Japanese submarines in the Indian Ocean.

The story about the U-boat's picking up a weather report from Duluth comes from Theodore Taylor's *Fire on the Beaches*, page 46. The account of trawler captains staying in port comes from the *GJ* on August 20, 1942.

The information about the Hodges family holiday gatherings comes from the *GJ*'s neighborhood sections for December 1942 and 1943. The descriptions of the quiet Christmases with mariners at sea came from numerous Mathews mariners. The descriptions of Captain Robert Gayle's Christmas came from a *GJ* story on December 26, 1985. Jack Rowe provided the account of Gayle's ship nearly colliding with a U-boat in the fog. Gayle's daughter Beverly described his personality. The *GJ* editorial about the holidays appeared on December 24, 1942.

Good descriptions of Roosevelt's and Churchill's discussions and strategy between North Africa and Sicily are in Churchill's *The Hinge of Fate* and Atkinson's *An Army at Dawn*.

The account of the *Collingsworth* sinking comes from NARA Record Groups 38 and 26 and the *GJ* on February 25, 1943. The account of the sinking of the *Roger B. Taney* comes from NARA Record Groups 38 and 26. The account of the sinking of the *Benjamin Harrison* comes from NARA Record Groups 38 and 26, as well as from the *GJ* on May 6, 1943.

The circumstances of Grand Admiral Erich Raeder's demotion are described in Samuel Eliot Morison's *The Atlantic Battle Won, May 1943–May 1945* (1954), page 57.

The descriptions of how castaways can read natural clues comes from Harold Gatty's fascinating *The Raft Book* (1943), pages 7–12 and 39–44. The captain of the *Roger B. Taney* paid attention to the natural signs as Gatty suggests, but he erred in thinking that the sight of a butterfly meant land was near. Gatty writes that butterflies, unlike shore birds, often stray too far out to sea and die.

The figure of 430 subs and the heavy toll on the two convoys in mid-March comes from Ed Offley's *Turning the Tide* (2011), pages 42 and 53. The account of the back-and-forth battles between U-boats and convoy escorts comes from Doenitz's *Memoirs*, page 328.

Doenitz's declaration that the attack on the two convoys was his greatest success comes from his *Memoirs*, pages 329–30.

The Allied counteroffensive against U-boats has been the subject of several books, including Michael Gannon's *Black May* (1989), Offley's *Turning the Tide*, David Syrett's *The Defeat of the German U-boats* (1994), and Vice Admiral Sir Peter Gretton's *Crisis Convoy* (1974). The counteroffensive has been described in numerous other books, including the British Ministry of Defence's history of the U-boat war, *The U-boat War in the Atlantic* (1989), Taylor's *Fire on the Beaches*, Riesenberg's *Sea War*, Lisle A. Rose's *Power at Sea: The Breaking Storm, 1919–1945* (2007), Clay Blair's *Hitler's U-boat War*, and Doenitz's *Memoirs*.

The contributions of British physicists to antisubmarine warfare in World War II are detailed in Stephen Budiansky's *Blackett's War*, notably on page 143. The significance of microwave radar is described in Barrie Pitt's *The Battle of the Atlantic* (1977), page 183. Doenitz's comment about aircraft being unable to destroy U-boats came from Pitt's *The Battle of the*

Atlantic, page 182. A U-boat's disadvantage against planes is clearly explained in Gaylord T. M. Kelshall's *U-boats in the Caribbean*, page 153. The advantages of new, more powerful depth charges set to explode at U-boats' maximum depth are described in Offley's *Turning the Tide*, page xiv. The advantages of the destroyer escort (DE) and escort carrier are described in Bruce Felknor's *The U.S. Merchant Marine at War*, pages 230–33 and Michael Gannon's *Operation Drumbeat*, pages 392–93. Morison's *The Atlantic Battle Won* describes how the DE came to exist, pages 35–36. Admiral Gallery, who led a hunter-killer group, describes such groups' structure and operations in his *Twenty Million Tons Under the Sea*. The fact that hunter-killer groups became the most prolific U-boat destroyers after mid-1943 comes from Gannon's *Operation Drumbeat*, page 392.

Raymond Hodges's letter to his parents was printed in the *GJ* on May 13, 1943. The account of Convoy HX-232 comes from British Admiralty records, and Records Group 38. Syrett's *The Defeat of the German U-boats* points out the paradox that each side was monitoring the other's messages while never imagining its own messages were being monitored.

The information about the mounting U-boat losses comes from the Ministry of Defence's *The U-boat War in the Atlantic*; Morison's *The Atlantic Battle Won*, page 11; and Blair's *Hitler's U-boat War*. Lisle describes the death of Doenitz's younger son, Peter, on page 319 of *Power at Sea*. Blair describes the fate of Doenitz's older son, Klaus, in *Hitler's U-boat War*, page 569. David Fairbank White describes Doenitz's personal attachment to his U-boats and crews in *Bitter Ocean*, page 232. John Terraine quotes Doenitz's decision to fight on in *Business in Great Waters* (2009), page 616. Rose describes Doenitz's decision to keep sending U-boats to sea in *Power at Sea*, page 319. Morison quotes Doenitz's upbeat message to his U-boat crews in *The Atlantic Battle Won*, pages 83–84, and Hitler's views on page 59.

Chapter Eleven: The Conveyor Belt

The account of the *Robert Rowan* sinking comes from an interview with Bernard Stansbury, NARA Record Group 38, and Wynn. The account of the disastrous Allied parachute drop appears in Robert Wallace's *The Italian Campaign* (1978), page 25.

Ernie Pyle's observations about the size of the Sicily invasion fleet came from *The Italian Campaign*, page 18. The account of the *Timothy Pickering* explosion came from Captain Arthur Moore's *A Careless Word*, page 281, and Felknor, pages 277–78. The description of Navy Armed Guard assignments as undesirable comes from Bernard Stansbury and from the August 7, 1943, *Collier's* magazine article, "We Man the Deck Guns," by Ensign Robert C. Ruark, USNR.

Doenitz describes his reluctance to send U-boats into the Mediterranean "mousetrap" in his *Memoirs*, pages 160–61 and 366. Herbert Werner's dispirited comment appears in his *Iron Coffins*, page 177.

The account of Captain Homer Callis's new ship and new assignment in the Mediterranean comes from interviews with his son Bill Callis and the Ship Movement Card for the *Cape Mohican* in NARA Record Group 38. Homer's granddaughter, Lisa Callis, provided the letter from Homer to Nancy.

The account of the torpedoing of the *Cape Mohican* comes from interviews with Bill Callis; NARA Record Group 38, including a Navy Armed Guard report; and the *GJ* on March 16, 1943. The fact that the torpedoing was the fourth for the *Cape Mohican*'s radio operator comes from the radioman's account on www.usmm.org.

Captain Herbert Callis's encounter with *Collier's* magazine writer Quentin Reynolds in Moscow is described in Reynolds's article, "It Happens in Moscow," on August 21, 1943. Accounts of Captain Callis's voyage to Murmansk on the *Thomas Hartley* come from an interview with Callis's daughter Joan Marble (who also provided a copy of the certificate Callis received for his ordeal) and from the Navy Armed Guard report of the voyage in NARA Record Group 38. The account of Callis's voyage to Murmansk came mainly from a Navy Armed Guard report. The fact that a crew member was put ashore as a "mental case" comes from the Russian Convoys file in NARA Record Group 38.

Accounts of the Germans' efforts to ruin the port of Naples to prevent the Allies from using it came from Rick Atkinson's *The Day of Battle* (volume 2 of the *Liberation Trilogy*) (2007), pages 2 and 242, and Wallace's *The Italian Campaign*, pages 77–78.

The account of the Allied mustard gas disaster at the Italian port of Bari is described in several books, including Gerald Reminick's *Nightmare in Bari* (2001).

The information on the increased production of Liberty ships in 1943 comes from Philip Kaplan and Jack Currie's *Convoy*, page 68. The statistic about the cargo numbers in October 1943 comes from Reminick's *Patriots and Heroes*, page 130.

The account of the mining and sinking of the *Delisle* comes from NARA Record Group 38. Paul Grubb's account of rescuing Captain Clendaniel on the *Delisle* appears in *GJ* notes and in a *GJ* story on November 18, 1943. Galza's account of rescuing Clendaniel—as well as a different one-legged mariner on a previous voyage of the *Delisle*—is described by the U.S. Maritime Commission in its narrative accompanying the award to Galza of the Distinguished Service Medal. Clendaniel's hometown paper, the *Brooklyn Eagle*, gave a different account of the return of Clendaniel's artificial leg in its February 27, 1944, edition. John Bunker's *Heroes in Dungarees* offers yet another version on pages 298–99. The background about Paul Grubb came from an interview with his younger sister Jane Grubb of Minnesota.

The account of the *Esso Providence* fire and Winder's heroics comes from *Ships of the Esso Fleet*, pages 486–91, and from the *GJ* on April 6, 1944, based on a war correspondent's reporting from Italy.

Jack White's experiences were described in the Mathews County High School newspaper, *Anchors Aweigh*. Jack Ward of Mathews described his experiences exploring inland Italy in interviews with me.

The Allied amphibious invasion at Anzio is described in numerous books, including Atkinson's *The Day of Battle*. Churchill's wry comment about the whale appears in his *Closing the Ring*, page 488. The descriptions of the terrifying German railroad guns come from *The Day of Battle* and Wallace's *The Italian Campaign*, page 179. The admiral's remarks to the merchant captains appear in Samuel Eliot Morison's *Sicily, Salerno and Anzio* (1954), page 370. Livesay's comments come from *GJ* notes.

The description of the disbanding of the airplane watchers and Eleanor Respess's christening of the *John Russell Pope* both come from the *GJ* on October 7, 1943. The account of the explosion at the mine depot comes from the *GJ* on November 21, 1943. The description of Paul Grubb's reaction to the explosion comes from an interview with his sister Jane Grubb.

The account of Bernard Stansbury's posting to the *Penelope Barker* and the ship's subsequent torpedoing on the Murmansk Run come from an interview with Stansbury; the *GJ* on May 3, 1944; and NARA Record Group 38, including a Navy Armed Guard report.

The account of stockpiling munitions at Anzio for the eventual Allied breakout comes from Wallace's *The Italian Campaign*, pages 187–88. The story of the *Paul Hamilton* explosion comes from NARA Record Group 38; the article "One Torpedo—580 Men—7000 Tons of Explosives," by Jim W. Dean, on www.veteranstoday.com, April 20, 2011; the *GJ* on May 10, August 17, 1944; and the family's remembrances of Billups in the Gwynn's Island Museum.

Bill Callis' experiences in the Normandy invasion came from an interview with him, and from the *President Monroe*'s Ship Movement Card in NARA Record Group 38.

The account of the capture of the U-505 comes from Daniel Gallery's *Twenty Thousand Tons Under the Sea*. The report that Admiral King was furious about the capture comes from Clay Blair's *Hitler's U-boat War,* vol. 2, page 553.

The captain of the Liberty ship *Cyrus McCormick*'s description of the crowded English Channel on D-Day comes from Bunker's *Heroes in Dungarees*, page 282. Doenitz's orders to his U-boats to defend Normandy against the D-Day invasion come from Werner's *Iron Coffins*, page 213, and Doenitz's *Memoirs*, page 422. The toll on U-boats on D-Day comes from

Doenitz's *Memoirs*, pages 422–23. Morison pronounces his verdict on the U-boats in *The Atlantic Battle Won*, page 63. The description of Randolph Payne's experiences on Omaha Beach comes from an interview with his daughter, Renee Arga-Bright. Bill Callis described his experiences at the port of Cherbourg in an interview with me. The total of supplies delivered to American troops at Omaha Beach in June comes from Bunker's *Heroes in Dungarees*, page 285.

Eisenhower's quote about the importance of the U.S. Merchant Marine to the Allied war effort comes from www.usmm.org.

The increasing losses of U-boats are described in Doenitz's *Memoirs*, page 420. The destruction of the U-107, U-515, and U-575 is described in Wynn's *U-boat Operations of the Second World War.*

Lester Smith's homecoming and his enthusiasm for returning to sea were described by his widow, Lottie Mitchem, in an interview with me. Raymond Hodges's son Bill described Raymond's suggestion that he join the Merchant Marine. Horace Hodges described his announcement to his mother that he was going to sea. Coleman's promotion to captain of the *Edward A. Savoy* was described by his daughter Betty Fernald. J. W. Corbett described his arrival and the *Edward A. Savoy* in an interview with me.

Chapter Twelve: War's End

My account of Coleman Hodges's achievement of his goal of becoming captain comes from interviews with his daughter Betty Fernald and J. W. Corbett, as well as the *Edward A. Savoy*'s Ship Movement Card in NARA Records Group 38. The description of J.W. comes from interviews with him and with other members of the Hodges family who knew him, including Brother Hodges and Jesse Carroll Thornton.

The statistics about the declining danger of the Murmansk Run came from the Masters, Mates & Pilots newsletter of July 1945. The account of the *Edward A. Savoy*'s voyage to Murmansk comes from NARA Records Group 38; records from the British Admiralty in London; Kemp's *Convoy!*, page 210–12; and interviews with J. W. Corbett and Coleman Hodges's daughter Betty Fernald.

The account of the Hodges anniversary festivities comes from the *GJ* on December 16, 1944, and from interviews with Jesse Carroll Thornton, Stormy Heart Romaniello, and Marlene Callis. Raymond's letter to Captain Jesse and Henny was provided by Jesse Carroll Thornton.

Jack Rowe described his meeting with Homer Callis Jr. in the Pacific in interviews with me.

The experiences of Captain Raymond Hodges and Captain Homer Callis in convoys come from NARA Records Group 38, including a Navy Armed Guard report.

The descriptions of the port of Antwerp come in part from Atkinson's *The Guns at Last Light: Volume III of the Liberation Trilogy* (2013), pages 330–32, and John Bunker's *Heroes in Dungarees*, page 287. J. W. Corbett described his experiences with V-1 rockets in Antwerp in interviews with me. Captain Rodney Callis's experience in Antwerp is described in the Naval Armed Guard report for his ship, the *Edward A. White*. The explanation of the origin of the "V" in V-2 comes from Richard Overy's *Why the Allies Won*, page 239. Atkinson describes the V-2 disaster at the movie theater in *The Guns at Last Light*, page 333.

The account of Raymond Hodges's first visit home since early 1942 comes from interviews with Raymond's son Bill Hodges, Jesse Carroll Thornton, and Stormy Heart Romaniello, as well as the *GJ* on March 8, 1945.

Bill Callis told me about his reaction after joining a ship and finding Lester Smith on the crew.

Bernard Stansbury described his reaction to his second sinking in a row.

The Masters, Mates & Pilots comment on Roosevelt's death comes from the MMP newsletter for May 1945.

A detailed account of the sinking of the USS *Monaghan* in Typhoon Cobra can be found in Bob Drury and Tom Clavin's *Halsey's Typhoon* (2007).

The description of kamikaze attacks in general, and specifically the attack on the USS *Hazelwood*, comes from Robin L. Rielly's *Kamikaze Attacks of World War II* (2010). Homer Sr.'s subsequent letters to his wife, Nancy, were provided to me by Homer's granddaughter (and Bill Callis's daughter), Lisa Callis. Bill Callis described his phone conversation with his mother regarding his brother's death.

Doenitz describes his unexpected discovery that he was the next führer, and explains his actions afterward, in his *Memoirs*. The sinking of the *Black Point* and its attacker is described in Lawrence Paterson's *Black Flag: The Surrender of Germany's U-boat Forces* (2009). The text of Doenitz's parting message to his U-boat commanders comes from Clay Blair's *Hitler's U-boat War*, vol. 2, pages 699–700. The account of a U-boat commander cutting his wrists in Boston comes from the *Virginian-Pilot*, via the Associated Press, on May 19, 1945. The account of the two U-boats fleeing to Argentina comes from Timothy Mulligan's *Neither Sharks Nor Wolves*, page 237, and from *Black Flag*. The text of the Bull Line's radiogram announcing the German surrender comes from Captain Walter Hudgins's son Elliott Hudgins, who has a copy of the radiogram. Elliott Hudgins also provided a copy of the U.S. Maritime Commission's radiogram explaining to mariners that Germany's surrender merely shifted the full focus of the war to the Pacific.

Accounts of the captured U-505 drawing crowds in Norfolk and elsewhere come from the *Virginian-Pilot* on June 30 and July 5, 1945.

Captain T. O. Rainier's experiences on the *Cape Victory* at the end of World War II came from interviews with his granddaughter Joan Marble (the daughter of Captain Herbert Callis, who was stranded in Murmansk with the Forgotten Convoy); in the *GJ* on November 16, 1950; and Paul Tibbets's *Return of the Enola Gay* (1998), page 187.

The account of William Franklin Hale's death on the USS *Indianapolis* came from his daughter, Betsy Stewart of Mathews, and from Richard F. Newcomb's *Abandon Ship! The Saga of the USS Indianapolis, the Navy's Greatest Sea Disaster* (2001).

The account of Mathews's reaction to the war's end comes from interviews with people in Mathews and from the *GJ* on August 16, 1945, the same day the editorial appeared.

The listed casualty rates of U.S. merchant mariners during World War II have changed over the years, reflecting the absence of a centralized records system and the frequent changes of crew on merchant ships. Immediately after the war, the Maritime Administration estimated the losses of merchant mariners at 5,638. Today the nonprofit group American Merchant Marine Veterans (AMVV) and www.usmm.org estimate that roughly 9,300 U.S. merchant mariners lost their lives in the war, including men who died after the war of war injuries. Using 9,300 as the total for losses, the Merchant Marine's casualty rate is slightly higher than that of the U.S. Marine Corps. The Merchant Marine and Marine Corps rates are much higher than those of any other branch of the service, although the Army lost by far the most men. The casualty rates of various branches of the U.S. armed forces in World War II come from Bruce Felknor's *The U.S. Merchant Marine at War*, page 331.

The information about the U-boat casualty rates comes from Mulligan's *Neither Sharks Nor Wolves*, page 251–52.

The figures on the U.S. Merchant Marine's accomplishments come from *The U.S. Merchant Marine at War: A Report of the War Shipping Administration to the President, January 15, 1946*. Admiral King's quote comes from www.usmm.org. The account of the parade comes from the *Virginian-Pilot*, through the Associated Press, on October 1, 1945.

Churchill's quotes come from *The Hinge of Fate*, page 125, and Stephen Budiansky's *Blackett's War*, page 141. Churchill's memorable quotes about U-boats also include, "The U-boat attack was our worst evil. It would have been wise for the Germans to stake all upon it. In politics, when you have got hold of a good thing, stick to it." And, less elegantly, "This mortal danger to our lifelines gnawed my bowels."

Rohwer's comment about the seriousness of King's error in failing to establish a convoy system sooner comes from Nathan Miller's *War at Sea*, page 296; Michael Gannon's comment is from *Operation Drumbeat*; and

Middlebrook's is from Alex Roland et al., *The Way of the Ship*, page 305. Blair defends King on page 692 of the first volume of his *Hitler's U-boat War*. Blair was so incensed by Gannon's criticism of King that he called out Gannon by name in *Hitler's U-boat War*.

The accounts of Raymond Hodges and other Mathews mariners quickly shifting to new cargoes after the war come from Brother Hodges, Bill Hodges, Benny Fitchett, Reginald Deagle, Pete Smith, and others in Mathews. The Maritime Commission's estimate that most of the war equipment in Europe would go to the Pacific came from the MMP newsletter of June 1945.

The accounts of Raymond Hodges's voyages to bring home U.S. troops came from interviews with his son Bill Hodges and the *Mormacmoon*'s Ship Movement Card in NARA Record Group 38. The description of Captain Frank Boyer's voyages comes from the Motorun neighborhood sections of the *GJ* between 1944 and 1946. The fact that the mariners also brought home the bodies of American service members came from Rick Atkinson's *The Guns at Last Light*, pages 639–40.

Brother Hodges described his encounter with his uncle Raymond in Odessa in interviews with me.

Chapter Thirteen: Legacy

The account of Jesse and Henny's move to Hudgins is based on interviews with Jesse Carroll Thornton and Brother Hodges and the *GJ* on August 30, 1945. The description of Captain Jesse Hodges's forced retirement from the sea came from Jesse Carroll Thornton, Brother Hodges, Stormy Heart Romaniello, Marlene Callis, and the *GJ* on August 25, 1957.

Jean Hodges described the family's retreat from the Hodges dinings. The account of the young seaman approaching Bernard Pierson's father comes from information provided by the Pierson family to the Gwynn's Island Museum, and from an interview with Jack Rowe of Gwynn's Island. The account of William Burton Gay's parents learning of his fate comes from the *GJ* on October 25, 1945. The account of Captain Otis Levering Callis's death comes from the *GJ* on December 6, 1945. The account of

Salome Hudgins's change of mind comes from an interview with her and her daughter, Vicki.

The accounts of the Nuremberg trials come from Ann and John Tusa's *The Nuremberg Trial*, in particular pages 355–60. Biddle's dissenting view is found on page 461. The description of Doenitz's attitude comes from *Collier's* magazine, September 22, 1945. Admiral Gallery's view is on pages 298–99 of his *Twenty Million Tons Under the Sea*.

My description of Travers Thompson's postwar career in the U.S. submarine service comes from an interview with him.

The account of Benny Fitchett's anxious visit to the old German battleship in Gdynia, Poland, comes from an interview with him.

My descriptions of Mathews's entry into the postwar world come from interviews and from the following issues of the *GJ* in 1946: January 24, January 31, February 7, February 28, March 21, August 8, August 15, September 13, October 3, October 11, November 6, and November 14.

The planners of the monument had few contacts in the Mathews black community and most likely were unaware that a black mariner from Mathews had been killed on the *Ruth*. Ashley Clinton Williams's family had moved from Mathews a decade before the war.

The story of Will Hunley's unusual way of wishing goodnight to his children comes from his son, Jimmy Hunley.

The account of the Mathews Day celebration in 1946 comes from the *GJ* on October 3, 1946. The *Richmond Times-Dispatch* editorial about Mathews was reprinted in the *GJ* on that day. The subsequent letter from the captain of the USS *Mathews* appeared in the *GJ* on November 14, 1946.

My account of Edna Hodges's unsuccessful efforts to have Dewey's death and the sinking of the *Onondaga* declared an accident comes from the *Virginian-Pilot* on February 17, 1948, and March 5, 1948; the written ruling by U.S. District Court Judge John Paul in *Hodges vs. New York Life Insurance Co.*, March 2, 1948; and an interview with Jean Hodges. The description of Edna's and her children's life after the war comes from interviews with Jean Hodges.

Details of Homer Callis's final days and his wife Nancy's life afterward came from Bill Callis and his daughter, Lisa Callis, who provided the letter from her grandfather.

The description of Eleanor Respess's life after the war came from interviews with Bill Callis and Eleanor's friend David Judson.

Lester Smith's widow, Lottie Mitchem, described his life after the war, with Jack Rowe and Bill Callis providing additional details. The description of Lester's last summer mornings with his daughter and granddaughter comes from the *GJ* on July 2, 1987.

Jesse Carroll Thornton, Jesse Hodges's grandson, described Captain Jesse's last days and his funeral, as well as Henny's decision not to attend.

My account of Raymond's days as a cruise ship captain comes mainly from his son Bill Hodges, who also provided a translation of an article about his father that appeared in *Critica*, the Buenos Aires newspaper, on February 16, 1955. Several articles about Captain Raymond Hodges also appeared in the Moore-McCormack company newsletter, the *Mooremack News*. The account of Raymond's final days and burial at sea comes from Bill Hodges.

The description of Coleman Hodges's short life after the war comes primarily from his daughter Betty Fernald, but also from a taped interview with his brother David and sister Louise, and interviews with Jesse Carroll Thornton, Brother Hodges, and Marlene Callis.

The account of Henny Hodges's death comes mostly from her grandson Jesse Carroll Thornton.

The descriptions of the physical remnants of the U-boat war came from my visits to those places. MIT spokesman Kurt Hasselbalch explained how the *Roper*'s anchor reached the school. Pete Smith described a cruise on the *Jeremiah O'Brien* and provided background documents.

The account of the explosion and deaths aboard the *Snoopy* came from the Associated Press on July 24, 1965. The account of the nonfatal torpedo discovery off Rhode Island came from the *New Bedford Standard-Times* on May 30, 1998. The story of the U-869 is beautifully told by Robert Kurson in *Shadow Divers* (2005). The story of Ballard's expedition and the

Navy's reconsideration of what sank the U-166 comes from the Public Broadcasting System's NOVA program "Nazi Attack on America," broadcast on May 6, 2015. The section about divers and government protection of wrecks is based on interviews with several wreck divers, including Jim Bunch of North Carolina; John Broadwater, former director of NOAA's Monitor National Marine Sanctuary; and Lauren Heesemann, research coordinator for the Monitor sanctuary.

The account of George Betts's sleuthing and his efforts to contact the families of men lost on the *Muskogee* comes primarily from a collection of Betts's personal papers. He donated the papers to the Independence Seaport Museum in Philadelphia, which keeps them in its archives. The collection also contains newspaper clippings and photographs.

In 2004 I communicated through an interpreter with a U-85 crewman's cousin, Dr. Hansjuergen Fresenius, in Northeim, Germany, about his views of the U-boat sinking. Fresenius was among those who made the trip from Germany to Hampton to visit the Germans' graves.

The information about the sinking of the HMT *Bedfordshire* comes primarily from L. VanLoan Naisawald's *In Some Foreign Field* (1997), which describes the sinking and aftermath in detail. I have attended the memorial service for the British seamen on Ocracoke Island, North Carolina, and also visited the graves of British seamen on Hatteras Island.

When I interviewed Jesse Roper Mohorovic in 2004 for a story for the *Richmond Times-Dispatch* about his lifeboat birth, I was surprised to discover that I had interviewed him a decade earlier while he was a shipping company executive. I had been writing a story about the decline of the U.S. Merchant Marine. Jesse did not mention his lifeboat birth to me at that time.

My description of the Merchant Marine's decline and its current state comes from my experience working at Maersk Line, Limited, of Norfolk, from 2009–2014, during part of which time the company was considered the largest employer of U.S. merchant mariners, and from an interview with Captain T. Christian Spain, national assistant vice president, government relations, for the American Maritime Officers (AMO) union in

Washington, D.C. I further consulted Maersk Line vice president David Sloane, Jeff Brandt of the U.S. Coast Guard's National Maritime Center, and Morris Harvey, president of American Merchant Marine Veterans (AMMV), a nonprofit advocacy group for merchant mariners. I also drew from Benjamin W. Labaree's *America and the Sea*, René De La Pedraja's *The Rise and Decline of U.S. Merchant Shipping in the Twentieth Century* (1992), and Alex Roland et al., *The Way of the Ship.*

The description of efforts to persuade Congress to grant mariners veteran status, and currently to approve lump-sum payments, comes from Morris Harvey and Saaren "Sindy" Raymond of AMMV, and H. Gerald Starnes's self-published book, *Torpedoed for Life* (2013).

Sonny Richardson provided a unique perspective on Mathews. He has roots in the maritime community—his middle name is Hudgins and his father was a docking pilot like Captain Willie Hodges; he has served in local elective office; and now he sells real estate in Mathews.

I have visited the Gwynn's Island Museum numerous times to examine its trove of photos and artifacts about the Mathews mariners in World War II. The museum was where I started. The Mathews Maritime Foundation museum is assembling its own collection of exhibits and artifacts.

The description of Bill Callis comes from numerous interviews with him and his daughter, Lisa. A fictional treatment of Bill Callis's life, and specifically his behavior when he came home from the sea, appears in the title story of Mark Richard's collection of short stories, *The Ice at the Bottom of the World* (1986). Richard gave the Bill Callis character the name Bill Doodlum, and Mathews County the name Doodlum County.

My descriptions of Mathews County men gravitating to the tugboat business come from interviews with Sonny Richardson, David Callis, and Jimmy Hunley in Mathews.

I have attended Hodges family gatherings at the invitation of Brother Hodges and Jesse Carroll Thornton, and have visited Gales Neck with Brother, Jesse, and Jean Hodges, and other family members, with the permission of the historic trust that now owns the property.

BIBLIOGRAPHY

Atkinson, Rick. *An Army at Dawn: Volume I of the Liberation Trilogy*. New York, Henry Holt & Company, 2002.

———. *The Day of Battle: Volume II of the Liberation Trilogy*. New York, Henry Holt & Company, 2007.

———. *The Guns at Last Light: Volume III of the Liberation Trilogy*. New York, Henry Holt and Company, 2013.

Bethell, Nicholas. *Russia Besieged*. Alexandria, VA, Time-Life Books, 1977.

Blair, Clay. *Hitler's U-boat War*. 2 vols. New York, Modern Library, 2000.

Blanchard, Fessenden Seaver. *A Cruising Guide to the Chesapeake, Including the Passages from Long Island Sound Along the New Jersey Coast and Inland Waterway*. New York, Dodd, Mead and Company, 1968.

Boyd, Carl, and Akihiko Yoshida. *The Japanese Submarine Force and World War II*. Annapolis, MD, Naval Institute Press, 1995.

Bradham, Randolph. *Hitler's U-boat Fortresses*. Westport, CT, Praeger, 2003.

Brennecke, Jochen. *The Hunters and the Hunted: German U-boats 1939–1945*. Annapolis, MD, Naval Institute Press, 2003.

British Ministry of Defence. *The U-boat War in the Atlantic*. London, Her Majesty's Stationery Office, 1989.

Browning, Robert M., Jr. *United States Merchant Marine Casualties of World War II*. Jefferson, NC, McFarland & Company, Inc., 2011.

Buchheim, Lothar-Gunther. *Das Boot*. New York, Alfred A. Knopf, 1975.

Budiansky, Stephen. *Blackett's War*. New York, Alfred A. Knopf, 2013.

Bunch, Jim. *Germany's U-85: A Shadow in the Sea*. Nags Head, NC, Deep Sea Press, 2003.

Bunker, John. *Heroes in Dungarees*. Annapolis, MD, Naval Institute Press, 2006.

Bunker, John Gorley. *Liberty Ships: The Ugly Ducklings of World War II*. Annapolis, MD, Naval Institute Press, 1972.

Butler, John A. *Sailing on Friday: The Perilous Voyage of America's Merchant Marine*. Washington, DC, Brassey's, 1997.

Carse, Robert. *A Cold Corner of Hell*. New York, Doubleday & Company, 1969.

———. *The Long Haul: The U.S. Merchant Service in World War II*. New York, Norton, 1965.

Cheatham, James T. *The Atlantic Turkey Shoot: U-boats off the Outer Banks in World War II*. West Columbia, SC, Wentworth Printing Corporation, Inc., 1990.

Chewning, Alpheus J. *The Approaching Storm: U-boats off the Virginia Coast During World War II*. Lively, VA, Brandylane Publishers, 1994.

Churchill, Winston. *The Hinge of Fate*. Boston, Houghton Mifflin, 1950.

———. *Closing the Ring*. New York, Houghton Mifflin Company, 1951.

Cremer, Peter. *U-boat Commander*. Annapolis, MD, Naval Institute Press, 1984.

Cruikshank, Jeffrey L., and Chloe G. Kline. *In Peace and War: A History of the U.S. Merchant Marine Academy at Kings Point*. Hoboken, NJ, John Wiley & Sons, 2008.

De La Pedraja, René. *The Rise and Decline of U.S. Merchant Shipping in the Twentieth Century*. New York, Twayne Publishers, 1992.

Doenitz, Karl. *Memoirs: Ten Years and Twenty Days*. Annapolis, MD, Naval Institute Press, 1959.

Drury, Bob, and Tom Clavin. *Halsey's Typhoon*. New York, Grove/Atlantic, Inc., 2007.

Duffus, Kevin. *War Zone*. Raleigh, NC, Looking Glass Productions, Inc., 2012.

Felknor, Bruce L. *The U.S. Merchant Marine at War, 1775–1945*. Annapolis, MD, Naval Institute Press, 1998.

Flaherty, S. J. *Abandoned Convoy*. Jericho, NY, Exposition Press, 1970.

Frank, Wolfgang. *The Sea Wolves*. New York, Rinehart & Company, 1955.

Freeman, Robert H. *The War Offshore*. Ventnor, NJ, Shellback Press, 1987. Contains *Eastern Sea Frontier War Diary* [National Archives & Records Administration].

Gallery, Daniel. *Twenty Million Tons Under the Sea*. New York, Warner Books, 1956.

Gannon, Michael. *Black May*. New York, Harper Collins, 1989.

———. *Operation Drumbeat*. New York, Harper Perennial, 1990.

Gasaway, E. B. *Grey Wolf, Grey Sea*. New York, Ballantine Books, 1970.

Gatty, Harold. *The Raft Book: Lore of the Sea and Sky*. New York, George Grady Books, 1943.

George, Rose. *Ninety Percent of Everything*. New York, Henry Holt & Co., 2013.

Gloucester County Historical Society. *History and Progress: Mathews County, Virginia*. The Mathews County Historical Society, Inc., 1982.

Gretton, Peter. *Crisis Convoy*. London, Pernell Book Services, 1974.

Groom, Winston. *1942*. New York, Grove Press, 2005.

Harris, Brayton. *The Navy Times Book of Submarines: A Political, Social and Military History*. New York, Berkley Publishing Group, 1997.

Hemingway, Ernest. *Islands in the Stream*. New York, Scribner, 1970.

Hemingway, Hilary, and Carlene Brennen. *Hemingway in Cuba*. New York, Rugged Land LLC, 2003.

Herbert, Brian. *The Forgotten Heroes: The Heroic Story of the United States Merchant Marine.* New York, Tom Doherty Associates LLC, 2004.

Hickam, Homer H., Jr. *Torpedo Junction.* New York, Dell Publishing, 1989.

Hoehling, A. A. *The Fighting Liberty Ships.* Kent, OH, Kent State University Press, 1996.

Hope, Stanton. *Tanker Fleet: The War Story of the Shell Tankers and the Men Who Manned Them.* London, Anglo-Saxon Petroleum Company, 1948.

Hoyt, Edwin P. *The U-boat Wars.* New York, Cooper Square Press, 2002.

———. *U-boats Offshore.* New York, PEI Books, 1978.

Ireland, Bernard. *Battle of the Atlantic.* Annapolis, MD, Naval Institute Press, 1993.

———. *War at Sea 1914–45.* London, Cassell, 2002.

Kaplan, Philip, and Jack Currie. *Convoy.* Annapolis, MD, Naval Institute Press, 1998.

Katz, Robert. *The Battle for Rome.* New York, Simon & Schuster, 2003.

Kelshall, Gaylord T. M. *The U-boat War in the Caribbean.* Annapolis, MD, Naval Institute Press, 1988.

Kemp, Paul. *Convoy!* Edison, NJ, Castle Books, 2004.

Knoblock, Glenn A. *African American World War II Casualties and Decorations in the Navy, Coast Guard and Merchant Marine.* Jefferson, NC, McFarland & Company, Inc., 2009.

Konstam, Angus. *Scourge of the Seas.* Oxford, Osprey Publishing, 2001.

Kurson, Robert. *Shadow Divers.* New York, Ballantine Books, 2005.

Labaree, Benjamin W. et al. *America and the Sea: A Maritime History.* Mystic, CT, Mystic Seaport Museum, Inc., 1998.

Land, Emory Scott. *Winning the War with Ships.* New York, Robert M. McBride Co., Inc., 1958.

Luthmann, William F. *At Liberty.* Chapel Hill, NC, Professional Press, 1995.

MacLean, M. Stanley. *13 Days Adrift.* St. Petersburg, FL, privately printed, 1943.

Mathews County Historical Society. *Mathews County Panorama.* Mathews County Historical Society, Inc., 2000.

Manolis, Nicholas. *We at Sea.* New York, Anatolia Press, 1949.

McCoy, Samuel Duff. *Nor Death Dismay.* New York, Macmillan Company, 1944.

McPhee, John. *Looking for a Ship.* New York, Farrar Straus & Giroux, 1990.

Miller, Nathan. *War at Sea.* New York, Scribner, 1995.

Moore, Arthur. *A Careless Word . . . A Needless Sinking.* New York, American Merchant Marine Museum, 1998.

Morison, Samuel Eliot. *The Battle of the Atlantic, 1939–1943.* Vol. 1 of *History of United States Naval Operations in World War II.* Annapolis, MD, Naval Institute Press, 1947.

———. *Sicily, Salerno and Anzio, January 1943–June 1944.* Vol. 9 of *History of United States Naval Operations in World War II.* Annapolis, MD, Naval Institute Press, 1954.

———. *The Atlantic Battle Won, May 1943–May 1945.* Vol. 10 of *History of United States Naval Operations in World War II.* Boston, Little, Brown and Company, 1984.

Moses, Sam. *At All Costs.* New York, Random House, 2007.

Mulligan, Timothy. *Neither Sharks Nor Wolves: The Men of Nazi Germany's U-boat Arm, 1939–1945.* Annapolis, MD, Naval Institute Press, 1999.

Naisawald, L. VanLoan. *In Some Foreign Field*. Raleigh, NC, North Carolina Division of Cultural Resources, 1997.

Newcomb, Richard F. *Abandon Ship! The Saga of the USS Indianapolis, the Navy's Greatest Sea Disaster*. New York, HarperCollins, 2001.

Offley, Ed. *The Burning Shore*. New York, Basic Books, 2014.

———. *Turning the Tide*. New York, Basic Books, 2011.

Overy, Richard. *Why the Allies Won*. New York, W. W. Norton & Co., 1995.

Parrish, Thomas. *The Submarine: A History*. New York, Viking, 2004.

Paterson, Lawrence. *Black Flag: The Surrender of Germany's U-boat Forces*. Minneapolis, MN, Zenith Press, 2009.

Pitt, Barrie. *The Battle of the Atlantic*. Alexandria, VA, Time-Life Books, 1977.

Powell, James R., and Alan B. Flanders. *Wolf at the Door*. Richmond, VA, Brandylane Publishers, Inc., 2003.

Reminick, Gerald. *Nightmare in Bari*. Palo Alto, CA, Glencannon Press, 2001.

———. *Patriots and Heroes*, Vol. 2. Palo Alto, CA, Glencannon Press, 2004.

Reynolds, Michael. *Hemingway: The Final Years*. New York, W. W. Norton & Company, 1999.

Richard, Mark. *The Ice at the Bottom of the World*. New York, Anchor Books/Random House, Inc., 1986.

Richards, Phil, and John Banigan. *How to Abandon Ship*. Baltimore, Cornell Maritime Press, Inc., 1942.

Rielly, Robin L. *Kamikaze Attacks of World War II: A Complete History of Japanese Suicide Strikes on American Ships, by Aircraft and Other Means*. Jefferson, NC, McFarland & Company, Inc., 2010.

Riesenberg, Felix. *Sea War*. New York, Rinehart and Company, Inc., 1956.

Rigge, Simon, with the editors of Time-Life Books. *War in the Outposts*. Alexandria, VA, Time-Life Books, 1980.

Rohwer, Jurgen. *Axis Submarine Successes 1939–1945*. Annapolis, MD, Naval Institute Press, 1983.

Roland, Alex, W. Jeffrey Bolster, and Alexander Keyssar. *The Way of the Ship*. Hoboken, NJ, John Wiley & Sons, Inc., 2008.

Roscoe, Theodore. *United State Submarine Operations of World War II*. Annapolis, MD, United States Naval Institute, 1956.

Rose, Lisle A. *Power at Sea: The Breaking Storm, 1919–1945*. Columbia, University of Missouri Press, 2007.

Schofield, B. B. *The Russian Convoys*. Philadelphia, Dufour Editions, 1964.

Sebag-Montefiore, Hugh. *Enigma: The Battle for the Code*. New York, John Wiley & Sons, 2000.

Snow, Richard. *A Measureless Peril*. New York, Scribner, 2010.

Spector, Ronald H. *At War at Sea*. New York, Viking, 2001.

Standard Oil Company. *Ships of the Esso Fleet*. New Jersey, Standard Oil Company, 1946.

Starnes, H. Gerald. *Torpedoed for Life: World War II Combat Veterans of the U.S. Merchant Marine*. New York, CreateSpace, 2013.

Stilgoe, John R. *Lifeboat*. Charlottesville, VA, University of Virginia Press, 2007.

Syrett, David. *The Defeat of the German U-boats*. Columbia, University of South Carolina Press, 1994.

Taylor, Theodore. *Battle in the Arctic Seas*. New York, Sterling Point Books, 1976.

———. *Fire on the Beaches*. New York, W. W. Norton & Company, 1958.

Terraine, John. *Business in Great Waters*. South Yorkshire, UK, Pen and Sword Military Press, 2009.

Tibbets, Paul. *Return of the Enola Gay*. Columbus, OH, Mid Coast Marketing, 1998.

Tusa, Ann, and John Tusa. *The Nuremberg Trial*. New York, Skyhorse Publishing, 2010.

U.S. Coast Guard. *Fire Fighting Manual for Tank Vessels*. Coast Guard Publication 329, January 1974.

U.S. War Shipping Administration. *The U.S. Merchant Marine at War: A Report of the War Shipping Administration to the President, January 15, 1946*. Washington, DC, 1946.

Vause, Jordan. *U-boat Ace: The Story of Wolfgang Luth*. Annapolis, MD, Naval Institute Press, 1990.

Wallace, Robert. *The Italian Campaign*, Alexandria, VA, Time-Life Books, 1978.

Walling, Michael G. *Bloodstained Sea: The U.S. Coast Guard in the Battle of the Atlantic, 1941–1944*. New York, International Marine/McGraw-Hill, 2004.

Werner, Herbert A. *Iron Coffins: A Personal Account of the German U-boat Battles of World War II*. New York, Da Capo Press, 1969.

Whalen, Jim. *Last of the Boom Ships*. Bloomington, IN, 1st Books Library, 2000.

White, David Fairbank. *Bitter Ocean*. New York, Simon & Schuster, 2006.

Wiggins, Melanie. *U boat Adventures. Firsthand Accounts from World War II*. Annapolis, MD, Naval Institute Press, 1999.

———. *Torpedoes in the Gulf: Galveston and the U-boats, 1942–1943*. College Station, Texas A&M University Press, 1995.

Williams, Andrew. *The Battle of the Atlantic*. New York, Basic Books, 2003.

Williamson, Gordon. *U-boat Tactics in World War II*. Oxford, Osprey Publishing, 1990.

Winton, John. *Ultra at Sea*. New York, William Morrow and Co., 1988.

Wynn, Kenneth. *U-boat Operations of the Second World War, Volume I: Career Histories, U1-U510*. Annapolis, MD, Naval Institute Press, 1998.

I found these Web sites especially helpful: www.usmm.org, www.ancestry.com, www.convoy.web, www.naval-history.net, www.uboat.net, and www.uboatarchive.net.

INDEX

W9-BTZ-270

Willy Remembers

ALSO BY IRVIN FAUST

Roar Lion Roar
The Steagle
The File on Stanley Patton Buchta

Willy Remembers

A NOVEL BY
Irvin Faust

ARBOR HOUSE
NEW YORK

MIDDLEBURY COLLEGE
LIBRARY

9/1972
Saul

PS
3556
A97
W5

Copyright © 1971 by Irvin Faust

All rights reserved, including the right of reproduction in whole or in part in any form. Published in the United States by Arbor House Publishing Co., Inc., New York, and simultaneously in Canada by Nelson, Foster & Scott, Ltd.

FIRST EDITION

Library of Congress Catalog Card Number: 79-157508
ISBN 0-87795-017-2
Manufactured in the United States of America

MIDDLEBURY COLLEGE
LIBRARY

for Kurt

"Fate has written our policy for us."
—ALBERT BEVERIDGE

"God takes care of sailors, drunken men and the United States."
—RICHARD HARDING DAVIS

"By Juniper, I'll have peace if I have to fight for it."
—UNCLE SAM

"You supply the pictures, I'll supply the war."
—WILLIAM RANDOLPH HEARST

"Bully!"
—THEODORE ROOSEVELT

Willy Remembers

I

A Call to Arms

MAJOR BILL McKINLEY WAS the greatest president I ever lived through. No telling how far he could have gone if Oswald hadn't shot him. He had wonderful hands. You can always tell a man by his hands. My father first taught me that when I was a little boy on Second Avenue. Taft had awful hands, one finger could hit three keys on a piano. He fancied himself as a golfer, but he had those terrible hands. Ike always won in golf because he had good hands, full of character, that is why he could beat Fatty Arbuckle in politics, too. Of course I voted for Taft in 1912, but that was because I didn't want communism, which in those days they called socialism, not for the mush on his wrists.

When I was born Rutherford Hayes was president, the same name as that town in New Jersey, having stole the office from Sam Tilden who stands up there in bronze on 112th Street, ten blocks south of where United States Grant lies in peace beside his beloved Julia. I gave a dollar fifty toward the building of that hallowed place and I never

9

regretted it to this day, as I have told many a reb. Each year when I come back for the parade I visit those two great Americans.

Tilden, you know, was an outstanding governor of New York State long before that office was stole by Rockefeller, who was very bright but completely without principle or honor. He had a tin stomach. Not gotten I can tell you from the canned beef which *we* had to eat in Cuba in the name of healthful army rations. You give that stuff to Garcia and believe me he will get the message and we will get the reds off our shores, a disgraceful condition I tell you after what we went through. Garcia had a bullet hole right in the middle of his forehead. I will always fondly remember General Nelson Miles, the head of the army and the man who conquered the Apache and Porto Rico, for properly calling our stuff embalmed beef and raising the right kind of Cain about army chow so that today our boys can get the very best. I'm beholden also to Mr. Sinclair Lewis for exposing the terrible maggoty conditions in meat.

A lot of Porto Rico natives in New York today. There wasn't a single one when I was a boy. Hungarians, Jews, Italians, Greeks and of course Germans. But not one person from Porto Rico. A Greek named Paul Tarussus froze to death outside my father's store in '88. You'll notice you do not see a single Apache in New York. Nelson Miles was big and puffy and full of himself, but he sure could fight the red man. Billy Baumgarden, who is an Indian War vet of a hundred and three summers, used to be my best buddy. He hated General Miles like poison because he says he stole all the credit for catching Geronimo from General Crook, who is JesusChristAlmighty to Billy. I used to kid Billy a lot, I would ask him so how come it took five thousand troops to capture twenty poor, starving Indians. Billy and me haven't talked in ten years.

My birthday is January 17, 1878. On that day the United States signed a treaty of amity and commerce with Samoa Island in the Pacific. I guess you could say that day kicked two squalling infants out into the world to assume a mountainful of responsibilities. Soon thereafter Pango Pango harbor was acquired as a coaling station for our navy, together with, as you would understand, a number of loose and dusky native maidens. Well that's the navy for you. My oldest boy, Henry, stopped off there in '44 on the way to the Philippines and he wrote me a long letter which I still have about how proud he was to carry on in my tradition. He served under a great man, Douglas MacArthur, who was something of a mama's boy, though it didn't hurt him too bad, and a hell of a lot thinner than my boss, General Shafter, who we used to hear was hoisted onto his buckboard with a block and tackle like an icebox. Henry and MacArthur finally defeated the Tagalogs under Aguinaldo, which was also a communist inspired insurrection. Arthur MacArthur died wrapped in old glory and that is going first class, but Doug needed his ma up at the Point. Well you've only got one mother.

I was three years old when President Garfield was shot by Oswald. He lingered on till autumn and I can recall my mother and father discussing it in soft voices in the dining room. He died in September, did not come *close* to a thousand days, and Chester Arthur was sworn in, the same way Roosevelt made it when Bill McKinley went. As did Truman, you know, the bullet having also got Tony Cermak, who was the mayor of Chicago, before the G-men could move in.

Garfield's murderer was hanged, electricity not yet being in common use. The supposed kidnapper of the Lindbergh baby was put to death in the chair, but that was a railroad job as the country was fiercely agitated against all things German, sauerkraut being liberty cabbage. Did you know Hauptmann's baby, Manfred, named for the ace of all aces, was himself the target of many kidnap threats? No, of course not, nothing was ever said about *that*. But a great many people in this country were sure surprised when the *Hindenberg* blew up and it certainly was very strange since it was filled with helium whereas the *Macon* and *Akron* were filled with hydrogen and I predicted to Helga and Henry they would go bye-bye. Hindenberg, in my humble opinion, was the best general they had over there, except for Eisenhower. The lousy reputation acquired by my outfit, the 71st New York, was caused by a damn balloon. There it was floating up above us as artillery spotter, like it was the *Hindenberg,* but in the process pinpointing us for the Spanish, neat as a telegram. Tom Whiston, Harry Barshinsky and Clarence Carstairs, all got delivery that afternoon because of that damn blimp. That is why Teddy got credit for San Juan Hill. The fact that we had old, black-powder Springfields instead of smokeless did not conceal us none either, but those were the problems a good many newspapers lost sight of. Old Joe Pulitzer, who was blind anyway, most of all. I waited an awful long time for him to get his, but the *World* finally went the way of all flesh, proving that the American public will not accept yellow, not in a belly or a journalist.

Now Mr. William Randolph Hearst, who had recently bought the *Journal,* was another story, for he was telling it straight. He was getting it, you know, from Señorita Eva Cisneros, a dark-tressed beauty who'd been held captive in a dungeon in Havana, and if he was having his fun who am I to cast the first stone? He was a true fighter against communism. He lived in a castle in California, brought over brick by brick, and he put Marion Davies in the movies, something Mrs. William Randolph Hearst never cared for as she was in the 400, so she turned to the milk fund for babies and put on some of the greatest fights of this century for the benefit of the little ones. Her loss, you could say, was their gain.

You know how Schmeling killed Louis, he had a little yid for a manager named Joe Jacobs, who always smoked a big cigar. No relation to Mike. He had store teeth. I saw Dempsey kill Carpentier in Boyle's Thirty Acres in Jersey City when Dempsey didn't have to pay a cent in income tax, but Carpentier was just a built-up light heavy and besides he was French and no fighter but a lover and frankly Mrs. Hearst would have been a lot better off with him than all her babies.

I used to go with a girl who looked like Marion Davies. Irene Flynn. Her father owned a bar on First Avenue and Tenth Street. My father cared very little for micks in those days so I think he was no little relieved when I went over to 14th Street and Broadway, with the *Maine* before and after blaring out at me from every store window, and joined up. The boys at the bottom of Havana waters or Pearl Harbor would never forgive me if I did not. A grand-looking soldier of the G.A.R. with gold buttons and a loop mustache was sitting on a stool in a tent in Union Square. By God I was on fire! I was twenty. I had missed all the fun. '61. The Indian Wars. Fuzzy Wuzzies in Africa. The damn century was nearly gone and I had seen nothing but German boloney. Well I was not missing this one. Especially not with the great news of Dewey's tremendous victory over the Spanish armada in Manila Bay. I was properly thrilled at the prospect of being on the same team with such a terrific fighting man. My father kept his bust in the dining room eleven years and I kept it in my house ten more till Henry knocked it over and busted his mustache. That man had my unqualified vote for president, but the politicians, sly creatures, dictated otherwise. It is a darn shame he had to settle for governor.

I told Irene of my plans and ideas as we walked back from *Tearing Down the Spanish Flag* on 14th Street and she presented me with a red flannel belly band which was guaranteed to ward off yellow, black or any other kind of jack. Though not a jill, which I did not tell her. She also gave me one heck of a kiss, which I saved up and carried to bed with me, my last night as a civilian, perhaps forevermore. "Now don't you forget me, Willy," she said and I promised I never would, although truly I was thinking a little ahead to Eva Cisneros, which I did not bring up.

The next morning, with my satchel, a new derby, my belly band under my pants, the blessings of a brother and sister and Marion Davies, my mother's tears and my father's pride and a Swiss cheese sandwich, I walked to the station at 34th Street and got aboard the train that would take me to Camp Black on the Hempstead Plains of Long Island and the start of my grand adventure, which was bound to change the course of history for this great country and get tremendous short shrift from all the professors of chair-borne infantry.

I I

The Great Adventure Begins

IRVING BERLIN WROTE *Yip, Yip, Yaphank*. My baby brother, Rudy, took the exact same train ride to Long Island in 1917 before he kept his appointment with Mr. Lafayette. I still say the sinking of the *Titanic* was a put-up job. Not that I am sticking up for the Kaiser, after all he was out to grab the Philippines. But I never trusted Lloyd George or de Gaulle either. Roosevelt lived out on the Island in Oyster Bay and he got over polio there after one of his African safaris. He sure was not crippled at San Juan. My oldest boy, Henry, took the same trip in 1943, only then it was called Camp Upton. And Irving Berlin was writing songs for Kate Smith.

Yip, Yip, Yaphank was a very successful army show. I'll tell you one thing, Bob Hope did not entertain us, nor did Lillian Russell or anyone else. Save local talent. The Floradoras were marrying too well to worry about Johnny Doughboy. *This Is the Army, Mr. Jones* was also successful. But too many entertainers got out of combat duty to cavort in these spectacles. Also baseball players, though I have great respect for Ted Williams and Christy Mathewson who died of weak lungs, but don't look for Cap Anson in Cuba.

> Oh how I hate to get up in the morning
> oh how I hate to get out of bed,
> then I'll amputate his reveille
> and step upon him heavily

His real name was Izzy Baline. Don't ask me why he changed it to Berlin considering the hot feeling against Germany. He was a little yid, a singing waiter in Chinatown, but he didn't smoke a cigar like Joe Jacobs. He married money, naturally, one of the millionaire Mackays. He wrote "All Alone by the Telephone" for her because her father hated singing yiddles. That is my wife Helga's favorite song. But she also liked "Stop, Stop, Stop!" by Norma Talmadge doing the slides in the nickelodeon. We sang "Tenting Tonight," which is my all-time favorite and "She's Not Colored, She Was Bawn That Way," although I also like "Over There" by George M. Cagney.

> Over there, over there,
> Comin' in on a wing and a prayer

Also "Praise the Lord and Pass the Ammunition" by a minister, I just hope and pray it is smokeless. We were on God's side, just ask Alvin York, who was a C.O. but then saw the light.

Elsie Janis was a wonder, she entertained the troops in all the camps here and in France and they were crazy about her. She sold a heckuva lot of liberty cabbage. Clark Gable's wife got killed on a bond tour at the peak of her career and he was all busted up, though he had an excellent war record,

much better than Chaplin. Dempsey too. Tom Mix got to
Cuba, although before he became a big shot.

Next to Elsie Janis I like Martha Raye even if she's got a
mouth like an open barn door, but she is regular and one
of the boys, and Mata Hari who was executed could park
her shoes and gauze nightgown under my bed any time, as
could Evelyn Nesbit who caused Harry Thaw to shoot Stan-
ford White on top of the old Madison Square Garden while
lolling about in a red velvet swing.

At Yaphank I got my first pay as a soldier, the magnificent
sum of $13 a month, with a supplementary addition of $1.30
for combat, which you were sure to get as not everyone was
in special service or ordnance, but you could at least buy
a schooner of beer for five cents and it wasn't three point
two and also the *Journal* for a penny, so don't belittle.

God that was comradely and carefree and full of great fun,
the life of a doughboy in an army camp. Chaplin and
Dempsey don't know what they missed. Sometimes now a
crazy incident just comes to me out of the blue, a joke or a
bunkie's face in the mess hall or on the latrine, and cheers
my whole day. Bunkie. Buddy was a Rogers who stole Mary
from Doug Fairbanks. All of it was such a beauty, with the
unknown stretching out before me, even to sleeping on straw
and a rubber poncho in the April wet. It did not faze me one
bit. White tents, they were like sails, soon to carry us off on
a great crusade, stretched out all up and down the dirt streets
far as you could see, and the blue uniforms set off against the
white and a red sky at sunset, ah it was an all-American camp.
And the bugles ringing in your ears from taps to reveille
which I would not amputate for all the money in the world,
though I sure groused then. Talk to Irving Berlin today and
he will tell you the same thing. I still get up at 5 A.M. like
clockwork, just as I did then, with my three bunkies in

number four tent of A Company, Tom Cooper, Mert Swenson
and Lister Colfax, all from New York and Brooklyn (Colfax),
all green peas, but gamely hustling out into the dark and
buttoning up their blouses and pants next to me at roll call.
Oh I have never felt so good, so possible. It was sixty years
between that feeling A and B, or rather two parts of the
same feeling, but I made it and everything in between is
just a big, fast dream.

We did everything together. As a team. From K.P. to
policing the company streets and giving fits to Sergeant Lou
Wimple from Paterson, N.J. But he gave us fits right back,
like all good top kicks should, like Sergeant Joey Bass in '17
and the notorious Benny of '43 who was no sergeant at all,
but called himself one and told the boys he wanted to see
nothing but asses and elbows on police duty. Oh that Benny.
He hated college men. But when the chips were down he
looked out for us as we were his boys. He stole us a real hotel
chef from B Company to run our Buzzacot oven, Jack
Bronsky, who had performed his culinary feasts at the Hotel
Knickerbocker in New York and made the best darn salad
you ever ate even if everything else tasted just like before,
except we knew it didn't because he was such a good chef.
Good old Lou, he even gave me a nickname which I now have
again and carried proudly through the campaigns. Germ. For
my country of descent.

Sergeant Lou and Lieutenant Harthwaite and Captain
O'Brien, a tough little mick from 103rd Street, sure did look
out for us. As good as my father. .They were all genuine
buddies and real leaders, not like much of the stuff that
passes muster these days, although Vinegar Joe Stilwell is
one glaring exception. Oh sure we beefed and groused
plenty, like doughboys immemorial, but just let an outsider
give us some heat and watch out for the fourth of July in

April! Henry and Rudy will tell you the same, as will Apache Billy Baumgarden, only don't tell him I put you up to asking, or he will clam up and stare out the window at the arroyos of D.C., the dumb kraut.

We got to know each other good and proper, like my friends on the east side, except in the shank of the evening my friends and I went our separate ways. None of that now. At night we would sing our camp songs and pass the bottomless pint around and then stagger off a couple of yards to lay down on our sweet straw, safe and sound and comfortable amidst our sarge, our lieutenant, our captain and our bunkies. Why it could have gone on forever, if it were not for our itch to see action. Add to that the pleasant company of the nearby townspeople and visitors from New York come to goggle at their heroes on parade and as Henry said we had it made in the shade. I met a girl named Laura Fistle from Oyster Bay, one day to be roughriding famous, and got me another belly band, this one trimmed in white lace, and also a heckuva reputation when Irene came out and I had to juggle her and Laura into my busy schedule. Don't tell me about Pig Alley or Monterey, I will tell you about Hempstead. I came up minus two buttons off my blouse, but ahead by four kisses. Also to be known as Liver Lips besides Germ, which really did not irk me even if I said it did.

Well came the inevitable day, as it must to all doughboys, when you pack up your gear, take a long sad-happy look around at a place you may never see again and leave for new pastures, maybe not greener, but with the promise of different adventure. That's the army for you. We put up our Merriam packs, the devil's own invention, rolled our blankets, stowed our whiskey and marched off to the train siding, where amidst cheering countrymen, we swung aboard, waved farewell and began the ride to New York, same as Rudy and

Henry and countless thousands in their time. Trains. That
is what we knew. That is what America was all about. Not
P-38s or Spads or B-17s or half-tracks, but the good old iron
horse. Crisscrossing this great land and providing honest
transportation. B and O's. Santa Fe's. Forty and eights. Or
eights and forties? Same difference. We were fifty men. No
horses, least not in our car, though Colfax was no butterfly.
We clanged and chugged past all the pretty Long Island towns
and waved at the hero-goggling folks like it was Château
Thierry here we come. 'Twas one heck of a victory ride,
believe you me, for victory it was sure to be, the American
people will settle for nothing less.

Till at last we pulled into the Long Island City yards,
the world's biggest and do not believe Chicago or L.A. There
to get another great hello. Tom Cooper's folks were present
and beaming and so were mine, but no Irene, for she had
smelled out Laura, well say la gear. Poor Tom, he was roaring sick drunk, so we kindly told his folks their darling was
on K.P. back at camp and would be along in due time. He
was behind a train puking up his shoe tongues, but Mert and
Lister were taking good nursey care of him, holding his head
like his own mama, which is what bunkies are for.

We then sacked in as best we could, considering all the
excitement. Only to be awakened by Mr. Berlin screaming
we hadda get up. We did. We rolled out, packed up the darn
Merriams and staggered over the tracks to the East River
ferryboats, which were lined up and waiting. We climbed on
board and started off down the river. As the morning rushed
in at us we sailed proudly down the line like we were on
dress parade, twixt Long Island and Manhattan, getting
salutes from tugs and steamer whistles and from the people
lining both sides and from our own drum corps playing
"When Johnny Comes Marching Home." Heroes, oh that is
what we were, the first in the East since '65 and so acknowl-

edged by the Brooklyn Bridge and its waving swarms as we passed proudly under and out into Buttermilk Channel on the way to glory.

2

We steamed west and humped up alongside our transport, a converted scow named the *Seneca,* after one of the Iroquois nations upstate; it was nothing to write home about. After climbing on we found out we were stuck down in the hold in bunks fitted out for baby soldiers, not the hero variety, also smelling like unwashed or powdered little ones.

We were four bunks deep. At that we were luckier than Rudy, who was five bunks and Henry at six. Still we were miserable enough, as is only proper in wartime. There were a thousand men on the *Seneca.* Not as much as on the *Queen Mary,* but sufficient so you could not move around in the hold or take a good unstinking breath. Also fitting. I tried going to sleep that night, but Tom Cooper next to me decided to continue his daytime activity and puked all over the place including yours truly and soon half the place is heaving, including truly yours. We got even sicker the next day as we tried downing the heated-up, or rather melted sowbelly they fed us in the name of rations. I puked mine. Then down to the latrine to lay a weary head on a cool urinal before releasing some more stomach. We asked very little, nothing really but three simple wishes: coolness, land, mama. We got sowbelly.

So it continued for what seemed like a month. And still the end would not come. So one weak morning I scraped together my remembered legs and tottered topside. I fully expected to see Cuba, or at the least Florida. What I saw was little old New York. 'Twas some wallop. Why we had not moved a blasted inch! My belly plunked into its socket and I walked up to a grinning sailor boy.

"What the hell is going on around here?" I demanded.

He looked at the blue scarecrow, which was me.

"Cervera (the Spanish admiral) is somewheres around here," he said, "and we got strict orders to keep you precious things safe and sound in the harbor."

So, by God, we had puked for no good reason at all and that is what hurt most. Next to the fact that Cervera and his U-boats never did show up.

I I I

New York, New York, Was a Wonderful Town

I WAS TEN in the blizzard of '88. Telephone lines in the snow like dead snakes. Stiff dead Greek. King of the Hill. Great fun. Well Benjamin Harrison beat Cleveland for president that year. Cleveland was a hopscotch president, in, out, in. Wasn't the best in history, but like my father said, he kept the People's Party out, and that was the main thing. They named a city after him. Grover, California. Also a great pitcher. He wound up in a flea circus. Cleveland beat Harrison in the popular vote. But Nixon got more states than Kennedy and Hayes jobbed Tilden. Joe Pulitzer never raked that muck. Roosevelt killed Landon every way and also the *Literary Digest*. But the Haymarket Riot killed the cops and you can't tell me those two wops were innocent anymore than Tom Mooney, although Izzy and Moe were honest as the day is long and nailed five thousand bootleggers, so not all cops were on the take, but Altgeld which

means Old Gold as in a carton of, though one heck of a
governor, should not have let the bombers go.

My father and mother got the milk through in '88. That
is how the business really got going. We kept all our new
customers that spring. And worked like hell. Just killed the
competition. Like John D. Only honest. Loose. The milk was
all loose. Glass came in much later. Paper? Forget it. Next
year the Kleinhans Dairy moved up to 23rd Street and
Second Avenue. Bertha was born and do not call her big
or she'll crack you. By '90 we were almost exclusive the
perfect food though not as yet discovered in all its true, complete value, and we still continued to carry some bread and
canned stuff which was not crawling with bacteria I can
tell you. I went to P.S. 4 on Lexington Avenue and 29th
Street and I had Miss McTaggerty in 3A and 3B and music
in 5B. She always hummed the pitch. Mouth like a fish
sucking air, toot toot toot. She marched in all the women's
parades on Broadway. She wore bloomers in 5B. Arthur
Fine and me would raise our hands to police the floor just
so we could look up and see the two sail boats. It was an
amazing sight. Rudy likewise when he came through in '02
as we tipped him off.

My father bought a bicycle in '92. He was a great sport.
Hans. He took lessons from a professional racer name of
Jimmy Hughes at the Michaux Club on 53rd and Broadway
who later won a six-day bike race at the old Garden defeating
all the wops they shipped over from Europe. Once my father
pedaled three-fourths of a mile through Central Park alongside of Marie Dressler when she was Marie Dressler and
not Tugboat Annie. She said: "You are a darn good bicycle
rider, Hans." He never forgot that. When he was sick and
dying he repeated what Marie said. He walked out on *Min
and Bill,* yelling it was a put-up job and who the hell were
they trying to fool that was Marie? Another time he took

me to the park to see Lillian Russell sweep along past the reservoir. I lay down beside him in the grass like we was sighting up Miss McTaggerty and then there she came, white dress shining in the sun, leg-of-mutton sleeves, gold bike, mother-of-pearl handlebars, her monogram in diamonds and emeralds, hubs and spikes inlaid with same. It was like a ship from Cathay, China. They don't make them like that anymore, but Diamond Jim is not around anymore. That was before she got fat. And smoked cigarettes in bed and sang coon songs. I like them thin. Like Frankie Bailey. And also Irene Flynn. I used to kid Irene a lot about Frankie who was then showing what she had at Weber and Fields' Music Hall and whose legs were on copyright at the Library of Congress in D.C.; well one day when we were munching a picnic basket under the Brooklyn Bridge and I was carrying on, Irene dropped everything, reached down and pulled up her dress right over her knees in front of God and every- body and said all right mister knowitall, I have heard enough, now what do you think of *these?* And so help me if she was not in possession of one of the most outstanding pairs of Frankies I had or have ever seen, including a set of neatly puckered knees. Little did I then realize I was gazing into two Herbert Hoovers, no, that was not discovered till much later and I myself checked that female trait right after the crash when I had Helga hike up her skirt on William Street where I got my bad news. Sure enough, the knees were Hoover. Do not let them kid you they are Eisenhower. He is babies. Check by looking into the face of the next tad you see. Dietrich had excellent Frankies too, but covered them up with pants, and Ann Pennington was tops also, however hers shook upstairs when she tapped, and they talk about Sally Rand's fans, I'll take her Baileys which I studied eight nights running at the Century of Progress in Chicago. Anna Held was not bad if French and Ziegfeld property and covered up. Of course she had to take it all off when she bathed in milk, thus getting my father's big OK and my mother's grudge. Our milk was the East River at 35th Street and as bareass as Anna. Not Turkish or tepid, but featuring Trojans, turds and Tidewater oil, yet it was our own true Riviera, yes it was. Soon as we got out of whatever it was we had to get out of, we would hustle our bustle over to the river, strip and dive off the wood piles. I had a beautiful backflip which was the envy of all, especially Irene. Besides Winging Willy there was always Arthur, Fritz Badlup and Jack Wallaby whose father worked the Astoria ferry. We would traverse a territory jealously guarded by Moses McGuire and gang and sometimes, even if he had no business there, Ettore Boronzi and company come up from Little Italy, looking for mischief, though they sure did not at Tobruk. Of course if the micks found the guineas first both would naturally forget their original purpose and wind up kicking the shit out of one another as we glided by hilarious. Mose thought he was Dempsey clobbering Bat Batalino. But don't forget how Jack ducked the Brown Bomber all those years, the latter being easily taken out by Schmeling who unfortunately had a glass jaw as demonstrated by Baer whose right came in from the bleachers for all to see except Max to his sorrow plus that of wife Annie Ondra, a cute blonde with movies on 86th Street. Pound for pound Sugar Ray was the greatest, just ask Marty Servo and his deviated septum. But Benny Leonard never had a hair out of place or broke a sweat and just between us I do not believe Jack Johnson is helping himself or the fight game any with this Black Muslim business.

Though it is true we played rough, we always played clean, about the worst of it being Jack Wallaby's eye which wound up on a trolley track at 21st Street and First Avenue.

I V

Oh My Papa

My father came over as a baby in 1848 and his boat was even lousier than the *Seneca*, nor did he have a fancy statue to welcome him, or Ellis Island. His mother, father, brother and he landed at Castle Garden, but all the hardship was worth it as Hans and my grandfather told me many times over. In the old country they lived in Geisenheim on Rhine, which is a very pretty river, but never in the least extolled by them, instead always lecturing me to be proud of and stick up for the East and North rivers.

They were dairy farmers in Geisenheim, although my father's grandfather, Erik, was one heckuva soldier, rising to corporal under Blucher at Waterloo. My father told me how it was lousy propaganda that Wellington, whose pants made him crap standing up, won that battle, but as is well known the English always fought to the last German.

My Uncle Konrad, who was my father's kid brother and stayed in Europe, took up where Erik left off by again beating hell out of Napoleon in 1870 at Sedan. Same way and

same place as the frogs got took in 1940 when they built
their fool Maginot Line up to that city but not one inch
further. Of course we had Bismarck calling the signals and
they had a general named Marie. Yes, Marie MacMahon,
and you will not win with a queer mick. The only man to
stand up to Bismarck was a yid named Disraeli who built
the British empire and was in seventh heaven when the
Kaiser dropped the pilot. The capital of North Dakota is
named after Bismarck, but it is a real kick in the ass for
herring.

When my father got drafted into the Union army he did
not resist or riot or shoot himself in the leg, he went. Unfortunately the war ended two weeks later, for he dearly
wanted to spit in Jeff Davis' eye. He really choked up when
he saw me in blue.

Well upon discharge, Hans went to work on a farm up
in Yonkers for a man named Philip Van Pelt who owned
five hundred acres or so that slanted down to the river.
He lived up there and slaved from reveille to taps for room
and board and fifteen dollars a month. But after five years
of that and the saving of a little capital he said to Van Pelt
this is it and hurried back to the city to live at home and
work as an apprentice glass cutter for Michael Flick who
was a glazier on the Bowery before that street became the
Bowery. But he did not care for Flick who was very arrogant
and overbearing like Wellington, so he quit and found a job
in a grocery store owned by Franklin Mayer on East Houston
Street, who had come over also in '48 from Mainz. That is
where my nephew on my wife's side, Sonny Schroeder, crossed
the Rhine in 1944, the old Mayer house being blasted by a
bazooka and a *Panzerfaust,* which is sure playing no favorites.

Mayer had a daughter named Brunhilde and before you
know it she and Hans were going hot and heavy and cul-
minating in wedlock in 1877. A year later I, Willy, came

along, as tads will, so with another mouth to feed Hans decided to leave his father-in-law and start his own store, which with Brunhilde's help and Mayer's anger he proceeded to do. However, he never, and I mean *never*, carried Bismarck herring.

> Hang Jeff Davis on a sour apple tree
> Down went McGinty to the bottom of the sea

V

Southward Ho!

TALK TO ME about Bobby Kennedy, I'll give you Abner McKinley. Oh he was one shrewd little pipsqueak, Abner, although in all honesty, he was not a skirt chaser on wheels like the president's brother-in-law, George Saxton, who shacked up with a dressmaker from Ohio and then gave her the old heave-ho, which she did not care for at all and to prove it busted down Georgie's door in Canton, O and raised all kinds of ned with the police, putting one heckuva millstone about the president's neck, which was already drooping low from his wife, Ida, who was always sick or fainting. That Abner was some promoter, living like an Astor at the Windsor on Fifth Avenue, not to mention a fancy summer place in P.A. Nothing was ever proved against him, of course, but you cannot tell me he was clean as a hound's tooth, lest that mutt was eating dirt. He had his mitts into any number of juicy little items like telegraph and rail bonds that turned out to be as valuable as reb money, but he always landed on his toes, the little sucker.

Still he never made attorney general or anything else official.
Everyone knew he was the busiest five percenter in D.C.
and so whilst we were puking up sow and our bellies on the
Seneca, the word was passed that this was one more of Ab's
shady deals, for ship's brokerage was right down his dark
little alley. Well our colonel also knew a thing or two and
was well connected in Washington and so he fired off a salvo
of missives to everyone who was anyone and lo and behold
twenty-four hours later we find ourselves in Hoboken, clean,
dry and ready to start living again. Especially when we are
back in a familiar rail yard surrounded by cake and lemon-
ade and pretty girls who are just dying to feed heroes. We
pleased them by eating like there was no tomorrow, nature's
compensation for gut-puking, and spent a lovely day making
them happy. Then at the witching hour, even while we are
still chomping, there comes a whistle, a toot, a bump, a buck
and a great cheer from without and within and once more
we are on the go, this time clacking properly south for Florida
and that darn elusive war.

We ducked our heads inside after waving farewell. The
car housing me and Tom, Lister and Mert and others of A
Company was an old coach stacked with grimy plush seats.
Much like the cars today. You turned the seats so they faced
each other and to make a bed with a mattress, lay your Merriam pack in between and 'twasn't bad at all. Sergeant Lou
told us the water cooler was out of bounds to bathing and
when Tom, who was a slick soldier when he wasn't a sick
one, grumbled, Lou said, "This is the army, mister," and
Tom shut up fast for in those days an order was an order.
As for myself, I was not too worried about personal hygiene;
I was too excited and happy to be off Abner's boat and
charging through the night. I looked out at the quiet little
towns and the dark countryside of Jersey and Delaware
brightened up by moon and stars and reflecting clouds and

I felt the lonely mystery of all soldiering from the first cru-
saders down to us. Just before I dropped off to sleep, charged
and happy, I made a promise to all those sleeping Americans,
same one I am certain Rudy and Henry made to sleepy
French hamlets and Luzon villages: I would be damned if
any dago was going to murder them in their beds, or defile
any woman, white or Cuban, in *my* presence.

2

Oh what a beautiful morning! Washington. Just perfect
before fighting a war. We were over in another siding and
a little ways off, pushing up over the early city was the lovely
dome of the capitol. No teapot, but the real McCoy. I still
look at it first thing in the morning and my day cannot start
till I make certain it is there. The day it ain't, we are in
big trouble. It was there and accounted for that morning,
all right, and a hop, skip away was our commander in chief,
William McKinley, Junior, surely already poring over his
war maps with General Miles whilst Ida lay slugabed with a
sick headache.

"Do you think," said Tom, "the president will come over
and see us?"

"Maybe," I said. "Maybe we'll go on parade down Pennsylvania Avenue."

"By God, my father marched down Pennsylvania and
across the Potomac with McClellan," said Lister. Oh what a
thrilling prospect!

Well we shined shoes and polished brass and got ready all
through the day. But alas 'twas not to be. The only parading
we did was down to the outhouses and over to the eating
shacks for sandwiches and coffee and night fell with us here
and McKinley and Miles there. And you know what they

were figuring out all day? I read it later in the *Journal*. It was strategy and tactics right enough, but of a most peculiar stripe. They were figuring how to get an army of blue down through the late Confederacy without starting another war, or worse, losing them states to the Democrats! Ah well, it must have been Mark Hanna's doing.

V I

In the Land of Cotton

As IS WELL KNOWN, the best laid plans of mice and maids and men and stuff etcetera etcetera and to that you can add politicians, even the world's best. Maybe Grant took Richmond, but did we? We did not. In fact we just chugged right past the erstwhile reb capital and our eager young faces caught nothing but steeples and spires and little black children waving shyly and looking bug-eyed. Cavalry Joe Wheeler made Major General and the good folks of the city piled up their fried chicken and hams and sweet potato pies and their blackbirds toted all down to the station, proving loyalty beyond a doubt, but not to our stomachs and we slid by unmixed, unawares, unfed. It is no wonder the G.O.P. did not crack the Solid South till Al Smith gave them rum, romanism and *raa*dio.

So down we sped, through Virginia and the Carolinas, through towns that contained but six houses and a name, past crossroad stores and water tanks, past miserable dirt roads and dust-dry countryside. Silent black faces. Curious

34

white ones. A wave and a cheer. Sleeping hound dogs and razorback hogs, for this was sowbelly country. And Stony Jackson and Jeff Davis country. I remember thinking: How could they fight so fierce over dust and dirt and shacks? But then, of course: Home is still sweet home.

In South Carolina, near Charleston, while on pisscall, Lister spies a collection of sawed-off hogsheads and a pump and putting two and two together we all pile out and peel and splash ourselves silly in them wood tubs whilst the whole (male) population of the county stares and the captain and colonel have fits for they are still scared of a Fort Sumter whereas Billy Yank is thinking only of aqua pura after two and a half prohibition days and Anna Held could not have felt better in her asses' milk, for there we were b.a. as the East River and it is the start of a real bareass war as Howard Chandler Christy so aptly portrayed at Daiquiri and other steamy sites. However, if anything, we cemented North-South relations with our homely gesture for we sure got a great cheer as we finally pulled out.

Still in all, Sumter darn near got fired off in Waycross, Georgia. That is where some John D. charged us TWENTY FIVE CENTS for a canteen cup of coffee and in a "white only" waiting room to boot! I tell you we were in a truce-breaking mood when the colonel himself took over and commandeered those urns, telling that cracker where to get off and supplying us the coffee free of charge which was government property anyway. No wonder there is a Truman committee. However, that was the only black-market operation against us, rather white-market. The following day we slipped over the border into Florida and if disappointed in the lack of Miami or bathing beauties, saw a plentiful supply of pine and hanging moss and swamp and shacks, all of which continued down the peninsula to Lakeland, which sounds pretty but was just another station with its ever-present white and colored,

two or three side streets with a house here and one there.
That is where we swung off. That is where we started to
train for war.

> The cluster'd spires of Frederick stand
> green wall'd by the hills of Maryland
> "Who touches a hair of yon gray head
> dies like a dog, march on," he said.

V I I

Early Days, Happy Days

ENTER 1894 AND RUDY right on New Year's morn, four A.M. He was some cute bug, covered with hair and fat and a real Katzenjammer. Did he ever break balls! Champion devil and whiner of all time. Did not have the least notion the world was here for others as well as him he was so spoiled, till at age six he clipped Bertha's curls while she was napping in the front room and she woke up and paddled his little can blue, white and pink as he squalled like a kitten in the alley and Hans held off my mother who was also bawling, calling out "He must learn, he must learn." After that the little brat started to come around.

With the three of us as economic assets in the form of child labor which I strongly favor to cure juvenile delinquency, we prospered in the dairy line and when I got out of the army and rebuilt myself from 94 dysenterried pounds up to 165 with Eugene Sandow's secret techniques, Papa scraped together his capital as he was a real hustler and bought a halfpint creamery on 97th Street and Third Avenue, north of the then beaten track, named it Farmbest Dairies and started home and store deliveries with two wagons equipped with rubber wheels. Which makes us the oldest in New York and that goes for Borden and Sheffield which are monopoly players anyway and should be investigated by the Interstate Commerce Commission. We still lived downtown, did not move up till '08 when two-ton Taft beat Bryan, thank God, and Arthur Fine's father bought a Model-T for $850.50 as a wedding present for Arthur and Irene Flynn and that was the Cohens and the Kellys. Black, it was black, as Ford would sell you any color long as it was black. I did not mind the dear Willy, I even went to the nuptials, which was Arthur's idea, not Irene's, at the Diamond Hall on Hester Street upstairs over the push carts. That is where I spied a big, red-faced, chesty girl with a carload of hair, standing in the corner, trying her darndest to look like Maxine Elliott and not making it. Well I was no Jack Barrymore; I walked up to her for I have always been a tit man, even in those days, and asked her if she would care to dance. She did not care to. I have never taken no for an answer, got that from my father, and in that respect was as spoiled as Rudy.

"Why not?" I said.

She got redder. I had her there.

"I don't know."

"There has to be a reason," I said.

You have to make them think, you see. While they are doing that and getting all mixed up, you make your move. I stepped in and took her around her boned-up middle and started out dancing. Poor thing, she almost fell down, but I grabbed on harder and could even feel some soft meat under the bone which inspired me and soon I had us whipping around to the strains of "If a Table at Rectors Could Talk."

"That is from the *Follies*," I said.

She mumbled something.

"It is a terrific show," I said. Which it was, but I was just giving her some bull. Did not see a Ziegfeld show till 1912 with Billie Burke starring and don't let them kid you that featherweight in the movies is Billie.

"I am Willy Kleinhans," I said.

"I know."

"You do? How? You see me off to Cuba? Or coming back?"

"No. You deliver milk to my father's restaurant."

"Oh."

She could have lied a little, but not that one, no sir. Never. Not even a little white lie. When our number was over I delivered her back to her corner. There to forget about her, and that night I took Janet Immendorf home and got a kiss and a feel, too, for this was postwar times and I was not settling for small apples. So with all that, it will be some surprise to learn Miss Tonguetied Truthful turned out to be Helga Brunkhorst, the daughter of Brunkhorst's Rathskeller on 14th Street and in three years and six months to the day she became my better half, though there were a few pebbles twixt the cup and the lip, but I will not go into that now. I kidded her for forty-one years about that first no.

Later the same year Hans bought a little house on 90th Street, right near the Ruppert Brewery which lived up to the old saying he smells like a brewery. I got friendly with Jack McTurk, who rolled the full kegs and I daily got a few on the house. I used to see old Jake Ruppert drive back and forth to his office, same Jake who later bought the Yankees and created a dynasty with Miller Huggins, Ruth and Murderers' Row. But my all-time favorite was Handsome Hal

Chase who was a ballet dancer around the initial sack and
do not tell me about Sisler or Terry, they were not in the
same ballpark, only Hal had a little of the Abner McKinley
in him, except not as shrewd in ducking the punch. As for
the present-day crop I lean toward the elder Dean, who pos-
sesses the true gashouse spirit and as Frankie Frisch says
in the *Journal*:

> Though I pitched you and I played you
> By the living God that made you
> You're a better man than I am
> Dizzy Dean.

For the Flash knows which side his bread is buttered on.

Still in all, oh that Babe! He made eighty thousand big
ones his top year, more than McKinley ever pulled down.
But then Mac could never hit the curve ball. Babe drove
old Jake wild, belting and balling till the wee small hours
and gulping hot dogs like Diamond Jim did oysters. One
time he ate so many he came down with the world's biggest
bellyache and missed a crucial game as a result. Jake got
so sore he docked the Babe and fumed all over every paper
in the country. In the end the Babe merely laughed, pointed
over the fence, blasted a shot to that spot and broke Charley
Root's heart as he trotted laughing around the bases on his
pipe stems. Proving once and for all the old adage: The Ruth
is mighty and shall prevail.

I watched the old Yankees at the Polo Grounds. They
had squatters' rights by the grace of the Giants and John
McGraw, the little Napoleon who thought he was Waterloo
and Sedan rolled into one. I took Rudy and sometimes Helga
when she started to talk and we rode the trolley up to
Coogan's Bluff with a picnic basket, which is now the dark-
town strutters' ball. Naturally with my background I favored
the Yanks and I made them do likewise, at least in my pres-

ence. How Rudy would wind up pulling for the Philadelphia As and Helga the St. Louis Browns, even with Sisler, is something I will never understand. Serves them both right neither team is in existence today and also John McGraw, whose great Giants are bye-bye, the little Napoleon.

But the Yanks are true blue, aren't they?

V I I I

A Black Day

Do NOT ASK about McKinley's dastardly murder. Suffice it to say that when that horse with the empty saddle and the turned-around spurs came into view I bawled like a baby. So did my father and mother. So did even Billy Baumgarden, and he voted for Bryan, the dumb kraut.

I X

A Debt Is Paid

THE YEAR WAS 1818. Fritz Kleinhans, age thirteen months, reached over and fell out of his little bed. For an entire year he did not crawl about or make tad sounds. He just lay in his tiny sack, his eyes two sad peeholes in the snow, his thin cheeks burning red. The Kleinhans line hung in the balance, for if he did not come around my father will not evolve or naturally me. Fritzie's father, Erik, untouched by Waterloo, was distraught by his baby's condition and brought in three doctors, one a yid from Berlin, but he sank even lower as they shook their heads and made doctor clucks over the still babe.

Get the picture?

OK. In the winter of 1819, Spain ceded Florida to the United States. So what? you say.

Well in March of that year little Fritz gurgled and waved a rooster arm. His eyes started to surface. Cheeks turned a healthy pale. By summer's end he was crawling and by Christmas breaking balls as normal tads should. He continued the upward climb, grew and thrived and hayed and milked and ran and jumped in the fields. He tarried here and there with a maid. In due time he married, turned his peppy eyes westward, felt the wind of hope and set sail for the new world to forge a link twixt that and the old. That is what. The end. All lived happily ever after.

Ah but. Yes, but.

The dago is shrewd. He builds armadas and when they break up in typhoons he drags his ass onto the nearest beach and populates the countryside. He hires a wop to discover America, then names the place after another wop. But most of all he remembers Florida, the place he ceded in 1819, and its great natural assets: lush orange groves, fountains of youth, fine hotels. So he digs in ninety miles offshore, tortures the *insurrectos,* strips women, blows up ships, rebuilds his armada and gets ready to pounce. And when he does, when he again grabs Florida, what will happen to that poor place?

It will be debauched by Alfonso, a bleeder, who would love nothing better than to upgrade his weak stock with strong American blood.

Sounds pretty bad, doesn't it? It surely does not sound good.

Well don't give up yet. Enter Bill Hearst. The same Bill who sent Fred Remington down to show the dago feeling up naked women. He dropped Marion Davies and rang the tocsin and the grandson of that reprieved baby, made whole in 1819, responded. For a Kleinhans always pays off in full. This young fellow in Yankee blue pitched his tent in the rugged Florida sun and dared hispaniola to enter. He got assigned to the famed Fifth Army Corps led by Major General William Shafter, fat like Taft, but tough as Ike. He dumped his Merriam pack and learned to make a soft shoulder roll. He drilled close order and skirmish line among the scraggly palmettos. Though he liked his bottle, he obeyed the letter of the dry Lakeland law, drank Stonewall Jackson milkshakes, General Miles grape juice. Did not even object to the nigger M.P.s. He was in spring training, but unlike the Dodgers, it was for keeps.

Assigned without a gripe to latrine duty, he developed General Goethal's eye for the straight, sheared side, the artist's knack for camouflage. He built a prize beauty, a real Calabra Cut. When Captain O'Brien came around on inspection, he looked around and then wham, he fell in. Climbing out, dripping from knee to ankle, the captain kicked a big one toward the Gulf.

"Who the hell built this latrine?" he bellowed.

"Kleinhans, sir," said three good bunkies.

He turned to the young Yank.

"That is one helluva latrine, soldier. I am putting you in for P.F.C."

And that he did. Proving that the young fellow and his leader sure knew shit from shinola. Which is more than you can say for King Alfonso and his covetous army.

X

Boy of Mine

My oldest boy, Henry, was the spitting image of Rudy and that was poetic justice because he was born the same year Rudy was killed, 1918. Rudy got the kiss of death in the Meuse Valley on November 7, the day of the fake armistice, though a true one for all time for my baby brother. I am proud as punch of Rudolph Peter Kleinhans, age twenty-four.

We waited some seven years for Henry and though it was well worth the sweat, I was starting to get a little worried. Not that we did not try. At least *I* sure did. Every mick and guinea in the neighborhood dropping them left and right and us drawing blanks. Helga's sister, Anna, has Sonny, my brother, Max, clicking with two girls then Vinny, Bertha and the twins, and we come up zero. It was embarrassing as well as frustrating and I was considering giving up the ghost, though I'm sure I never would. Till this time when I go downtown with Jack Wallaby and Jack McTurk and we wind up over on Tenth Avenue with a couple of live ones and several bottles and I get so worked up that in the middle of all I charge home, wake up Helga and then pass out cold. When I come to, she is bareass beside me, hair down to her hips, with a neat smile, sponging off my forehead as well as my youknowwhat and though she would never admit to anything, nine months later, bingo!

He was something. Popped out a mile a minute like he couldn't wait to see what it was all about. Ten and a quarter pounds. Stood up in his crib at eight months, walked at ten, hardly ever crawled, and that always straight ahead. Never cried, never. Always smelled like grade A. Not punky, like the other babies, Mrs. Hearst would have loved him. Better looking than Sonny Schroeder by a mile when he was three weeks old. My father called him Rudy half the time. He didn't mind, little Mr. Sunshine, he knew what the old man meant. And he broke the ice; one year later Margaret came along and after her Frank Joseph, although the less said about him the better.

God he was smart. Talk about Kieran and Information Please, or the Quiz Kids, even Joel, I'll give you Henry. At age four he was correctly identifying every car on the road. He would stand out there with me on Lexington Avenue, plant his little legs and I would say OK, Henry, on your mark, set, go and he'd point a chubby finger and his squeaky little voice would pipe right up: "Fordmodel T. Nash, Packard. Caddy. Shivvy. Booick. Hudson. Reo. Stupidaker." Oh that was the best of all and he broke me up every time, for which I would buy him a Breyer's cone as we were not yet in that line. Stupidaker!

And his sayings. Sweet Jesus he knew them all. We would visit his Aunt Bertha and the guinea she married, Salvatore Arculeo, and he'd knock and say, "I hope there's no one to home here, I hope I hope I hope." Whenever my brother Max and me were arguing about business or the Yanks and Giants, he would breeze into the room, he was ten at the

time, point at us and say, "Let's you and him fight, I'll
hold yer coat." Nipping all right in the goddarn bud. Or
he would say to Maxie's wife, Clara, on the phone, "Come
on over for a duck dinner, you bring the duck." I'd be on
the floor and even Helga would giggle and she hated to encourage him in any of that stuff.

Right after the crash, he started up with the Little King.
The one with the robes dragging on the floor. He would
sail into the office with a curtain over his shoulders and a
pie plate on his head. I would stop yelling at Lugenstein,
my stupid broker, hang up, lean back and say, "Your majesty,
what do you think we should do about the international
economic crisis?"

He'd screw up his face and consider. "Nov shmoz ka pop,"
he'd say.

And the street could go to hell.

Or: "Your majesty, what should be our policy toward
France, now that she will not pay her war debts?"

He'd shrug. "Nov shmoz ka pop."

I only wish Hoover could say that instead of moratorium.

Or the topper: "Your majesty, what should be our posture
now that your colleague has abdicated and married Wally
who is divorced?"

"Hmmmm. Kop pop na shmoz."

Christ, roll and butter around the floor!

And he had this God-given gift with his teeth. I never
saw anybody else who had it. He could tap out any song
by clicking his teeth together. He could hit the tempo and
pitch right on the button. He could do "Lucky Lindy," or
"Yes We Have No Bananas," or "Barney Google," or you
name it, just on his teeth, in front of company or anybody.
I tried to get him on the Amateur Hour, but that was a
put-up job and I never got an answer as all they cared for
was one-man bands.

Radio songs? Are you kidding?

> "When the world should all be sleepin
> and a melody comes creepin
> They're crispy, they're crunchy the whole day through
> Jack Armstrong never tires of them
> and neither will you
> Arf says Sandy
> Don't despair
> use your head, save your hair."

If they sent it out, he could sing it. Jesus. He would do number-one on Helga's hit parade, next to "All Alone by the Telephone." She would go all dreamy eyes as he'd pull his chin in, lower his voice and let go:

> "Jump on the Manhattan merry go round,
> The low down, the show down of New York Town,
> Broadway, the Bowery, and Park Avenue,
> new songs and blue songs, they're all for you.
> So smile and brighten up your faces,
> HOT CHA CHA, WE'RE GOING PLACES,
> and we won't get home until morning
> on the Manhattan merry go round!"

And he did not need a megaphone or a mike.

What a kid. And we were the best of pals, the real McCoy, not like Max and Vinny which was simply a matter of biology. I was always present at his stickball games or real tackle where he could dodge the other kids out of their drawers. I bought him the first basketball on the block in 1927 and he developed the best two-hand set shot into the sink since Nat Holman even if it drove Helga nuts. I would let him, *encourage* him, to belt me shot after shot in the stomach and unlike Houdini, I would *never* flinch, much less keel over.

Yet with it all, he always got AA in school. I had only

one major rule: I don't care what you get in work because God gave you your brains and you cannot get blood out of a stone, though with your inheritance that is no problem, but conduct is another story and there I will accept nothing but the best. And the best is just what he gave me. At P.S. 14. At Stuyvesant, the only kid in the whole family to make it there, he was great in math and science and they begged him to go to Rensselaer and I said are you kidding? He was driving at thirteen, handling a truck at fourteen and at sixteen working the platform for me and doing a better job than my regular crew which was union. I am positive he was laid by the time he was fifteen, but equally sure, like his father, he never paid for it in his brief but meteoric career.

He graduated Stuyvesant in '36 and I said to him what do you want for a present? Anything in God's world, I said, you just name it. The Olympics, he said, just like that, without hesitating. I said sold American, we can even visit Geisenheim. I left my foreman, Al Fino, in charge and the kid and I went over first class on the *Bremen* which was the Olympic ship. And who was the hit of the week? Why Henry, of course. More popular even than the team itself. Eleanor Holm gave him the big hello, so did Archie San Romani. He helloed right back. Eleanor was OK. She got a real lousy deal, just for popping some champagne. And Harding stays in office, that's justice for you. I never did know what she saw in a little yid like Billy Rose, still anybody can win the world's shorthand championship with a pencil in a potato has to have something. Including lead in his pencil. Henry always thought highly of Billy Rose, so I did too. We also met six black auxiliaries on the boat, including Owens and Corny Johnson. Very pleasant fellows. I have always liked and gotten along with them. One of my best friends was Alonzo Starr, who chased Villa with Blackjack Pershing on

the Mexico border; I called him a black auxiliary for eleven
years. Last year he just clammed up, like Billy Baumgarden.
Dumb nigger.

We landed in Hamburg. I took the kid to see a few things,
though not what you think. Then I rented a Mercedes, the
world's best car after the Packard and drove to Geisenheim.
We got a fine hello from the Burgomeister, Heinz Flugel,
who was very good friends with my cousin, Ernst, son of
Konrad of Sedan, who had an important governmental job.
The mayor liked our family with a special fondness for he
used to get candy from Konrad as a baby. His mother was
a yid, making him officially yiddle, yet there he was mayor
of a German town which shows you how truthful the propaganda was. So what if he lost his job a year later? It was for
juggling the books. Jimmy Walker also got the ax for being
a crook, does that make this country anti-mick?

Geisenheim turned out to be a nice place to visit, but.
After a big blowout in a beergarden specially rented by
Ernst, we bade everyone a fond farewell and took a train
that was clean, new and on time to Berlin. Mussolini could
not have run it better, though he would have wound it up
in Frankfort.

Berlin was some town. Clean wide streets, clean sidewalks,
flowers, banners, friendly faces everywhere. Not a single jack-
boot, not a black shirt, nor a foot of barbed wire, not one
busted jaw. So much for all the bullshit.

We took a clean bus to the *Reichsportsfeld* and it was a
beauty. It even had television outside in case you couldn't
get in. *In 1936.* And the Olympic village was better than
Levittown, I only wish I had the milk concession.

And we saw all the great ones. Thorpe, Cunningham,
Nurmi, Weissmuller. Just as my father and I had seen them
at the old and the new Gardens. Chesty Joie. Peerless Paavo.
He always peeked at his wristwatch before breaking your

heart. John Paul Jones, not the navy man. Charley Hoff clearing 13-6 for a new world's record. Billy Bonthron, who had
some kick for a Princeton man and Cunningham who had
burned legs and a bigger kick. The wop, Luigi Beccali, who
won the '32 Olympics, but flopped at the Garden. Naturally.
We saw Jim Dandy beat Gallant Fox.

> There never was a handy guy like Sande
> For bootin them babies home.

However, I have always liked Banana Nose.

Truth to tell, despite all the auxiliaries, Germany won
the Olympics. Which was quite a feat as the blackbirds have
an extra inch in their Achilles tendon giving them a terrific
advantage. Naturally the dagos did not win a thing.

We returned home on the *Berengaria* after a wonderful
month that was both inspirational and educational. Henry
clicking again, especially with a girl named Arlene Lorentz
from Fort Worth, Texas, who wrote to him for three years
and would have left the corral in a minute if he had whistled
which he did not.

We were not home a month when Henry walked into my
office. Eloise the girl was clackety clacking in the outer office
and she gave him her patented grunt as he breezed through.
I hired her in '34. She was weaned on a pickle, but one
heckuva secretary. A grunt from her was like two months'
concession. Henry came straight to his point, like always.

"I think," he said, "we should go to homo."

You might suspect he was referring to Frank Joseph or
queer milk, but he was not, just the homogenizing of the
latter. Everybody and his uncle knew how I felt about that.
But nobody except the kid had the guts to try me. Eloise
the girl perked up an ear as she clacked.

"Milk should not be tampered with," I said.

"We pasteurize it," said the wise one.

"And that doesn't help it any, it was much better loose. But it's the law and I respect the law."

"The public wants homo."

"The public don't know what's good for them. The public eats canned meat. Milk is already the perfect food."

"Make it more perfect."

"Do not screw with nature. That is a cardinal principle. Never."

Oh but he was shrewd, that one, he could have taken on Leibowitz. He gives me Rudy's million-dollar smile.

"I've been looking at some catalogues," he said. "I think I'll go to Purdue."

There it is. The old one two.

"Jesus, don't start that again," I said.

"What good is staying around here? You never listen to my advice." He has stopped smiling. The last time he stopped smiling he hit me with Texas A. & M. "You might as well turn it over to Frank Joseph," he said.

"Sure, and go bankrupt in three months. You gonna drag him out of the village?"

"He's basically very bright."

"That's right. So is Dillinger."

He shrugged and got up.

"Jesus, where are you going?" I said. "Can't you stick around a little and talk business."

"I already talked business. You want to live in the past. Be happy, go lucky." He turned. I can already see Betty coed, whose dress I guess is black for old Purdue. What can I do?

"All right," I said. "What's the deal?"

He swung back and sparkled on me.

"We go to homo as of next week and I'm in charge of converting. You won't be sorry, Pop."

How could I be sorry? Nature versus Henry, nature got to lose. Not fair or square, but what is in business? I got up from that chair, put my arm around the kid and said you did it again you little s.o.b., come on, I'll buy you a beer. And me and that great kid walk out of there arm in arm past Eloise the girl who almost smiled except her face would crack. We walked down to 86th Street and I bought us five beers, imported, at the Lorelei, and then we walked home, kings of the hill, to get holy ned from Helga as we breeze in singing three widda fishies in a iddy biddy poo. Jesus, but you could have fun with that kid.

My word has always been my bond. Next week we began to switch over, with Henry in charge, Betty coed's loss was the milk industry's gain. I sent Frank Joseph instead, for all the good it did him, and Regensberg U., which was the only place I could get him in and that thanks to pull. Business increased 17 percent by the end of the year. In three months my brother Max on Staten Island had converted to homo, with Henry showing Vinny the ropes, naturally. I wound up giving him a bonus of five hundred dollars, every cent of which he earned. God what a business man that kid was, and could have been, were it not for that fuckin bullet with his name on it.

> So smile and brighten up your faces,
> Hot cha cha we're going places.

But I am proud as punch of Henry Paul Kleinhans, age twenty-six.

X I

We Don't Forget

FOR TEN YEARS, starting in 1920, Lister Colfax and I went on a pilgrimage. Every Christmas to Florida. We would leave the wives home, put our foremen in charge and take off for the southland. We took the train for five years, then in '25 I bought a Packard and we drove down Route One, parallel to our original crusade. That was a great treat for two dough-boys as we could stop off and explore the sites once denied us in the name of duty. Washington. Richmond. Petersburg. Charleston. Then the trip would get very serious as we landed and explored the sacred places. For a starter, Lakeland. There to check into the Bluewave Hotel and go over all the old landmarks. True to the pledge we made on the first pil-grimage, we never touched a drop in Lakeland, same as '98.

Then on to Clearwater, outside of Tampa, and the Gulfo Inn, which had a room ready and waiting. We drank there. Next thing we would do was hire a fishing boat and sail out onto the beautiful, placid waters we had once plied as con-querors. Then back for a quick one and a change and dinner looking out at the setting sun. And then to the main business at hand. We would take a taxi over to Tampa and start on the rounds of that fabled city, including a Cuba Libra on the veranda of the Tampa Bay Hotel, from which vantage point Richard Harding Davis figured he was running the war. We would continue on, to prowl about our old haunts in Ybor City where at Pablo's Palace we had another drink and ate an uncanned sirloin steak for the boys of A Company. We had ten such great trips, but it all ended in '29, and with it an era. In that year, Lister, who manufactured Splendid Yeast, a competitor for Tasty Yeast, except it was strawberry, went kaput in the market. He sprinkled some rat poison on his product, sat down for a bite and he did not get up.

I never drove down again.

Now we did not especially look for it, but if we hooked on with a couple of live ones, well we were free, white and over twenty-one and away from home. But '98 was a whole different ballgame, for us at least, if the same ballpark. They had a cat house in Tampa named *La Luna Linda,* which featured a daily lineup of every fellow you could name, minus two. They all figured it was last-chance hotel on this earth, but I could never buy that bill of goods. Nor should any doughboy if he wishes to see it through and tell the tale. Besides I understood what could happen as Arthur Fine, who knew all and told you, had scared the beJesus out of me. Just as I did Rudy and Henry, and don't let anyone kid *you* it is just like a bad cold. Take care of your body, I always say, and it will take care of you, just like a good car. Abuse it, you will need a ring job, points, plugs, the works. But you could not convince those dying fellows busting down doors. Well you pays your money and takes your choice.

We had shipped out of Lakeland to Ybor City, a dinky town located outside of Tampa Heights. That's where we got our 45-caliber ammo and our Springfields and learned how to balance a target on the sight and squeeze off the shot, getting some sore shoulder in the bargain. We were now Fifth Army Corps, the outfit that was to hit Cuba, First Division, First Brigade, and we had to get ready to do a job. I dug my Panama Canal specials. We got pup tents and learned how to sleep in the field. At night we continued to train by getting passes into Tampa where most of the boys made a beeline for the above described location, but where Lister and I knocked around, as we did a quarter-century later, soaking up sights, sound, color and bourbon, for the local option was wet. It was a real army town, prices up, service down. Joplin. Liverpool. Paris. Manila. Seoul. You name it, they all see you coming. But as long as we had three hots and a flop, who cared?

Each day the transports pulled into the docks. And navy vessels scooted up and down the nearby waters, waiting for Cervera to come out and to knock his block off. He did not show anymore than in New York. Finally in June, McKinley or Alger (not Horatio, but the war secretary) decided to make a move as the American public was getting as itchy as we were. Orders were cut. We packed up, marched, piled on wagons and rolled out through the city to Port Tampa and the waterfront. There, which is the army for you, to wait some more. Nights we slept on board the boats, days we practiced amphibious landings out in the islands of the bay, charging the crabs, getting bit by them and the sun. Still waiting for Cervera. The fancy-Dan newspapermen were living on Easy Street at the Tampa Bay, overseeing all from the veranda with bourbon highballs in hand. As Joe Pulitzer would have at Waterloo. I didn't mind. I was making history, not Joe.

At long last the word ran up and down the line: Cervera was over in Santiago Bay. Which meant the navy could bottle him up and he could not do us any harm, which was fat chance anyway as the dago fleet was about on a par with

Mussolini's. But finally we could move. I took another last
look around, a soldier's constant gesture, this time at the mainland and I waved a farewell to the folks up in New York.
Then with my buddies of A Company, I marched toward our
transport, the *Yucatan*. We thought we were all set, but a bird
in hand is still worth two in the bush, for who should be
standing amidst all the unholy confusion and blocking our
colonel's way, none other but Colonel Teddy Roosevelt,
replete with polka-dot kerchief and teeth. At that point in
his life he was about middle rung, but that never stopped
T.R. I saw it all. The colonel walked up to him and said
I am loading my troops on our transport. Teddy gave him
enamel and said, but we already have it. He then preened,
spun on his heel and walked on board to join his Rough
Riders and Leonard Wood, all of whom were what they were
courtesy of R. H. Davis. He leaned over the side and surveyed
the scene below, and a wild mess it was, like he was about
to fire when ready, Gridley. The colonel stood there eating
crow, also the captain, so naturally us. From that day on
Teddy was on my list, why I even voted for him holding my
nose. And I gave him one big horselaugh when in a remark-
ably short time, as army time goes, we wind up on the
Vigilancia which was bigger, newer and better by far than
the *Yucatan,* so to blazes with him and his teeth too.

   We piled onto the *Vigilancia*, number 24 in the line, and
off we sailed to liberate Cuba, avenge the *Maine* and protect fair womankind.

> Splendid Yeast will please you
> Try a single pack
> If you're not delighted
> Take your money back.

So long, old pal.

X I I

A Pleasant Voyage

I WAS NOT SEASICK a single minute, though others sure were. Oh those blue glass waters, those pure, clean, soft days, the creamy nights pierced above by a million stars. As in a lazy dream we just slid down that Caribbean lagoon, ready enough to do our duty, but cushioned by tropical beauty before making *Cuba libre*. We sang our songs far into the night; days we would sit around and gab or play a little poker and look out at the flying fish, which do not fly at all but leap up off muscles as powerful as any black auxiliary's, and gaze out at the far horizon, just as the boys at Vera Cruz did in '46 and Henry in his turn. He was up there overhead was Henry, watching every move I made so I had to be extra careful to do the right thing before my unborn son. Likewise Konrad and Erik Kleinhans. And of course, far off to the north, my commander in chief, if only Ida would leave off a bit.

Talk about Omaha and Utah Beach and D days and LCTs and LCIs, hell we invented amphibious landings! 15,000 men, 55 transports. Stretched out in a deadly line, with the

PT boats hustling up and down like worried sheep dogs, taking excellent care of us and our precious heavy stuff that included field artillery, Gatlings and a dynamite gun. No rockets, no big Berthas, no mustard gas, just human-type warfare.

We steamed south past Key West. So long, Harry Truman, in your flower shirt. *Adios,* mainland. For two weeks we will float on the blue cushion, suspended twixt peace and war, till we will pull into Santiago Bay, which we are sure to find as we have American captains. We ran blacked out, but so what, our wake curved behind us like a shiny white tail linking us on to the next ship, and that to the next, while all the voyage the moon and stars were on our side. In my humble opinion there is nothing like a Caribbean cruise before starting a war.

Till finally we saw land. Gentle at first. Then higher and greener and blue and lush and then rugged. I stared. Oh it looked peaceful and pretty enough, but Eva Cisneros was a prisoner in a dungeon somewhere in there and all that cute scenery was just filled with pointing guns, itching fingers and squinty eyes. Yes, Toral was in there and Yamamoto and all the red legions, and Rommel too, the poor misguided bastard, behind his bristling pillboxes. Throwing down the gauntlet to me and Henry and all the embattled, shivering doughboys riding in with democracy on our backs. It was time to wake up from the beautiful dream. I sat myself down in a corner and wrote a letter:

> Dear Mother and Father,
>
> Well it is close after dawn here. We are all staring out across the surf at the Sierra Maestra Mountains. We cannot guess what is in store for us but in a very short while we will leave our shipboard home and storm the enemy's shore. I can only say we are ready to do our duty by God

and country. You may not hear from me again, but if so remember I went out here so all of you could be safe in your house from the cruel Spaniard and downtrod people could be free of hateful masters. Pray to God for me and give my loving regards to Rudy and Bertha. And also the fellows in the neighborhood, of which I am the first to be here.

Your loving son,
WILLY

I gave the letter and fifty cents to a cabin boy who promised to see it through. Then I got up.

"Where you goin?" said Tom Cooper.

"Down to see the chaplain," I replied, "to get baptized."

X I I I

A Friend Indeed

MY FATHER and Gerhart Brunkhorst, Helga's dad, became great friends. Social as well as business. They played pinochle together and took Turkish baths on 14th Street and went up to Saratoga every season for the horses and the water. In 1910, leaving me to mind the store, they took a trip to the old country. Making the grand tour, they sailed up the Rhine far as Cologne, bought a carload of Eau de, visited the cathedral which Papa said compared favorably with St. John's, drank up all the beer in Munich, all the wine in Salzberg and all the *shpritz* water in Bad Nauheim. Then they gave a lot of Yankee dollars to both families. When they got back to the first greatest country, speaking highly of the second, Helga and I found out our troth had been plotted.

Truth to tell, though I played it a little coy, I was not that much put out. Nothing at all like the federal case Henry made when I tried to set him up for life with Dora

Schroeder in '38. I had to pull back, but my father did not, well it was a different operation. Actually Helga and I had got to know each other pretty well and I found out she could talk, though not day and night, which was a great relief after Irene Flynn, who was now chewing Arthur's ear off, which he asked for and I never briefed him on, why should I? I took her to see some ballgames at the P.G. and a six-day bike race and a Harrigan and Hart show where the krauts kick hell out of the micks and in general we were getting along quite well when Hans sprung his proposition on me. It was not too bad. Brunkhorst would kick in with a dowry of eight thousand plus the wedding and Hans would make me a full partner in Farmbest. A week later I popped the question. She got all red, but finally stammered out a yes and we got married at the Bavarian Gardens on 25th Street and Third Avenue and it was some affair—Brunkhorst catered it himself—topping by far the Fine-Flynn nuptials.

However, with my long-term future in the bag, I now ran into some trouble with my short-term. Namely the honeymoon. Which suddenly loomed very large, for Helga had sat up the whole damn wedding night, crying. You would think I was a raping dago the way she carried on and you can well believe I sat up on my side of the bed thinking whatthehell have I got myself into? Or not into. So the honeymoon was the only way I could figure to save the deal. I brought it up next morning at breakfast. Suddenly she is not bawling or terrified.

"Out West," she said. "I want to go out West."

Well OK, why not? Everybody went to Niagara Falls, including Arthur and Irene, this had possibilities. I said that is a great idea. So all seemed settled and most promising. That is what you think, for there was a slight catch. Seems Helga had this bosom buddy, Fanny Kronheim, who

was a nurse in Bellevue and the two of them had invented
friendship. Fanny was to come, too.

"What is that?"

"Fanny comes along or I don't go. She wants to see the
West also."

"Well let her go out and see it."

"No. With us."

I ranted and raved. She started to get red and to cry. My
own Niagara. Plus coughs and choking all over the place.
You have easily guessed the outcome. Fanny came along. At
least they gave me a concession: We started out in separate
trains, for how would it look for a combat vet and an up-and-
coming businessman to be chaperoned by Clara Barton?

We started out from Grand Central and we circled up by
way of Albany, where we all got back in the same car, and
thence on to Chicago. We had a layover in the windy city
and I took the Bobbsey twins out to see where they slaughtered
all the maggoty meat I ate in the war. Nurse got sick.

Then on to St. Louis and another change of train and
out into Apache and General Crook country, with the ladies
cooing and goggling and me staring out the window at the
red canyons and mountains and tablerock towns which under
different circumstances would have been inspirational, but
were now giving me the horselaugh. I was married ten days
and had ought to show except timetables.

We ended up in Santa Fe at the Hotel La Fonda, a lean,
leathery place at the end of the old Chisolm Trail. If I had
any hope 'twas the beginning of mine, I was doomed to dis-
appointment. The Dolly sisters took one room and I another.
And that was about the size of it as we went out on sight-
seeing trips, visiting the governor's house and the nearby
Indian reservations and saw much wild dancing that was
supposed to do something to the blood, but did nothing to

Helga's. I bought some wampum and beads and plates with Santa Fe stamped on them and I gave my traveling companions one heckuva time. As for me, I was more down in the dumps with every passing day. Staring out from D.C., Billy Baumgarden would be in seventh heaven.

That is how my honeymoon-so-called—went. Till the afternoon of the big, black-haired, bushy-mustached fellow. At least that is how I think of that day in my memory book. Sometime after breakfast I became aware that this *hombre* was hanging around, a few paces back, wherever we went in that town. We would be here, he would be there, rolling a cigarette, lounging against an adobe wall, spinning a lasso neat and tricky. Finally, at the Dancing Lady Wild West Chuck Wagon, I said to myself this is too much, murmured excuse me, got up and walked out to where this fellow was lounging.

"Good afternoon," I said.

"Howdy," he replied.

"Well now, you have been following us about the good part of the day and do not deny it. I would like to know the reason," I said.

"Those are eastern women you are with?"

"Yes, they are."

"Hot damn," he said, slapping his quirt against his leg.

"Is that right?" I said. "And what of it?"

"I figgered they was," he said with a smile.

"Who are you to figure that, or to worry about the women I am escorting?"

He rolled a cigarette and lit up by flicking the matchhead with his thumb.

"I am just a fellow from Virginia," he said quietly.

"I did not ask where you are from, but who you are."

"Well that is who I am."

"Is that a fact?"

"Yes it is. An eastern fellow wrote a book about me. Did you read it by any chance?"

"What is it called?"

"Why *The Virginian.*"

"Heckyes, I read that. It is all about a reb in the Wild West."

"That's the one."

"Was it really about you?"

"Sure thing. Except that Molly business. He made that up."

"Well," I said, "that part did not ring too true."

"Pardon me," he said, "but the light-haired lady you are with from the East, is she a schoolmarm?"

I knew he meant Fanny, for Helga had black hair.

"Why?" I said.

"Well ever since he wrote that stuff about me and a schoolmarm, well . . ." and he stopped and gave me a wink.

I began to put two and two together.

"You mean now you go for them?" I asked.

He shrugged. "You might say that."

"Well, yes," I said, "she is, in a way."

"Ah," he said. Just ah. I get the glimmer of an idea.

"How would you like to meet her?" I said.

"It would pleasure me."

"OK. What is your name besides Virginian?"

"Sam Constanty, with a C."

"Put her there, Sam. I am Willy Kleinhans."

We shake. "Howdy, Willy," he said.

"When you call me that, smile," I said.

"What is that?"

"When you call me that, smile. Didn't you read your own book?"

"Oh sure. Sure. Sometimes I forget. The way that really come about was one night during a card game. I looked at the other fellow and said, 'When you smile like that, call.' But you know how writers are."

Recalling Richard Harding Davis, I said, "I sure do." Then, "Come on, Sam, I'll introduce you."

So I took Sam into the chuck wagon and introduced him all around. He made an instantaneous hit, especially with Fanny, for she was a great reader, especially when he kept on saying, when you call me that, smile. Well putting one little word after another, starting with that night Sam Constanty showed us the *real* Wild West, not the dime-novel version, and that included a genuine saloon off the tourist trail, his very own set of pinto ponies and carved saddle given him by a Mexican *padrone*, and to top it off an authentic, working bunkhouse. All of a sudden prim little Fanny begins acting like I never knew she was capable of. That Sam sure had a way with eastern schoolmarms. For the very first time, I noticed she was not at all a bad looker, especially when all dolled up, as she now always was, and without breaking balls.

So it went, Sam doing a very fine job as tour leader and everybody getting into the spirit of the Old West which was sort of wide open and devil may give a damn. Until this one night when the tour leader directed us into the aforementioned bunkhouse. This time the boys, who were genuine types, were in town making whoopee and we had the place all to ourselves. We had some coffee out of a tin pot that sat on the stove, which is what they always do in bunkhouses as you no doubt know from seeing Buck Jones or Art Acord and then Sam hauled out a bottle and told us to try a nip.

"What is it?" I said.

"Tequila; you drink it like this." And he put some salt on his wrist, licked it off and took a slug.

"Oh let me try," said Fanny.

"Sure," he said and handed her the salt and the tequila.

She did the routine very neatly. "Mmmm," she said, "that is better than tizwin."

"What?" said Helga.

"Indian juice," explained Sam, looking at Fanny with a new gleam in his eye.

"Let me try some," said Helga. Next thing I know she is licking salt and slugging. Well heck, then, so am I. It was pretty darn good, not at all like bourbon, but who wants bourbon in a bunkhouse? Around the circle we go. And then around again. Fanny begins to say call me and smile, then smile me and call and finally smile darn you smile and Helga begins opening her jacket for suddenly it is quite warm. The next thing I know, I look around and Fanny and Sam have disappeared and Helga and I are apparently all alone in that bunkhouse, chock full of empty bunks and a single, dim lantern. Hell, I did not hesitate one minute and neither did she. In two shakes of a lamb's tail her Maxine Elliott hair is down around her hips and we are rolling about in a lower and I am making my way post haste through whale bone and metal and all other sorts of impedimenta.

At the end of the trail I at last accomplished my honeymoon mission.

Shortly thereafter, one day to be exact, three happy dudes said their good-byes to a town that will always rate aces high in my account book. By every standard it had been a wonderful and educational trip to a splendid section of this great country and lounging in the picturesque station against an old steamer trunk was the fellow who had just made it all possible. *Con mucho gusto.* As we started out, he waved us a lazy-circle farewell and I and my eastern ladies, especially a certain schoolmarm, did likewise. Then we quickly ducked our heads inside and the snorting iron horse began its gallop across the wild mesa. Well. Right then and there Helga said will you please excuse us, Fanny, and Fanny, getting the message, left for another car. When we are *todamente* alone, Helga hauls forth a bottle of tequila and some salt and before you can say Bat Batalino we are continuing in that Pullman car right where we had left off the night before; nor did we stop, except of course for coffee, till we reached New York town. And then only until we got installed in our new house which Hans had bought and Brunkhorst furnished, all *dinero* on the line. As for Fanny, well she got married very *pronto* to Jack McTurk, who had a medium mustache, which soon thereafter turned into a Kitchener. Heck, people can say what they want to about the South, as far as I'm concerned I will always be indebted to Sam Constanty, known to the outside world as the Virginian. But my good friend. And one heckuva ramrod.

X I V

Cheek to Cheek

Now FRED ASTAIRE and Irene Castle were a wonderful dance team. They did the "Texas Tommy" and the "lame duck" and the "half and half" in the Castle House across the street from the Ritz-Carlton. Irene bobbed her hair and wore a rubber girdle and silk bloomers that gave you a heckuva lot better view than Miss McTaggerty. Helga put them on in 1919. I gave her holy hell. But she was a mule, so I got used to them.

Barney Baruch's brother won a dance contest in Madison Square Garden. His name was Sailing. Barney is telling Wilson how to run the country and Sailing is doing the "turkey trot." Well to each his own. I preferred Bert Williams. But Bojangles was also fine, especially when he tapped up and down the steps with little Miss Marker, and Georgie Raft was the world's fastest dancer until he started flipping coins. But the greatest was Maurice, the Apache, who danced at the Cafe de Paris. He had this blondie doll who jumped at

the end and hooked onto his middle like a pair of gorgeous
scissors and he whirled her about till Saturday. You could
see the start of her cheeks. It drove Lister Colfax nuts. He
sent her flowers three nights in a row and Stage Door Johnnied
four more. She gave him a smile and he moaned and groaned
for a month and then moved back in with his wife. Maurice
was not a red-man Apache. He was not even French. He was
just a west side slum kid. Like Sigrid Gurie was supposed
to be Marco Polo's piece and was that a put-up job, she was
from Brooklyn, N. Y. Along with Theda Bara, who was Death
Arab like fun, just a liddle yiddle. As Texas Guinan always
said, there's one born every minute. But he was some gigolo,
you could use his hair for winter driving.

In March of 1920 I took Helga to see the *Ziegfeld Follies*,
words and music by Izzy Baline. There was some excellent
hoofing, but the best number in the show was "Leg of
Nations" which was easily won by Germany, as you can understand if you saw *Blue Angel.* But don't laugh at Jannings,
you would blow your cork too if Dietrich waved her Frankies
under your nose. The next day Helga came to me and out of
left field says she wants to take dancing lessons. I got up
off the floor and naturally asked why. Because I want to,
that's why. But *why?* I want to, and I want you to. Hah,
we are not exactly spring chickens. All the more reason.
But *why* dammit? You never do what I want. What does that
mean? It means you never—Oh Christ, all right, but not in
Castle House, understand, for I am not made of money. She
sighed and went back to the kitchen, but that night she
made me *kartuffel* pancakes.

So next afternoon I consulted Bill Hearst's *Journal* and I
spotted an ad for *Charles Carstairs' Studio Dansant—Home
of All Refined Steps—*on 73rd Street and Madison Avenue. It
sounded legitimate, no Apache dancing, for I would not

abide the thought of Helga hooked onto my middle and whirling into seventh heaven, nor Irene Castle, but Dietrich with her eyes closed was a different story. I found out Carstairs had taught dancing with his partner, Adele, on the *Leviathan* as "The Waltzing Wonders" and that was not a bad credential, either. So Friday night I took Helga up to his place.

He was quite a clean-cut fellow, though he and Adele could write *Life Begins at,* and he spoke very soft and pleasant even if you could not catch every word. But enough so that I wound up buying a package for the two of us that covered fifteen weekly lessons on the two-step, the waltz and the "Castle walk." Going home that night, to my surprise Helga asked if we might stop off at my speak, Hugo's, on 84th Street and Lex, which had just opened two months before, as had all the others courtesy Mr. Volstead. I said sure and we went down and she ordered tequila and they brought us gin, so what? She was happy and all because I had done a simple thing which is the secret, she won't forget it, you won't regret it. And on Monday we started out on our dance careers.

Carstairs had what he called a confidential approach to terpsichore, which meant individual rooms to save embarrassment, and your own steady partner. I drew Dolores. No last name, that was the custom, Zorina being the exception that proves the rule. When I asked if she was a dago, Carstairs gave me a polite look and said no, Mexican, which was Jake with me, though nix on the former, as was widely known. She was probably a put-up job from Tenth Avenue anyway like Sigrid Gurie, but trying to make a living, so why should I complain about the kid? Well a bit more than a kid, twenty-five I would say, though at night it is difficult to tell and if you've seen a live one in a saloon at 11 P.M. and again at 11 A.M. you will know what I mean. Hair blonde, bobbed of course, black skirt, always black like a Model-T, up above the knees, excellent Frankies, her upper lip always shining with a line of beaded sweat after one go-round. Helga got some skinny little fellow with hair by Vaseline and we retired to our separate studio rooms.

I did not let on I knew a thing or two on the dance floor, as that is how I conquered Helga, but played it real dumb. She took my hand right away, with no phony boloney, stood beside me and said let's walk. Walk? Yes, walk. OK. So we proceeded to manipulate our pedal extremities in such a fashion as to produce forward motion, hand in hand to "Alexander's Ragtime Band," by you know who.

"You walk very well, Mr. Kleinhans," she said.

"Willy. Thank you. So do you."

You never miss the opening, for it might not come again.

Well we walked for half an hour and then she stood in front of me, pulled my hand firmly about a tiny, soft middle, not a whalebone in sight, held her other hand up and to the strains of "Sweet Marie" we started out one and two and onetwo, one and etcetera. I faked a little clumsiness, not too much, but soon was gliding about the room very neatly which was very easy for she was a feather on wheels.

"You're doing beautifully," she said.

"I got a beautiful teacher," I said, adhering to my policy.

"Thank you," she said without a miss, adhering to hers.

And around we go to "Charmaine" and "Roses of Picardy" and sometimes with no Victrola at all but Dolores singing the lyrics and tapping out the time on my shoulder. Nice Sen-Sen breath. Her upper lip glistening like Steffi Duna's, who also was no dago. Yet 100 percent American. More Judy Garland when she was and there I am, Gene Kelly, though not shooting myself in the leg to get out of service,

hellno, but the smiley hoofer, for how could I step around
with a slug in my knee? Ask Ruth Etting singing her heart
out in some crummy rub joint.

> All you need is a ticket,
> Come on big boy,
> Ten cents a dance.

Who winds up with Moe the Gimp and you know he is
nothing out on the floor. But they will do anything for a
career. So after an hour of ungimpy gliding, Ruth looked
up at the clock, sighed and said oh where did the time go?
Search me, I shot right back. She shook her bobbed head
very cutely and without dropping her hand from my shoulder
walked us to the door, one and two and onetwo. Does she
then drop her hand? She does not. We just stood there with
the sweat on her lip. I was tempted to take out my handkerchief and mop it up, but she flicked her tongue like a little
garter snake and did the job for me, leaving a damp place,
but not beady and that I could take. Only then did she
drop her hand and say, most sincerely, good night Willy,
I really enjoyed it. So did I, I said and as I did her eyes,
which had been boring into mine, suddenly bounced over
my shoulder. I know eyes, being in the business world, so
turned, and sure enough in walked her target, Joseph Hayseed, hair parted in the middle with a ruler, sleeves over
the wrist like Dopey the Dwarf, the whole shooting match.
Naturally I was disgusted, and I showed it, and I was 100
percent positive she gave me a silent sigh, but Ruth Etting
had to go on with her job, crummy as it mainly was. I felt
very sympathetic and patted her cheek and said good night,
kid. Then I walked out and fetched my missus and we walked
home for it was a splendid New York night. On 86th Street,
as I watched the greenhorns on a pogo stick up in Coblenz

Hall, I told her, Helga, you know you had a darn good
idea there?

We worked through the two-step in a lesson and a half,
the waltz in two and the "Castle walk" in three. We also got
friendly. The poor kid was from outside Mexico City and
had a rotten old man who squandered all the family's
money and then took off for parts unknown, the old lady
died milking a cow, so she left school and came to town and
waited table and then won a dance contest in Tiajuana and
came to New York via New Orleans and Knoxville where
she also had tough sledding, but in the big town she intended
to get on Broadway if Ziggy or Frohman had any sense which
they did not, or at least form a dance team and play the
smartest night clubs here and abroad and she thought I was
the best student she ever had. It was b.s. propaganda of course,
all except the last part for didn't I finish the prescribed course
in half the time? Still I had plenty of practice lessons left and
was looking forward to brushing up. Dolores had other ideas.
The eighth week she said, Willy, you are doing so well, why
don't you come twice a week and learn the tango, it will
not cost that much more and you are just right for the
particular movement the tango requires. We were walking
to the door, arms about middles as she said it, so I considered briefly and said sure thing, not, you understand, that
I had any idea of being Velez to her Yolanda, still we did
do a very nice job together as the mirrors on the wall showed.
I especially like to check her round little can as she stepped
backward and I charged forward and I will match hers against
Josephine Baker any time.

I told Helga I was working on a tough business deal
Wednesdays which in a sense I was and in two shakes I was
dipping and swooping like the goddarn sheik and Dolores

was assuring me that Joe Hayseed would never even get past
the two-step. My fourth tango lesson I bent her elastic middle
far back, leaned over, looked in the mirror and liked what
I saw, then kissed her. She snapped up into me, kissed back
and placed both arms about my neck. So holding tight, I
returned us to the upright and began a little roman hands
and russian fingers. She smiled and swerved away very neatly
and said, Willy, you know you could learn the "Texas
Tommy" in no time.

"I could?"

"Yes you could. You have real ability. Suppose I sign you
up for one more night."

I guess I was getting a little heated up for I made a grab
at her. She ducked and I missed by a mile. Canzoneri had
nothing on her.

"All right, Willy?" she said.

"Sure, sure, all right."

Her head came around and zonk, she gave me a good
hard one, a little wet, a trifle deep, and then pushed me
away ever so gently as I came back for seconds, and said,
let's dance, hon, all right?

All right and how! We danced. Arms all entangled. And
we kept on dancing. I told Helga business was turning into
a real headache because of prohibition and she said why is
that and I said because people were drinking milk instead
of booze and she said oh. And I added Thursday night to
my agenda. And followed this by asking Dolores if she would
care for a drink after work at a speak I knew and she replied
it was against the rules, how would I like to learn the "lame
duck" in four more lessons? I would like that. And so she
went with me to Hugo's and after that we always finished
up there except of course on Helga's night, and with the
further addition of the "half and half" I got to take her

home over on First Avenue and 45th Street. It is easy to see
I was getting involved with this kid.

And that was the rub.

Because of my darn lousy conscience. You see it really
started to bother me. For I had never fooled around in New
York since I got married, out of town naturally being a different story, as was getting loaded with the boys. But dancing
with Dolores and taking her home and getting a kiss, then
a feel topside which was small but pointy and hard after we
began the "Peabody," well it just bothered me. Coming
home to Helga, trustworthy and innocent, did not help my
condition, either. That is when Jiminy Cricket really gave
me the business. Not that I was Catholic or anything, but I
did have my principles and this was turning into a genuine
case of I love my wife but oh you kid. Helga was such a
darn good woman, too, why she even helped me over the
place, going through the books and the mail as she was a
whiz in math and had a beautiful handwriting and therefore rubbed some more salt in the wound. In fact I started
to get a good case of acid stomach and some bean-busting
headaches; that Mexicali rose was sure getting under my
skin. And I began to think, in spite of myself. What did I
think? Well that maybe, just maybe, the two of us could
hook up and make a go of it, not like Moe and Ruth, that
was a punk relationship, but perhaps like the Castles, all
sunshine and class. True enough I was over forty-two. But
when she hit sixty-three I would only be eighty, as Chaplin,
Daddy Browning and the King of Bavaria proved.

Those lousy thoughts kept on plaguing me even when I
ordered them not to. But this was not the army, Mr. Jones.
And my insubordination got worse. And things were not
improved any when after eight rides home, Dolores finally
invited me inside her room on the assurance of a fifty-dollar

loan for a proper pair of dancing shoes and then on a hundred more for a proper new dress, I got into her bloomers
on her teddy bear and panda bed with the white satin
coverlet. That is when my stomach went from bad to worse,
not at all helped by citrate of magnesia, and I had this darn
feeling my fly was unbuttoned as I walked through the streets,
though on repeated inspection it sure was not. It got so I
was starting to resent her for all I was suffering. Compared
to her, Helga was a real doll baby, and as fine a mother to
Henry and Margaret as you could desire. Oh if only she had
been rotten, but with my luck she never was. Mornings after
the night before I was sure I should go on and make the
break and hook up with Dolores, afternoons I was back with
Helga, my old self again, wondering how I could be such
a pushover and by evening I was thinking ahead to my
temptress and what tie I should wear.

Such was my dilemma as I worked in the office one day,
side by side with Helga who was going over the books, when
she said something and I said uh-huh and she replied quite
loud, is that all you have to say? Something clicked and
though deep in a dream I roused up long enough to say,
about what?

"I said I'm leaving you, Willy."

This time I carefully lay down my receipts, for they are
a mess if out of order, and I answer, come again?

"I'm leaving you," she said. "I'm going away with Arturo."

"Who?"

"Arturo, from the Studio Dansant. My teacher."

I looked at her. She was very calm.

"You're leaving me for a *dago*?"

"Arturo is from Venezuela."

"I don't give a shit where he's from," I yelled, getting up
out of my chair. "What kind of bull is this?"

"It is no bull," she said quietly and I knew that voice.

"I have thought it over very carefully." She got up and walked to the door and opened it and said come in, *me karo,* or somesuch, and in he walked, uglier and skinnier than I remembered, hair worse than ever, having struck oil. He bowed far over and said, "Good afternoon, señor."

"Get that dago out of here," I yelled.

Helga nodded her head. "I hoped you would react differently," she said in that voice. "I should have known better."

"What kind of better?" However, I was not yelling for I could see this was not going my way at all.

"I want to leave on good terms," she said. "I would like to be friends."

"Are you kidding?" I said. "Any dame who walks out on me is no friend of mine."

"Well then there are things to consider."

"I'll say there are things to consider. My poor brother is not yet cold in his grave and you go and pull this."

"Pardon me, señor," said forty weight. "I love your wife with respect."

I kept myself from looking at him and that was smart for I have a terrifically short fuse. Soft but firm I said, "Will you please tell that dago to keep out of this? This is between two married people who only death can do part."

She sighed. I knew that sigh.

"You are the mother of two babies," I said.

"I have thought of all that."

"You have? Have you thought of what I am going to say when they are old enough to understand? Your mother ran off with a fuckin dago?"

"All right," she sighed, "that's enough."

"You think they could ever live that down?"

"Pardon me, señor——"

"You keep outa this or I'll kick your ass back to Madrid!"

I walked to the door and closed it as Etta, Eloise the girl's predecessor, had rabbit ears. I walked back to Helga and sat down very quietly beside her. "Why?" I said.

For the first time she began to fill up a little. She glanced at Pennzoil. "He dances with me," she said.

"He's *paid* to dance with you."

"No," she snapped. "No. He dances with me on his night *off*."

". . . What night is that?"

"Wednesday. While you're so busy making money."

"You mean while I am so trusting, you are running around with this gigolo?"

"Only on Wednesday. Plus my regular lesson. But you are so busy you don't even notice."

"I'm busy for *us*. For our family. So we can be better off in life."

She shook her head. "It is no life if you do not care for me."

Now she was spilling over, but not one goddarn sob.

"*Care* for you," I said. "I *love* you."

She brushed her eyes. "How can you love me when you never once danced with me after we went to the studio together to learn how and took lessons for fifteen weeks?"

"Oh Jesus," I said.

"Arturo takes me dancing on his night off."

"Jesus."

As if I don't have enough of a headache, I heard: "I love Señora Kleinhans, but with much respect." But I shook it off. I looked at Helga. Her chin was down. I reached over and raised it.

"Tonight is Wednesday night," I said with a smile. "We are going dancing at Castle House."

"*I* am taking the señora dancing tonight."

"Kiss off," I said.

"Señor, I——"

"YOU HEARD ME."

He looked at her. "Please," she said and sighed, but better.

"Yes," I said. "And every night this week. And every Saturday night from now on."

The room was quiet, holy Hannah was that room quiet. Finally I heard the three little words. "You mean it?"

"Helga, have I ever broke my word to you?"

"No," she said pushing through the clouds at last. "That is one thing you have never done."

"And never will do. You can make book on that."

Well the wheels, round and round they goes, where they stop nobody knows. After sixty years, at last. Lemons? Ah. She got up. I knew that face. She walked over to latins are lousy lovers; no doubt he was a bleeder, but I kept my mouth shut. "I have decided to give my husband another chance," she said, which I swallowed, "Thank you for everything," which I also ate. *"Por todos,* Arturo. *Muchas grácias."*

I was doing one heckuva discipline job on myself, and while I did, cucaracha took her hand, bent and kissed it. Tonight, Gre-Solvent. "Ah señora," he said. *"De nada.* You have made me happy for a little while, even if now you break my heart. *Mi corazon.* But," he shrugged, "I respect your wishes." He turned and faced me. *"Adios,* señor," he said crisply. "She is yours for the moment." He bowed again and slid out.

I was surrounded by the typewriter and the afternoon trucks. Finally: "Just whatinhell did he mean by that?"

"Nothing. It is his pride. *Machismo."*

"If he comes around here I'll kick his ass down the stairs. I have some pride too, you know."

"Willy!"

"Well I do."

"Willy!"

"All right, all right."
(*Come hit the timber.*)
We were alone now, at long last, my wife and I. I took
her in my American arms and kissed her good and hard, but
dry. "Jesus, Helga," I said, "do not scare me like that again.
You were kidding, weren't you?"
"No."
I examined her. No is no. I was a clam. I walked to the
door, locked it and then pulled down the shades. I returned,
picked her up, which at the least ruptures Alfonso, and car-
ried her to the sofa. Very gently I put her down. God, but
she was suddenly a knockout. "Take your hair down," I said.
"I can't. It is bobbed."
". . . Sure it is. And it looks great."
"You really like it?"
"Sure I do."
(*Loosen up and start to limber.*)
I started to unbutton her.
"Not yet," she whispered.
"OK," I whispered back.
"First dance with me."
"Now?"
"Yes, now."
"Sure."
(*Listen to that hot marimba.*)
I quickly buttoned her back up. She arose and we began
to dance. Not the two-step or the waltz or the "Castle walk,"
heck no, but the tango, which that bastard must have taught
her, but my lip was buttoned. And so was hers. We swooped
and glided and dipped all over the office and when we were
both panting and dizzy, I twirled her over to the sofa and
we resumed the angle, and I swear she was a thousand times
better than what's her name. Who by the way I did not ever
see again except briefly in 1927 on the Third Avenue El with

a baby who had the eyes of a bleeder. I looked right through them to the river. Nor did I answer the frantic phone calls which in due course petered out. That very day I got in touch with Carstairs and told him I was not taking lessons anymore, but that he could keep the money. Like magic, my stomach and fly cleared right up.

We went dancing that night. And true to my vow, we went dancing every Saturday night thereafter. Till at the age of sixty-two Helga fell and broke both Herbert Hoovers in Roseland. And between you and me and the lamppost, in all that time I never more had occasion not to trust her.

LET YOURSELF GO!

X V

Are You Brown from the Sun?
No, I'm Smith from the Telegram

GIVE ME ERNIE PYLE, I'll give you Steve Crane. He wrote
the *Open Boat* while we were plunging toward war. His
famous *Red Badge* came straight out of his head, but not
the *Boat;* he lived that one while running guns, and he also
saw the real McCoy with the marines on Guantanamo, just
as hot as Guadal, and also in the fighting for Santiago. As
did the slew of other big-time reporters, such as Richard
the Lion Harding, beau ideal of the Gibson girl, poor silly
creature, Sylvester Scovel, a writer not a lover, and Ed
Marshall, a grand fellow from the *Journal,* who got his back
shattered by a real bullet. Crane helped him out, but not
Dickie boy. He was too busy making Teddy into a hero.
He called himself a descriptive writer. That's what he told
Shafter when the general ordered all reporters to stay on
the ships. I don't give a shit what you call yourself, said
Shafter, I treat you all the same. Dickie sharpened his pencil

84

and from then on Shafter got the shaft. I'll take Marshall.
He knew his onions about how soldiers really die, not with
the blind staggers, or flung arms, or tossing coins, but *chug*,
down and out. One minute full of piss and vinegar, at the
top of the ladder, next, bang, nothing. Zero. I think of my
poor Henry. Happy-go-lucky, cracking wise. One minute
saying, you know Parkyakarkas's first name? It is Takeachair-
and. The next minute, chug, he is gone. Fuckin bullet. I will
never know why Steve Crane wound up with Lana Turner,
for he was much the bigger shot, even though she was a
looker when all dolled up. Must have been the silk bloomers.

We were to go after Santiago. Everyone knew that. From
Shafter and the hot correspondents down to Garcia with the
bullet hole in his forehead. Teddy the Terror and the
Rough Riders, led by Wood and *not* Teddy, knew it. Hell
they wanted to do the whole darn job themselves. They
landed at Daiquiri, not yet a drink and that frozen in hell,
near the road to the city and they got themselves ready for
heroism while we hove to near Siboney, not yet a song. You
want to know about the Rough Riders, go read Teddy's
book; I'm talking about the 71st.

To make sure the enemy did not know our landing plan,
the navy pounded the whole stretch of coast. We crowded
the decks to see. Nothing to worry about from the Spanish
warships. A frog likes his cognac, a limey his rum, but the
dago sticks to port. We poured it on, did we ever. Normandy
and Iwo could not lord it over that ploughed up shore. We
even pointed Captain Zalinski's dynamite ship, the *Vesuvius*,
at the island and let go with an eruption that could have
won the Nobel prize. Tore a hole big enough to drop in the
Flatiron Building. Mert yelled, "Give it to them, you big
sonofabitch," and we all joined in the refrain for it sure
was something grand to see, all that thrilling and chilling
American power sounding off. Do troopers cheer today in

a barrage? I guess not, they are too busy belittling. And
Sampson gave us something to be real proud of, even if all
he hit was dirt and deserted blockhouses.

Then the pounding ceased and we knew it was our turn.
We formed up, one, two, three. God I was so excited I could
have drunk a quart of milk, acidophilis or grade B. But nix
on the white stuff, and I mean *nix*. And that goes for any
other refreshment. Or any other action. For what did we do,
we waited. Hurry up Yost would have had kittens. Yours
truly was shitting a brick, but there was nothing for it.
Ask me why and I will tell you. OK, because of horses and
mules first, that's why. They led the frightened buggers
pared down to ribcages from the long voyage, up to the deck
and over to the cargo ports and slapped them right over the
side. No cargo nets, no choppers. Just a crack, a snap and
over they went as if deserting a sinking ship. And started
swimming for it. In their weak condition, some panicked and
started swimming in circles. I recognized big, brown Hunky
Dory who was hell bent for South America, when suddenly a
bugler on shore blew "Boots and Saddles" and "Charge" and
old Hunky swung around and made a beeline for the enemy.
We cheered like he was winning the derby. But perky, frisky
Battles, everybody's pet, was not so lucky. I saw his head
go bobbing and I thought uh-oh, water in his ears, when that
happens they are goners. Sure enough, his eyes got white
and he thrashed about crazily as if looking for solid ground
in the quicksand and though we yelled like mad, he plunged
into a ship's propeller and under he went in a mass of bright
red water. I will never forgive them for Battles.

But then at last it was time for the two-footed variety.
I could see lines of ship's boats flowing past, filled to the
gunnels with doughboys and towed by navy launches. We
looked thirstily at the captain and he broke into a smile.
Then barked out orders. I thought, God, this is it. We

snapped to at the end of his words like they were a whip and lined up at the gangway. "ALL RIGHT MEN, COUNT OFF." Numbers ripped down the line. "LET'S GO." And down we went along that dark and slippery chute to war, guided neatly by the sturdy sailor boys. I was loaded down with equipment, but light as a newborn feather. When I reached that last step, leaving America behind, I said to myself, oh Mama, Papa, Rudy and Bertha pray for me and don't stop.

The boat was jampacked with my buddies of A Company and there was a light sea, but not a one got seasick as in some invasions I could mention. Heck we had serious business ahead. Had to plunge America into world powership. Our eyes and bodies strained for the shore which was fast coming up in the starry night. It was Yankee weather. Some hundred feet out we stopped. No fancy LCIs or Ts, shoot, it was over the side, boys, and keep your powder dry. We did not hesitate. We got up as one and in good order, trusting to God and the captain, we stepped out. Neither let us down. The water just came over my leggings. I held my rifle high and splashed in fast as I could kick through that warm tropical water. It was a real bright night, nature providing its own milky flares, but helped out by ships' searchlights, and in the glow, bareass fellows down at the waterline held out their hands and pulled us up. Then we were on the sand; Christ, enemy soil! Hardly believing, I looked about. If Lafayette and de Gaulle were not present, neither was Rommel; a few little brown scarecrows gazed with no comment, for the rest it was Saturday night in town. Naked troopers gaily jacking supplies, others running and splashing about in the surf, others singing and dancing like Crazy Horse around the campfires. Lister, who was always a great party man, took one look, pointed a beak to the moon and started to yowl. The urge bit me and soon I was baying and bawling and feeling like a million, and we were shortly followed by the whole shooting match. We yowled ourselves silly and why not? The first invasion since Vera Cruz and we were it. So it was our night to howl. And as we did the Baskerville, far up in the hills, Dick Davis, come up from Daiquiri with the Rough Riders, looked down on us from his eminence and wrote it up. 'Twas in the scrapbook my father kept entitled *The Wartime Adventures of Willy T. Kleinhans*, which I read in the fall. The descriptive writer said, though with much more flower, just about what I did, but compared the scene to Coney Island, only louder. Well I have news for the Gibson Guy: You run around bareass in Coney Island, you are sure to get pinched!

OK. Sergeant Lou yelled nobody peels, get me? We got him. Then he cracked out orders. Alas, I and my buddies were sent down to a rusty machine shop on the beach and that's a real laugh if you know anything of foreign mechanical skills, Ford and Stupidaker have peanuts to worry about. But we were not laughing. Instead of hunting dago, we found ourselves jacking supplies from the boat to the shop. I said to the sarge, can I dig my specials instead, he said you heard me, do it in the bushes. So we sweat and strain the whole night through, and though we were tempted to join the splashing puppies, we knew better with the sarge around, even if our uniforms were weighted down with water and b.o. Ab McKinley must have cornered the blue flannel market.

Through all our first night in Cuba, we were kibitzed by no less than Tracy Beecy, who you never heard of and that's not surprising as he was just second string on the *Brooklyn Eagle*. Tracy sat on a busted winch, smoked his pipe and told us what was what. He covered the Nez Percé and Geronimo and would be dearly loved by Billy Baumgarden as he too thought General Crook was God. All reporters being generals, he told us how the Apache would take the high ground and pour holy Ned down on us and he expected the Spanish to do the same. I could tell him a thing or two if I was not so busy getting ruptured, like the dago was not anywhere near the American Indian upstairs, but I did not. Tracy was a bean buster anyway, always belittling; figured he should be with the Rough Riders, but being just a middle shot, got us. Tough apples. Still, though I would not let on, I was ticked off, for while we were humping it there to here, Teddy's Terrors and the big three were off to see action. How did I know? Don't be stupid, who else would get the first licks except those with pull?

Seems they had landed up the line at Daiquiri, with Joe Wheeler, the new reb general everyone and his brother knew was itching to pull the first trigger. As luck would have it, he found his target far back in the hills at Las Guásimas and sent the Rough Riders after them, naturally, as if no one else could do the job. That Teddy was some persuader, especially with a big stick, just ask the mosquito, who laid down and played dead for him in Panama.

Suddenly Tracy jumped up and yelled, "Jesus, there they go!" And he was right, only more like here they come. They crashed right past us in the firelight, the whole wild pack, Wood, Teddy, the cowpokes, the fancy Dans, Dickie Dare and his Arrow collar.

"Holy jumpin catfish," said Sergeant Lou, "They ain't got no point!"

We could hardly believe it, but it was true, as you well know. They were careening hell bent for glory without a single goddam scout! Even Henry playing Boy Allies knew better. Yet they were moving out and here we are working like niggers. And kept on working very close to dawn, when all of a sudden the bugles started blowing, and not reveille, and the sergeants were yelling to drop everything and fall in.

"What's up, Germ?" said Lister.

"Search me. But if we get out of this detail I won't complain. What's happening, Tracy?"

"Dunno," he said, "but I'll sure find out," and being an invisible beetle, scooted off on his little Brooklyn legs.

I started to think. Maybe we were moving to another camp site, but just *maybe* we were going to see a little action. Well I was ready for that. I ducked behind the shop and like lightning changed into the new white underwear my mother had given me. Just in case I was wounded and succored by a beautiful señorita. That done, I fell back in. Where in hell you been? said the sarge. Back in the bushes like you said, I replied. All right, all right, don't give me no lip. Then: "All present and accounted for, sir."

"Count off. Columns of four."

We holler out and form up.

"Let's go!"

And we started hiking. Guess where? Sure. Right up the same patch the Rough Riders had taken a few hours before.

"Are you thinking what I am thinking?" said Lister, swinging along beside me.

"Yep, I sure am," I said with a wink and a grin.

And like a dot after the sentence, along came Tracy busting with the news. "Rough Riders . . ." he gulped, "are . . . in trouble . . . and need help!"

"Is that a fact?" said Lou. "Tell me another. Now you just fall in there, Mr. Beecy, and keep your brains down and your ink wet and maybe you'll get a story." And he winked at us. Well we gave Tracy the horselaugh, but he was too zipped up to even notice and he charged down the line asking how we felt on the verge of battle. When he got to us, Lister told him, just great, we are going to save the

Rough Riders' ass. In the *Eagle* my father sent me, it came out, "I'm a bit scared, all right, but I hope I can do the right thing before my bunkies."

Well truth is no stranger to fiction.

2

The path soon narrowed and the column of fours pinched into twos. That jungle tightened about us like a hairy rope and please don't tell me about New Guinea. We still humped our way up, now in single file, now scrounging to see a bunkie's back. Ab's blue flannel shirts pulled in the morning sun, soaking my fancy underwear, ah well, Eva, a man sweats. At least my campaign hat did a job, not like the foreign legion my Uncle Otto wore at Second Bull Run. We kept on pushing. Tongues hanging out, legs groaning. Still no one dogged it. The whole march I never saw no one dog it. No combat fatigue. No need for Shafter to slap a doughboy. Don't ask me about San Juan; there were reasons. Arthur Fine's kid cracked up on the train to Upton. Whole world is 4F. We slugged our way up. Tarzan could swing out of that jungle, he'd get a kick in the balls. Onward and upward. The light brigade had horses, we had shank's mare; those odds were Jake with me. We reached a blockhouse, deserted, naturally. Then, like a wonderful reward, we busted clear onto the top. The top was clean, no Teddy, no dago. OK, the book said take ten, but not our captain and not us. We formed into fours again and took off, now quick time and the word was passed down the line; Gismo? No, Quasmas. You know it now as Las Guásimas, but Johnny on the spot does not have all that hindsight. He is too busy spoiling for action.

Then we heard it.

Soft at first, like faraway thunder and lightning. Then, like a Stromberg Carlson tuning in, it came loud and clear. The dull heavy whomp of the big guns, the whine and pop of the rifles. Playing serve and catch, us to them and back again. No radio program, no *Red Badge,* no story in the *Journal.* The real McCoy. I looked at Lister. He looked at me and reached over. Silently we shake. We have come a heckuva long ways for this; Konrad and Erik were smiling, so was Henry up in the clouds. And it was only the beginning, only the beginning. We plunged forward, double-time now. I tell you I was itching for the fiendish enemy. He was Fu Manchu, Tojo and Sitting Bull. My clever mind reached up and plastered the face of Evangelina Cisneros under my hat and also the naked ladies getting felt up by greasy hands. That is the way to get up for a battle, I only wish the boys at Kasserine Pass knew the trick. I strained ahead for the sight of dago, but caught only vines and trees and under-growth. The whomp and the crack, the singing whines grew louder. Now into the symphony the bugles screamed. Column right. We broke into a grassy field and moved ahead. I glanced back. The second battalion. Well this was it, all right. We were formed for attack, first battalion firing line, the second in support. Again the bugles. We stopped and gathered for the rush.

And we waited.

And waited.

And while we waited, slow but oh so sure, that marvelous thunder and lightning began to fade. I wanted to jump over the trees and pull it all back, but I was not Buck Rogers. I could do nothing but wait and fiddle my diddle. We peered out and then at one another and we said, Jesus, whathehell is this? And no one could answer.

"REST."

Oh no. Oh *yes*. We were at the top of the peak, at Marshall's chug point and . . . rest! We flung our cheated bodies down in great disgust and we stared up at that smirking tropical sky. I heard a shout and sat up. Wouldn't you know, here comes a Rough Rider on a mule, his legs dangling to the ground. Those legs, they are bloody. Lucky bastard.

"The sonofabitch got me," he yelled, as if we didn't have eyes. "But I got mine. Now you git yours." He waved and strutted on downtown. Then a few more straggled by, equally blooded. Siboney would be impossible to live with tonight. I heard Tracy's pipsqueak: "Hey, that is Jackson." He hopped up and rushed for a trooper with his arm in a sling. Would that it was his ass. However, we knew he was a reporter, for they recognized each other even if Chinese and they were thick as thieves. The two of them gestured and their mouths flapped and Tracy jumped up and down like a grasshopper with a hot foot. He came charging back.

"It's all over. Jesus. A helluva fight, but the Rough Riders charged and they broke and ran. Ham Fish got it. So did Ed Marshall. His back was pierced. It's a great victory." And he hopped about in a circle, punching his palms and looking at the sky and saying damn, damn, like he had just struck out with the bases loaded. *He* struck out? Heck, we were in the park, but not on deck, in the hole or even shoveling coal. I looked disgusted at my buddies and they looked likewise back at me. What is the sense of hoping? It must be true all right, with our luck. And it was. We found out soon enough, as did the world. Just when the point-less Terrors were getting their biggest lumps, the dopey bastards charged, that's right, charged, and the dago who is not too bright, thinking the whole damn army was following, why else charge? turned and chased his nose. Fish, of the bigwig Fishes, was killed right off. Marshall was thought to be done for. It turned out he was not; foreign correspondents have too many grand rainbows to chase in their pith helmets to ease off for a bullet. Joe Wheeler returned to days of glory and yelled: "WE GOT THE DAMN YANKEES ON THE RUN." What a heavenly madhouse it must have been, and wouldn't you know the Rough Riders would luck it out? And now with Dickie and Teddy in cahoots, Jesus, they were shooting straight up their ink-stained way to the glory road.

And us? What of us?

Why, the king's horses, the king's men, they marched up the hill and they marched down again, the king's horses. And the king's men.

X V I

An Enigma Wrapped
in a Conundrum

WE WERE SUPPOSED TO RETURN to normalcy under Harding.
Yes, well anybody passes *that* name onto his baby is not
setting the kid up as Joe Smith, American. And if the kid
becomes president, heaven help the working man. So naturally the country had teapots and domes and Harry Sinclair
and I had Frank Joseph, whose tough luck it was to be born
in 1921, but it couldn't be helped since I was now clicking
like Papa Dionne.

Oh he looked normal enough at the start, though he was
no Charley Paddock in the hundred coming out of Helga's
Gate; came out feet first like he was testing. He had a ring
of blond hair and nice fat and two lungs that produced a
high-pitched shriek that sounded like "Charge!" I called
him Bugle for six months but Helga made me cut it out.
He was fairly cute, as are all tads, it's their natural state, his
face was Ike in pain, but Baby LeRoy, not to mention Henry,

had nothing to fear from this kid. We once entered Henry in the *Daily News* Beautiful Child contest and he got local honorable mention which I told them to stick, it was strictly a put-up job, but when Helga suggested we enter Frank Joseph I told her, are you *kidding*? Not that I ever compared the two, I was most careful not to and to give each his just due. Trouble was there was not a heckuva lot you could ante up for dues. Where Henry walked, he crawled, sometimes sideways like a land crab. Where Henry clearly said ma-ma, da-da, he let go with something between ugh and e-e-e-, sort of a Mauser bullet whining in slow motion. He spoke late and when he did had very little of real substance to say, like his mother in her early days. Mainly he liked to look into people's faces with his big serious eyes. Just look like the mystery of King Tut's tomb was to be found there. It bothered me no little, till I got used to it, though not altogether. Now it's true you should always look someone straight in the eye, Dale Carnegie could tell you that, although frankly I have been shafted by some of the steadiest eyes in the business. However, Frank Joseph, though he seemed to peruse you, did not look in your *eyes*, and worse, did not seem to be listening to you and that burned my bubble. You would explain something to him, say how a carburetor works, and he would go into his staring act and when you were finished, he'd pause and say but how does a carburetor work? So of course I yelled, but I never smacked him.

I began to wonder if he was all there. Helga's sister's third kid, Hildegard, pissed in her pants all her life and still does, but Helga has a crazy uncle; everybody on my side is OK, so that was out. I decided he was just lazy. He just got through grammar school all right, though nothing like Henry, who did? So when he neared the end of 8B I sat down with him and asked him what he wanted to do. How do you mean? he said.

"Well, you're getting on and it is time to make a few basic decisions. What do you like?"

"Stuffed cabbage."

"No, not to eat, what do you like to *do*? Henry liked math and science so I sent him to Stuyvesant, now what about you?"

He started to stare.

"Well? Dammit."

He kept on staring.

"Well? For crissakes say something."

He swiveled his eyes like he just woke up. "What do you want to know?" he said.

"I just told you, dammit. What do you want to do?"

"What do I want to do?"

"Yes."

"I . . . don't know."

I looked at my kid and I suddenly felt awful. I could see his whole future laid out, unskilled, untrained, a pushover for any con man. Or woman. It gave me a heckuva jolt, for I can think of nothing more fearful than not knowing where you're going in life. They send crazy people up in an airplane to snap them out of it; OK, I was Eddie Rickenbacker.

"Frank Joseph," I said, picturing a life for which he had no preparation, "what is the most frightening thing in the world?"

He relapsed. But I waited patiently, Helga always said be patient. This time it paid off. He came to. "What am I scared of the most?" he said.

"Yes, son."

"Turning to stone."

"What . . . ?"

"Benny Plofsky. From Gary, Indiana. I read it in the *American Weekly*. He is turning to stone and nobody can stop him."

"No," I said, still gentle. "I don't mean in your health. I'm talking bigger. Think hard now. What is the most frightening thing in the world? When you think ahead to your life, to that tough world out there, the way you're going, what frightens you the most?"

"A vacuum in space."

"Whathehell is frightening about that?"

"Well if you try to think of that it will drive you crazy. Just try it and you'll see——"

"Never mind. Now I'm talking to you. You have very few interests. You're going into high school. Pretty soon, before you know it even, you'll go out where it's dog eat dog. It is a tough world. What frightens you about that world?"

He glazed over.

"Wake up, will you?" I said. *"Please."*

"What frightens me?"

"Yes, Frankie."

"A fer-de-lance."

"Go on up to your room! Read something. Read *A Message to Garcia*. Henry! Come here. We're going down the corner for a Pepsi!"

That is how it went with my albatross. McKinley had Ida, I had Frank Joseph. He was some dreamer. Dream when you're feeling blue, dream that's the thing to do, dream, dream, dream. He would go bye-bye between shoes, between socks, between the fingernails on one hand and those on the other. Once he was on the pot so long I thought he fell in, but no, when I came in he was staring into space, and when I had inspected, had done no business. But then every so often he would come to and when he did, look out. For then all that dream power would pour into being an opposite. Don't ask me how he found out about things with all the lapsing he did, but he would pick up the opposite side and could never give you a reason, you could eat your heart out. Thus he stuck up for Buster Crabbe instead of Johnny Weissmuller, don't ask why. Jackie Searle instead of Jackie Cooper. Ramon Navarro instead of Doug Fairbanks. Clarence Chamberlain instead of Lindy. Navy instead of Army. Buzz Borries instead of Monk Meyer. The Strand instead of the Roxy. Corn Flakes instead of Wheaties. Seabiscuit instead of War Admiral. Bettina instead of Sonja Henie. Sitting Bull instead of Errol Flynn. Gene Sarazen instead of Olin Dutra. Bomba instead of Tarzan. Firpo Marberry instead of Johnny Murphy. Dracula instead of Frankenstein. He even rooted for the limey challenger over Rainbow! That drove me nuts. To top it off, in '24, when he was just three, somehow or other he found out who was running for president and went around chanting, Day-biss, Bwy-an, like he was Edwin C. Hill or somebody, knowing of course how I felt about those two names. Male tads have a sixth sense about what will burn their old man. Arthur Fine explained that to me and he knew everything. However they do like their old lady. In fact, since around 1910 they want to lay them. Now that is a shocking idea at first. But not when you think about it a little. If I was Lillian Russell's kid I would want to get into her bloomers. Or Sally Rand, which would be even better as I could see her bareass all the time around the nursery. Of course if Frank Joseph ever made a pass at Helga I would break his balls. But no danger, he would never stop staring long enough to concentrate on laying his ma.

Well by the time he was thirteen it was clear he was racing downhill like an express train. So before he was a goner, I

decided to take the bull by the horns. I enrolled him at
Commerce High School on West 63rd Street, thinking that
at least a business education would never hurt. Not that I
could ever trust Farmbest to him, but with Henry's help we
might keep his nose above water and if anything happened
to me he would be equipped to earn a living. I hope I hope
I hope. He did not kick. Never did. Just examined my face
like he had never seen it before and went along. So next
fall he traveled off through Central Park to high school and
surprise, he got through his first year, true by the skin of his
teeth, but he made it. The next term, around Christmas, I
decided I should have a talk with his grade adviser to see
if I could tip the scales a bit upward as I was getting very
tired of 65s.

Going over school was nothing new to me. I had done
it for Henry in 5A. He had Mr. Pilsud, who made them
build a book house out of all the books they read. Each book
was a brick and the kid who built his house first got a pair
of Chicago skates. Henry slaved for those skates, read till
Helga made him sack in, then, with my help, smuggled in
some more books. One day he came to me in tears. Whatheheck
is the matter? I said to my boy. He finally stopped sniffling
and told me the story. He had read all the *Tarzan* books,
the whole *Boy Allies* series, all of *Tom Swift,* all the *Rover
Boys,* enough for a Chrysler Building. What did Pilsud do?
He gave Henry *one brick for each series.* Now that was shit
for the birds and no kid of mine was going to sit there and
take it. I went up the school. Pilsud was a Polack who was
certainly Pilsudsky, and a fag, what kind of job was that for
a man, teaching 5A? But he was quite the boy as he put
up with me. Very patiently, for you catch more flies with
honey than vinegar, I told him how much time and effort
the kid had put into his reading. Pilsud said yes, but we do
not pay off for effort, Mr. Kleinhans, commendable as that

may be, it is results that count. He has read seventy-three books, I said. Well yes, but he must broaden his range, the books he has read do not have too much merit. I have read *Tarzan and the Jewels of Ophir*, I said, and found it very interesting; it tells a lot about Africa, and the description of the jungle is very good since I was there and can vouch for it.

"You were in Africa?"

"No, Cuba, and we had plenty of jungle. In the Spanish-American War. Were you in the World War, Mr. Pilsud?"

". . . Yes."

"Where?"

"Oh . . . France."

He was a fuckin liar, and we both knew it. The army does not take fags. Well we chatted a little more and I smiled very politely from on high and in no time at all he had given Henry *two and a half* bricks for each series, and thrown in a brick and a quarter for *A Message to Garcia* as it is a preachment as well as a book. Betty Finestone won the skates, naturally, being a girl and yiddle, but Henry learned his old man could be surely counted on, in school as at Las Guásimas.

As now Frank Joseph would learn the same lesson. Mrs. Illowhite, his grade adviser, reminded me a lot of Miss McTaggerty, toot toot toot, but naturally I did not check the drawers department. She also taught English. The very first thing she said after hello was I had a very interesting boy there. I did? Yes indeed. I always knew he had ability, I said, we have many interesting discussions around the dinner table, but for some reason he just has not been able to bring it out in school. Oh I wouldn't say that, she said, he is different, but he has quite unique talents. Read this. And she handed me a piece of yellow composition paper. At the top was his name in a handwriting that slanted back and forth like grass in the wind, but that is the Palmer method for you. Gradually I made out the rest.

OH HAIR

Oh hair is there and everywhere,
Oh hair is quite gregarious.
Oh hair is there and everywhere,
Oh hair is multifarious.
Oh hair is there and everywhere,
Oh hair will ever stick to us,
Oh hair is there and everywhere,
Oh hair is quite ubiquitous.

"Well," I said, "it rhymes."

She got extremely serious. "Not only that, Mr. Kleinhans. This has a mellifluous feel for language. Frank has a marvelous ear."

"My Frank?"

"Oh yes."

"You mean he is a good listener?"

"He's better than that. He *absorbs* language like a sponge."

"Mrs. Illowhite," I said, looking at her in a new light, "let me tell you something. I notice Frankie likes to stare a lot. You talk to him and he stares at you like you're a wonder. But do not tell me he is listening when he does that. Because he does not hear a word you are saying. Believe me, I know."

"Oh dear, Mr. Kleinhans," she said with a little chuckle. "That's because he is so busy *studying* you, studying in particular a certain feature. He loves to look at mouths."

"He loves to look at mouths?"

"Yes indeed. He is fascinated by them. We've had several long talks about that."

"He talks to you?"

"Why yes. We've had some very good talks. He is absolutely fascinated by mouths. Their different shapes and sizes and textures. The way they contract and expand and click and dentalize and aspirate. Thus producing words. And language."

"He likes that."

"More than like. It captures his imagination. He is particularly taken by the way mouths move at a distance, when two people converse and he cannot hear what is said, they are practically independent agents as it were and he is just delighted."

"Hmmmm," I said, thinking of Captain O'Brien talking to the colonel up near the San Juan River and wondering if my fate was being sealed. Meanwhile I was looking at her mouth. The kid had a point. "They really interest him?"

"They. And language."

"Let me ask you a question, Mrs. Illowhite. Can that do anything for him? I mean in a career sense? In the world?"

"Why of course it can. There are a whole host of possibilities. Speech therapy and pathology. Dramatics. The field is wide open."

"I see." I stood up. "Mrs. Illowhite, I want to thank you for your time and trouble. You have been very helpful and I'll be sure and tell your principal."

"Oh that's very kind of you, Mr. Kleinhans, but totally unnecessary. I only wish more fathers took an interest in their sons' education."

I walked right out and into her boss's office and I told him what an excellent worker he had there and he was delighted I was not belittling. The next day I also sent her a case of pints. You can never be a piker.

That night I walked up to Frank Joseph's room. Sure enough he was listening to the radio, for all I know seeing mouths in the loudspeaker. He didn't even know I was there until I sat down. Then he snapped to and lowered the volume.

"Hello Frankie."

"Hello."

"Is that a good program you were listening to?"

By God she was right. He was zeroing in on my mouth like a dentist. I tried to speak very distinct though it was not easy with him staring. Oh well. "Did you like that program?" I said, flapping away.

". . . Was it a good program?" he said.

"Yes, sonny, did you like it?"

". . . Yes I did."

"What was it?"

"The program?"

"Yes the program."

"The Kellogg's *Singing Lady,* Irene Wicker."

"The Singing LADY?"

". . . Yes."

"She's a singer?"

"You mean does she only sing?"

"Well yes, Frank."

"No. Mainly she does voices. She imitates other people and ducks and geese and like that."

"You like it?"

"Ducks and geese?"

"No, all the voices she has. Do you like those voices? Frank? . . . Frank?"

"Her voices?"

"Yes Frankie."

"They're OK."

"Sure they are."

I walked to the door and yelled down the hall. "Henry. Come here a minute." Then I walked back and sat down and looked gently on my kid. He studied me and I smiled with my mouth. Just then Henry breezed in, full of beans. "Yeah, Pop?" he said, looking from me to Frank and back.

"Henry," I said, "do Roosevelt. Now Frankie, you watch Henry and listen to him."

Henry curled his lip back and shoved out his teeth. I held up my hand. "No, Henry, the other one."

He uncurled and pulled in his chin. Then he booms out, *"I hate war."*

"Now you say that, Frankie. Frankie."

"What?"

"Repeat it."

"What Henry said?"

"Yes, what Henry said. Do it just like Henry."

He did not do much with his chin, but he said, "I . . . hate war."

"That's fine, Frankie. OK, Henry."

"Eleanor hates war."

"Go on Frankie."

"The same thing?"

"Yes, the same thing."

"Eleanor . . . hates war."

"I hate Eleanor," says Henry.

". . ."

"Go ahead, Frankie."

". . . He's married to Eleanor."

"That's OK, Frankie. Just say it."

"If they both hate war, why would he hate her?"

Henry's eyes were rolling. "Just say it, sonny. Don't think about it. Just say it like Henry. Go on, sonny."

He began to fade.

"Frankie, say it. Frankie. You can do it. You got a very nice voice. You could do it good as Henry. Say it, Frankie. I hate war, Eleanor hates war, I hate Eleanor."

He was staring at me. At my fuckin mouth. It was suddenly tingling. So was my hand. It was itching to slap that kid silly. But it did not, it *dare* not. Instead I just got up

and patted his face. "That's perfectly OK, sonny," I said.
"It's OK. You go ahead and listen to the Singing Lady. It's
OK. Come on, Henry."

Henry and I walked downstairs. He said, "Mah friends——"
and I held up my hand. "Not now, Henry," I said. "Go back
upstairs and finish your homework. OK? That's a good boy."
He walked right up, asked me no questions, I told him no
lies. I heard him saying mah friends and you are mah friends,
how do I know you are mah friends? And the door closed
softly, leaving me all alone with my problem, but all of a
sudden with some brand new and unique thoughts on the
subject.

The very next day I started asking around. What did I ask?
Why where the kid can get a radio audition. There was
absolutely no reason we could not some day have the Frank
Joseph Hour. I could even sponsor him. Or he could do the
fights with Sam Taub, the hell with Angelo Pullangi. Or
announce *Manhattan Merry Go Round*. He could become
the *Singing Gent*. We could develop a trademark good as
you wanna buy a duck. Maybe even his cute trick of asking
the same question you ask him. Like Illowhite said, there
was a whole host of possibilities, including being a host. So
I looked into the matter. And finally I came up with an
answer from, who else, Arthur Fine. He could get an audition
on WNYC, which was a city station and you do not need
pull, just write away. I had listened to NYC, not too much
as they did not have advertising, but to La Guardia reading
the comics to Lew Valentine and I voted for him even if
he was a guinea, at least his hand was not in the till and
he was not laying any showgirl. That is something I held
against Harding. It's OK for King Carol to screw Madame
Lupescu, but an elected official should keep his pecker in
his pants.

So I wrote away. Sure enough they sent me back a very polite letter giving Frank Joseph a six-minute audition in three weeks. Now to go to work. First thing I did was pick out his material. To show off his variety I chose his own piece, "Oh Hair," followed by "Flanders Field," "Trees," "The Shooting of Dan McGrew" and winding up with "Columbia the Gem of the Ocean" in that order. Then I got hold of the kid and began to work him. I saw right off what Ziggy and Belasco had to go through. He was very shaky, you would think he was trying out for *G.W.T.W.* But now I knew a thing or two. See, first I went through his routine myself, hypnotizing him with all my sounds and shapes, until he was cobra to my mongoose and quite pliable for action. Then I put him in front of a mirror and let him watch himself go to town and that clinched it. He was fascinated, as are all hams, by his own clicks, shapes and clacks and in amazingly little time he memorized (with feeling) his act. Proving once and for all that he could do the job if only he would shake his ass, as I told Helga. Naturally I was prejudiced, but to me he sounded like Brokenshire in his palmy days.

Well came the big day. Or night. I dressed him up in his new blue suit and a reversible coat, herringbone side out, for if you look the part you can play it, and I took him downtown in a taxicab. First we went out for chink's on Mott Street so he would have his strength but would not be too filled up, then checked him into the Municipal Building and took an elevator up to the fifteenth floor and the station. A very nice pear-toned young fellow greeted us and explained the setup. Which was a large room with a glass partition, and a microphone and that was it. You just walk in, said the young fellow, and begin when you feel ready. Frankie was starting to gaze at him so I pulled him to one side and said OK, you go in there now and do it just like we rehearsed, practice makes perfect. Am I supposed to go in there? he asked. That's right. *That* room. Right there. And I will be nearby, so don't worry. Now you go in there and do a job for your future and your family. I shook his hand which was soft and clammy and gave him a little push. He wound up a few feet inside the door, looking at me. I smiled and motioned at the mike. Very slowly he turned. Then slowly he walked over to it. Meanwhile the pear stuck his head out of another door and motioned for me to follow him. I closed the door before Frank could see and walked around to what was a glass booth and entered and sat beside him. He leaned into a box and said you can start anytime, Mr. Kleinhans.

Frank gave a little start and turned around. He saw us and I winked. He turned back and saw the mike and examined it. I began to sweat. All of a sudden I heard booming out, "Oh hair is there and everywhere." We were off and running.

I leaned back. And I took a peek at the young fellow. He was Helen Wills Moody. I swiveled back to the kid. He had paused. Then he started up again: "In Flanders Field the poppies grow, between the crosses row on row," and so on and so forth and in my humble opinion did a terrific job. A little fast, but with tons of expression. He stopped and looked around. Then turned back and did "Trees." When he finished that he blinked a few times and sailed into "Dan McGrew." And halfway through he stopped. Cold. I could hear his breathing; he was staring at that mike like it was all mouth. I looked at Major Bowes. He had folded his arms. Back to Frankie. He was turning around and starting for the door. Excuse me, I said, and jumped up and ran out and made it there just as he was about to exit. He looked like Clarence Carstairs when the dago big guns opened up.

"Get back in there," I whispered.

He began to push at me. I gave him a good shove.

"That's all right, Mr. Kleinhans," boomed a voice. "He can leave if he's finished."

"Oh he ain't finished, sir," I yelled. I grabbed the kid and walked him back in. Clarence made it, Bill Terry kept Clydell Castleman in through fourteen runs; if I let go now the kid was a goner.

"Frankie," I whispered, "you got to stay there and finish. You got to."

He started to cry.

"Frankie," I said, "Please, you just got to. There's no two ways about it. Do it Frankie. For *me*."

Slowly he turned and looked at me. His crying started to stop. I smiled and nodded. It was touch and go. Then he turned back and trudged the last mile to the mike. Hauptmann could not be sadder. And he did not have Leibowitz to talk to. Poor little bastard. Very softly, so as not to tip him over, I walked to the door, eased it closed and ran back to the booth. Christ it was Siboney in there. The governor and warden peered out. Frankie licked his fingers and was wiping his eyes. He stared, *glared* at the mike. Suddenly he started on "Dan McGrew." From the very *beginning*. He charged right through without a single fluff. Then on up to "Columbia the Gem of the Ocean." Christ, strong and tough. McKinley would shiver in his spine. When he finished he looked at that microphone like it said made in Spain. Then he boomed out, "Oh hair is there and everywhere——" Warden Lawes bolted upright and leaned into his box and said, "That is all right, Mr. Kleinhans, that is all right. *Mr. Kleinhans.*" Frank came to and stopped booming. Major Bowes cut his throat with his finger. Frank blinked like he just woke up. The young fellow turned to me and he was *smiling*. And holding out his hand. I grabbed it. "Thank

you, Mr. Kleinhans," he said. "I enjoyed it." "Thank *you*,
sir," I said right back, "we enjoyed being here."

I got up and walked out of that booth on cloud nine and I
floated into the studio and shook my boy's hand. It was all
wet. Proudly I turned him around and steered him out. He
threw up in the men's room, but so does Freddie March, and
then I took him out for a black-and-white ice cream soda.

He was at the peak, King of the Hill, he had covered himself with glory, old and new, and next morning, chug, he
did not get out of bed. Helga came downstairs and said
Frank is sick. What with? I don't know, he can't keep anything down. It was one thing after another. I swallowed my
coffee and walked upstairs to his room. Hello, sonny, I said.
Hello . . . , he said and vomited into a basin. I held his head.
It was wet and hot. But he did not look yellow. Something
hurt, Frankie? He shook his head and heaved again, hard,
like he had just eaten melted sowbelly. I fetched a cold rag
for his head, lowered the shades and went back down. It's
just an upset stomach, I said, you know how kids are. And
I went over the place.

That night he was still heaving. And the next day. Till
the yellow I was looking for on the outside started to come
up. We gave him rhubarb, peppermint and soda and calomel
tea and he shpritzed that up. So finally I gave in to Helga
and called up Weinmeister. He jumped in that night as they
used to be human. Well, he said, I don't know, his neck is
funny. I'll leave you some powders, give them to him three
times a day. It runs in the family, I said, my grandfather
had this in 1818. I'll drop in tomorrow, he said.

Well tomorrow and tomorrow and tomorrow. He retched
up the powders and kept fading away. Finally Weinmeister,
who had been doing the doctor headshake, said well he may
have a touch of meningitis. Helga grabbed her mouth. We'll

see tomorrow, he said, giving me a look. Outside: I'll get a bed ready just in case.

The next day was Friday. All day. And the mail came early for that was human too. And in the mail was a letter from WNYC. I ripped it open. It was a mimeographed letter. Cheap wop. "Dear sir," it said. "Thank you for your recent audition at WNYC, your city station. We shall be unable to make use of your services. Very truly yours. Joe Blow or somebody."

"Whathehell is this?" I said.

Henry read it. "He flunked his audition," he said.

"But the guy *loved* it. He told me."

"Well," he said, "that's not what it says here. I gotta get ready." He wiped his mouth and went upstairs.

"A goddam form letter," I said. "I should have voted for the mick."

"What did you expect?" said Helga.

"What did I expect? I'll tell you what I expected. I slaved over that kid, not you."

"Don't aggravate yourself."

"Shit. You ever listen to La Guardia? *He's* got talent? He owns the fuckin station, that's how he gets on."

But she was not listening to me. I could always tell. I shifted around. Frank Joseph was creeping down the stairs. He was bent over like a little old man, but on his feet. And not puking. His bathrobe hanging down off his piperack shoulders. He crept up to us.

"I flunked?" he said.

"Yes, Frank," said Helga.

He sat. Helga went over to him. "Frankie, can you eat something? Oatmeal or Cream of Wheat?"

"Would I like something to eat?"

"That's what she said."

"All right. Kellogg's Corn Flakes with raisins."

Helga fixed it, with warm milk. He dipped in and ate, *wolfed* it down. I waited a minute. He did not puke it back up.

"Jesus Christ," I said. "Christ. You're all better now."

"Leave him alone, Willy."

He started in to gaze.

"That's right. Look at me a little. Look. I'm the seventh wonder of the world. Look. You could've had a terrific career. You could have done something with your life, instead of looking." I knocked his Corn Flakes box over. "You could have sold this shit, or any other. But no, not you. You think you can make a living staring in somebody's tonsils?"

"Willy!"

"Willy, shit."

I got up and I threw down my napkin. "I bust my bananas and what do I get? Looks and vomit. Is this what I made America a world power for?" I walked to the stairs. "Henry!"

Henry stuck his head out of his room.

I looked at Frank Joseph. He's got no monopoly. "Henry," I yelled, still looking, "come down here and do Charles Laughton and the goddam Gettysburg address!"

> Hello nephews, nieces mine
> I'm glad to see you look so fine,
> How's Mama, how's Papa
> And how's your radio?
> This is Uncle Frank, your Uncle Frank
> Hello little friends, hello.

Oh shit.

X V I I

As We Charged
To Meet the Foe

SONNY SCHROEDER LANDED on Omaha Beach. Lew Schroeder was lucky. His kid magnetized no bullets. Don't ask me what Lew did to deserve such luck, he was a thief, in business and in life, whereas I have always been on the up and up. Mc-Kinley was another nice guy. Sonny's bunkies landed on Utah Beach. The frogs never forgave us for plunking America down on their sacred soil. Wellington they can take, but not Sonny. Not now. But they were sure happy then. Why not. He saved their ass. Iron Pants only beat it. Fireman save my child, ooooh you nasty man. But back then Sonny got champagne and Calvados and zig-zig and sixty-nine; froggies in American suntans and Ikes and smiles held out their hand like it was Siboney. Six weeks and Gamelin was kaput, also Weygand. We got *insurrectos*. Practically b.a. Not one Anna Held. Gold teeth. Bimbos were paid in Mauser bullets. Try that in Pig Alley. Lister and I had two real live ones in Havana in

'28. Pack up all your summer clothes, see you down at Sloppy Joe's. Batista ran some whorehouse. Now Lola Montez is a cobra woman. The King of Bavaria fucked himself into the grave. They had dirt baked into the dirt. The men played soccer with lopped-off dago noggins. Throw an American kid Pancho Villa's head and he will catch it, even without a glove. Throw Pancho at a garlic, he will kick it back at you. The bullet that got Henry came from the Second Avenue El.

They cadged cigarettes. No gum chum, no candy Andy. Not that we had that much. By San Juan some of the fellows were smoking horseshit. And begging themselves. But we handed out what we could. Zonk!

"Jesus, is this what we are fighting for?" said Tom.

"Give them a chance," says I.

So we gave them a chance. You know that gallant caballero smoking a Murad? Forget it. They pounced, they squatted. All over the camp. Sucking in heaven. Smiling and nodding. The hell with cancer. You tripped over them, over legs and arms, slipped on their shit. If so, watch out, you'd be stripped of Made in America faster than Talon zippers. Well a gook is a gook.

Six days we laid over in Siboney, swatting off the squatters. Plus other squatters who we could not swat, much as we wanted. The great newspapermen come for the big Santiago show. All the five-star finals. Tracy of course, still hustling and whining. Frankie Norris. Remington. Christy, Jimmy Creelman of the *Journal,* who got it like Marshall, playing Steal the Flag. Silly Scovel, who turned the tables on Patton by taking a poke at General Shafter. And died broken-hearted. For you do not sass the brass. Canucks. Limeys. Not Churchill. He'd covered the dago side, naturally, and taken off for Africa before we got there. Why not with his pull? Ben Lyon and Bebe Daniels made theirs in the U.S. of A., then took off for limeyland. They can stick *Hell's Angels*. Churchill's old man had a dose.

Willie Hearst. He came down to the war in his private yacht, the *Silvia*, named no doubt for his latest dark-tressed beauty in a dungeon. Could have named it the *Gloryosky* or *Eva* or *Marion*, but why ask for trouble with Mrs. H. Joe Pulitzer on the other hand was accounted for but not present. He couldn't even stand the crackle of his own newspaper, much less our rifles. Pulitzer was no prize. He paced his cork office, gnashing teeth as Bill scooped him. And lived through Steve Crane. Who had his own troubles with his kid knocking off Johnny Stomp in Lana's boudoir.

Meanwhile Sampson and Schley were strutting about in the beautiful water outside the harbor, neat, clean, just waiting for Cervera to stick his neck out, then whack, another soccer ball. The navy got the headlines while we got mud, gooks and mosquitoes. Thus be it ever for the dogface, Lafayette Escadrille please note.

Well on the seventh day we did not rest. The bugles shrieked and we woke up. Henry woke up to the "Song of India," we to the song of Berlin. We broke camp in two shakes. And we knew this time it had to be the real McCoy, just *had* to be. A limey reporter told us. All of a sudden I got terrible excited. Like the time I waited for Joie Ray to beat Nurmi; I hoped this would turn out better. I ducked behind the machine shop to my canal and did some healthy prewar business, just as I did at the Garden, changed into my special B.V.D.s and wrapped up in my two red flannel belly bands. Laura was the face in the misty night, goodnight Irene, Irene goodnight. Then we packed up, including five days' rations, counted off and lit out down the Aguadores turnpike which was no Lincoln Highway. Toward Santiago. Thataway. Trudging through muck and mire and if you say hello muck

I'll say hello Meyer. Stepping on each other's heels we were so eager to eat garlic.

And who should we run into, why none other than the one publisher with guts, Bill Hearst. Who put his mouth where his money was and planted himself there at the side of the road on his horse. He and his ace, blackbeard Jimmy Creelman. We yelled and they waved and said "Good luck boys" as we swung past. Now there was an American for you. Stuck right up for an American outfit when that hunky gave us the shaft. Where he put his pecker was his business.

Up ahead, thunder? But it was not raining. That is *it*, said Lister, eyes smoking. The knowledge rippled down the ranks like a great wave. I felt the wallop of that marvelous fact. I turned for a last look at New York. OK, Bill, you supply the words, we'll supply the war. Give our regards to Broadway, remember us to Herald Square. Also Marion. Knighthood is in Flower. Peg O' My Heart, I love you. Lister broke out into the "Old Gray Mare." Not "Armentieres," not "Dirty Gerty from Bizerty." We all joined in and the thunder drums rolled in the foreground, mixed with hail and the *ssss* of angry lead insects. Then our artillery opened up and sure enough they left a calling card of white smoke; it hovered over the road like our own little mushroom. Down in Nagasaki where the men chew tabaccy and the women wicky wacky woo. The garlics obliged with smokeless, now what American traitor slipped them that know-how? Gompers? Tom Mooney? A smart captain at least told our guns to shut up.

Now as per recipe we hurried up and waited. And ditto. And et cetera. And putting one little foot agonizingly after another, where were we headed? Not El Pozo. Not El Caney. Not Kettle Hill. But the big H. That's right, *San Juan Hill.* Us. Not Teddy bear. Not the swells and finaglers and connectors. Not Dick Daredevil. But old cotton-haired General Hawkins and his First Brigade: the 6th, the 16th *and* the 71st.

Yorkers. Volunteers. Strictly. Toward our Suribachi. Over hill, over dale, hard against that muddy trail. Hawkins and General Kent had made the decision. Baby Ike down in Abilene, face of Phil Sheridan, would have nodded and said yes, that makes tactical sense, even if Kent did have nicotine stains in his pants. So we plunged down that road, corduroyed now.

"Whatinhell is that?" said Mert pointing.

I stared up. Why it was the *Graf Zeppelin*. Hanging up there on a sky hook, telling Kent below what to do. Also telling the dago by means of the trail rope, which arrowed straight down to the troops. There we were, *Just Kids,* attached to our speech blimp which said SHOOT ME. So naturally they did. Just in front of me, in a ragged column of four, Clarence Carstairs slapped his neck and said, damn mosquitoes. He scratched and the blood spurted out round his fingers and he walked three more steps, his hand covering the hole, and toppled, looking around very puzzled. Tom Whiston said what is it, bunkie? And bent over Clare, and as he did his back started to pump red and he fell over on his bunkie. I looked at both those fellows and I said to myself, is that all there is? Practical Lister said out loud, come on! and he and Harry Barshinsky and I pulled both of them off the road and Harry let out a scream and grabbed the back of his head which was now partly gone. Some of his hair had slapped me in the face. He sat down and then lay down and Lister and I broke open our kits and bandaged up what was left as best we could. Lister give him a plug of Piper Heidsick which he could handle as his front was OK, and said you'll be all right Harry, we'll git a dago for you. Don't leave me, said Harry, please don't, I've been a good friend, which was not the truth as we were just in the same company and only sang camp songs together. But a fellow with half his head gone will say things. Poor doughboy. As we slugged off down the road we could hear him screaming to the column not to leave him.

He lasted the night like that. Oh that Kent and his fucking balloon.

We pushed on ahead. Now Colonel Derby in the basket of that thing was pointing. If you looked real hard you could see a break in the jungle, a trail cutting off sharp to the right. 'Twas almost hidden to us, but Derby could see it like a slash on a relief map. And Kent could see Derby. Suddenly we were plunging column right, straight into that slash, surrounded by underbrush, vines, trees and mud and without benefit of an *insurrecto* machete. Little did we then know something was rotten in Denmark, rather in Kent's head, or guts. For neither the 6th or the 16th veered onto that trail, before us or after. And Hawkins had to go it alone without a full force, as now we had to, and even Gamelin knew divide and you are conquered. Joe Pulitzer, please copy before you make your yellow-bellied, corked-up charges!

We had to squeeze down to single file. Like a stream of Pebeco, with Kent squeezing the tube from the road, we slithered out on that trail. It was dappled with sun and clouds and jungle and wet, and dago lead zipped and buzzed and stung. Then courtesy of Colonel Blimp the shells began to drop. It felt like the San Francisco earthquake. One fragment skimmed over my head and slammed into a tree. But another hit Sergeant Lou just up ahead and he dropped. Tom and I wrestled our way through to him. His arm was dangling half off at the shoulder and his blouse was soaking red. We kneeled over him, but he pushed us off with the good arm, God he was strong. "Go on, dammit, get goin. They'll find me." We looked at one another and he yelled again. You do not argue with the sarge, so with tears in our eyes we took off. They found him all right, and he survived, and he was called Wingy the rest of his unnatural life. Kent.

My back began to hurt fierce and my stomach got funny and so did my legs as we hunkered along. Damn legs were almost ready to give out but were saved by the bell and the order to lie down. Somewheres up ahead at the river there must have been one great traffic jam, why not with the cop we had? So I burrowed into that mud like the three little pigs and would have nosed down to China if I could. But then came the "Forward!" and the boys ahead of me were up and moving and, thank God, so were my legs.

I tried looking about for my bunkies. All I could see was Mert. The other faces were strange. "Where you from?" I asked the trooper behind me. "Second Infantry," he said. "First Brigade?" "No, Second. You too?" "Heck no, the First." "It's a holy mess all right." "You can say that again." And again and again and again. Our boys will not go off to war. At that point the orders started flying like the bullets. "F Company forward!" "C Company here! *Here* dammit." "Captain Jimson's men over here!" Where? Here. Whothehellareyou? Whothehellareyou? And without getting answers we would crash forward, except someone would fall like he had tripped, but when you offered a hand up he was gone. Another would twitch and slap off a lead mosquito and then collapse and we'd have to shove him aside, else what life remained would be stomped out. Please do not come the little war with me. I will match that holy hell with the Argonne. And Chancellorsville. And Vera Cruz. And Bunker Hill. And Wounded Knee. And Bastogne. And Inchon. And Lundy's Lane. And St. Lo. And Shiloh. And Anzio. And Saratoga. And Okinawa. And Quebec. And Cassino. And you name it. Ask Clarence.

We who were there, and left, plunged on. I could see none of my company now. But I could hear cursing that would make Vinegar Joe blush; did Henry hear that? Yet somehow it was a comfort. The mud was not; it was sucking at my shoes like a thousand fish mouths. I looked down. The stuff was red, as if the pirates of the deep had stripped our feet.

I tore away from the sight, only to be commanded to hit the deck. I folded. Nose dived into that bloody muck. It had a sharp, bitter smell which I will never forget if I use ten tons of Aqua Velva. The hard tack began to travel upward, but I pushed it back. Then it was leap up and bang ahead.

About my fourth catapult I heard a cheer. The fellows ahead of me were pointing up. I looked to heaven and so help me, God was a fair C.O. It had taken the dago a mighty long time, as might be expected, but at last he had connected. The balloon was flopping and folding in on itself and swaying downward amidst our cheering. Served it right. And our combined breath helped blow it down. Till fast as we cheered we clammed up. Why? Why the sonofabitch had the last laugh by nestling in the branches, mortally wounded but still pointing our way. Greaser bullets came thicker and harder and surer if that was possible, the wonder being that some of us were not hit. I did not at all feel like moving, but the press behind me was irresistible; Kent was squeezing like a boa, and so I crashed on ahead, whatheheck you do not hear the one that gets you. Ask Henry. Ask Rudy.

I passed under the monster and drove ahead like Red Grange carrying the ice, and thanks to the lord and Mama and Papa I did not have to dive till I was clear of the deadly pylon. When I was and the order came to drop, I did so gratefully, red ooze or no, double grateful when the flat man alongside me turned out to be Mert Swenson, giving me his sly grin.

"Jesus bunkie," I said, "Whereinhell you been? Mert, it's Germ. Mert?"

He kept looking at me all right, and smiling the Mert smile, but he said not a word. I wondered if his nerves had snapped. Then I saw them. His eyes. They were wide open and covered with crawling ants. I looked at that sight for a hundred years, then like a dago shell had shot me up from

China, I rose, and all the dead soldiers in history were screaming in my ears. The growing grass was thunder. I could feel
the crush behind me, or my body and legs could, and they
did not hesitate. They plunged me off sideways into the
jungle, away from the screaming, away from the chugging,
away from the sucking red, away from Mert and his eyes.

This person who surely was me, I freely admit it, charged
off, careening into bushes and trees and hollering up to
heaven to clean the sound of hell out of his—*my* ears. And
also dug at my eyes to release them from Mert. Deeper and
deeper in I ran. Once my pack caught and I began screaming
to please let go, I'd be good, and wrestled so hard that I left
it behind as I floundered away; when I peeked back it was
in the clutches of a greasy tree. I left it there. And I kept on
flopping about though I know it must have been in circles,
for that's what you do when the demons ride your back. But
at least and at last the bugles inside my ears grew blessedly
fainter. Oh they were still there all right, but not sending
such hot streaks through my head. And a good thing too, for
I was suddenly growing very weak, losing whatever starch
had brought me this far. When I crashed into a tree, I hung
on before staggering ahead. Still in all I kept on going, somehow, judging progress only by the lowering of the volume
in my head, as if my giant hand was reaching up and turning
the dial of Papa's Victrola: Strongheart was fighting me off,
but slowly I was winning. In and further in I pressed, fighting
the battle of the dial, and I thought surely these legs and this
body must faint, but the picture of Mert struck me like a
whip and I screeched and plunged on.

> Nights are long since you went away
> I think about you all through the day

Till finally this poor broken doughboy, this *me,* could
take it no longer and sank down in the mud, even with Mert

staring, hoping never to rise again; and the mud was black and clean!

I do not know how long I lay there, shivering and breathing in the earth. I do know that gradually Strongheart shrank down to size and gradually I heard the insects and birds. And then in the cleaned-out space about me I heard someone say, "Hello Willy." Just the one time. I made myself roll over and saw him leaning against a tree in front of me. I sat up. Then quick as I could I reached down for my gun, which strange to say I hadn't thrown away. I couldn't locate it.

"Oh so now you want it," he said.

Somewhat embarrassed, but relieved he was surely no garlic, I dropped my head.

"What company you from?" I asked.

"Your company."

I looked up and peered in closer. The latticework jungle was slatting the sun across his face and 'twasn't too easy to see, but it showed me enough. "I never seen you before," I said. "As a matter of fact," and this time I spotted the rifle and grabbed it, "I don't even recognize the uniform. You Cuban?"

"Nope. I'm your Uncle Erik."

I looked extra careful at him.

"Erik of Waterloo?"

"The same."

"What are you doin here?"

"Trying to keep you from making an asshole of yourself."

I lowered my head. But even then his voice kept coming in at me. "Even the Imperial Guard stood their ground," he said. "And they were frogs."

I brought the head back up. "How about the frogs at Sedan? They ran."

He shook his head gently, the way my grandfather used to when I pulled his beard.

"That is Konrad's concern," he said. "I don't know about
them."

I swiveled quickly about. "Is he here too?"

"I haven't seen him. Maybe. Most likely he's staying away
so he won't be recognized as a relative."

"You ain't afraid of that, I see."

"Well I am not *proud*, Willy, of that fact. No sir. It's just
that I think you can do it. I *know* you can."

I stared at mud. Mud stared back. "I'm not so sure."

He was silent. I stared an awful long time. Finally my throat
let out a deep sigh and I looked up. He was not against the
tree. "Over here." I swung about. It wasn't Erik. I could see
that. "Uncle Konrad?" I said, a little sheepish.

"No."

"Uncle Otto?"

"No."

"Stop playin games, goddammit. You don't want to tell me,
don't."

"OK. It's Blucher."

"Who?"

"Don't act stupid. Erik's C.O. If you won't shake your ass
for him, do it for me."

"I . . . I just can't, General."

"Of course you can. It's an order. Move your ass out of
here, soldier."

I tried picking up a leg. It wouldn't budge.

"You heard me," he said. "Are you gonna pull this in front
of Wellington and the whole goddam limey army?"

"Jesus, I don't *want* to."

"Well then, *move*."

"I told you I *can't*. And you got no authority to make me.
And don't be such big apples after the way you folded on
the western front."

"That was Ludendorf——"

"I don't care who it was. Don't pull rank on me. A general got me in this fix."

"And a general will get you out."

It was not Blucher's voice. I gazed at this fellow. He had a beard like Grandpa. Oh no. "Do not tell me to slug it out if it takes the whole summer," I said, "because I am not falling for that banana oil."

"All right, soldier. I understand. Now just get ahold of yourself and do the right thing. *For your country*. You hear?"

Oh God. "Yes I hear, I hear, but how? Gimme a drink, sir, please!"

"The hell I will. You got to do it on your own."

"Fuckin brass. You're all alike."

"I could court-martial you for that, soldier."

"Fuck you, you rummy bastard. If the South had a few more men you wouldn't be here now. Go on, steal some more funds."

He drew his saber and I pulled my shirt open. He stuck the weapon against me and I swear I was a goner. Then he shook his head and turned and walked into the woods, still shaking. Christ I was tired, so damn tired. So I made a little pallet with leaves and lay down. I dozed off, I don't know how long. I do know I woke up with somebody's hand on my fly. I snapped up and pushed it away. I saw something with a soldier's hat on, but whatever it was was also wearing a dress. "Whathehell——" I said.

"Yes?" it said with a big smile.

"What's goin on here? Don't tell me you are a dago."

"Oh no."

He or she or it got up and gave me a fancy salute.

"General Marie MacMahon. At your service."

Funny thing was he—*it*—does not have an accent. Spoke perfect English.

"Where did you learn to speak English like that?" I said.

He shrugged his shoulders. And pulled his dress up. "Andersonville," he said.

He was wearing absolutely nothing. Instead of a pecker he had a huge cunt and it was spurting blood.

"Christ," I said. "You will bleed to death."

He looked down. Then back at me. "Not if you take care of me," he said.

"Listen," I said. "Pull your goddam dress down and get out of here. You're pickin on the wrong army. Go back to Paris. I wouldn't touch you with a ten-foot pole."

"Ah," he said.

"You heard me."

He pulled the dress down. "Do you think you're better than me?" he said with a smile.

"You are goddam right."

"Then what are you doing here?"

Uh-oh. I look around. "Don't look around," he said. "How does it feel?"

"What?"

"Running like hell. While your bunkies are back there." He came up close. "It's all right, Willy. I know how you feel."

"Stay away from me," I said, holding the gun up. "Take one more step and that cunt will have lots of company."

"Ohhh so brave."

"Stop it, I tolya."

But he kept on coming. He took off the dress and he kept coming, with just his kepi on and that spurting cunt. I pulled the trigger. It was point blank but I missed. I shot again and we were surrounded by white smoke. "Listen," I yelled into the smoke. "Kent is back there up the line. He is your speed. You two will hit it off just great!"

It was suddenly all quiet on the southern front. I was alone.

I sank down on my hands and knees. I checked my fly. OK. "Now I lay me down to sleep," I said, looking up and then I finished. Then I got a terrific urge. I tried to move off into the bushes, but I could not. So I dropped my pants right there and took a dump. Right in the middle a hand tapped me on the shoulder. I looked around and it was Eva Cisneros. I turned away. "Excuse me," I said, "I'll be through in a minute."

"I will wait, Willy," she said.

I knew I should be embarrassed as hell, for once Mama walked into the w.c. by mistake when I was on it and I couldn't look at her for a week, but now I was quite cool, calm and collected. I finished and used some leaves and covered up my business with dirt.

"*Buenos días,*" she said.

"Hello Evangelina."

"You know my name?"

"Sure I do. I read the papers. Is Bill Hearst laying you?"

"Why do you want to know? Are you jealous?"

"Bill is a good fellow. But when this is over he'll have bigger fish to fry."

"That is sweet. You are worried about me."

"You have been having a rotten time of it, that's all."

"Ah sweet. Willy, would you like to rape me?"

"What? Jesus, whatayou think I am? Some greaseball?"

"You can, Willy."

"No, Eva."

"You *can.* I *want* you to."

She came toward me and grabbed me and kissed me. I threw her down on the ground and she screamed no, no, but she was clutching me around the neck, God she smelled beautiful. I pulled up her dress as she kept panting no no no. She was wearing white bloomers, satin. I pulled them down and it was all there, just as I had dreamed it, not like Mac-

Mahon, but beautiful like Lillian Russell. In a jiffy I was out of my shoes, leggings, pants and shirt. She looked up at me and said, "I like your underwear."

"Brand new," I said, "special just for you."

"Ah sweet."

Then she made a strange wild sound and reached up and ripped away at my fly, all the time keeping on with the "no" business, till at last I was as exposed as on piss call. She rolled over on her back and I yelled out, "Not there!" "Why not?" she said. "I just dumped there!" "It is *your* dump, Willy," she said. "No. No." She sighed and said, "All right." Then quick as a cat, dump or not, she reached up and pulled me down on top of her. No, oh no, she said spreading wide open. I started in just like I read in Arthur Fine's book.

"You are not up," she said.

"Never mind," I said.

"You cannot rape me if you are not *up*."

"Well *get* it up, darnit."

"No. *Cubana* does not do that. Frog women do that."

"Eva, sweetheart, please," I said. "You got to. You just got to."

"I am royal stock, soldier. I will not do what you cannot."

She pushed me away and sat up. Very neatly she put on her bloomers, rearranged her dress and stood up. She was one handsome woman looking down at me. Her hair seemed to pile up to the treetops.

"You are nothing," she said with a sneer. "*Nada.*" She spit down on me and I noticed she had two gold teeth in front. "I will find Richard Harding Davis," she said. "He will know how to rape." And with that she spun on her tiny spiked heel and switched off through the jungle. "Hah," I yelled, "he won't even take his pith helmet off!" But she was gone. I brought my knees up and clutched them; at least my legs could do that. Maybe I could not get it up, but I did not have

a celluloid collar down there. I looked about me. This time
I was all alone. She won't be back, even when she gets the
heave-ho from Davis, she is too proud. Well it did not feel
right being in my underwear in the jungle, so I put my
clothes back on. I wondered how many days I had been here.
Two? Three? The afternoon sun was just coming off center.
It was cool. It was really not so terrible. I could even hide out
several years. By the time I got back no one would recognize
me. Or care. If they cared they wouldn't have sent me out
here, and that went for Mama and Papa, though they meant
well. But what did they know, what did any of them know?
Jesus, McKinley should know. I will send him an unsigned
letter and tell him what's going on. But he sent me *out* here.
So it must be right. Well then, that's it, I had to lay low.
Somehow or other I would reorganize my life; that was the
main thing now. If only my goddam legs would work. I
heard a twig snap. I picked up my rifle.

"OK, step out. You're covered."

He stepped out, hands up.

"Were you watching all that time?" I said.

"Yes."

"You goddam peeping tom, I oughta blow your brains out."

"Why? Just because you couldn't get it up? I know you
can."

"Who are you, God?"

"No. I just know what you can do and cannot do."

Oh Jesus I was suddenly so weary. "Look," I said, "just get
the hell out of here and leave me alone. I have had all the
shit I can take."

"No sir," he said.

"Look mister, *I* got the weapon."

"You haven't used it a heckuva lot."

"I didn't get the chance to."

"You won't use it now."

"No? I told you mister, catch air."

"I can't."

"Oh no? Just why the hell not?"

"I'm your kid."

I got up. I leaned forward and examined the claim. Now in '98 I wasn't even married, nor as was plain, had I ever been laid, and those are items you do not forget, war or no war. Still I did not say the obvious; it just did not occur to me to say it. I merely looked at that doughboy and sure as I am me and you are you, *he* was Henry.

Suddenly I cannot take it any longer. I bent over and started to cry. I had not cried since I was twelve and Papa called me a rotten kid for ripping my pants. But I made up for lost time now. It was like I wanted to throw up but instead of puke only tears retched out. All the time I am sobbing and choking and jerking he says not a word. Just stands there. Making me cry all the harder. Till at last there is nothing left in the well. I pulled myself together and straightened up my shoulders. Darn if he does not reach over and wipe my face.

"Don't do that," I said.

"Why not?"

"Never mind. Don't. I just don't want you to see me like this." And I took a deep sigh; I can still taste the tears. "Well," I said, "you did. Now what do you think of your old man?"

"It's all right, Papa. You did your best."

"Sure."

"You did, Papa."

"Don't give me no applesauce," I said. "I'm still your father."

"All right," he said. "All right. *I think you are a goddam yellow belly. I only wish to God a dago had fucked my mother instead of you!*"

My head slammed back like a bullet had struck. In that same moment the emptiness around me faded and the noises of war barreled in. But wonder of wonders my insides did not turn to Redi-whip. And my left leg stepped forward, followed by my right.

"Fifty-four forty or fight," I said.

"We have met the enemy and they are ours."

"Don't give up the ship."

"YOU MAY FIRE WHEN READY, GRIDLEY."

I jumped straight up. Even while in the air I was turning. I landed and before anything or anyone could stop me I was charging back through the jungle toward the sounds of hell. If anything they were worse now. I could hear the tat tat tat of our Gatlings mixing with their heavy thuds and the zing and spit and thock of all that hot, angry lead. Still I kept running toward the magnets. I had to have them, just had to. I was all alone, sure, but I knew darn well he was watching all right all right.

Well I kept on going. Straight back toward Bloody Ford. Where you could have any color long as it was red. And even at that crucial moment, even as I was returning from up shit creek, from hell, with my whole future in the balance, I knew that never in my life would I or mine ever smoke a Kent, buy suits at Roger Kent, clean them at Kent Brothers, see a Kent Taylor picture or God forbid, play an Atwater Kent!

We will always remember, how they died for liberty
Let's remember Mert Swenson˙and go on to victory.

X V I I I

The Fear of a Fer-de-Lance

A HUNKY ARMY OFFICER killed himself by eating a tube of toothpaste. General John J. Pershing would wrap up in Old Glory and pull the trigger of his service revolver like a man. Or launch himself from the Washington Monument. He'd never eat toothpaste. He was born in 1860. When he was one year old Sumter was fired on. He was the son of a poor railroad foreman in Missouri. He attended Normal School in Kirksville, Missouri, but he was anything but normal. He taught colored children and learned they have ten fingers and toes like the rest of us. He wanted to be a lawyer but took the test for West Point and passed, luckily for this country. Jack Pershing was a great bareback rider, fencer, a keen shot and an all-around top sportsman. He graduated the Point in '86, molded by the long gray line. He went out to fight Geronimo and marched his troops 146 miles in blazing heat and got commended. He then saved some cowboys from crazed Zuni Indians. In '98 he was captain of the 10th Cavalry, a colored outfit and they would go to hell and back for him

131

and did. He was upped to colonel and sent to the Philippines to suppress the Huks, which he did, earning their respect and affection. He made governor of the Philippines long before McNutt and was given the greatest jump in rank in history by T.R., who at least was not nearsighted in this case. He chased Pancho Villa back to Mexico and earned the respect and affection of the peons. He led the A.E.F. and said Lafayette we are here. Pershing was a real American in that he had a keen sense of humor, loved practical jokes, always had a twinkle in his eye off duty and laughed with gusto.

One day I asked Frank Joseph what was frightening about a fer-de-lance. He told me of this man who had read a book about them. That night in bed he rolled over and saw two blazing lights staring at him in the dark, certainly a fer-de-lance. Next morning they found him dead. The doctor said he had died of fright. So what did the blazing eyes turn out to be? Just the two ends of a pair of shoelaces gleaming in the reflected streetlight! That is how frigtening a fer-de-lance can be. Well Pershing would have tossed *it* and the shoelaces in the garbage can.

The first marine went over the top, parlay voo

The Prince of Wales was fucking Lily Langtry long before he met Wally. I waited two and a half hours to see *The German Side of the War* at the 44th Street Theater. Naturally a general named French was the head of the limey army.

The second marine went over the top, parlay voo

Harry Richman had his fun with Clara Bow who then married Rex Bell and flipped. Pulitzer fired Crane and with all his domestic troubles. Pershing was called Black Jack not because of a weapon, cards or complexion, but because of his way with colored troops who adored him. Do anything to a

blackbird but do not kick him in the shins. They are his
weak spot. Houdini's weak spot was his belly. Henry could
hit me all day in the belly.

> The third marine ate the beans,
> farted all over the submarines

Henry could do Coolidge. He'd sit in my rocker and look
at you for fifteen minutes and say that's Coolidge. To me a
cobra is much more frightening than a fer-de-lance. Henry ate
a hot dog then went to see *The Speckled Band* and vomited
all night. Yelled "band speckled." The next night Mrs.
Hackitay died. She had walking pneumonia and Helga took
care of her kids all the time she was sick. Hackitay always used
my phone and never paid. Also my pool table. He broke up
home and the kids went to Glens Falls, New York, with a
grandmother.

> Theirs not to reason why
> theirs but to do or die

Cecil Rhodes was the one good limey. Besides Cobber Cain
who was an Aussie. When they asked Rhodes as a kid what
he wanted to do he said to do or die. Also wanted to annex
the stars. He would have made a great president. As would
Pershing. A boa can't bite you to death but has to squeeze.
Also the python. I would rather be squeezed to death than
bitten. A cobra has that hood but it does not mean beans
to the mongoose. The Spanish-American War could just as
easily have been called the First World War with the First
being the Second and so on, as we became a power while
the whole world watched. But Pulitzer got enough publicity
out of two wars without handing him another. My favorite
picture of all time was *Ben Hur* starring Chuck Heston and
Francis X. Bushman who made a comeback. Hollywood is
controlled by yids and griks. Zukor and Skouras. A lot of

hustle. Skouras' kid is deathly sick so what good is all his
money? What does one grik say to another when they meet?
How's your location. George Givot always said How *do* you
do? *Birth of a Nation* was also good. I saw it in 1914. But
not on 125th Street. They broke Griffith's beans so he made
Intolerance. "A golden thread binds the four stories—a fairy
girl with sunlit hair—her hand on the cradle of humanity—
eternally rocking—"

It was a lemon. Roxy liked any letter long as it was R.
Mabel Normand was a peach. Ben Turpin was funnier than
Chaplin. His eyes rolled me in the aisles. Long as Frank
Joseph stared so, I figured I could cross his eyes and make
his fortune. It never worked. Fatty Arbuckle fucked himself
right out of pictures. I'll never know how a Wampus baby
star could take all that weight. Man Mountain Dean was
no relation to Dizzy. Jimmy Londos could take them both.
Gino Garibaldi was OK, but Abie Feldman hit him in la
bonza with his head and that was that. Jackie Coogan was
almost as cute as Henry. He's some dog now.

> Moppin up soda rickey
> to our hearts' delight
> Dancin to swingeroo quickie

That was Henry's favorite. Doug Fairbanks was great, but
Doug Jr. was a stiff. Same thing with Tarzan and the Son
of Tarzan and Kong and the Son of Kong. As Bob Armstrong
said, he was only a patch on the old man's pants. Jack Johnson lay down with a glove shielding his eyes from the sun,
smiling. White women were crazy about him. Why not?
His dong was two feet long. Barney Ross was a tough little
yid, he saw his old man killed in a candy store. But Al Singer
ran all the way home against Canzoneri, a wop, but a good
one, who had the Herkimer Hurricane's number. As Louis

said, you can run, but you can't hide, a piece of advice I
gave Frank Joseph which he never took.

> It's so easy to call pet names
> when you listen to the trumpet of Harry James

Margaret's favorite was the "Tenement Symphony" as sung
by Tony Martin.

> The Cohens and the Kellys
> The Jones and the Vermicellis

Frank Joseph's favorite was "You Call It Madness, Ah but
I call It Love." Funny song for a boy. Henry made Arista.
I made Helga see *Traffic in Souls* three times at Joe Weber's
Theater. It was educational. But I did not let her see *Where
Are My Children* as it was about abortion with Ty Power
who was also in *Son of Fury* and much cleaner.

> We love to hear that tenor croon
> whenever the Inkspots sing a tune

Shirley Temple was actually a midget. If you looked closely
you could spot it. But Jane Withers was normal. Broncho
Billy was OK but could not sit a horse like Pershing. Chaplin
made six hundred big ones in a single year and is not even a
citizen. I didn't begrudge Little Mary her million, she was
a darn hard worker. And wonderful to her family. Don't tell
me about dope, Wally Reid was taking that stuff before all
these cokies were a gleam in their old man's eye. Myrna
Loy used to play chinks, well she has a chink name. I don't
care for Roosevelt but any man has a tough time with his
kids I feel for. He lost Quentin in the war. But Sisty and
Buzzie were OK.

> Goodman and Kaiser and Miller
> help to make things right
> mixin hot licks with vanilla

Oh Henry. Harold Lloyd was terrific. Real American. But *Hold 'em Jail* was good too. Frank Joseph liked Barry Wood instead of Albie Booth. Then he went on the Hit Parade. Lanny Ross was OK, but not as good as the Street Singer. Marta, rambling rose of the wildwood. If a rattlesnake bites you, or for that matter a fer-de-lance, cut an X in the bite and suck out the poison. I would not mind the job if Sally Rand got bit in the ass. Henry was a genius with *I'se a Muggin.* 1,2,3,4,5,6,uh uh,8,9,woof woof. Also, 66,uh uh, 68, 69,uh uh woof woof,uh uh,uh uh,uh uh,uh uh,uh uh,uh uh,uh uh,uh uh,uh uh,woof woof.

X I X

A Day To Remember

On December 7, 1941, I came home from the place at one o'clock in the afternoon sick and tired and full of aggravation. I walked in the door and through the living room, past Henry who was reading the paper on the sofa and up the stairs to the bedroom. I slammed the door and lay my aggravated self down. I waited a few minutes, staring up at the ceiling that showed a water spot in one corner; Angelo had only fixed it a month ago; nobody did a job anymore. *Nobody.* The 83rd Street sounds were low and calm, a real New York Sunday. No tenement symphony. No fine confusion where I dreamed of a grand illusion.

"Henry," I yelled.

No answer.

I yelled again. No answer, no *real* answer. But whispers in the dark. The high-level conference. Henry and Helga on "him" and what was eating "him" this time. Sure enough.

"Can I do something?" Helga.

"No. I said Henry. I want *Henry.*"

"Do you want some tea?"

"I told you what I want. Now you get up here, Henry."

More whispers, clacks, hisses. Kellogg-Briand in my own house. Finally. OK Pop; she is letting him out into no-man's land. I closed my eyes and waited and at last I heard his presence; it's been ten years since I called. I took *my* time, then opened my eyes. He was standing there in the doorway in a green corduroy shirt and white ducks. I said I am glad you could make it. Ah don't be like that, he says, I was doing something.

"What?"

Reading the paper. What paper? The *Times*. What's wrong with the *Journal*? Nothing, I like the *Times*. Ochs was laying low while Hearst was ducking hot lead in the war. I know Pop. Don't humor me. OK Pop. You heard me. OK, OK, how are the Giants doing? How do I know, I'm not in love with Tuffy Leemans. OK, Pop.

"Well come in. Don't stand in the door. She's listening."

He walked inside. He sat down. I could smell his Vitalis. Some neck, thick and absent, like my Uncle Otto.

"Well," I said, "they've been breaking balls all day."

"Who?"

"Benny."

"Benny the wop?"

"Yeah. He's starting up with paper again."

He said nothing. I do not like it when he says nothing. It means he does not agree with me. I don't like a Hollywood yes man, but I do not want a kid of mine to disagree. I said don't give me no silent applesauce, Henry, I heard it all from Benny.

"Everybody and his cousin has converted to paper," he said.

"Not me."

"It's much more sanitary. The cartons are disposable."

"Tell me something I don't know."

"There's no danger of communicable disease."

"I boil my bottles in 220 Fahrenheit." I sat up in the bed, carefully watching my feet; Helga got wild with dirt on the bedspread. "What about the wax?" I said. "There's loose wax in all paper cartons."

"They'll overcome that. They're working on it." Expert.

"You'd want your baby to eat wax?"

He sighed.

"Don't sigh. Your mother sighs. Where's Margaret?"

"I don't know. Out somewhere."

"With the Arab?"

"He's Armenian."

"Arab, Armenian, is that who she's out with?"

"I don't know. I think so."

"That bastid is out for one thing; I know Arabs."

Again the accordion.

"Stop sighing."

"OK, OK. . . . You were the same way with homo, you know," he said.

"Don't bring up history. Homo is homo, paper is paper. Milk has to be seen. That's part of the pleasure. It is pure and looks pure. You ever hear the saying pure as the driven snow? That's milk. In glass. What're you reading in the *Times?*"

"Just current events."

"What do you want with current events? Stuyvesant was a math-science school."

"I don't go there anymore. I live in the world, don't I? I have to know about it, don't I? I have to understand what's happening, don't I?"

"What's happening? The wops are getting their ass beat in Africa and we're saving their ass."

"I wish you wouldn't say *we.*"

"What should I say? Thee? Thou? Are you ashamed of your grandfather and great-grandfather?"

"No. But these are Nazis you're talking about when you say we. These are evil people. They really are, Pop."

"Is that a fact?"

"You saw them beat up that guy in the Garden."

"He was a nut. It's all they understand."

"Fritz Kuhn is not a nut?"

"He forgot more than you'll ever know."

"Jesus H. Christ. Pop, read the papers will you. Stop, look and listen."

"Balls, Henry. You believe that crap? It's all b.s. propaganda so Roosevelt can get us in the war. I know the Roosevelts. You believe what Heatter and Hill and the rest of them b.s. artists tell you you'll wind up crazy. Like Frankie's vacuum in space."

"Jesus Pop, even Hess saw the light."

"If he's in England I'll kiss Churchill's ass in Macy's window."

His head swiveled on that no-neck. "Pop," he said quietly, "they do have concentration camps."

"Go back to school. The *limeys* got concentration camps. You're talkin about the Boer War."

"Oh for cryin out loud Pop, a Jew cannot be a professional man in Germany today. Everyone knows that. He can't own a business. He couldn't own this business if it was in Germany."

"Jews don't go in the milk business. They're too good."

"See? See? That's what I mean."

"What's what you mean?"

"That . . . attitude."

"What attitude? I stated a fact. Ask a Russian Jew about a German Jew, he'll tell you the same thing."

"That is an anti-Semitic statement."

"Don't hand me that crap."

"It *is*."

"Don't you tell me my own feelings."

"Well then just *look* at your feelings."

"I look plenty."

"Oh yeah, I'll bet."

"Some of my best friends are kikes."

He got up.

"Where you goin?"

"Downstairs. I want to finish the paper."

I swung out of bed. I put my hand on the kid's shoulder. "Come on," I said. "Whathehell are we fightin for? Don't be that way. Come on. Give me Mussolini."

Again the swivel and the sigh. "I don't feel like it, Pop."

"Come on."

"I'm not eleven, Pop."

"You did Mussolini when you were eighteen."

"Well I don't feel like it now."

"Henry, didn't we have a great time at the Olympics? Henry?"

"Yes, Pop."

"Wasn't Jesse Owens great?"

"Yes, Pop."

"I think he's the greatest runner in the world. And he's colored."

"OK, Pop."

"You wanna go again, Henry?"

"They were canceled. Last year was the year. They've been called off. There's a war on."

"It won't last forever. They'll start up again in forty-four. How about it?"

"I don't know . . . maybe, Pop."

He started for the door. Moppin up soda pop rickey started

for the door. "Henry," I said, "Can you still do 'Brother Can
You Spare a Dime'? Once I built a railroad, made it run, made
it race against time. Henry?"

"No."

"Sure you can. Once I built a tower to the sun." I held
out my clasped hands. "Brudder, can you spare a dime?"

Ah that golden sunlight through the clouds. The Henry
sunshine. Pure cream. "You won't budge on paper?" he said,

"Now I told you I wouldn't."

"I'll go to Ohio State."

"You're too old."

He grabbed me around the neck. I grabbed him.

"Al Capone," he said.

"Watch that. Make it Arthur Flegenheimer."

"Oh you con man."

We walked to the door, arm in arm, my kid and I.

"Hey do me a favor," I said. "Go down the place and check
on things."

"I thought Al was there."

"Al is Al. You're the boss's son. There's a world of difference. I don't wanna get stole blind. Here's the keys, take my
car."

"You trust me not to go down to Hester Street for lox and
bagels?"

"Vy not? You should eat and be healthy. Now get the hell
out of here."

He shot his fist out and clicked his heels. Fuckin wise-guy
kid. I should only have a dozen of them. Then he walked out.
Christ he forgot more about Mussolini than Jack Oakie ever
knew.

I went straight to sleep and did not have a single goddam
dream. When I woke up it was three o'clock. I put on my
shoes, smoothed out the bed, washed up and went downstairs.

Helga was in the kitchen. Margaret back yet? No. Henry? No.
I knew where Frank Joseph was, out in Regensburg, Ohio,
dreaming. Where are you going? Down the place. You were
there all morning. Well I'm goin again. Don't stay all day
and night, I'm not running a cafeteria. I never said you were.
And before she could answer I skipped into the hall, put on
my sheepskin lumberjacket and hurried outside to the pickup
truck. I got in and shoved the floor shift around and clashed
a few gears and drove down the place double-clutching all the
way, my hand on the stick like it was a live one's knee.

I parked on 97th Street, sat and looked at the place for a
good five minutes, then got out and walked around the back
to the platform. Gregory the day man was checking in a tank
with the driver. How much water they put in, Gregory?
None, they better not, Mr. Kleinhans. You tell em, Gregory.
I smacked him on the can and walked into the office. Henry
was there all right. And Al Fino. And so was Benny Martinelli.

"What's he doin here?" I said.

"Hello Willy," Benny said, "I was just talking to Henry
and Al."

"What's he doin here, Al?"

"Talkin. Like he said, Mr. K."

"We already talked." I looked at Henry. "What's goin on
behind my back?"

He gave it the eyeball roll. "Nothing Pop. Not a single
thing. We were just talking, that's all."

"That's right Willy," said Benny with a big smile. "After
all it *is* a free country."

"Don't tell me about this country, you swamp guinea. I
wanna know what you're doin here."

"Hey wait a minute, Willy. Now just watch your language——"

"I wanna know *whathehell is goin on behind my back.*"

Henry looked at Al.

"And I don't want looks!"

"Take it easy, Pop. We were talking about paper."

"I *told* you about paper. I told *him* about paper. I made that clear, Al. So what's he doin back here?"

"OK, Mr. K, OK. I didn't think there was no harm——"

"*You* didn't think. You're not sup*posed* to think. Thinking is my department." I turned to Henry. "Is this how you look out for things when I'm not here?"

"Oh forcrissake," he said.

"Some answer. *Some* answer."

Benny got up and smiled at Henry and Al. "It's all right, fellas." He smiled on me. "It's my fault. *I* came back. Al didn't tell me to. Or Henry. I just wanted to talk a little plain common sense to you. I didn't think you gave it enough chance. I thought you were here, that's all, Willy."

"We *talked*."

"I know we did. But you're not seeing this thing in perspective. You are gonna lose a lot of business, Willy. Now Willy, you are a lot of things, but stupid is not one of them." He gave me a Chaplin smile that hiked up his mustache, then he looked at Al. "This man," he said, "knows more about the milk business than Sheffield and Borden put together. You cut this man's wrists and he'll bleed milk."

"Shit me easy, Benny," I said.

"It's true. The truth is the truth. Plain and simple. That is why for the life of me I cannot understand you deliberately cutting your own throat. I just cannot understand it."

"You don't hafta understand it."

"But I *want* to, Willy, I *want* to."

I looked down at him. "I'll make you happy. First you pasteurize it. Then you homogenize it. Now you embalm it."

"We what?"

"Ask Armour. Ask Sinclair Lewis. And don't tell me about progress. I know all about progress."

He flipped eyes at Al; Al shrugged.

"Willy, you got it all wrong. We are *saving* the product. Pepsi-Cola and Coca-Cola and Mission Orange they're killing this product. We are saving it. It so happens, Willy, this *is* progress."

"I could put horseshit in those cartons. Who would know?"

"*You'd* know, Willy. You couldn't do it. Not in a million years."

"*I* wouldn't. But what about my competitors?"

He gave me Henry Armetta's shoulders. "It's just not realistic, Willy." He sprayed the area. "You fellas know that. Willy, *you* know that. Look." He whipped out his order pad and a pencil. "Look at this. Dairylea, twenty gross. Mueller's thirty five. Silvercrest fifteen and they're half your size." He started figuring. "Take a measly five thousand. I can get you a point off."

"No."

"Three thousand."

"No."

"A thousand."

"Stop tryin to Jew me down. The answer is no. N.O. It's been nice talkin to you."

He squeezed his shoulders inside all the padding and pulled his jacket down like it was a corset. He looked at Henry and Al and they looked back and he shook his head.

"You dago sonofabitch," I said, "with your looks. I'll give you looks." And I took a roundhouse swing at him. He flicked to one side and I staggered and almost went down. "Hey," he said, "you crazy in the head?" I straightened up. "I'll show you who's crazy, you spaghetti burner." I stepped in and swung again. He was a little mongoose. He ducked and ran behind the desk. "Now you cut that out, Willy. I don't like that." I went after him. "I don't give a good goddam what you like." And I got on my bicycle and he got on his and around we go, only now I am Canzoneri and he is Al Singer. "Hey, whatsamatter with this man? Hey, he's crazy. Hey this man wants to *kill* me."

All of a sudden my arms were locked in iron. And my neck. "Take it easy, Pop, take it *easy*." "Yeah, calm down, Mr. K."

Hell it took the two of them, full strength.

Benny stood out of range, breathing in and out like the Street Singer. He pointed a fat little finger at me.

"That man is . . . a . . . fuckin . . . *lunatic*!"

I broke away and lunged. He jumped like he was goosed, turned and rushed out the door. *"Lunatic,"* he yelled over his shoulder. Then it was quiet, with only the breathing. I leaned against the doorway trying to nail down my breath but it was just out of reach. I turned around and walked inside and plopped down on my chair. The fifth column was studying the wall. Finally Al said, "Well I hafta check up on Gregory," and without a single look he padded out. Henry glanced longingly after him, shook his head, then slumped down on the leather sofa. I finally pounced on a breath and caught it and then some more. I packed them all down hard and sat on them.

"Well?" I said.

"Well what?"

"You couldn't wait, could you?"

At the ceiling he looked, at the Sistine Chapel, head waggling.

"You're gonna get it all some day anyway," I said. "What's your hurry?"

"Ah hell Pop, will you stop it already?"

"A daughter who lets an Arab get away with who knows what. One son in dreamland. Another a double-dealer. Who used to be with me a hundred and ten percent. Some team I got now. Some loyal team."

"Ah shit."

"You work your ass off. You build something. Out of a couple of cows and a can of milk. Something solid and substantial. Willy, *du bist ferrickt.*"

"I'll never talk to him as long as I live. I'll never talk to anyone without written permission from you. OK?"

"They couldn't even beat the fuckin cannibals in Ethiopia. Now they're experts on milk. They don't even *drink* it."

"All right pop, I *heard* you."

"They drink guinea red all day."

"That's *enough.*"

He got up and threw my keys on the desk.

"Where you goin?"

"To jump off the Queensborough Bridge."

"Don't talk like that. I don't like you to talk like that."

He scooped his suede jacket off the chair, put it on and zipped up hard. "I'll see you," he said.

"Wait a minute."

He stopped and half turned. I got up and walked around the desk to him and held out my hand. He looked down at it. "Go on," I said, "it won't bite you. Go on. I'll forget it this time." He shook his head even while he was shaking my hand. "That is a damn poor fish," I said. He shook a little harder, not much; this was the same kid that would dive through the window and come up whistling "Yankee Doodle" for me. "OK," he said in that lately discovered voice, "I'll see you for supper."

"Hey," I said. He shifted. "Hey, how about goin out for a little ride?"

You would think I was Lepke. ". . . Where? . . ." he said.

"Hell anywhere. Like we used to. Over to Jersey. Staten Island to see Max and Vinny. It's a beautiful day. Come on, you can drive."

He just stood there considering the enormous proposition. For a rotten minute I thought he was going to say go to hell, in which case I would have to beat him up. But then, holding his mouth the way he did at six with the dislocated thumb, he sighed and said, "All right, let's go."

I had him drive through the park at 97th Street. . . . *Remember I used to hit you fungoes out here?* Yes. . . . *You could never play the sun till I showed you how to hold your glove against it?* Yes. . . . *I showed you how to hook slide right over there, you got as fancy as Ben Chapman.* Yes. . . . On Central Park West I said turn right and we drove north into Harlem. . . . *Joe Louis country; boy you stay out of here when he fights, they'll tip your car over.* Uh-huh. . . . *I'll never understand why Conn got cute, he could have had the title today, do you know?* Nope. . . . *Thick mick* . . . Turn left on 125th . . . *Father Divine owns half this. Boy there is one smart nigger. But don't look for him with the 10th Cavalry on Kettle Hill; Peace, brother.* Uh-huh. . . . *Let's take the ferry across, it's a great day for a ferry ride.* He shrugged and slid into line and drove onto the boat. . . . *C'mon, let's get out.* We got out and walked to the front of the boat and leaned against the wind. . . . *This is one great river.* . . . *Remember the Rhine?* Yes. . . . *Well this is just as impressive, isn't it?* Yes. . . . *And don't let anyone b.s. you about the Golden Gate, I'll take Mr. Washington's bridge right up there.* Mmmm. . . . *What do you think about a trip to California next summer?* Maybe. . . . *Well it can't be any better than this town, look at that view, isn't that something?* Yes. . . . *This is some town.* Yop. . . . The boat edged into the pilings, we got back in the car and I had him drive out and up through the Palisades to Fort Lee. . . . *Boy now you can really see it, with the sun shining on the buildings, but keep your eye on the road.* Uh-huh. *Go left on 23, I'll show you a few things.* He turned west and we drove through the woods and hills of Jersey. . . . *Mayor Hague owns half this; he's a bigger thief than Jimmy Walker, but he gets*

the graveyard vote out so Roosevelt takes care of him. Uh-huh.
*. . . And they say Hauptmann was a criminal. . . . They should
have followed through on Irving Bitz and Salvatore Spitale,
they would have taken the G-men straight to the Black Hand.*
Mmmm. *. . . Jafsee was sick in the head.* Mmmm. *. . . So was
O'Brien.* Mmmm. *. . . Willentz was out for blood, and don't
say I'm prejudiced.* OK. *. . . Joe Louis trains out here in
Pompton Lakes . . . Schmeling could have finished him in
five, but carried him . . . Baer was a national disgrace . . .
Tami Mauriello was a goddam cripple, could only go forward
. . . Smell that? That's rubber, from Butler, one of the biggest
rubber plants in the world. They get the latex from South
America, they slash the trees like for a rattler bite and collect
the sap in buckets and boil it and make balls of rubber and
ship it up here. . . . They say ersatz rubber is almost as good,
don't you believe it. . . . That is Bomba the Jungle Boy country
down there, Frankie was in love with Bomba, but you stuck
to Tarzan. . . . There was no comparison. . . . Vinny spent six
months in that C.C.C. camp. Just to build himself up. . . .
He's still not as tall as you, is he?* Just about. *. . . I don't think
so, you slouch too much, we won't drive to Staten Island, it's
too late. . . . Paterson is over that way. . . . It's the silk capital
of the world. . . . The Japs grow the worm, but naturally we
make the finished product.* Uh-huh. *. . . The worm spits the
silk out of his mouth and makes a cocoon and wraps up in it.
Then he turns into a butterfly. He's no good for anything
after that.* Uh-huh. *. . . Rayon will never replace silk. . . . I'd
never bail out in a rayon parachute if they gave me a million
dollars, would you?* Nope. *. . . Your grandfather worked like
a slave to start Farmbest and just for one thing, his kid. And
I'm doing the same.* All right. *. . . There's just one thing that
he asked and it's all I ask and that is loyalty; it's the only thing
that counts; without it we're all goners. . . . You understand
that, Henry?* Yop. *. . . .*

We drove back to New York. Me staring out my window. Him hunched over the wheel.

It was eight o'clock by the time we reached the house and parked. *Your mother's gonna kill us, well I'll take the full blame.* Gary Cooper said nothing, not even nope. OK, so we walked into the house. Helga was sitting on the couch. And so was Eloise the girl.

"Hello Eloise," I said. "I kept us out," I said to Helga. "It was my fault."

She got up. For a minute there I thought she had on her Edna Wallace Hopper's White Youth Pack. She did not; she was just pale.

"Take your jackets off," she said.

We took them off and hung them up.

"Sit down."

We sat down.

"All right," she said to Eloise the girl.

Very thin, very tight, she folded her hands on her lap and looked straight ahead and said, "I'm pregnant. He is the father." And she unfolded and pointed a long finger at Henry. Then she refolded. He turned red, hot and blue.

"Well?" said Helga. "Well, is she right?"

His eyes suddenly filmed over. I had not seen that since he was five, not even with the snapped-in thumb. I was damned if he was going to cry now, in front of the whole wide world.

"Wait a second," I said. "*Just a second.* What is this, a lynch mob?"

"I don't want any smart remarks," said Helga. "I want to know if what she says is true. You keep still."

"Like hell. She just can't walk in here, point a goddam finger and——"

"Is she right, Henry?"

"You don't have to answer that, Henry. You don't have to say a goddam thing. You're not on the witness stand."

"Henry?"

"Hell, a half a dozen guys could have banged her. Al Fino is always screwin around with her."

"They didn't," said Eloise the girl. "Al didn't. He did."

"Henry, you keep your mouth shut. Look," I said in a very nice way to her, "how much do you need? I'll let you have whatever you need."

"Drop dead."

"She's right," said Henry. He studied the floor.

"Howinhell do *you* know? Will you keep quiet and let me handle this?"

"She's right."

Helga got even whiter. She walked over to him, picked up his chin and for a terrific moment I thought she was going to crack him; I could feel it down to my toes. She did not. She said, "I never told you to do this or do that, you always did whatever you wanted and your father let you get away with murder and I never said a word, *but you don't shit in your own front yard.*"

"Helga!"

I jumped up and ran and grabbed her and wrestled her away before she did something stupid in front of an outsider. She jerked her arms loose and said aach and walked across the room and sat down and looked out the window.

"Jesus," I said, patting the air, "don't get so cockeited." She looked briefly at me, then back to the window. If looks could kill. "Now," I said, "let's just look at this calmly. OK? OK." I walked over to Eloise the girl, pulled up a chair and sat down next to her. "Are you sure?"

She almost laughed in my face. "Of course I'm sure."

"What about your family? Do they know?"

"She doesn't have a family," said Henry in his concentration camp voice.

"OK," I said quickly, "I believe you. Now. I said I'd give

you whatever you need. You said no. OK. I'll play it any way
you want. You go somewhere and I'll take care of everything."
    "I want him to marry me."
    "I knew it," said Helga.
    "Oh no, Eloise," I said. "No ma'am. That is the one thing
he doesn't do. Anything else within reason I'll go along. But
not that."
    She got up, very prim, very proper. She wasn't even bulg-
ing yet. Where a kid could maneuver in all those sharp angles
I'd never know, but that was his problem. She walked to
Henry. "That's what I want," she said, looking down at him,
"and that's what you said before you got cold feet." He rubbed
the back of his neck. I began to get pins and needles. He had
concentration camps on the brain; last week he had lectured
me on Georgia chain gangs for fifteen minutes. He looked up
at her. I said very fast, "Henry, this time I mean it. You keep
your mouth shut." He looked at me. "Eloise," I said, "you
know that's out."
    "I'll kill myself," she said.
    He got up. "Jesus Christ," he said and started to walk
around the table. "Je-sus Christ." He kept walking and Christ-
ing and her eyes followed him every inch of the way. I knew
those eyes; they were smelling a win. I got up. I walked to
him. I grabbed him and twisted him around.
    "You got yourself into this pickle," I said, "and Jesus Christ
ain't gonna get you out. Now be a man, goddammit!" I then
looked sweetly at her. "How do you wanna do it? You want
my car keys? You drive around the back into the garage, close
the door and pull up all the windows. Just keep the motor
running." I took the keys out of my pocket and threw them
on the table. She stared at them. "How about some rat
poison?" I said. She looked up at me. "Henry, go upstairs
and get my gun."

"Pop . . ."

"Go get it!"

Head down, massaging his neck, he walked out and upstairs. I folded my arms; she got her tough look, the one she gave salesmen; Helga sat in a solid bunch. He came back down holding my .38 by the barrel. He gave it to me. I took it and flipped it, catching it by the barrel. I held it out to her. She looked hard at it. "Go on," I said. She reached out and took it with two fingers, then held it out away from her like a live snake. Then she dropped it; it's a good thing the safety was on. I picked it up and shoved it into my belt. "OK," I said, hooking my belt with my thumbs, "so much for the bullshit. Now," and I took her arm, "you sit right here." I walked her to the table and sat her down. "Helga, you make some coffee. Henry, you sit here with Eloise and see she's OK."

Everybody moved.

I walked out to the kitchen with Helga and whispered make it good and strong. Then I got on the phone and called Weinmeister. I got him in . . . I have to talk to you, Klaus, this is very important . . . I don't give a *shit* about Pearl Harbor, I got a real problem, now listen to me. . . . That's right. . . . Yeah . . . I know you don't do anything like that, I'm asking you who *does*. . . . The *hell* with your license; you wanna keep my place? I can give it to ten other doctors, they're dyin for the job. . . . Yeah. . . . Yeah. . . . I jotted down the number. . . . All right, you call him and tell him about me, but don't use my name. Tell him I can take care of him. Tell him tonight. . . . That's right, to*night*. Don't give me any bullshit, they do it for appendicitis. Then call me back and I'll talk to him. . . . OK, thanks, Klaus, I won't forget it.

I hung up and smiled at Helga who was *really* looking at me.

"Here Willy," she said, "drink your coffee."

She ranted and raved. I let her. Then I said there's no other
way is there? And at last she started to cry. I let her get it
out of her system and Henry held her hand and patted it
and Helga made her drink more coffee and eat some cake.
Finally she swallowed the sobs, drew herself up and said all
right, let's get it over with. Now you're talkin, I said: I'll say
one thing, she had more guts than General Kent.

Helga insisted on coming along. Well why not? A half an
hour later the four of us were driving downtown on Second
Avenue. The traffic wasn't too bad and I was down at the Man-
hattan Bridge in two shakes. I crossed over the bridge into
Brooklyn and then down Flatbush Avenue Extension past the
Brooklyn Paramount which was showing *Hearts Divided* with
Dick Powell which was a put-up job as it was about Napoleon
instead of Flirtation Walk. I found a parking spot near Atlantic
Avenue. I said now you stay here, I'll be back as soon as I know
what's what.

I got out and walked into the Long Island Railroad Station.
It was eleven o'clock on the dot, as per orders. Two winos were
asleep on a bench. A dozen or so people were sitting around
like people do in stations. A few were wandering through, including a cop who tapped the winos on the soles of their feet
and as they came up mumbling, told them to beat it. I looked
at the clock, took my hat off and put it on, then took it off and
put it on again. I went through the routine three times and I
was going to call Weinmeister when one of the wanderers on
the other side of the station took his hat off and put it back
on. So did I. So did he. I walked slowly across the station. He
took out a timetable and began to study it, meanwhile looking up and down at the clock. When I came up alongside I
faced in one direction and out of the other side of my mouth
said, "Are you Charlie?"

"Charlie who?" he whispered.

"I don't know. They didn't tell me."

"Well I don't know if I'm Charlie."

"You goddam well better know."

"Well if I am Charlie, do you have the money?"

"If you're Charlie, I got the money."

". . . Where are you parked?"

"Around the corner from Atlantic Avenue."

"OK. I'll take a chance on you. I'm two blocks away. A blue '37 Olds. I'll drive around the block. When you see me, pull out and follow me."

"No. I get in with you. Somebody else will drive my car."

". . . The girl?"

"Never mind."

"What is this anyway?"

"This is the way we're doin it, Charlie."

"Doctor X won't like it."

"Fuck Doctor X. I got a .38 in my pocket."

"Are you a cop?"

"Don't be stupid. Let's go."

"You sure you got the money?"

"You want me to show it to you right here?"

"Shit, no."

"All right then, let's go."

He looked up at the clock and set his wristwatch and said out loud, "Harry couldn't make it but said to go ahead and start without him." And we walked out. He kept pointing at the timetable and said no, no, the heavy type is P.M., you have to change at Jamaica, but if you take the Hempstead train get off at Stewart Manor and the track is right there, only coming back, get off at Floral Park. He was some actor. Then we were outside and walking casually to my car. He looked around at the buildings while I leaned in and told Henry to drive and follow us in a blue '37 Olds which would be coming around in a minute. He patted Eloise the girl's hand and nodded. I turned around and walked back to Charlie who said I think it's that way, Lou, and together we walked calmly down Atlantic and around the corner.

"That's a goddam army you got there," he said.

"Don't worry about it," I said. "Is that your car?"

"Yeah. Doctor X is just expecting you and the girl."

"She got a big family and they're all concerned. Get in."

"You sure you got the money?"

"Get in."

Shaking his head and smiling, his Oscar performance, he got in. I held the door and hopped in beside him. "OK," I said, "around the corner and in front of my car. When I say all right, you take off, but if I say wait, double park and wait till he catches up and when we take off you better not lose him, understand?"

"Yeah. Shit."

He started the car and drove slowly around the block and past Henry. "Stick out your hand," I said, "and wave him out." He did. I looked in the mirror and saw Henry pull into the traffic. "OK, go ahead, but don't lose him." "Jesus," he said, "I heard you the first time." And keeping at an even thirty we drove through out through Brooklyn. I recognized Red Hook and Greenpoint, we had a good route in Greenpoint. On Driggs Avenue he said, "Doctor X is a terrific guy."

"Is that right?"

"Yeah. If he was in politics he would be president of the United States."

"He's a bright man."

"Bright bullshit. He's *brill*iant. And a million-dollar personality to go with it."

"Why does he do this?"

"What business you in?"

"Milk."

"You like it?"

"Sure."

"Well he likes his business."

I said I can understand that and we continued on through Pete McGuinness's town. With Henry keeping two car lengths behind. Even down by the refineries, where it was practically deserted, he kept his distance. He was doing a darn fine job, considering.

"Does he know his onions?" I said.

"Are you serious? He's a fuckin artist with the knife. I been with him twenty years and in all that time he only lost one client and she was half gone when she came in. He only took her as a personal favor to a very big man in Albany. If I told you who it was you'd faint."

"He's well known in his field?"

"You ask the biggest cunt men in Hollywood about Doctor X. They'll tell you."

"Well that's just fine," I said.

We crossed into Williamsburg and through the rabbi section. On the other side of it he drove around the same block three times. Then he stopped. He waved Henry on ahead. Henry parked a few houses up.

"Go get her," he said. "But just the girl. Not the whole *mishbooka*."

"*You* get her."

"Gee you'd think I was a common thief."

"Go on, Charlie."

Still belittling, he got out and walked to my car and stuck his head in the window. Then Eloise the girl got out and they walked back toward me. What an actor. He started weaving all over the place like a drunk Leon Errol; she had to hold him up. As soon as they staggered past the Olds I got out and followed them. He clutched her arm and leaned on her, but all the time he was bearing towards a tenement that was even

dirtier than the others on the block. They made it up the
steps and I walked in after them. It smelled of cats and baby
carriages and piss and was lit by a bulb down the hall and
the mailboxes were hanging open.

"I don't like this," she said.

"Don't worry," he said. "This is just the outside."

He pressed a bell three times, then twice, and without waiting for an answer pushed in the door which was unlocked. We
followed him and walked up three flights, then down another
hall to a back door every bit as *shmutzik* as the ones downstairs. Charlie took out a key and let us in. We walked through
another flaking, streaked hallway into a kind of waiting room.
I could tell that is what it was from the worn leather chairs, the
worn end table and the dog-eared *Lifes* and *National Geo-
graphics* on the table.

"Just make yourselfs comftable," he said and disappeared
through a gray door. Eloise the girl said Willy I don't like this
and I replied let's just give it a chance, OK? and at that moment Charlie came back. With him was a small, white-haired
fellow in a white coat who looked like he was born scrubbed
and clean, like Timmy Kidmesty in the 71st who always won
the soldier-of-the-month award.

"This is Doctor X," said Charlie.

The doctor held out a gloved hand; it looked like he had
on five Trojans, but he did not. I shook it. The hand felt
pretty mushy for his line of work. He turned to Eloise the
girl.

"Ah," he said, "Miss Sanger."

"That's not her name," I said.

"I call all my patients Miss Sanger," he said, "as a tribute to
the concept of family planning."

She gave me a look and I nodded. "Can we get started?" I
said.

"Of course. May I have my retainer?"

I took out the envelope. It held a cool two hundred. I gave it to him and he slid it into his back pants pocket.

"Aren't you goin to count it?" I said.

"Of course not. Your references are impeccable."

"See? See?" said Charlie.

"Now just make yourself comfortable, Mr. Jones," said the doctor, "and we'll get on about our chores."

"All right," I said.

"Charlie?" And he took her by the arm.

"Hey," I said, "is he goin in there?"

"Of course. Charlie is my right-hand man."

"Willy . . . ," she said.

"Ixnay with the amenay. You just go on in there with the doctor. Everything is gonna be all right."

"You sonofabitch," she said.

I smiled at Doctor X. "She is a little upset," I said.

"And understandably so." He looked at her. "You have been used and abused. Your innermost self, that sacred being in all of us, has been violated. Of course you're upset."

She stared at him.

"Come along, my dear."

He offered her his arm. She took it and like they were going to the class reunion they walked through the door, with Charlie bringing up the rear. I sat down and picked up a 1938 *Life*.

She was through in twenty-five minutes. Charlie on one side, Doctor X on the other. She looked a little woozy.

"She's just fine," said the doc. "She was a real little trooper." And he patted her hand. She nodded weakly. "Let her stay in bed tomorrow and give her one of these before each meal." He gave me a bottle of pills. "Just finish this bottle and she'll be

as good as new." He held out his hand; he still had on the
Trojans. I shook them. "Good-bye and good luck, Mr. Jones."

"A great man," breathed Charlie.

Eloise the girl was now leaning hard against me. "You OK,
girlie?" I said.

"I . . . think so."

"Of course she is," said Doctor X. "Her personal self has
been wounded, that has been the principal damage. But with
an understanding of the situation, that too will heal."

"That sonofabitch will never touch me again," she whispered.

"I'll take it from here," I said quickly.

"I'll help you," said Charlie.

"No, it's OK, I don't need any help. It's *OK*."

"Miss Sanger," said the doctor, "aren't you going to kiss me
good-bye?"

She stirred; I held her back and considered. After all here
she was all scooped clean of trouble and complications and
Henry and Helga had been giving me their old-time looks.

"She ain't gonna kiss you," I said, "but I am." And I
grabbed him and planted a big smack on his forehead.

"Why thank you, Mr. Jones," he said with a grin. "You are
experiencing a great catharsis and a sense of control, but it is
still very kind of you."

"Yeah yeah," I said. "Well so long now, don't do anything
I wouldn't do."

He bowed. I walked us to the door and through it and down
the three flights of stairs. The street didn't look quite so bad
as we walked back to my car. Henry jumped out and helped
her in.

"Henry," I said, "you stay in back with her. Helga, you
sit up front with me."

They hurried into position. I started the car. "There's a

great chink's on Fulton Avenue," I said, "we're gonna stop there, yours truly is starved."

Well she stayed out the one day. Sure enough, the day after, she came back to work, a little pale maybe, but just as efficient and grouchy as ever. In a family council I called, Helga pleaded with me to get rid of her, but I said, are you crazy? she has got to stay, we *owe* her that. Henry came into my room that night and silently shook my hand. I told him I was going to give her a raise starting next week and he filmed over; I did not tell him I was already trying to fix her up with Jack McTurk's kid, a no-good banjo player. It never worked out and she stayed with us eight more years until she walked in one day and said I'm going to Arizona, I'm sick and tired of New York. What I did tell him was OK now, you just keep it in your pants where she is concerned, you hear? Don't worry, Pop, he said, I have learned my lesson where they are *all* concerned. Well, I said, have your fun but just keep yourself covered, you know? I know, he said, with a pre-b.s. smile. And he was as good as his word. From then on he was nothing but polite around her, although frankly I am not so sure he could even have gotten a smell after her session with the doc who I would hire as a route manager any day in the week. And he never said another word about paper; I held out till '47 when I took it in his memory, and not because Benny and the Mafia were leaning on me. What a kid! What a day!

Joe Joe DiMaggio
we want you on our side.

X X

The Real McCoy

WHEN MY FATHER used to send me out for a pail of beer, he would always say run like hell and stay in the shade. Well that is exactly what I did on the afternoon I charged back to the war. In that return to duty and honor my body bossed itself and became my personal machete, slashing me through the jungle toward the thud of the big babies, the pop and hiss and zing of the rifles and the tat tat tat of the coffee grinders that stitched the battle together. I was filled with remorse and the overpowering urge to make up for lost time as I headed post haste for where my sense told me Bloody Ford should be, not that any part of me had any exact idea where that was. I just kept on running toward the action, as if it had tossed out a giant lariat and was pulling me in. I bounced off trees like a ball of latex and I fell down and once thocked myself so hard with my rifle butt that I saw a star-spangled sky, but I rolled over and up onto my feet and kept going. I kept going until I saw the fresh gleam of water.

When I saw that I yelled for pure joy; I broke out of the

jungle onto what had to be the San Juan River. I mean I knew that subsequently, as Andy always said, but right then I just knew it meant the Spanish-American War. Even though the war itself was not yet accounted for, being somewhat up ahead, beyond the curve of the river. Tingling, hurting, yearning, wishing, dreading, thrusting, I stepped in, not knowing if I would flounder, sink in quicksand, drown or do all three. Well Mama and Papa were still watching out for their sonny boy, for I sank only to my knees and then, happily, I was kicking and splashing up to the bend and around it, directly under the zinging lead that was crisscrossing the water like hot telegraph wires.

Our boys were sure enough fording the river up there, in a place wider and less red than old Bloody, but plenty active in its own right. I kicked through to join them. When I drew nigh I was mildly surprised to recognize absolutely no one, so as I splashed alongside a serious doughboy I asked who he was with. The 16th, he spit out, without turning his head. Well whatayou know? I had completely outflanked my outfit and had found the rest of the brigade under General Hawkins and they were far out in front which was just Jim Dandy with me! I asked no more questions, I just ducked under the incoming fire and splashed high for the shore. Just in front of me a trooper gamely dragged a bleeding leg after him, leaving behind a swirl of red water. On the far bank two bodies lay in the water, one facing the Spanish, one twisted back with the head half in the river as if he was drinking, but never more in this world would slaking coolness run down that bent throat.

Then I was up and over the bank. Once more to find myself in the fine agony of confusion and death. Officers and noncoms yelling orders and charging about trying desperately to form us up, crumpled bodies, frozen into ragdoll sleep. All of it under a sheet of fire that was heavier even than

Bloody Ford. Remembering the dirty deal my legs had pulled, I looked down and checked: They were holding their ground, gripping it, even with every reason to break my previous record in the hundred.

I looked calmly around. We had a bit of cover, several bamboo trees and a second bank that had been cut at high tide and troopers were crowding into both. The Spaniard of course smelled out our pickle and zeroed in on the area and in no time at all it had earned its nickname of Hell's Pocket. The book, Wellington, Weygand and Toral knew we could not possibly break onto the plain and take out for the dago safe and snug on his hill.

The hell with all that!

Even as we hunkered down and bodies folded and the book spelled out its history lesson, an American officer leaped up out of our pitiful cover and stood straight and clean against the sunlight. Obviously he couldn't read or know history or take orders. In one hand the fool waved a sword, in the other a pistol. His name rippled through us. Not Roosevelt. Not Wood. But something close to "Ought." Who? I asked the fellow beside me. *Ord,* the crazy sonofabitch, he said with a smile before he went down. And then I recognized him. Heck, our quartermaster, a shavetail, Lieutenant Ord, a pleasant young fellow, a nice young fellow, suddenly a great, splendid fool.

"Come on! Come on!" he yelled. "We can't sit here all day!"

And he turned and charged!

When I heard that voice and saw that man go, every muscle in me erupted, like I was San Francisco and this was '03. By the time I came down I was outside our cover and eating up the ground between us. And at that moment I was aware that the plain on all sides was also erupting and the stupid, il- literate doughboys were following us across that flatness, hell-bent for the foot of San Juan Hill. All about me boys were dropping, but I—and the rest— kept charging, the hell with the hedgerow zigzag, 'twas a straight line for the enemy. As luck— or Henry—would have it, no lead had my name on it and I hit the hill right behind the glorious Ord and started up on his heels. Suddenly it was quiet and someone yelled out, holy shit, they're on the real crest! By God yes, they had no angle on us from up there at the top! Had they been down on the military crest, some thirty feet below, we'd have been dead meat. Well the book did not tell you to fight the dumb dago.

Filled with this knowledge, I dug into the hill like my shoes were spades. I thrust dirt and scrub grass and rock back under me and away and before I had time to think of the great thing we had done, I was up at the military crest. With the top of the hill just thirty feet up. I saw garlics jumping out of their trenches and lighting out for Santiago. Others, either ringers or blind deaf mutes, stood their ground; too bad for them.

I pulled my spilling-over self together for the final charge into the history books. As I did I saw the lieutenant take a flying leap over their first trench; he was spread-eagled against the sunlight, like Luz Long in the Berlin Olympics. Alas he set no record. Or could he beat Jesse Owens. At the peak of his jump he stiffened and then lost all control, like a bird pierced on the wing. While we watched, helpless, he crumpled and dropped, his hat fluttering down after him like a broken feather. All was silent; even the Gatlings were quiet. Then with a great, terrible roar two other boys and I dashed forward up to the crest to our leader.

'Twas too late; he was twisted into the sleep of heroes.

A high, endless keening beat around me. I looked back. The screaming troops were leaping for the trenches, shooting point-blank, thrusting bayonets and madly clubbing. The enemy's face was a flash of terror and wonder as he dropped. The lucky ones, with loaded pants, barely made it back to their lines. Standing there, astride their trench, breathing like a great bellows, I could make out the red tiled roofs of the city. Then I looked down. Ord and his murderer lay side by side.

Suribachi. Balaklava. King Mountain. San Juan. The book said it could not be done, so did the watching world, so did the experts, so did "they." Well we had done it. Ord and the 6th and the 16th and truly yours. Not the Rough Riders. Not Teddy bear. Not all the ink in China. Jules Ord never became governor or president, he never became anything but Flanders Field where poppies grow, between the crosses row on row.

Yes, but Daddy, did the Rough Riders do *any*thing in the great war? Sure they did. When the 10th Cavalry under Pershing took Kettle Hill, they were their white auxiliaries.

OK, Henry?

X X I

An American Hero

ARTHUR MACARTHUR WAS BORN ON June 2, 1845, in Chicopee Falls, Massachusetts. His father, Arthur, was a lawyer and a judge and a lieutenant governor of Wisconsin, where the family had moved after young Arthur's birth. He was educated in the public schools of Milwaukee and grew up with the beer industry. He learned democracy firsthand. In 1862, at the age of seventeen, he was commissioned a first lieutenant in the 24th Wisconsin Volunteer Infantry, having strained for service during the intervening year. By the time he was twenty he had been promoted to colonel, a spectacular rise even in those days of instant promotion. His regiment gained fame in Phil Sheridan's division and Arthur became known as the Boy Colonel of the West. He was wounded three times, brevetted four times and cited for gallant and meritorious service at Perryville, Stone's River, Missionary Ridge, Pesaca, Dalton, Jonesboro, Kenesaw Mountain, Atlanta and Franklin. He was awarded the Medal of Honor for seizing the regimental colors at a crucial moment and planting them on the captured crest of Missionary Ridge. At the war's end he entered the regular army since he had shown such an affinity for military life and for twenty years fought in the Indian campaigns of the Southwest. He was married in that period and fathered two sons, Douglas and Arthur. The former, an army brat all the way, was born in 1880 and graduated West Point at the head of his class in 1903 although his mother lived outside the gate. He saw duty in the Philippines and the Far East, including Korea, all of which served him in good stead after firing on the Bonus marchers. The other son went into the navy. When the Spanish-American War broke out, MacArthur was appointed a brigadier general and as Shafter had Cuba, Miles Porto Rico, he was assigned to the Philippines command. His brigade was instrumental in capturing Manila, thereby fulfilling his pledge to return. He was again cited for gallant and conspicuous service. When the Huk rebellion broke out, he was a major general and commanded the main column that defeated the insurgents. He moved up to the command of the 8th Army Corps, then the Army of the Philippines and finally became military governor. In that capacity he laid the foundation of a modern and democratic Japan, introducing writ of habeus corpus, establishing a free public school system and revising ancient dago law. During the Russo-Japanese War he was a special observer and very helpful to Roosevelt who won the Nobel Prize and later used his knowledge when we went to war. He became a lieutenant general and senior officer of the army in 1906. He retired in 1909 and thereupon became commander of the Loyal Legion. On September 5, 1912, MacArthur attended a regimental reunion and as he addressed his old comrades he dropped dead, a patriot to the end. They wrapped him in an American flag.

Brandeis was Wilson's payoff to Barny Baruch. Baron Von Cramm was the only one of her husbands who could handle

Barbara Hutton. But his tennis game went to hell. Judge Crater was bumped off by Mussolini along with Carlo Tresca. He knew too much. Kayo slept in a drawer. Judd Gray was some sucker. So was Albert Snyder. If Helga and Arturo conspired to knock me off neither would have lived to tell the tale. Wall Street laid some egg. Tommy Manville was only married to seven women. He married number four twice. *The American Weekly* was our reading habit. Puck said what fools these mortals be. Margaret liked peculiar fellows beside the Arab. Gable Goldberg and Tod Winoker to name just two. Pilsud could have played Humphrey Van Weyden in the *Seawolf* as he was also a fag. But all the Anacin in the world would not have helped Wolf Larsen's headaches. Kenesaw Mountain Landis was named after one of MacArthur's victories. He and Carole Landis are not related. He did not save baseball, the Babe did. Cincy would have taken the Black Sox dive or no dive and Arnold Rothstein knew it. Go see *Greed*. Attorney General Mitchell, no relation to Billy, took care of all the bolshies. The first time my father caught me jerking off he beat me black and blue and I never did it again and neither did Henry. But he never had to as he was getting plenty. Frank Joseph never jerked off in his life. Jay Berwanger, a kraut, won the first Heisman trophy. Then Chicago discontinued football. Draw your own conclusions. I knew that Orson Welles broadcast was bullshit and I told Helga so as she shivered in the kitchen. But she nevermore made Campbell's soup. When Albie Booth, Larry Kelly or Clint Frank had a big day, Henry would sing *Bulldog, Bulldog, bow* wow wow, E-li Yale. It was written by Cole Porter. That was his real name. I like "On Brave Old Army Team." I trained Margaret very early to swim the English Channel but she couldn't even do the dead man's float. Frank Joseph was in love with King Kong Klein. I liked Pudge Hefflefinger. So did Walter Camp. You cannot tell me Amelia

Earhart and Wiley Post are not shacking up somewhere in Pango Pango. Everybody in Chicago got knocked off except Johnny Torrio. He was one smart wop. Max's wife Clara went around saying day by day in every way I'm getting better and better. When you asked her how she felt she said terrible melancholy. Darrow made a monkey out of Bryan. But he should not have taken Leopold Loeb. They should have strung them both up by the balls except they had none. You're wondering why Eddie Robinson kept washing his hands in 5 Star Final. It's because the character was based on Pulitzer. Lefty Gomez was the one good dago. He liked to watch airplanes. Flint Rehm was a fuckin screwball. Hubbell's arm was a pretzel. Dempsey wore patent leather shoes in the shipyard. But Tunney did all the dancing. Muni Weisenfreund wrote *I Accuse* because they always stick together. Harding thought he was the Prince of Wales. But Nan Britton was no Lola Montez. It is my considered judgment that my brother Rudy is the Unknown Soldier. Helga was crazy about *Myrt and Marge*. Also *Helen Trent*. Just a little love a little kiss, just an hour that brings a world of bliss. But Drew Sinclair, the noted director, was a prick for screwing around with Helen while his wife was in the funny farm. I made Frank Joseph join the Boy Scouts and worked like a slave with him on the Beaver Patrol cheer, but he could never remember it. Herman Brix was a great shotputter. The *Graphic* was a b.s. paper, but not the *Mirror*. If you think Roosevelt is dead you're crazy. *No* one ever saw his body. All these years he's been in the looney bin, as cuckoo as Drew Sinclair's wife. Arthur MacArthur was idolized.

> Elamem
> Elamem
> Elamem diego, san diego
> Ish kiddy boom boom
> Ice kiddy I sky

Chicka boom bah
Teddy roo one two
Teddy rah one two
Teddy rubby dubby, flubby dubby
Sis Boom bah
Beavers Beavers
Rah Rah Rah!

XXII

A Busted Cherry

I WAS DRIVING THROUGH the Holland Tunnel in 1937 which is a giant latrine under the North River on my way to visit my brother Max socially since I hadn't seen him in two months and as usual when away from the business I was worrying about Frank Joseph and his future when I started to look around and to think. I thought: Holland. And Goethals. And Roebling. And Hoover. And W. Kleinhans digging straight, smooth canals. And Frankie and his clay; when I forgot to bring it home when he was sick with the grippe he'd cry like a shell-shocked soldier.

Engineering

With that settled, I drove over to Max and had a nice visit with him and his foreman Lupowiscz and then drove back to Manhattan and straight down to Kleich's Toys and Sporting Goods on 14th Street. After batting the breeze with Herman, whose father was great bunkies with my father, and testing the pocket of a Goose Goslin glove and smelling it, for I love the smell of freshly oiled leather, I bought a senior Erector Set that contained an inspirational guide book and directions by A. C. Gilbert, inventor and developer of Erectors and a Bulldog Bow wow wow and a self-made man. Then over to the place and home.

That night after supper I went upstairs with the set for a nice fireside chat with Frank Joseph who was now sixteen and a half and simply had to make some basic decisions. Henry was all set. Margaret was a girl. But Frank just had to straighten out; there was no two ways about it. After having had several talks with Mrs. Illowhite, I was much better attuned to his delicate internal machinery, which apparently was like a good link conveyor belt, so I hit him very easy. Even so, he got his glazed cobra look even though I carefully avoided the mongoose weave, and when I was finished his head was waving gently like there was a wind in the house, and I said softly well then, what do you think?

"You mean about what you just said?"

"Yes. Now what did I just say, Frankie?"

"Well, then, what do I think?"

"No. The *thing* about which what you think."

". . . You know an engineer . . ."

"Not exactly, Frankie. Although I have known a few in my time. What I want to know is what do you think about becoming an engineer?"

"What do *I* think?"

"Yes."

"I don't know."

"You like clay, Frankie."

"He was a great compromiser."

"It, Frank, it. There's no compromise here. You're an engineer or you're not. Hoover was an engineer."

"Before he caught Dillinger?"

"That's right. *I* think you also have the stuff. But I want you to prove it to yourself."

And I picked up the Erector Set and handed it to him. He looked at it. "Go on, it's yours," I said. He took it onto his lap and sat very straight and stared down at it. "Now," I said, "you take your own sweet time. Look through the book of directions at the different bridges and buildings and things and read what A. C. Gilbert has to say because he knows his onions, and then you can build whatever you want. I won't say a word. OK, Frank?"

". . . You want me to build a bridge?"

"Only if you want to, sonny. You can build the Chrysler Building or the Taj Mahal if you want."

With that I patted him on the back and got up and left and went downstairs in time for Chandu the Magician.

I left him completely alone. Just as Illowhite had said. No pressure, no push, no pull. I wanted to let him mull it over and make the decision strictly on his own hook, although I was on pins and needles (and I don't mean the commie play) to see what he would come up with. At fourteen Sonny Schroeder had made an Ivory soap carving of the League of Nations in Geneva and I never heard the end of it. I stayed out of the picture for a good two weeks. I was getting darn edgy and I was gritting my teeth for a third; that Friday Eloise the girl buzzed and said the high school was on the line. I swept up the phone. "What's wrong?" I said.

"Is this Mr. Kleinhans?"

"Yeah. What's the matter?"

"The father of Frank Joseph?"

"Yeah, yeah, what's he done?"

"Oh dear, Mr. Kleinhans, oh no, this is Mrs. Illowhite."

"Yeah? What's wrong?"

"Why is it that whenever the school calls, you people always think something is wrong?"

"Because there always is. What is it this time?"

"This time it's something different."

"What's he done? Or what hasn't he done?"

"Mr. Kleinhans, I must tell you I'm delighted. Absolutely delighted."

". . . About Frankie?"

"Yes, about Frank."

"Has he written some more poems?"

"No. Not just now. Although he's written some good ones since we last talked. He did one on the wind——"

"What? What?"

"Take a guess, Mr. Kleinhans."

"What?"

"Take a little guess."

"Jesus, Mrs. Illowhite, I can't. Come on, what is it?"

"Try."

"Oh Jesus. I don't know. He made a speech."

"Oh no. That's nothing new."

"Please, Mrs. Illowhite. What?"

"All right. He's taken up pole vaulting."

". . . What do you mean?"

"Just what I said. He told me yesterday. I saw him climbing an imaginary rope in class, like those darling little Indian boys? I asked him, just in fun you know, was he a swami? He said no, a pole vaulter. I let him continue to climb, but the very next period I asked Mr. Bernier, our track and field coach, and he told me yes, he's been at it for a *week*. Isn't that marvelous?"

". . . But he got weak arms. You ever look at his arms? They're two pipe stems."

"That makes no difference. Not when there's intrinsic motivation. And this will help build him up physically, which is a very important matter to the adolescent boy. I'm just delighted, aren't you?"

"Sure. OK, Mrs. Illowhite, thanks for calling——"

"Thanks? Goodness I get my thanks from watching a boy like Frank reach up and grow like an unfolding flower. That's a teacher's pay."

"Well you earned your money. Thanks again——"

"Nonsense. He might even write some poems about the experience. But I won't push him. You shouldn't either."

"No I won't. Well you've been very cooperative, Mrs. Illowhite——"

"Oh no, *you* have. I only wish more fathers——"

"Hell he's my kid. Well thanks again."

"I simply *had* to call you."

"Well you call anytime . . ."

"And *you* feel free to do the same, Mr. Kleinhans. I'm free the second period, 8:56 to 9:32."

"OK, I got that. Well thanks again . . ."

"I'm so pleased. I think we're seeing real daylight, Mr. Kleinhans."

"Yeah. Thanks. So long . . ."

"Bye now."

I went straight home. I didn't say a word to Helga. I waited in his room. He didn't show up till four o'clock.

"Where you been?"

"In school."

"*Since* school."

"Since I got out of school?"

"Yes."

"Before I came home?"

"Yes."

"Well I took a bus after I got out and then another bus and——"

"After you got out and between the goddam buses."

"Oh. Over in River Field."

"What doing?"

"In the field?"

"In the field."

"Practicing."

"Practicing what? And stop makin me be a goddam dentist."

"I'm not making you a dentist. You'd never like dentistry——"

"Forget it. Practicing what?"

"Over in River Field?"

"Yop."

"My pole vaulting."

"OK. Whathehell do you know about pole vaulting?"

"What do *I* know?"

"There's nobody else here."

"What I read."

"Read where? And give me an answer."

"In a book."

"What book."

"A. C. Gilbert's book."

"*Gil*bert's book? His book is about Erector Sets."

"His other book."

"What other book?"

"The one I sent for."

"Whatayou mean sent for?"

"Well I read the first book, like you said . . ."

"Yeah? And?"

"He told how he was a pole vaulter at Yale and how much he got out of it and if any red-blooded American boy was interested in learning his techniques he would send him his illustrated book. So I sent for it."

"You didn't tell me."

"You didn't ask me."

"OK, OK. Is that the book?"

"Yes."

"Is that Gilbert?"

"Yes."

"How high is he going?"

"Eleven six."

"I saw Charley Hoff do thirteen six at the Garden with your grandfather."

"Well George Varoff did fourteen six and a half last year. And he's American. Charley Hoff was Norwegian."

"I know what Charley Hoff was. At least his drawers weren't down to his knees. How high do you go?"

"Me?"

"Yes you."

"I just started."

"Don't be a Philadelphia lawyer. How high?"

"Four ten."

"Four feet ten inches?"

". . . Yes."

"Jesus Christ I can *broad*jump higher than that."

"I bet you can't."

"Well I can high jump higher."

"Yes, but with a pole?"

2

He didn't touch the Erector Set and I'd paid ten dollars for it. Every day he came home a little later. I finally gave the goddam thing to Elmer the night man's kid and went up the school and walked into the gym office, appointment or no appointment. Bernier was a real load. He was drinking coffee and smoking a cigar; he couldn't do 3-6. I said who I was and all and he said oh sure, Frank Joseph's father. How's

he doin? I said. *He's the hardest working kid I ever had.
Frankie has always been a hard worker, at home, in my plant,
every place; is he on the team? Well he's not exactly Bill
Sefton. But you didn't cut him? I never cut any boy who
works, I don't believe in it; let's just say he's on the squad.
But he can't get in any meets? Well no. How does he make
the team? Well as I said, he's on the squad——The hell with
the squad, how does he make the team and compete? Well he
has to break his novice. What's that? Well it's, well it's, well
Mr. Kleinhans, it's like when a girl who has never . . . well
when she——You mean he has to bust his cherry? Yeah like
that. How does he go about it? He has to do it at the Manhattan Novice Meet next month, but realistically speaking
he's only up to five one. You mean he's already* OVER *five feet?
That's right, but he hasn't exactly been invited to the nationals
——That's OK, thank you very much, Mr. Bernier, if I can
ever be of any help in the milk line, give me a ring.*

I walked out. It was 1:30.

I checked up on a few stores and came back to the school
at three on the dot. When he walked out, all alone, I honked
my horn and waved at him. He looked all around except at
me for they just love it when they find you up at school, but
I kept honking and finally yelled. That did it, they love that
even more. He walked across the street.

"Get in. I'll drive you over the field."

"Don't you have to be at the place?"

"No. Get in."

"I can walk."

"Get *in*."

He slouched in and slammed the door. We drove the few
blocks without talking and I parked. He got out, and without
looking at me, walked quickly into the field house; (I should
only pull that on *my* father). I walked over to the pole vault
pit and watched kids doing push-ups, sit-ups, and jogging

around the track in twos and threes while Bernier jotted on a
clipboard and smoked his stogie. Then he came out. He was
wearing a gray sweat shirt and long blue drawers and also had
on a pair of high Keds. On his shoulder was balanced a bamboo pole, about the thickness and length of Helga's rug beater.
*Where are your track shoes? I don't have any. Why not? I'm
not on the team.*

Very tenderly then he lay his pole down beside the runway
and started to jog around the track. Alone. Looking down.
He did one quarter, then walked to the head of the straightaway and holding one arm out in front and the other crooked
behind, gripping the imaginary pole, he sprinted fifty yards
or so, that is, tried to sprint, for he did not get much forward
motion out of the shoulder wobble and foot chop he featured;
he looked like a slow-motion Twinkletoes Selkirk. He was
surely not the white hope Jesse Owens would lose any sleep
over. (Not that he had to worry about them either, for although the nigger can jump like a fiend under his own steam,
he does not have the coordination to handle a pole. Nor for
that matter the endurance for anything over a half.)

Three times he twinkled down his dream runway. Then he
jogged over to the pit. I was the only father there. Bernier
never even looked over, naturally a.k.'ing Dick Merriwell and
Jack Armstrong. I didn't say a thing. He picked up his pole
and walked to the head of the runway, turned and faced the
pit. He wasn't looking down anymore, looked, in fact, wide
awake. His hands clasped and unclasped the pole, squeezing
hard on the black tape near the end. For the first time I
noticed he didn't have on his glasses. He squinted as he
examined the (enemy) imaginary bar. Then he took a little
skip and started down the runway in that itty bitty chop chop.
Halfway down he picked up speed, or as much as he could
find, and with the pole straight out in front like a lance, he
ran right through the pit, staggered, almost fell as he ploughed

into sand, but caught himself and came pit patting out the other side and trotted around in a big circle back onto the runway. I kept my mouth shut.

He walked to the plant box, stared down at it, then shoved his pole in. He packed the dirt to his satisfaction, now thrust again and ran up hard against the pole and as it straightened, bounced backward, and almost fell down. He did this a few more times, each time flailing about and catching himself just in time. Then he nodded and back to the head of the runway. The little hop, skip and down the pike, this time stabbing hard for the box. He missed. The pole skidded off to the side and he sprawled head first onto the sand. I didn't make a move.

He lay there for a few seconds. Then he rocked back onto his feet. He walked to his pole and picked it up.

"You don't have your steps," I said.

He looked over. "My steps?"

"Sure. You have to mark them off. Didn't A. C. Gilbert tell you that?"

". . . I didn't get that far."

"Your steps were way off, that's why you missed the box."

He walked over to me, squeezing the pole with both hands, holding it on his shoulder.

"That's how Charley Hoff did it," I said. "I watched him. Go get your towel." He trotted over to his towel, picked it up and brought it back to me. "OK," I said. "We'll make three check marks." I took off my tie and my belt. "Now you walk down the runway with your pole, stretch out to a running step, about, oh three feet." He turned and jogged to the head of the runway, then walked back, stepping long. He had to do it four times and we moved his start up and back before his left foot was planted alongside the jabbing pole. "OK, we put the towel up here, that's checkpoint one, the tie about halfway and the belt here. Now run through, but don't plant. Just hit everything with your left foot. Keep thinking, left." He did it twice and I made a slight adjustment each time. Then, suddenly, he was hitting the box perfectly, planting the pole and running through. "Before you knock off today, get a tape measure from Mr. Bernier and measure off your check marks. Also count off your steps. Write that down and keep it with you. When you come out tomorrow you'll know where the hell you are." He squinted at me. "It's all yours." And I walked off to one side.

He hesitated, then picked up the crossbar and set it on the standards. It came about up to his chin. I could see Charley Hoff gazing up at the Garden ceiling. He jogged past me. "How high?" I said.

"Five two," he said, looking straight ahead.

He ran to his starting mark at the end of the runway. Turned. Examined the crossbar for a good minute, skipped and chopped down. He hit his marks perfectly, planted the pole, swung on it, his arms hanging straight down like two short, skinny pendulums and as he cleared the ground, jackknifed his knees. He passed under the bar. As he did, his pole knocked it off. He went into the pit on his face and he lay there without moving. When Charley missed 13-6 he lay like that. I didn't make a move. At last, very slowly he got up, brushed himself off, reset the crossbar, picked up his pole and walked back. Sand streaked his hair and caked on his neck.

"You hafta swing through without the crossbar," I said.

He turned.

"To get the rhythm. When you get it, put the bar up and just do the same thing."

"Is that how Charley Hoff did it?"

"Yop. And it's also common sense."

He hefted the pole from one shoulder to the other. Then he walked to the pit lifted the bar off and set it down. And trudged back up the road. He bustled down and hit and swung through with his half jacknife, sailed out in a nice broad jump and landed near the end of the pit, his back to the standards, but at least without killing himself. Charley, and everyone else I ever saw, swung and pulled up like he was chinning, thrust his feet straight at the sky, practically stood on his hands and at that moment twisted around and draped over the bar, then dropped down facing it, landing on his can looking up, at 13-6 crying for joy. The trouble with Frankie was those two short pipe stems. Don't ask me what they were built for, but it wasn't pole vaulting.

Anyway he went over the imaginary bar six times, clearing about four feet. Then came the main event. He set the bar up chin high and jogged back. He ran down. And he stopped. He walked back and ran down again. And stopped again. The third time he studied that world's record height, skipped and came down. Planted. Swung. Lifted his knees. And cleared the bar by a good foot, landing going away, flinging the pole behind him and trying to catch up to his body. He didn't make it. He flopped on his chest and face outside the pit. I ran over to him, lifted him up and pointed him at the firm, unshivering line.

"It's a new IC4A record," I said.

He examined the bar and shook his head.

"No," he said. "But it's my all-time personal best."

3

I took him down to Kleich's and bought him a pair of Spot Bilt spikes, a decent jock, athletic sox, white shorts with a blue stripe, an athletic shirt (white) and an all-white lamb's wool warm-up suit. Also a genuine leather blue duffel bag and a steel, wind-up tape measure that stuck its tongue out fifty yards. I had Herman order two bamboo poles from a plant in

Jersey and threw in six rolls of friction tape. Maybe he wouldn't look like Charley Hoff, or even A. C. Gilbert, but he wouldn't look like Ish Kabibble either. To make doubly sure of that, I sent away for Charles Atlas's course in Dynamic Tension and set him up in the basement along with a chinning bar over the door, plus a bag full of sponge balls for his grip, which made Tunney what he was. To make sure he was not goldbricking, I kept track of his daily workouts and progress with a huge wall chart and blue flags: He was the Fifth Corps and I was McKinley.

Each day I went over the field with him. With all his modern equipment, techniques and coaching, in three weeks he was up to 6-4, or well over his head. If Gary Cooper grew a crossbar out of his hair, this kid could vault over it. And now he was warming up with another athlete, Normie Levinson, who ran the 180 lows when he wasn't knocking them over and whose father was a butcher and never showed up for practice.

The Manhattan Novices. Saturday, May 15. That morning I got him up at 6:30, fed him Wheaties, fresh strawberries and grade A, one slice of Silvercup toast (each loaf had a whole cup of milk) and another cup of grade A mixed with Coco Malt and for dessert a Fleischmann's yeast cake. Then I drove him and Normie, whose father was in *shul* instead of with his kid, up to Van Cortlandt Park. I shook hands with both cherries, wished them well, then walked to the stands in front of the pole vault pit. A few kids were already doing their sit-ups and push-ups and side-straddle hops. One smart little ass with red hair and a mick face was walking on his hands. I gave them all Jimmy Grippo's evil eye.

In a few minutes Frankie and Normie came out, chatting calmly, their mouths flapping in the distance with those magical motions that used to fascinate the kid so. I could see why. They jogged side by side, still flapping, and suddenly it was the deepest, most important conversation in the world, even though I knew it was kid b.s. Down the straightaway and around the turn they jogged, in perfect stride. Frankie holding a track shoe in each hand as if it was ballast. (Normie held nothing.) Never once did Frankie look down; if he looked anywhere it was off into space with Charley Hoff's eyes. Now and then he turned to Normie and smiled as he flapped. Twice he spit out of the side of his mouth, thin and hard.

They patted around three times, then broke for the infield and lay down on their backs and humped up into bicycle kicks. They really spun it out. Then they rolled down and onto their feet, patted each other's fannies and trotted to their specialties. Normie ploughing into and over a single hurdle. Frankie walking back to the field house and emerging with his two poles neatly bound in white adhesive tape at each end. He walked across the infield, rather *stepped* across, to the runway and carefully set his bundle down. Then he swung into his dynamic tension routine, his sit-ups and push-ups (he could only do six and that with a little cheating), but no handstands; I made a note of that.

The sprints got started, but let them. I had my eyes on the two judges who walked to the pit and handed numbers to the kids which they pinned on each other's backs, Frankie and the mick doing the honors. They all gathered around the judge with the clipboard and I heard him call out names and the kids say here. When he got to Kleinhans, Frank said Yo! My hands began to sweat.

They then measured off their check marks, or some of them did, including the Yo. Most trusted to dumb luck. Well their old man was in *shul*. One kid measured with one foot in front of the other. The mick used a cloth tape measure. Frankie's steel tongue gleamed in the sunlight. "That one is my kid," I said to the man next to me. "Uh-huh," he said. He had red hair. Dumb mick.

They all got in line and ran through the pit. Three times without the pole, three times with. Then three into the box and three over the bar at the warm-up height. He even pulled up a little and landed facing sideways.

"Hey," I yelled, "How high?"

A judge turned and held up five fingers, closed the fist and held up three more.

"Whatayou startin at?"

He held up the five fingers and one finger of the other hand. No sweat. Then he blew a whistle. I took out my handkerchief and wiped my hands. The kids gathered at the head of the runway and the judge called a name. A tall fat kid took off his warm-up suit and picked up his pole and waddled up the runway. He hadn't marked off a thing. Without talking to himself, without studying the crossbar, he shlumped down the runway full tilt. Near the box he minced his steps, thocked his pole in and flung himself at the bar. He rolled over, arms and legs flying madly, pole bending and creaking. He tipped the bar and he landed on his hands and knees, but it stayed up. He bounced out of the pit, picked up his pole, clumped back to the grass and spit and lay down. The judge barked again.

Seven out of fifteen kids missed that first go round. Including Frankie. He came down on top of the bar and broke it and they had to send to the field house for another. The mick on his hands took a bye. Frankie missed his second try, also, this time kicking it off on the way up, although his form was pretty good. Only one more kid made it that time.

As he set up for his third try I prayed to Mama, Papa and Bill McKinley. He studied that crossbar like it was a math regents, then the skip and he was off. I closed my eyes. When I opened them he was face down in the pit and the bar was still up. And stock still. I said to the bricktop, "Did he go under?" "No," he said. "Cleared it OK." I sat back.

He made 6-6 on his first attempt. An all-time personal best.

The fat kid made it on his third try, hitting the bar so it couldn't possibly stay up, but it did. That kid could fall into a barrel of shit and come up roses. Ah, and now the mick consented to jump. He pranced around the infield like Gallant Fox, picked up a pole twice as long as anyone else's, shoved it into the box and whiplashed back a good eight, nine feet. You'd think he was performing in front of the Millrose crowd. He took up a very short, quick run, snaked the pole in, swung up, thrust his legs at the sky, let go of the pole and continued to sail upward. He cleared the bar by at least three feet, twisted as he did, then floated down onto his feet and backside, properly facing the runway and smiling. I saw Frankie shake his head.

He still had the hangdog as he prepared for the next height. I willed him to cut it out. But his head was still wagging as he ran down. Naturally he tried to stop before the plant, couldn't, knocked the bar off with his pole. Another kid made it. His second try he sailed right into the bar, no pull up, no form. A thin, tall kid who was all arms and legs and could have stepped over, made it. The third time I couldn't even close my eyes. As he planted, the pole slipped through his hands, knocked the bar down and he flipped sideways into the pit. I got up and walked out.

I had three beers in a kraut bar on Broadway and then drove down to the place; hell, he could make it back on the I.R.T.; the mick Charley Hoff probably lived on the subway and his old man was loaded every night; didn't hurt *him*. I heaved a few cases around myself and bawled everybody out, till Eloise the girl told me to go to hell. I said all right, let the place fall down and I went home. I stayed up in the bedroom till supper, then without washing my hands, which would kill Helga if she knew, I came downstairs. I sat down without saying a word and began to eat. They all knew enough not to touch me with a ten-foot pole, bamboo or otherwise. Not him.

"What happened to you?" he said. "I looked for you after the meet."

"I had to get back to the place."

He looked bright-eyed around the table. "How do you like this?" he said and he reached down and picked up a small box and passed it over to Henry. Henry opened it and made a very impressed face. "Hey that's all right," he said. "Congratulations." And he passed it over to Margaret who oohed and ahhed.

"Let me see that goddam thing," I said.

She handed it over. I looked down at a thick bronze medal. Raised up from the background, good and solid, was a man down on his mark. Across the bottom, next to Dieges and Clust, who had the medal monopoly, it said *P.S.A.L. Manhattan Novice 1937*. Above the medal was the triangle of red, white and blue silk. I ran my fingers over the silk and the medal. I looked at Frank.

"You went out at seven two," I said. "I saw you."

"Yes, but I got fifth on fewest misses." He held out his hand and I passed his medal over to him. He propped the open box alongside his soup. He looked around the table. "I broke my novice," he said.

He was issued a uniform. And he lived at the track. And also on his hands. Where he used to examine your mouth when you talked, now he would dive down and do push-ups. And by the senior indoor season, after months of buckling and landing on his head, I had him up into a clean handstand. After that there was no stopping him; he did handstands all over the house, including on the arms of my personal Morris chair and the john. In the outdoor season he did eight feet in a meet with Seward Park, got a fourth, and did 8-8 against George Washington for a third. Everybody including the papers was watching Leslie MacMitchell—you would think he had Harding Davis for a press agent—but I concentrated on the pole, where Frankie was dueling, of all people, the red-haired mick. He won it at 10-6, why not with his form and beer-barrel arms? He turned out to be Red Tannenbaum, but I know plenty of yiddles who drink and do manual labor, they're not all Einstein. Same kid broke the city schoolboy record at 11-8 in June. By the time he graduated high school he had done 12-4 and got a track scholarship to N.Y.U. along with MacMitchell. He was killed on Tarawa, don't ask me why he wasn't playing it safe as company clerk. But he was one less thing for Frankie to worry about. By the senior outdoors Frankie was doing 8-10. I went up to see Bernier.

"Can he get a track scholarship?" I said.

"For eight ten? You're out of your mind," he said.

"What does he need?" I said.

"For what college?" he said.

"Where do you have connections?" I said.

"Well you have to make up your mind," he said. "You want him to be a big fish in a little pond or a little fish in a big pond?"

"A big fish in a little pond," I said.

"How about Transylvania?"

"Who goes there, Dracula?"

"It happens to be a very good little liberal arts college in Kentucky," he said.

"I don't want people coming up to him and nipping his neck the rest of his life. What else you got?" I said.

"How about a nice Lutheran college?" he said.

"Like what?" I said.

"Oh Regensburg," he said.

"That's in Germany," I said.

"No, it's in Ohio," he said.

"You got an in there?" I said.

"Well I could always do *some*thing," he said, "if only Frankie could go higher."

"How high?" I said.

"Oh nine six for admission, ten six for scholarship," he said.

"Let's settle for admission," I said. "I don't want to put too much pressure on the kid."

"OK," he said.

"What happens when he gets in and he don't do nine six?" I said.

"He got a muscle pull," he said. "Don't worry, once he's in, he's in."

I got up and held out my hand. He shook it and sucked up the fifty dollars.

"I'm sure we can work something out, Mr. Kleinhans," he said.

He took up weight lifting and by graduation he could press sixty pounds. In June at a P.A.L. development meet at Victory Field in Queens he broke the nine foot barrier, took second and won a silver medal which he wore in bed for a month. In September I drove him out to college. While he was getting squared away in his room and with his program I went over to the phys. ed. office and had a nice talk with Herb Macintosh, the track coach, and told him just how to handle the kid, plus my office and home numbers, any time day or night. When I said good-bye, very concerned about how the kid would make out away from home the first time in his life, he was chinning on his dorm room door.

He made it through his freshman year. Just. And he was number two vaulter on the freshman team. They had two vaulters. In April I drove out for the Ohio All Comers meet and he did 9-2 for 14th place. The next year he maintained his D plus average and on the varsity took two fourths in dual meets. He also wrote letters for the first time in his life. Here is the one he wrote in June:

Dear Pop,
    After the last meet I measured my biceps bracchi and discovered they were six inches in circumference, a gain of one-quarter inch since high school. Also my latissimus dorsi have a two-inch flare which is also an advance. Chip Meltzer and I drove to Columbus last week and I saw Bill Graber do 14-3. Coming home we had a big argument as as to who will do 15 first. Chip says the Japs. I say never, my money is on Meadows or Sefton. I have to pick a major for next year and I picked pole vaulting.

Your son,
FRANK

I drove out to Ohio.
"What do you mean pole vaulting?"
"Well they asked me for a major."
"But that's no major."
"It's the one I want."
"It's not a question of what you want."
"Well they *asked* me what I want."
"I don't gave a shit what they asked you. It's what's *available.*"
"This is available. I do it all the time."
"You can't earn a living pole vaulting."
"Why not?"
"There are no jobs in pole vaulting. Except for coaching. You wanna coach?"
"No. I want to pole vault."
"There's no *call* for pole vaulters. Believe me, I'm in the business world, I know."
"Well they didn't ask me all that. They just asked what I wanted to major in."

"Whathehell are you gonna do when you're sixty, pole vault?"

"Yes."

I walked out and into Macintosh's office.

"I know," he said.

"Well?" I said.

"Well what?" he said.

"What are you doing about it?" I said.

"I talked to Dean Venty," he said. "We'll call him a physics major."

". . . He stinks in math," I said.

"Oh he won't need math," he said. "Just a little work in fulcrums and torque."

"Wait a minute," I said. "You mean you're letting him get away with it? What kind of place is this? Bernier told me it was on the up and up."

"Mr. Kleinhans," he said, "this is the kind of place where we endeavor to meet the individual needs of each student. And we have a very good batting average in that regard. Good afternoon, sir."

He graduated in 1942 with a B.S. in pole vaulting. At ten feet even. The army was now staring down our throat, Henry was already in, but he could take care of himself. I talked to Vic Lummler at Bell Telephone who owed me a few and I got Frankie into the Signal Corps, where at least he would not be a mud slogger. So what did they do? With his pole vaulting background, they made him a telephone lineman and sent him out to Camp Crowder in Missouri for training. The first time he climbed a pole he froze and they had to haul him down with a block and tackle, so they transferred him to the infantry and he was shipped out to the 65th Division as a repple depple and he slogged it through France and Germany, including Regensburg, and wound up in a castle in Linz,

Austria, hooking up with the bolshies. He had liberated a set of weights in Bad Tolz and a bamboo rug beater in Wiesbaden and by V-E Day was up to 10-6 outside the castle, also easily clearing the moat. That's just what I wanted to hear, especially with Henry getting pierced by the Second Avenue El outside Manila. When Frankie came home I couldn't look at him.

"It's not his fault," said Helga.

"I suppose it's my fault."

"It's nobody's fault," said Helga.

"Tell it to Henry."

"Well you can't take it out on Frank Joseph," said Helga.

"Don't tell me who I can take it out on."

"He's your flesh and blood, too," said Helga.

"Oh boy and didn't I give him blood?"

"You're his father," said Helga.

"Listen, Churchill's father never even looked at him. You know that? And he had a *dose*. While I have always kept myself clean. Immaculate. Now look at Churchill and look at my kids!"

She sighed and walked into the kitchen.

He took a room at the McBurney Y on 63rd Street and joined 52-20 and spent a lot of time in Central Park. Margaret told me, also that Helga was slipping him a few dollars, which I did not forbid as she said he was awfully thin. He didn't work for a year, except on readjusting, moved to a place across from Penn Station and then down to 15th Street and Ninth Avenue. That winter he vaulted in the armory on 168th Street and went out at ten feet. In May I gave Margaret fifty dollars for him and the next month he entered a junior AAU meet at Ohio Field in the Bronx and did 10-2 for a fifth place. In July 52-20 ran out and I went down to see him. He had the carved-out look of all track men and something of the vaulter's chest, not too much. His hair was getting thin on top. He still wore his steel-rimmed G.I. glasses and the lenses were Coca-Cola bottoms. I noticed khaki underwear scattered around the room.

"Well are you ready to come home?"

"No."

"How you gonna live?"

"I'll get a job."

"What doing?"

"I don't know."

"You wanna go back to school? I'll pay for it."

"You don't have to pay. I got the G.I. Bill."

"Well, so take it."

"No."

"You plan to keep living on top of that pogo stick?"

"Yes."

"What for?"

"I want to do eleven eight."

"Why?"

"A. C. Gilbert did eleven six in my book."

"Big fuckin deal. What then?"

"Twelve feet."

"I really don't know what to tell you," said Mrs. Illowhite.

"You know him."

"Yes, but I haven't seen him in eight years," said Illowhite.

"He always talked to you."

"Yes and no. What's he like now?" said Illowhite.

"Well at least he don't answer a question with a question. And he don't look in your mouth when you talk, he looks at your forehead. Otherwise he's Frankie."

"Have you ever considered help for him?" said Illowhite.

"Whatayou think I'm *try*in to do?"

"I mean out*side* help," said Illowhite.

"So I'm *asking* you."

"I mean psychiatric help," said Illowhite.

"That kid ain't crazy. He's nuts, but he ain't crazy."

"No one is saying that," said Illowhite. "He simply needs some help in finding himself and in gaining some needed insights. How old is Frank Joseph now?"

"Twenty-six."

"Well he *could* use some career guidance," said Illowhite. "After all, you won't be around forever."

"Christ, don't I know it? That's what's killin me."

"Frank," said Illowhite, "do this for me."

"Who'll pay for it?" said Frankie.

"Your father, of course," said Illowhite.

"How much will it cost him?" said Frankie.

"Believe me an arm and a leg," said Illowhite.

"I'll do it," said Frankie.

Dr. Emmanuel Wiseflash said: "His bamboo pole is a penis extension."

I said: "You mean he's vaulting on his own private?"

Illowhite said: "I think the doctor may very well have a point."

Frankie said: "He just sits and looks at me."

Wiseflash said: "In a sense yes, but only in its erect state."

Frankie said: "Once he fell asleep."

Wiseflash said: "He takes the pole with him wherever he goes. He fondles it."

I said: "He never pulled off in his life."

Wiseflash said: "He also *tapes* it."

I said: "That's so he can get a decent grip on it."

Wiseflash said: "Very good."

Illowhite said: "He always did keep to himself a lot."

Wiseflash said: "Also he is binding the wound."

I said: "What wound?"
Wiseflash said: "The wound and the bow."
Illowhite said: "We all have it."
Wiseflash said: "He puts *baby* powder on his hands."
Frankie said: "He repeats whatever I say."
Illowhite said: "Oh dear, I hope he's not regressing."
Wiseflash said: "You are the crossbar."
I said: "Christ, once he fell on top of the bar and broke it."
Frankie said: "What's wrong with the way *I* say it?"
Wiseflash said: "See?"
Frankie said: "Well it's *his* money."
I said: "What about his career? I won't be around forever."
Illowhite said: "He writes creative poetry."
Wiseflash said: "Never. I see something with much more security. This boy needs oceans of security. Civil Service work. I recommend the post office."
I said: "Over my dead body."

4

In September, '47, he entered Delehanty's and started studying for the letter carrier's exam. We told him there was plenty of outdoor work, the bags were good and heavy for his biceps bracchi and he could even trot from house to house. Of course I picked up the tab. In December he took the test and passed with flying colors and was assigned to a route in the Bronx. He moved into a furnished room on Tremont Avenue, which was still civilization, and Margaret helped him fix it up. He seemed to be very contented. He even talked to me a little. In the next depression, I said, you and the teachers will have it made.

Six months later he failed to show up for work. He was pole vaulting in McCarran's Park, Brooklyn. He finished seventh and got bawled out. So a month later he went to Philly for the Pioneer Club Invitational and missed a day and a half. Then it was Newark for the Jaycees and Travers Island for the NYAC Handicap and the 69th Armory on 25th Street and Lexington Avenue for the Mayor's Citywide and he was fired.

"He certainly has stick-to-itiveness," said Illowhite.

Vinny was managing my brother Max's place on Staten Island. Sonny Schroeder was out on his own as a patent attorney. In 1951, two weeks after his thirtieth birthday, Frank pole vaulted 10-6. The world record was 15-7¾, set by Corny Warmerdam and not a Jap, thank goodness, in 1942. It was to last fifteen years. Frankie was now working in Alexander's basement on the Concourse and still living in the Bronx. Because, Vinny said, he didn't want to live in the same borough with me. The planet earth he could accept. Margaret was another one. Since '48, when Truman destroyed the *Literary Digest*, she and the Arab were in California and she was whelping like crazy. Why not? He was the most fertile fella ina da whole Napa Valley. Also the thickest. No wonder the yids take them every day in the week including Saturday. She never wrote. Raise kids. So I had Vinny keep tabs on Frankie and also slip him a couple of dollars which I always reimbursed double. I asked Vinny if the kid was going with anybody and he said only if she was in track and field and I said you can forget it then as they all have dongs longer than Jesse Owens. Helga went up the Bronx once a month even though I forbade it, but I never made a federal case because she could always throw things up that would stab you right through the heart and then rub salt in the wound.

But then in 1952 Helga suddenly stopped talking. To me, that is. With everyone else she was Ma Perkins and Super Suds. I thought maybe she had had a stroke and I talked to

Weinmeister, but no, you can't have a part-time stroke. Well
since I had to communicate with *some*body, I went to Wiseflash, but Frankie was right: If he didn't fall asleep, he only
said what I said, so I wound up talking to Illowhite. She was
retired now and living on a pension I paid for so I figured
she owed me some conversation at least. I spent a lot of time
over her place in London Terrace on West 23rd Street and
believe me they really live, I don't care what you say about
a fixed income. We talked about the old days before the war—
World War II, not the Spanish-American—when things were
still normal, no thanks to Harding, and naturally Frankie was
the center of interest, especially his poetry, some of which she
still had, including "Hair" and "Night Goes into Day" which
she tried to change to *turns* into day, but he said uh-uh and
I said boy, that is Frankie all right. I used to love to look at
her talk and sure enough, just like Frankie said, toot toot toot.
But then in '54 she had to go and die on me.

For an entire year it was h. on w. with Helga. Admiral
Byrd at the South Pole had better company. At least a penguin
struts around a little. She sat and stared. By this time Al Fino
had retired and the union had pushed a thief down my throat.
He and Moscowitz, my accountant, got me indicted on price-
fixing and by the time I had kicked both of them in the ass,
I was out five thousand dollars plus my good name. Through
it all Helga never once gave me the right. But the law of
averages catches up with you and so does God. In May of '55
I got a phone call. It was Frankie.

"Something's happened to Mama."

"What?"

"She was saying good-bye and turned to leave and tripped
over a lamp."

"She fell in forty-nine and broke both her knees."

"This is worse."

"How worse?"

"Her hip. It's shattered. They have to operate and put in a plastic joint."

"She's in the hospital already?"

"Yes."

"What hospital?"

"Fordham."

"I don't want my wife in no mick hospital!"

"Don't start that, Pop."

"Don't Pop me. I want her in a yiddle hospital where at least they know their ass from a hole in the ground. Weinmeister's kid is connected with Mount Sinai. I'll make all the arrangements. You get up to her and have an ambulance ready and when I call, sign her out. Then get her down to Mount Sinai, understand?"

". . . Yes, Pop."

We worked it all out to a T and they operated the same night and at least the surgeon wasn't stinking drunk. The operation was a complete success, he was Yehudi Menuhin with the knife. They had her on her feet the next day. I practically lived at the hospital, along with Frankie. I did everything. I lifted her out of bed; I fed her; I took her to the john, I sat her down on it; I wiped her ass. And she never said a word to me. To the nurses, the gray ladies, the candy stripers, the nigger ward boys, yes. Not to me.

A week later she fell again at five o'clock in the morning when I wasn't there and she tried to get out of bed. They called me and Frank and when we got there she was talking very funny. To him, not to me. And to her father, Brunkhorst. Weinmeister's kid thought it was a stroke, but neurology said no and they took some more tests and said it was kidneys. I was relieved, but Helmut said don't be. He was right. She lasted two more days, talking to Frankie and Henry and her mama and papa and never to me. She went at three o'clock of a bright afternoon with the kids playing noisily across the street in the park. At the end she just stared up at me.

I remembered how she hated Campbell's soup since Orson Welles, so I called Cook's and ordered the best in the house. Then I called her family and my family and everybody else I could think of. She had a wonderful turnout, including Dolf Zilfuss, our assemblyman and Jerry Jackson, commander of my post and a nice fellow even if he saw all his combat on Governor's Island. The only one who didn't show up was Margaret; she sent a fifteen-cent card. Then around midnight, when they had all gone, Frankie and I walked to the coffin and looked down at her.

"She looks natural," I said.

"They gave her too much color."

"They always do that."

"Yes. Oh well . . ."

"She was a good woman."

He began to sob.

"She got one lousy deal," I said. "One kid killed in a war. The other a million miles away and doesn't even call. It's a good thing you're here."

His shoulders jerked up and down. I let him get it out of his system. Finally he calmed down and wiped his face with his handkerchief.

"I was pretty lousy too," he said.

"Nah don't be silly. You had your own eggo needs to take care of."

He put the handkerchief away and looked at me.

"You were in the process of finding yourself. She understood," I said.

He kept looking.

"You're gonna be at the funeral tomorrow?" I said.

"What time?"

"We'll leave from here at one o'clock."

"I have a track meet in Queens."
I swallowed very hard. "Well," I said, "You do what you have to do."

He got out to the cemetery at 2:45, in time for the end of the service. *How did you make out? Third. How high? Eleven feet. Isn't that an all-time personal best?* He nodded and looked down at the grave. *I did it for her.*

All of a sudden he started to come to himself. Not in a great overwhelming rush, but enough so you could notice. And three months after Helga I went out to see him in a track meet. It was the Junior Olympic Development Meet at Randall's Island, although he was now thirty-five years old. I sat in the familiar spot next to the pit and watched as he warmed up and swung through his practice jumps. He had the run we had blocked out pretty good, even if he still chip chopped down the line. He had the plant and pull-up, the thrust and the reverse drop, all surprisingly neat and clean. He just couldn't go very high. Not with those short, weak arms and the body that said uh-uh to his yes-yes. And he still had the bamboo pole even though all the others had aluminum. But he did 11-2 that day for a sixth place. And I took him out for supper afterward at the Cafe Geiger in Yorkville, just like Henry in the old days.
"Would you like an aluminum pole?" I said.
"You'll buy me one, right?" he said.
"That's right," I said. "It's no crime for a father."
"No thanks," he said. "I'll stick with bamboo."
"Why? Because I'm buying?" I said.
"No. It's like unpasteurized milk. It's purer," he said.
"You talk like Henry," I said.
"No," he said, "that's what you said."
"I did?" I said.

"Yop," he said.
"How would you like to come home?" I said.
"No thanks," he said.
"You sure?" I said.
"Yop," he said.
"You can come and go as you please," I said.
"No thanks," he said.
"Don't do me no favors," I said.

After two months I began to follow him around the circuit. I even got to know the kids he competed against and they turned out to be pretty good bunkies, giving both of us a very nice hello. Little by little I started to let the business go, the union was stealing me blind anyhow. I really didn't give a shit: paper, skim milk, ersatz whipped cream. How could I ever explain to Papa? In 1957 he said, Pop, this is no life for you. I know it, I said, it's rotten, even Benny Martinelli is living like a king with his daughter. Why don't you sell out? he said. What would I do? You don't want me. He smiled and shook his head. Why don't you go into the Soldier's Home in Washington? You'd put your father in a home? I said. Come on Pop, you always loved the army, you still have your campaign hat and Uncle Rudy's puttees. In a million years, I said, I never *once* dreamed of putting my parents into a home.

In 1958, at the age of eighty, I reentered the army. After sixty years as a civilian. Borden's had bought me out for a song, but so what? I had three hots and a flop. I had the flag, I had the bugles and I had my bunkies even though Billy Baumgarden turned out to be a stiff. And for the first time Frankie and I really got close. My C.O. was not at all chicken shit, like Tom Cooper when he made first sergeant, and long as I toed the mark I could get a pass any time I wanted. So I would come up to New York for the meets and in between times, when he wasn't working out, he would come down. We would sit and watch TV together: Ed Sullivan, who got his start on the bullshit *Graphic,* Uncle Miltie, a new face of 1937, and best of all *Your Hit Parade* featuring Snookie Lamson. I liked Snookie, but he wasn't in the same league as Lanny Ross. Uh-uh, he said, Barry Wood, and we were off to the races. And it was really something when we got down to the special bonus songs. I stuck up for "Chapel in the Moonlight," which was number one for twenty-two straight weeks, while he went for "Deep Purple," claiming twenty-five weeks and a reappearance as a bonus. So we had our fun. Even when Borden's bought out *Your Hit Parade* and Snookie went back to Ray Noble, we had our fun. And to tell the truth it seemed to be very good for his pole vaulting. Every year or so he added an inch on to his all-time best and he got up to A. C. Gilbert's 11-6, although with the new fiber glass poles they were now doing around 17. He stuck to bamboo.

In '66 I came up to New York for a Memorial Day Parade on Riverside Drive and the next day went up to Yonkers to see him in the Mets. He was now forty-five, very thin on top and with flesh-colored glasses which he taped to his head. They started at 11 feet just for him and all the fiber glass boys byed. They moved it up to 11-3 and he made that. They moved it up to 11-6 and he made that. All on his first try. By this time the boys had all gathered around the pit and were beginning to yell with every vault. And I started to get my Van Cortlandt hands. He was still vaulting against himself and I heard the judge say, what do you want, Frank?

"Eleven eight," he said.

"Yeah, Frankie," I heard. They moved it up and he adjusted the standards very carefully, then walked back up the runway. He missed by a mile his first try, kicking the bar up to the bleachers. On his second vault he ticked the bar. He landed on his back and stared up. The bar shivered, then lay

still, just as I ordered. The crowd around the pit went wild.
Corny Warmerdam shook every hand and got his rump patted
good and proper. My eyes started to bother me. I turned to the
fellow beside me and was about to say that's my kid, but at
the last minute didn't. And now he was holding up ten
fingers, then two more. They whooped. Boys and girls in
warm-up suits and shorts came running from all directions.
I heard "Go, Frankie, Go" and "Jesus man, twelve feet."

He walked to the standards and glared up at the crossbar.
Then he turned the knob at each upright to move the bar in,
glared up, moved it out, then was reasonably satisfied. He
poked his pole into the box and measured against the bar, let
the pole fall and caught it near the end. He jammed the pole
into the box, ran up on it and sprang back—without falling—
and I thought of Red Tannenbaum under a Mogen David in
Tarawa. Then very slowly, calmly, holding his pole precisely
at the midpoint, he walked back up the runway, looking
straight ahead. Oh God! Charley Hoff. And A. C. Gilbert. And
Helga. He walked past all the thin, whiplash fiber glass poles
laying there like fer-de-lances beside the runway. He didn't
blink. When he reached the end, he turned. He crouched. He
studied. Then, although no one else could catch it, he glanced
at me. I *know* he did.

He jumped into his little hop, skip and was off. Chopping
down the runway, holding his private straight out in front,
but not playing with it. He hit his marks perfectly and slid
into the tough little cunt and arced up, swinging on those
stubby arms. Oh Henry and Margaret, you should only see
your baby brother! His form was great. He jacknifed perfectly.
And he hit the bar on his way down; it fluttered beside him.
The crowd moaned.

He bounced up. Re-measured and walked softly back. Again
he gave me a glance, then pounded down. This time he hit on
the way up. The guy in front of me said he's pooped.

This time he did not look at me. That's OK, he needed all his concentration. The crowd was one big hush. But when he kicked off they began to yell and that yell fed him and he fed it till they were like one as he chopped along. He missed his second check mark and I thought this is it. He just stretched out and hit the last one and his poor little arms almost came out of their socket as the pole caught and he jerked up. Suddenly you could hear a pin drop. He reached the top of his arc and twisted. He was over the bar by six inches and he hung there and in that moment he glanced at me and smiled. Then his pole snapped. He came down clear of the bar and onto the bottom half of the pole. It thrust up through his stomach and came out his back. He dropped straight down into the pit with bamboo sticking through his body, still holding the upper half of the pole, still smiling.

> So long for a while
> That's all the songs for a while
> We hope that our hit review
> Brought a measure of pleasure to you . . .

X X I I I

History's Child

I FOUND NO THRILL on Misery Hill. I found my outfit. And misery. And by that I do not mean Teddy the Terror, although his proximity at Fort Roosevelt plus his press agent did not help my stomach any. Don't rush me. He got all the history books, I got this page. What about my company? All right, according to Lister, my company with the captain and lieutenant still in charge, but without Sergeant Lou who was back in Siboney in a thing called a field hospital, actually some muddy ground, had finally squeezed out of Bloody Ford. From there it was but a hop, skip and jump up San Juan Hill, not, and I repeat NOT captured by T.R., but now free and clear of garlics thanks to the 6th and 16th and us mavericks. Now although we were just a thin blue line we held on tightly to our hill, despite the vote of General Kent for retreat, which was told to us by Chub Stollis, a headquarters orderly and the biggest gossip in Cuba. Thank God Shafter's pants were not filled with the brown stuff and we stood pat, else we would never have heard the last of it from the navy which had just smashed Cervera, from the folks back home, from Hunky Joe and most of all from *ourselves*. Hell. Not only did we not retreat, we *advanced*. That is correct, sir. During a hot tropical rainstorm, very late at night, when the world should all be sleepin, that is when we came a creepin. Down our hard-won hill and up the next, the one that got named Misery and fully earned it. When dawn broke, there we were, dug in next to the Rough Riders and the aforementioned fort. And looking beyond them, another batch of blue. Beyond that, yet another. Sure. This was it. The siege line around Santiago, ready to pull tight for the hanging.

"Hey."

I looked up from the latrine. 'Twas none other than a skinny blue scarecrow named Lister Colfax. I used a handful of leaves, hitched up my britches and ran over to him.

"Je-*sus*, bunkie," I said, "you are a sight for sore eyes. I thought sure you didn't make it."

"I thought *you* didn't," he said.

I sat down beside him and overlooked the city. "I darn near didn't," I said. "Remember the mess we were into down at old Bloody? Well in the middle of it all three dago sharp-shooters dropped out of a tree right on me. Right *on* me. Georgie Doyle had missed these birds, but they sure didn't miss *me*. Well I got one, but the other two overpowered me and drug me off into the jungle, there to do God knows what. I played possum all the way and when we got near their lines which I could tell from all the jabberin, I suddenly reared up and bayoneted both of em before they had a chance. Well——"

"You mean you still had your gun?"

". . . Yep. Now wasn't that dumb of them? Well after they were down and out I took off and circled back through the woods and came upon the sixteenth and we went up San Juan."

"Jesus, Germ, you were with Ord?"

"Yep."

"Jesus. Ord."

"Yep. He was a man's man."

"I'll say. Boy, that's something to tell your grandchildren, Germ."

"You're darn tootin."

"All we saw was mud and blood."

"Heck, don't I know? Believe me, it was worse than Hell's Pocket and that was God awful. Before I got captured I saw poor Mert."

"So did I. It's really something when your own bunkie gets it."

"You can say that again. How did Tom come out?"

"Jesus, don't even ask."

"Why not?"

"He's new top sergeant."

"Well Tom is a good boy, what's wrong with that?"

"I'll tell you what. You'd think he never even *knew* us."

"Uh-oh, one of those."

"Yep, one of those. Only worse."

"Well don't forget, bunkie, the war won't last forever."

"Oh I won't forget."

And he grins and twists the neck of the chicken.

Captain Waterman of the 16th gave me the go ahead to rejoin my outfit, which I did. And was Lister ever right! If it is true that absolute power corrupts absolutely, then Tom was Mussapoleon. The most chicken shit topkick in the whole First Brigade. Why when the Y.M.C.A. came through with a huge tent where the enlisted men could write letters and take life easy, chicken shit Tom, sucking up to the brass and the chaplain, *personally* kept us out. Don't think we took it lying down. Lis and I kept track of all and sundry in the margin of *Little Susie's Prayer*, one of the Y books we did not use for toilet paper, and after the war, which sure as shooting did not last forever, we set out to settle accounts. We called a big reunion in Brooklyn, near Lister's house, and we got good and ready to take care of our forgetful bunkie, when just like that, he reverts and turns back into good old Tom who was the best guy in the world and who could get sore at that? So instead of revenge, we wound up feeling no pain and had ourselves a memorable reunion along with a couple of Flatbush Floogies with the floy floy, floy doy, floy doy, floy doy.

Anyways Tom was just one of many miseries. There was the dago taking pot shots, and though we didn't even duck for if it's got your number, it's got your number, some did. There was the hot rain, steaming up clothes, trenches and latrines like Papa's Turkish baths. There was the hardtack which was hardtack. Soak it in river water, swell it up to a dumpling, it was still hardtack. There was our pot bellies, just like chowhound Congo pygmies had, only with us it was the hunger hump. There were the latrines spilling over into high tide, spiked a bright red. There was the awful smell, like all the I.R.T. toilets rolled into one. Miss Clara Barton, all starched and bushy-tailed, charged in to help out and did what she could before the overpowering whiff sent her back down the hill. Too bad, as we were much worse than the limey nurse put up with in the Crimea.

Of course after a while it didn't smell funny to us. In fact when I went back to h.q. on message duty, *that* smelled funny. So I hustled right back. Not that there was that much to hustle back to. Just on guard duty and off. And getting hungrier, wetter, thirstier, turning into a man with a shredded asshold. Poor Tracy Beecy. All he could do was bend over and hug his gut like Harry Wills had plugged him right up to the wrist. The only recreation was watching the waltz of the generals. That was pretty good, if not the "Castle walk." Each day from Shafter to Toral and back, the tall white flags flowed, bowed and dipped.

Shaf: "Say uncle or I'll blow you into the sea."

Toral: "*Caramba!* In two weeks your troops will melt into brown jelly."

Shaf: "Pshaw! I have thousands of fresh troops on transports out in the bay. Look for yourself."

Us: "Oh slick Billy! He's got Miles out there, destination Porto Rico, but don't tell that to the dumb dago!"

So it went, up back and around the mulberry bush and in the end Toral got faked out of his drawers, as if he was Harvard and Shafter was Albie Booth, only don't compare weights. And Toral said uncle. But he still had his *machismo*, see, unlike most bums of the month, so he made this deal. Whereby Shafter told Captain Capron to lob a few shells into Santiago so garlic could give up like a man, but for God sake don't hit anything.

Capron, who had lost a son at Guásimas, handled the gun himself and laid a few stingers onto their barracks. Then yelled like crazy at the insubordinate piece, meanwhile winking at us. He was a hundred percent, Capron, much less chicken than Tom and drowning his sorrow in a bottle every night like a real man. Little did I dream, or nightmare, I would one day be in his shoes. All I can say is if *I* had the Japs next door . . . Well, thank God for Harry Truman even if he was a Democrat. And Billy Mitchell. Of course if Roosevelt had done the job with the fleet in '08 like he was supposed to, Henry would be here today, well better late than never. . . .

They sent a few shells back and we both kept up the game for several days. And then, just like that, it was over. July 17, 1898. Put that in your pipe and smoke it. Add on to November 11. V-E. V-J. We who had kept Uncle Sam's win streak intact, had in fact shut out the opposition, unlike some other home teams I could mention, we climbed up out of our trenches. And let go with all the strength left in our soupy bodies. Capron's boys fired off twenty-one rounds. My ears waved. So did my belly. The rest of me looked around at the historic scene. Lister. C.S. Tom. The lieutenant. The captain. Trenches stretching right and left. Blue scarecrows popping up and cheering along with the raggedy gook. But no Ord. No Allyn Capron. No Ham Fish. No Mert. No Clare. No Harry. No Sergeant Lou. Tell *them* it was a neat little war.

MAINE EXPLOSION CAUSED BY BOMB OR TORPEDO?

The Nation's Grief

By Fate unwarned
In death unafraid

Cuban crisis
close at hand

Wrecked by Mine
M'Kinley knows

The doom-host of the darkness freed,
The mine that splits the maine;
The white hot wake, the 'wildering speed—
The chosen of the Slain!

THE WHOLE COUNTRY THRILLS WITH WAR FEVER

WAR!   SURE!

The Union
Ablaze
with Patriotism

War—Spanish
Warship
Approaching

"The *Journal* is neither surprised nor affected by the abuse heaped upon it by newspapers whose owners either live in Europe, or being native there, came to this country too late in life to absorb the spirit of American Institutions or the temper of the American people."

DESTRUCTION OF THE MAINE BY FOUL PLAY

Armed Intervention at Once!

It is no longer the time for debate . . .

In the name of humanity,
In the name of civilization . . .

I ask the Congress to authorize and empower the president . . .

"To whom would it bring honor,
to whom honor with death,
to whom would the chance come
and who would seize it when it came,
and who would make it come?"

"In April
everywhere
over this
good
fair
land
flags
were flying . . ."

HOW I COULD DRIVE SPANIARDS FROM CUBA WITH THIRTY THOUSAND INDIAN BRAVES
by Buffalo Bill Cody

Order the Squadron except Monocacy to Hong Kong. Keep full of coal.

A Soldier's Farewell

"About 11:30 the entrance to the bay can be seen. Two dark headlands— one on either side of the entrance— show up gloomy. . . . In the space between a smaller mass shows where dreaded Corregidor lies . . ."

What Did Dewey Do to them?

GREAT VICTORY AT MANILA

How did Dewey Do It?

A DEWEY COCKTAIL, PLEASE

"I heard somebody dying near me. He was dying hard. It took him a long time to die. He breathed as all noble machinery breathes when it is making its gallant strife against breaking, breaking. But he was going to break. . . . He was long past groaning. There was only the bitter strife for air which pulsed out into the night in a clear penetrating whistle with intervals of terrible silence in which I held my own breath. . . . I thought this man would never die. I wanted him to die. Ultimately he died."

"In all the armies of Europe there are no better soldiers man for man, than those of the United States Infantry . . ."

"Down here we are sweating day and night with the thermometer 98 in the shade . . ."

"But Mr. Davis has had his portrait published as a war correspondent, attired in a Norfolk jacket with 24 pockets, golf trousers, cavalry boots, hat and gauntlet, a field glass, a note-book, a revolver, a cartridge belt, and a practicable flask."

A
B
O
U
T

T
O

S
T
R
I
K
E

T
H
E

D
E
A
T
H

B
L
O
W

"... The abundance of greasy pork and beans."

"The U.S. troops sweat day and night in their cowboy boots, thick flannel shirts and winter trousers."

"Worst confusion yet."

"Railroad system is utterly mismanaged."

THE WORLD CON FESSES TO STEALING THE NEWS!

THE PURPLE BUTTON OF FEAR
By Craven Steen

Prut-prut-p-r-r-r-ru t! Pop-pop-poppety pop!

"Then came the landing, the long strings of ships' boats."

"Soon the sea was dotted with rows of white boats."

VIVA CUBA LIBRE!
VIVAN LOS AMERICANOS!

"Then the noise ceased, and out of it came the strains of the Star Spangled Banner."

"Chug came the bullet and
I fell into the long grass ...
There was no pain, no surprise ..."

214

My country tis of thee
Sweet land of Liberty

"The private soldiers go around half naked, their clothes worn to shreds."

"It was simply a gallant blunder."

"Lt. Col. Roosevelt's Rough Riders, who were ambushed yesterday, advanced at daylight without any particular plan of action as to how to strike the enemy."

"Always eating."

HOW DO
YOU LIKE

THE JOURNAL'S
WAR?

"Its great glistening bulk hung just above the tree tops . . ."

"The attack on Santiago is to begin in a few hours."

"It begins as corn begins to pop."

"Give them hell boys, they've been doing us dirt all morning."

"The sound was like the sound of wild animals in agony . . ."

"His face the color of wax."

Journal's Editor describes the capture of El Caney

"Dirty hands hooked like a buzzard's claw."

AN AWFUL TRAGEDY OF THE SPANISH WAR

"The balloon was dying,
dying a gigantic public
death."

CER
VER
A'S

"The volleys
rolled
like
a
surf."

FL
EE
T

THE 71ST NEW YORK
DEMORALIZED

SM
A
SH
ED

S
L
U
R
S

O
N

O
F

T
H
E

B
O
Y
S

O
N

T
H
E

O
F

B
R
A
V
E
R
Y

T
H
E

7
1st

THE
FLEET
UNDER
MY
CO—
MM
AND
OFF
ERS
THE
NA
TION

By God, there go our boys
up the hill!
Yes they were going up the hill
up the hill
It is very gallant, but very
foolish
It is slaughter
It was the best moment of anybody's
life

I want ye! I want ye! I want ye! I want ye!

AMMUNITION!

AS
A
FO
UR
TH
OF
JU
LY
PRE
SEN
T

Stars and stripes
the Spanish

Well they got me.

waved over
stronghold

AMMUNITION!

"We are in the face of possible disaster."
"We cut their heads off, of course."
"The city may fall tomorrow."

NOW
WHAT
DEWEY
THINK
OF
SAMPSON?

"Schley   *Comida!*   is as much   *Comida!*   the
hero   *Comida!*   of
Santiago as   *Comida!*"

Two of a kind—the *Herald*
and the *World,* traitors . . .

Only a step   *to Santiago*

PRESIDENT McKINLEY PRAISES
THE CUBAN EDITION
OF
THE JOURNAL

```
H  H     A     I  L
H  H    A A    I  L
H  H   A A A   I  L
H  H  A     A  I  LLLL
```

```
CCCC  0000  L     U  U  M   M  BBBB  I     A
C     0  0  L     U  U  MM MM  B  B  I    A A
C     0  0  L     U  U  M M M  B  B  I   A A A
CCCC  0000  LLLL  UUUU  M   M  BBBB  I   A     A
```

XXIV

Occupation

It was all over but the shouting and we were the Charley Paddock of the world's armies. But. Sonny Schroeder had himself a little strength through joy in Graz; Vinny had some slanty poontang in Osaka. Clara Barton and Joe Wheeler's daughter to the contrary notwithstanding, we had fever. And the runs. And rubber joints. And doughboys dropping left and right. The bugles for the troops who would never see home began to fade into each other like a roundelay. It got so the general forbid volleys and taps lest we would keel over from fright, that is if we were still standing. Then the bugles went dead because the buglers were. What the dago couldn't do with guts and guns he tried with bugs. And he darn near made it.

Each day I found myself going downhill. Harder and harder to climb out of my slimy sack. By noon, with the temperature 100 in the shade, I was Greely of the Arctic. By nightfall, with a drop of 50 degrees, I was Chief Gotzongoo. We ate shit and I dreamed of Mama's *gedemftefleisch*. And Lister and Wally

Spivwak, who had replaced Tom as the third musketeer, and I told each other tales of mahogany bars and tubs of pickles and sour tomatoes and beer and grape juice and cider and Liebfraumilch. Shafter had champagne for his gout, we got river water for our runs. Well R.H.I.P.

Till came the day a voice at half mast said: "I want a detail."

Into the upright I rolled. There was Captain O'Brien, weaving but vertical.

"What fer?" said Lister.

"Go . . . into . . . Santiago. Get supplies off . . . the . . . *Vigilancia.*"

"Why not?" says Wally.

"Me too," says Lister.

"Me three," says I.

He combed the whole company and found eight or nine more who were still human and we started out. The lieutenant was camped on the larry, Tom was doing the San Juan rock, 'twas just the cap and us. We staggered down at attention. But I tell you one thing, we looked mighty tough; ragged and filthy and stinking and tough. And the dago soldiers peeping out of their barracks, as well as the gook civilians, were scared as shitless as we actually were.

We tottered on down, through the suburbs, which were not New Rochelle, past the adobe houses, past the barracks that Capron had stung, past the opera house where the 9th Infantry was doing all the singing, past the archbishop's palace which was the best house in town, but don't look for the archbishop, down along the waterfront and alongside the carriers and the torpedo boats, down to number 23 in line, the good old smelly *Vigil,* and there behind an iron shed, where no one could see, we collapsed.

We stayed out for half an hour and the captain gave us another hour to come to ourselves. Then he proceeded to get us organized which took another hour. See we were doing everything halftime. Charley Post, a New York artist, but 100 percent, volunteered as cook and the rest of us started jacking supplies off the boat and that included a beautiful Buzzacot oven, Pillsbury's 3XXX fine white flour, canned beef and fish which had escaped the mortuary, real roasted coffee, Worcestershire sauce, ketchup, lime juice for scurvy and a twenty-pound case of Piper Heidsick plug, unrotten. Don't ask me why or how or what all that stuff was doing here while we were hardtacking out there, maybe Ab McKinley had a hand in transport, too. But whichever, in two shakes Charley had a pair of gooks doing K.P. and pots and pans and water detail and that night we ate like there was no tomorrow. For Lincoln Cruikshank there wasn't. He died then and there. The rest of us got sick unto death. The closest thing to it being the eight hot dogs I ate at Asbury Park in '27, then taking the loop de loop with Lis and two live ones who came through just fine but had to carry me back to the hotel where I passed out cold in the midst of poontang on the half shell.

This time I stayed conscious, just. And after puking went back for more. As did all the others. Except Linc, of course. And the captain. But then he was a West Point man. Finally we got some kind of temporary balance in our fevered systems and we set up a slow-motion train back to the outfit in order to share the wealth, for Secretary Alger sure wouldn't. The captain even allowed us to bunk down in the iron shed on the pier; it was not bad duty at all, though hardly Graz or Osaka. Or Asbury Park. The third night, as we prepared to sack in, Wally said let's get something to eat.

"We just ate," I says.

"Nah," says he. "I mean something to *eat.*" And he does a figure 8 with both hands.

I looked at my smiling bunkie and then over to Lister. He was also grinning from here to there. And all of a sudden

I got it; when fellows live together and shit, shave, shower and shampoo together, words are not a necessity.

"Check and double check," I says. "How?"

"Just leave it to me," says Wally.

He rolled onto his feet and stepped outside the shed and I heard slushy whispering and t's and *si,* no, *si,* no, SI. Then Wal was giving us the high sign. We got up and followed him outside. One of the gooks was standing there with a can of tomatoes and fondling same like it was Dolores Del Rio.

"Girl-o?" says Wally.

The gook nodded.

"Where-o?"

The gook hunched his shoulders.

"Where. *O?*"

He shook his head.

"*Donde?*" says Lister.

He smiled and motioned with Dolores Del Rio and took off into the night. We fell in behind him. We walked along the waterfront. Past other sheds. Past Hood's Immunes, who had just been vaccinated and were letting the whole world know; you would think they were Carl Hubbell with bone chips. We walked on past and out into town which was just as poor by night as by day; in the States at least sometimes you got a whole new ballpark when darkness descended. Then out to the outskirts. And to a shanty in old shanty town. And sure enough to a queen waitin there in a rockin chair, though not blowin her top while the gators stare. She was cool, calm and collected. What she collected was a big hunk of Piper Heidsick which she started chewing good as Red Lucas ever did and spitting even better.

"*Señorita,*" says the gook to us.

"*Si, si,*" says Wally. "Scram-o," and he points down the road. The gook takes off. The queen, definitely not Eva Cisneros, continued to rock.

"Wally," says Lister, "I ain't so sure about this."

"Why not?" says Wally.

"I don't like her looks," says Lister.

"What's wrong with them?" says Wally.

"I just don't like them," says Lister.

"Hell. What about you, Germ?" says Wally.

"Well she ain't Lily Langtry," says I.

"And you ain't the Duke of Paducah," says Wally.

"Maybe I ain't, but I know what I like," says I.

"You fellas," says Wally, "you talk like you're on Broadway and Forty-second Street and eatin steak every night."

"Well," says Lister, "Why don't you go on, Wally?"

"Listen," says Wally, "I got a cousin in the navy. You oughta see what *he* takes."

"That's OK," says Lister. "You go right ahead, Wally."

"All right. I darn sure will," says Wally.

And he walked up on the porch. More a couple of planks than a porch. But don't look for a swing. He tapped the lady on the shoulder and she stopped rocking. "You. Me-o. Inside-o," he says. She held out her hand. He shook his head and reached into his shirt and pulled out another can which he handed over. She took it, got right up and walked inside. Saluting us from the nose, Wally followed after.

Lis and I sat down on a broken step. All around us in the gook night we could hear the language of romance and barter and once: "My vaccination! My vaccination!" which made you stop and think. We peered out into the dark, occupied with our own thoughts, like the fellows in the novels of Ned Buntline. Finally Lister says, "Well Germ, here we are."

"Yep," I says.

"In Santiago, Cuba," says Lister.

"Who'da thunk it?" says I.

"We won a war," says Lister.

"We sure did," says I. "We made history."

"It ain't very historical," says Lister, "sittin on the steps of a whorehouse."

"Well I don't know about that," says I. "My uncle made history in seventy-five and he had a Frenchie outside Sedan."

"He did?" says Lister.

"Yep," says I. "You know the Frenchies."

"I bet she smelt bettern this one," says he.

"Don't bet on it," says I. "She most likely covered up the smell with perfume and that's the worst smell in the world."

"And how," says Lister. "I knew a girl in Coney Island did that. It smells worse than niggers."

"You can say that again," says I.

"Wally ain't no rose," says he.

"You can say *that* again," says I.

"I hope he don't take all night," says Lister.

"I can't see why he should. The way he's talkin it oughta be wham, bam, thank you ma'am," says I.

"Hey here she comes," says Lister. "You're right."

She came all right. Down the steps, steaming and sizzling in their jabberwocky, pointing inside, sizzling some more.

"Hold on there," says I. "Whatsamatter-o?"

She keeps on rattling away. I grabbed her skinny arm and said, "Where is soldier-o?"

"*Que passa?*" says Lister.

She laid her face on her hands and started to snore.

"Holy Jesus," says Lister. "He went to sleep on her. And after all that."

"Oh no," I says, doubling over and grabbing my poor, weak belly. "Oh that's rich."

We both just grabbed and rocked till our puffabellies could take it no longer. She stared at the two coconuts, stomped back to her rocker and plopped down and rocked and spit a mile a minute. At last we uncurled. "Oh boy," says Lister. "I needed that."

"It's better for you than black molasses," says I.

"Come on," says he, "let's go get Romeo."

We walked past the rocking chair lady and into her house-o. It smelled of her and piss and soldiers and burned garbage. In the middle of the room was the bed, with believe it or not Ripley, a fancy brass top and bottom. And there corked off was lover boy, his ragged blue pants floating around his knees. We doubled up again for that was the sight of the night. Then we walked to the bed and shook him. He was some sound sleeper.

"I wish we had some cold water," says Lister, looking around. "But I wouldn't trust *that* stuff. It must be piss."

I bent over and sang in his ear: "Come and get your beans, boy, come and get your beans."

"If that don't do it, nothin will," says Lister.

"Hey wait a minute," says I.

I pulled back one of his eyes. He stared up at me. I let the eye go and it crawled together. I bent over and laid an ear against his chest. I jumped back like it had burned me.

"Oh God," I says. "He's dead."

"You're kiddin me," says Lis.

"No I ain't. He got no heartbeat," says I.

Lister bent over him. Then straightened up.

"She murdered him," he says. "That dago sonofabitch."

I looked around. I took a burning candle to the bed and inspected it. "I don't see no blood," I says.

"That's true," says Lister.

We stood beside the bed, looking down at our bunkie. He was very peaceful.

"The fever," says I.

"It got him, the poor bastard," says Lister.

"I wonder if he even got in," says I.

"Oh Jesus, I hope he did, the poor bastard," says Lis.

"Well," says I, "he woulda caught something and suffered

the rest of his life and finally gone crazy. It's better this way."

"You are right," says Lister.

We took off our greasy campaign hats and stood at attention. Then we put our hats back on and saluted our fallen bunkie. Then we picked him up and walked back to the outfit.

> Day is done
> Gone the sun
> From the lakes
> From the hills
> From the sky.
> All is well
> Safely rest
> God is nigh.

I wrote his mother he was killed in action.

X X V

The Fruits of Victory

WINFIELD SCOTT SCHLEY. He got a royal screwing. Margaret's Arab name is Karkatunian. He had a great Civil War record. She took first prize in shorthand at Julia Richman. He was cited for gallantry in action. Weinmeister's kid, Helmut, was sweet as sugar on her. Conspicuous bravery. She had a real head on her shoulders. He rescued Greely in the Arctic in '84. Not Horace. It was very hazardous duty. She made a very nice appearance. They gave him command of the Flying Squadron in '98. Ships, not planes. We didn't have planes yet. He was senior to Sampson, yet Sampson had pull so got overall command. She went with one yiddle who was at C.C.N.Y. and another who was at Brooklyn. Schley destroyed Cervera in Santiago Bay and Sampson had the nerve to say *he* presented the Spanish fleet to the nation as a Fourth of July present. That wasn't enough for her, she had to go and get hot pants for the Arab. I know just how he felt. So does Jules Ord up in Valhalla. His father had a rug store on 80th Street and Amsterdam Avenue. Mainly second-hand. They

called a Court of Inquiry to look into the conflicting claims
after the war. He went to N.Y.U. nights. The court screwed
Schley. He picked her up in the prehistoric hall of the Museum
of Natural History. Dewey was the only one with guts enough
to stick up for him. Probably felt up her ass in a crowd. Like
the way I picked up Freida Janaway who carried a mattress
on her back in Chicago in '33. I offered to take him on
behind the museum. Roosevelt put the stamp of approval
on the court. Of course. I said don't let the glasses fool you.
Roosevelt knew what a Court of Inquiry could do to *him*.
He walked away. She tried to tell me how much his family
had suffered from the Turks. Shit, the Turk was the sick
man of Europe. Also the fag. Ask Lawrence of Arabia. He
also lived in Washington. Helmut wound up with Kleich's
daughter, who was thick as this wall and twice as homely.
He died from apoplexy, why not, with all his aggravation?
She made her bed, now let her sleep in it.

Madison Square Garden Bowl was like the son of Kong;
neither one could cut the mustard. Henry could shag like
sixty. He used to shag all over Farmbest. Peary could also
have discovered the South Pole, but he wanted to be nice
to the Swede. Even Eloise the girl had to smile. Why he took
Matt Henson with him on the last dash is beyond me when
he had five good white men with him. Don't tell *me* Frankenstein is the doctor. Maybe he was a nigger lover. One of the
main problems with kids today is they don't teach *A Message
to Garcia* in grammar school anymore. Champ Clark got
some hosing in 1912. *Congorilla* was better than *Bring 'Em
Back Alive*. How anyone could vote for a Woodrow over
a Champ beats me. Bertha loved the Sisters of the Skillett.
Maxie's wife, Clara, loved the Happiness Boys even though
she was always melancholy. Jack Pickford was mighty lucky
he had a sister. I wonder if he called her sis. Pius had Al

Smith in his hip pocket. Arthur Fine had some looker for
a mother. Oswald took a pot shot at Roosevelt in 1912. She
complained to my father that I always looked at her ankles.
With his luck Teddy just got winged. He made me promise
not to do it anymore, so I always looked at her chest which
was out to here. KDKA wasn't a bad station. Dillinger busted
out with a potato pistol dyed in iodine. Frank Joseph loved
California Syrup of Figs. He was a funny kid. In 1916 I
told everybody and his uncle Pétain was shit for the birds;
in 1940 I was proved right. Clara Bow had it, Ann Sheridan
had oomph, Chili Williams had polka dots and Mabel Normand had grief. *Trader Horn* was better than *Congorilla;*
try to tell that to Edwina Booth. The soy bean is the bean
of the future. Disraeli, one smart yid, could teach us a thing
or two:

> "We don't want to fight, but by Jingo if we do,
> We've got the ships, we've got the men,
> We've got the money too!"

Hauptmann gets the chair and Bill Haywood is innocent.
Figure that out. Enzo Fiermonte couldn't punch his way out
of a paper bag, but he sure could ahfongoo society dames. If
they ever nail me on bombing or murder one, get me Darrow.
Especially if I'm guilty. Kids today don't read *Hiawatha* or
Uncle Remus. Frank Joseph was scared shitless when we saw
White Zombie. Believe it or not Ripley, Joel Chandler Harris
was as white as you or me. When he said it's getting serious,
I knew I better get him the hell out of the Orpheum. When
the Great White Fleet went around the world in '08, they
could have saved us a lot of aggravation by knocking out
Russia, Japan and Spain. Harriman was a helluva railroad
man, but he had to go and get mixed up with the bolshies.
We used to belly wop on 14th Street. Mighty Joe Young was
a laugh compared to King Kong. My first drink after repeal

was Old Overholt. Valentino's sideburns could stab you to death. Phainting Phil Scott was a limey laugh, so was Jack Doyle. Kid Lewis was really a yid named Mendeloff. Carpentier was a put-up job by Tex Rickard. Paulino Uzcudun was a bum of the month. As were hunkies Charley Retzlaff and Johnny Paychek. J. P. Morgan had the beak of the week. Don't let them kid you that he liked midgets; he liked pieces of green paper with pictures of dead people. Henry got nothing but the best: Flexible Flyers, Chicago ball bearings, Ivor Johnsons, Keds, Bumble Bee salmon. Dutch Schultz spilled his true guts on his deathbed: Roosevelt and Howe controlled all the bootlegging in the country; repeal was a cover-up; Litvinov was futzing around with Eleanor; she had turned the banks over to Stalin; the two wops were guilty as hell and he could prove it and the Bible predicted everything if only you could read. He died peaceful. Frank Joseph would have been world champion in 1898. Well that wasn't a bad year. The picture in the *Graphic* of Valentino and Caruso up in heaven together was a phony. Roosevelt screwed Taft in '12 and thereby the country. Naturally. Cagney had a skippy ticker in *Ceiling Zero*. Also ice on the wings. They never have ice on the wings anymore. Rudy Vallee sang through his nose. Not Gene Austin. Marty Servo would have made a great singer after Sugar Ray got through with him. Harriet Beecher Stowe may have started the Civil War, but her brother, Reverend Henry Ward Beecher, was some cunt man. The frogs tried to build the canal, but were beaten by a mosquito. My father only smoked Murads. Also, the engineer was screwing around with Loretta Young and Annabella. When they went out of business, he stopped smoking. Goethals stuck strictly to his knitting. Henry liked Crosby. Frank Joseph liked Ish Kabibble. Margaret liked Bon Bon. Jimmy Walker and Sloan Simpson, Bill O'Dwyer and Betty Compton; a mick is a mick. My father touched up his hair with shoe polish. I never touch my hair. Those workers in the watch factory who put the radium brushes in their mouth get a sentence of death. When King Gillette got fancy he lost me. Radium was discovered by two frogs. Owney Madden was the only smart mick and don't tell me about Billy Conn. Walter Huston ate a frog in *Of Human Hearts* and I understood why even if Jimmy Stewart didn't. Helga walked into the w.c. while Frankie was on the pot. He said excuse me and locked himself in for three hours. When Khrushchev came to America, his favorite city was San Francisco. The first name of the man who runs Spain is Francisco. Draw your own conclusions. Farmbest is now a playground for poor kids. Well Nelson Miles just had to have Porto Rico.

X X V I

Hail and Farewell

It RIPPLED THROUGH THE WATERFRONT and back to the hills
and back to the waterfront. Fellows flat on their ass struggled
up and mouthed it and sank back. One boy said it and died
saying it. Little Jelly Doxson, of our detail and Staten Island,
ran all the way back to Misery singing it and collapsed
there and they carried him back down to the general hospital
mumbling the word. The magic word. Say it and you get
a bonus. *Home.* That was the word. We were going *home.*
You're dreamin. No I ain't. You're crazy in the head. Go
to hell. Well how do you know? Joe told me. How does he
know? Jack told him. How does he know? Pete. And Tubby.
And George. And Rip. And Bill Shafter. Two-ton? How
does he know? Alger. Oh shit. Yeah, McKinley.
                    Jesus, Yes!
   So we packed our gear. A bag, B bag, down to the station,
ain't just goin home on rotation. Or what gear was left
after stuffing in the Worcestershire and canned fruit and
chocolate and plug. Henry stuck Oh Henrys in his gas mask.

He had a C.O. from Louisiana who would yell, GACE! Oh Henry bars. We sat and waited a day for our regiment. And then there they came, every man jack of them who could walk, crawl or creep, britches up, down, floating around, and that included Sergeant Tom who came lugging in, sprung, between two corporals, both of whom had once looked much better. For if you got sent to a general hospital, forget it. The doughboy's Bellevue. Didn't Jelly know it? Sure he did, there he came, Creepy Crespi, in the arms of two bunkies, whilst two others provided camouflage. At "Fall out," they all did. Each one collapsing onto his horse collar, but happy for a little while, eyes and cheeks aglow with the healthy color of fever. Same way Marge died with Myrt hovering over.

Next A.M. Izzy Baline gives us the early-bird jive and we get up and choke down a ration and struggle out and on board our troop ship. A froggy named the *Grande Duchesse.* Very very. And too too. Brass. White paint. Swabbies sloshing down same. And we dirty bums spoiling all that spick and span. Ah. Hey ixnay with the iplay. Bare boards. And bare floors. For bunks. Not a single land crab, except what we brought inside our drawers. I was assigned a cabin in B deck along with Lister, Jelly, Hap Day and Jed Polansky, members in good standing of the heat and ice brigade. Jelly and Hap were worst off so they flopped in the bunks while Lis and Jed and I sacked out on deck. In my four square feet I produced *Sailor Jack's Homecoming,* a Y book, and I ripped out two chapters apiece for toilet paper. Same way I handled *The Rough Riders* in '07.

For three days we hove to. Doughboys dropping left and right all over the boat. Yes, swabby, *boat.* On deck, those that could, crawled like wounded worms port to starboard, crab racing the tracking, stabbing sun. Medicine? Forget it, buster. Sternberg, the surgeon general, had. And one latrine. One. *Uno.* For one thousand enlisted men. Yes. Whose dream of heaven was a giant white pot in the sky. So some genius stuck two six by sixes out over the fantail and made a floor in between and that is where we camped out, pot shotting the fish. Tracy almost fell in. As did Jed.

Finally somebody or other in Washington blew the whistle. We watched vacant-eyed. Winches groaning, heaving; chains clanking, horns honking. Noisy, so noisy. My ears felt like Joe Pulitzer. But at last the *Grande Duchesse* gathered her froggy skirts, picked up and glided down the line. Lis and I heaved ourselves up off the deck and tottered to the rail and looked out at our fuckin erstwhile home. Still smiling with innocence. Just like the first time we had seen it, a hundred years ago, full of piss and vinegar. Well we had left that down here, along with brown guts and good boys. History books lay scattered in those pleasant hills and lush jungles and fords and whorehouses and graves. Henry was out there. So was Rudy. Ah yes. Sonny, Vinny, James, Elliott, John and Franklin Jr. were not. Nor Churchill. Quentin was, I'll give him that. Out in the harbor we passed some more history. The sunken *Merrimac*, Hobson's choice. The remains of Cervera's fleet; Christmas in July. The silent *morro* forts. Jesus, is that all there was to history? Then out into the beautiful blue Caribbean. We shook our two heads, took off our red belly bands, fed them to the fish and slumped to the deck against the rail.

Puking, running, yellowing, moaning, bitching, leaking, clutching, dribbling, rocking, wetting, twisting, farting, gasping, jerking, burning, freezing, shivering, steaming, crawling, stealing, staring, begging, scratching, drowsing, leaping, dropping, dying, we cruised homeward.

Third day out a storm came up, a hot, driving twister. We deck hands staggered below. "Where's Jelly?" I said.

"Latrine," mumbled Hap.

"On the fantail?"

"Search me."

"When?"

"Jesus Christ, I don't know. I ain't his mother."

"Fuck you. Come on, Lis."

We walked topside and fought our way to the stern and looked out at the potting shed. No Jelly. I pointed down. Lis nodded. We weaved our way back to a gangway and struggled below. We caught our breath there, then inched forward to the e.m. latrine, each of us holding our nose. Don't tell me about getting gassed at Belleau Wood, please. Fellows were lined up on the floor of the passageway, waiting to crawl in. Some couldn't wait. We stepped over and around and some boys cursed and a few took weak swings. They were like flies brushing your leg. We kept on going. Once inside the black hole, we carefully checked every bowl and every trooper. Well we found him, all right, dead, pushed out of the way under a washstand, twisted into a little yellow ball. Not a one gave him a second look. We gathered ourselves, let go our noses, picked him up and carried him out of the stench and moans up to the infirmary into some more stench and moans. Lister said, here you sonsofbitches, now *do* something. They did. Buried him at sea next morning. Poor little Jelly, about the size of a bird dog under the flag. I only wish Hunky Joe, who loves to knock New York troops, could see that sad sight. I told Henry and Rudy not once but a thousand times, you have got to be all wool and a yard wide to overcome the bad reputation New York soldiers have due to Joe and Kent and of course greenhorns.

The fifth night out, under the white arch of the milky way, I had me a dream of Eva Cisneros. At the crucial moment, which was a great surprise to me in my weak condition, and although it didn't seem to bother her one bit, I exercised some tough dream control and got so ashamed of what she was seeing, hearing and smelling, I ordered her right off the boat.

By the sixth day we had eaten through our rations. So those of us who could, went below and busted into the holds. All is fair in love and war, as I taught Henry. I also taught him the cabinet using St. Walpinac: State, Treasury, War, Agriculture, Labor, Post Office, Interior, Navy, Attorney General, Commerce. That's before they threw in everything but the kitchen sink. We found toilet paper. By now we weren't hungry anyway. And didn't have the strength to use the paper. So we just lay slugabed about, staring up at that yellow bowl in the sky, not even crawling away from its stabbing finger. The only genuine satisfaction was Tracy, two bodies away from me, doing Libby Holman's "Moanin' Low." As for this corner (Bill Corum always said this corner), we (Dan Parker always said we) thought mainly of a pack of Clara Bartons, all white and starchy and smelling of Life-buoy, gently lifting me onto a latex-springed ambulance, with horses on velvet hooves and carrying me silently off into the cool evening. Don't ask where, just off. I thought of that a thousand hundred times and it is true what they say about mind over matter for it gentled down the chill and held off the heat and the shivering. Just like Frankie, down with scarlet fever in '37, thought of Marjorie Gestring diving in slow motion in the Olympics and it pulled him through.

One day, just like any other day, Lister says to me, "Hey I see a long purple shadow out there. I think it is land." "Tell me another," I said.

"I think it is, Germ," he said, "I think it is."

"Well well and two more holes in the ground."

"Is that all you have to say? Home is just around the corner, bunkie."

"Yeah?"

"Yeah, dammit!"

"Well," I said, "just get me to a hospital."

"Are you crazy in the head? You wanna go to Bellevue?"

"I don't care."

"Germ, listen to me. You ever read 'The Pit and the Pendulum'?"

"Nope."

"Well in that, Edgar Allan Poe was sick unto death also."

"Not as sick as us."

"Sicker! But by the end he wound up without the pit and without the pendulum."

"Was the pit cool?"

"I don't know. Probably filled with snakes."

"Snakes are cool. And soft. I bet they make a good mattress."

"Oh *shit*. I'm tryin to *help* you."

"Thanks."

"I oughta known better. God helps those who help themselves."

"Is that a fact?"

"Yep, that is a fact. Even Tracy Beecy is on his feet lookin at the land."

"Where?"

"Right over there."

I rolled onto my side. Tracy was looking all right. I grabbed that goddam rail and hauled myself up. I leaned against it and caught my breath. I saw the long, low shadowy hump. I looked over at Tracy. "What's he sayin?"

"Land."

I punched the air with my fist. "Land," I croaked. "Land ho."

2

DISCOVER A WHOLE NEW WORLD AT MONTAUK LONG ISLAND NEW YORK. Enjoy fun-filled activity or carefree relaxation . . . it's all here in the fishing capital of the world! Guest accommodations to meet ALL requirements, with Dining and Cocktail rendezvous to satisfy any palate. Teeming with practical, recreational and esthetic assets amidst Real Estate offerings and investment opportunities. Our beaches transform cares into sand castles. . . . So make Montauk Your Vacation Paradise . . . THIS year . . . EVERY year.

A Coney Island sidewheeler. She puffed up alongside. Alongside the *Grande Duchesse*. Coney Island sidewheeler. Henry loved Luna Park. My father loved the Wooden Elephant. She made fast. We looked down at her. We took the steamboat at the Battery and sailed straight down the harbor. The hell with gear. We lined up, hanging on to one another and to the rail. The Cap said Go and we started. A hundred miles down the gangplank. Hap Day was in front of me. Three steps along and he sank down in sections and was about to ooze into the water when a sailor caught him and carried him down. Bertha had a bathing suit up to here and Papa tore it up. I let Margaret wear anything she wanted. I began to slump and another sailor caught me. "I'm OK," I said. *Sure* you are. And he carried me down to the Coney special, dumped me and returned for another liar. Arthur Fine and his family always went to Brighton Beach. Irene Flynn's old man hung out at the Sheepshead Bay race track. They say he dropped dead there. In the paddock. I sat down on the tiny deck. Too much. I lay down. All about me the fellows were doing likewise. Except Lister. He was a horse. He kept on sitting up. Made me hurt to watch him. Flat out then, our heads twisted around, we churned toward the U.S. of A. Some grass. Sand. A little dock. Ambulances. Frank Joseph never learned to swim because he couldn't stand an all-wool bathing suit. Even if it was a Jantzen.

Crunch. Lister tugged at me. We both got me upright. At the Cap's order we stepped out on the runty dock and then onto the sand. Oh that was rough. It heaved like the *Grande Duchesse* in heat. Rudy got seasick on the trip to Coney Island in '05. I sank down. Nope, I did not kiss it like the Movietone News fourflushers. I just lay there panting like a hungry bird. At long last the sand calmed down a little and I heard voices. Clean soldiers walking my way. With a . . . *stretcher*. Lis was digging me in my poor ribs. Oh I longed for that stretcher. Shut me up in a drawer with Kayo. Lis bunked me again. Asleep on a pile of white shirts. No starch. Again dammit, in the ribs. I struggled up. I smiled. The orderlies passed me up and packed Hap onto their pallet. He's a goner, Lister whispered. He's *lucky*. Cut that *out*. OK, just don't yell, I ain't yellin. OK, OK.

An ambulance frisked up. Oh no. Oh yes! "All you men who can walk, get up there." Lis got on and then pulled me in like a sack of flour. Boy it stunk in there. We took off. No rubber joints on that buggy, no velvet hooves. Stone, it was made of stone, like Benny Plofsky. We charged up the hill in the stone. Stopped short and my belly did the Castle Rock. "Let's go, men." We rolled off. Rolled. Down onto the grass and sand. The stone ambulance clanged away. Up ahead, tents. Row on row. Down below the bay and more doughboys staggering off the boats. Henry and I camped out on the Palisades in '32. He made a tremendous Hunter's Stew. The Hudson gleaming down below. We flopped on our backs and stared up at the sky. Well, said Lister, here's our camp.

From the moment you arrive you will DISCOVER THE MAGIC
OF MONTAUK . . . a truly Utopian Vacation Paradise . . .
where the glistening, sandy beaches are second to none!
Your cares will vanish as you enjoy the cool, cool breezes
of the blue Atlantic—soak up the sun—splash in the surf.
Little Wonder Why Montauk is now the Mecca of Sun
'N Fun Seekers.

It was named Camp Wikoff, that is what it was named.
After a gallant colonel who fell on the charge up San Juan
Hill. No, not that colonel. He only fell on the way to the
front page. We landed at 9:30 A.M. At 7:30 P.M. we got into
quarters. On a stretcher. Yep. Lis hovering over me. Making
darn sure they weren't sneaking me to the hospital. They
scooped me off and onto sand. That was our floor. Clumps
of grass. Not as soft as snakes, but not too bad. Lister and
me. Jed Polansky. And sitting on camp stools, playing whist
or whatever bluebloods play, polka-dot kerchiefs, healthy as
horses, two Rough Riders. Straight from stateside duty. Truf-
fle troopers. I sat up. I shoved an iron bar up my spine. I
was goddamned if they would see me cash in my chips.

That night we got our first meal. A pail of slops from
our nurse. Not Helen Hayes. Not even Walt Whitman. He
was about ninety. But the only one who cared. For he came
thereafter noon and night with more of the same. Just him.
We swabbed out our mess cups with grass after each feast and
got set for the next. Capone on the Rock was better off. So
were the poor lads of Andersonville. Warden Lawes could
have written a hundred books. Mornings, the kerchief kids
waltzed to the mess tent and ate eggs and caviar and drank
champagne and then came back and talked about it all till
lunch. They never lowered themselves to talk to us. Jake with
me. The roughest ride they ever had was on top of Mrs.
Astor. Fourth day, Lister hiked to the mess tent and brought

back squab, pheasant and champagne straight from Mr. Van-
derbilt's kitchen. Yop, the 400 were taking care of the boys.
With friends like that, who needs dagos? I got sicker. A year
later, New Year's Eve 1899, Irene and I welcomed the new
century at her friend Tina O'Hanlon's house, and I didn't
drink a drop of champagne and was called a party pooper. I
didn't touch the stuff till prohibition, July 17, 1926, at a
milk convention in Albany, where I celebrated the armistice
with Trudy Van Heyden, a Dutch live one, whose cheeks
were apples upstairs and down. They carried poor Jed away
that night. Dead.

Ab McKinley finally caught up with us now we were back
in the cool North. Took away our heavy flannels and replaced
them with nice light duck. We froze our ass off. Well business was still business. Then an orderly came in out of the
blue and decided to stuff me into a pair of pajamas, which
somebody, maybe old Abs, had dumped onto the sickest. Lis
and I wrestled him down and kicked his ass out of there,
for in pajamas you could never make it out of the pit, how
would that look? Suit yerself, he yelled. So I did. Flannels
under my ducks. And still froze. And burned. And froze.
Sand in my shoes, sand from Havana. I got some quinine
from the nurse and a blue mercury pill that could choke a
horse. I puked it all up. All that is real is the feel of the
sand in my shoes.

Next day they brought in Toby Tillyou. He had the
whole package and a busted leg to boot and stunk like embalmed beef. Champagne was the undoing of John L. Sullivan. The Fag Riders wrinkled their little noses. With Lister's
help I did all my duty in the corner of the tent. Toby did
his where he lay. Mr. Sandman, send me a dream. Next day
the two dear boys cleared out. Make her complexion like
peaches and cream. Even with Toby the tent smelled better.

You've never known such luxurious comfort as our new 2½ room Park View Executive Suite with adjoining large bedroom. From the deep-down relaxation derived from sleeping on our Beautyrest mattresses to the grace and charm of the decor and furnishings, you'll be refreshed daily and ready for the vast selection of healthy activities available nearby, should you choose to investigate.

Well that night the rains came. But don't look for Ty Power. The thunder rolled like all the bad little boys in the sky were knocking heads together. That's what I told Frank Joseph and he finally stopped shivering. No blue rain shinin down on my window pain. A snare drum on the roof. Then a bunch of bass drums. I sat up and took notice. Lister. He was up too, pushing against the front tent pole. I sighed and crawled forward to the pole and clawed my way up its greasy length and then pushed along with him. In the corner, Toby was staring at us both, not seeing a thing. Well it was like Indian-wrestling Sandow: The harder we pushed, the harder the pole pushed back.

"Come on," yelled Lister, "let's get out."

"I can't," I yelled back.

"Don't argue."

"I ain't arguin."

While we were not arguing, the pole gave way and the tent came down on top of us. Like a load of Mama's wet wash. I couldn't move. And if I couldn't, imagine poor Toby. Then I felt a scrabbling to the south of my feet. Good old Lis. He was pulling at my legs, trying to save his bunkie. Hell, the least I could do was help out. Between the two of us then I began to slide out into the night. Which was no great bargain. But at least it made me stand up out of the mud. And slapped me awake, since the stuff was cold and hard, not like gook rain. 'Twas a scene out of the *Old Dark*

House; good thing Frankie was not present, he would have whimpered it was getting serious and made me take him home. It was serious, all right. All around us lightning ripping the sky. The little buggers were hitting spares and strikes. A tent picked itself up and went sailing down the street, neater and faster than Kent's balloon ever did. All the other tents in our street were down.

"Let's get to headquarters," I shouted.

"What?"

"Headquarters." I pointed.

"You crazy? They won't do nothin."

I did not tell him two negatives made a positive.

"Well," I yelled, "we can't stay here."

"Follow me."

"Where?"

"Just follow."

"Toby is still inside."

"We can't help him now. Maybe later. Come on."

He grabbed hold of my arm and yanked me after him. I was too weak to hang back and we leaned into the rain and fought our way down the street. Other boys were also dancing to the storm. But nobody was singing, I'll tell you that. We stepped over canvas mush. Once it groaned and I hotfooted across. Now Lis was pointing. A big solid tent loomed ahead. Barnum and Bailey always said under the big top, but it was always in Madison Square Garden.

"Mess tent," yelled Lister.

I nodded. We struggled forward and reached the big top. It had steps and a wood floor. Guarding same was a wild-looking fellow holding a meat cleaver We held up.

"You not come in here," Cookie bellowed.

"Why not?" yelled Lis.

"Dis my tent."

"The fuck it is. You don't own it."

"Yes. Dis my tent."

Lis turned around.

"You hear that? He's up there on Easy Street," he yelled. "And says we can't come up. And we fought the fuckin war for him."

The yell was thunder on thunder. We went up those steps like he was the San Juan blockhouse. We knocked him on his lardass and then picked him up and tossed out into the mud. We charged around that place, ripping blankets off bunks, ripping our own duds off, wrapping up in front of the pot belly, all the while hypnotizing the two goggling K.P.'s.

"Coffee," Lis commanded.

Coffee it was. We drank more coffee that night than Bill Hart and Ken Maynard put together. Then we sacked in alongside the stove. You can have the Waldorf; I'll take that mess tent. And we actually lasted till nine o'clock, when a surgeon and his chicken sergeant came roaring in and tossed us out. Darn Sternberg, if only he'd stuck to Dietrich instead of medicine. We slugged through the mud back to our street and our load of laundry. It looked like Johnstown. When we dug Toby out, he was gone.

Each unit has been carefully designed for your maximum relaxation and privacy. All are equipped with wall-to-wall carpeting, a small electric refrigerator, a coffee maker and a television set. Each unit has its own private balcony or terrace squarely facing the ocean and directly on the beach. The view from your room across the beach to the surf is superb, through sliding glass doors. The entrance to each unit is at the rear, on the opposite side from the ocean and beach. The heating system is designed so that each guest may control the temperature in his quarters. The efficiencies have a complete kitchen unit, consisting of a stove, refrigerator, kitchen sink and all the equipment required for cooking and eating.

Mama told us never to get our feet wet. Never. Bertha
and I always listened. But that Rudy. He went out to Central
Park in '03 during a rainstorm and sloshed around in the
lake. Said it was wet anyway. The little bugger never even
sneezed. While I, I faced the truth and paid the consequence.
After that storm my fever came back triple. I was now in
another tent, equally deluxe, flat on my ass, of which there
was now very little. Lister did not look so hot either. We
lay side by each whilst a corporal from East Harlem, white,
which they all were in those days, came and went without
much notice of us. After all, we were just combat vets. Well
at least he was not an R.R. We heard other comings and
goings. More men piling off the transports. Thirty thousand?
Christ. Somebody was making a fuckin fortune on canvas.
Ab? Mark Hanna? Maybe Pat Gleason, as crooked a mick
as Jimmy Walker, but a little smarter. Not too. Alger? Nah,
too dumb. Here he came on inspection, frock coat and goatee.
The camp all combed down and curried. All the shit buried.
And the boys. "How are you, men? Anything we can do for
you men? Come, Captain."

What was that? Passes to New York? You're kiddin. No,
it's true; but you gotta walk to the railroad station. That's a
fuckin mile away, I knew there was a catch. . . . Shit. . . .
Go on, Lis, you can make it. Nope. Don't be stupid, get out
and tell Hearst what the hell is goin on out here. Nope.
You're a goddam fool, but thanks, bunkie. . . .

The door flap flips back. A tall officer. He is leaning over
me. God, not Sternberg. *Wie getz, Willy? Wha? Ah du bist
sie krank. Wha? Lister, get this old fart out of here. He's
yer old man, Germ, Wha? Yah, Willy, it's me. You're a fuckin
officer. Ah such language, they teach you such language in
the army? He's sick in the head, Mr. Kleinhans. Wha? I
bought dem clothes, Willy. Whothehell are you? I told you,
kinde, Papa. Wha? Du kumst, we getting out of here. Uh*

uh. Why not Willy? Not . . . without Lister. OK, we take him too. Wha?

I felt myself rising. Like Mama's strudel. I was bouncing on a shoulder. Lister? Yeah Lister beside me. Upside down. Tent upside down.

"Can I give you a hand there, sir?"

"No sergeant. I do it. At iss."

"Yes sir . . ."

He walked softly and my head saw Camp Wikoff bounce away. Then I was floating in a wagon. No an ambulance. No a wagon. *Wha's goin on here? Neffer mind, you hold his head, Lister.* We were off, stepping gently on the dirt road, every pebble a boulder. Ocean and sand. Siboney? *Hey, Lis, we save their ass at Guásimas. Sure thing, bunkie. Fuckin right. Aaach such language. Wha?* Then it was quiet. And empty. I woke up. Noise. and pulling. *Careful, Lister dot's it. Christ, you been in the country forty-five years, can't you speak English? Don't mind him, it's the fever. Himmel, what they done to him? Ah fuck you, what were you doin while I was fightin your war? Himmel. Whu he say? This Richmond, bunkie? No, Montauk. Montauk? Yep. Pullman we want. Tree for Pullman. Speak English damn you. Aaach. Yes, sir. Hey where we goin? Take it easy, bunkie.* Steps, up steps. Through a car. Ladies. *Fuck you, Mrs. Astor.* Parting like the Red Sea. *Wha you holdin your nose?* YOU *stink.* Officers. *Hey Major, you charge the Flatiron Building? Pipe down, Germ. Wha? He got the fever, he don't know what he iss saying.* . . . Fading, I was fading.

I woke up on a seat. Papa holding my head up and tilting a flask at me. *Don't want no champagne. Milk. Drink, Willy.* Ah cool. And soft. More. I started choking. They sat me up and whacked me. Fading. Clangs, chugs, hisses, looks, faces, noses, t's, s's; Frank Joseph would be in heaven. *He's coming to. Issy Willy. Gott he's a sick boy.* The bench was

stone. Rocking through my bones. Loop de loops. No, telegraph wires. Rising, hitting, drooping, looping, rising. Must
be moving. When they do that, you're moving. I watched
those wires. Ah, Marjorie Gestring in the Olympics. Frankie
was not as dumb as he looked. New Jersey? Delaware. Maryland. *Don't worry, ma'am, any dago tries to rape you, I'll
cut off his balls. If he got any.* The bench was hard, so hard.
*Papa, put me on the floor. Nein, sonny. Yes, Papa, I can
stretch out, it's got a carpet. I think he got a point, Mr.
Kleinhans. OK. Hey you, moof ofer.* I was eased down and
smoothed out. My legs pulled straight. Ahhh. *My neck, Papa.
Ya Willy? Straighten out my neck, it's in the river. How's
dot? His neck, Mr. Kleinhans. Ya, OK. Gay shloffen, kinde.
Yes, Papa* . . .

   Wha in hell? Eva Cisneros. Coming down off the telegraph
wire. Thanks Willy. *Heck, for what?* For telling me about
Richard Harding Davis. *Shucks.* I should have listened to
you, Willy, he does not like women. *Well live and learn.*
Thankkkssss. And she was off with a tall fellow in blue.
Ord? Very handsome couple. GET THAT FUCKIN BALLOON.
*Issy sonny, go issy, here try a little milk. Wha? Here Willy.
That's good, Papa, you ain't leavin me? Nein, I ain't leavin
you. Where's Lister? Right here, bunkie.* Ah. *Hey what
about Mert? He's in the next car, bunkie. How's his eyes?
Fine, Germ. He got ants on his eyes. No longer, bunkie, we
cleaned them out, his eyes are clean as a whistle.* Ahhhhh.

   Grant, he came by and shook my hand. Well done, soldier.
Thank you, sir. You can keep your horses for spring planting.
Thank you, sir, I'm sorry I called you a rummy. Forget it,
soldier, let us have peace. . . . Erik? and Konrad? You did
good, son. *I did?* Yes. *You SURE?* Yes, we are sure, you are
a credit to us. Ahh. . . . Hey we stoppin. *Lakeland? No
bunkie, Jamaica. Don't go to no whorehouse, bunkie, you'll
ruin yourself for your wife and kids. I won't, bunkie. Get*

a whore for Teddy. OK, bunkie. High society loves their whores. You can say that again. . . . Sir, one of your generals is a yellow belly, I don't want to name names, sir, but don't believe everything you read. The 71st New York is true blue. I know that, soldier. *And sir, don't trust a certain colonel, he's out for your job.* Thank you, son, I'll keep an eye peeled. *. . . Wadayou think of your old man now?* I got the greatest father in the whole cockeyed world. *You'll tell that to your kid?* Darn tootin I will. *Ah that's a good boy. . . .*

"How's it goin, bunkie?"
"Lis?"
"Yeah, bunkie. How's it goin?"
"Pretty good."
"We're in Long Island City."
"We gettin on the transports?"
"Nah, we're taking a ferry to New York."
"Don't put me on the *Seneca,* bunkie."
"I won't, bunkie."
Yelling. Cheering.
"They're on the real crest, the dumb bastards."
"Himmel."
"Yeah bunkie."
"Come on, Lister."
"OK Germ."
"I didn't run, Lis."
"Course you didn't."
"Anybody tells you that, he's a fuckin liar."
"Sure, bunkie."
". . . Whatheheck you doin here, Papa?"

I weighed a thousand pounds. Boy is this what Shafter feels like to himself? Poor bastard. Now I was up. Three people hefting me. Floating along like Houdini said the magic word. That was Papa. And Lister. Je-sus. *I don't want Tom, bunkie, he stinks on ice. He sure does.* I floated. Henry floated in '31. Almost the dead man's float. Got hit in the head playing tackle. Delirious three days and nights. The fourth day he sat up and said who won? That kid. Arthur Fine's tzotzkola only played touch. We were walking up a gangplank. Uh-oh, I says to myself, that is the *Seneca,* don't shit me. I squirmed loose. *Hey grab him. Gott he hit his head.* I DON'T WANT THAT FUCKIN BOAT. *It's OK, bunkie, I swear it is. You swear to God? I swear. Kiss your finger up to heaven. OK. Satisfied? Yeahhhh.* . . . . They lifted me up and carried me on and stretched me out on deck. Horns, cheers, whistles, throbs under my bones. Oh my bones. Oh Jesus. The clouds over the rail were moving. No, *we* were moving. Henry aways ran to the bow when the ferry started; he was nuts about the Staten Island ferry. Frank Joseph sat in the car and got pale. *That dynamite gun makes a lot of noise, but we gotta do all the work. Ain't it the truth.* Clara Barton in starched white. Mert said she became a war nurse to see our peckers; I didn't believe him. I believe she was sincere, although you never can tell. Now if you told me Lillian Russell or Lily Langtry, I would say definitely. Sally Rand, I don't know. But I would not look at her ass or tits till I got well. When Henry and Sonny saw *Snow White* they came home singing heigh-ho, heigh-ho, we're off to Minsky's show, we pay two bits to see two tits, heigh-ho, heigh-ho. It was Sonny's doing, but I lectured them both. I felt a grinding. My bones? No, the boat. More yelling. More floating. Sideways. Forward. *Where are we, Lister, Montauk? No, East 34th Street.* Now all around me hands, faces, voices, buildings. I was down amongst buildings and faces and floating over cobblestones. Horses out there. Christ Frankie was scared shitless of horses. He was afraid of his own shadow. But not with a pole in his hand. He even got seasick on trolley cars.

You feelin besser, sonny? Yes, Papa, how is Mama? Fine,
effrybody iss fine, you see, you be fine too. Yes sir, but don't
put me in Bellevue. Nein nein. Jesus Christ don't put me
in Roosevelt! Mein gutt, don't worry kinde, gay shloffen yetz.
Yes sir. . . . Ah the floating again. I wonder, did the
Dutchman float in '35 when they riddled him full of holes
in the Palace Bar? I always told Frankie, if you figure out
the motion, you'll never get sick. That kid just would not
listen. Dutch said, a boy has never wept, nor dashed a thousand
kim. Those are awful sad words. Buildings again. Wheeling
about me, turning, twisting. Walking down the street, the
Woolworth Building was very tall. Illowhite told me a hundred times you couldn't say that. Well floating down the
street, all the buildings *were* very tall. She was OK, although
toot toot toot.

We had stopped, I was heavy again. I heard Mama's voice.
Mother is the best bet, said the Dutchman, and don't let
Satan draw you too fast. And Bertha. And that little cockroach
of a brother, squeaking all around me. Dutch carried on all
day and night. Not like '32, when the Japs beat us in swimming and I snapped back with Stanback. Well Roosevelt
has been carrying on for twenty-six years. I was on terra firmer
and the firmer the terra the better. Putting one foot in front
of the other in such a way as to produce forward motion.
I was through the door and smelling the house. Such a
beautiful smell. Oh we were so happy then. What a family
I had, all for one and one for all. Home. My blue heaven.
Mid pleasures and palaces. Not one discouraging word. Henry
loved Castoria, but he never cried for it.

THE END

PS
3556
A97 W5

Faust, Irvin

Willy remembers

PS3556 A97 W5
+Willy remembers; +Faust, Irvin.

0 00 02 0208705 2
MIDDLEBURY COLLEGE